The Imperial Russian Air Service
Famous Pilots & Aircraft of World War One

Alan Durkota

Thomas Darcey   Victor Kulikov

Three-View Scale Drawings by

Ian Stair   Harry Woodman

Illustrations by

Alan Durkota   Terry Waldron   James Dietz

Flying Machines Press
Mountain View, CA

> **This book is dedicated to our families.**

© 1995 by Alan Durkota

Published in the United States by Flying Machines Press, Mountain View, California and Stratford, Connecticut

Color aircraft profiles and color section design and layout by Alan Durkota

Sketches and uniforms by Terry Waldron

Paintings by James Dietz

Three-view scale drawings by Ian R. Stair and Harry Woodman

Book and cover design, layout, and typesetting by John W. Herris

Text edited by R.D. Layman

Printed and Bound in the United States by Walsworth Publishing Company, Marceline, Missouri

All rights reserved. No part of this publication may be reproduced, stored in a retrieval system, or transmitted in any form by any electronic or mechanical copying system without the written permission of the publishers.

ISBN 0-9637110-2-4

Publisher's Cataloging-in-Publication Data

Durkota, Alan 1960–
The Imperial Russian Air Service—Famous Pilots & Aircraft of World War One

Bibliography: p.544

Contents:
1. Russia - Armed Forces - medals, badges, decorations, etc.

2. Aeronautics, Military - Russia- History - World War, 1914–1918

I. Title

UG1185.G3026 1995   358.4'11342'0943   95-083553

Flying
Machines
Press

Contents: The Imperial Russian Air Service

Introduction iv
Acknowledgments vi

Section 1: Overview of the Main Branches of Imperial Russian Aviation 1
The Imperial Russian Army Air Services 2
The Imperial Russian Navy Air Services 22
The EVK (*Eskadra Vozdushnykh Korablei*, or
Squadron of Flying Ships) 32

Section 2: The Russian Aces 41
Introduction 42
Pavel d'Argueeff (Argeyev) 43
Juri Gilsher 49
Nicholai Kokorin 54
Alexander Kozakov 58
Yevgraph Kruten 72
Ernst Leman 79
Ivan Loiko 82
Donat Makeenok 86
Ivan Orlov 90
Alexander Pishvanov 95
Mikhail Safonov 98
Alexander Seversky 102
Ivan Smirnov 112
Valdimir Strizhesky 122
Grigory Suk 127
Konstantin Vakulovsky 131
Vasili Yanchenko 134

Section 3: Aces In Foreign Service 141
Introduction 142
Louis Coudouret 145
Victor Fedorov 153
Maurice Gond 158
Georges Lachmann 165
Eduard Pulpe 174
Charles Revol-Tissot 178

Section 4: Distinguished Russian Pilots 183
Introduction 184
Ivan Bagrovnikov 185
Jezups Bashko 187
Jaan Mahlapuu 197
Petr Nesterov 201
Alekei Pankrat'yev 205
Marcel Plait 215
Boris Sergievsky 218
Alexander Sveshnikov 228
Olgerts Teteris 231
Vyatcheslav Tkachev 234
Peter Tomson 239
Victor Utgoff 243
Pioneer Women Pilots 258

Section 5: Famous Russian Aircraft Designers 265
Introduction 266
Dimitry Grigorovich 268
Igor Sikorsky 284

Section 6: Russian Aircraft Manufacturers . . 331
Introduction 332
The Rossiya B 336
Anatra 338
Dux 345
Lebedev 359

Section 7: Colors and Markings 375
Appendices 441
Appendix 1: Lighter Than Air Aviation 442
Appendix 2: Imperial Russian Awards and Orders . . . 459
Appendix 3: Combat Victory Lists of the Aces 467
Appendix 4: Aircraft of the Pilots 485
Appendix 5: Aircraft Scale Drawings 487
Glossary 543
Bibliography 544
Index 546

Introduction

This book is about an air service during the First World War, more specifically about the aviators and aircraft that made it a success despite all the social and logistic problems it faced during its short existence. All things considered, it is remarkable that these men and women accomplished as much as they did while their entire world dramatically changed before their eyes. In short, it is a book about human devotion, sacrifice, and—above all—courage.

Considering the chaos of the Russian civil war and the closure of historical archives under the Soviet government, it is not surprising that an official Russian history of its air service during World War I does not exist; until there is one, much that happened will remain unclear. None the less, it is possible to arrive at a basic narrative of events and to make some effort at describing them, especially when comparison can be made with Russian, German, and Austro-Hungarian sources.

To do justice to this vast subject, each chapter of this book would warrant a volume several times the size of this study. Generalizations and simplifications of some questions and problems and the omission of others of lesser consequence are therefore inevitable. Despite these limitations, imposed mainly by space considerations, the book represents the first work to cover the history of the Imperial Russian Air Service.

Air warfare was perhaps the most important military development arising from World War I. However, war in the air was not entirely new when hostilities started in August 1914. Aerial observation by balloon had been practiced for more than a century, and the first anti-aircraft fire in history was as early as 1794, when an Austrian cannonball nearly hit the bottom of a French balloon-basket. In effect, however, military aviation began less than eight years after the Wright Brothers' first powered flight: on 22 October, 1911, an Italian Nieuport made the first official military reconnaissance flight in the Italo-Turkish war, and days later, on 1 November, an Italian Etrich *Taube* dropped the first bombs in action.

Clearly, these early episodes helped to stir interest in aviation and ensured that aviation would have a place in warfare. Consequently, at the outbreak of World War I, each of the major powers had at its disposal fleets of aircraft that reflected the importance placed on military aviation. Russia (which had virtually no independent national aircraft industry) had nearly 250 machines, Germany about 230, France some 130, and Britain managed to assemble about 60.

If any doubt still existed about aircraft, it clearly faded in the early months of the conflict, when the ground war became increasingly static and cavalry patrolling impossible. By early 1915 aerial reconnaissance became the most reliable method of obtaining information on enemy movements, and by mid-1915 aerial cameras were able to produce photographs of outstanding clarity that presented a view of enemy positions never before available to a general. In fact, by war's end, nearly two-thirds of all intelligence was gathered by this means. Airborne artillery spotting had been made effective by the development of wireless telegraphy. Aerial bombing assumed increased importance as the war progressed and strategic bombing was made feasible by the development of longer-range aircraft capable of carrying a larger bomb-load.

Russia's air service possessed all these capabilities and in many cases was the first to introduce them. By 1916 the Russian navy possessed the world's second most powerful seaplane carrier force, outmatched in size only by that of the Royal Navy. However, the Russian navy surpassed the Royal Navy in efficiency and aggression. The Russian aviators Nesterov, Kruten, and Orlov had each produced technical manuals to teach aerial tactics to fledgling pilots well before the other air forces considered it necessary. In matters of strategic bombing, the EVK units, operating with Sikorsky's giant Il'ya Muromets bombers, were second to none in effectiveness throughout the entire war.

My first aim in writing this book has been relatively straight-forward: to fill a significantly large gap in aviation history of the First World War. In preparing this work a great amount of effort was put into correction of errors and inaccuracies that have found their way into print. As a result, the second objective of this book was to correct some of the lingering myths that have surrounded Russia's air service.

A brief explanation is in order concerning the manner of presentation of this book's contents. The photographs represent years of collecting, and the photo captions are longer to allow the inclusion of sufficient information to make the photos more meaningful to the reader. This same purpose was also in mind when writing the paragraphs of text accompanying the color illustrations. The illustrations themselves are of crucial importance in correctly portraying aircraft, uniforms, and awards, as well as aiding in the description of the Russian system of coloration, national markings, and serial number identification system.

For the reader unfamiliar with the role of Russia's air service in the First World War, the brief overviews covering the army, navy, and EVK may prove useful before reading the main body of text concerning specific aviators and aircraft types.

In each section of the book, and again in the appendices, the aviator biographies are arranged alphabetically. Russian name forms are used for the sake of uniformity and because Russian was the official language of the empire. For the sake of simplicity, the names of decorations are given in English. The first time any rank is mentioned it is translated into an English equivalent. An English-to-Russian glossary has been provided as a quick reference guide to most commonly used terms.

We have used the transliteration system from Cyrillic script of the United States Board on Geographic Names, except for names that have acquired a familiar transliteration—Sikorsky, for example, instead of Sikorskiy.

All dates have been converted from the Julian calendar to the Gregorian. Before the revolution of November, 1917, Russia followed the Julian calendar, which in the twentieth century was thirteen days behind the Gregorian or Western calendar. Similarly, we have converted the old Russian system of measurements of weights and distance to the metric system.

Wherever they were appropriate, the aviators' original letters and combat reports have been included to allow the fliers to speak for themselves. In some cases they have been abridged to make the narrative more coherent.

To avoid confusion, it was decided to retain the city name St. Petersburg throughout the text. The second term requiring explanation is *detachment*. It was decided to use *detachment* as the translation of the Russian word *otriad*. Historically, *otriad* was the smallest basic organizational and tactical aviation unit in the Imperial Russian Air Service.

To supplement the chapters concerning aircraft designers and manufacturers, a large set of technical drawings has been assembled.

Appendices include information on the Aeronautical 'Balloon' Corps, awards and decorations available to Russian aviators, and the most detailed victory lists yet compiled for each Russian ace.

This book represents ten years of research and contains mostly new material and photographs that have never appeared in print before. Main sources of information were the military and other historical archives throughout the world, but primarily those in Russia, Romania, Germany, Austria, and the United States.

I started my investigation in 1985 while conducting a two-year general research into World War I aviation. In 1987 I met with a fellow researcher/writer, the late Dr. Martin O'Connor, to discuss gaps in information. The next month I spoke at length with fellow historian Tom Darcey, who agreed to assist with the project. The third member of the team—Victor Kulikov—joined the project in 1993.

Besides being the primary researcher, writer, and artist of this book, I felt my role also included that of team leader, responsible for keeping the project on track, and coordinating and overseeing its growth. Although I played a major role in the book's final format, I should acknowledge that Tom Darcey alone suggested a foreign service section and for the most part worked alone to bring it to fruition. Tom's major writing also included the manufacturer sections, lighter-than-air appendix, and several pilot biographies. Although Victor Kulikov did not participate in the writing phase of this book, he was instrumental in obtaining information and photographs. Without his help this book would not have been possible.

In the course of researching and writing this book, much help has come from many people. The 14 persons whose photos are included in the Acknowledgment section are those who continually supported me for many years and without whose help this book could not have been completed. Many others who deserve recognition are also included.

Alan E. Durkota
Stratford, Connecticut
September, 1995

Acknowledgments

The authors wish to extend their deep and sincere thanks to the many people who were helpful throughout this research project.

Ian R. Stair was born in London, England, in 1921. After serving in the British army during World War II, he began a successful career as an engineer/architectural draftsman. Since retiring in 1986, Ian has devoted much of his time to creating highly detailed and accurate technical drawings of World War I aircraft. At present, more than 200 of his line drawings have been published in various journals, magazines, and books.

Ian's support was of key importance to this project, having provided drawings that represent 39 different aircraft types. Each of his drawings is a work of art and we are very grateful for the long hours he spent creating them.

Harry Woodman was born in England in 1929. He retired in 1987 after a series of careers which included merchant seaman, Royal Air Force, and civil service.

Harry has published more than 130 articles on model building and aviation history and authored two books, *Scale Model Aircraft in Plastic Card*, published by Argus Press in 1975 and 1977, and *Early Aircraft Armament: The Aeroplane and the Gun Up to 1918*, published by Smithsonian Institution Press in 1989. Since the early 1980s, Harry has been actively researching the early career of Igor Sikorsky and the development of aircraft armament in World War I. He has been an armament adviser to the RAF Museum at Hendon, England and the National Museum of Science at Ottawa, Canada.

We are indebted to Harry for the use of his beautifully executed technical drawings of the Sikorsky Grand and Il'ya Muromets type V bomber. Harry's knowledge of the EVK is enormous and we are very grateful for the valuable information he supplied.

Acknowledgments vii

Terry Waldron was born in Connecticut in 1959. A self-trained artist, Terry has been primarily a historical portrait painter for the past 20 years. In high demand, she continuously displays her work throughout the New England area and operates one of the states most respected art studios. Although Terry's interests in aviation art is relatively new, she quickly produced several prints and is involved with illustrating several books.

Terry labored with excellence and dedication to produce the outstanding portrait sketches and color uniform illustrations used in this book.

James Dietz was born in 1946 and was graduated from Art College of Design in 1969. He began to specialize in aviation and military art in 1978, and has quickly gained international recognition. Jim's originals are found in many private collections and museums, including the Smithsonian's National Air and Space Museum. He has exhibited at the EAA Museum, the San Diego Air Museum, and the Naval Air Museum in Pensacola, Florida.

The EAA presented Jim with the title of Master Artist after he won best in show in three successive years in the EAA Aviation Art Show. He was awarded the People's Choice Award by his peers at the American Society of Aviation Artists Forum, and received Best in Show in the Franklin Mint Artist Show. He is an Artist Fellow of the American Society of Aviation Artists.

Jim created three wonderful paintings for this project. His unique ability to link aircraft with people creates settings that are truly outstanding.

Sergei I. Sikorsky was born in New York City in 1925, the eldest son of aviation pioneer Igor Sikorsky. Sergei grew up to witness the construction of his father's famous Clipper Ships which pioneered the trans-Atlantic and trans-Pacific passenger services, and the first successful Sikorsky helicopter, the VS-300. Sergei actually flew in the VS-300 as a passenger with his father at the controls.

During World War II, Sergei served in a joint U.S. Coast Guard / Navy Helicopter Development Squadron. In that role he was involved in many of the world's earliest helicopter search and rescue missions and was a key contributor to the development of the first helicopter rescue hoists and medevac systems.

Sergei retired from the Sikorsky Aircraft Corporation in 1992, as vice president of special projects. He is the recipient of numerous aviation awards and honors.

We are especially grateful for the never-ending support and encouragement Sergei has given us throughout this research project. Besides writing the epilogue for the Igor Sikorsky chapter, his knowledge of aspects of his father's early career in Russia and the overall operation of the EVK helped to make those sections as accurate and detailed as they are.

Olga (nee Bosse) Svetlik was born in Grigorjevka (now Donetsk), south Russia in 1917. Olga has been an educator and technical translator of Russian, German, French, and English for many years—language teacher at the University of Kharkov, 1939–41; language professor at Oberschule, West Berlin, Germany, 1945–46; adjunct assistant professor at the University of Bridgeport, Connecticut, 1951–79.

Olga was the chief Russian translator on this project and labored for years to provide us with thousands of pages of needed material. Clearly without her help this research project would not have been possible.

Jack Herris was born in California in 1946. He was graduated with a B.S. in aeronautical engineering in 1971. Jack served in the United States Navy, first as a nuclear reactor operator instructor and later as a pilot, flying P-3s out of the US and the Far East. He then joined the Laser Fusion Program at Lawrence Livermore National Laboratory. Later, while working as a marketing engineer for a Fortune 100 electronics company, he started Flying Machines Press to provide aviation enthusiasts with a source of high-quality books.

Jack's primary function on this project was publisher; however, his continuous support and friendship made him much more. His own knowledge of World War I aviation is substantial, and he has been an aviation history consultant to the USAF Academy. His expertise and creativity enabled him to contribute significantly to this book's final format.

Photo by John Alves

ACKNOWLEDGMENTS   ix

Captain Vadym V. Utgoff (U.S. Navy, ret.). Capt. Utgoff was born in Sevastopol, Russia, in 1917, the son of Imperial Russian aviator Victor Utgoff.

Capt. Utgoff is a 1939 graduate of the U.S. Naval Academy, and a postwar graduate of M.I.T., and the Armed Forces Staff College and Naval War College. He commanded a squadron of PBY Black Cat seaplanes in the southwest Pacific area during World War II and was awarded the Legion of Merit with combat V, the Distinguished Flying Cross, and the Air Medal with gold stars. His squadron was awarded the Presidential Unit Citation.

Capt. Utgoff commanded a squadron of PBM Mariner seaplanes in the Korean conflict and was awarded a Commendation Medal. His naval service also included a tour of duty on the carriers Yorktown, Wasp, and Valley Forge, as deputy director of the Naval Weapon Laboratory at Dahlgren, Viginia, and as commanding officer of the U.S. Naval Air Facility at Sigonalle, Sicily. In 1964 he became a civilian professor of aerospace engineering at the U.S. Naval Academy, and shortly after retiring he was named professor emeritus.

We sincerely appreciate the help and guidance Vadym afforded us on his father's career and naval operations in general. The generosity and friendship he and his family has shown us over many years are memories we will cherish always.

Martin O'Connor was born in 1942 in New York City. He obtained a doctor of medicine degree from New York University and became a diplomate of the American Board of Diagnostic Radiology in 1974. Marty's main aviation interest was the study of Hapsburg aviation. He provided consultant services to the National Air and Space Museum in Washington, DC, Champlin Fighter Museum in Mesa, Arizona, and the USAF Museum in Dayton, Ohio. He published numerous articles on model building and aviation history and authored one book, *Air Aces of the Austro-Hungarian Empire 1914–1918,* published by Champlin Fighter Museum Press in 1986 and reprinted by Flying Machines Press in 1994.

Marty's knowledge of the Austro-Hungarian Air Service was second to none. He was a continuous wealth of information and support to us from the start of this project until his untimely death in 1994. He was our mentor and dearest friend.

Friedaricke Seidl dePierro was born on a small farm in Osterhofen, Germany, in 1923. During World War II Frieda was a train conductor on the Munich-to-Landshut route. After traveling abroad with her husband, who was attached to the United States Army, Frieda and her family settled in Stratford, Connecticut. She was well known throughout the community for her efforts in caring for injured domestic and wild animals.

Frieda was the chief German translator for this project until her untimely death in 1994. During her battle with cancer, she labored intensely to help us on this project. She was a gracious, generous, and gentle person whom we will always remember.

Lobov Stellizky was born in Woznesensk, Russia in 1917. She lived in Italy during 1920–28, Yugoslavia during 1929–44, and Austria during 1944–50. During World War II Lobov served as a technical draftsman for the Yugoslavian railroad. She moved to the United States in 1950 and in 1954 became a founding member of the Rodina Russian Military Museum. As chief curator of the Rodina Museum, she labored many years to maintain the museum's collection and to educate those interested in Russian history.

Lobov's continuous efforts to answer our many questions was of key importance in understanding and developing the Russian awards and uniform sections. Her encouragement and generosity was unparalleled. We will always remember our visits to Rodina.

Margaret E. Mokin was born in Yekaterinodar (currently Krasnodar) Russia in 1912. She moved to Germany during World War II and the United States in 1951. She is the assistant curator at the Rodina Russian Military Museum.

Margaret provided her unique knowledge of Russia's armies and their operations in World War I. For her many years of endless support, we are truly grateful.

Johan Visser was born in The Netherlands in 1934. His interest in aviation developed during World War II while watching the large Allied air formations flying overhead. Since that time, Johan has collected photographs of various aircraft.

We greatly appreciate the many rare and valuable photographs Johan provided, which helped to bring this book to life.

Sherwood Merk was born in 1937. His interest in photography has spanned more than 35 years. We are grateful for the photographic work Sherwood provided for this project and his endless efforts to insure the highest quality.

We would also like to thank the following people and institutions for their help. All are owed our deepest gratitude.

Appearing in alphabetical order:

Manfred Albrecht; Andrei Alexandrov; Prof. Valeriu Avram; a special thanks to Frank Bailey for information he provided on the foreign service pilots; Pamela Berthiaume; August Blume; Carl Bobrow; Bureau Central d'Incorporation et d'Achives, France; Central State War Historical Archives, Moscow; Paul Chuhnov; Curtiss Museum, Hammondsport, N.Y. and its curator Lindsley Dunn; Jerzy Cynk; Jim Davilla; Frank Dorber; the late Boris Drashpil; a special thanks to Donna Durkota for transcribing data from various sources and her efforts on naval research; Ed Ferko; a special thanks to Allan Forsyth for information on his uncle, Imperial Russian aviator Boris Sergievsky; Foundation for Aviation World War One, Princeton N.J.; Helena Fuentes; Helsinki University Library, Finland; Dr. Mark George; Dr. Thomas Goworek; Anda Grasis; Robert Gretzyngier; Peter M. Grosz; Jon Guttman; Adam Hochschield; Ray Holland; Hoover Institution, Stanford, California; Institute for History of Science and Technology, Russia; a special thanks to Joan Kerkin of Gecko Graphics, Albuquerque, N.M., for making the two maps in this book, a special thanks to R.D. Layman for editing the text and for helping to inspire this project; Bruce Laskey; the former Soviet Central Ministry Archives, Moscow; de l'Armee de l'Air, France; National Military Museum of Romanian Archives; Nick Mladenoff; Thomas Nilsson; a special thanks to Neal O'Connor for information on Russian awards; Leo Opdycke; Johanna Pankow; Gennadi Petrov; a special thanks to Nicholas Pishvanov, the son of Imperial Russian ace Alexander Pishvanov; Rodina Russian Military Museum, Howell, N.J.; a special thanks to Michael Safonov, grandson of Imperial Russian ace Mikhail Safonov; a special thanks to Victor Sheppard for his information on Russian awards; Igor Sikorsky Jr., the late Rudolf Simecek, World War I Austro-Hungarian aviator; Sikorsky Historical Archives and directors, Harry Pember and Phil Spalla; Service Historique de l'Armee de l'Air (SHAA); Smithsonian Institution's National Air and Space Museum and staff members Russell Lee and Von Hardesty; Dimitry Sobolev; Ellic Somer; United States Air Force Museum Dayton, Ohio; United States National Archives; a special thanks to Dr. Christine White for information on Women aviators; Charlie Walthall; and Yale University, New Haven, Connecticut.

xii THE IMPERIAL RUSSIAN AIR SERVICE

Aircraft Scale Drawings in Appendix 5 (1/48 scale unless otherwise noted)

Lebed VII..487
Anatra D (Anade)..488
Anatra DS (Anasal)..490
Curtiss Triad..492
Curtiss F Boat (1914)...494
Curtiss F Boat (1913) (1/72)...496
F.B.A. Type C (1/72)..497
Deperdussin TT...498
Grigorovich M-5 (1/72)..500
Grigorovich M-9 (1/72)..501
Grigorovich M-11 (with skis)..502
Grigorovich M-15...504
Maurice Farman MF.11 (Landplane and Floatplane) (1/72).......................506
Henri Farman F.22 (Landplane and Floatplane) (1/72)................................508
Lebed XI...510
Lebed XII..512
Morane Saulnier G...514
Morane Saulnier H...515
Morane Saulnier L..516
Morane Saulnier I...518
Morane Saulnier N...519
Morane Saulnier P..520
Nieuport 6 M (type 4)..522
Nieuport 9..524
Nieuport 10 (wheels & skis)...525
Nieuport 12...527
Nieuport 11 & 16 (wheels & skis)...528
Nieuport 17 (wheels & skis)..529
Nieuport 21...530
Nieuport 23...531
Spad A.2 & A.4..532
Spad 7..534
Vickers F.B.19..535
Voisin LAS (1/72)..536
Sikorsky S.12..538
Sikorsky S.16..540
Sikorsky S.20..541
Sikorsky S.10 Hydroplane (1/72)..542
Sikorsky Great Baltic (The Grand) (1/72)..........................Foldout
Sikorsky Il'ya Muromets Type V (1/72)..............................Foldout

Section 1

Overview of the
Imperial Russian Air Service

The Imperial Russian Air Service
An Overview of the Army Air Units

Russia's army entered aviation when it established a special school for balloonists at Volkov Field, near St. Petersburg, in 1885. By the outbreak of the Russo-Japanese War (1904–1905), the Russian army was well-practiced in aerial observation and successfully fielded a balloon company in support of its army units during the conflict. Based on those results, in 1906 the decision was made to form ten aeronautical balloon battalions. A year later, Russia had an aeronautics training park, three eastern Siberian field aeronautic battalions, two fortification aeronautic companies, and six aeronautic fortification detachments. Consequently, for two more years, Russia's interest in aeronautics was apparently dominated by lighter-than-air technology. However, with Louis Bleriot's historic flight across the English Channel in 1909, the Russian army quickly turned to the airplane through the guidance of several key supporters.

An army kite balloon ascending at Volkov Field, circa 1913.

Grand Duke Mikhail Alexandrovich, cousin to the Czar.

Without question, the most significant of those supporters was Grand Duke Mikhail Alexandrovich, a cousin of the Czar. Considered Russia's first major air theorist, the Grand Duke immediately understood the military implications of Bleriot's flight and quickly began to stimulate interest in aviation throughout Russia.

As a direct result of his activities, in January 1910, the Department of the Air Fleet was created under a special committee. The department would soon be known as the Imperial Russian Air Service (IRAS) and was chaired by the Grand Duke himself. His first efforts were to raise money from public donations to buy French aircraft— Bleriots and Farmans.[1] Next, the Grand Duke dispatched a number of military officers to France for flight training.

The army, already committed to its own ballooning program, at first displayed some reluctance to embrace the Grand Duke's ideas. Nevertheless, by 1911 the old Volkov Field, which had been used to train balloonists, was expanded by the army to include a heavier-than-air section, and soon after the army purchased its first aircraft for testing—a Bleriot. That same year the Russians held the "First All-Russian Aeronautical Exhibition." Hailed as a major aviation event, it attracted a significant number of foreign aircraft manufacturers and exhibitors, and in many ways signaled Russia's official entry into the aviation community.

From this small operation the Russian army subsequently opened the Gatchina military flying school, 25 miles outside St. Petersburg. Unfortunately, each year the Gatchina school fell victim to the long Russian winter and flight training was restricted by snow and severe cold. To solve this problem, the Grand Duke opened the Sevastopol School of Aeronautics, located in the Crimea

---
(1) He already had at his disposal two million rubles collected through public donation during the Russo-Japanese War, intended to finance construction of torpedo boats for the Imperial Navy. The Grand Duke used this sum as '"seed money" for the aviation fund.

Above: A Bleriot aircraft, circa 1916. The Bleriot design was the first aircraft type accepted and purchased by the Russian army for testing in 1911. This type remained in military service as a trainer until 1917.

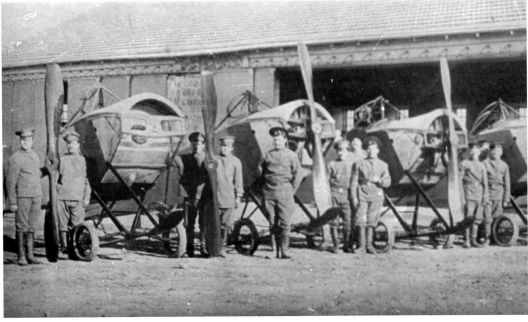

Nieuport IVs at one of the aviation companies, circa 1913.

on a plateau overlooking the Katch River. The Sevastopol school boasted a grand total of eight aircraft when it opened, but most significant was its ability to maintained air operations year-round, which afforded training to both army and navy officer cadets.

Simultaneously, the Russian army devised an ambitious plan in 1911 to organize trained aviators into functional groups that called for ten fully-staffed and equipped aerial detachments by the end of the following year. Although the number of officers recruited in 1911 did not support the plan's requirements, the army rectified the problem by authorizing non-commissioned officers and soldiers of lower ranks to be trained as pilots. To screen, accept, and organize these men into groups, the first recruitment detachment was established at the Siberian Aeronautics Battalion on December 31, 1911. Following the success of the program, a second recruitment detachment followed in June 1912 and was formed as the 7th Aeronautics Company in Kiev. Weeks later, on July 30, a separate aeronautics department was

A line up of Nieuport IVs of a typical army air service detachment, circa 1913.

Morane-Saulnier type Gs and Hs at the Fourth Aviation Company, Lida, circa summer 1914.

formed for the army and linked to the General Staff in hopes of optimizing the army's growing aviation program.

Although the Russian army had only eight air detachments on January 1, 1913, it had already gained an appreciation for aircraft's potential use during pre-war artillery spotting and reconnaissance exercises. This is illustrated by the army's expanding aviation requirements established in March 1913, which called for a grand total of 63 aviation detachments and nine aviation parks.[2] This plan was confirmed by the army's General Staff on March 4, 1913, and called for the following detachments and pilots:

37 Field detachments
10 Army detachments (one attached to each army)
8 Fortification detachments (one attached to each major fortification)
8 others (for special assignments)

(2) The aviation companies (also know as air parks) were responsible for supplying equipment, manpower, and repairs for the air units located in their assigned combat sector.

Fortification detachments staffed by:
  9 pilots (6 officer and 3 soldier) and
  8 aircraft
All other detachments staffed by:
  7 pilots (5 officer and 2 soldier) and
  6 aircraft

The plan's total aircraft requirement: 394
The plan's total pilot requirement: 457

By August 1914, Russia's growing frontline strength seemed impressive—some 250 aircraft divided into 40 detachments and manned by more than 200 trained pilots (164 officers and 36 NCOs) and 100 observers. In detail, the units were divided into the following groups:[3]

Eight Fortification Companies—each having one detachment

Name	Location
1. Brest-Litovsk	Warsaw
2. Ossovietz	Warsaw
3. Novo-Georgevsky	Warsaw
4. Kars	Caucasus
5. Vladivostok	Caucasus
6. Koven	Vilna
7. Grodno	Vilna
8. Sevastopol	Odessa

Six Aviation Companies:

1. First Aviation Company was based St. Petersburg and serviced the following aviation units: 1st, 5th, 16th, 18th, and 22nd corps detachments.
2. Second Aviation Company was based at Warsaw and serviced the following aviation units: 14th, 15th, 19th and 23th Corps detachments.
3. Third Aviation Company was based at Kiev and serviced the following aviation units: 3 field squadrons

(3) The eight fortification detachments were under the command of the fortress staff, while the 32 Field and Corps Detachments were under the command of the military district commanders.

Deperdussin TT, circa 1914.

and the 9th, 11th, and 12th corps detachments.
4. Fourth Aviation Company was based at Lida and serviced the following aviation units: 2nd, 3rd, 4th, 6th, 10th, 20th, and 21st corps detachments.
5. Fifth Aviation Company was based at Bronnitsy (near Moscow) and serviced the following aviation units: Grenadier, 13th, and 17th corps detachments.
6. Sixth Aviation company was based at Odessa and serviced the following aviation units: 7th, 8th, 24th, 25th, 1st Siberian, 4th Siberian, and 5th Siberian Corps detachments.

The unusual armament system used on an Deperdussin TT is clearly illustrated in this photo. The large metal plate placed directly in front of the observer was intended to guard against enemy gun fire.

Clearly, at the beginning of the war Russian military aviation compared favorably in size with Germany's 230 operational machines and the 130 mobilized by France. However, what is not evident from such statistics is that the aircraft used by the Russians were for the most part old and poorly maintained, making them barely fit for the service now required of them. To make matters worse, a majority of the Russian detachments were composed of a large variety of older foreign designs, notably Farman, Morane-Saulnier, and Voisin, which would still be in use three years later. Ultimately, this meant that Russia's air units went into action flying a large variety of aircraft types which other belligerent countries had often abandoned as out of date, and for which a large inventory of spare parts was required and invariably unobtainable.

Perhaps a greater concern for Russian air units in 1914 was the damage sustained through normal use and friendly fire.[4] Several reports by Russian commanders drew attention to the unfortunate fact that Russian planes were continually fired upon by Russian troops. By the end of 1914 most frontline detachments had to be sent to the rear because many aircraft had sustained serious damage or were worn out from normal use in a war which lasted longer than expected.

To make matters worse, domestic aircraft manufacturing was able to sustain an inventory only slightly larger than its pre-war total. By the fall of 1914 chronic shortages of aircraft and aero engines forced many detachments to be re-equipped from of the meager stocks available. A lack of technology and proper quality control

---

(4) Incidents of air-to-air combat were rare during 1914–1915. Nevertheless, even without enemy action, planes still crashed on takeoff or landing, and like other belligerent countries, Russia had vastly underestimated the wastage that would be incurred under normal war conditions.

The Imperial Russian Air Service

Scheme of Subordination of Air Units and Institutions in the Army in the Field by the End of 1916

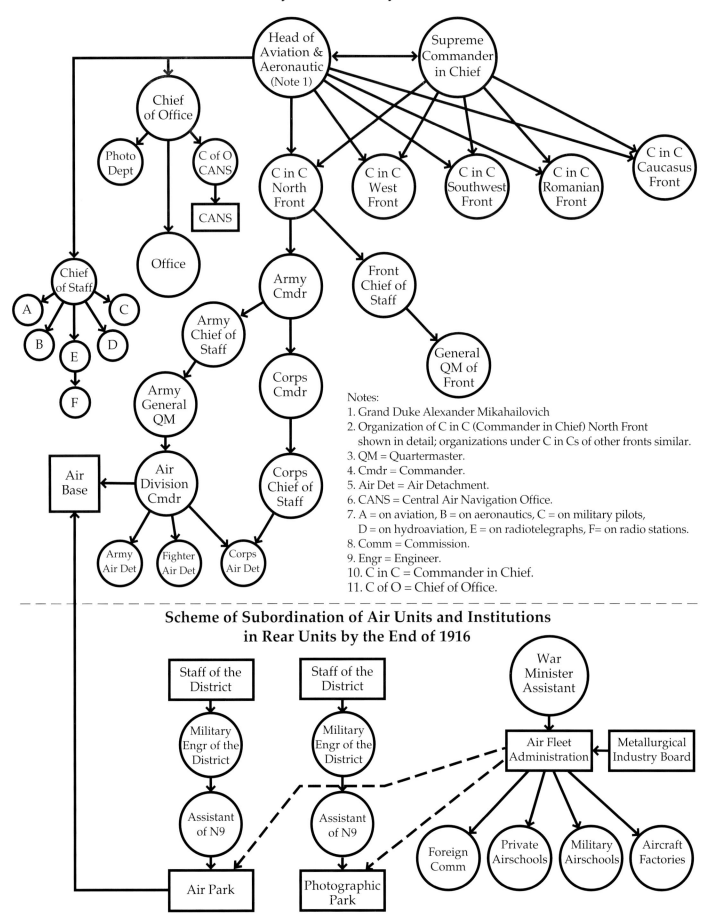

Notes:
1. Grand Duke Alexander Mikahailovich
2. Organization of C in C (Commander in Chief) North Front shown in detail; organizations under C in Cs of other fronts similar.
3. QM = Quartermaster.
4. Cmdr = Commander.
5. Air Det = Air Detachment.
6. CANS = Central Air Navigation Office.
7. A = on aviation, B = on aeronautics, C = on military pilots, D = on hydroaviation, E = on radiotelegraphs, F = on radio stations.
8. Comm = Commission.
9. Engr = Engineer.
10. C in C = Commander in Chief.
11. C of O = Chief of Office.

Scheme of Subordination of Air Units and Institutions in Rear Units by the End of 1916

Organization of Aircraft and Aeronautics in the Army in the Field by the End of 1917

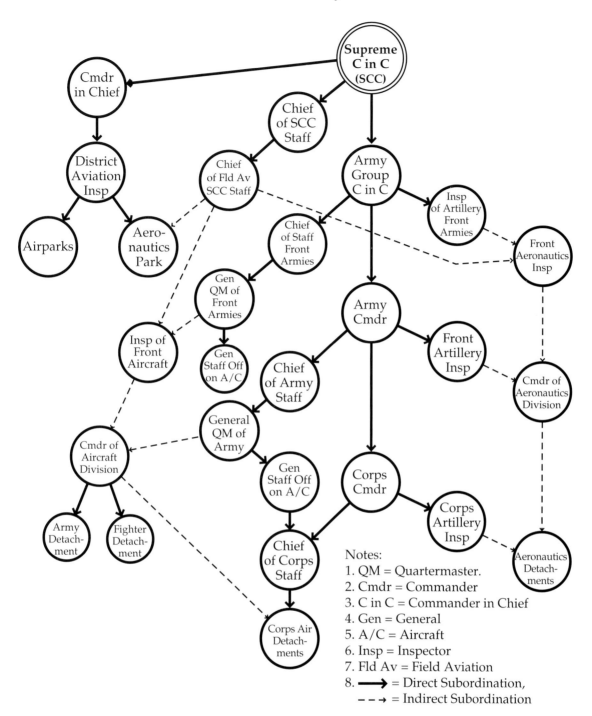

meant that many newer machines were actually less effective than some of the pre-war imports of 1914. Throughout the war, Russian pilots endured an unending series of faulty, inadequate, and even hazardous machines inflicted upon them by a military command which, in view of the shortage of aircraft, was reluctant to dispense with even the most unreliable machine.[5] Consequently, units were generally refurbished with an ever-increasing variety of aircraft types, which at times included captured Austrian and German machines, hastily repaired and thrust upon them. The whole procedure was in fact, rather haphazard, but it did at least allow the majority of air detachments to return to active duty by the spring of 1915.

---

(5) A report from the United States War Department dated August 24, 1916, stated in part: "The great majority of Russian machines are very dangerous to fly, due to lack of proper over-hauling and having been tinkered with by inexperienced men. Lack of spare parts induced the Russians to fit magnetos and sparking systems to motors for which they were not built, and this makes the wear and tear excessive all around."

Organization of the Aircraft and Aeronautic Units and Institutions in Rear Units of the Russian Army at the End of 1917

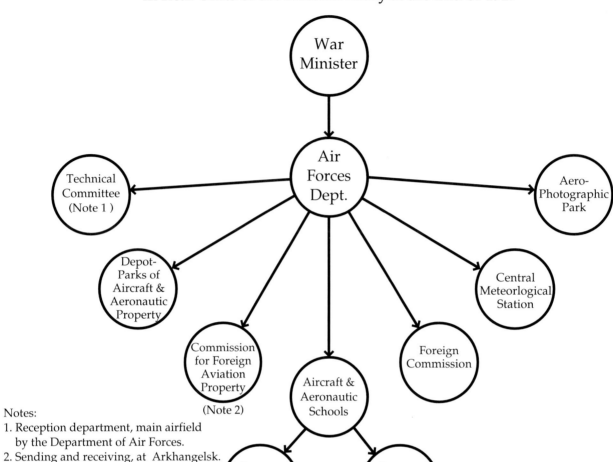

Notes:
1. Reception department, main airfield by the Department of Air Forces.
2. Sending and receiving, at Arkhangelsk.

Six months later, the Russian frontline strength was only 553 aircraft, being divided between an estimated 58 units which included: 1st–13th Army Detachments, 1st–37th Corps Detachments, 1st–5th Siberian Detachments, 1st–2nd Guard Detachments, and the 1st Turkestan Detachment.[6]

Despite its material shortages, the IRAS achieved great success in training pilots and observers. By early 1916 Russia had 12 military flight schools offering a well-conceived and efficiently run program of primary and advanced training.[7] Wartime requirements dictated strict criteria of recruitment for pilot training, which stressed merit rather than family background or wealth. As a consequence, the pool of military pilots in 1916–17 was decidedly less aristocratic in background than during the pre-war years. The Imperial Russian Air Service remained elitist and self-conscious of its special status, but as the war persisted its membership became increasingly mixed with representatives from all classes of society. Throughout the war Russia always had more pilots than aircraft.

May, 1916, is a typical month for operations. Table A shows 2234 missions were flown, lasting a total of 3101 hours. This was a daily average of 72 missions totaling 100 hours. However, by this time the Russian front stretched for more than 1000 kilometers. Seventy-two missions per day averaging 58 minutes duration each were hardly enough to provide adequate air cover for ground forces on all sectors of the front.

To some extent the problem was solved by means of a partial reorganization of the IRAS into special detachments. Although many units remained a collection of various types for reconnaissance and bombing, more thought was given to the possibility of better organization of aerial combat units. With the arrival of fighter aircraft from France, the Russians formed 12 offensive fighter

---

(6) The 13 army detachments were formed between February and May, 1915. During this same time, most of the fortress units were regrouped (i.e. the remnants of the Novo-Georgevsky Detachment were regrouped into the 33rd Corps Detachment).

(7) Training aerodromes were situated in the following places: St. Petersburg, Gachina, Tsarskoe Selo, Kolomiagi (near St. Petersburg), Riga, Warsaw, Kiev, Moscow, Bronnitzy (near Moscow), Odessa, Sevastopol, and Tiflis.

The 21st Corps Air Detachment based near Lida, circa fall 1914. The unit's mix of aircraft included at least two types—Henri Farman 20s and Lebed VIIs.

detachments between April and August 1916. Several months later, the Czar officially approved a report by aviation authorities which argued that large German fighter groups must also be opposed by similar IRAS units. As a result, four combat air groups were formed in the summer of 1916, not only to prevent enemy reconnaissance maneuvers but to pursue and destroy aircraft.

At the end of 1916 the IRAS had a frontline strength of nearly 800 aircraft divided between an estimated 74 units which included: 1st–12th Fighter Detachments, 1st–13th Army Detachments, 1st–37th Corps Detachments, 1st–2nd Guards Detachments, 1st–4th Artillery Detachments, 1st–5th Siberian Detachments, and the 1st Turkestan Detachment.

Throughout the final year that Russia was in the war, the military authorities continued to depend upon the Allies for machines and especially engines. Even the majority of aircraft built in Russia were powered by foreign engines.

In February 1917, when the Kerensky government took power, the Russian army had a frontline strength of 1040 aircraft divided among an estimated 74 units. To support the air units of the Provisional Government, imports continued to arrive from allied countries, particularly in the first half of 1917. At that time the French government shipped a large batch of Nieuport 17s, Spad A.2s, and Spad A.4s. Although the Nieuports were welcomed by the Russian pilots, the unusual seating arrangement for the observer/gunner in a vulnerable nacelle in front of the propeller made the Spad A.2s and A.4s unpopular. The French army had quickly withdrawn the type from its service, but Russian fliers had little option but to use it, for the IRAS was desperate to keep its air arm operational.

Perhaps feeling guilty for shipping the Spad A.2s and A.4s, the French government sent the Russian military a consignment of 43 Spad 7s in late spring 1917. Unlike the "nacelle" Spads, this popular fighter plane, only eight months old on the Western Front, helped to supplement or replace Nieuports and Moranes in Russian service until the second revolution in November 1917 ushered the Bolsheviks into power.

The general inability of Russia's industry to meet the material demands of a long war of attrition was magnified by the industrial and social revolutions of 1917. Estimates of total domestic war production to the February 1917 revolution vary between 4000 and 5000 aircraft, comparable to the production of the Austro-Hungarian Empire and clearly well below the other main belligerent countries. More serious than the lack of aircraft, engines, and spare parts was poor maintenance. More aviators died accidentally in faulty machines that were forced upon them by the Russian military command than died in aerial combat.

In the end, despite all the deficiencies, army air units remained intact and continued to fight while most of the army around them had disintegrated. Aviators of the Imperial Russian Air Service were estimated to have shot down nearly 200 German and Austro-Hungarian aircraft, a considerable achievement considering the conditions.

Table A: **IRAS Flights, August 1914–September 1916**

Month	No. of IRAS Pilots 1914	1915	1916	No. of Missions 1914	1915	1916	Flying Time (Hrs.) 1914	1915	1916
January	—	148	196	—	725	944	—	674	1331
February	—	169	165	—	967	728	—	965	882
March	—	180	201	—	1021	1230	—	1123	1816
April	—	183	231	—	1526	1454	—	1912	2059
May	—	193	256	—	1713	2234	—	1954	3101
June	—	191	265	—	1603	1441	—	1728	2592
July	—	202	299	—	1841	1347	—	2150	2440
July–August	129			1162			1151		
August	—	192	369	—	1597	2116	—	1672	3444
September	90	189	—	369	1231	—	409	1762	—
October	96	181	—	506	1040	—	521	1377	—
November	117	176	—	720	842	—	695	975	—
December	117	169	—	472	732	—	412	873	—
Annual Total	549	2173	1982	3229	14838	11521	3458	17165	20315
War Total	4704			29588			40938		

Source: General N.N. Golovin, *Voennyia Usiliia Rossii v Mirovoi Voine*, Paris, 1939, Vol. 2 p.48.

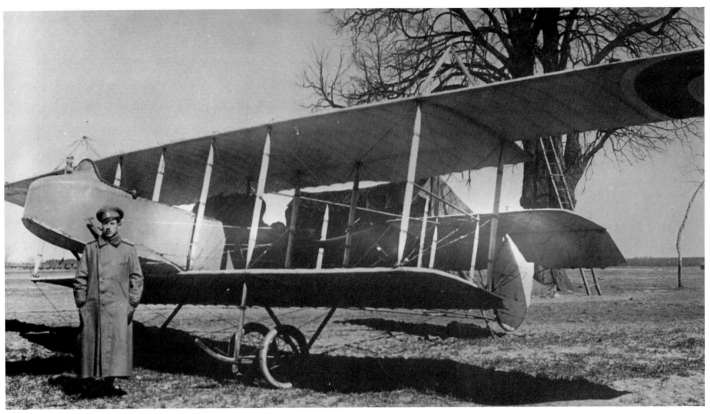

Above: Henri Farman 20 from the 21st Corps Detachment, circa fall 1914.

Right: Deperdussin TTs remained in active front service during 1916, and then retired to various flight schools for cadet training.

A standard forward area army park showing aircraft being repaired for their return to service with frontline detachments. A captured Albatros is in the foreground, with a Morane-Saulnier L behind it. Nieuport IV fuselages and Voisin nacelles are also visible.

Voisin LA with pilot Jan Dzikowski. This type of aircraft was produced in many Russian factories and also imported from French manufacturers.

The cockpit of a Voisin showing the wicker pilot's seat and the wooden bench for the observer. The addition of a gun ring is experimental. Instrumentation is sparse. A clock is mounted forward on the port side. A wireless antenna reel is attached to the port side in the rear area and is locked in place by a hook over the handle. The device in the foreground attached to the starboard top edge of the cockpit opening is probably the telegraph sending unit. The throttle quadrant is next to the pilots seat.

Left: Soldier inspecting the cannon mounting on a Voisin.

Right: Another view of the same Voisin with its unique armament mounting.

Morane-Saulnier L of the 1st Corps Detachment, circa 1915. The overall covering of this machine was plain linen.

Above: Morane-Saulnier L built by the Dux aircraft manufacturer. The overall color of this machine was light gray. Russian cockades appeared on the upper and lower surfaces of the wing, both sides of the fuselage, and the wheel covers.

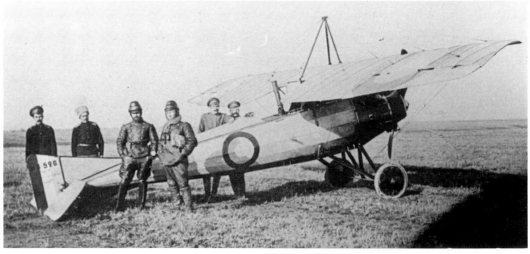

Morane-Saulnier P (serial 526). The French supplied a large number of these machines in 1915. Overall finish in plain linen. Metal panels and wheel covers are finished in red.

Above: Morane-Saulnier I from the 4th Corps Detachment, circa winter 1915.

Morane-Saulnier N. Russia received a substantial number of these machines in 1915.

Left: Dux-built Nieuport 9.

Above: French-built Nieuport 10 (serial 221) of the 4th Corps Detachment, fall 1916. The observer's position was in the forward position, the top wing having an opening to allow the observer to stand up through it and fire a rifle.

Above: Nieuport 10 equipped with a machine gun, circa spring 1915.

French-built Nieuport 10 (serial 348).

ARMY AIR UNITS 15

Right: French-built Nieuport 10 (serial 621) equipped with a Lewis machine gun. Photo: H. Woodman.

Below: A Nieuport 10 being prepared for flight by the pilot and ground crew. This machine is in plain finish with clear doped linen and natural aluminum cowl and panels.

Above: A typical Nieuport 10 of the Army Air Service. The dark color of the fuselage indicates that this machine is finished with a single opaque paint scheme, probably green or reddish-brown.

Above: Close-up of a Lewis machine gun in the observer's position on a Nieuport 12.

Left: French built Nieuport 12 (serial 1043) flown by Shiukov of the 3rd Corps Detachment. This machine is armed with a Mk.I Lewis machine gun. The aircraft is finished in a two-tone green and red-brown camouflage pattern. Undersides are plain linen. Wing edges are trimmed in light blue.

Above: French-built Nieuport 11 (serial 1502). This aircraft is finished in a two-tone green and brown pattern, while having undersurfaces of wings in plain linen. Flying surfaces are trimmed in light blue and the cowling remained silver. Cockades appear on lower surfaces of wings.

Above and left: Dux-built Nieuport 16. The overall color is light gray. Cockades appear in 14 different locations.

French-built Nieuport 17 (serial 3224). Overall finish of this French-supplied machine was silver.

Below: Nieuport 21 on skis. The men are holding the aircraft until the pilot signals he is ready for takeoff.

Right: The same aircraft in flight moments later.

Above: Lineup of Nieuport aircraft at the front, circa 1917. From right to left—Nieuport 23 (dark rudder with white number 9), French built-Nieuport 21.

Right: Nieuport 24bis in Bolshevik markings. Small numbers of this type appeared in late summer, 1917.

Below: French-built Spad A.2 (serial 67). The French sold their entire stock of Spad A.2s and A.4s to Russia after deciding the type was not adequate for frontline service.

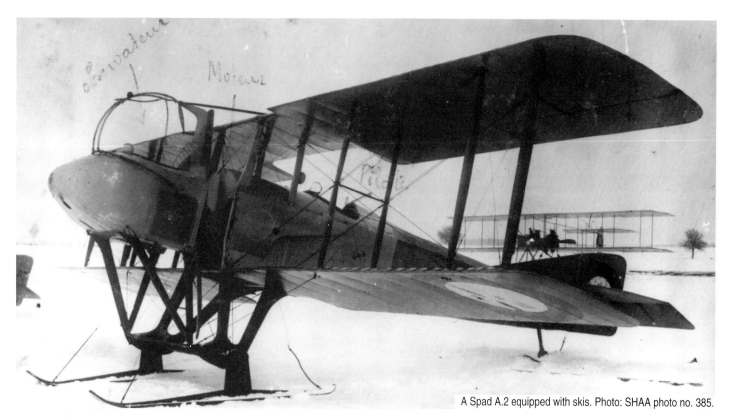

A Spad A.2 equipped with skis. Photo: SHAA photo no. 385.

Closeup of the observer's nacelle on the Spad A.2. The nacelle pivoted around its lower attachment points on the landing gear, thereby allowing maintenance of the machine's 80 hp Le Rhône engine. The small screen at the rear of the cockpit was designed to protect the observer from the propeller.

Closeup of the Spad A.2's power plant—a 9 cylinder, 80 hp Le Rhône 9C rotary engine. With this power plant the aircraft could reportedly reach a top speed of 100 mph.

Starboard view of what is believed to be the rare Spad G.1 multi-gun fighter. The French developed this type in 1916, reportedly with Hotchkiss guns; however, only a photo of a concept prototype existed. The aircraft carried the guns and ammunition in the forward nacelle instead of an observer. This machine, serial S.97, may be a modified Spad A.4, but the three machine guns in the forward nacelle are undoubtedly Colts.

Left and above: Two views of the nose of S.97 showing the detail of the Colt machine gun installations. The port and starboard guns have been set into deep cutout areas in the nacelle. Each gun was equipped with approximately 250 rounds. With all this added weight, no crew member occupied the nacelle. The guns were fired electrically. The SPAD logo on the nose indicates the nacelle is factory built, not a field modification.

French-built Spad 7 (serial 1471) after being captured by Germans on November 11, 1917. This aircraft has its rudder marked with a red-blue-white band. The fuselage also has a red band running round it.

Spad 7 finished in Bolshevik markings. A large number of these machines were delivered to Russia in the summer of 1917, and were quickly taken over by the Bolshevik forces during the civil war.

The Imperial Russian Naval Air Arm
An Overview

The Imperial Russian Navy became interested in aeronautics shortly after the acceptance of the observation balloon for army service in 1885, and by the early 1890s had established 'aeronautic parks' on the coasts of the Baltic and Black Sea. Shipboard aeronautics started in 1904, when a balloon was operated from a steam cutter, *Diomed*, and later from transports and the armored cruiser *Rossia*. These trials were for evaluation of air-to-sea communications during operations that involved mine laying, mine detecting, and spotting naval gunfire against shore targets.

During the Russo-Japanese War (1904–05) a variety of Russian naval vessels were equipped with observation balloons, but contributed little during operations against the enemy. From May 9–11, 1904, the balloon carried on the cruiser *Rossia* during a raiding cruise into the Sea of Japan made 13 successful ascents from the warship before the balloon's mooring line broke loose and the balloon was seriously damaged upon landing on the sea. Although the *Rossia's* balloon activities were short-lived, this was the first attempt by a warship to utilize a balloon in a wartime high-seas operation.

The Russian navy entered heavier-than-air aviation in March 1910, with the dispatch of eight personnel to flight schools in France—four navy officers for pilot training and four non-commissioned officers for training as aviation mechanics. Later in 1911 the first aircraft were ordered from France—ten Voisin Canard amphibians.

During World War I the two major theaters of airborne operations for the Russian navy were in the Baltic and the Black Sea. Although each theater had a Russian air wing that conducted similar tasks, the enemy forces that they opposed were considerably different. In the Baltic the opponent was the German navy and its well-equipped air service, while in the Black Sea the main fight was with Turkey. Throughout the war, the German navy was able to maintain a strong presence in the Baltic Sea and frequently used ships to support their land forces. In the Black Sea, Turkey's naval presence was weak compared with the Russians, but bolstered by German support that included two modern cruisers[1] and a moderate number of U-Boats. The enemy seaplanes in the Black Sea were all German in origin.

Operations: The Baltic Sea

At the beginning of the war, Russia controlled the coastline from St. Petersburg to the German frontier in the southwest. The number of Russian coastal naval air stations in the Baltic was moderate at the beginning of the war, but continued to increase as the war progressed. Some stations were quite extensive, with concrete ramps and metal hangars, while others were nothing more than a wooden dock with a shed or tents. Nevertheless, by spring 1917 naval flights had been established at the naval base at Revel and the islands of Dago and Oesel covering the entrance to the Bay of Riga, and the southwest coast of Finland and the Aland Islands.

At the start of hostilities, the Baltic Fleet had 8 fully-trained pilots and 4 student pilots. By January 1915 the number had grown to 21 pilots and was divided between three air groups.

One of these air groups was on board the *Orlitza*, a cargo-passenger liner that had been converted to a seaplane carrier in February 1915. Capable of carrying and deploying a small number of aircraft while at sea, the *Orlitza* served mainly in the Gulf of Riga area during 1915–17 and was active in defense against German naval operations around Moon Sound, the Straits of Irben, and Oesel Island. Her 4–9 aircraft, sometimes based on the coast or on inland lakes, were also active against the German army on the Courland coast.

In 1916 the Baltic Fleet's three air groups were re-organized into an air arm consisted of two air brigades. Each air brigade controlled three air divisions; in turn each division controlled three detachments—the equivalent of a flight consisting of six aircraft with some in reserve when up to full strength. By the summer of 1917 the Baltic Fleet's air group consisted of approximately 50 pilots and 70 aircraft.

In 1914–15 Russian aviators were very active in this theater conducting reconnaissance patrols and bombing enemy vessels. After the German navy established coastal air stations in the spring of 1916, combat with enemy aircraft increased considerably. Two Russian naval officers reached ace status before war's end.

Operations: The Black Sea

At the start of hostilities in 1914, the Black Sea Fleet's air arm possessed approximately 12 pilots divided between two air groups—one in Kilen Bay, and the other at the large naval base at Sevastopol. The Russian Black Sea Fleet was mainly concerned with supporting shipping activities, the defense of Russian ports and military installations, and attacking enemy vessels and coastal installations (especially the coal ports). To support the first two activities the Russian navy needed efficient reconnaissance reports, so aircraft became the eyes of the fleet. For the later activity, the Black Sea Fleet utilized *gidrokreisera* (hydro-cruisers, a uniquely Russian designation for seaplane carriers) to extend the operational range of aircraft. Eventually three Russian ships were in commission in addition to three ex-Romanian auxiliary cruisers impressed into service as carriers.[2] By 1916 the Russian navy possessed the world's second most powerful seaplane carrier force, outmatched in size only

---

(1) The battle cruiser *Goeben* and the light cruiser *Breslau*, renamed *Sultan Yavus Selim* and *Midilli* in Turkish service.

(2) A few proposals for aviation vessels had been advanced before the war and there had been a number of experiments to test the possibility of operating seaplanes from ships.

by the Royal Navy. However, the Russian navy surpassed the Royal Navy in efficiency and aggression.

In operations against the Turkish and Bulgarian coasts in 1915–16, the Black Sea Fleet created the world's first carrier-battleship task force, with the capital ship subordinated to the carriers as the main striking arm of the combination. These operations clearly refute the myth that the Russian navy of World War I was an inefficient military force that did not understand the potential of air power.

The first attack by Russian ship borne aircraft took place between March 15 and 17, 1915, when flying-boats from the carriers *Almaz* and *Nikolai I* conducted a reconnaissance mission and dropped bombs on Turkish coastal targets. This operation and others, up to the arrival of the first M.5s at Sevastopol in the summer of 1915, were carried out by Curtiss type "F" boats.[3]

The entry of Bulgaria into the war in 1915 (on the side of the Central Powers) made little impact on naval operations in the Black Sea. However, it allowed the port of Varna to be used by German U-Boats.[4] On October 14, 1915, a Russian force led by

---

(3) During 1912–14 the Black Sea Fleet was composed largely of Curtiss floatplanes and flying boats. However, in 1915 these types began to be phased out in favor of the indigenously designed and manufactured Grigorovich M-series flying boats, which constituted the main strength of Russian naval aviation throughout the remainder of the war.

(4) The German *UB-7* (Lutjohann) may have been the submarine bombed and reportedly sunk by a Russian flying boat in October 1916, but its loss to aerial attack has never been confirmed. *UB-7* had been slightly damaged in a skirmish with Russian flying boats in February, 1916, when it unsuccessfully attempted to attack the hydro-cruiser *Imperator Alexandr I*.

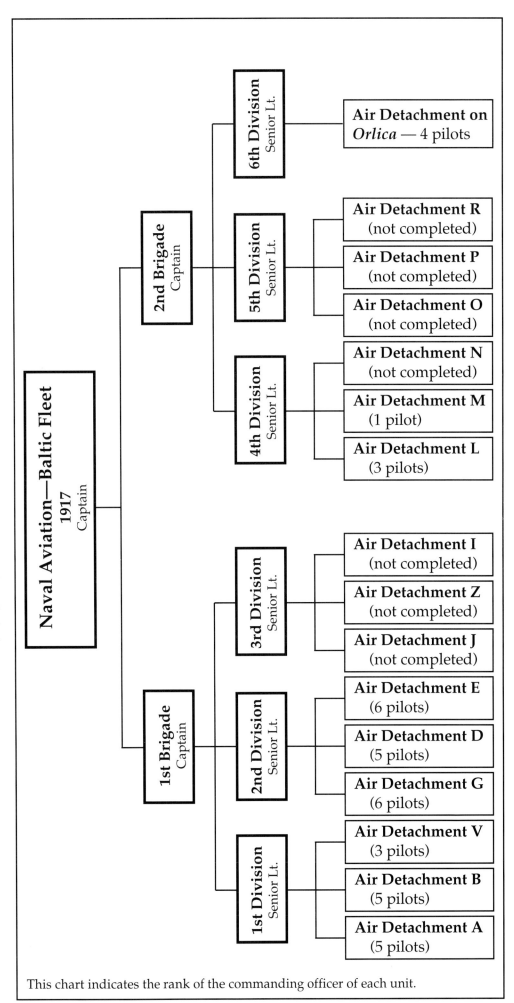

This chart indicates the rank of the commanding officer of each unit.

the carriers *Almaz* and *Nikolai I* with their complements of M.5s bombed the port's facilities.

After Romania entered the war on August 27, 1916 (on the side of the Allies), Russian naval aircraft were able to use the important port of Constanza as a staging area to attack Varna, but the port fell to German/Bulgarian forces on October 10, 1916.

In 1916, the Black Sea Fleet's air arm consisted of two air brigades, each having three air divisions. Two of the air divisions controlled three detachments—the equivalent of a flight consisting of eight pilots and 16 aircraft. The other four air divisions were of varying sizes and were mainly on board the carriers *Almaz*, *Imperator Alexandr I*, *Imperator Nikolai I*, and *Romania*.

The *Almaz*, a hybrid cruiser/yacht, was initially rated as a third-class cruiser and intended to serve as a viceroyal's yacht. In early 1915 the *Almaz* was outfitted for use as a seaplane carrier and equipped to deploy 3–4 seaplanes by a boom on her mainmast. As the fastest of the Black Sea Fleet's carriers, she took part, independently or in conjunction with other carriers, in operations off the Bosporus and Turkish European coast from March to May 1915 and in raids on Varna, Bulgaria in October 1915 and August 1916.

The *Imperator Nikolai I* and the *Imperator Alexandr I* were sister ships. They had been cargo-liners before the war and were converted in early 1915. Able to carry 6–8 aircraft each, they turned out to be the most efficient carriers in rapid launching and recovery of seaplane. From March 1915 they were active in numerous operations against shipping and ports on the Turkish European and Anatolian coasts, and took part in raids on Varna in October 1915 and August 1916. On February 6, 1916, their aircraft sank the Turkish collier *Irmingard*, the largest merchant ship lost to air attack in World War I.

The *Romania* was one of five merchantmen of the Romanian State Maritime Service which served as auxiliaries with the Black Sea Fleet after Romania became a co-belligerent in August 1916. She was rated as a *gidroviotransport* (hydroplane transport) and carried up to four flying boats.[5]

By late 1917, just before the Bolshevik Revolution in October, the Black Sea inventory comprised approximately 50 pilots and 150 aircraft. The equipment consisted mostly of Grigorovich M.5, M.9, M.11, and M.15 flying boats, with a few Nieuport fighters.

(5) Other known Romanian vessels capable of carrying aircraft included auxiliary cruisers *Dakia* and *Imperator Trayan*, three aircraft each; mine-layer *Regele Carol I*, one aircraft; and the net-layer *Principesa Maria*, one aircraft.

Russian transport *Kolyma* preparing to loft a spherical balloon at Vladivostok, late 1904. Photo: R.D. Layman.

Armored cruiser *Rossia* at Vladivostok in 1905 with the kite balloon she employed operationally. Photo: R.D. Layman.

A closer view of the kite balloon riding over *Rossia's* quarter-deck just before the start of the raiding cruise of May 1905. Photo: R.D. Layman.

Orlitza, the Russian navy's only Baltic Sea carrier, with covers furled on the aft hangar and down on the forward hangar.

Orlitza in 1917. An FBA flying boat is in the forward hangar.

The seaplane carrier *Almaz* carried up to four aircraft on her deck. Photo: R.D. Layman.

Table A
Aircraft Used In The Baltic Sea:

Accepted 1913 – 1917:
Sikorsky S-5a (Tactical Nos. unknown)
Sikorsky S-10 (Tactical Nos. unknown)
Sikorsky Ilya Muromets
FBA Tactical Nos. 4, 5, 7, 17 (Others unknown)
Maurice Farman type 11 Tactical Nos. 7, 8, 14, 11, 25, 26, 31 (Others unknown)
Henri Farman type 22 Tactical No. 2 (Others unknown)
M.2 Tactical Nos. 2, 3
M.4 (Tactical Nos. unknown)
M.9 Tactical Nos. 16, 21–38, 43–58, 60–69, 102 (Others unknown)
M.11 Tactical No. 4 (Others unknown)
M.12 Tactical No. 18 (Others unknown)
M.15 Tactical Nos. 1–15
M.16 Tactical No. 16 (Others unknown)
Nieuport Fighters Tactical Nos. 1–10 (Others unknown)

Table B
Aircraft Used In The Black Sea:

Accepted 1913 – 1914:
Voisin Carard (Tactical No. 1)
13 Curtiss Triads (Tactical Nos. 2–13)
7 Curtiss F Boats (Tactical Nos. 14–20)

Accepted Spring 1915:
4 FBAs (Tactical Nos. unknown)
20 Curtiss F Boats (Tactical Nos. 1–28) *assumed Tactical Nos. from Triads
2 M.2s (Tactical Nos. 29, 30)

Accepted August – September 1915:
10 Curtiss F Boats (Tactical Nos. unknown)
4 Curtiss K Boats (Tactical Nos. unknown)
2 M.4s (Tactical Nos. unknown)
19 M.5s (Tactical Nos. 31–49)

Accepted January – February 1916:
8 M.5s (Tactical Nos. 50–57)

Accepted May – August 1916:
21 M.5s (Tactical Nos. 58–78)
20 M.9s (Tactical Nos. 100–119)

Accepted September – December 1916:
10 M.5s (Tactical Nos. 79–88)
17 M.11s (Tactical Nos. 1–17) *assumed Tactical Nos. from Curtiss F Boats
17 M.9s (Tactical Nos. 120–136)

Accepted January – April 1917:
4 M.5s (Tactical Nos. 89–92)
28 M.9 s (Tactical Nos. 137–165)
9 M.11s (Tactical Nos. 18–26)

Accepted May – July 1917:
7 M.5s (Tactical Nos. 93–99)
34 M.9 (Tactical Nos. 166–200)
2 M.15s (Tactical Nos. 201, 202)

26   THE IMPERIAL RUSSIAN AIR SERVICE

Table C

Aircraft Losses Due To Enemy Action

Baltic Sea:

Date	Type	Crew	Reason
22 June 1915	FBA #7	Seversky (P) Blinov (O)	Shot down, aircraft destroyed by explosion of own bomb. Observer killed, pilot wounded.
26 July 1915	FBA #4	Galibin (P) Ivanov (O)	Damaged during attack on German cruiser *Roon*. Crew POW.
28 July 1915	FBA		Aircraft destroyed by German warships at Cerel during bombardment.
28 August 1915	FBA #17	Zverev (P) Kavelin (O)	Aircraft was damaged during bombing raid at Vindaa. Crew sank aircraft. Crew POW.
4 March 1916	MF	Mustiac (P) Unknown (O)	Missing after reconnaissance flight in Shwern area.
12 May 1916	MF	Misinsky (P) Unknown (O)	Crash-landing. Aircraft sank.
21 June 1916	M.9 #14	Sizvekov (P) Nazarov (O)	Shot down by German aircraft. Aircraft lost and crew killed.
4 July 1916	M.9	Zaicevsky (P) Stankevich (O)	Shot down by anti-aircraft artillery during bombing mission against German warship. Aircraft lost, crew rescued.
20 July 1916	MF #25		Aircraft destroyed by German warship bombardment at Arensburg.
3 August 1916	M.9		2 M.9s were destroyed at Runo by enemy bombardment.
22 August 1916	M.9 #16	Trofimov (P) Tarakanov (O)	Aircraft damaged during bombing mission in Irben area. Observer wounded.
13 September 1916	M.9 #8	Garkovenko (P) Unknown (O)	Shot down by enemy aircraft. Both crewmen killed, aircraft lost.
13 September 1916	M.9 #39	Safonov (P) Orlov (O)	Pilot wounded. Returned safely.
17 September 1916	M.9 #40	Nagursky (P) Rusakov (O)	Observer wounded in battle. Returned safely.
5 may 1916	M.9 #32	Rumiancev (P) Khramcov (O)	Shot down by enemy aircraft. Aircraft lost, crew rescued.
28 May 1917	M.9 #26		Destroyed by German bombardment.
28 May 1917	M.9		4 M.9s destroyed by German bombardment.
31 May 1917	MF #8		Destroyed by German bombardment.
10 June 1917	M.9	Matveev (P) Iakushin (O)	Crash-landed at own base after battle.
19 June 1917	M.9	Lubushkin (P)	Aircraft sank with pilot after battle, pilot killed.
12 August 1917	M.9	Baruzdin (P) Unknown (O)	Pilot wounded in air battle.
20 August 1917	M.9	Elizarov (P) Unknown (O)	Aircraft sank with pilot after battle. Pilot killed, observer saved.
31 August 1917	M.9	Makarevich (P)	Killed at Abo Station.
1 October 1917	M.9	Baruzdin (P) Unknown (O)	Aircraft damaged by enemy aircraft at Cerel.
1 October 1917	Nieuport	Fillipov (P)	Missing after flight at Kuyvasta.

Black Sea:

Date	Type	Crew	Reason
Unknown date	M.5		Captured intact—Turkey.
Unknown date	M.9 #110		Lost in Romania.
Unknown date	M.9 #112		Lost in Romania.
21 May 1917	M.9 #161		Captured intact—Romania.

An FBA flying boat attached to a hoisting boom on the *Orlitza*, circa 1917.

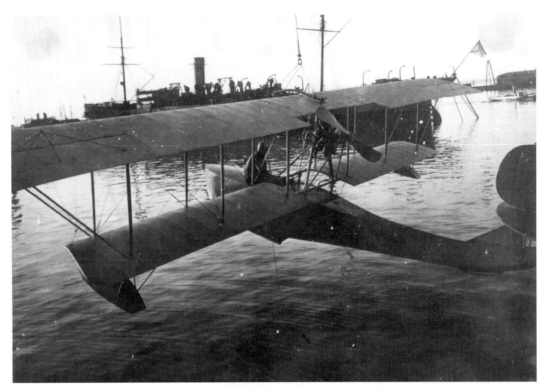

Imperator Nikolai I, at Sevastopol. She is distinguished from her sister ship, *Imperator Alexandr I*, by a dark band on the funnel. Photo: R.D. Layman.

An aerial view of a metal hangar at Sevastopol, circa 1913. A Curtiss Triad is positioned on the concrete dock/ramp.

Romania was the best-equipped of the aircraft-carrying Romanian merchantmen that joined the Black Sea Fleet. She is carrying three Grigorovich M.9 flying boats aft and amidships. Photo: R.D. Layman.

Curtiss Triads (1911 type E) tactical numbers "3" and "4," on the concrete dock at Sevastopol, circa 1913. Each aircraft's tactical number was on an anti-skid panel located near the engine bay. The tactical number refers to 'Fleet Number.' Up to October 1916, the tactical numbers were re-allocated to new machines from existing machines which had been scrapped or lost. For example, the original tactical numbers 2–26 were allocated to the Curtiss floatplanes and flying boats in the Black Sea Fleet purchased before 1916. However, the same numbers were then re-allocated to new M.11s received in October 1916.

Carpenter shop inside one of the hangar facilities at Revel Air Station, Baltic Sea, circa 1914. The air stations at Revel and Sevastopol were both equipped with elaborate machine shops to repair aircraft.

Michman Alexander Mihailov at Sevastopol, circa 1916, with what almost certainly is a radio transmitter-receiver. Antenna wires can be seen on the right rear wall.

Right and below: FBA flying boat (tactical no. 48) of the Black Sea Fleet, circa 1915. This type was used in large numbers by both fleets in 1913–16. The rudder of this machine displays the naval Cross of St. Andrew (light blue cross on a white field).

A Maurice Farman Shorthorn (M.F. 11) at Revel Air Station (Gulf of Finland), winter, 1915. This type was used by the Baltic and Black Sea Fleets.

The nacelle of this Maurice Farman displays tactical no. M 14, Baltic Sea, circa 1914. In addition to having tactical numbers applied, many Maurice Farmans in the Baltic Fleet also had the Cyrillic letters M (em) and ∞ (eff) added as a telegraphic code symbol for an MF aircraft.

Below: Henri (Anri) Farman H.F. 22 with floats (tactical no. 2), circa 1914. In addition to the tactical nos. applied to the Anri Farmans in the Baltic Fleet, several machines also had the Cyrillic letters A (ah) and ∞ (eff) added to denoted an AF type aircraft. A unique telegraphic code symbol of Russian letters also appeared on Sikorsky, Grigorovich, and Nieuport aircraft used in the Baltic Sea Fleet.

Curtiss Triad (tactical no. 7) of the Black Sea Fleet, Sevastopol, circa 1913. During 1912–14 the Black Sea Fleet was composed largely of Curtiss seaplanes and flying boats. *Michman* (Ensign) N. Ragozin is standing second from right.

Maurice Farman Shorthorn floatplane (tactical no. 7), Revel Air Station, winter, 1916. It was common practice to launch floatplanes from inland lakes after ice formed in the winter months.

Nieuport 9 fighter of the Baltic Fleet. Both the Baltic and Black Sea Fleets were equipped with a small number of Nieuport aircraft (types 9, 10, 17, and 21).

The *Eskadra Vozdushnykh Korablei* (EVK) or Squadron of Flying Ships

The Original Organization

The success of the pre-war Il'ya Muromets led to the War Ministry issuing an order to the Russo-Baltic Wagon Works (*Russko-Baltiisky Vagon Zaved* or R-BVZ) of St. Petersburg for ten Murometsy to be delivered by March 15, 1915. In July 1914, the War Ministry issued an order creating combat units (*Boyevye Otryady*-Combat Units) of Il'ya Muromets (IM) and stated that ten such aircraft were being built and were to be fully equipped. Staff Captain G.G. Gorshov (staff officer, Aviation School Gatchina), was instructed to recruit staff and draw up regulations for operation of the aircraft. At the same time, the Main Artillery Administration was requested to develop bombs, bomb sights, mechanisms to drop bombs, and defensive gun-mounts for the IMs. At the outbreak of war, Igor Sikorsky was the sole test pilot for the giant Il'ya Muromets aircraft. He alone assumed responsibility for training the seven officer candidates selected in late August 1914.

The original organization stated each IM should be considered a single combat unit and they would come under the command of the appropriate administration of *Stavka* (the headquarters of the Supreme Commander-in-Chief), who happened to be the newly-appointed Grand Duke Nikolai Nikolaevich. However, in the field they would be under direct control of the various army and corps commanders. The original scheme called for each IM combat unit to be supported by three scout aircraft for liaison and training purposes. The unit commander, who was to be a military aviator, and personnel under him were to be divided into two divisions—one flight and one ground. The flight division consisted of the IM commander and deputy, mechanics for in-flight repairs, an artillery officer for observation and bombing, a photographic specialist, several machine gunners, and three officer pilots for the scout aircraft. The ground division consisted of a supply officer and about 40 ground troops. Their equipment consisted of several tent hangars (one large tent for the larger aircraft and smaller tents for the scout aircraft), a mobile photographic laboratory, an automobile unit, a mobile stores unit, a meteorological section, and a mobile repair shop. The mobile repair shops were located a mile from the unit, along the nearest railroad. It consisted of a train of ordinary box cars fitted for that service. The repair shop car contained hand and foot power lathes, drills, forges, etc. Within hours, the needed supplies and spare parts were sent by car or truck to the airfield.

Summary of EVK Operations

Unfortunately, at the outbreak of the war only two of the original ten IMs ordered were nearing completion. The first two IMs (*Ship I* and *Ship II*) left for the front in September 1914. *Ship I* left on September 12 for the

The Il'ya Muromets (*Ship I*) with crew members of the EVK, based at Yablonna, near Warsaw, 1915. Photo: United Technologies Corporation.

The huge hangar at Lida that once housed Russian airships is shown with an Il'ya Muromets inside, July 1915.

Galician front in the area of the Russian 3rd Army. After several mishaps en route, *Ship I* reached Brest-Litovsk. *Ship II* also made an attempt to reach the front by air. However, while it was over Rezhitsi, Russian troops opened fire on it and forced the machine to make an emergency landing. The crew of *Ship II* decided to complete the journey to Brest-Litovsk by rail.

Between October 21, 1914, and January 10, 1915, *Ship I* conducted a series of reconnaissance missions. However, the flight commander of this ship felt the Il'ya Muromets did not perform well. After a scathing report was submitted to *Stavka*, the commander of the north west front refused to accept delivery of *Ship II*, which was on its way. Faced with this news, and additional recommendations from army officers that no more IMs should be ordered, *Stavka* canceled all orders.[1]

After hearing the army had canceled the IM program, R-BVZ director Shidlovsky made a personal appeal to *Stavka*. One must wonder what was on his mind at that time. Although considered by most a steadfast patriot, he was, after all, the director of the R-BVZ, and he was also acutely aware of the financial loss the company would have assumed should the orders stay canceled. Whatever the reason, Shidlovsky stated the IMs had the ability to help the army, but the original scheme established for the

(1) Apart from the army's original request for ten IMs in the spring of 1914, four additional IMs were requested in July, and 32 more had been ordered on October 2, 1914. The July and October orders were canceled.

operation of the giant aircraft was unsatisfactory. He recommended they be formed into a special unit under the direct control of *Stavka*.

Although the cancellation order was not rescinded, Shidlovsky's operational suggestions for the aircraft were adopted. Soon afterward the single IM units were abandoned and one centralized base for all the IMs was created at Yablonna, about 25 miles north of Warsaw. *Ship I* and *Ship II* were transferred there in January 1915, and joined five other IMs. The centralized unit was known as the Squadron of Flying Ships (*Eskadra Vozdush-nykh Korablei*, or EVK). The commander of the EVK was none other than Shidlovsky, who had been appointed to the rank of major general.

The base at Yablonna had been selected for its strategic position between Warsaw and the fortress of Novogeorgyevsk. At the time the EVK was formed, only seven of the contract IMs had been completed; five were "B," but two were of the newer type "V," equipped with Argus engines. The newer type "V" machines were referred to as the *Kievsky II* and *Ship III*.

The first war flight of the EVK was carried out by *Kievsky II* on February 15, 1915, when its crew flew over enemy territory and bombed enemy trenches. This prompted the Germans to notice the aerodrome at Yablonna and to bomb it regularly.

From February to May, *Kievsky II* and *Ship III* carried out a number of long-range reconnaissance and bombing missions for the Russian 1st Army and the command of the northwest front. Perhaps as a last chance for the giant aircraft, one daring mission was designed specifically to destroy a railroad station. In the end, all the flights were very successful, and the army commanders soon began to change their opinion of the IM. The cancellation order by *Stavka* was rescinded and the request for 32 aircraft was restored in April, 1915. As continued success with the IMs was achieved, a further order for an additional 30 was placed on July 4.

By the summer of 1915, even the Germans realized the importance of the large Russian aircraft. The decision by the Germans to send their 'R' planes to the "quiet Eastern Front" for evaluation in late 1915 might have had a morale element connected to it. The vision of large Russian aircraft continually flying over the German troops, apparently unaffected by gunfire or aircraft, was hardly good for German troop morale.

The arrival of replacement IMs at Yablonna permitted a section of the unit to be detached for operations elsewhere. The first of these combat detachments was formed on May 1, 1915, and consisted of two aircraft—*Kievsky II* and *Ship III*. The First Combat Detachment proceeded first to Lemberg, then Lublin, and eventually Wlodowa, starting reconnaissance missions from there on June 12.

On one such mission (July 6, 1915), the overconfident crew of the *Kievsky II* decided to carry one machine gun and a rifle. Well inside enemy territory the IM came under attack by four German aircraft from *Feldflieger Abteilung* 21 based at Lipnicki. In the ensuing battle the IM was seriously damaged and several crewmen were wounded. The aircraft made a forced landing several miles behind the Russian front lines and sustained more damage. This was one of only three occasions when an IM was shot down by enemy action. *Kievsky II* was written off and serviceable equipment was removed and installed on other IMs then located at Lida.

At the same time (July of 1915), a combined German-Austrian offensive had forced the main EVK unit to leave Yablonna. It moved first to Brest-Litovsk, then to Lida, and by late August had moved again to Pskov, which became the main base for the next year.

In September 1915, while the EVK was at Pskov, the Second Combat Detachment was formed consisting of nine "V" type ships (No. I, II, IV, V, VI, VIII, IX, X, and *Kievsky III*). This detachment was stationed at Zegewold, about 30 miles from Riga.

The Second Combat Detachment conducted a series of missions that involved several IMs in flight at one time. One such mission took place on October 18—*Ship III*

Bombs being loaded onto an Il'ya Muromets. Depending on fuel and defensive armament loads, the bomb load of an Il'ya Muromets varied between 1,150 and 2,200 pounds. The upper machine gun position is visible near the fuel tanks. Photo: United Technologies Corporation.

raided Tukkum, while *Kievsky III* bombed Shavli, and *Ship II*, *Ship V*, and *Ship IX* raided Fredrichsdorf.

Soon afterward (November 15, 1915), *Ship III*, which alone remained at Wlodowa after the destruction of *Kievsky II*, was hit by German anti-aircraft fire and went into a flat spin from which its crew never recovered. *Ship III* crashed near Priluki, killing all but one crewman.

At the end of 1915 the Russian army was preparing for an offensive in east Galicia. To support it the EVK was ordered to send a detachment to this sector. *Kievsky III* and *Ship II* were grouped into the restructured First Combat Detachment (later joined by *Ship XIII*) and proceeded to Tarnopol. For several months this group provided valuable reconnaissance information.

Back at the Second Combat Detachment, *Ship I* carried out the first night raid for an IM when it successfully bombed the railroad station at Mlava on February 8, 1916. Several months later, the Third Combat Detachment was formed at Pskov and left for the area of Minsk on June 17. On September 26, 1916, the Third Combat Detachment lost *Ship XVI* after it was attacked by the full force of *Feldflieger Abteilung* 45 based near Bogdanov.

At the end of 1916 it was decided to send an IM unit in support of Romania, which had decided to enter the war on the side of the allies. The Fourth Combat Detachment was formed at Vinnitsa in January 1917 and left for

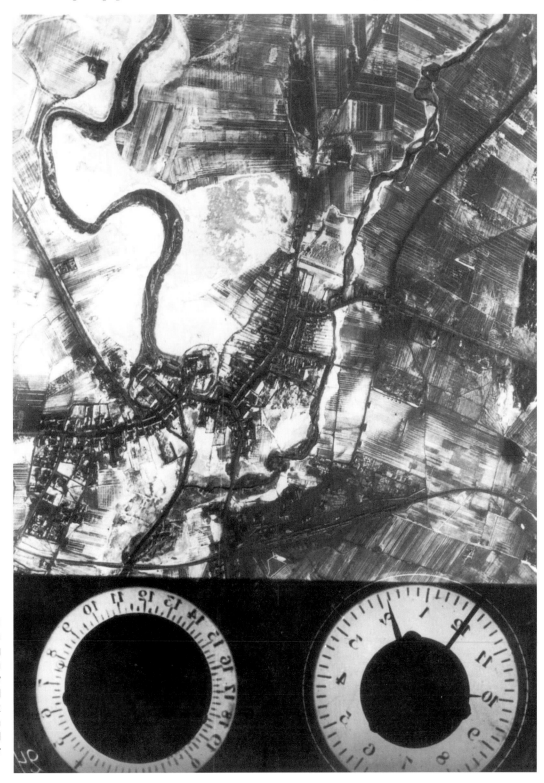

An aerial reconnaissance photo taken through the observation window of an Il'ya Muromets during a bombing mission. The Ulyanin camera used on many of the IMs simultaneously recorded the object of interest and also an aneroid-altimeter and clock on the some photo plate. A mirror in the camera caused the altimeter and clock to be photographed as a mirror image.

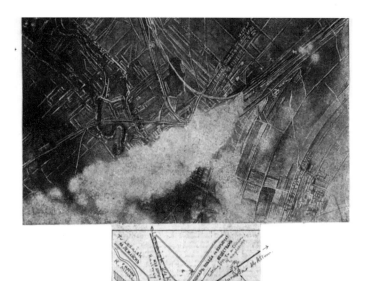

The EVK developed very advanced aerial photography techniques during World War I. The upper photo shows explosions at the Przerorsk railroad station after bombs from an Il'ya Muromets were dropped. The lower sketch (usually created by the IM's artillery officer) shows the photo interpretation of the railroad bombing, and clearly indicates the accuracy of the mission. Once created, these sketches were supplied to field officers to indicate points of interest.

Belograd, Romania, in March. The group consisted of two type "V" aircraft (*Ship III, Ship IV*), and the newer "G-2" type (*Ship V*, and *Ship IX*).[2]

Although the EVK represented an impressive aerial unit in early 1917, by February the Czar abdicated and the Provisional Government took over the country and the war effort. One of the first moves by the Provisional Government was to dismiss Shidlovsky and certain other officers from the EVK. Many officers complained and suggested future operations by the EVK would be difficult. Nonetheless, the war minister, Alexander Kerensky, was determined to launch an offensive in April 1917, and he wanted the EVK to support this effort. The Third Combat Detachment (*Ships IV, XVII, XIX,* and *Kievsky VI*) was based at Buzcac near the army HQ and by the end of May 1917, the First Combat Detachment (*Ships III, XV, XIV,* and *XVIII*) was based at Jagelnitsa.

Meanwhile, on April 28, 1917, *Ship I* of the Second Combat Detachment crashed in an accident, killing all six crew members. The subsequent court of inquiry reached no firm conclusion, but sabotage was suspected.

During the Russian offensive and subsequent retreat, the First and Third Combat Detachments were at times combined into one large unit and shared a field with Alexander Kozakov's 1st *Aviagruppa* (First Fighter Group). On many missions the IM units combined their efforts with Kozakov's fighters. On one noted occasion seven IM bombers were escorted by 26 fighters.

In September 1917 there were four IM detachments still in place; however, military activities had basically stopped. As the Germans advanced many of the IMs were destroyed on the ground. After the October revolution the Bolshevik government surveyed surviving military aircraft (this did not include surviving IMs held by

---

(2) By the end of 1916, the EVK had received many replacement ships, mostly the newer G type.

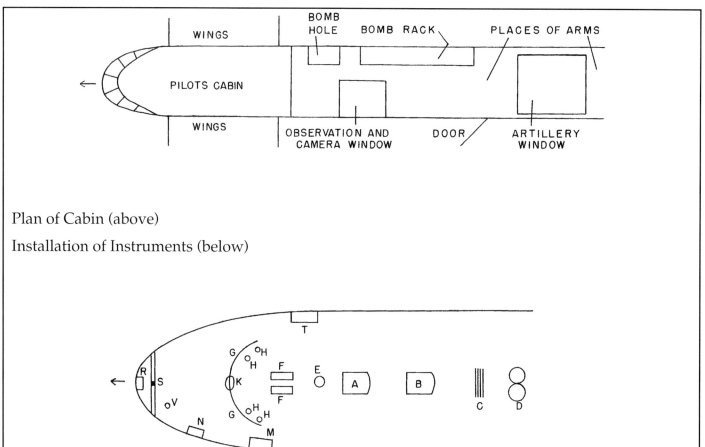

Plan of Cabin (above)

Installation of Instruments (below)

Ukrainians at Vinnitsa). The list included 15 IMs, most of which were located at either the R-BVZ factory or at the Korpusnoi airfield. A number of these were employed by the Red air force and served into the 1920s.

Performance figures calculated during March 1915 suggested the "V" type IM was capable of a five-hour flight with a payload of up to 640 lbs. When extra fuel tanks were installed, the flight duration could be extended up to ten hours. When equipped with a crew of three, and two defensive machine guns, the same IM easily lifted a half ton of bombs. The usual operating height was 8000 feet at a maximum speed varying between 62 and 70 mph.

The Russian army ordered a total of 76 IMs. The EVK considered 38 IMs combat-worthy and accepted those by February 1917. During 1915 the EVK carried out more than 100 missions and dropped an estimated 4700 lbs. (2135 kg) of bombs. By the end of the war, the EVK had carried out more than 400 missions and dropped 44,000 lbs. (20,000 kg) of bombs.[3]

Installation of Instruments & Plan of Cabin

Based on the "V" type Il'ya Muromets, the cabin was divided into the pilot's cabin and the observer-artillery cabin. The pilot's cabin contained the pilot's seat, the co-pilot's seat, and all the instruments required. The observer-artillery cabin was located just behind the pilot's cabin and was separated from it only by guy wires and supports. The general plan of the two cabins was as shown in the upper sketch on page 36.

The pilot's cabin was arranged as follows:
A = Pilot's seat
B = Assistant pilot's seat
C = Small vertical latter to roof and gun position
D = Two compressed air tanks. They were charged by wind-driven generators while in flight and were used to restart a motor while flying if necessary.
E = Small compass, mounted on the floor.
F = Two ratchet controls for feet, which controlled the rudders.
G = A large steel arch, hinged at its two ends, which controlled the stabilizer.
H = Four revolution indicators, one for each of the engines.
K = Control wheel, set on the arch G, which controlled the warping of the wings.
M = Barometer and watch, set on springs and hung from the wall of the cabin.
N = Speed indicator, which looked like a thermometer. Filled with liquid, the level would change with changes in speed.
R = Direction indicator—a simple needle which moved over an arc showing degrees to right and left.
S = Lateral stability indicator—a ball in a glass tube.
T = Switch board indicator, connecting with the artillery officer. It was a simple signal board, arranged with

---
(3) The 400 mission total includes reconnaissance and bombing missions. Depending on fuel and defensive armament loads, the bomb load of a type "V" and "G" Il'ya Muromets was up to 2,200 pounds (1,000 kg).

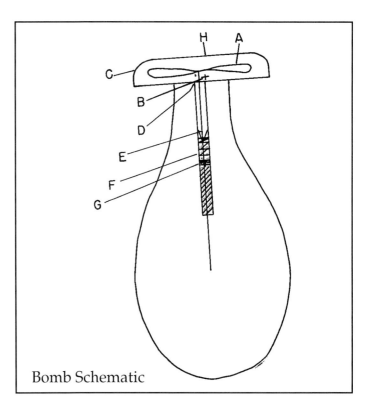

Bomb Schematic

buttons and small lights (18 total), each button and light indicated a prearranged signal, such as "bomb dropped."
V = Small red light , indicating that a bomb had been dropped.

Bombs

The first bombs were developed by the Main Administrator of Artillery and were divided into three categories, depending on the explosive used: dynamite for the heavier demolitions; toluene and troctile for lighter demolitions and incendiary effect; and fragmentation bombs filled with iron slugs.

All the bombs were of the same construction. The detonators came in two sizes—for large and small bombs. They screwed into the bomb case at (D). The simple catch (B) pulled out, allowing the plunger (E) to rest on the spring (F). While the bomb was falling the wind wheel (A) held the plunger up. When the bomb hit, its plunger went down onto the detonator (G). The object of the cylinder (C), supported by skeleton frames (H) and (I) at the top and bottom, is to guard the wind wheel (A).

In this section, bomb weights are given in Russian (*pud*) units. Conversion of *pud* to metric kilogram (kg) is as follows: 1 *pud* = 16 kg.

Conversion of *pud* to English pound (lb) is: 1 *pud* = 35.3 lbs.

Lighter demolition bombs were produced in weights of: 1, 1.5, 2, 3.5, and 5 *pud*.

Heavier bombers were produced in weights of: 10, 15, and 25 *pud*.

Fragmentation bombs were produced in weights of: 1, 1.5, and 3 *pud*.

All the bombs (except the 15-*pud* missile) were carried internally in wooden racks running along the starboard side of the cabin and ending at the bomb hatch. Each rack

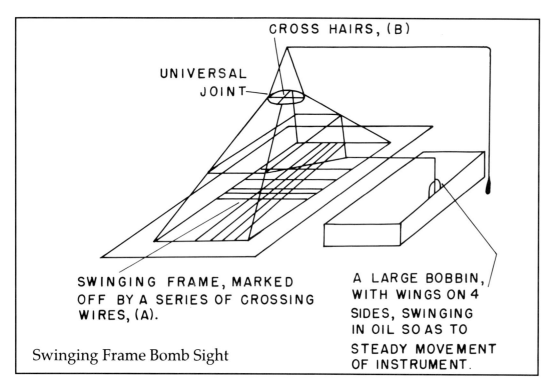

Swinging Frame Bomb Sight

held several bombs at one time to allow a long salvo to be released.

Bomb Sights

There were several bomb sights used by the Il'ya Muromets crews. The simplest, best described as a swinging pyramidal frame, was designed by Igor Sikorsky and found on several "B" type aircraft.

The observer simply looked down through the cross hairs (B) and the squares of the frame (A). He released his bomb when the cross hairs (B), matched a certain crossing of wires on frame (A). Corrections were made for height, speed, and wind from a chart.

The newer "V" type aircraft were equipped with a small bomb sight that stood only about 12 inches (30 cm) high and corrected for lateral wind, speed, height, and head wind, basically everything that effected the flight of the bomb.

For readers in search of basic theory, the following is offered:

Ignoring corrections, the bomb had to be dropped when vertically over the target. This vertical line was determined by means of the plumb bob (E), swinging backward and forward in the narrow, oblong cup (J). On the upper end of the plumb bob was an indicator arm (N). The observation glass (B), through which the artillery officer looked, pointed vertically down. When the plane of glass (B) came into the plane of (N) and (E), the electric light turned on at (C), which indicated the bomb should be dropped.

For those in search of detailed theory of the instrument, here is additional information:

Corrections from the vertical (everything which affected the flight of the bomb in the plane of the line of flight) were done through several steps. To correct for lateral wind, head (I) was rotated (which moved the whole instrument and therefore the line of the glass (B)) to the right or left. To correct for speed, height of the aircraft, and head wind, a certain offset number was selected on the scale (G). This worked in the following way—the ring (H) was turned, until (F) was set equal to (G). Then, as the glass (B) followed the approaching target, the drum (A) revolved under the arm (N). When the true vertical was reached, a catch inside the drum (Y) did not allow the drum (A) to revolve further without moving arm (N) with it. This connection threw on an electric current, which lit a small light (C). The correction used on scale (G) was taken from a plotted chart once speed, height, and wind were entered. The electrical connection made at (C) turned on a small red light in the left eye of the artillery officer, who immediately pulled a cord at his right hand and released a bomb. The handle (K) was attached to the glass (B), and swung to the left or right. To correct for aircraft direction, a scale on handle (K) indicated degrees. The observer read the true course to the pilot, who would steer directly for the target.

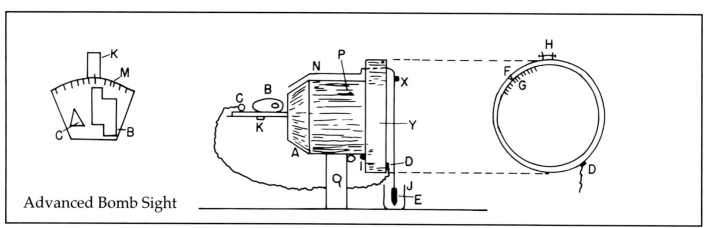

Advanced Bomb Sight

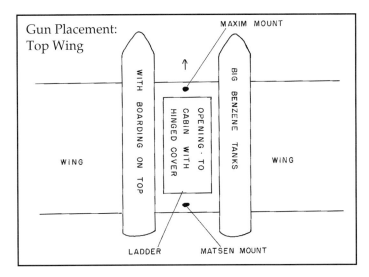

From the time the target was sighted until the photos of the bursting bomb were taken, the artillery officer would lie on his stomach behind the bomb aiming instrument. At the same time, one of the observers would work the camera (lying behind it). At the right hand of the artillery officer was a cord that connected with the bomb rack and released the bombs. The bombs in the rack moved automatically forward until they came up against a catch directly over the bomb hatch. At the right hand of the artillery officer was also the signal board, which he used to signal the pilot. The artillery officer's left hand was free to move handle (K) of the bomb sight. The window in front and below the artillery officer's face was only partially taken up by this instrument, and afforded a large field of view.

Assuming that a prearranged aircraft speed and height for the bomb run had been reached, the artillery officer plotted off corrections for lateral wind and sighted the target. Next he aimed glass (B) at the target, by means of the handle (K). If he noted by scale (M) that the course of the aircraft was off in degrees, he would have signaled this to the pilot by means of the signal board and secured a course which would have carried the aircraft as nearly directly over the target as the lateral correction on the aircraft would have allowed. Once (K) was centered on scale (M), the artillery officer would have signaled the pilot to hold a steady course. At this point he would have plotted off correction from a chart (altitude, speed, and head wind) on scale (G), and followed the target with the glass (B). Once the red light (C) turned on, he would have pulled the cord with his right hand, releasing the bomb. At that same instant two other red lights would have turned on—one in front of the pilot and the other in front of the camera operator. When the pilot saw the bomb light he would have held a steady course for at least 35 seconds, to allow a photo to be taken and the fall of bombs to be observed. The camera operator would have snapped either a given number of seconds after the red light appeared, or after the operator saw the bomb explode. The artillery officer would also have observed the explosion and corrected for any bomb aiming error.

Armament

The Il'ya Muromets usually carried four or five crewmen on a 3–4 hour flight. As the bomb load varied, so did the number of machine guns carried. In most cases, at least three guns were on board. Maxim, Madsen, Lewis, and Colt types were usually available. Although one IM was initially equipped with a 37-mm Hotchkiss cannon for shooting down Zeppelins, it proved impractical and was soon removed.

Bombs dropped from an Il'ya Muromets explode on an Austro-Hungarian railroad line, showing the accuracy achieved by the crews.

EVK crew member displays one of the larger bombs dropped from the Il'ya Muromets bombers.

Section 2

Ace Pilots
of the Imperial Russian Air Service

The Ace Pilots

Contrary to popular belief, the designation *ace* was not started by military authorities but by political bodies for the benefit of the general public at home, desperate for some information about the heroic exploits it had been taught to expect in past wars—the heroic exploits that would keep the populace interested in and supportive of a war that was killing its young men at an astounding rate.

Even today aviation enthusiasts are drawn to the stories of ace pilots. Perhaps this is based on the false perception that the ace, or *knight of the air*, most often is associated with heroism and chivalry; that he alone was operating in an environment separated from the mass killing on the ground. Strangely, the airplane alone, unlike other modern weapons used in World War I, maintained a distinctly romantic aura about it, which only added to the ace myth. This romantic aura may be related to the new dimension of the first war in the air, the terrible fate that awaited so many aviators shot down in flames, and the fact that so many pilots flew single-seaters and depended on their skill (as well as luck) for their success and survival.

In reality, there was nothing chivalrous about the air war or the ace pilots. The act of providing first aid to a captured enemy pilot after being brutally shot down and just prior to his interrogation is one of many acts historians all too often mislabel as chivalrous.

It is true that pilots just waved at each other in a friendly manner during the war's first aerial encounters, but that did not last very long. War was too serious a business even for the air, and the man in the other plane was soon transformed from fellow aviator to enemy. Throughout World War I the methods required to dispose of the enemy aviator remained a major objective and various alternatives were tried and quickly perfected.

Perhaps the number of aircrew dying each day was insignificant compared with the losses on the ground. But infantrymen were often hit by bullets that traveled 500 yards, whereas pilots were frequently hit by bullets fired from only 20 to 50 yards and traveling at maximum velocity. Furthermore, aviators were sometimes hit with a combination of several tracer, armor-piercing, explosive, burning phosphorus, and expanding bullets. In many cases the air war was more brutal.

There is one area where aces undoubtedly merit the recognition they have received. In terms of military effectiveness, aces contributed far more than their share to the air war. Statistics indicate that Russian aces accounted for about 40 per cent of the enemy aircraft shot down, a tally far out of proportion to their small numbers.

All things considered, it took a courageous man to go up day after day knowing the odds against long-term survival. In the final analysis, when one puts aside the myths, clearly what remains is a small group of extraordinarily brave and talented flyers who obtained remarkable success while operating under desperate conditions.

Aerial victories compiled for this book and listed in Appendix 3 are believed to be the most complete and accurate ever assembled for the ace pilots of the Imperial Russian Air Service and for the foreign service pilots. The Imperial Russian Air Service had a general policy concerning the crediting of victories based loosely on that of other Allied air services. Each crew member of an aircraft which significantly contributed to the defeat (not necessarily the destruction) of an enemy airplane, balloon, or airship received credit for one full victory. Those flyers with five or more confirmed victories were considered aces. Victories scored as a fighter pilot, two-seater pilot, or aerial gunner all counted equally.

A Deperdussin TT takes off for a patrol.

Pavel Vladimirovich Argeyev

Capitaine Pavel Vladimirovich Argeyev in a postwar photograph proudly displays his awards. Russian awards: Order of Saint George, Fourth Class; Golden Sword of Saint George; Order of Saint Vladimir, Fourth Class with Swords and bows; Order of Saint Anne, Second, Third, and Fourth Class; Order of Saint Stanislas, Second and Third Class. French awards: *Chevalier de la Legion d'Honneur*; *Croix de Guerre* with 8 palms.

Pavel Vladimirovich Argeyev was born into a military family on March 1, 1887, in the coastal city of Yalta, located on the southern tip of the Crimea Peninsula (60 miles east of Sevastopol). The son of a military officer, his career was clearly established at birth. With little choice, he developed a healthy respect for the armed services by attending various military schools for boys. His final infantry training was obtained as a young adult at the Odessa Military Academy. He was graduated in October 1907 with the rank of *Praporshik* (Ensign), and plunged into an aggressive military career. On November 14, 1910, he was promoted to the rank of *Podporuchik* (2nd Lieutenant) and assigned to the 184th Infantry Regiment of Warsaw. Several months later, on May 12, 1911, he was transferred to the 29th Infantry Regiment of Chernigov with special assignments. Then on December 12, 1912, Argeyev was promoted to the rank of *Poruchik* (Lieutenant) and for the next year and a half he traveled abroad for the Russian army.

Argeyev happened to be in France studying when war was declared in August 1914. Like most of his generation all over Europe, he was eager to see active service. He quickly contacted the Russian Embassy in Paris, and expected to be sent back to Russia. However, much to his surprise, he was assigned to the French service. One week later, on August 30, 1914, Argeyev was commissioned a lieutenant in the French Army. On September 12, he was dispatched to the Western Front with the 331st Infantry Regiment.

Argeyev was wounded on September 23. However, he returned to the front with the 5th company of the 131st Regiment on October 19. Within weeks most of the officers of his company had been killed in intense fighting. Because he was not French, there was some reluctance about placing him in command. Nevertheless, owing to a severe shortage of French officers, on November 5, 1914, Argeyev was placed in command of his company with the rank of Captain. He quickly showed his ability to lead men in battle and by January 9, 1915, he had been awarded the French *Croix de Guerre* with two palms. Several months later, on May 7, 1915, he was also made a *Chevalier de la Legion d'Honneur* (member of the French Legion of Honor) with the following citation: "A Russian national who took command of a company in November. Has shown by his actions great alacrity and the highest energy. He has complete authority over his men. He was lightly wounded on April 17, 1915, but retained command of his company."[1]

Soon afterwards, on May 2, 1915, Argeyev was wounded again, this time so seriously that he was declared unfit for infantry duty. Undaunted, his response was to request a transfer to aviation.

It might seem that Argeyev had seen enough action and that he should have requested a desk job for the duration of the war. Perhaps by today's standard, he would be judged a war lover. Yet his decision was not at all unusual for a young man of that generation in Europe. From age ten he had been schooled in the life of a career soldier, with its Spartan discipline and sense of duty. It was the only life he knew.

On July 17, 1915, he reported to Dugny aerodrome for basic flight training and moved on to Avord aerodrome for advanced training on October 22. He was awarded his military pilot's license *(brevét* #2573) on January 30, 1916. On June 1, 1916, he was assigned to the French *escadrille* (squadron) N.48.[2]

---

(1) Argeyev gallicized his name to d'Argueff in 1915.
(2) French *escadrilles* (squadrons) carried a prefix to indicate the type of aircraft they flew. The "N" in *escadrille* N.48 indicates *escadrille* 48 was equipped with Nieuport aircraft.

Argeyev and other pilots of French *escadrille* N.48, June 1916. Argeyev is standing fifth from the left. (SHM photo B89/1275.)

Although Argeyev had successfully transferred into a French aviation unit, problems apparently existed between him and the French officers. To make matters worse, as a foreign subject in France's service, his future was very limited. French laws of the time would not allow him to receive a promotion to the next highest rank nor the possibility of commanding a French air detachment. Consequently, Argeyev served only two months with N.48 before he transferred to the Russian Front.

Whether or not Argeyev transferred for personal glory and recognition, his personal courage was second to none. Just flying in those days posed a constant danger due to mechanical faults. In combat those risks were magnified. It took a courageous man to go up day after day knowing the almost inevitable odds against surviving for any length of time. The fact that he transferred from perhaps the best equipped air service at that time into the poorly-equipped Russian Air Service says as much for his mettle, grit, and determination as any information we have.

Upon his arrival in Russia, Argeyev contacted the Ministry of Foreign Affairs. In a report he stated: "I am informing your Excellency that I arrived in Saint Petersburg and I have delivered the military mail to the office of the Ministry of Foreign Affairs. Herewith I am submitting an application for my employment in the Russian Army, in the field of my profession, which is aviation. I have served in a fighter squadron of the French Army, till the 1st of August of the current year. The French Government provided me with a private plane of the newest system (Apparatus—Nieuport Fighter—type 17). In addition I was dispatched to Russia, supplied with a 110 hp Le Rhône engine, spare parts and motor, and also a Vickers machine gun with 500 bullets."

By an imperial order dated October 22, 1916, Argeyev was reinstated in the Russian Army in the rank of *Stabs-Kapitan* (Staff-Captain). On November 2, 1916, he was transferred to the 12th Fighter Detachment and on December 2, 1916, he was reassigned to the 19th Corps Fighter Detachment and placed in command, directly under *Stabsrotmistre* (Cavalry Staff Captain) Alexander Kozakov.

Kozakov described Argeyev as "An excellent officer and pilot. Knows his business and likes it. Works hard on the military activity of his detachment. Industrious. Is familiar with business arrangement of French aviation, having served in a detachment in France."

Argeyev lost little time in setting the pace for the rest of the detachment and on January 10, 1917, he obtained his first aerial victory. Although enemy machine-gun fire tore through his aircraft and he was slightly wounded in his right arm, he quickly attacked and shot down a two-seater. Once the victory was confirmed by Russian troops, he was awarded the Order of Saint Vladimir, Fourth Class, with Swords and Bow

In February 1917, the Russian Army's First Combat Air Group and its detachments were transferred by train into Romania to support military operation. The 19th Corps Detachment was positioned near the town of Jassy.

In Russia with members of the 19th Corps Fighter Detachment. Argeyev is standing at left of photograph. Kozakov is standing 4th from left.

A Nieuport 17 of the 19th Corps Fighter Detachment, nicknamed the "Death or Glory" detachment because of the unusual unit markings (white or black skull) applied to the rudder of each aircraft.

However, the aerial activity appeared slow and bad weather generally hampered flying operations for the remainder of the month. Several weeks later the detachment was moved 180 miles north to the town of Stanislav. Argeyev was up whenever possible and contacted the enemy more frequently. On April 21, 1917, Argeyev was awarded the Golden Sword of Saint George for his second aerial victory over an enemy two-seater.

On May 6, 1917, Argeyev teamed with Kozakov and *Podporuchik* Zhabrov on a patrol flight. Argeyev's combat report states: "I took off with detachment personnel consisting of the commander, *Stabsrotmistre* Kozakov, *Podporuchik* Zhabrov, and *Praporshik* Leman at 0920 hours. South of the village Shebalin, Kozakov and I chased an enemy plane down to 1800 meters, but he escaped. Next we moved north and gained altitude. At 0940 we attacked two Albatros aircraft coming from the east. One Albatros started a battle with me. After a short engagement he quickly descended. Although I chased him, I had to stop the pursuit at 1400 meters because of artillery fire at the line of trenches. I fired 430 bullets."

According to Russian troops the enemy aircraft, Brandenburg C.I 26.51 from Flik 1, crashed while on fire in Lysonsky woods, north of Brzezhany. Both the machine and its Austro-Hungarian crew, pilot Parcny and officer observer Ferstel, were captured.

On May 17, 1917, Argeyev and Kozakov combined efforts again to shoot down an Albatros two-seater over

A Nieuport 17 from the 19th Corps Fighter Detachment.

the village of Bozhikul, to the southwest of Podgaytsy. The enemy, *Leutnants* Witgen and Bode of *Flieger-Abteilung (A)* 242, were busy photographing the Russian trench system when they were suddenly attacked by the two Russian pilots. Minutes later, both enemy airmen were wounded and crash-landed near Russian troops.

By the time Argeyev and Kozakov reached the crash site the usual crowd had gathered and administered first aid. The four airmen conversed politely, and the two Germans complimented Argeyev and Kozakov on their shooting and attack. It was remarkable that the two Germans had not been more seriously wounded or killed in the battle. The aircraft had taken some 60 hits and much of the cockpit area and its instruments were shot to pieces. For this victory, his fourth, Argeyev received the Order of Saint Stanislas, Third Class.

One of the most important tactical developments in the use of air power in World War one was the close support of ground action through low-level strafing and bombing along the front lines. Of equal importance were attacks on troop concentrations, artillery positions, and supply dumps in the immediate rear. Some of the more adventurous pilots took on these hazardous jobs in between their regular duties.

On the night of May 30, 1917, pilot *Stabs-Kapitan* Argeyev and observer *Stabsrotmistre* Starskii made a night raid near the town of Stanislav and bombed a vital enemy train yard and troop center. Although they came under accurate enemy anti-aircraft fire, they escaped to their own lines successfully. Then came the tricky business of a night landing, something Argeyev had never attempted before. Starskii leaned far out of the cockpit and over the side to pick up the ground as they glided down. Luckily no trees appeared and they landed safely.

On June 8, 1917, Argeyev and Kozakov shot down an enemy aircraft for Argeyev's fifth victory of the war. Although the enemy plane, Brandenburg C.I 63.75 from Flik 25, crashed on fire west of Vikturovka and was destroyed, the crew, officer observer Paylay and pilot Kimmel, were not seriously injured and were easily taken prisoner. Argeyev had reached "ace" status and was awarded the Order of Saint Anne, Fourth Class, for this victory.

Argeyev's sixth and last victory in Russia was obtained on June 20, 1917. Together with Kozakov, Argeyev attacked an enemy aircraft moving along the Drestr river near the city of Tarnopol at 0900 hours. After a short battle both Germans, *Leutnants* Bolweg and Deter, were seriously wounded and crash-landed north of the village Mihaylovka. The plane, Rumpler C.I serial 4739/16, had more than 50 bullet holes and sustained serious damage to its fuselage, propeller, and lower wings upon landing.

Argeyev's long service was clearly recognized and on November 13, 1917, he was awarded the Order of Saint George, Fourth Class, perhaps one of the last to be given during the war. Soon afterwards the Bolsheviks withdrew Russia from the conflict. Although many Russian officers were now drawn into a civil war, Argeyev chose to return to France and departed Russia in April 1918. Argeyev was a Russian to the marrow. He loved his Czar and homeland, and his heart followed the military tradition that demanded his patriotic duty and his aid in defending his country. However, like many Russian soldiers at the time, Argeyev found it impossible to fight against fellow Russians.

Argeyev arrived in France in early May and quickly volunteered his services. Accepted, he was assigned to *Groupe de Combat* 21 (Combat Group 21 or GC 21), and placed with *escadrille* Spa.124.[3] On May 25th, Argeyev's unit was sent to the front and stationed near the city of Reims. Two days later, the Germans began the battle for the Chemin-des-Dames, better known as the Third Battle of the Aisne.

The German 1st and 7th Armies attacked along a 25-mile front between Berry-au-Bac and Anizy with 19 divisions and tanks. The initial attack was a complete success, and in seven days the Germans had advanced as far as Chateau Thierry and had taken about 65,000 French and British prisoners. However, as with the prior two assaults, the initial progress was finally contained.

The *escadrilles* of GC 21 had participated in many

---

(3) *Escadrille* SPA.124 was equipped with Spad aircraft.

Argeyev's 6th confirmed victory—Rumpler C.I, serial 4739/16. Argeyev teamed with Kozakov to shoot this aircraft down near Tsmenitzi, Romania, June 20, 1917.

combats during the battle and performed admirably. Argeyev contributed on June 1, 1918, by shooting down an enemy machine over Pusieux-Beaumont. However, he was slightly wounded during this battle.

For its part in the defense of Reims, GC 21 was cited two times. Officially the unit flew 209 missions and conducted 36 combats. Four enemy balloons and 12 enemy airplanes were destroyed as a result. To immortalize their heroic participation in the defense of Reims, the commander of Spa.124, Capitaine d'Humieres, decided to place the squadron under the patronage of Saint Joan of Arc. By his order, the helmeted head of the heroine was copied from the statue in front of the cathedral of Fremiet and painted on the sides of the squadron's aircraft.

On June 2, 1918, GC 21 was reassigned from the 4th French Army to the 6th French Army. As a result the squadron was transferred to Francheville, near Coulommiers. There it remained for the rest of June, defending the Villens Cotterets/Dormans Front.

In the months to come, Argeyev became Spa.124's champion pilot, although, like many aces, he was not quite a team player. One of his squadron mates, Marcel Robert, provided this description of Argeyev during an interview with a fellow historian:[4]

"*Capitaine* d'Argueff wasn't a refined pilot. Very rough in his piloting—we tipped him off to it at the time—but an extraordinary warrior and hunter.

"He only liked to fly and fight alone. Considering his background, our squadron commander left him entirely free to fly when and as he pleased. Being of Slavic temperament, he had fits of passivity, sometimes waiting

(4) This interview was conducted between Marcel Robert and Jon Guttman.

numerous days, just watching us fly or sleeping in the sun. Then, when the fit passed, he would go off alone to hunt. D'Argueff had the 'eye of the hunter' to an extraordinary degree, discovering game when we couldn't find it. As soon as an adversary revealed himself, he would charge at full speed, diving to break everything, without making the slightest maneuver, and would not fire until he had closed to point-blank range. And thus, he had more victories than any of us over 'the idiotic Boche,' as d'Argueff called the enemy.

"*Capitaine* d'Argueff was obviously older than the band of little junior lieutenants of which I was part, and besides, he was our superior officer. He was nonetheless quite close to us, liking to joke around and let himself be kidded and joked with, particularly on his errors in French, which he spoke a bit approximately.

"We liked him very much, but I never had any serious conversations with him. It was with our squadron commander, his contemporary *Capitaine* d'Humieries, that he spoke intimately, particularly of his past in Russia."

In addition to his victory of June 1, 1918, Argeyev shot down a Rumpler on June 13, followed by another German two-seater the next day. On June 26, his score reached ten with yet another two-seater.

On July 3, 1918, GC 21 was reassigned to the 4th French Army and moved to the Somme-Vesle/Champagne Front. On July 9th, the commanding General of the 6th Army issued order #600 which cited Argeyev for his fourth victory in France.

From August 16 through August 30, 1918, the pilots of GC 21 hit a dry spell. Although the unit undertook 323 missions, its pilots engaged in combat only 15 times and no victories were claimed.

The situation changed in September. Argeyev resumed

Capitaine Argeyev (or d'Argueff, to use the French spelling) beside his Bleriot-built Spad 13, No. 19. The aircraft of each pilot in Spa.124 was identified by a white number on either side of the fuselage, midway between the cockpit and the white band. The numeral was repeated in white on the upper right side of the upper wing and in black on the left lower wing. Argeyev's aircraft had the numeral 19. Every *escadrille* in *Groupe de Combat* 21 (GC 21) was identified by a diagonal band on the rear fuselage. Spa.124's band was plain white, as were the cowlings of the unit's Spads. Over the white fuselage band was a helmeted bust of Joan of Arc. (SHAA photo B87.3829.)

his scoring with a Fokker D.VII north of Cernay on September 27. Not many pilots could claim "ace" status in more than one air force, but Argeyev could. The Fokker D.VII was his fifth victory in France and his eleventh of the war.

The next day Argeyev accounted for two German two-seaters, one over Manre (at 1010 hours) and the other near Sechault (at 1520 hours) for his 12th and 13th confirmed victories. In early October, the commanding general of the 5th Army issued order #142227 which cited Argeyev for his 13th victory in France. The citation described Argeyev as an "Officer full of initiative and bravery. An excellent pursuit pilot, who has showed courage and exceptional ardor. On September 27th during the course of a combat against eight enemy scouts, he downed one of them in flames northeast of Cernay."

Then on October 5 Argeyev was credited with a two-seater over Orfeuil, and a probable victory over a two-seater at 1125 hours northeast of Autry. His 15th confirmed success, and last of the war, a two-seater east of Quatre Champs on October 30, was also the 26th and final confirmed victory for Spa.124.

Argeyev was cited by the French Army for the 8th time in General Order #12.239 "D" for his 15th confirmed victory. It honored him in a simple statement "A Russian officer, who at the start of the campaign, commanded a company where his superb bravery was particularly remarkable. Badly wounded and inept for the infantry, he entered aviation. Pilot in a French *escadrille*, besides in Russia where he downed six enemy aircraft, came to France at his own request to the French Mission and resumed aviation service where he continued to astonish his comrades with his courage, spirit, and good humor. Has downed nine enemy aircraft, bringing to fifteen the number of his victories. *Chevalier de la Legion d'Honneur* for feats of war."

On November 1, 1918, SPA.124 was moved to a quiet sector near Machauht/Lenincourt. However, this not deter Argeyev from attacking the enemy. He was credited with two probable victories on this date, the first over a two-seater in the Quatre, the other over a fighter near Noirval.

By the time of the Armistice on November 11, 1918, Argeyev had been wounded five times. Although he survived the war, he did not long survive the peace. On September 1, 1922, he joined the commercial airline company Compagnie Franco-Romaine to fly the route between Prague and Warsaw. On October 30, 1922, he became disoriented in bad weather and was killed when his plane crashed into a mountain near Trutnow, on the German-Czechoslovakian border.

Juri Vladimirovich Gilsher

Cornet Juri Vladimirovich Gilsher during the fall of 1916. Gilsher's awards include the Order of St. George Fourth Class; the Golden Sword of St. George; the Order of St. Vladimir, 4th class, with swords and bows; the Order of St. Anne, Fourth Class; and the Order of St. Stanislas, Third Class. The Nikoliavsky Cavalry School badge is next to the Order of St. Vladimir. The lowest badge is an early aviation badge.

Juri Vladimirovich Gilsher was born into Russian nobility on November 27, 1894, in what was then considered the cultural and spiritual center of Russia—the historic city of Moscow, located in the center of the great Russian Plain between the Rivers Volga and Oka. A gentleman by birth, his religious exposure to the Orthodox faith was balanced with social obligations that required he receive the best education available. He was reared a loyal Russian subject, expecting to serve in the army; however, to the bewilderment of some, and in contrast to most young men of his social standing, he did not consider a military career in his early years, and instead entered the Alexejevsky Commercial School of Civil Engineering, located in Moscow.

Gilsher was undoubtedly intelligent and clearly understood this was one of the most opportune times in Russia—the midst of its Industrial Revolution. Moscow had become a center of rapid growth, and there were plenty of opportunities for gentlemen with the correct educational and social backgrounds. Clearly, Gilsher would have done quite well as a businessman with an engineering degree, especially when compared to the crude Russian businessmen then working within the system.

Apparently, many of the industrialists lacked the interpersonal and communication skills needed to formulate and maintain a cooperative work force, and the workers, mostly peasants, were still bound by certain ties to their villages and in constant protest of their socially and economically troubled environment. The poor working conditions, long hours, and low pay definitely helped to lay the foundations of socialism within the new working class.

Gilsher was graduated from school in early 1914. He was highly motivated and clearly showed his ability to inspire and lead people. Unfortunately, his industrial activity was short-lived. War clouds had loomed over Europe for some time, so the outbreak of war in August 1914, was no surprise. Gilsher knew he and his brethren were expected to serve after the start of hostilities, and so on December 13, 1914, at the age of twenty, he fulfilled his obligation by entering the Nikoliavsky Cavalry School in Moscow.

Gilsher was first exposed to aviation in the spring of 1915, while he and the other cavalry cadets trained on the open airfields near his school. On occasion and without warning, an aircraft flew over the columns of mounted cavalry cadets with startling effects. The images of scattered columns, thrown riders, and men angrily shaking their fists skyward apparently had a great impact on Gilsher, who requested a transfer to an aviation unit immediately after graduation from his cavalry school with the rank of *Praporshik* (Ensign) on June 14, 1915.[1]

Accepted, Gilsher was sent to the Gatchina flight school on August 29, 1915. Although he was temporarily transferred to a special air detachment established for the defense of the Czar's Imperial Residence at Czarskoe Selo (near Saint Petersburg), he soon returned to Gatchina, and quickly completed his required flying test for pilot on September 22, 1915.

In early October 1915, Gilsher was sent to the 4th Army's Aviation Air Company, located southwest of Minsk. The air companies were responsible for supplying equipment, manpower, and repairs for the air detachments located in their assigned combat sector. Upon arrival he was assigned to the newly-formed 4th Army Air Detachment, and dispatched to the front on November 9, 1915. Unfortunately, his flying activity with this group lasted only several weeks, ending when his left hand was seriously injured by an airplane's rotating

---

(1) Gilsher was assigned to and actively served with the 13th Dragoon Cavalry Regiment until his transfer.

A Sikorsky S-16 fighter. A mix of national markings can be seen on individual aircraft—cockades on the upper and lower surfaces of the top wing, and pennants on the fuselage and rudder. Gilsher was shot down in Sikorsky S-16 serial number 201.

propellor blade. Although he was not hospitalized, the injury kept him grounded until he was ordered to the Odessa flight school (located near the Black Sea), in early 1916.

After finishing the advanced pilot training at Odessa, Gilsher returned to the front with the rank of *Cornet* (Cavalry 2nd Lieutenant) on March 21, 1916, and was attached to the Army's Third Aviation Air Company, located in Kiev.[2] He was placed under the command of *Podporuchik* (2nd Lieutenant) Ivan Orlov, and was stationed with the newly formed 7th Fighter Detachment, located near the village of Tarnopol, on April 5, 1916. Within weeks of his arrival, Gilsher's unit was required to perform daily reconnaissance flights in preparation for the next Russian offensive, which started on May 1, 1916, under the command of General Brusilov. As the battle continued along the front, many of the pilots were in the air several times each day and frequently engaged in combat with enemy aircraft.

On May 9, 1916, Gilsher was flying one of these long-range missions with observer *Praporshik* Kvasniko when his Sikorsky S-16 aircraft was attacked by several enemy fighters and seriously damaged. Gilsher nursed the damaged machine into Russian territory, but while over his own airfield it suddenly fell into a spin and crashed. The impact was severe. Kvasniko was killed and Gilsher's left leg and foot were crushed. Once removed from the tangled debris, he was sent to a field hospital and his lower left leg was amputated.

Gilsher's wounds should have resulted in an extended recovery period and a discharge from the service.

Presumably, he would have been able to continue his earlier work in industry; having been decorated for the air battle which cost him his leg, he would have returned to civil work a war hero. Nonetheless, to the amazement of fellow officers, Gilsher decided to return to the front and fly operationally again.[3]

While Gilsher forced himself through a very quick and painful recovery that required walking on his prosthesis by mid-summer 1916, he persistently badgered the local commanders about returning to active duty. Although resistant at first, the authorities most likely decided Gilsher's determination and spirit would serve as an excellent example for others, and finally agreed to his request. On November 13, 1916, Gilsher arrived at the front and was placed in temporary command of the 7th Fighter Detachment, relieving *Podporuchik* Orlov, who was sent to France for training.

Within days of his arrival Gilsher built an elaborate cockpit trainer of his own design, which allowed him to determine his physical limitations while safely on the ground. Once convinced that he could control an aircraft, Gilsher began short flights over his own airfield. On November 22, 1916, he flew his first long-range reconnaissance mission with observer *Stabs-Kapitan* (Staff-Captain) Michael Medel. Although he was under heavy anti-aircraft fire, he maintained control of his machine and completed a successful mission. Photographs taken by Gilsher's observer helped to verify several new enemy artillery batteries.

Gilsher's flying abilities quickly returned, and he

---

(2) The Russian Army restructured its aviation sections into four major air companies.

(3) Gilsher was awarded the Order of Saint Vladimir, 4th class, with swords and bows, for the air battle which cost him his leg.

Gilsher in his cockpit trainer, November 1916. While using this elaborate device he became accustomed to flying with his prosthesis.

routinely performed reconnaissance and fighter patrols throughout December 1916. In a letter dated December 24, 1916, he vividly described his daily activity to his sister, Irina Vladimirovna Gilsher.

"Our life is very interesting and intense. Our quarters are not big. It is a landlord's house with a veranda. Many of us live there: two detachments and a division—something like a big main detachment, consisting of six usual ones. My whole detachment was placed in one room. There was a time when ten people lived in one room.

"We get up at 0800 hours and run to the airfield to check the machines and try the motors and machine gun. If everything is all right, we drag the machines to a launching position, and then we sit down on a bench and listen. One can pick up the sound of an airplane by ear, sooner then one can see it. Our comrade observers pass by in their huge heavy machines. They fly off the ground and circle slowly to pick up speed; then they depart in the direction of the front. After a while, one can see the Germans put them under artillery fire; the machines are very often tangled in black smoke. When white puffs of smoke appear at the horizon, it means our artillery has put the German plane under fire, and we have to ascend. We get into our 'BeBe' fast, take off, and start the battle. Last time I was 80 meters away from the German, but my machine gun jammed and I hardly escaped his bullets. The cracking of enemy machine guns is very unpleasant.

"When one's aircraft is in bad order and unable to fly, one can often see how the German circles over our airfield. First, moving away he would position himself against the wind, and then slowly move above our heads and across the airfield. At this point it is necessary to escape, he is ready to drop his bombs. Everybody runs away to hide, in a second one hears the whistle of the falling bomb. One has only a single thought—fall down to the ground as soon as possible. Then…Bang!…deafening thunder, splinter, more whistling, screams of the wounded, and a lot of noise in general. We threaten the German with our fists, and hobble away in flocks. Lately there is a lot of dangerous work.

"In bad weather we go horse riding in the morning. Later we disassemble the machine guns or motors, and we practice machine gun shooting, or we use our rifles.

"We are trying to get all kinds of newspapers and magazines; we all are very interested in politics, everybody without exception."

After a relatively quiet winter of 1916–1917, Gilsher relinquished command of the detachment to *Podporuchik* Ivan Orlov, who had returned from France on March 17, 1917. Within weeks the front was active, and Gilsher was spending more time flying with his fellow pilots, *Praporshik* Vasili Yanchenko and *Poruchik* Donat Makeenok in particular.

Gilsher, Yanchenko, and Makeenok formed as a well-orchestrated team that attacked the enemy frequently, as illustrated on April 13, 1917, when they intercepted two enemy machines that were conducting an artillery observation flight.

The enemy—Austro-Hungarian crews from Flik 7; *Oberleutnant* Roman Schmidt, and his pilot, *Feldwebel* Paul Hablitschek, flying in Brandenburg C.1 67.03, had just crossed the Russian lines with their escort of Brandenburg C.1 67.04, flown by Sergeant Alexander Klefacs and observer Heinrich Szeliga, when the three Russian pilots brutally attacked from out of the sun.[4]

Caught by surprise, both enemy crews desperately tried to evade the Russian fighters, but failed. Quickly, Yanchenko and Gilsher swooped down on the enemy machine flown by Klefacs and Szeliga, who in attempting to avoid them, accidentally turned directly into Makeenok's machine gun fire. Makeenok was an excellent shot; at such a close range he clearly observed bullets hitting and seriously wounding the observer, Szeliga. As the machines tried to descend, Makeenok followed and continued firing on the aircraft. Soon the enemy machine rolled over onto its wings and crash-landed in thick woods.

The other enemy crew of Schmidt and Hablitschek bravely continued their mission, only to be attacked again by Gilsher and Yanchenko while over the village Posechi. While the enemy crew desperately tried to out-maneuver Yanchenko's fighter, their machine was attacked by Gilsher, who, unseen in the sunshine, approached in his Nieuport to a point of 15–20 meters before opening fire.

---

(4) *Oberleutnant* (First Lieutenant) Roman Schmidt would later become an ace with six confirmed victories to his credit.

Gilsher sitting with his dog and unidentified personnel of the 7th Fighter Detachment, winter 1916. The aircraft is a Nieuport 10 fitted with skis. The pilots are wearing heavy wool leggings to combat the freezing temperatures.

The attack was sudden and savage. Bullets from Gilsher's machine gun tore into the Austro-Hungarian aircraft and seriously wounded its pilot, Hablitschek, who, barely able to maintain control, spiraled down in a tight circle while Gilsher continued shooting in close pursuit. Only after realizing the aircraft was seriously damaged did Gilsher stop firing. Minutes later the enemy machine crash-landed with a somersault on the field of Austro-Hungarian Balloon Company 14, near Lesiowka. Gilsher did not see the enemy aircraft crash, but confirmation for both victories was received from the Russian 12th Army Corps—8th Army South West Front at 1525 hours.[5]

On May 15, 1917, Gilsher detected and attacked an Austro-Hungarian aircraft over the village of Bolshovtse at 0820 hours. While he maneuvered his Nieuport fighter into position, he noticed the enemy crew firing both rockets and bullets with luminous trajectories, but luckily none hit his aircraft. Apparently Gilsher's aim was better; bullets from his machine gun had either wounded the crew or severely damaged their machine. Shortly afterwards, the enemy observer stopped shooting and raised his hands in a sign of surrender. Gilsher held his fire as the man pointed down to the ground to indicate a landing zone. He truly believed both crew members were still alive as the aircraft crashed landed south of Bolshovtse. However, Russian artillery had quickly fired on the downed aircraft and scored several direct hits. When Russian troops finally approached, they found Oeffag C.II 52.52 from Flik 11 totally destroyed. The pilot, officer Pius Mossbrugger, was alive but seriously wounded, and the observer, First Lieutenant Julius Hochenegg, was dead. For this victory, his third, Gilsher was awarded the Order of Saint George, Fourth Class.

By late May 1917, Russia's military services had been considerably weakened by political and economic developments. By the end of June, many Russians believed Russia should stop fighting and end the war. Unfortunately, Alexander Kerensky, a politician turned Minister of War, ordered *General* Brusilov (Commander-in-Chief of the Russian Army) to make one more attempt to keep Russia in the conflict. Brusilov's offensive of July 1, 1917, was Russia's last of the war, and launched the Russian Armies of the Southwest Front into Galicia. The Russian Army's early gains were absorbed by the Germans and Austro-Hungarians, who then counter-attacked on July 19, 1917, driving the dispirited Russians out of Galicia and into a full retreat.

The air fighting had been exceptionally fierce during Brusilov's offensive and the enemy counter-attack. The pilots from the Russian 7th Fighter Detachment had flown into battle several times each day, against overwhelming odds. Heavy losses were inflicted on both sides.

---

(5) Gilsher, Yanchenko, and Makeenok each received credit for two victories.

Nieuport fighters of the 7th Fighter Detachment just before take-off, Vikturovko airfield, near Tarnopol, early June 1917. Gilsher is standing sixth from left. Detachment commander Ivan Orlov is fifth from left. The center aircraft is Gilsher's mount, a French-built Nieuport 11, serial number 1232. The other two aircraft are French-built Nieuport 21 fighters in the standard factory finish of overall silver.

On July 4, 1917, the 7th Fighter Detachment was deeply affected when its commander, *Podporuchik* Ivan Orlov, was killed in combat with two enemy fighters. Luckily, Gilsher was highly respected by the enlisted men and officers alike. Appointed as the new commander of the detachment, he had a direct and important impact on the morale of the men. Under his leadership the detachment remained intact and continued to fight while most of the Russian army around it had started to disintegrate.

Gilsher obtained his fourth aerial victory on July 17, 1917, after he viciously attacked an enemy aircraft near the village of Posuhov, (located south of Brzezhany). During the attack the enemy machine lost power and was forced to glide into its own territory before crashing. Once again Russian artillery confirmed Gilsher's victory after firing several rounds on his victims. Later that day he was awarded the Golden Sword of Saint George.

By July 18, 1917, Gilsher was clearly concerned about the detachment's aircraft. The continuous flying required throughout the Russian offensive and enemy counter-attack had clearly pushed many of the machines beyond their normal life span, but unfortunately no replacements were available. In a letter he states "Air fights are going on day and night, but my old Nieuport is not reliable as before. My worn out Le Rhône engine is very dangerous and my Lewis gun is breaking all the time."

Two days later, on the evening of July 20, 1917, Gilsher, Yanchenko, and Makeenok had taken off to intercept a formation of seven enemy aircraft that were heading for the city of Tarnopol. As the three ascended, Makeenok was suddenly engaged in a vicious battle, forcing Gilsher and Yanchenko to continue alone. They intercepted the first formation over the city, only to be surprised by a second formation of eight aircraft that appeared from the opposite direction. Although outnumbered 15 to two, the Russians decided to engage and quickly shot down one machine on their first attack. However, while they positioned themselves for a second attack at least one enemy fired on Gilsher's aircraft and caused it to break up in the air and crash. Yanchenko clearly observed the motor from Gilsher's aircraft tear off its mount and fall out; seconds later the wings folded up.

Unable to continue the battle alone, Yanchenko landed near the wreckage of Gilsher's aircraft and removed his body, which was sent to Tarnopol and placed in a coffin. The next day he was buried in a solemn ceremony in the town of Bugach, in Galicia.

Both Gilsher and Yanchenko received credit for the enemy aircraft shot down. This was Gilsher's fifth confirmed victory. The official report from the 7th Fighter Detachment stated "Our valiant commander entered the battle and was shot down by numerous enemy, while being attacked from several planes simultaneously. In the person of *Cornet* Gilsher the detachment lost their second commander, who carried out his duty for his Fatherland piously, heroically, and with moral intelligence. Let the deed of this military pilot serve as an example to all fighting men, of boundless devotion to Russia."

Nikolai Kirillovich Kokorin

Nikolai Kirillovich Kokorin proudly displays his non-commissioned officer's awards—the Cross of Saint George, Fourth, Third, and Second Class, fall 1915. The Arabic numerals of the 4th Corps Air Detachment are clearly displayed on his shoulder boards.

Nikolai Kirillovich Kokorin was born into a poor working class family on May 21, 1889, in the town of Khlebnikovo, located in Russia's central region. In his youth he attended a small Orthodox school and received what was considered an elementary education. As with most young men in his position, he ventured into the workforce at an early age and began a series of extremely laborious jobs. Although he was noted for his productive accomplishments and energetic behavior, due to his limited education and poor social background his future offered only two solid career choices: a factory worker or a soldier. Presumably, he considered the latter held the possibility of a long productive career that might elevate him into positions of higher standing. On December 23, 1910, he volunteered for the army and was assigned to the Vislyanskaya Mine battalion.

Kokorin's interest in aviation was probably sparked by news of Russia's expanding military air power. By mid-1911 several flying schools had been established and were actively recruiting a small but steady stream of military officers for pilot training. Fortunately for Kokorin, the number of officers recruited did not meet the ambitious requirement that called for ten fully-staffed aerial squadrons by the end of 1912. To meet those needs, the Russian army authorized the acceptance of soldiers of non-commissioned ranks and lower to be trained as pilots. To screen, accept, and organize the soldiers into groups, the first recruitment squadron was established at the Siberian Aeronautics battalion on December 31, 1911.

In January 1912, Kokorin was a mere *Starski unteroffizier* (Sergeant) and clearly looking for an opportunity. Considering his adventurous nature and the fact his present situation offered little hope of change, he successfully requested a transfer into the Siberian Aeronautics Battalion in June 1912. But his aspirations were abruptly brought to a standstill. Within days of his arrival he was informed he was not selected for pilot training and was instead assigned to the battalion's motor section.

For the next 18 months, Kokorin continually applied as a candidate for aviation school. In one of his many letters he states "For over one year I have continued to perform my assigned tasks with zeal. I believe I would provide useful service if I may use my time in learning to fly airplanes. I hope you will look favorably upon this request and kindly send me to an aviation school for pilot training."

On January 21, 1914, Kokorin's persistence apparently paid off. With the formation of additional squadrons, he was finally accepted as a pilot trainee and temporarily attached to the newly formed 5th Siberian Corps Air Detachment. In the winter of 1914 he was given the rank of *Feldwebel* (Sergeant-Major) and, with other members of his unit, sent to the Sevastopol Military Aviation School. He successfully passed the required exams on the Nieuport type 4 aircraft and was given the rank of military pilot in August 1914. Undoubtedly, he learned this trade the hard way.

Kokorin received his first frontline assignment when he transferred to the 4th Corps Air Detachment shortly after the declaration of war. After flying actively with this group for the next nine months, he was sent to the Moscow Aviation School for advanced training. He arrived on July 19, 1915, and flew newer aircraft designs then being introduced—the Morane Saulnier type L, and the Henri Farmans. He returned to the 4th Corps Air Detachment with the rank of *Podpraporshik* (Warrant Officer) on September 4, 1915, and quickly displayed his aggressive nature in numerous combat missions. By December 1915, he had been decorated three times with Cross of Saint George awards (the Fourth, Third, and Second Class medals) for successful reconnaissance flights.

The winter of 1916 was uneventful for Kokorin; however, on April 15, 1916, he encountered and attacked an enemy machine while flying a reconnaissance mission

Kokorin seated in the cockpit of a Henri Farman F.22 aircraft while several bombs are loaded on board, winter 1915. An automatic pistol was the armament.

with observer *Podporuchik* (2nd Lieutenant) Belokurov. The Russian crew directed their aircraft to close range in order to fire their only armament—two automatic pistols. Unfortunately, the enemy crew was better equipped, and as a result seriously damaged the Russian aircraft and wounded Belokurov with accurate machine gun fire. Although forced to withdraw, Kokorin maintained control of his machine and returned Belokurov safely to their airfield. For the aggressiveness displayed by Kokorin in this action he was awarded the Cross of Saint George, First Class.

Several months later, in August 1916, the 4th Corps Air Detachment was attached to the Army's First Combat Air Group and placed under the command of *Stabsrotmistre* (Cavalry Staff-Captain) Alexander Kozakov. Kokorin was promoted to the rank of *Praporshik* (Ensign), and sent with his detachment to the city of Luzk, located north of Tarnopol. As key railway centers, Luzk and Tarnopol were prime targets for enemy aircraft, who aggressively bombed the area on a regular basis.

In the defence of the cities, Kokorin was in numerous combats. But his unit's aircraft were inferior to enemy machines in maneuverability and speed, as illustrated on November 10, 1916, when he was flying a Spad A.2 with observer *Poruchik* (Lieutenant) Grigoryev.

A German aircraft was in the region of Lockachy village when Kokorin spotted and attacked it. Conducting a sharp turn, he directed his machine toward the enemy aircraft as Grigoryev fired from a distance of less than 50 meters. However, no clear results were obtained and, having a superior speed, the enemy crew quickly turned their machine toward their own lines and disappeared.

Only after his unit was re-equipped with fighter aircraft did Kokorin's luck change. Flying a Nieuport fighter on November 25, 1916, he suddenly encountered an enemy machine which quickly placed him under heavy machine gun fire. Banking his aircraft around in a tight turn, Kokorin maneuvered into position and fired on the enemy aircraft at point blank range, wounding its pilot, who crash-landed moments later near the village of Rozitze. For his first aerial victory, Kokorin was awarded the Golden Sword of Saint George.

On January 2, 1917, Kokorin scored another victory. Flying a Morane Saulnier type H fighter, he surprised the crew of an enemy aircraft who, totally absorbed in their reconnaissance mission, failed to evade Kokorin's machine gun fire as he swooped down. At a range of less then 50 meters, bullets from his machine tore into the enemy aircraft and crew. Soon afterward the machine turned over and headed straight down from an altitude of 2200 meters. It crashed near the villages of Vulka and Porskaya. Russian troops easily confirmed the victory for Kokorin, and he was awarded the Order of Saint George, Fourth Class.

On January 19, 1917, Kokorin was again in combat with enemy aircraft. Although no results were obtained, weeks later he was awarded the Order of Saint Anne, Fourth Class, for his aggressiveness.

French-built Spad A.2 fighter fitted with skis, winter 1916. Kokorin flew this type of aircraft during fall 1916. Armament was a Lewis machine gun mounted in the front observer/gunner's pulpit.

Below: Kokorin in the cockpit of his Morane Saulnier H. This was the machine Kokorin used to obtain his victory of January 2, 1917.

In February 1917, the Russian Army's First Combat Air Group was transferred by train into Romania to support military operations. The 4th Corps Detachment was positioned near the city of Monastyrzesko. Shortly after his arrival, Kokorin was given the title of military pilot.

Kokorin obtained his third victory on April 14, 1917, while flying a joint mission with *Feldwebel* Zemblevich. Patrolling the front lines in Nieuport fighters, the two Russian pilots engaged two German crews flying Albatros C.IIIs near the city of Kozov. Zemblevich, the first to attack, quickly forced one German crew to leave the battle. Seeing their companion fly away, the second German crew decided a retreat was in their best interest, and turned into the sun's glaring rays to make good their escape. Fortunately, Kokorin had anticipated this possibility and slipped directly behind them. At a distance of less than 30 meters, his machine gun fire easily hit the machine and forced it to crash-land with a somersault near Russian troops. Although still alive when captured, both Germans were seriously injured.

Kokorin engaged the enemy one more time during April, but no results were obtained and the enemy crew successfully escaped. Then on April 20, 1917, he was sent on leave and did not return to the front until May 23, 1917.

The next day, May 24, 1917, Kokorin attacked an enemy aircraft over the village of Shibalin. The battle was short but vicious. Although he lost sight of the enemy machine as it descended, he believed it was seriously damaged, crash-landing in its own territory. Unfortunately, the battle was over enemy territory and Russian troops could not see the battle nor confirm the victory for Kokorin. However, a review of Austro-Hungarian reports confirms Brandenburg C.I 64.62 was attacked by a lone Russian fighter in that same area. Its crew, pilot Knotis and observer Franz Fasching from Flik 11, were both seriously wounded and forced to land in their own lines. This crew most likely engaged Kokorin that day.

The next morning, May 25, 1917, Kokorin and Zemblevich both attacked Austro-Hungarian aircraft over the city of Kozov. Flying Nieuport fighters at a height of 2800 meters, the Russians engaged and quickly shot down the enemy machine, which fell on Russian territory near the village of Teofipulka. Russian troops confirmed the enemy aircraft was Brandenburg C.I 64.51. Although the machine was discovered intact, its crew from Flik 9, pilot Lager Anton and observer Willibold Patzert, were both dead.

This was Kokorin's fifth victory of the war, but it was also his last. He was killed three days later, on the morning of May 28, 1917, after he became involved with five enemy fighters near Podgaytsy. The most likely victors were the German pilots who claimed a Russian Nieuport east of Podgaytsy that day—*Leutnants* Grybski and Quest of *Feldflieger Abteilung* 242.

The 4th Corps Air Detachment filed a report with Army Headquarters. It simply stated, "Five enemy aircraft appeared above Podgaytsy at 0400 hours and dropped some 40 bombs, which caused no damage. Our flyers fought them, but in the course of the action our illustrious flyer *Praporshik* Kokorin was killed."

Praporshik Kokorin is shown with the officer's award—The Order of Saint George, Fourth Class, which he received for his aerial combat of December 20, 1916.

Kokorin standing in front of his third aerial victory; a nosed-over German Albatros C.III which crashed near Uvse village on April 15, 1917. Kokorin can be seen standing in front of the aircraft (center of photo wearing a light-colored fur hat).

Alexander Alexandrovich Kozakov

Alexander Alexandrovich Kozakov. His major awards included the following: Order of Saint George, Fourth Class; Golden Sword of Saint George; Order of Saint Vladimir, Second Class, with Sword; Order of Saint Vladimir, Third Class, with Sword and Bow; Order Saint Anne, Second Class, with Sword; Order Saint Anne Third Class, with Sword; Order Saint Anne, Fourth Class, with Sword; Order of Saint Stanislas, Second Class, with Sword and Bow; Order of Saint Stanislas, Third Class, with Sword; British Distinguished Service Order—George 5th; British Military Cross—George 5th; British Distinguished Flying Cross—George 5th; French legion of Honor; French *Croix de Guerre* with one palm.

Alexander Alexandrovich Kozakov was born a gentleman on January 15, 1889, in the Kherson province of Russia. From birth, he was nurtured in an environment that supported a strong belief in the Orthodox faith and a sincere devotion to the Russian throne. He was described as exceptionally honest, highly moral, but—most of all—very conservative in his views.

Kozakov's education had been very strict because his parents had entered him in various military schools while he was still a young boy. As a teenager, his studies continued at the Vorohezch Military School. Upon graduation he quickly enrolled in the Elizabethgrad Cavalry School in June 1906. Kozakov completed this phase of his military training on June 28, 1908, with the rank of *Cornet* (2nd Lieutenant-cavalry). The next day he was appointed to the 12th Belgorod Uhlan Cavalry Regiment.[1]

By military standards, Kozakov's service in the 12th Uhlan regiment was short—ending five years later in late 1913, due primarily to his growing interest in the rapidly expanding air service. Like many at that time, Kozakov had developed a fascination with aircraft and requested a transfer. Accepted, he was sent to the Katchinsky military aviation school, near Sevastopol, on January 14, 1914. His aviation training started in February, with courses on the basic principles of aerodynamics. Having mastered these requirements by late July, he began actual flights on the school's Henri Farman type 4s just as war was declared in August 1914.

Kozakov was graduated on October 6 with the rank of *Poruchik* (Lieutenant). The next day the title of "military pilot" was conferred upon him and he was assigned to the 4th Corps Air Detachment.

When Kozakov reached the front, the 4th Corps Air Detachment was stationed north of Warsaw, Poland. The unit's primary function was to conduct aerial reconnaissance and bombing support for the First Russian Army. It was equipped with the Morane Saulnier type G.

Many pilots referred to the Morane G as a "tiny two-seater" because the observer was required to sit immediately behind the pilot on a single, elongated seat. Nevertheless, this monoplane was quite maneuverable and had considerable strength. Normally equipped with a 80 hp Gnome engine, it could obtain top speeds nearing 70 miles per hour. The first of these machines, introduced into Russian service in 1913, were French built; however, soon after, the Dux aircraft factory in Moscow started building a large number of this type under license. In fact, by the fall of 1914, nine Russian air units were equipped with Morane Gs as their primary aircraft.

Kozakov started flying reconnaissance and bombing missions in the little monoplane in late December 1914. With the aircraft's ability to carry several small bombs, he successfully attacked enemy encampments and artillery units throughout the winter months. However, for encounters against enemy aircraft, Kozakov and his observer usually carried only a pistol or rifle. The results were typical for the time—one or two shots fired with no result and the enemy aircraft continued to fly on.

To rectify this situation, in early 1915 several aviators attempted to install more effective armament. Perhaps one of the most interesting ideas of the entire war was Kozakov's concept of using an explosive entanglement system which he dragged by cable below the fuselage of his Morane G (serial number 316). In detail, the concept first required the unreeling of a small sea anchor while in

---

(1) The 12th Belgorod Uhlan Regiment was one of 11 non Austro-Hungarian regiments placed under the honorary commander of Austrian King Franz Joseph I. As a result, on December 2, 1908, Kozakov and other officers of this regiment received the Austro-Hungarian Bronze Commander's Jubilee Medal for Foreigners which celebrated the 60th anniversary of Franz Joseph's reign.

Morane Saulnier G aircraft. This type was used by Kozakov during the first year of the war.

Below: V.V. Iordan's system for mounting a Maxim machine gun on Nieuport 10 serial number 222. Photo: H. Woodman.

flight. Next, mobile blocks packed with gun cotton were released to the cable's end. Finally, after diving down onto an opponent's aircraft and snaring the machine with the anchor, the gun cotton would explode and destroy the enemy machine.

Kozakov successfully tested his invention by hooking a heavy rope stretched between two trees in late March 1915. Days later, on the morning of March 31, he took off in eager pursuit of an enemy aircraft. The flight ended 30 minutes later, with Kozakov crash-landing near his own airfield at Guzov.

Once removed from the wreckage, Kozakov explained to fellow officers, "The damned anchor got caught and was dangling under the bottom of the enemy plane, so I decided to strike across the upper surface of the Albatros with the undercarriage of my plane. I pushed the elevator downwards and collided. My landing gear folded up into my fuselage and then something blew up with a loud whistling noise. Seconds later, a piece of the Morane's wing struck my elbow. The Albatros rolled first to one side, then folded its wings and dropped like a stone. I had switched off the engine, because one blade of the propeller was missing. Having lost my bearings, I began gliding. It was only owing to the shrapnel bursts that I could guess where the Russian front was. At first I went down in a spiral and even turned upside down, but near the earth I was able to correct my flight and landed safely."

Although Kozakov had caused the destruction of an enemy aircraft, clearly his explosive entanglement system had failed. To make matters worse, his Morane G had sustained serious damage in the collision and subsequent landing. It was amazing he had not been killed. Under the those circumstances, it was not surprising that Kozakov tried to play down the incident in his report: "Took off at 11 o'clock with the purpose of chasing German apparatus. Sunny, hazy. Landed at the airfield at 11:30. Duration of flight 30 minutes."

Kozakov's method of attacking the enemy plane could be considered peculiar even by 1915 standards, but few could argue the high level of courage he displayed by executing it. In the end, his comrades admired him for his daring encounter. In fact, the commanding officer of the 4th Corps Detachment filed a more detailed report with the Russian First Army. It stated in part, "The German apparatus was returning from the side of Grodisk and

Kozakov seated inside his Nieuport 10. The gun's muzzle can be seen extending up through the front edge of the top wing.

Below: Kozakov seated in his Nieuport 10 serial number 222. His hand is on the Maxim's standard trigger button.

while flying over the Russian airfield near Guzov, its crew dropped three bombs, evidently having the intention of hitting our kite balloon. Approximately at this time *Poruchik* (Lieutenant) Kozakov deployed his anchor equipment and began to move near the German plane, chasing it from the back. *Poruchik* Kozakov saw that the observer of the German plane turned back and began to shoot. At this point *Poruchik* Kozakov noticed that the anchor did not catch onto the enemy apparatus and he swooped down into the upper surface of the German plane, switching his motor off at the moment of collision. Soon after both planes separated and began to fall down. *Poruchik* Kozakov leveled his apparatus and landed near the airfield at Guzov. The enemy plane—an Albatros— crashed near the bank of the Visla river, killing both crewmen. *Poruchik* Kozakov's apparatus suffered a broken propeller and damage to the right wing. This deed of selfless courage, with the aim of bringing down a hostile plane, is an unusual example equal to the example of bravery shown in the heroic death of *Stabs-Kapitan* (Staff-Captain) Nesterov and must be regarded the pride of Russian military aviation."[2]

With little choice, Kozakov returned to the more traditional methods of engaging the enemy. On April 18, he conducting a successful reconnaissance and bombing flight. The next day he took off to chase a German aircraft which was seen in the region of Sokhachev. Although he forced the German crew to fly back into enemy territory, the battle was indecisive. Five days later, on April 23, Kozakov was awarded the Order of Saint Anne, Fourth Class, with the inscription "For Bravery." Soon after he also received the Order of Saint Anne, Third Class.

The following week, on May 2, 1915, the first phase of a new Austro-German offensive began under the command of General Machensen near the region of Tarnow (200 miles south of Warsaw). Because of the remarkable success of the attack, the Russian armies to the north of Tarnow feared a similar assault. To prepare for the worst, Russian aviators around Warsaw began flying an increased number of reconnaissance missions in the hope of obtaining information on enemy troop buildups or movements. As part of that effort, Kozakov detected and bombed a newly located heavy artillery battery (south-west of Boliliv) on June 5, and spotted several large columns of enemy transport vehicles moving toward the front on June 19.

Other Russian aviators were equally successful in detecting enemy buildups and reporting details. However,

---

(2) In July 1915, Kozakov was justly awarded the Golden Sword of Saint George for his first aerial victory.

Believed to be Kozakov (standing in center) with a Nieuport 10 belonging to the 19th Corps Detachment. All others unidentified, circa spring 1916.

Kozakov poses with his Nieuport 10. The top wing has a V-shaped cutout to allow fitting of the Maxim machine gun. An Imperial Russian crest can be seen on the cowling.

Pilots of the 19th Corps Detachment circle an unexploded bomb which landed at their airfield at Dvinsk on July 29, 1916. This same day, Kozakov obtained his third aerial victory during an engagement that involved 24 aircraft. In the photo from left to right: Lieutenant Korzhenko, Lieutenant Huber, Second Lieutenant Karpov, Ensign Bashinsky, Secretary Golovanov, Staff-Captain Kozakov, Second Lieutenant Kirilov, Second Lieutenant Shishkovsky, Volunteer Shaytanov, and Ensign Bratolyubor.

Detailed illustration of the Imperial Russian crest placed on the cowling of Kozakov's Nieuport 10.

when the second phase of the German offensive finally began near Warsaw, on July 13, the Russian armies appeared stunned and unable to react.

By the end of July, Lublin and the fortress of Ivangorod had fallen to German troops. Warsaw followed on August 5, and on August 19 the German 9th Army took the fortress of Novo Georgievsk, inflicting 80,000 Russian causalities. By the beginning of September, German armies were entrenched in the soil of Mother Russia and elected to halt the advance along a line running from Dvinsk to Khotin on the Dniester River only because of inclement weather.

Except for Russia, never have the armies of one nation owed so much to inclement weather. Naturally, Russian air units viewed the weather differently from the ground troops, because they were unfortunately required to continue daily reconnaissance and bombing missions to track and disrupt the movements of enemy troops near the front. If one considers that just flying at that time posed a constant danger due to the delicate nature of the aircraft, then the Russian pilots were justified in their attitude when poor weather magnified those risks. Kozakov's flight on August 29, 1915, clearly illustrated this risk when his Morane G unexpectedly encountered heavy winds and quickly dropped in altitude. Tragically, Kozakov's mechanic, Peter Kirs, was not secured to his seat and died after falling out of the plane at an altitude of 500 meters.

That flight was also Kozakov's last with the 4th Corps Detachment. Three days later, on September 2, 1915, he was transferred to the 19th Corps Detachment. He arrived the following week and on October 1, 1915, was given command of the unit and the rank of *Stabsrotmistre* (Staff Captain-cavalry).

Initially the 19th Corps Detachment was equipped with Morane Saulnier type Ls (also referred to as the Morane Parasol). Like the Morane Gs, these aircraft also suffered from insufficient armament as illustrated by Kozakov's combat flight on October 29, "Second flight with observer Huber for photographing of enemy positions. Route: lake Dvinsk—Sveten—lake Ilzen, at an altitude of 1900 meters. After photographing the region a German apparatus was observed nearby. We approached the German apparatus and then *Podporuchik* (2nd Lieutenant) Huber opened fire with a Mauser pistol with little effect. Determined, we tried a second attack on the German apparatus, but again with no effect. After our second attack, we discontinued the chase because our apparatus lacked gasoline. After landing we presented the ten photographs we had taken of the region to the staff with explanations."

Nieuport 10 of the 19th Corps Detachment on its back in 1916. The aircraft's Colt machine gun can be seen lying on the top wing. The unit's skull insignia is on the rudder. The 19th Corps received a large number of these machine in 1916.

Ensign Bashinsky standing in front of a Spad A.2 from the 19th Corps Detachment. Bashinsky and Huber operated this aircraft on September 6, 1916, to assist Kozakov in shooting down a German two-seater from *Feldflieger Abteilung* 46. This was the first aerial victory involving a Russian-operated Spad A.2.

In a new attempt to rectify the armament problem, Kozakov approached the head of the 8th Army Air Detachment—V.V. Iordan, an engineer, whose creativity had been responsible for mounting machine guns to several Voisin and Farman aircraft. Kozakov requested Iordan's help in mounting an automatic weapon on a French-built Nieuport 10 (serial number 222), which the 19th Corps squadron had obtained on October 30, 1915.

The result was a Maxim machine gun extending out from the front cockpit at a 24° angle, so the gun muzzle went up through the front edge of the top wing and fired above the propeller arc. An ample supply of ammunition, nearly 700 rounds, was stored in the forward fuselage of the aircraft and automatically fed to the gun by a belt once the gun's standard trigger button was engaged.

The modified Nieuport 10 returned to the front on February 3, 1916. Two days later Kozakov unleashed the new weapon on an enemy Albatros with great expectations. Unfortunately, no clear results were obtained, because aiming a tilted gun was harder to master than Kozakov had expected. Throughout March, April, and May of 1916, Kozakov attacked numerous aircraft without success, but in each case he improved his skills with the new weapon system. Finally, on June 27, Kozakov attacked and shot down an enemy aircraft in the region of lake Drisviaty (near the villages Skipki and

Russian pilots Kozakov, Huber, and Bashinsky pose with POWs, German Lieutenants Mueller and Bergen, whom they shot down on September 6, 1917. Standing from left to right; POW Mueller, unknown, Kozakov, Huber, POW Berger, and Bashinsky.

Shoukteli). Although no other details are known about the battle, Russian troops confirmed the victory for Kozakov—his second.

Victory number three followed on July 29, 1916, after Kozakov teamed with eleven other Russian pilots to engage an equal number of German aircraft that had just dropped 40 bombs on Dvinsk and the 5th Russian Army. In perhaps one of the largest aerial battles on the Eastern Front, Kozakov (flying Nieuport 222) managed to single out and shoot down another enemy plane above lake Drisviaty. The victory was quickly confirmed by order #696 of the 5th Russian Army.

The next month the 19th Corps Squadron was withdrawn from the front as part of an effort to restructure smaller air units into larger air groups. On August 22, the 2nd, 4th, and 19th Corps Air Detachments were assembled into the First Combat Air Group and placed under the command of Kozakov. The unit returned to the front on September 2, 1916, and was positioned at the town of Lutsk.

Lutsk was an important railway junction on the southern front and a prime target for enemy aircraft attacks. To counter that activity the First Combat Air Group was supplied with a large number of Nieuport 11 and Spad A.2 fighters obtained from France.

The Spad A.2 was clearly one of the more unusual aircraft designs of the war, with the observer/gunner positioned in a pulpit forward of the machine's engine and propeller. This aircraft was designed before reliable gun synchronizers had been demonstrated in action. It might be difficult to understand why the French government sold a large number of these inferior machines to Russia. Nevertheless, the Russians were desperate for fighters and in the end the Spad A.2 became an effective combat aircraft in the hands of skilled pilots.

The 19th Corps Detachment clearly supported this assessment on September 6, 1916, when *Podporuchiks* (2nd Lieutenants) Bashinsky and Huber, flying a Spad A.2, accompanied Kozakov (flying a Nieuport 11) in a battle against a German two-seater 3000 meters above the town of Lutsk. Kozakov drew the enemy's attention away from the other Russian aircraft, which then approached to close range and opened fire. Within moments the enemy crewmen were both wounded and their aircraft crash-landed in flames near Kozakov's own airfield. Although the enemy machine was destroyed, its crewmen, *Lieutenants* Mueller and Bergen from *Feldflieger Abteilung* 46, were not seriously injured. The victory was Kozakov's fourth and the first involving a Russian Spad A.2.

Two days later, on September 8, Kozakov engaged a group of seven enemy aircraft 2800 meters above the railway junction of Kovertsy-Rozchishe. In the ensuing battle his machine gun fire hit two aircraft, the second of which began emitting heavy smoke and quickly turned

Kozakov poses with *Leutnant* Franz Weigel, an Austro-Hungarian from Flik 10. Kozakov shot down Weigel's aircraft, Brandenburg C.I 27.14, on December 21, 1916, for his fifth victory.

Below: Aircraft of the First Combat Air Group lined up in Galicia, April 1917. The first four machines (Nieuport 17, Spad 7, Nieuport 10, and Dux-built Nieuport 17) were used by Kozakov and have rudders decorated with dark skulls on white backgrounds, opposite of other aircraft in the 19th Corps Detachment.

west. Kozakov was unable to follow his adversary, but he clearly observed the machine losing altitude as it flew away. It was very likely the enemy crew was forced to crash-land in their own territory; however, this was not observed by Russian forces and never confirmed.

Freezing rains and heavy snow greatly reduced flying on both sides for the remainder of the year. Nevertheless, Kozakov managed several short flights and obtained his fifth victory over Lutsk on December 21, successfully attacking a group of three enemy aircraft from Flik 10. The victims, *Leutnant* Franz Weigel and his pilot, *Feldwebel* Johan Koeble, were flying calmly in Brandenburg C.I 27.14, until two bullets from Kozakov's machine gun tore into Koeble's back and head. Weigel, suddenly aware of the attack, could do little to defend himself while desperately trying to maintain control of the aircraft from the observer's station. Moments later he crash-landed in Russian territory and was captured. For this combat Kozakov was awarded the Order of Saint George, Fourth Class.

In early February 1917 the units of the First Combat Air Group were transferred by train to the Romanian front. In transit, the units were re-equipped with Nieuport 17s and 21s, Spad 7s, and Morane Saulnier type I fighters. The group reached its destination in March 1917 and was initially located in a snow-covered field near the town of Jassy. However, aerial activity was slow and in April 1917 the group was moved north to the town of Stanislav.

From this new location, Kozakov obtained his sixth victory on May 6, 1917, while flying a morning patrol with three other pilots: *Stabs-Kapitan* Argeyev, *Podporuchik* Zhabrov, and *Praporshik* Leman. At 0940 hours the four Russians were flying Nieuport 17 fighters in formation 3800 meters above the village Shebalin when they spotted a pair of enemy aircraft. Although one enemy crew managed to escape, the Russian pilots simultaneously hit the other with machine gun fire. Within seconds, the enemy aircraft was engulfed in smoke and quickly lost altitude. The Russian pilots followed the damaged machine down to 1400 meters, then leveled out because of intense enemy anti-aircraft fire. The enemy machine, Brandenburg C.I 26.51 from Flik 1, crash-landed on fire in Lysonsky woods, north of Brzezhany. Both the machine and its Austro-Hungarian crew, pilot Parcny and officer observer Ferstel, were captured.

Four days later, on May 10, Kozakov obtained another victory during a patrol with *Stabs-Kapitan* Polyakov and *Praporshik* Leman. Flying at 3800 meters, the three Russian pilots attacked three enemy aircraft above the trench system near Sarniki. During the ensuing battle the Russians isolated and attacked what they later described to be a "single-seater Fokker monoplane." After a very

German Rumpler C.I 4739/16 from *Feldflieger Abteilung* 24. Kozakov and Argeyev shot this machine down on June 20, 1917, for Kozakov's 11th victory.

Right: The remains of Brandenburg C.I 63.75 from Flik 25. Kozakov shot down this machine for his ninth confirmed victory on June 8, 1917.

quick battle the enemy machine crash-landed west of the village Sarniki. Russian troops confirmed the victory for the 19th Corps.

On May 17, 1917, Kozakov and Argeyev cooperated to shoot down an LVG two-seater over the village of Bozhikul, to the southwest of Podgaytsy. The enemy crewmen, Lieutenants Witgen and Bode of *Flieger-Abteilung* (A)242, were photographing the Russian trench system when their aircraft was attacked by the two Russians. Within minutes the German LVG had taken some 60 hits and much of the cockpit area and its instruments were shot to pieces. Both crewmen were wounded and crash-landed near Russian troops, who confirmed the victory.

Kozakov's ninth victory followed on May 25, after he engaged and shot down an enemy aircraft north-west of Konjukhi village. Another victory followed several weeks later, on June 8, 1917, after Kozakov and Argeyev shot down Brandenburg C.I 63.75 from Flik 25. The machine crashed on fire west of Vikturovka and was destroyed. Although the crew, officer Paylay and pilot Kimmel, escaped serious injury, both were quickly taken prisoner.

On June 10, 1917, Kozakov attacked two enemy aircraft and forced one to land near Mechischeu. Unfortunately, the victory was not confirmed. Likewise in battles of June 11 and 14, Kozakov forced enemy aircraft to land at Bzhezhany and Stavetyn. However, in both cases confirmation was not obtained.

Kozakov's luck returned on June 20, 1917, when he and Argeyev attacked an enemy aircraft flying along the Drestr river, near the city of Tarnopol. During the engagement both Germans, *Leutnants* Bolweg and Deter, were seriously wounded and crash-landed north of the

village Mihaylovka at 0900 hours. Their plane, a Rumpler C.I (serial 4739/16), had more than 50 bullet holes and sustained serious damage to its fuselage, propeller, and lower wings upon landing.

The following week, on June 27, 1917, both Kozakov and Leman took off in Nieuport 17s to pursue enemy planes 3400 meters above Podgaytsy. Kozakov's report stated "After my ascent with *Praporshik* Leman at 1700 hours to the North of Podgaytsy, three enemy planes were noticed, that were moving from Plotych to Podgaytsy. I attacked the closest enemy plane and after a short battle it started descending to the west. However, I did not see it crash. Immediately, I attacked the second enemy plane, which after a short battle also started going down fast. I noticed it was only at an altitude of 200–300 meters when over Stavetyn woods. Evidently the enemy observer was killed or mortally wounded, because he did not shoot, and as far as I could notice he was reclining inside the plane. The pilot of the plane also seemed to be hit or wounded, judging by his uncertain operation of the plane. Because of that I stopped firing, but when I saw that the enemy plane tried to cross the line of trenches to the North of Stavetyn at the Krosnopolye installations, I attacked it once more over the line of foremost trenches at the altitude of 200 meters, but because of the breakage in the machine gun, I

Kozakov (third from left), posing with the crew from German Rumpler C.I 4739/16—POW Bolweg (fourth from left), and POW Deter (extreme right).

stopped the fire and flew back. The enemy plane was descending but I did not see its final fall or landing. I suppose that the troops could have seen the battle and would give the information. I fired a total of 270 bullets."

Russian troops confirmed the victory for Kozakov, his 12th, just as he and Leman landed. Several hours later, at 2100 hours, Kozakov and Leman took off again to engage another group of enemy aircraft. The subsequent report stated "At an altitude of 3400 meters, *Praporshik* Leman and I came across three enemy planes moving to Buchach. We attacked the two planes that were in the rear from a distance of 50 meters. During this time I was wounded in my arm from enemy gun fire. Because of the wound, I stopped the battle and descended to the airfield successfully. My aircraft received six bullet holes." Moments after Kozakov was wounded, Leman managed to hit the same aircraft with machine gun fire. It crash-landed at Nizhnev, near the Dniester river. The enemy crew and their plane—a Rumpler C.I from *Feldflieger Abteilung* 29—were captured intact and Kozakov and Leman were credited with a victory.

Kozakov's wound was not serious, but it caused a considerable amount of pain throughout the summer of 1917. In fact, several historians have incorrectly tried to associate that issue with a incident that occurred on July 24, 1917. Kozakov's report stated, "During a reconnaissance flight I saw the battle of *Stabs-Kapitan* Modrah and the enemy fighter to the east of Tysmenitzy. Afterwards the enemy plane fell down to the east of Tysmenitzy—near the edge of the forest. I quickly noticed the enemy pilot trying to run away into the forest, so I fired at him from the air. I almost hit him with my gun fire, but he unfortunately managed to escape." The simple truth is Kozakov's actions were quite normal for that time, especially in a war that had nothing to do with chivalry.

On July 27, 1917, Kozakov resumed his scoring with the help of *Esaul* (Cossack Captain) Shangin, by shooting

Kozakov with Austro-Hungarian officer (observer) Theodore Fischer from Flik 18. Kozakov shot down Fischer's aircraft, Brandenburg C.I. No. 269.18, for his 18th victory on September 11, 1917. Several hours after the battle, Kozakov picked up Fischer and Fritz Weber (Fischer's pilot) in his staff car and then took both prisoners to his airfield for interrogation and first aid treatment. An armed guard stands nearby with rifle and bayonet!

Spad 7 used by Kozakov and *Esaul* (Cossack Captain) Shangin. Kozakov flew this machine on several occasions, but never obtained an aerial victory in it.

Left: Austro-Hungarian pilot Rudolph Simacek (to left) and pilot Kopenstein on the Eastern Front in 1917. Simacek was shot down by Kozakov and Shirinkin on September 23, 1917.

down an enemy aircraft over the village Obertyn.[3] The following week, on August 2, Kozakov teamed with Shangin again to attack Brandenburg C.I 64.67 from Flik 26 over the village Hotyn. In the ensuing battle the enemy pilot was wounded and crash-landed his machine near the village of Dolinyany. Russian troops quickly seized the aircraft and its crew, pilot Corporal Traian Varzanon (who later died), and officer observer Franz Slivik. Confirmation reached Kozakov just as he landed his Nieuport 17.

During August 1917 Kozakov obtained two additional victories. On August 8 he shot down an enemy aircraft near Ivane-Pusto village, and on August 29 he shot down a German two-seater for his 17th confirmed victory.[4] Kozakov's report stated, "I met the enemy plane and attacked it over the village Lapkovzy at 1100 hours. After a short battle the enemy plane was shot down between the villages Danjuki and Lapkovzy. The Albatros was from the 24th German Squadron. It was smashed in the crash. The officer pilot, Kaushalter, and officer observer Frenzel, were also completely smashed."

In addition to the two confirmed victories for August 1917, Kozakov teamed with Ivan Smirnov on August 24 to attack an enemy aircraft in the Gusyatin region. After both Russians hit the enemy aircraft, it escaped to its own territory trailing smoke. Unfortunately, no confirmation was obtained.

(3) The enemy aircraft was most likely Brandenburg C.I 26.27 from Flik 20. The crew of Parcny and Ferstel were reported shot down and captured that day.
(4) Kozakov was wounded in his right leg during the battle on August 8, 1917.

Another non-confirmed combat followed on September 7, 1917, after Kozakov and other pilots of the 19th Corps forced down an enemy aircraft near Tlustenky. Kozakov's luck changed on September 11, 1917, and he shot down Brandenburg C.I. 269.18 for his 18th victory. The crew from Flik 18, officer observer Theodore Fischer and pilot Fritz Weber, were only slightly wounded and managed to crash-land near Kutkovez. Several hours after the battle, Kozakov picked up both crewmen in his own staff car and took them to his airfield for interrogation and first-aid treatment.

On September 23, 1917, Kozakov attacked a group of four enemy aircraft in the region of Smotrych. During the battle he was joined by an unidentified Russian pilot flying a Nieuport 17 marked with a black rudder. While Kozakov drew enemy fire toward him, the other Russian pilot moved into the middle of the formation and hit one aircraft with machine gun fire. Moments later the damaged machine—Brandenburg C.I 269.26 from Flik 36—crash-landed near the village Shidlowze, south of Gooyatin. The enemy crew, pilot Rudolph Simacek and observer Leo Onciul, were captured by mounted Cossacks.

Kozakov continued the battle with the three remaining aircraft, but all crossed safely into their own territory, south of Scala. Upon landing he described the bravery of the unknown pilot who assisted him in the

Alexander Alexandrovich Kozakov, circa fall 1917.

Below: Kozakov (first row, fifth from left) posing with other members of the Slavo-British Detachment, circa 1918.

Kozakov shortly after receiving the British Distinguished Flying Cross. Although Kozakov is in British uniform, he still displayed an Imperial Russian double-headed eagle badge on his hat. April 21, 1919.

British soldiers take Kozakov's body to a medical tent after his fatal crash on August 1, 1919.

battle. By commenting on the Nieuport's black rudder, the pilot was later identified as officer Shirinkin from the 7th Fighter Detachment.

In November 1986, the author met with former Austro-Hungarian pilot Rudolph Simacek, who was then residing in Long Island, New York. When asked about the battle of September 23, 1917, he replied in a serious tone "I remember the battle very well. It was the only time I was ever shot down in my life! Our group of aircraft had just crossed into enemy territory when we were attacked by a single Russian Nieuport. The Russian didn't care about being outnumbered so we knew he was good. He hit us with several bullets very quickly and then moved off out of range. I thought his gun might have been jammed, because he just followed us at that point. Unfortunately, while we were all looking at the first Russian fighter, a second Russian fighter came out of the sun and attacked us. I remember bullets hitting everywhere. I was scared to death. I don't remember the marking of the first Nieuport, but I remember the second Nieuport had a black rudder. We crash-landed soon after and were captured by a Russian cavalry unit. I wasn't injured in the air battle, but soldiers from the cavalry unit bayoneted one of my legs so I wouldn't try to escape. If you ever find the Russian who shot me down—tell him to go straight to hell!"

By November 1917 most of the Russian armies had fallen apart and others increased their demands for an armistice. Participation in aerial combat during that time was generally avoided. Nevertheless, on November 26, 1917, while conducting in a joint mission with Ivan Smirnov, Kozakov was involved in four attacks on enemy planes in the region of Skolat. One of these planes was forced down to ground level and suddenly crash-landed at the enemy's front lines. Russian troops confirmed the victory for Kozakov—his 20th and last of the war.

On December 4, 1917, the Soldiers' Revolutionary Committee gave Kozakov the rank of *Palkovnik* (Colonel) and temporary command of the 7th Air Division. However, this group also issued a decree that stated all battle flights must be discontinued. Obviously the persistent combat and stress related to the uncertain future drained Kozakov's spirit and health. He resigned the command soon after and on January 2, 1918, left the front for a field hospital and needed rest.

Although the Bolsheviks continually requested Kozakov's services, he elected to join the British military forces at Murmansk in June 1918. He was given the rank of major and appointed commander of the Slavo-British air detachment stationed at the airfield at Benezniky. Kozakov flew continuously for the next six months. However, during a bombing mission in early January 1919, he was badly injured by a bullet that entered his chest at an acute angle and came out his shoulder (via his lung). He was hospitalized until March 1919.[5]

By the time Kozakov had returned to the front, the situation for the British forces had become serious. As a result, their military units started evacuating Murmansk at the end of July 1919. Although Kozakov was offered a post in England, he refused it. The following week, on the evening of August 1, he took off in a Sopwith Snipe and was killed moments later when it crashed.

Several British officers commented that Kozakov appeared very gloomy and upset before take off. Furthermore, once in the air, he had made no attempt to gain altitude until suddenly going straight up as if to loop the aircraft. However, at the highest point of the maneuver, the aircraft stalled and fell vertically into the ground. Kozakov died before help could reach him. Several days later, on August 4, 1919, he was remembered as his nation's greatest fighter pilot and buried with full military honors in a small chapel in Berezniky. He was almost 31 years old.

---

(5) Kozakov was awarded the British Distinguished Flying Cross on March 20, 1919, for the air battle in which he was wounded.

The funeral procession for Kozakov on August 4, 1919. He was buried in Benezniky, Russia.

Yevgraph Nikolaevich Kruten

Yevgraph Nikolaevich Kruten. His awards include: Order of Saint George, Fourth class; the Order of St. George, Third Class (posthumously); Golden Sword of Saint George; Order of Saint Anne, Fourth Class with Swords and Ribbon; Order of Saint Stanislas, Third and Second Class.

Yevgraph Nikolaevich Kruten was born in Kiev on December 29, 1890. His father, Nicholas Yevgrafovich Kruten, was a colonel in the Russian army, and his mother, Caroline Karlovna (nee Zenkievich), was the daughter of an army colonel. True to family tradition, in 1901, at the age of eleven, Yevgraph was sent to the Kiev military Cadet Corps.

While at school Kruten developed an interest in technical machinery and horseback riding. To pursue those interests, he transferred to the St. Petersburg Artillery School's Mounted Division in 1908 with the rank of *Praporshik* (Ensign). He received the rank of *Podporuchik* (2nd Lieutenant) after graduation from artillery school in 1911, and in April, 1912, he was transferred to Kiev, where he was given the rank of *Poruchik* (Lieutenant) several months later.

As part of a study conducted by the Russian army in June 1913, five airplanes with pilots, led by Petr Nesterov, were sent to Brovary to conduct Russia's first artillery spotting exercise. Kruten became deeply fascinated with aviation after he was selected as an artillery spotting officer for this event and required to participate in several flights.

Kruten requested additional aviation duties and was quickly directed to the 3rd Aviation Company stationed at the Sviatoshinsky airfield, near the western suburbs of Kiev. Shortly thereafter, in August 1913, he participated as an officer-observer during maneuvers of troops of the Kiev military region. At first he was assigned to military pilot V.G. Sokolov and flew with the 9th Detachment in the region of Vinnitsa. Later, Kruten flew with Petr Nesterov and the 2nd Detachment near Gadjach. While with Nesterov, Kruten performed six flights in very rainy and foggy weather, including one at night.

Kruten and Nesterov developed a close friendship, and Nesterov provided Kruten with a signed letter of recommendation that strongly suggested the army transfer him into an aviation school. A few days later Kruten observed, with other on-lookers, Nesterov perform the world's first successful loop of an aircraft.

Although Nesterov's recommendation carried considerable weight, many early military aviators were in fact artillery and ordnance officers because the army believed they were more prepared technically. In January 1914, Kruten was ordered to the Katchinsky military aviation school, located near Sevastopol. A pre-acceptance examination by the school's physicians required the applicant only to state if he was healthy. Upon answering yes, the applicant received a certificate of health and was enlisted into the school.

At the school, students were instructed in various topics. In the theory courses students dealt with theory of flight, how it effected various aircraft mechanisms, and how to avoid major malfunctions while in flight. They were trained to fly in Henri Farman type 4s. These machine were very basic in design—no cockpit, only an indicator of altitude, which was tied to the leg of the student pilot, and the dropper to control motor lubrication. Initially, the trainee sat behind the instructor and watched the operation. The training took only 3–4 hours and provided the basic skills needed for the student to take off, stay in the air, and land. After several flights with the instructor, the trainee would solo. It is not surprising that, after such perfunctory training, there were many accidents.[1]

Kruten learned to fly quickly and was regarded as a very talented pilot who always had perfect command of his aircraft. This fact is illustrated on August 23, 1914, when he climbed to 2000 meters and performed two "Nesterov loops." After that he switched off power to his

---

(1) By 1915 the level of training had improved considerably.

A Voisin LA. Kruten's first victory was obtained in this type of aircraft on March 6, 1915. This photograph shows the unusual firing position the observer used to aim behind the aircraft.

machine and spiraled down several hundred meters before landing safely.

Before his graduation from the school, Kruten was sent to the Lebedev Aviation plant to accept Voisin LAs being built under license. On his return trip he received the news that Nesterov had died in an aerial battle. Kruten took the death of his friend and teacher very much to heart. In a letter to a St. Petersburg newspaper Kruten wrote "The first battles in the air have begun. He happened to be the foremost fighter as well as the Russian hero, the bearer of the crown of glory for the first loop—Petr Nikolaevich Nesterov. Glory to the Russian Hero. Thank God that Russians are this sort of people!"

Kruten was graduated from the school in September, 1914. He was given the title of military pilot and attached to the 21st Corps Detachment. This unit was equipped with Voisin LAs and supported the 2nd Russian Army by conducting reconnaissance and bombing missions. Kruten reached the front in October, 1914, and by late February, 1915, he had flown more than 40 reconnaissance and bombing missions. However, he had not seen any enemy aircraft and each of the flights ended without incident.

This changed the following month, when on March 6, 1915, Kruten was joined by staff officer *Kapitan* (Captain) Ducimetier on a long-range reconnaissance flight over the regions of Sohachew and Ravka. While over enemy territory, the Russians were attacked by an enemy plane. Luckily, after Ducimetier returned gun fire, the enemy aircraft made a steep turn to the ground. On the return flight the Voisin was placed under heavy anti-aircraft fire and severely damaged. Soon after, the Voisin's engine stopped and Kruten was forced to land just inside Russian territory, near the 2nd Caucasian Corps. Several days later he was awarded the Order of St. Anne, 4th Class with inscription "For Bravery" for shooting down the German airplane. Although the two Russian pilots did not see the enemy aircraft crash, apparently *Kapitan* Ducimetier believed it did. Because he was an officer on the staff of the general commanding the 2nd Army, few would argue with his opinion, and this became Kruten's first victory.

Kruten continued to fly extensively, logging more than 25 long-range missions in April, 1915. The mission report for April 18, 1915, read "In late evening, fall of dark, all three Voisins of the Detachment, led by *Stabs-Kapitans* (Staff-Captains) Grezo and Pudi, with *Poruchiks* Shebanin and Kruten, flew out to bomb the village of Sanniki. They separated because of clouds, dropped bombs; Grezo—two (36 lbs.) bombs on the bridge at the town Plotsk; Kruten—one (72 lbs.) and four (36 lbs.) bombs on reserves in trenches in the eastern region of Bauri; and Pudi—five (36 lbs.) bombs on Sanniki. This was the unit's first night bombing mission."

In late May, 1915, Kruten was appointed senior officer of the 2nd Army Air Detachment for his outstanding skills as a pilot and for his bravery. These were displayed one week later, on June 5, 1915, when Kruten was conducting another reconnaissance mission with *Kapitan* Ducimetier. Upon landing Ducimetier filed the following report; "The motor of our aircraft went out of order over the enemy territory, the propeller began to wobble with such power that the whole cabin was shaking under such conditions that the motor could have fallen out. In spite of that, *Poruchik* Kruten indicated he had no desire to become prisoner. He did not switch off the motor until it stopped by itself at the altitude of 300 meters, then he crossed over the Vistula under violent fire and machine gun shooting by the enemy just below us, which made holes in many places of the apparatus. It continued about 20 minutes, and all that time he kept cool, and did not loose presence of mind, and performed a successful forced landing inside our lines." The report followed with a recommendation to promote Kruten to the rank of *Stabs-Kapitan*.

One month later, Kruten received the promotion and was awarded the Order of Saint Vladimir, Fourth Class,

The Moska-MB-bis. Kruten evaluated this type of aircraft in April, 1916.

with Sword and Ribbon. The citation read; "From March 22 to July 5, 1915, officer Kruten has dropped 100 bombs with a total weight of 2500 pounds and 16 incendiary shells. He has carried out three air attacks against enemy aircraft, each time starting the attack by himself. On April 18 and 20, 1915, he participated in night bombing flights alone, while under enemy projectors that illuminated the sky and placed him under heavy gunfire."

In the beginning of 1916, Kruten's detachment was equipped with Nieuport type 11 fighters. Although he mastered the machine in a short time, he realized many pilots were unprepared for aerial combat. Deeply concerned with instilling the necessary skills in other pilots, Kruten began to write the first of what later became a series of six theoretical booklets. In the first, he strived to develop rules for conducting a successful air battle. He defined the classical sequence of attack as: altitude—speed—maneuver—fire. This booklet also provided key information Kruten had obtained from Nesterov and other famous pilots.

In April, 1916, Kruten was sent to Smolensk to form one of the new Fighter Groups. As part of this activity, he was ordered to Moscow to conduct trial flights on foreign-designed aircraft being built under license and a new all Russian-built fighter—the Moska-MB-bis—to determine the flight qualities of each.

On May 20, 1916, Kruten returned to Smolensk and on June 6 was appointed commander of the 2nd Air Combat Group, consisting of the 3rd, 7th, and 8th Corps detachments. Unfortunately, as usual there was a shortage of planes and pilots, and the 2nd Fighter Group did not reach the front until late July, 1916.

On August 7, 1916, the unit established a base near Nesbizh. On August 10, Kruten conducted the first battle flight for the unit. Flying Nieuport 11 (serial 1137) at an attitude of 2800 meters, he tried to intercept an enemy

Kruten entering his Nieuport 11 (serial number 1137). The fuselage, wheel covers, and upper wing surfaces of this French-built machine were finished in a two-tone camouflage pattern (green and brown). The cowling was silver and the under-wing surfaces were plain linen.

Kruten's Nieuport 21 (serial number 4572) decorated with a helmeted medieval knight.

aircraft, but was unsuccessful. The next day, Kruten was in pursuit of an enemy aircraft, but his Nieuport 11 was accidentally placed under artillery fire by Russian troops and he was forced to withdraw.

Kruten's luck changed the next day, August 12. While flying his Nieuport 11, he engaged an enemy aircraft 3000 meters above the village Svoyatichi. His report stated in part: "I discovered the German plane over the village Svoyatichi, I attacked it and discharged the cartridge clip of my Lewis machine gun—47 cartridges. The German flew away somewhere to the side. When I changed the cartridge, I could not find him any more and returned home." Although the enemy crew had escaped Kruten's second attack, their machine, Albatros C.III No. 422, had been severely damaged in the first attack and forced to land near the 9th Army Corps position. The crew and aircraft were quickly captured by Russian troops and the victory was confirmed for Kruten—his second for the war and the first for the 2nd Fighter Group. The Albatros C.III was only slightly damaged—one bullet had broken the fuel line at the carburetor, which made its engine stop, and another bullet had broken the rudder cable. This machine was repaired and used by the 2nd Army Detachment.

Kruten's third victory followed two days later, on August 14, 1916. His detailed combat report states; "Flying my Nieuport 11 (No. 1137) above the airport I saw in the village of Malevo the German plane was flying over Togoreltsy. I flew up to Zamirye; from there I speeded up and kept chasing the German along the railroad beyond station Stolby. I overtook the enemy plane above Negoreli, and cut off his way to his position. He tried to get away from me by diving under my plane. I thrust at him, and discharged one clip at him, but missed. Immediately, I turned after him, and renewed my pursuit, cutting off his retreat while I changed the clip in my machine gun. I managed to approach him from the front over Nesbizh. Again he tried to dive, but I flew at him and discharged the second and last clip, hitting several vital parts of the plane. However I had difficulty noticing it, and the German gained altitude as it moved homewards. I began pouncing on him continually from the top and from the front forcing him to go down to 1400 meters altitude. I noticed that the water in his radiator was boiling over and the motor had stopped. It was clear to me that the German was hit. He landed at the hamlet of Nesbizh and tried to burn his plane, but failed. The two Germans were hardly able to extinguish their own clothing, which was also on fire. I circled over them until the Cossacks and an officer approached them, then I returned to my airfield." The enemy pilot had been wounded in the neck and arm. The fire in the enemy machine, Rumpler No. 615, was extinguished by the Russian troops. Like the Albatros C.III Kruten shot down, this machine was also only slightly damaged. Later it was transferred to the Russian First Corps Detachment.

On November 13, Kruten was selected to join a group of officers being sent to France in the hope they would become acquainted with tactics used in other air services. Kruten was sent to the airfield in Pau, France, in January, 1917. Soon after, he was transferred to the school at Cazau. In early February he was assigned to the famous *escadrille* N.3 and placed under the care of French aces Guynemer and Heurteaux.

In February 1917, a telegram sent to the commander of the Southwest Front stated Kruten had shot down a German plane and had been awarded the French *Croix de Guerre* with palm.

In early March, 1917, Kruten was in Paris preparing to return to Russia when he received news of the Czar's abdication. He called it "the saving thunderstorm that liberated Russia from the Czarist regime." Although many have suggested it was Kruten's democratic attitude coming through, perhaps it was more of his growing anger at the Russian army, which stemmed from decisions made in 1916.

In 1916, the attrition rate of aircraft used by Russian units had increased considerably and a severe shortage of aircraft and spare engines developed. Surprisingly, military commanders viewed increased demands for needed materials as an excuse for not fighting, and in 1917

Members of the 2nd Combat Group, spring 1917. Kruten is standing to right. Boutzillo is standing third from left. All others unknown.

Russia requested French pilots to support its own air service. Although the performance of the French pilots was in many cases very heroic, nonetheless, many Russian pilots resented the 'foreign invasions.'

Kruten wasted little time in voicing his opinion. While in Paris, he met with a new group of Russian pilots on the way to the front. During this meeting Kruten stated, "There is nothing about flying that we could learn from foreigners, and nobody dares approach us in our ability to fly." Kruten returned to Russia on March 24, 1917 and finished his next booklet—*Invasion of Foreigners*.[2]

In early April, 1917 Kruten assumed command of the Second Air Combat Group. The unit was equipped with a mix of Nieuport type 17 and 21 fighters. Kruten's two aircraft—Nieuport 17 (serial 2232) and Nieuport 21 (serial 4572) were both adorned with personal markings—the image of a medieval knight.[3] The practice of applying personal markings was common in France, and clearly met with his approval.

In mid April, 1917, the Second Combat Group was moved to Plotych village, 10 kilometers to the north of Tarnopol. Kruten wasted little time setting the lead for the other pilots. He was flying intensely, safeguarding the unit's airfield from enemy air attacks, carrying out missions to adjust Russian artillery fire, and flying beyond the front lines to support Russian photo-reconnaissance aircraft. In his efforts to intercept enemy aircraft, he was second to none, as illustrated on May 30, 1917, when over Tarnopol he engaged in six different battles during one mission. Unfortunately, the outcome of each was indecisive.

The next day, Kruten spotted an enemy aircraft conducting a reconnaissance flight over Tarnopol at 0750 hours. Flying at an altitude of 4000 meters, he managed to

---

(2) Kruten is better remembered as a tactician than an 'ace' pilot. His booklets were by title: *First Theorist in Fighting Aviation; Air Combat; Military Aviation of France; Manual of Fighter Pilot; Type of Fighter Apparatus; Creation of Fighter Groups; Invasion of Foreigners; Glaring Necessities of Russian Aviation.*

(3) The medieval knight most likely represented the legendary Russian warrior Il'ya Muromets. Il'ya Muromets, as a warrior, embodied the ideals of heroism and courage, a defender of Russian lands against its enemies.

The remains of Brandenburg C.I 64.55. Kruten shot this machine down on June 6, 1917, for his seventh confirmed victory.

overtake the enemy machine northeast of Brzezhany and engaged its crew in a quick combat. After his first attack the enemy plane caught fire and one wing fell off. Moments later the machine hit the ground in the region of Vymyslovka village, not far away from Taurov and Russian troops. The machine, Brandenburg C.I 69.78, was destroyed and both crewmen were killed. This victory was Kruten's fifth.

On June 5, 1917, Kruten was again over Tarnopol when he attacked an enemy machine. He later stated: "I attacked the enemy in the air two times. Evidently, after I fired one Lewis charger clip at him, the enemy observer was killed in the first attack, because one could see the way he fell to the bottom of the gondola and stopped firing. During the second attack over enemy territory, the German plane went down to 1500 meters altitude. However, my machine gun failed at this time. When I fixed my machine gun the enemy had moved far away." Surprisingly, Kruten was credited with a victory for this battle, his sixth.[4]

---

(4) Apparently the Russian Army credited Kruten with an aerial victory for this combat. Resume #3746 for the Staff Southwest Front, June 6, 1917, states Kruten had three victories in the course of this week.

The next day Kruten was descending to his airfield from a height of 1500 meters when he noticed signals indicating three enemy planes were nearby. Despite his low supply of fuel, he immediately started chasing them. Kruten's report stated: "Over the village Mariauka to the east of Denisov, I managed to overtake and at a close distance attacked one of the enemy apparatus. Unfortunately my supply of benzene (fuel) came to an end, but I managed to attack when gliding down for landing. The enemy pilot was badly wounded, but the observer was only slightly wounded and was bringing the plane down for landing. They both capsized at the village Marianka, I got in close to them, and found out that it was a Brandenburg. The second artillery squadron brought me the fuel for my aircraft." This was Kruten's seventh victory. According to the Austrian archives, the plane was Brandenburg C.I 64.55 of Flik 18, crewed by *Oberleutnant d.R.* Willibald Patzelt (observer) and *Korporal* (Corporal) Anton Lager (pilot).

On June 19, 1917, Kruten was returning from a flight when his Nieuport 17 suddenly went into a spin over his own airfield and crashed. He was removed from the shattered plane and died in the hands of his close friends.

An official telegraph stated, "On June 19, 1917, *Kapitan*

The remains of Nieuport 17 (serial number 2232). Kruten was killed in this machine on June 19, 1917.

Kruten of the 2nd Army died in a plane crash at 0925 hours on his return from guarding the picture-taking plane, because his aircraft went into a spin after a sudden turn at the low altitude of only 20—30 meters. In illustrious fights with Austro-Germans, he shot down six enemy aircraft, which fell on our territory." (Apparently one of his victories was not counted in this message.)

Palkovnik (Colonel) V. Tkachev (commander of the Imperial Russian Air Service), followed with a news report: "On June 21, 1917, with deep sadness I found out about the death of highly-respected and beloved Yevgraf Nikolaevich Kruten. In this person, the Russian aviation service lost one more precious jewel, a sincere and honest friend who has gone to eternity. He was an ideal battle commander and a modest hero. He was the bearer of inexhaustible energy, noble impulse, and limitless devotion, and working enthusiasm. May you rest in peace, dear comrade."

Kruten was posthumously promoted to the rank of *Podpolkovnik* (Lieutenant Colonel) and presented with the Order of Saint George, Third Class. His remains were sent to Kiev and buried on the slopes of Dreper, near the wall of Nicholsky Military Cathedral. In 1930, his remains were transferred to Lookyenovsky cemetery.

Yevgraph Nikolaevich Kruten beside his Nieuport 17. This original oil painting is by aviation artist James Dietz.

Ernst Krislanovich Leman

Ernst Krislanovich Leman in the cockpit of his Nieuport fighter. His awards included: the Order of Saint George, Fourth Class; Order Saint Anne, Fourth Class; Order of Saint Stanislas, Third Class with sword and bow; and the Soldier's Cross of Saint George, Fourth Class. This original charcoal sketch is by Terry Waldron.

Ernst Krislanovich Leman was born in Lithuania in 1894. Apart from knowing he had come from a middle-class Lutheran family, no information is available concerning his private life. His military life began with his enlistment as a *Nijnichin* (Private) on November 14, 1914. His first assignment was to the Odessa Aviation School, which might suggest he had a knowledge of automobiles and perhaps engines. Working his way up through the system, by the spring of 1915 he was accepted into flight school. He was graduated a pilot on June 29, 1916, with the rank of *Podpraporshik* (Warrant Officer). One month later, on July 28, Leman was assigned to 19th Corps Fighter Detachment, located near the town of Lutsk.

In August 1916, the 19th Corps became part of the army's First Combat Air Group and quickly developed a reputation for having Russia's best pilots among its ranks. Leman wasted little time in supporting that claim. On August 22, he engaged an enemy aircraft spotting artillery fire on Russian troops. Although the ensuing battle was considered indecisive because the enemy machine withdrew safely, clearly the Russian troops who were in the process of being bombed appreciated Leman's efforts.

An official army communiqué released that day, stated in part: "To Pilot Leman—Hunter of the 19th Corps Detachment. A message of thanks is expressed on behalf of the Army."

Throughout the remainder of 1916, Leman had continued to display heroic behavior during aerial engagements. As a result he was awarded the Cross of Saint George, Fourth Class, on January 9, 1917.

In late February 1917, all the detachments of the Russian army's First Air Company were positioned near the Romanian town of Stanislav. Throughout March and April, Leman was in the air whenever possible, engaging the enemy frequently in what were described simply as intense aerial combats. Although victories continued to elude him, he was again acknowledged for his continuous service with a promotion to *Praporshik* (Ensign) in late April, 1917.

Leman obtained his first victory on May 6, 1917, while flying a morning patrol with three other pilots: *Stabsrotmistre* (Cavalry Staff-Captain) Kozakov; *Stabs-Kapitan* (Staff-Captain) Argeyev; and *Podporuchik* (2nd Lieutenant) Zhabrov. At 0940 hours the four Russians were flying their Nieuport fighters in a formation 3800 meters above the village of Shebalin when they spotted a pair of enemy aircraft. One of the enemy crews quickly realized the situation and managed an escape to their own territory. The other crew, apparently trapped, elected to stay and battle it out. Considering the odds and the gallantry displayed by that crew, many people would have expected a chivalrous response, but the reality of warfare was quickly expressed by the Russians, who simultaneously hit the enemy aircraft with machine gun fire. Within seconds the aircraft was engulfed in smoke and quickly descended. The Russian pilots followed the damaged aircraft in hot pursuit and stopped only because of intense enemy anti-aircraft fire at 1400 meters. The enemy machine, Brandenburg C.I 26.51 from Flik 1, crashed on fire in Lysonsky woods, north of Brshegan. The machine and its Austro-Hungarian crew, pilot Parcny and officer observer Ferstel, were captured.

Four days later, on May 10, Leman obtained his second victory during a patrol with Kozakov and *Stabs-Kapitan* Polyakov. Flying at 3800 meters, the Russian pilots engaged three enemy machines above the trench system near Sarniki. The Russians isolated and attacked what they later described to be a "Fokker type with a single seat and one wing." After a short battle the enemy machine crash-landed west of the village Sarniki. Russian troops confirmed the victory for the 19th Corps.

On June 26 Leman was given the title of military pilot. The next morning, June 27, he and Kozakov took off at 0850 hours in Nieuports to chase three German aircraft reported over the region of Nijilov. Fifty-five minutes later the Russians reached an altitude of 3600 meters and engaged the three German planes positioned slightly

80 THE IMPERIAL RUSSIAN AIR SERVICE

A Dux-built Nieuport 16 finished in pale gray and standard markings for the 19th Corps—skull and crossbones. Leman used this type of aircraft to obtain most of his victories.

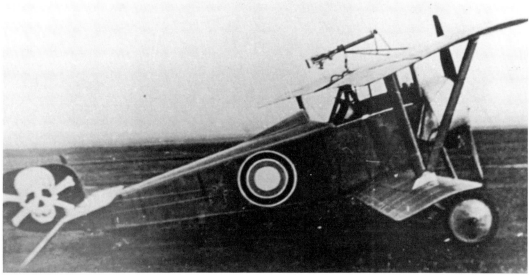

below. In a report Leman stated, "I attacked the rearmost machine. Diving down on top of the German and firing 100 bullets at a very close range, the enemy aircraft emitted gray smoke from the cabin area and went down fast. At this time another German attacked me. I maneuvered to fire, but after a short burst of five shots my machine gun jammed. After fixing my gun I went after my adversary but he lost altitude and escaped to his own territory. I did not notice the first enemy aircraft hit the ground. Perhaps it fell in Tsmenitzi or Nejnilov area. My machine has four bullet holes in two areas." Russian troops confirmed the victory and Leman was awarded the Order of Saint Anne, Fourth Class.

From July to September 1917, Leman was in daily air battles. His fourth aerial victory was obtained on August 16 with Smirnov, and he was awarded the Order of Saint Stanislas, Third Class, with Swords and Bow, on September 20.

The following week, on September 26, Leman and *Praporshik* Krisanov simultaneously attacked an enemy two-seater near Gusiatina. During the ensuing battle Krisanov's aircraft went out of control and soon crashed in enemy territory. Moments later, Leman and the enemy crew were simultaneously hit by each other's gunfire. Leman maintained control long enough to see the enemy machine fall near Krisanov's. Russian troops confirmed Leman's fifth victory and the loss of Krisanov.

The location and extent of injury caused by the bullet that hit Leman is unknown but required long hospitalization. Several weeks later, perhaps fearing his poor state of health, Leman and his fiancée, Lydia Vilensky (a nurse at the hospital), were married at his bedside on October 7, 1917. After the wedding service Kozakov left the front for two weeks to attend a Georgievsky Duma Conference. Clearly Kozakov thought highly of Leman and expressed this in the form of a recommendation to the Georgevsky Council, which awarded Leman the highest honor possible—the Order of St. George, Fourth Class, on November 13, 1917.

Leman appeared to recover from his wound and was finally released from the hospital on November 22, 1917. Although back with the 19th Corps, he was physically very weak and did not fly. No military reports pertain to him until December 17, 1917. On that day, in the early morning, he is reported to have attempted suicide by shooting himself in the head. He died in the hospital several days later with Lydia Vilensky Leman at his side.

Although the Provisional Government under Kerensky had some measure of control during the summer of 1917, the revolution could not be contained. September brought a time of uncertainty; demands for an armistice became more insistent and December brought a revolution in full swing, as the Soldiers' Committees condoned the murder of officers at the front. The Bolsheviks probably noticed the Georgevsky Council's recommendation that bestowed the Order of Saint George on Leman and made him a role model for others. Unfortunately, receiving this award most certainly started the Bolshevik plot to eliminate him and resulted in his death. One should note that during this same time pilots Smirnov and Lipsky of the 19th Corps were also slated to be shot by the Bolsheviks, but they anticipated the plot and deserted the unit.

Members of the 19th Corps Detachment boarding a train near the Romanian town of Stanislav, early March 1917. Standing in the first row (right to left): Leman is second; Argeyev is fourth; Smirnov is fifth; Lipsky is seventh. Kozakov is standing second from top. All others unknown.

Members of the 19th Corps Detachment standing with POW German observer Witgen who was shot down by Kozakov and Argeyev on May 17, 1917. Standing left to right: Lipsky is second; Argeyev is third; German Prisoner is fourth; Kozakov is fifth; Leman is sixth; Smirnov is seventh. All others unknown.

Ivan Alexandrovich Loiko

Ivan Alexandrovich Loiko. His awards included: Order of Saint George, Fourth Class; Order of Saint Vladimir, Fourth Class with Sword and Ribbon; Order of Saint Anne, Fourth Class; Order of Saint Anne, Third Class with Sword and Bow; Order of St. Anne, Second Class with Sword; Order of Saint Stanislas, Second Class with Sword; and the Romanian Order of the Star. Original charcoal sketch by Terry Waldron.

Ivan Alexandrovich Loiko was born into a middle-class Orthodox family on February 6, 1892, in the capital of Byelorussia—the ancient city of Minsk. For the working class, the city represented the region's biggest industrial and scientific center; for the wealthy and socially elite it also represented the region's largest cultural center. Many people settled throughout the communities surrounding Minsk and as a result, endless opportunities existed for the working class. Unfortunately, Loiko's aspirations were higher than the opportunities at hand. Although he had been graduated from the Minsk Technical High School, his family had no means to support additional studies. Most likely bitter, Loiko turned to the army.

His training began with his entry into the Alexeyevsky Military School for young men in 1909. Known for its strict discipline, the school's atmosphere contributed to the Loiko's ideals and beliefs. He was graduated with the rank of *Podpraporshik* (Warrant Officer) in 1912 and was assigned to the 59th Infantry Reserve Battalion. An early report from his unit indicated Loiko had a meticulous nature and that his organizational and leadership skills were superior. These efforts resulted in his rapid promotion to *Praporshik* (Ensign) by mid-1913.

An additional facet of Loiko's personality is revealed in the early months of the war. His promotion to the rank of *Podporuchik* (2nd Lieutenant) on October 14, 1914, was supported with a report commending his courage and bravery in leading men against enemy troops. The adventurous side of his personality is highlighted one month later, when he requested a transfer into the aviation section. Perhaps he was making up for lost opportunities in his earlier life.

Accepted, Loiko was assigned to the Sevastopol Aviation School on December 10, 1914. He finished his pilot training on April 5, 1915, and became a member of the 30th Corps Detachment several weeks later.

When Loiko reached the front on May 1, 1915, the 30th Corps Detachment was stationed near Przemysl. The unit's primary function was reconnaissance support for the Russian 8th Army. To fulfill that role Henri Farman 22 and Voisin type 3 (also known as the LA) aircraft were readily available. Pilots preferred the Voisin because of the superior features it offered—a range of more than 300 miles, a maximum speed of nearly 74 miles per hour, and the ability to carry more than 100 pounds of bombs and a single machine gun for defense. As fragile as the Voisin LA looked, it was surprisingly strong and was considered the backbone of Russia's Air Corps units. Loiko performed his first reconnaissance flight in a Voisin on May 5, 1915.[1] By June 1916, he had safely completed more than 100 missions in the delicate looking machines.

Although Loiko was placed in command of the 30th Corps Detachment on July 20, 1916, to his delight that position was short-lived. Within weeks he was selected to organize and command the newly created 9th Fighter Detachment.

Loiko obviously had the necessary flying skills to lead, but more importantly the Russian commanders believed he possessed the necessary grit. A character reference in 1916 described Loiko as "...an excellent officer and superb pilot. He has total command of the detachment and maintains discipline. He is respected by his comrades and subordinates." Clearly, if Loiko's stern expression did not convey the need for respect, his methods of commanding demanded it and insured he received it.

The simple fact is that Loiko applied techniques which were not generally used in other Russian units. One rule suggested that the most aggressive pilots would receive the best aircraft. Another implied a pilot who

---

(1) Several weeks later, on May 30, 1915, Loiko was awarded the title of military pilot, which entitled him to wear the breastplate badge.

Pilots of the 30th Corps Detachment. Loiko is seated on extreme left with a pipe in mouth. Karl Skaubits is seated, holding a violin; all others unknown; circa spring 1916.

fouled up could easily end up with a less than desirable plane, regardless of rank or title.

Under Loiko's command, the 9th Fighter Detachment set out for the Romanian Front on September 2, 1916, to help support Romania, which had declared war on the Central Powers on August 27, 1916. By early October the detachment was located near Okna (northwest of Focsani) and prepared for action.

Loiko acquired his first taste of combat on October 26, 1916, during a patrol flight with *Praporshiks* Vinogradov and Aleljuhin. Above Mamalyga Station and countless Russian army units at 1200 hours, the three Russians intercepted a single enemy aircraft. Loiko was the first to attack and quickly hit the enemy with machine gun fire at point-blank range. Soon afterwards the machine turned over on its side and crashed near Russian troops, who confirmed the victory for Loiko.

Although Loiko's victory was a joyous event for the unit, by this time the Allied armies were in a full retreat along the Romanian Front. The Germans' beautifully orchestrated three-pronged offensive had placed their units in arms reach of the Romanian capital and sealed the country's fate. By December 6, the Romanian army, having lost an estimated 350,000 troops, desperately tried to link up with Russians to the northeast. To support this effort, the 9th Fighter Detachment intensified its efforts to attack enemy aircraft.

On December 27, 1916, Loiko took off in a Nieuport 11 to intercept an enemy aircraft that appeared over the Komaneshty airport. His combat report stated "at an altitude of 3500 meters, I overtook him south of Okna. Coming close to him in the direction of Poyana—Sereth, I fired my machine gun. The enemy also fired a burst of machine gun fire, but then descended quite low and flew back to their territory. When I turned back to Okna, I noticed another enemy aircraft flying from Okna to Oneshty; I overtook him fast and fired machine gun shots from a distance of 50 meters. The enemy tried to fly away to the south of Oneshty descending very fast, but seeing the uselessness of his maneuver, he turned in a direction to confront me. I opened the fire again; however, after the 15 shots there was a jam in my gun. I had to threaten the enemy with maneuvering, and he was forced to fly around my position. That was a two-seater apparatus, probably a Brandenburg type, with one machine gun on the immovable control surface."

Later that same day, Loiko performed a second patrol and attacked an enemy machine dropping bombs on the airport of the 28th Corps detachment. Loiko stated "after a short time I approached the enemy from the front and I fired 150 shots. Soon after that the enemy machine made a sharp turn downward and quickly disappeared near our lines."

The enemy aircraft—Brandenburg C.I 63.79—crash-landed near Onesti. Its pilot, Jambor, and officer-observer, Haindl, both from Flik 13, were captured by Russian troops. Loiko's victory was confirmed within hours.

By early January 1917, the weather had deteriorated to a point where flying on both sides was minimized. Loiko referred to the winter months as "an empty and dreary time, that clouds a soldier's mind and numbs his skills." Despite the weather, Loiko participated in several patrols each month, but they were of little value.

In April 1917, the 9th Fighter Detachment renewed its activities along the front. On May 11, Loiko and *Praporshik* Strizhevsky attacked one of two enemy aircraft over Sooshitsy valley. During the battle the enemy aircraft became wrapped in heavy smoke and then descended between the river Kasin and Put, east of the Romanian border and just inside enemy territory. Unfortunately, the victory was not confirmed.

On June 13, 1917, Loiko narrowly escaped serious injury after he flipped a Morane Saulnier H during a landing.[2] Although his injuries were minor, the aircraft was severely damaged.

(2) Morane Saulnier H serial No. 732.

Voisin LA. Although the aircraft appeared fragile, its structure was quite sturdy by 1915–16 standards.

More bad luck followed on July 18, 1917, when Loiko, *Praporshik* Vladimir Strizhevsky, and *Podporuchik* Koklin attacked an enemy plane over the village of Vermeshty. Loiko clearly observed bullets hit the cockpit of the enemy two-seater, but not before Strizhevsky had been wounded with two bullets in his leg. To make matters worse, as the smoking machine started going down, it was lost in clouds. Due to heavy clouds, Russian troops could not see the battle nor confirm the victory.

A review of Austro-Hungarian records indicates Brandenburg C.I 67.52 from Flik 39 was attacked and forced to land near Comanestie on July 18. Its pilot, August Novak,[3] was severely wounded and its observer, Franz Firtos, was killed. Perhaps this crew engaged Loiko and Strizhevsky that day.

Loiko finally achieved his third confirmed victory on September 4, 1917. Flying with *Praporshik* Grigory Suk, the two Russians attacked an enemy plane flying 3000 meters above the village Yaslovet. Loiko and Suk simultaneously opened fire at a distance of 150 meters and continued uninterrupted until only 20 meters away. The enemy crew was apparently caught by surprise and did not return fire until both Russians were only 30 meters away. The intense fear the enemy crew must have felt in the first moments of the attack was surely intensified greatly after their machine gun jammed. The enemy observer was now forced to shoot at the two Russians with a carbine. The Russians, realizing the situation, continued to hit the enemy aircraft with machine gun fire at point-blank range. Loiko believed bullets tore into the enemy pilot, because the plane went into a straight dive. Moments later, Loiko and Suk saw the enemy machine shatter as it hit the ground near the river village of Auchavita, between Radautz and Wolowets.

On September 6, 1917, Loiko and Karklin were on a patrol in Nieuport 17s when they noticed an enemy plane flying from Falticeni to Gura Gumora. At an altitude of 4300 meters over Boteschi, the two Russian pilots attacked. While returning fire, the enemy aircraft suddenly made a sharp turn and with great speed headed downward. Both Russians followed in hot pursuit and continued to fire until both their guns jammed.[4] Moments later the aircraft crashed near Teodoreshty village. Confirmation for the victory came from the staff of the Russian 29th Army—region of the 1st Division, which had observed the enemy crash. For this victory, his fourth, Loiko was awarded the Order Saint Vladimir, Fourth Class, with Sword and Bow.

On September 7, Loiko was flying a Nieuport 17 at 1800 hours when he spotted and attacked an enemy two-seater flying 3000 meters above the villages of Arbora and Glit. Loiko quickly surprised the enemy crew and fired 150 shots at them. However, their skillful flying allowed their escape near the town of Raduatz. Climbing back to altitude, 15 minutes later Loiko attacked another enemy aircraft near Radauts at 3500 meters. As before he fired 150 shots at the enemy machine as he swooped over it, but this machine also disappeared. Then at 1845 hours, a third enemy aircraft was observed over the town of Sereth under anti-aircraft artillery bursts. Loiko attacked it two times at an altitude of 3500 meters in the region of Gadifalva, but his gun jammed and the enemy escaped.

The next day, September 8, 1917, Loiko was flying a Nieuport 17 at 1230 hours when he observed an enemy aircraft spotting artillery fire between the villages of Arbora and Glit. Seeing Loiko, the enemy fired several hundred rounds at him and then made a sharp turn away. At 1305 hours, Loiko spotted another enemy plane in the region of Gadikfalva village. However, his attacks were inconclusive and the enemy flew away.

---

(3) Feldwebel Augustin Novak would later become an ace with five confirmed victories to his credit.

(4) During the battle, Loiko had fired 260 rounds and Karklin had fired 250 rounds.

Nieuport 17 fighter being positioned on the airfield for a mid-day patrol. The Nieuport was a very light aircraft and easily moved by several men as illustrated by this photograph. Loiko obtained four of his confirmed victories in this type.

At this point Loiko's aircraft required refueling and rearming. Having just landed at his own airfield, to his amazement, another enemy machine appeared—this one directly overhead. Quickly, he and *Praporshik* Suk took off. Thirty minutes later, the two Russians overtook the enemy machine at 3300 meters above the village of Balkauts. Their first two attacks were inconclusive; however, during the third attack the enemy observer suddenly stopped shooting his machine gun, apparently because it jammed. As he was hitting the gun with his fist the plane started to dive down. To prevent the escape, Loiko turned into the enemy machine and attacked a fourth time at close range. Moments later the enemy machine glided down and crashed near the village Unter-Gorodniki and well within enemy territory. Loiko's fears were realized upon landing—the victory was not confirmed.

The following week, on September 12, 1917, Loiko conducted a patrol with pilots Suk and *Podpraporshik* Sapozhnikov. Over the region of Sereth their group spotted and engaged what they later described as a Brandenburg C.I. Although the Russians had the advantage of altitude, the enemy crew appeared determined and returned well-aimed fire. To avoid being hit, Loiko was forced into a spin and the other Russians swooped up and past the enemy machine. Loiko recovered from the spin and attacked the enemy from below, firing 350 bullets into the underside of the enemy aircraft. The machine quickly turned over and landed soon after. Loiko noted the time was 1030 hours.

Thirty minutes later, at an altitude of 3200 meters, the three Russians regrouped and simultaneously attacked another Brandenburg C.I over the villages of Burla and Yaslovets. At very close range each Russian fired more than 100 bullets into the enemy machine, which by this time was covered in smoke and began to lose altitude. The three Russians followed the damaged aircraft to 1700 meters. Moments later it glided into enemy territory and landed in the town of Raduatz. The enemy crew, both from Flik 44, had escaped death. Officer pilot Georg Altadonna was badly shaken up, and his observer, Adalbert Kuneze, was shot in the neck. Russian troops confirmed this victory, Loiko's fifth, and he was awarded the Order of Saint George, Fourth Class.

Loiko's sixth confirmed victory came on October 3, 1917, with the help of *Podpraporshik* Sapozhnikov. At 1200 hours both Russians engaged an enemy machine over the town of Yaslovets. Loiko was the first to attack, but after 50 well-placed shots his gun jammed. Sapozhnikov attacked next and hit the enemy crew with a burst of gunfire. Soon after the machine turned over, breaking its wing and throwing its observer out into the air. The observer and plane hit the ground near Russian troops, thereby allowing a quick confirmation.

Loiko's military records list him with the unit throughout October 1917. His activities and fate after this time are unknown.

Donat Aduiovich Makeenok

Donat Aduiovich Makeenok. His awards included: the Order of Saint Vladimir, Fourth Class, with Sword and Bow; Order of Saint Anne, Fourth Class; Order of Saint Anne, Third Class, with Sword and Bow; Order of Saint Stanislas, Third Class, with Sword and Bow; Order of Saint Stanislas, Second Class, with Sword; and Soldier's Crosses of Saint George, Fourth, Third, and Second Class. Original charcoal sketch by Terry Waldron.

Donat Aduiovich Makeenok was born into a peasant family on May 19, 1890, in the village Dambovka, located in the Osvedsky region of Polish-Russia. He was Polish by nationality and Roman Catholic by faith. Both of these facts were most likely drilled into him daily, as he was educated in a local parish school. The remainder of his education included three years at a parish trade school.

In Makeenok's youth there was no independent Polish state, save the satellite Duchy of Warsaw. In fact, there had not been one since 1795, when the old kingdom's territory and people were partitioned between 'parent' countries—Austria, Prussia, and Russia. Naturally, each of the 'parent' counties believed people in their newly acquired segment could serve as a buffer against invading armies. To encourage those thoughts within the territories, each of the three counties publicly claimed to embrace the Polish people, despite the reality that each established rules aimed at destroying any nationalism that might have existed. Perhaps Russia's half-truths of helping Poles were more believable than those of Austria and Prussia. Why not—Russia was the self-proclaimed guardian of the Slavic nations. In any case, all three counties failed to convert Poles, and in the end a strong Polish nationalism survived.

Makeenok was, like many in Polish-Russia, proud of his heritage and resentful of Russian control. Unfortunately, these same people needed work and the Russian army was often their only choice. Makeenok was no exception, and he enlisted in the Russian army on November 20, 1911, and was assigned to the 97th Livland Infantry Regiment.

By late 1911, Russia's army was expanding its air power. The plan called for additional aviation units to be fully staffed with pilots by late 1912. However, difficulties were soon found in recruiting officers for pilot training. After much consideration, this problem was alleviated by also opening applications to enlisted men.

Seeing an opportunity, Makeenok requested a transfer to the air service in December, 1911. His application was approved in the winter of 1912, and on April 4 he was transferred to the newly formed 3rd Corps Detachment, located in the southwest.

On June 10, 1912, Makeenok was sent to the Sevastopol Aviation School for pilot training on the Nieuport type 4. He was graduated on March 7, 1914, with the rank of *Starski unteroffizier* (Sergeant) and returned to the 3rd Corps Detachment in April, 1914. On the eve of war he was promoted to *Feldwebel* (Sergeant-Major).

Before the start of hostilities in 1914, many Poles were torn between Polish nationalism and military obligations to a "parent county." With the understanding that Poland would be one of the main theaters of the conflict, and as nearly one million Poles were mobilized by one side or the other, the importance of Poland was clearly recognized. To counter anti-Russian sentiments encouraged by Germany, on August 14, 1914, Grand Duke Nicholas issued a proclamation calling all Poles to support Russia and promised in return a united, free, and democratic Poland under the Russian crown. In Polish-Russia the educated opinion as a whole was now enthusiastically for the war. The fact that Russia had England and France on its side seemed the main guarantee for the fulfillment of the Russian promise.

In September, 1914, Makeenok was sent back to flight school for training on the Morane Saulnier type L. These machines were ordered in large numbers from France and later built by the hundreds in Russian factories. Generally, the Morane Saulnier type L was not a particularly remarkable airplane. Its most important features were its 150-pound bomb load and the stable platform the aircraft offered during photo-reconnaissance. In addition, the type L offered a maximum speed of 72 mph and an endurance

The Nieuport IV. Makeenok flew this type of aircraft during the first months of the war.

of 2.5 hours. Although crewmen tried to mount a single machine gun, the aircraft's structure usually limited its use, and as a result carbines were normally carried.

Makeenok passed all training requirements by November 19 and returned to his unit in December, 1914. After a relatively quiet winter, he began to fly combat patrols daily in the type Ls. On June 19, 1915, he was promoted to the rank of *Podpraporshik* (Warrant Officer) and awarded the Cross of Saint George, Fourth Class, for his battle services. By August 1915, the Crosses of Saint George, Third and Second Class, were also presented to him.

For the next ten months, Makeenok continued to fly with the 3rd Corps. Although he had distinguished himself with a further promotion to *Praporshik* (Ensign) on October 3, 1915, and received the title of military pilot in January, 1916, by spring he was clearly looking for a career change.

Timing is sometimes everything. Fortunately for Makeenok, his was perfect. His desire for transfer peaked in the summer of 1916, while the Russian army was reorganizing its air units.

Makeenok requested a position in one of the newly-formed fighter units and was immediately accepted. He was sent to Odessa for advanced pilot training on the Nieuport type 11. He was graduated on August 12 and promoted to the rank of *Podporuchik* (2nd Lieutenant). In December, 1916, he was placed under the command of Podporuchik Ivan Orlov and was stationed with the 7th Fighter Detachment, located near the village of Tarnopol.

Pilots of the 7th Fighter Detachment possessed generally similar personalities—quiet, reserved, and modest on the ground, intensely aggressive and determined in the air. For the most part, Makeenok was no different. A report concerning him issued in 1917 stated in part: "*Praporshik* Makeenok fits in quite well. He is a pilot of extreme courage; he not only excellently fulfills the tasks directed to him, but volunteers to undertake difficult flights, and carries them out superbly. He also understands very well the technical side of the flight. Loves his work. Has quiet disposition. He is the best person for fighter aviation, though he carries out just as well all other tasks."

By early February, 1917, Makeenok had been involved in several intense combats, but in each case the enemy managed to escape. Determined to score a victory, he soon realized his chances would improve greatly with a dependable and courageous companion. It should be no surprise he identified with *Praporshik* Vasili Yanchenko, a seasoned veteran with three confirmed kills to his credit.[1] Within a short time, the two pilots were discussing various methods for destroying an adversary, and in the process developed an exceptionally strong friendship.

By late February, 1917, Makeenok and Yanchenko had fine-tuned their tactics and were clearly waiting for an opportunity to present itself. Fortunately, the wait was a short one. On March 7, 1917, while flying a patrol with Yanchenko 2200 meters above the village of Svistelniki, the two Russians spotted and quickly engaged an enemy machine. In the ensuing battle the enemy aircraft was seriously damaged and raced for safety. Makeenok and Yanchenko followed it down to 400 meters and attacked it again just over the enemy's first trench system. Moments later the aircraft crash-landed just inside enemy territory, near Lipitza-Gura. Russian troops confirmed the victory for both pilots—Makeenok's first and Yanchenko's fourth.

On April 13, 1917, Makeenok and Yanchenko teamed up with fellow pilot *Cornet* (2nd Lieutenant, cavalry) Juri Gilsher to intercept two enemy aircraft reported in Russian territory. By Makeenok's own account, "At 0845 hours our group flew up to pursue two enemy planes in the region of Stanislavov. We attacked them in the region

---

1) Vasili Yanchenko finished the war with 16 confirmed victories.

Morane Sauliner L. Makeenok performed more than 100 missions with this type of aircraft. Although the Morane Sauliner L was well received by pilots, it required continuous maintenance. This photo shows ground crews adjusting the support cables that ran from the center pylon to the wing.

of Lysets. I stayed lower in altitude than the other pilots. During our battle, military pilot *Praporshik* Yanchenko, in a Morane Monocock (sic), attacked the enemy from above and forced him to descend to my altitude, which helped me to attack successfully. After my attack, the enemy started to fall down, rolled over the wing to the west of Maydansky Buda. Not reaching this area, it fell into the woods catching fire."[2]

This enemy machine was Brandenburg C.I 67.04 from Flik 7. The pilot, *Feldwebel* Alexander Klefacs, escaped serious injury. However, his observer, Heinrich Szeliga, had been wounded by Makeenok, and their aircraft was destroyed.

The other enemy machine, Brandenburg C.I 67.03, was also from Flik 7. Its crew of *Oberleutnant* Roman Schmidt and his pilot, *Feldwebel* Paul Hablitschik, were still being attacked by Gilsher and Yanchenko. Within moments, Hablitschek was also wounded and he was barely able to maintain control. His machine spiraled down in a tight circle and crash-landed in enemy territory near Lesiowka.

Confirmation for both victories arrived by Russian 12th Army Corps, 8th Army, Southwest Front, at 1525 hours. Makeenok, Yanchenko, and Gilsher each received credit for two victories.

On April 16, Makeenok obtained his fourth victory after a quick battle above the region of Yamritsa. Russian troops confirmed the enemy aircraft crash-landed in the region of Kozeyarki.

Two weeks later, on April 29, Makeenok attacked a plane near Kosjarko. After his first pass, the enemy aircraft rolled over, dove down to Kosjarki, and crash-landed there. Unfortunately, this victory was not confirmed.

By late May, 1917, the Russian army under General Brusilov was preparing for its next offensive. As large numbers of Russian troops assembled near the front, the most serious concern was to remain undetected from the air. To minimize that threat, the pilots of the 7th Fighter Detachment were to intensify their activities to intercept enemy aircraft.

As part of this effort, on June 29, 1917, Makeenok attacked an enemy plane above the region of Potootory station. After a short battle it descended and crash-landed beyond the enemy trenches near Martchenuva village. This was Makeenok's fifth victory; he had reached 'ace' status.

Three days later, on July 1, 1917, the Russian army launched its offensive. The air fighting was exceptionally fierce during the battle and heavy losses were inflicted on both sides. On July 4, *Podporuchik* Ivan Orlov, commander of the 7th Fighter Detachment, was shot down and killed in a battle against four enemy fighters, and Juri Gilsher assumed command.

On July 6, 1917, Makeenok teamed with Yanchenko to conduct a reconnaissance of enemy positions. While the two Russians were photographing artillery batteries north of Brzezhany, an enemy aircraft attacked Yanchenko's Nieuport 17. Fortunately, no damage was caused and Makeenok responded very quickly. He maneuvered his Nieuport 17 behind the enemy machine and hit it with machine gun fire. As the enemy descended to 1400 meters, both Makeenok and Yanchenko attacked a second time. Within minutes, the aircraft turned over and hit the ground just inside enemy territory, near Lapshin village. The victory was confirmed by Russian troops.

Five days later, on July 11, 1917, Makeenok joined

---

2) Morane Monocock is referring to a Morane Sauliner type H.

Makeenok, standing second from left, scored several of his victories in this Nieuport 17. This machine's unusual markings included a rudder adorned with a white owl on black shield. The side of the fuselage has a painting depicting a young girl in white dress, carrying a sword and cross. An unfurling flag is located diagonally from her right arm and flowing down across her feet. The flag's colors are unknown but presumed to be Polish in nature. Reportedly, this image was applied to both sides of the aircraft.

Yanchenko again and attacked a group of four enemy planes above Brzezhany. In the ensuing battle the two Russians isolated one machine and, after a short fight, caused it to descend while emitting thick smoke. The machine crashed soon after, marking what was probably the last lucky day of the war for the pilots of 7th Fighter Detachment.

In the late evening of July 20, Makeenok, Yanchenko, and Gilsher took off to intercept a formation of eight enemy aircraft heading for Tarnopol. However, minutes into the flight, Makeenok was attacked and forced into battle with a single enemy fighter. Although Makeenok managed to escape, the intensity of the battle drew him away from Yanchenko and Gilsher, who continued on to intercept the larger formation alone.

Later that night, Makeenok discovered that Yanchenko and Gilsher were surprised by a second formation of enemy aircraft. In the ensuing battle, while out-numbered 16 to two, *Cornet* Juri Gilsher was killed after his aircraft fell apart in the air.

Several weeks later, on August 5, 1917, Makeenok and Yanchenko spotted an enemy aircraft attacking a Russian reconnaissance machine photographing the enemy trench system. The two Russians dove down onto the enemy aircraft and quickly hit it with machine gun fire. Soon after, it turned over and crashed near Brzezhany.

Although Russian troops confirmed the victory for Makeenok, his eighth, he had been seriously wounded in the battle. He was sent to a hospital at Sevastopol to recuperate from his wound. While there he was promoted to the rank of *Poruchik* (Lieutenant) on September 27, 1917.

On November 8, 1917, he returned to the front. However, by this time most of the Russian military units had ended all hostilities.

Makeenok returned to what was German-occupied Poland in 1918. After World War I ended, he learned that the remnants of the Russian-Polish army were reforming. Makeenok offered his services and in 1919 was elected to a commission responsible for selecting a plant to produce aircraft in Poland. The commission selected the Plage and Laskiewics factory in Lublin, which started with license production of Ansaldo planes soon after.

Makeenok was given the command of the 3rd Polish Squadron just before the Russo-Polish war of 1920. Poland started the war to preempt a Russian attack to expel Polish nationals from disputed frontier territory. The Poles stopped the Russians' advance in the battle of Warsaw in August 1920, and defeated them again at the battle of the Niemen and Schara in September, 1920. Hostilities ended with an armistice on October 12, and by the Treaty of Riga on March 18, 1921, Russia agreed to all of Poland's territorial claims. Poland had finally gained its independence.

Makeenok survived the Russo-Polish conflict and remained commander of the 3rd squadron until the end of 1921. Unfortunately, no further information on him is available after this date.

Makeenok's skill as a fighter earned him eight confirmed victories, ranking him fifth among the aces of the Russian Empire. Furthermore, he has the unique distinction of being the only Polish air ace of World War I.

Ivan Alexandrovich Orlov

Nijnichin Ivan Alexandrovich Orlov, September 1914. The Arabic numeral of the 5th Corps Air Detachment is clearly displayed on his shoulder boards. The Cross of Saint George, Fourth Class, is the uppermost award attached to the left breast of his shirt.

Ivan Alexandrovich Orlov was born into Russian nobility on January 19, 1895, in the capital of St. Petersburg. St. Petersburg was not only the center of power—housing the Czar's residence and the great offices of State—but also the splendid repository of art. It was in St. Petersburg that Russia's modern literature and ballet was born, and it was also the home of the Faberge craftsmen who created exquisite objects for the collections of royalty and millionaires.

Unfortunately, in the twilight of the Czar's empire, it was in St. Petersburg that troops were ordered to disperse a workers' demonstration on Bloody Sunday in 1905, and here, too, the fate of the 1917 revolution was finally sealed when the Provisional Government was ousted from the Winter Palace, and the Bolsheviks took over the capital and the country[1].

To understand and appreciate Orlov's life, one has to look at these links. His was the opulent world of silver spoons that tarnished and quickly faded before his eyes.

(1) St. Petersburg was renamed Petrograd from 1914 until 1924.

In his youth, Orlov's life was carefree. After attending a local air show he developed an interest in aviation. At first, his family perceived this as the latest in a series of short-lived hobbies. However, to their amazement, his interest in aviation did not fade; in fact, it became an obsession.

From a generous allowance bestowed upon Orlov by his father, he purchased all the required materials and built several gliders as a boy. Then in 1913, he built his own powered aircraft and christened it "Orlov Number 1." Soon after, he became a member of the All-Russian Aero Club of St. Petersburg, receiving his pilot license (No. 229), on June 13, 1914.

Luckily for Orlov, as a gentleman his interest in aviation was balanced with social and family obligations that required he receive the best education available. He attended the Imperial Alexandrovsky Middle School and later studied law at the University of St. Petersburg. Unfortunately, he never finished his studies. With the outbreak of war, he quickly volunteered his services to the Imperial Russian Air Service. Three days later, August 2, 1914, *Nijnichin* (Private) Orlov received his first frontline assignment when he transferred to the 5th Corps Air Detachment.

Considering Orlov was a mere *Nijnichin*, it is more than likely that individuals from less prestigious backgrounds found pleasure in ordering the young nobleman about. Perhaps his overly-aggressive nature was an attempt to prove his worth to fellow soldiers. Whatever the reason, he had clearly developed a fearless nature. By October 3, 1914, he had been promoted to *Feldwebel* (Sergeant-Major) and decorated three times with Cross of Saint George awards (the Fourth, Third, and Second Class medals), for a series of dangerous reconnaissance flights.

On December 19, 1914, Orlov was sent to the St. Petersburg aviation school for advanced training on the Voisin aircraft. He returned to the front as an officer with the rank of *Praporshik* (Ensign) on February 21, 1915, and was attached to the First Army Air Detachment.

The winter of 1915 was uneventful for Orlov; however, on April 4, 1915, he was awarded the Order of Saint Anne, Fourth Class, for reconnaissance flights in enemy territory. On June 1, 1915, he was given the title of military pilot.

During World War I both sides used aircraft in a combat role with increasing effectiveness. However, for the Russians, the primary role of the airplane was reconnaissance. On no front was this so important as the Russian, with its vast length and widely scattered areas of intense combat. There was a continual need to know the enemy's movements along a zone that stretched from the Black Sea to the Gulf of Finland (approximately 900 miles). Bombing and air-to-air combat were secondary to the principle mission of reconnaissance.

Above: The Orlov Number 1. There is very little information about this monoplane. However, it is known that the fuselage and the undercarriage were all made of welded steel tube, but neither was covered nor wire-braced. The wing and tailplanes were made of wood and power was provided by a 35 h.p. Anzani engine. Control was by means of a control column and pedals.

Left: A Russian Voisin LA, winter 1915–1916. Orlov conducted most of his reconnaissance missions in this type of aircraft.

Praporshik Orlov clearly illustrated this on August 11, 1915, when he and his observer, Gatovsky, conducted a reconnaissance of enemy fortifications in the region of Bausk and Birzhi. Despite severe damage Orlov's Voisin received from violent ground fire, he and his observer managed to take several photographs of the enemy fortifications and created a sketch-map of important positions. Thanks to the information obtained, the Russian 37th Army Corps and its Third Cavalry Squadron were able to establish a point to attack and reduced their own losses during the ensuing battle.

On August 28, 1915, Orlov earned the Order of Saint George, Fourth Class, for another reconnaissance. The citation read in part: "Flying near Fridrichstadt with extremely bad weather conditions of heavy raining and clouds at the altitude of less than 300 meters. He fearlessly ignored the danger of violent gunfire that already had caused several holes in the apparatus. In accordance with his assignment, he carried out two flights over enemy positions, and during those he discovered considerable enemy reserves hidden in the woods. Thanks to the bravery of the pilot and his timely report to the commander of the 37th Army Corps, successful measures were taken to stop an enemy breakthrough, which in combination with a forced river crossing would have been of great strategic importance to the enemy."

Two days later, on August 30, he was awarded the Order of Saint Stanislas, Third Class, with Sword and Bow, for another flight over enemy territory. Then on November 2, 1915, he was awarded the Order of Saint Vladimir, Fourth Class, with Sword and Bow, after he had photographed German positions between Lakes Swenten and Lisen. As before, his report supplied valuable information, but at the expense of a seriously damaged aircraft.

An Austro-Hungarian Flik photographed from the air. The Brandenburg C.I (located in front of the lower two hangars), and the seven canvas aircraft hangars might indicate the type and strength of this enemy unit—valuable information to a Russian commander.

By late November 1915 the severe Russian winter had set in and many of the air crews minimized their activities. Orlov however, continued to volunteer for flights into enemy territory. A report dated November 30, 1915, states in part: "Knowing the air temperature at ground level was only -15° Fahrenheit (-26° centigrade), and knowing the temperature while flying would be much worse and difficult to fly in, *Praporshik* Orlov conducted a bombing mission in which he navigated under heavy artillery fire. At a very low altitude he managed to break through the extremely close artillery explosions on the way to Novo-Alexandrovsk, where he dropped five bombs and blew up an enemy artillery depot."

Several days later, on December 4, 1915, Orlov was promoted to *Podporuchik* (2nd Lieutenant) by an imperial edict and sent to Odessa aviation school to become acquainted with the new Nieuport fighters arriving from France. He was graduated on January 10, 1916, and sent back to First Army Air Detachment. However, soon afterward he was transferred to the Third Air Company located in Kiev and assigned the task of forming the 7th Fighter Air Detachment under his command.

The commander-in-chief of the Russian Air Service, General V. M. Tkachev, commented about Orlov: "He impressed me as a very reckless, unrestrained young man. I noticed that both the Grand Duke Alexander Michaelovich and his right-hand man, General Vogel, regarded this young officer with great favor and they patronized him. Even during the days of his service as a pilot of a reconnaissance detachment, Orlov displayed remarkable bravery. Evidently the display of this bravery motivated the Grand Duke to entrust with Orlov the command of the first detachment being raised."

The 7th Fighter Detachment was located near the village of Tarnopol, in Galicia, on April 5, 1916. On May 1, 1916, the next Russian offensive started under the command of General Brusilov. As the battle continued, many pilots were engaged in daily combats.

Orlov described the frequent encounters in one of his many reports: "On May 22, 1917, I was flying a Nieuport *BeBe* when I saw an enemy Albatros flying towards our positions in the vicinity of Ribno village. I attacked him and shot off 15 cartridges, causing him to dive away towards the village of Muzhilov. I continued patrolling and moments later I spotted two more enemy planes. One of them was large, with two machine guns. I attacked him

Spad 7 of *escadrille* N.3. While in France, Orlov flew this type to obtain his fourth victory.

in the Prisup area. He did not retreat and did battle with me. After my second attack, the enemy craft descended to the west at the inclination of 8–9 degrees to the south of Yasen village. I continued the pursuit at a low altitude until I was shot at by enemy artillery".

Orlov obtained his first victory on June 8, 1916, while patrolling at 2500 meters near the village of Petlikovtse. After seeing an enemy two-seater conducting a reconnaissance, he swooped down and approached in his Nieuport to 35 meters before opening fire. Bullets from Orlov's machine gun violently tore into the enemy aircraft and its observer, who reached for his chest before falling into the plane. As the enemy pilot descended to 500 meters in an attempt to escape, Orlov followed and continued firing. Soon afterward, the enemy aircraft crossed into its own territory and crashed on the edge of a forest near the region of Chertkov city. Russian troops situated in the front trenches observed the battle and confirmed the victory for Orlov.

According to Austro-Hungarian reports, approximately at the same time and location, Lloyd C.II 42.21 from Flik 9 was shot down by a lone Russian fighter. Officer observer Walter Schmidt was mortally wounded in the chest and neck and the pilot, Karl Rumiha, crash-landed his damaged aircraft behind his own trenches. This crew most likely engaged Orlov that day.

Orlov obtained his second victory on June 25, 1916, while flying a joint mission with *Praporshik* Vasili Yanchenko. Orlov had already made nine combat flights that day without success; however, during his tenth mission, he and Yanchenko intercepted an enemy machine over the village of Podgaytsy.

Caught by surprise, the enemy crew desperately tried to evade the Russian fighters, but failed. Orlov and Yanchenko both fired at point-blank range until the aircraft rolled onto its side and crashed near Russian troops.

The enemy was an Austro-Hungarian crew from Flik 27—*Oberleutnant* Gustav Wangler and his pilot, *Feldwebel* Friedrich Schallinger. Both were seriously wounded and taken prisoner, and their machine, Aviatik B.I 33.30, was captured.

From July through October 1916 Orlov hit a dry spell, but the situation soon changed. On November 4, 1916, Orlov resumed his scoring after he and Yanchenko jumped a German two-seater near Brzezhany.

Yanchenko forced the enemy crew to maneuver into a position that placed Orlov directly behind them and less than 30 meters away. Orlov opened fire, and easily hit both crewmen. Within seconds the aircraft began to fall, leaving a long trail of black smoke. It crashed in enemy territory, but Russian troops confirmed the victory.

On November 13, 1916, Orlov was sent to France to become acquainted with the military experience of French pilots. Assigned to the famous *escadrille* N.3 for several months, he was under the instruction of French aces Guynemer and Heurteaux.

While in France, Orlov prepared to explain his findings to fellow pilots. Like Russian ace Evgraph Kruten, Orlov compiled his suggestions into a small booklet. However, Orlov's booklet, *Ways of Carrying Out an Air Battle*, did not deal with the problems of French aviation, but instead described the techniques learned from the French. First, he described what he believed to be the most correct and least dangerous method of attack.

Although this method required great precision,

knowledge, and aerobatic skills, Orlov used it to shoot down an enemy plane near Fresnoy Les Roye on January 24, 1917, for his fourth victory.[2]

The substance of that method recommended that the pilot: "Go into a power dive from the protection of the sun, perpendicularly to the line of flight of the enemy plane. Swoop under it, then begin a loop. Finish it by flipping onto the wing, at the same time balancing under the enemy plane, or in immediate vicinity to it."

For pilots who had no experience of air combat and no skill in aerobatic flying, Orlov recommended an easier method in his booklet: "The pilot descends from the tail towards the enemy in a zigzag motion until he takes the necessary position under the enemy tail."

On March 17, 1917, Orlov returned to a different Russia—Czar Nicholas II had abdicated and the 300-year-old Romanov dynasty had ended. Russia had become a republic.

Under considerable pressure, the Provisional Government propelled the forces of social change. Unfortunately, the political moves had eroded the discipline and authority necessary for an effective military organization. That Orlov maintained control of the 7th Fighter Detachment and it effectively engaged the enemy says a lot for his personal courage and determination.

Orlov became an ace on May 21, 1917, after he attacked an enemy airplane in the Prysup region. The plane, an Albatros two-seater from *Feldflieger Abteilung* (A)242, crash-landed to the west of Yasen village and was captured by Russian troops.

Although Orlov was not hurt in the combat, his aircraft was slightly damaged by enemy artillery as he followed the Albatros down. Considering that his Nieuport 11 had already been pushed well beyond its normal life span, the damaged aircraft should have been removed from frontline service. Unfortunately, no replacement aircraft were available. He would write in a letter: "We are stealing many parts from old aircraft to keep a few airworthy. Clearly we are all tempting fate day after day."

On July 1, 1917, General Brusilov (then commander-in-chief of the army), launched Russia's last offensive of the war. The air fighting was exceptionally fierce during the battle. Pilots from the 7th Fighter Detachment flew into battle several times each day against overwhelming odds.

Three days later, on July 4, 1917, *Podporuchik* Orlov was killed in a battle against four enemy fighters. While he was maneuvering, the lower starboard wing came off his old Nieuport and he crashed from a height of 3000 meters. After a solemn ceremony, the young nobleman was buried near the Czar's imperial residence at Czarskoe Selo (near St. Petersburg).

Ivan Alexandrovich Orlov. His awards included: Order of Saint George, Fourth Class; Golden Sword of Saint George; Order of Saint Vladimir, Fourth Class, with swords and bow; Order of Saint Anne, Fourth Class and Third Class with sword and bow; Order of Saint Stanislas, Third Class, with sword and bow; Soldier's Cross of Saint George, Fourth, Third, and Second Class; French *Croix de Guerre* with palm.

---

(2) Orlov was awarded the French *Croix de Guerre* with one palm for this victory.

Alexander Mikhailovich Pishvanov

Alexander Mikhailovich Pishvanov. His awards included: the Order of Saint George, Fourth Class; Order of Saint Vladimir, Fourth Class, with Sword and Bow; Order of Saint Anne, Fourth Class, Order of Saint Stanislas, Third Class; and Solider's Cross of Saint George, all four classes. Original charcoal sketch by Terry Waldron.

Alexander Mikhailovich Pishvanov was born on October 21, 1893, in the Crimean city of Novocherkassk, north of the Sea of Azov. He and his twelve brothers and sisters lived on the family's large farming estate north of the Don River. Wheat was the farm's main agricultural product, but was secondary to horses, which the family raised for the Russian Cavalry.

Sources suggested Pishvanov greatly disliked horses and farming in general, and preferred tinkering with mechanical devices. The fact that he did not study agriculture, and instead obtained a degree in engineering, supports this. His interest in aviation started while he attended engineering school and continued after graduation. He obtained his first airplane ride at the Odessa Air Club in the summer 1912, and his pilot's diploma in October of the same year.

Pishvanov's activities from 1913 to the start of the war are unknown. He enlisted as a *Nijnichin* (Private) shortly after the start of hostilities in 1914, and by mid-1915 had received all four Crosses of Saint George. In the summer of 1915, he was accepted for pilot training and assigned to the Odessa Aviation School. He was graduated in April 1916, with the rank of *Podpraporshik* (Warrant Officer).

In May, 1916, Pishvanov was attached to the 27 Corps Detachment, which in turn transferred him to the Moscow Aviation School for advanced pilot training. Pishvanov completed the program on Nieuport fighters on July 9 and prepared to return to the 27th Corps. However, it appears that *Poruchik* (Lieutenant) Belov (commander of the Moscow Aviation School) reported Pishvanov's superior skills to fellow officer and friend *Esaul* (Cossack Captain) Belofastov (commander of the 10th Fighter Detachment). Belofastov immediately requested that Pishvanov be transferred into his unit. Apparently Belofastov outranked his counterpart at the 27th Corps, because Pishvanov reported to the 10th Fighter Detachment on August 5, 1916.

This new detachment was attached to the 10th Russian Army and located at Gnidava airfield in Romania. Pishvanov assumed this location was a hotly contested battle zone and eagerly awaited his first patrol flight. The wait was longer than expected. His first operational flight occurred almost two months later, on October 2, 1916. During that month Pishvanov made nine combat patrols totaling more than ten hours of flying time without seeing a single enemy aircraft. By early March, 1917, Pishvanov's flight log recorded 50 patrols totaling more than 80 hours of flying time, and he had still not seen a single hostile aircraft.

At this point, Pishvanov must have assumed the probability of seeing an enemy machine was quite low, and as a result, on his patrol flight of March 21, 1917, he casually approached what he believed was a Russian reconnaissance plane over the region of Galatz. He later stated "I moved to a very close distance—thinking the aircraft was one of ours returning from a patrol. Unfortunately, they began firing at me before I realized what had happened."

Luckily, Pishvanov reacted by turning his Nieuport 11 around and onto the tail of the enemy machine. At a distance of less than 30 meters he opened fire and quickly hit the enemy observer, who fell into the cockpit. The enemy pilot headed for his own lines with Pishvanov in hot pursuit. At this point Russian pilots from the 29th Corps joined Pishvanov and forced the enemy aircraft to crash-land on its own territory. Pishvanov's first victory was soon confirmed by Russian troops.

The next week, on March 28, at an altitude of 3200 meters, Pishvanov in a Nieuport 21 joined an unidentified French pilot and attacked what he later described as a German Aviatik south of Galatz. Pishvanov and his French comrade attacked the German six times. Later Pishvanov reported, "After the first attack the German

Pishvanov seated in the cockpit of his Nieuport 17 fighter, circa summer 1917.

machine was puffing black smoke. We pursued the German, who in a critical moment used clouds to hide. Then he descended and crash-landed in Beldoneshi." Several days later Pishvanov's victory was confirmed. He was promoted to the rank of *Praporshik* (Ensign) and awarded the Order of Saint Anne, Fourth Class.

Another combat followed on April 15, 1917, when Pishvanov and an unidentified Rumanian pilot both attacked a hostile aircraft in the region of Galatz, above the Sereth River. During his first attack, Pishvanov clearly observed bullets from his machine gun strike the fuselage of the enemy machine. It went into a steep dive and landed near Braila. However, Russian troops were unable to confirm the victory.

Throughout May and early June 1917, Pishvanov engaged several enemy aircraft, but none of the battles were decisive.

Then on June 26, 1917, Pishvanov attacked four enemy aircraft above the village of Iveshti. Unfortunately, during his first pass Pishvanov's machine gun jammed. Considering the odds, it was surprising that he elected to stay and continue the battle. The enemy crews quickly realized his situation and converged on him. Pishvanov's aircraft was hit with gunfire, but he managed to clear the jammed cartridge before serious damage was caused. Although the four enemy aircraft were now in a close formation, Pishvanov turned into the group and concentrated his attack on one machine. As Pishvanov's aircraft passed near the group, one of the enemy observers threw four grenades that exploded in the air with huge puffs of white smoke. Pishvanov stated they "resembled the bursts of shrapnel." At this point, two French fighters arrived, one from Galatz, another from Tucuci, and supported Pishvanov. Together they attacked one hostile aircraft and clearly damaged it; the observer had fired off two signals of white smoke from a pistol, and then the machine quickly descended to Putna where it crash-landed. Next, Pishvanov's group split up and attacked two of the remaining enemy two-seaters. After Pishvanov opened fire on his target, a grenade was again thrown at him. It exploded very close to Pishvanov's aircraft and distracted him long enough to allow the enemy to escape. In all, Pishvanov made seven attacks. The battle was clearly observed from the ground. The enemy machine that crash-landed was confirmed for his third victory. Soon after, he was awarded the Order of Saint Stanislas, Third Class.

During the warm summer of 1917 Pishvanov, according to his son Nicholas, conducted one of the most bizarre missions of the war. He filled a large watermelon with vodka and secured it to the outer wing strut of his Nieuport. He had been scheduled for a mid-day patrol and believed the cooler air encountered while flying would refrigerate the vodka-filled melon and create a wonderful snack after landing. Unfortunately, as Pishvanov crossed over the enemy's first trench system, he was surprised by anti-aircraft fire that made him maneuver his Nieuport in a manner that accidentally released the melon. Moments later it hit the enemy trench. As the story continues, later that day the 10th Russian Army sent a communiqué to Pishvanov's detachment. It stated in part; "The Russian army praises your pilot for his brave attack. Although the large bomb did not explode, it appears to have caused a great deal of confusion."

Pishvanov's fourth confirmed victory occurred on the morning of July 4, 1917. This patrol resulted in five consecutive combats. The last took place over the River Sereth (near the village of Endependante). At a distance of less than 40 meters, Pishvanov surprised the enemy crew with his machine gun fire, which hit the fuselage, engine, and perhaps the observer, who only returned one short burst of fire and then hid in the cockpit. Soon after the enemy machine lost control and crash-landed on a farm field within enemy territory. For this combat, Pishvanov was awarded the Order of Saint Vladimir, Fourth Class, with Swords and Bow.

According to Austrian archives, pilot *Oberleutnant* Rupert Terk and observer *Oberleutnant* Josef Brunner were flying Brandenburg C.I 68.54 over Endependanze on July 4, 1917. While adjusting their radio they were attacked, and after a short combat shot down. Enemy fire damaged the propeller and cooling system of their machine.

Three days later, on the morning of July 7, 1917, Pishvanov flew to attack a group of hostile aircraft that were supporting artillery fire in the region of Latinul village. Accompanied by *Podporuchik* Desino, Pishvanov forced the enemy aircraft to withdraw. Moments later, he engaged a second enemy two-seater. The enemy, not wanting to fight, quickly dove from a height of 4400 meters. Pishvanov dove after him persistently, pursuing to an altitude of 1200 meters. At this point one of the explosive bullets from the observer's machine gun burst in Pishvanov's cockpit and tore into his right leg. Despite the pain, Pishvanov closed in and at point-blank range hit the enemy crew with gunfire. The machine hit the ground near the second line of trenches. Russian artillery units—the 3rd Battery of the 30th Artillery Brigade and 3rd Battery of the 4th Mortar Division—shelled the wreckage for good measure. This was Pishvanov's fifth confirmed victory. Several days later he was awarded the Order of Saint George, Fourth Class, and given the title of military pilot.

The next week, on the morning of July 11, 1917, Pishvanov encountered a hostile aircraft over the region of Tutor-Vladimiresku Village. He attacked it from above and opened fire at a close range, but his machine gun jammed. The enemy used this opportunity and returned

Alexander Pishvanov, circa late 1920s.

fire. One of the bullets hit Pishvanov's right hand and tore off two of his fingers. In spite of the wound and misfire of the machine gun, Pishvanov did not retreat. He removed the jammed cartridge in the gun, attacked the enemy, and forced him to withdraw to his territory. Pishvanov returned to his own airfield, where he damaged his aircraft slightly during landing.

The loss of several of his fingers grounded Pishvanov until late September, 1917, but by that time his unit ended all hostile activities. In December, 1917, Pishvanov flew to Novocherkassk and joined the Volunteer Army under command of Generals Denikin and Wrangel. Several years later he joined the British air force as a pilot instructor. He emigrated to the United States in 1926 and worked as an engineer for Igor Sikorsky. He became an American citizen in 1928, and in 1931 joined the Seversky Aircraft Corporation. Pishvanov's close relationship with Alexander Seversky lasted many years and involved highly diverse activities. Perhaps the most significant was his work with Alexander Seversky and Walt Disney in 1942 to produce the movie *Victory Through Air Power*. Pishvanov died in 1966. He is survived by one son, Nicholas, a retired U.S. military officer.

Mikhail Ivanovich Safonov

Mikhail Ivanovich Safonov. His awards included: Order of Saint Vladimir, Fourth Class, with Sword and Bow; Order of Saint Vladimir, Third Class, with Sword and Bow; Order of Saint Anne, Fourth Class; Order of Saint Stanislas, Third Class, with Sword and Bow. Original charcoal sketch by Terry Waldron.

Mikhail Ivanovich Safonov was born on November 13, 1893, in the town of Ostrogozhsk in Voronezh province. He was Russian Orthodox by faith and a nobleman by birth. He was graduated from the Ostro-gozhsk gymnasium (comparable to high school and junior college in America).

He entered the Imperial Naval Academy at St. Petersburg on September 20, 1909. His shipboard training included cruises with the training ship *Vernyi* (Faithful) in 1910, schooner *Zabava* in 1910, cruisers *Bogatyr* (Epic Hero) in 1911 and *Russia* in 1911 and 1912, training ship *Voin* in 1912, and cruiser *Oleg* in 1913.

On February 21, 1913, Safonov received the Bronze Medal celebrating 300 years of the reign of the House of Romanov, and in April 1913 he was awarded the Bronze Medal celebrating the 100th anniversary of the Fatherland War.

In May 1914, Safonov was graduated from the Naval Academy and promoted to the rank of *Michman* (Warrant Officer) on July 29, 1914. He was appointed to the battleship *Gromoboi* (The Thunder) on August 2, 1914, and transferred to the battleship *Sevastopol* on September 30.

Safonov served on the *Sevastopol* during the first year of war, and then in September 1915 requested a transfer to the aviation section of the Baltic Fleet. His request was approved and on November 24 he was placed under the command of the Officer's School of Naval Aviation for the Baltic Fleet.

Safonov was set to the Polytechnic Institute of Emperor Peter the Great in St. Petersburg, where courses in aerodynamics were taught. After completing this course of study he was sent to the Baku naval station (winter branch of the school) and passed all examinations for pilot. His first solo flight was made on December 1, 1915.

Safonov was attached to the Baltic Fleet's Liaison/Signal Service Corps on February 24, 1916, and completed his pilot training at the Revel naval air station of the Baltic Fleet in March, 1916. Days later he was assigned to the Baltic Fleet's Third Air Station, located on the coast of the Gulf of Riga. This unit was equipped with variety of aircraft, Safonov being assigned a Maurice Farman type MF.11 with floats (serial number 31).

The following month, on April 2, Safonov was given the rank of naval pilot and a yearly salary of 920 roubles.

During the summer of 1916 the Baltic Fleet's Air Arm was restructured into two Air Divisions. Safonov was assigned to the Second Air Division and placed in its First Air Detachment, "Glagol," on August 11, 1916.

The First Air Detachment, "Glagol," was equipped with the newer Grigorovich M.9 flying boats. Generally well liked, these aircraft allowed the Russian crews to carry a larger bomb load, but more importantly a single Madsen machine gun for defense. Considering that during the summer of 1916 aerial activities had increased considerably as German ships and aircraft extended their range of operations, the arrival of the M.9s allowed the Russian air crews to engage the enemy on basically equal terms.

An aerial battle on September 9, 1916, clearly illustrated this fact. "During the day, enemy aircraft appeared several times over the Irben strait and engaged in combat with our flyers. Notwithstanding the enemy superiority in numbers, the enemy was, each time, chased away. During a dogfight between five Russian seaplanes and five German aircraft over the Mikhailovsky Lighthouse, the crew of Mikhail Safonov and his mechanic/gunner, Orlov, attacked a German plane that then made a sharp turn and glided on to the Irben River. Safonov's flying boat (Tactical number 29), received 4 holes and its radiator was damaged too." For his courage and success in this engagement, Safonov was awarded the

Maurice Farman MF.11 floatplane. Safonov flew MF.11 (telegraph/serial number MF-31) in 1916.

Order of Saint Anne, Fourth Class, with the inscription "For Bravery," on September 19, 1916.

The following week, on September 26, 1916, while flying a patrol off Runo Island, *Lietenant* (Lieutenant) Garkovenko with gunner Zaitzevsky (in M.9, serial number 8) and *Michman* Safonov with gunner Orlov (in M.9, serial number 29) made an excursion toward the German base at Lake Angern in the hope of bombing it. While over the base, the two Russian crews were met by a superior group of enemy aircraft (estimated at 20 machines). During the battle several German crews focused on Safonov, wounding him in the leg and seriously damaging his machine. Garkovenko saw Safonov's situation and bravely went to his aid, but exposed himself to enemy attack and was soon shot down and killed.

Safonov, now alone, was forced to withdraw. He landed safely and resumed flying the next month.

On October 19, 1916, Safonov was awarded the Order of Saint Stanislaus, Third Class, with Swords and Bow, and on November 14, by order Number 380 of the supreme commander-in-chief of the Navy Staff, was awarded the Order of Saint Vladimir Fourth Class, with Swords and Ribbon, for his excellent service.

Safonov was involved in several battles in early 1917, and although the outcome in each was indecisive, he was awarded the Order of Saint Vladimir, Third Class, with Swords and Ribbon, on February 5, 1917.

On July 10, 1917, Safonov was promoted to the rank of *Lietenant* (Lieutenant). Four days later, on July 14, he assumed command of the air detachment "Glagol," and together with another pilot took off in Grigorovich M.15 flying boats to intercept a German plane approaching Arensburg. During the encounter, Safonov attacked the German aircraft from a distance of 100 meters and it began to lose altitude. Although the aircraft was not observed to crash, Safonov was given credit for a victory.

Safonov's third victory followed on September 7. The report stated "at 1140 hours a mixed flight of five Russian planes (Nieuport fighters and Grigorovich M.15 flying boats) attacked three German aircraft over Arensburg. A two-seater enemy aircraft was shot down by Safonov (Nieuport fighter—telegraph/serial number NR-1) who attacked the enemy from the tail at a distance of 50 meters. Safonov fired only 10–15 bullets."

On October 25, 1917, Safonov was promoted to the rank of *Starschi-Leitenant* (Senior Lieutenant) and granted a short leave, during which he married Ludmila Tschebotarioff.

Safonov returned to the front soon after, and on November 14, 1917, assumed command of the Second land fighter detachment, located at Kuivastoin.

Two days later, on November 16, German air crews conducted a large number of reconnaissance flights in the area of Moon Island. Safonov flew up from Kuivastoin in a Nieuport fighter (telegraph/serial number NR-1) to intercept an enemy airplane at 0915 hours and shot down one German plane that fell onto Moon Island.

The next day, November 17, in the early morning a large number of enemy aircraft dropped bombs on the Russian ships at Moon Island. At 0900 hours Safonov took off in a Nieuport fighter (telegraph/serial number NR-1)

Grigorovich M.9. Safonov flew at least two M.9s during the war. Their telegraph/serial numbers were SchS-18 and SchS-29.

Below: Grigorovich M.15 used by Safonov.

from Kuivastoin and intercepted a German twin-engine bomber over the Gulf of Riga. During Safonov's attack the enemy aircraft began to smoke and moments later fell into the water. This was Safonov's fifth and last victory of the war.

Although Safonov's military activities had ended, he remained listed as an Russian officer until he was discharged on March 19, 1918, by Bolshevik decree.

The chaos caused by the Bolsheviks in 1917 brought about Poland's declared independence as well as Finland's. Like Poland, Finland had been a part of Russia (as an semi-autonomous grand duchy) until declaring its independence on December 6, 1917. At this time a considerable number of Finnish merchants and craftsmen lived and worked in St. Petersburg. Within their community an activist group tried, after the revolution, to recruit White-minded officers of the Imperial Russian Air Force who were willing to defect to Finland with their aircraft. Safonov was among a group of five Russian pilots rather obscurely promised 25,000 roubles, Finnish citizenship, and possibility of serving as a pilot in the Finnish air force under General Mannerheim.

After one of the Russian pilots defected to Finland in a Grigorovich M.9, the other four (including Safonov) secretly intended to make a joint defection the next day. Using four Nieuports—two type 10s and two type 17s—

Safonov and his wife, standing next to the Nieuport 10 (in Finnish markings) which they used for escape from Russia in 1918.

Safonov with other pilots in Finland. Safonov is seated in first row, second from left.

the four left from Komendantsky airport on April 11, 1918. Safonov flew one of the two-seater Nieuport type 10s with his wife as a passenger.

The Finnish authorities believed that it would be more expedient and safer for the Russian members of the new air force to assume Finnish names for the duration of hostilities, so upon landing Mikhail Safonov became Mikko Vuorenheimo.

The Russians were immediately assigned reconnaissance flights during the Finnish civil war. But despite all their efforts and recommendations, the Russians were under a considerable amount of suspicion by the Finnish authorities. By the summer of 1918 Safonov realized the Finnish authorities were unwilling to fulfill any of their earlier promises. He managed to obtain all the necessary papers to travel through German-occupied Russia.

By 1919 Safonov had joined General Denikin's White Army near Novocherkassk, Russia. Later, Safonov (with his wife) traveled to Persia and India, were he joined the Royal Air Force. In 1924, Safonov (with his wife and two children) went to China, were he was contacted by the Chinese navy to organize a flying school for naval officers and to aid in the construction of flying boats. He was killed in an accident in May, 1924, while testing a newly-built flying boat on the Ming River.

Safonov's wife and their two children would settle in the United States years later. He is survived by grandchildren living in the United States.

Alexander Nikolaivich Prokoffiev de Seversky

Alexander Nikolaivich Prokoffiev de Seversky in Washington, D.C., 1918. His rank of *Kapitan 2. Ranga* is indicated by the gold strips embroidered on the cuffs of his dark blue uniform. Above his left breast pocket is the Order of Saint George, Fourth Class. His other Imperial Russian awards included the Golden Sword of Saint George; Order of Saint Vladimir, Fourth Class; Order of Saint Anne, Fourth, Third, and Second Classes; Order of Saint Stanislas, Third and Second Classes.

Alexander Nikolaivich Prokoffiev de Seversky was born on June 7, 1894, in the city of Tiflis in Georgia. Without doubt, his earliest aviation influence was his father, Nikolai Prokoffiev Seversky, who had been one of the first pilots to own a private airplane in Russia. By the time Seversky was fourteen (in 1908), his father had taught him all the basic skills required to fly this aircraft. That same year he entered the Imperial Russian Naval Academy in Saint Petersburg. Considering the thrilling images that Nikolai Seversky must have planted in his young son, and combining it with the boy's apprenticeship at the Korporusmy Military Aerodrome while a naval cadet, it was no wonder he would write, "I would watch aircraft in amazement, and at times was allowed to sneak a ride on an experimental test flight to act as ballast. I wanted to fly more than anything else in the world. It was the ultimate adventure."

Seversky was graduated from the Naval Academy with the rank of *Michman* in early 1914. Although he requested an aviation assignment, he was sent to sea with the Baltic Fleet. As months passed, his dreams of flying were stirred by exciting news of developing aerial technology. Finally, with the start of World War I, the navy requested applications from its officers interested in a flying assignment. Without hesitation Seversky asked to be relieved of his shipboard posting and requested a transfer into the aviation program.

Seversky was accepted and initially sent to the Saint Petersburg Institute of Theoretical Aviation, where a broad knowledge of the principles of flight and design was taught. After successfully completing the four-month aeronautical course, he was transferred to the Gatchina flight school, 25 miles southwest of Saint Petersburg.

Gatchina was the largest of four primary flight training centers in Russia. Seversky arrived there in late March, 1915, and quickly completed his basic flight training on the Farman 4. Next, he entered the Russian Naval Aerial Combat and Gunnery School and learned to fly the more

Seversky in the cockpit of a Farman 4 aircraft while at Gatchina flight school, spring 1915. With his brother as his instructor, Seversky required less than four minutes of training before being pronounced ready to solo. An Imperial double-headed eagle is embroidered on Seversky's sweater.

The Seversky family at the Gatchina flight school in June 1915. From left to right, George (Alexander's older brother), Nikolai (Alexander's father) and Alexander Seversky. Both Nikolai and George were flight instructors at Gatchina when Alexander Seversky arrived for flight training in March 1915. All three men wear the rank of Leitenant on their shoulder boards. The circular pilot's badge is clearly shown on George's and Alexander's left breast pockets.

advanced Voisin aircraft. Upon graduation in late June 1915, Seversky was promoted to the rank of *Leitenant* and assigned to the Baltic Fleet's air arm.

Although this air arm was officially organized in mid-1912, it was clearly inadequate at the start of hostilities in 1914. Many of the permanent shore installations designed as service and flight centers for naval air reconnaissance were unfinished and understaffed. In June, 1915, when Seversky joined the Second Aerial Bombing-Reconnaissance station, located on Oesel Island in the Gulf of Riga, he was one of only twelve pilots available to the entire Baltic Fleet.

Unfortunately, Seversky's career with this group lasted only a few days. It ended during his first mission on July 15, 1915. Piloting an FBA flying boat, on that evening's flight over the gulf, he and his observer, Quartermaster Blinov, sighted and attacked a German destroyer.[1] Although maneuvering under heavy anti-aircraft fire from the ship, Seversky believed his initial pass produced two hits on its vessel's stern. On his second pass his aircraft was hit and heavily damaged by the destroyer's intense machine-gun fire. Continually loosing altitude, Seversky decided a safe landing must be attempted, but while alighting on the water one of his externally-mounted bombs exploded through the starboard hull of the flying boat, instantly killing Blinov and severely wounding Seversky.

In the fading twilight the explosion was clearly seen for miles, causing several nearby Russian patrol boats to investigate. They found Seversky barely clinging to floating debris. Doctors at the Kronstadt naval station discovered his right leg had been shattered. Considering the severity of the wound, he was immediately transferred to a hospital at Saint Petersburg, where the leg was amputated below the knee.

Recuperating through the fall of 1915, Seversky began to re-evaluate his personal goals and objectives. He eventually requested a transfer back to frontline duty, and pleaded his case personally to Alexander Touchkoff, the commander of the Baltic Fleet's air arm. Seversky could obtain only an appointment as chief inspector of naval aircraft for the Saint Petersburg district. Nevertheless, he eagerly accepted the task, working with crutches until his prosthesis arrived.

Seversky had a high level of energy and enthusiasm, but more than that he possessed a boundless love of

---

(1) The Franco-British Aircraft flying boat that Seversky flew on that mission was serial number seven.

An FBA (Franco-British Aircraft) type C flying boat, with a 130-h.p. Clerget engine, Baltic Sea, circa fall 1915. Saint Andrew flags are attached to the outer wing struts. Photo: Rodina Russian Naval Museum.

A Russian-built FBA flying boat, Revel Air Station, circa fall 1915. It was powered by a 130hp Clerget engine, which was fueled by a gravity fuel tank attached to the top wing. The two occupants were seated in tandem. Light colored bombs have been attached to each side of the hull. Photo: Rodina Russian Naval Museum.

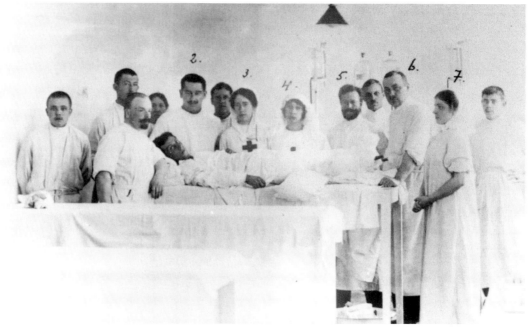

Alexander Seversky prior to his leg amputation, Saint Petersburg, July 17, 1915. Nikolai Seversky is standing behind his son, and is indicated by a number 2. Photo: Rodina Russian Naval Museum.

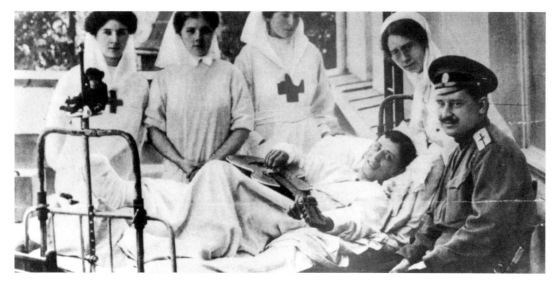

Seversky recuperating at Saint Petersburg, fall 1915. Nikolai Seversky is seated at the right.

A Grigorovich M.9 flying boat number 161, powered by a 140hp Salmson engine. Seversky flew M.9s on numerous missions, and scored four of his confirmed victories in this type of aircraft.

Grigorovich M.9, number 161, circa 1917. Twin fuel tanks are mounted between inboard interplane struts. The hull's wood surface has been painted with a light gray marine paint just below the water line.

flying. With his continued requests for frontline duty denied, the spirited Seversky decided to prove once and for all that he was still a capable flyer. In May 1916, he learned a local military aerodrome had arranged an air show. Seizing an opportunity, he slipped into an airplane during the show and performed an impressive, but unauthorized, aerobatic exhibition. Upon landing, he was arrested and confined to his quarters to await punishment. As fate would have it, news of his daring episode spread through Russia, and Czar Nicholas II asked the Navy Ministry for a full report. Although the Czar normally deplored any breach of discipline, he apparently viewed Seversky's enthusiasm positively, and recommended that Seversky be restored to full flying duty.

Seversky returned to the front on July 1, 1916, and scored his first victory three days later. Flying a Grigorovich M.9 flying boat, he attacked a German seaplane over the Gulf of Riga and sent it crashing into the water. For the rest of the month, Seversky made continuous reconnaissance flights from Oesel and Runo island, and reported several engagements with enemy fighters, but scored no additional victories.

The summer of 1916 was marked by increased aerial attacks as both sides actively searched for and bombed opposing ships and fortified installations. For the Russian air crews, the German seaplane base at Lake Angern became a prime target. Although heavily defended, it was frequently bombed by Russian aircraft.

One such attack was scheduled for August 15, 1916, by two Russian aircraft flown by *Leitenants* Seversky and Diderichs. Apparently, the mission, a surprise bombing-reconnaissance attack, was successfully executed and several aircraft hangars at Lake Angern reportedly hit with bombs. However, the two pilots were themselves surprised when seven German aircraft intercepted them far in enemy territory. Instantly, the Russians placed their Grigorovich M.9s in an evasive criss-cross pattern, which nearly caused them to collide several times while trying to avoid German aircraft. Every aircraft appeared to receive hits from opposing machines, but as the battle continued, Seversky's mechanic managed to concentrate fire on two enemy aircraft, forcing each to withdraw and make emergency landings.

At this point, Diderich's gun jammed. Seversky later noted, "The moment Diderich tried to clear his gun, all eyes seemed to be focusing upon him." As Diderich's observer feverishly attempted to dislodge the jammed cartridge, the remaining German aircraft converged on him. Realizing his companions' desperate situation, Seversky quickly turned into the enemy group and attacked. His aircraft almost rammed a German seaplane

Seversky displays his black leather flying suit after a reconnaissance flight over the Baltic, circa summer 1916.

as his mechanic fired a long burst of machine-gun fire at a range of several yards, severely wounding or killing both its occupants. The enemy machine turned over and plunged to the ground. The remaining German aircraft broke off their attack, allowing the Russian crews to return safely to their base.

The bitterly fought battle had lasted more than an hour. Seversky's airplane was found to have 30 bullet holes in it. As the first Russian pilot to obtain three victories in one day, the quality of Seversky's service was well recognized.[2] He was promoted to the rank of *Starschi-Leitenant* and awarded the Golden Sword of Saint George, the second highest award the Russian Empire could bestow on a junior officer. To Seversky this award was his most cherished, for Czar Nicholas II presented it to him personally.

Seversky and other pilots continued flights over the Gulf of Riga throughout the summer and well into the fall of 1916. However, as winter approached, the Baltic Sea's stormy weather forced the Russian navy to reduce the number of reconnaissance missions. For pilots having to endure high winds and freezing weather with unreliable engines, the prospect of crashing in rough seas was very immediate. Once immersed in freezing water, a person's survival time would be measured in minutes.

By late November 1916 the pilots were restricted to missions near the coast. As the flying gradually decreased, many spent their time repairing equipment and preparing for another spring campaign. Seversky lost little time in putting his energy and inventiveness to work. Realizing the need for all-weather capability, he devised and installed a set of skis on a Grigorovich flying boat. His concept of using skis was not an original one. It was his universal mounting design that was innovative, being the first that could be quickly connected to any Russian flying boat, thus allowing takeoffs and landings on snow and on ice. In late December 1916 Seversky was assigned to the Shchetinin aircraft factory in Saint Petersburg as a technical adviser. He monitored the manufacture of his ski design and its installation on the newly-developed Grigorovich M.11 flying boat.

In February 1917, Seversky, like most officers, became uneasy with the news of the revolution and the establishment of the Provisional Government. Wanting to remove himself from Saint Petersburg's political chaos, he requested a transfer back to frontline duty; it was accepted and he was assigned the command of the Second Naval

(2) Seversky's three victories are based on Russian and British reports.

Grigorovich M.11 flying boat mounted with the ski apparatus designed by Seversky, winter 1917.

A Nieuport 21 fighter used by Seversky and his detachment, Oesel Island, summer 1917. A small Saint Andrew's cross has been painted on the side of the fuselage. The serial number "3" is the same red tone as the fuselage cockade. Photo: G. Petrov.

Fighter Detachment on Oesel Island. Unfortunately, before leaving he was injured in an unusual accident. He slipped under the wheel of a horse-drawn lorry which rolled over his good leg, breaking it and temporarily eliminating his hopes of a command.

After recuperating until May 1917, Seversky was sent to Moscow as a technical adviser, assigned the dual responsibility of instructing new pilots in combat techniques and examining new aircraft designs being accepted by the Baltic Fleet. In addition to flying each aircraft, Seversky studied and recommended ways of improving their flight characteristics.

In late July 1917 Seversky was appointed commander of a fighter detachment stationed on Oesel Island[3] to defend its fortifications from aerial attack. As fate would have it, Seversky arrived at his station only days before Russian intelligence suggested a large German assault on Riga and the Baltic islands would start soon.

To avoid a German trap, the Russians began a gradual withdrawal of their forces southeast of the Dvina River. Each of the Baltic islands was left with a small defensive force, whose main objective was to mislead German intelligence through light, but effective, confrontations. When the coordinated German attack on Riga finally came in September 1917, the Germans claimed the operation's impressive success was due to their new tactical method

---

(3) Seversky's detachment on Oesel Island was equipped with four Nieuport fighters, one Grigorovich M.9, and six Grigorovich M.15 flying boats.

Seversky's detachment on Oesel Island was equipped with a mix of Nieuport fighters and Grigorovich flying boats. This Grigorovich M.15 is a typical example. It has been painted overall light gray and has a black number "5" painted on the nose of its hull.

German naval seaplanes returning to their base at Windau after a raid on Oesel Island, October 8, 1917. The aircraft are Gotha WD 11, Friedrichshafen FF 33H, and Albatros W.4 fighters. Photo: Edgar Meos.

Below: A German Friedrichshafen FF39, Two Sablatnig SF5s, and a Friedrichshafen FF33 seaplane at Windau, Courland, October 1917. Photo: Egar Meos.

(the storm battalions). However, it can safely be said that Riga and the Baltic islands were not taken in this manner. Except for the courageous actions of several small defensive units, these locations were given away by the Russians, who had withdrawn a full month earlier.

Seversky's detachment had remained on Oesel Island during the German assault, reporting daily combats as enemy aircraft increased activity before the amphibious landings. Seversky claimed several victories, but with most of the Russian troops gone, none was confirmed until October 10, 1917. Intercepting a large formation of enemy aircraft that day, Seversky shot down a German fighter and a bomber. This time Russian troops viewed the combat clearly and confirmed both victories, his last of the war.

Seversky's detachment finally left Oesel Island on October 14, 1917, after its aerodrome and hangars were destroyed by gunfire from the German fleet and shortly before enemy troops arrived. As Oesel's remaining aircraft were flown to Kuiwast, Seversky's plane developed engine trouble, forcing him to land behind enemy lines. After removing a machine gun and several instruments, he burned his plane and headed on foot to the front, about 10 miles away. With the large number of German troops advancing rapidly through the area, a general state of confusion existed. This allowed Seversky to elude detection and return safely to the growing nightmare on the Russian side.

Once he was known to be safe, Seversky was summoned by naval officers, who to his surprise awarded him the Order of Saint George, Fourth Class, for his courageous defense of the Baltic islands while cut off by German forces and under continuous attack from the air and sea. In addition, Seversky was promoted to the rank of *Kapitan 2. Ranga,* and given a new appointment as assistant naval attaché at the Russian Embassy in the United States.

Seversky arrived in Washington D.C. in March 1918, and was placed under the command of Victor Utgoff, a Russian naval officer and pilot. Seversky was part of a team that tried to develop an aircraft bombsight with the United States government, but after months of

A photo taken to help sell war bonds in Washington, D.C., 1918. Russian naval pilot Victor Utgoff is in the back row, third from right. Alexander Seversky is in the back row, third from left. Both men have the Order of Saint Stanislas, Second Class, around their necks and the Order of Saint George, Fourth Class, on their right breast pockets. Photo: Cradle of Aviation Museum.

unsuccessful tests the funds supporting this effort ran out and the Russian Embassy prepared to close.

Seversky was suddenly without a country or work, so he volunteered and was accepted as an aeronautical engineer and test pilot for the United States. While serving in this capacity he flew as a member of the Allied Acrobatic Team for the promotion of Liberty Loans, organized the Sikorsky-Hannevig Aircraft Corporation, and in 1921 acted as a consultant for General William (Billy) Mitchell's airplane versus battleship test. As a result of his service, Seversky was appointed consulting engineer for the United States Air Service by the Secretary of War in 1921—an unusual tribute for a person not yet an American citizen.

Shortly after being appointed, Seversky was assigned to the flight test branch at McCook Airfield in Dayton, Ohio. This elite group included such aviation greats as Jimmy Doolittle, W.C. Mosley, Muir Fairchild, Ralph Lakewood, and Archie Smith, the pioneer American air mail pilot. While in this position, Seversky obtained the U.S. rights to the failed bombsight he and others had worked on in 1918. After months of continued work, he produced a workable system and sold the patents to the U.S. government. The money from this sale allowed Seversky to develop his own company, the Seversky Aero Corporation, in 1922.

In 1927 Seversky became a naturalized U.S. citizen and joined the Army Air Corps Reserves.[4] In 1931 Seversky organized a new company with Wall Street backing. In addition to being elected its president and director, he was employed as general manager and chief designer.

Although Seversky initially designed a series of all-metal amphibian airplanes which he used to set numerous world speed records, he is best remembered for several military aircraft built by his company. These include the BT-8 basic trainer of 1935, which became the first all-metal monoplane accepted by the Army Air Corps for training; the P-35 fighter of 1936, the U.S. Army's first all-metal, cantilever, stressed-skin monoplane; and the P-43 of 1938, the first fighter with an air-cooled, supercharged engine to provide greater high-altitude performance. The P-43 led to the very successful P-47 fighter, which was produced in great numbers during World War II.

Seversky had advocated a long-range escort fighter, and believed the P-43 would have provided it. But the government did not subsidize the project and formally rejected the plane for large-scale production. Undaunted, Seversky planned for the future of the United States, and against the wishes of his company's financial backers decided to invest the firm's money. The cost of the plane was enormous, and the Seversky Aero Company soon ran into financial difficulties. In February 1939, while Seversky was in Europe negotiating sales of new aircraft, the company's board of directors voted him out of office and changed the firm's name to Republic Aircraft.

Republic Aircraft made millions of dollars on the "unwanted" plane during the war. Although Seversky filed a lawsuit (which was settled in 1942), it is interesting to note that a citation was presented to him towards the end of the war, signed by President Roosevelt. It read in part: "He foresaw the necessity for the long-range escort fighter and devoted himself single-mindedly to its development. As a result, our country was prepared to apply these principles against the enemy at the crucial moment, thereby winning the control of the air which guaranteed victory."

After Seversky left his company in 1939, he embarked on a career as a free-lance aeronautical consultant, writer, and speaker crusading for air power, enlightening the American public on the role of air power in modern warfare. His views were considered controversial at the time, but most were confirmed in action during the war. His 1942 best-selling book, *Victory Through Air Power*, and its serialization in newspapers, reached millions of people.

(4) While serving in the United States Air Corps Reserves, Seversky rose to the rank of major.

Seversky's first job in the United States was to test fly SE-5a fighters while in Buffalo New York, 1918.

Seversky (left), General William "Billy" Mitchell (center), and an unidentified officer of the United States Air Corps, circa 1921.

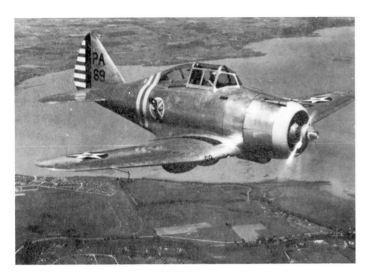

The P-35 fighter was widely advertised as America's first 300 m.p.h. fighter. P-35s were active in the defense of the Philippines until the surrender of Bataan.

The P-43 fighter. Used in small numbers, it lead to the famous P-47.

During World War II the P-47 Thunderbolt was credited with more than 7000 air and ground victories in the European Theater of Operations. Photo: USAF.

Alexander Seversky, circa 1939.

Later, the book was animated by Walt Disney in a Technicolor movie that played a crucial role at the Quebec Conference in 1943, when British Prime Minister, Winston Churchill, requested that it be shown to President Roosevelt. After viewing it, the Combined Chiefs of Staff decided to give aviation the necessary priority to guarantee control of the skies before undertaking the European invasion.

World War II ushered in a highly technical aerial war, and the American government felt that Seversky clearly understood the immensely complex global issues. His ability to analyze problems was matched only by his ability to foresee future issues. In 1945, Seversky was appointed as special consultant to the Secretary of War and went to both the European and Pacific Theaters to analyze employment of air power.

Although Seversky's career as a crusader for air power became more controversial in the postwar years, he was continuously requested to discuss his views. In 1955 he was appointed lecturer to the Air War College, and in 1959 the U.S. Air Force presented him with the Air University Award for his efforts.

Seversky remained active until his death in 1974. In the end he was credited with hundreds of aviation-related designs and inventions. He was the recipient of two international Harmon Trophies (1939, 1947), and held two honorary Doctor of Science degrees. Seversky was a trustee and vice president of the Air Force Historical Foundation, a fellow of the New York Academy of Sciences, honorary member of the Air Force Association, member of the National Aeronautics Association, member of the Society of American Military Engineers, and was elected to the Aviation Hall of Fame.

Seversky will be remembered as one of the true greats in the history of aviation. Ever outspoken, he broke loose from outmoded views, and, with clear insight, influenced and shaped the view of air power of millions of people around the world.

Ivan Vasilievich Smirnov

Nijnichin Ivan Vasilievich Smirnov, fall 1916. The Cross of Saint George, Fourth Class is displayed on his shirt. His other awards included: Cross of Saint George (Third, Second, and First Class awards); Order of Saint Stanislaus with sword, Third Class; Order Saint Anne, Fourth Class and Third Class with sword; Sword of Saint Anne; Order of Saint Vladimir with sword, Fourth Class; Golden Sword of Saint George, Fourth Class, Golden Sword of Saint George; Order of Saint George, First Class (special award established by the Kerensky government); Serbia's Order of the White Eagle; and France's *Croix de Guerre* with Palm.

Ivan Vasilievich Smirnov was born into a peasant family on January 30, 1895, in the farming province of Vladimir, 120 miles east of Moscow. Cast into a system reminiscent of ancient serfdom, he was legally bound to his community and its land. Like most peasants, he labored daily to preserve his potential rights to a small allotment of cultivated land. Smirnov had no formal education and little hope of improving his social situation. Hopes of improving his financial situation were equally bleak. Peasants who worked in country factories for higher wages were still required to farm land for the community in which they lived. Few searched for financial opportunities without special permission. Clearly the system destroyed most dreams of a better life. Had it not been for the outbreak of war in the summer of 1914, Smirnov's future would have offered little hope.

Luckily for Smirnov, it was natural in Russia for young men to fulfill their patriotic duty by defending their country. Traditionally, many communities called their able-bodied men to arms. The province of Vladimir was no exception. Shortly after the start of hostilities, 90 of its peasants volunteered for military service and were granted admission into the army. Smirnov was among the first to join the Vladimir Contingent.

Smirnov's unit was attached to the 96th Onsk Regiment and stationed with the 2nd Russian Army, located near the town of Lodz in late September, 1914. It arrived at the front with only basic infantry training and days before a new Austro-German offensive started on September 28, 1914. The offensive centered near the town of Lodz and continued until Russian troops evacuated it and stabilized their lines eastward on December 6, 1914. Characterized by a series of reckless clashes fought in heavy snow, this offensive clearly illustrated the mass slaughter of men. As each side desperately tried to out-maneuver the other, entire units were caught by surprise and destroyed.

Ironically, many of the peasants in Smirnov's unit volunteered for the army as a means to improve their future, but as Smirnov states "We were thrown in as mere gun-fodder against the well-trained and well-equipped German troops. After one night of hand-to-hand fighting and heavy machine-gun fire, the Vladimir Contingent had only 19 men left of the 90 who had started."

On October 24, 1914, *Nijnichin* (Private) Smirnov was recommended for his first decoration—the soldiers Cross of Saint George, Fourth Class. This was the first decoration bestowed on a member of the Vladimir contingent, and most likely its last. Within days, Smirnov was the only one left fighting.

Weeks later, on December 8, 1914, Smirnov's right leg was seriously injured by enemy machine-gun fire. He spent the next five months in a hospital in Saint Petersburg. While recuperating, he became interested in aviation. With the aid of his nurse and her influential father, he transferred to the aviation school in Saint Petersburg on August 7, 1915, and then moved on to the Moscow flying school in the winter of 1916[1]. On August 25, 1916, he was given the title of pilot and sent to the 19th Corps Fighter Detachment, located near the town of Lutsk.[2]

Throughout the fall of 1916, Smirnov received advanced pilot training on Nieuport aircraft while at the front. On December 21, he made his first combat flight under the watchful eyes of his commanding officer, *Stabsrotmistre* (Staff-Captain, cavalry) Alexander Kozakov. Smirnov was flying a Nieuport 10 with observer *Stabs-Kapitan* (Staff-Captain) Pentko when Kozakov shot down an enemy aircraft for the education of the fledgling hunters. The enemy machine, Brandenburg C.I 27.14 from Flik 10, crashed south of Zabocol Village. This was Kozakov's fifth confirmed victory.

Twelve days later, January 2, 1917, Smirnov and his observer, Pentko, were flying a Nieuport 10 when they

---

(1) The nurse's father was a General on the staff of the Grand Duke Alexander.
(2) In August 1916, the 19th Corps Fighter Detachment was attached to the Army's First Air Company.

Cadet group at Moscow flying school, summer 1916. Smirnov is laying down in first row, third from left.

Right: Smirnov (second from left) and Lipsky (third from left) at the Moscow aviation school.

Morane Saulnier L, winter 1915. Smirnov trained in this aircraft while at the Moscow aviation school.

Deperdussin TT of the 19th Fighter Detachment, fall 1916. The black Roman numerals XIX and serial number 2 are clearly visible on the fuselage. The small manufacturer's serial number (43) is visible on the rudder. Although no other markings are present, it is believed Russian cockades were applied beneath the wings.

encountered a German aircraft in Russian territory. Although the Russians were equipped only with rifles, they quickly engaged the enemy machine and severely wounded its crew. The German machine crashed near the town of Lutsk. Russian troops confirmed the German aircraft, Aviatik C.1 serial C2775/16, was destroyed and both crewmen were dead. For his first victory, Smirnov was promoted to the rank of *Starski unteroffizier* (Sergeant).

In February, 1917, the Russian Army's First Combat Air Group and its detachments were transferred by train to Romania. The 19th Corps Detachment was located in a snow-covered field near the town of Jassy. However, aerial activity was slow and several weeks later the detachment was moved 180 miles north to the town of Stanislav. To counter the enemy's aerial activity in this sector, Smirnov flew daily patrols under hazardous conditions. On April 29, 1917, he was awarded the Cross of Saint George, Third Class, for his aggressive behavior.

Three days later, May 2, 1917, Smirnov earned the Cross of Saint George, Second Class, for his second victory. Flying a Morane Saulnier I, he attacked a German Albatros from *Flieger Abteilung (A)* 220 near the village of Guilche. Although Smirnov initially caught the enemy crew by surprise, after a short burst of gunfire his weapon jammed. Forced to maneuver under enemy fire, he quickly repaired his gun and attacked the enemy machine a second time, apparently with better aim. Within moments a white jet of smoke appeared from the damaged aircraft and it crash-landed nose down. Although one German jumped out and attempted to set the aircraft's wing on fire, the plane and both crewmen were quickly captured by the 3rd Caucasian Corps.

Smirnov was promoted to the rank of *Praporshik* (Ensign) on May 13, 1917. On May 18, 1917, he had a brutal battle with an enemy aircraft at 0900 hours north of Bolshovtse. Smirnov believed the enemy machine was hit several times before its pilot made a steep descent to his territory and landed; however, because Russian troops did not observe the battle, no confirmation was given. A Russian report indicated Smirnov's aircraft was severely damaged by the enemy's fire.

On June 3, 1917, Smirnov was sent on leave and did

Nieuport 10 aircraft of the 19th Fighter Detachment, Galicia, fall, 1916. The second aircraft from the right of photo is serial number 720. Smirnov scored his first victory in a Nieuport 10 on January 2, 1917.

German Aviatik C.I, serial number C2775/16, which Smirnov and Pentko shot down for their first confirmed victory, January 2, 1917, Lutsk.

not return to the front until July 3, 1917. At the beginning of August he was conferred the rank of military pilot. Two weeks later, on August 16, 1917, he obtained his third victory during a flight with *Praporshik* Ernst Leman. Both Russians sighted and attacked two aircraft over the front lines. Although the first enemy machine escaped in the region of Skala, the second was shot down at Melnitsy.

One week later, on August 23, 1917, *Praporshik* Smirnov teamed up with *Poruchik* Huber, to obtain his fourth victory. Flying Nieuport 17s at 3800 meters, both Russian pilots were involved in six consecutive fights with various enemy aircraft in the Gusyatin-Gorodische area. The last machine was chased down below 400 meters and crash-landed near the village of Ludwipol. Smirnov's combat report stated "The plane nosed over on landing. One of the pilots got out of the aircraft, the other remained there being badly wounded or killed. Evidently, the radiator and motor were punctured judging by the amount of steam coming out."

On August 24 Smirnov flew a patrol with Kozakov in the Gusyatin region. Both Russians attacked an enemy plane that left a trail of smoke as it went down, but no

The detachment's Halberstadt C.I. This heavily armed machine is equipped with three machines guns; a fixed forward-firing Colt, a Lewis mounted on the top wing, and a German Parabellum in the observer's position. *Stabs-Kapitan* Pentko is standing at right.

Above: Smirnov with other unidentified pilots of the 19th Fighter Detachment, Lutsk, winter 1917. Smirnov is second from left, with the Soldiers' Cross of Saint George, Fourth Class, on his left breast.

Smirnov with POW German pilot Herman Lader from *Flieger Abteilung (A)220*. Smirnov shot down Lader for his third victory on May 2, 1917.

confirmation was obtained. More bad luck followed on August 29, when Smirnov attacked a pair of enemy aircraft north of Skala at 1915 hours. Although he hit one machine on his first pass, both escaped across their own lines. Finally, on September 8, 1917, Smirnov's luck changed. He shot down an enemy aircraft in the Gusyatin area. This time Russian troops clearly observed the action and confirmed the victory, Smirnov's fifth.

Smirnov scored his sixth victory in a Spad fighter on September 24, 1917. Flying over the village of Balin with *Praporshik* Longin Lipsky, both Russians swooped down onto a German reconnaissance aircraft from *Flieger Abteilung (A)240* and mortally wounded its observer, Paul Thierfelder, with several bullets to his head. Although the pilot, Herman Utsch, was unharmed, apparently the sight of his observer convinced him surrender was in his best interest and he quickly landed his machine. Russian troops captured the slightly damaged Albatros C.III, as well as the pilot. For his sixth victory, Smirnov was awarded the Golden Sword of Saint George.

Smirnov's accomplishment in scoring six victories cannot be overstated. Considering that the equipment used by the Russian pilots was generally out of date and not well maintained, it was an impressive feat. A machine gun that jammed in battle could have disastrous consequences for a pilot. Smirnov clearly explains the problem: "On October 2, 1917, I encountered ten enemy planes in a quick succession, but I had to carefully

Smirnov scored at least two confirmed victories in his French-built Nieuport 21, serial number 1514. This machine's unusual armament is a Madsen machine gun (fixed in position) and supplied with ammunition from the belt. Discharged cartridges are held in the canister located on the gun's right side.

Aircraft of the 19th Fighter Detachment lined up at Guilche airfield, Galicia, April 1917. The mix of Nieuports (types 10, 16, and 17) are both French- and Russian-built. The Morane Saulnier I was used by Smirnov to score two victories. Standard detachment markings were black skull on white rudder or white skull on black rudder.

Left: Smirnov in the cockpit of his Morane Saulnier I, April 1917.

Below: A Spad A.4 of the 19th Corps Fighter Detachment, Jassy airfield, Romania, February 1917. Smirnov (center of photo) and Lipsky flew several missions in this aircraft.

Bottom: Smirnov with pilot Alfred Heft from *Flieger Abteilung (A)*240. Smirnov shot down Heft's aircraft for his fifth confirmed victory, August 23, 1917. Although both men are standing in front of Smirnov's Morane Saulnier I, combat reports indicted Smirnov shot down Heft while flying Nieuport 21 serial number 1514.

Smirnov with his Spad 7, summer 1917. He scored seven confirmed victories in this aircraft.

Praporshik Longin Lipsky. After the war, Lipsky emigrated to the United States.

maneuver around each, because the machine gun was jammed again. One machine fired eight rockets at my aircraft—fortunately without results! The next day, I attacked an enemy plane south of Skala, but after I fired 90 bullets at him, my machine gun jammed again. While I tried to clear the jammed bullet my fuel tank was shot through. Luckily, there was no explosion or fire, and I returned to my airfield unharmed." Fortunately, not all of Smirnov's combats involved jammed machine guns. He scored his seventh victory on October 24, 1917, by shooting down German pilot Helmut Tehsenvity over Kowel.

Besides faulty equipment, Smirnov had to endure political unrest. Although the Provisional Government under Kerensky had some measure of control during the summer of 1917, the revolution could not be contained. The period from September to October was a time of uncertainty as demands for an armistice became more insistent. At the front, the Soldiers' Committees condoned the murder of officers. In addition, one of the first acts of the Bolsheviks was a cessation of the war. On November 8, 1917, they issued a decree of peace and ordered soldiers to stop fighting. Just flying at all during this time, much less flying successfully against the enemy, took more than a little fortitude.

Smirnov clearly conveyed his attitude to the political war on November 11, 1917. Teamed with Lipsky, they scored their first double victory of the war. The enemy machines, Brandenburg C.Is from Flik 9, were photographing the Russian trench system when the Russians attacked at 1700 hours.

Praporschik Longin Lipsky with his Nieuport 17. Lipsky teamed with Smirnov to obtain several victories.

The first machine was hit by machine gun fire from Smirnov's Spad 7 and quickly exploded into flames. As the machine descended, it rolled inverted and dumped both crew members out. They struck the ground only seconds before their machine, Brandenburg C.I 269.08, crashed into the trenching wire near the village of Zelena.

The second enemy machine, Brandenburg C.I 269.68, with pilot Josef Ryba and officer observer Josef Barcal, concentrated their gunfire on Smirnov's aircraft, only to be surprised by Lipsky, who dove his Nieuport 21 down on top of the enemy crew and quickly hit them with gunfire. Within seconds the enemy machine was in flames and, with a sharp turn, crashed between the trenches south of Zelena. Russian artillery promptly shelled the second aircraft to insure its destruction, while the crewmen of a third machine safely descended into their own lines. As Lipsky passed overhead, he observed shells burst on top of the fallen machine.

Smirnov's combat report stated; "After three enemy planes were reported. Lipsky and myself immediately started the motors. Lipsky's motor failed, therefore I decided to launch by myself. I happened to be 200 meters higher than the enemy planes that were doing reconnaissance. I approached one of the enemy planes and opened fire and I noticed that I hit it, though I was shooting from a limited distance. The enemy began to glide like a leaf, suddenly his plane exploded in fire and fell down leaving a long black oily tail of smoke. I turned towards the other plane, but when I attacked, my machine gun was jammed. I became helpless. I could only circle over it, and it would be crazy for me to attack it being armed only with my revolver. Suddenly I saw Lipsky. I continued to distract the attention of the German (sic) circling around so that Lipsky could approach me unnoticed. Before the German realized what was going on, Lipsky dove firing a whirlwind of bullets at him. The German caught fire fast and went down following his comrade."

Two days later, on November 13, 1917, Smirnov was awarded the Order Saint George, Fourth Class.[3] Another victory followed on November 23, 1917, as Smirnov brutally attacked an Austro-Hungarian aircraft south of Letovo village. After a short but vicious battle, Smirnov killed both crewmen with gunfire and shot down the enemy machine. Russian troops confirmed the fallen aircraft was a Lloyd C.V, serial 46.22, from Flik 18.

Smirnov scored his 11th and last victory on November 26, 1917, while participating in a joint mission with Kozakov. The Russians conducted four separate attacks on enemy planes in the region of Skolat; one of them was forced down to ground level and crash-landed at the enemy's front lines.

General Vyatcheslav Tkachev, commander-in-chief of the Russian air force, noticed the activities of the pilots and sent a telegram to the 19th Corps Fighter Detachment. In addition to praising Smirnov for his continued success over the enemy, the telegram read in part "During the days of terrible devastation and deathly danger for our long suffering country, your actions insure us that our glorious pilots will fulfill to the end their duty, and they

---

(3) Smirnov and Lipsky each received credit for two victories.

Smirnov in his RAF uniform, Upavon airfield, England, 1918.

would remain at their difficult, but glorious posts, winning new crowns of laurels for our fine native aviation."

Although this telegram was well intended, it unfortunately caused the Bolsheviks to take note of Smirnov. Perhaps fearing reprisals from German troops, the Bolsheviks viewed Smirnov's actions in a different light and decided he was to be shot with other officers in the unit. Luckily, he anticipated the plot and deserted the unit before it could be carried out. Joined by Lipsky, and Sikakovon (another officer pilot), the three men made their way out of Russia in early 1918.

After the end of the war, Smirnov was appointed assistant air attaché and chief test pilot for the White Russians in Paris. He served as a member of the Slavanic-British aviation detachment during the Russian civil war and as a member of the RAF, instructing pilots at England's Upavon and Netheravon air bases. In 1920,

Smirnov standing in front of a Fokker F-3 aircraft, 1922. Smirnov was employed with KLM (Royal Dutch Airlines) as a commercial pilot.

Smirnov joined the Belgian airline SNETA (preceding Sabena), where he flew D.H. and Spad aircraft. In 1922 he began a long and brilliant career with the Royal Dutch Airlines (KLM) as a commercial pilot. During World War II he flew with the Netherland's East Indies Army Air Corps, obtaining the rank of captain. He was shot down and seriously wounded on March 2, 1942 by three Japanese Mitsubishi Zero fighters. He stopped flying in 1949 and died in Majorca in October 1956.

Vladimir Ivanovich Strizhevsky

Vladimir Ivanovich Strizhevsky. His awards included: The Soldier's Cross of Saint George, First, Second, Third, and Fourth Classes; and the Romanian Crown with Swords. Charcoal sketch by Terry Waldron.

Vladimir Ivanovich Strizhevsky was born on December 26, 1894. He was a nobleman from Mogiljevsky Province and a member of the Russian Orthodox church. Strizhevsky attended the Petrograd Polytechnical Institute, majoring in electro-mechanical engineering. Little else is known of his early life.

On October 14, 1914, he volunteered for the Russian air service. Four days later he was sent to the St. Petersburg Polytechnical Institute to take a course concerning theoretical aviation. He was graduated on January 2, 1915, and sent to Gatchinsky Military Air Force School. He passed examination for the title of pilot on July 29, 1915, and was appointed to the 16th Corps Squadron on August 10.

Strizhevsky arrived at the 16th Squadron on September 5 and was promoted to the rank of *Podporuchik* (Warrant Officer) on September 14. Between his arrival and January, 1916, he made 43 battle flights with a total duration of 65 hours and 44 minutes. By early 1916 he had received all four classes of the Soldier's Cross of Saint George, and was promoted to the rank of *Praporshik* (Ensign) on February 10, 1916, for his distinguished combat service.

On March 9, 1916, while on a routine patrol from the village of Touritche to the town of Kamenets-Podolsk, Strizhevsky crash-landed and was seriously injured. A report concerning the incident stated *"Praporshik Strizhevsky of the 16th Corps Detachment and his mechanic were injured because the motor 'Gnome' in his Morane-Parasol type L malfunctioned. Strizhevsky was badly wounded in his face and his right leg. The mechanic received several contusions. Strizhevsky will be out of service for several months. The apparatus is broken completely."*

Strizhevsky was hospitalized until June 24, 1916, and then sent to a therapy center in Odessa until July 1916. He returned to the front on August 24, 1916, with a transfer to the 9th Fighter Detachment.

Probably due to his poor health, Strizhevsky's first assignment with the 9th Fighter Detachment was manager of the photo lab. His first combat patrol occurred in December 1916, in a Dux-built Nieuport 11 (serial 1016). From January to March 1917, he slowly increased the number of missions he performed as his strength returned.

Strizhevsky's first confirmed victory occurred on March 17, 1917, when he shot down an enemy plane that caught fire and went down near the region of Herzh. The subsequent report stated, "An enemy plane was noticed in the valley Oytoz. Having overcome the enemy fast, in my Nieuport 21 (serial 1719), I attacked him and fired at him almost point blank, while swooping over him from the back. During my second attack the enemy plane was going down fast, but it opened fire on me. In spite of that, I approached it once more from the back and fired at it again. I was following the enemy who continued going down. Probably the damage was serious, because it forced him to go down fast. While recharging my machine gun, I lost sight of the fast descending enemy as he flew to valley Oytoz." Although Strizhevsky did not see the enemy aircraft crash, Russian troops did and confirmed the victory.

After his first victory, Strizhevsky really hit his stride as a fighter pilot. In April, 1917 he made 12 battle flights totaling more than 23 hours flying time and scored four victories, three of which were confirmed.

Strizhevsky's second confirmed victory came on April 11, 1917. According to the Russian air force communiqué to the Romanian Army General Headquarters; "At 0940 hours four Russian planes flew over the town of Kezdy-Vasarhely to reconnoiter the enemy positions and drop bombs on the ammunition dumps at the town's outskirts and on the barracks inhabited by the Austro-Hungarian troops. Having taken off from the airfield by the town of Siret, the four planes were strongly strafed by the enemy anti-aircraft artillery located around the target. The 105-

A Spad 7 preparing for takeoff. Strizhevsky used this type of aircraft to obtain three of his seven confirmed victories.

mm guns discharged on them hundreds of shells that forced our pilots to rise to 3,700 m (12,100 ft). Several shells splintered and struck the fuselage and wings of our machines without succeeding in preventing them fulfilling their mission. The bombing was successfully accomplished and a fire was spotted in the northwestern part of the town, where the troops' barracks and dumps were concentrated. On their return flight, our planes, accompanied by a Spad 7 fighter plane manned by pilot officer Vladimir Strizhevsky, met two German scouting LVG planes, accompanied by a Fokker E.III fighter. Our planes, as well as the enemy's planes, dispersed, surprised by the unexpected meeting, and afterwards regrouped to face the attack wherever it came from. Pilot-officer Strizhevsky attacked the enemy fighter and chased it away from the front with machine-gun fire. Damaged by our fighter's bullets, the German plane retreated to its lines leaving behind the two LVGs that, having remained on their own, organized themselves fairly well to be able to elude and even answer the attack of our fighter or of one of our scouting planes that had participated in the bombing mission. Pilot officer Strizhevsky attacked one of the enemy planes by coming to it up front and then, negotiating a turn, swooped down after it, closing at approximately 80 meters. Thus, having come from behind, he had the possibility to fire on the LVG for about 7–8 seconds, a long round of tracer bullets that closely besieged the enemy plane. It turned its tail, zigzagging and hoping to escape its pursuer. But our fighter pilot, proving his great skill at flying, succeeded in catching up with the enemy plane and firing several rounds at it. The enemy gunner had been killed by the bullets because pilot officer Strizhevsky no longer encountered the shooting resistance from the enemy plane. This gave Strizhevsky the possibility to administer a death blow in the fuel tanks. The LVG took fire and began to spin to finally fall down and crash in the Romanian lines, in the 5th Infantry Division's sector. The Romanian officers that witnessed the air fight confirmed our pilot's courage. Upon landing, the engineers found two enemy bullet marks on our plane's fuselage that, however, did not inflict great damage."

Strizhevsky's next victory, which was not confirmed, came on April 16, 1917, during an effort to support several reconnaissance flights being performed for the 2nd Romanian Army, whose front lines ran from Bitca Carelor to Iresti. Of special interest was a stretch of 33.6 km. that ran from Magura Casinulin to Miniia Hill. The Romanians expected an attack in this area and it was being watched carefully. Unfortunately, for aerial reconnaissance the only scouting unit the Romanians had was a Farman detachment.

To ensure a successful mission, pilots from the Russian 9th Fighter Detachment were required to fly escort for the Farmans. The official report for Strizhevsky's mission of April 16, stated; "Our aircraft took off at 0830 hours from the Airbocamul airfield, a scouting and light bomber plane (F.40) serial number 3204 (pilot, officer Popa, observer, officer Sanatescu) directed itself towards the front area, accompanied by a Russian fighter plane manned by pilot-officer Strizhevsky of the Russian 9th Fighter Detachment. During their mission the two planes were attacked by a K.D. Austro-Hungarian fighter.[1] In the beginning, the enemy fighter rushed to the scouting F.40 that avoided the attack, its pilot, officer Popa, having skillfully maneuvered and dodged the enemy bullets. Situated slightly higher, at 2,900 meters (9500 ft.), the Russian pilot came in a gentle dive and attacked the aggressor, enabling the Romanian F.40 scouting plane's departure and retreat towards its airfield. The fight was an extremely tough one, gunfire storming both ways, the two pilots highly skilled in the art of flying. Each of them evaded the direct confrontation, looking for an opportunity to administer a final blow. The firing continued for well over 10 minutes with no outcome. The Austro-Hungarian K.D. withdrew from the battle, creating the impression that it was going back to base. But that was only a trick, because, having flown off for just about 700–800 meters, it took a sharp turn and, enjoying a higher position, dashed at the Russian pilot that was on his way towards his airbase. Dodging the direct attack, pilot-officer Strizhevsky turned and finding the correct moment, stuck the enemy with several bullets in the fuselage, near the cockpit, and the Austro-Hungarian pilot was forced to flee the fight because some of his controls were damaged." Although this was not a confirmed victory, Strizhevsky certainly got the best in this combat.

Strizhevsky's third confirmed victory came the next day, April 17. Again according to the official report: "Our fighter pilots Suk and Strizhevsky during patrol flights attacked two enemy planes in the Keyupul region going to Radautz. The enemy planes flew at 4000 meters altitude; when they noticed our pursuit, they turned to the south of Toyoy. The pilot Strizhevsky attacked the back plane of the enemy group and, maneuvering skillfully, fired at him from a very close distance with two machine guns in sequence. The enemy plane began a steep descent, moving irregularly up and down, and the pilot was throwing some kind of objects out of the plane. Our second pilot, *Praporshik* Suk, was attacking the other plane, that tried to help the first plane, but he was forced to go down. Pursuing the enemy, *Praporshik* Suk saw how the enemy plane that had been shot by *Praporshik* Strizhevsky at the altitude of 700 meters, went into a spin and crash-landed in the woods at Rakoas." This victory was confirmed by Suk and Russian troops.

Strizhevsky had become a formidable fighter pilot and he quickly scored another confirmed victory, his fourth, on April 23, 1917. The 2nd Army's report stated: "Detachments from the First Air Force Group carried out several reconnaissance and bombing missions on the Oituz Valley and over the Hirja village and in the 71st German Infantry Division sector. Our planes were

strongly shelled by the anti-aircraft artillery situated on hill (K713), to the north of Poiana Sarata and on mark (1038) to the east of it. The guns' bore seemed, according to the black smoke of the shells, 105-mm. On the morning missions of April 23, three Russian planes also participated—two scouting and one photographic. One fighter was flown by pilot-officer Strizhevsky of the 9th Fighter Detachment, whose airfield was located near the town of Sereth. Having arrived over Aura Humorului, in the front area where the Austro-Hungarian 7th Army units were located, the Russian planes began to photograph the enemy positions. After an interval of about 20 minutes, during which the enemy anti-aircraft artillery had shelled the planes with dozens of heavy caliber shells, when the mission was almost completed and the allied crews were preparing to go back to base, from somewhere to there left there appeared a formation of four German scouting LVG and Albatros planes that had carried off a reconnaissance mission to our lines. The Russian pilots abandoned their business and flew towards the enemy formation that was slightly lower. In the beginning the German crews did not notice the fact that the Russian planes had turned their way and were continuing on the way to base unaware of the danger threatening them. They saw their opponents only when those were already at about 200 meters from them. The Russian pilots' attack began by harassment, the last plane in the formation's tail being the one they attacked. Pilot-officer Strizhevsky dodged in time a round of tracers, shooting sharply upwards. This maneuver made him lose his ground for a short interval, an advantage he had won with great effort. The German pilots were very sure of themselves and, having organized, embarked on a coordinated defense action, re-grouping and answering with precise fire. After taking a rather sharp turn the Russian fighter pilot rose in height and attacked the enemy formation that was also being harassed by the crew of flying officer Llya Gurkov and observer *Kapitan* Vasiu Antonov. The other Russian crew withdrew from the battle as their plane had been badly damaged and its controls deranged, and flew to base. The other two allied planes continued to fight. Pilot-officer Strizhevsky attacked a LVG on the same level and in front of him. He fell easily on it, converting his 100 meters of altitude into speed and placing himself exactly behind it, in the dead angle, unnoticed by the German crew. The Russian fighter pilot opened fire and the enemy plane got seriously struck in its controls. The damaged plane started with disordered movements towards the ground to finally have a crash landing near Gura Humorului." This victory was confirmed by 2nd Russian Army troops.

The Romanian Army General Staff report of the same battle read: "In Gura Humorului an enemy plane has been knocked down during a fight with a Russian Spad fighter manned by the pilot-officer Strizhevsky. The two German pilots taken prisoner stated that they belonged to the 42nd Squadron and that one section of this was located at Toplița. The 42nd Squadron's main location was in Focsani and it was equipped with no fighter planes and only scouting and bomber planes of Albatros, LVG, and

(1) Officially designated the Brandenburg D.I.

Pilots of the 9th Fighter Detachment, early spring 1917. Strizhevsky is standing in first row, center. All others unknown.

AEG type. The prisoners stated that they had been on their fifth mission over the Romanian front and that they had photographed several positions of the Romanian and Russian armies on the Oituz valley. They also pointed out the fact that in Focsani there was located as well the 20th squadron, that possessed DFW and AEG scouting and bombing planes, and that soon there was also expected to arrive here one more squadron from the French front. The prisoners also related having seen many wounded soldiers that belonged to the 182nd and 252nd German Infantry Regiments of the 76th and 216th Infantry Divisions."

On May 11, 1917, Strizhevsky attacked an enemy plane in the region of the village Bogda-Neshti. After several attacks the enemy plane was wrapped in heavy smoke and crash-landed in enemy territory. No victory credit was given to Strizhevsky for this combat.

The next week, on May 17, 1917, Strizhevsky obtained his fifth confirmed victory . The 2nd Romanian Army's report read: "The enemy scouting aircraft have lately intensified their activity entering our lines and trying to photograph the fortification works, the lines of communication, and the troops' movements. The First Air Force Group (Romanian Air Unit-Bacau) has received the order to intensify its activity; above the front lines there are to be permanently present two scouting planes, accompanied by a fighter plane. Because the stretch of the front is rather great, a cooperation with the 9th Fighter Detachment is to be maintained so that missions would be carried out with the direct participation of the Russian fighter aircraft, since the First Group possesses just one fighter squadron and a small number of planes and pilots. On May 17, 1917, a F.40 plane belonging to First Air Force Group (crewed by pilot Popa and observer-officer Petrescu Serbau) received the order to do the ranging for a battery on the 2nd Army front. The F.40 was escorted by a Spad fighter-plane, manned by pilot-officer Strizhevsky, that ensured its protection. During the mission an enemy K.D. fighter attacked the Romanian scouting plane that had, for a short time, to interrupt its activity. The Russian pilot started the fight with that plane and after some firing, the enemy plane flew from the fight, having been badly damaged in its engine, and afterwards fell to the ground where it crashed. On its way back, the Romanian F.40 was straddled by the shelling from several enemy artillery batteries and was hit in full. The crew crashed in the Caflin area and the two Romanian pilots died." This victory was confirmed by the 2nd Army.

Strizhevsky 's sixth confirmed victory came on June 17, 1917. The Romanian Army General Headquarters News Office reported for that day: "The 4th Russian Army's communiqué no. 1/3752 indicates that at 6 in the morning, six enemy planes flew over Tecuci dropping several bombs, but without causing too much damage. Our, as well as the Russian, destroyers (fighter planes) have driven away the attacks of the German scouting and bomber aircraft. During one of the air fights that took place during the day the Russian pilot-officer Strizhevsky knocked down a German Fokker fighter plane. Having gone at noon on an escorting mission with two Romanian F.40 scouting planes of the First Air Force Group that had the mission to photograph the enemy positions of the First Austro-Hungarian Army, our formation was attacked by two German Fokker E.III fighter planes. Their target proved to the scouting planes, whose crews were not impressed by the attack on them. The observer gunners on the F.40s opened a precise fire and kept the aggressors at a distance, then pilot-officer Strizhevsky managed to chase a Fokker away. After one enemy retreated to his lines, Strizhevsky valiantly attacked the remaining one. The enemy pilot was a greatly experienced flier because he succeeded in eluding the Russians pilot's direct attacks. The fight lasted well over 15 minutes and, taking advantage at one moment of the fact that the German pilot had lost altitude, the Russian pilot managed to shoot a round that struck the other's engine. Black smoke began immediately to come out of the plane, the enemy pilot took a turn and tried to fly back to his airfield. But the Russian pilot caught up with him and gave the plane the finishing stroke, the German Fokker crashing on the Uzul Valley." Strizhevsky's victory was confirmed by the Romanian army and the 4th Russian Army.

The next day, June 8, 1917, Strizhevsky conducted two combats with enemy aircraft over the valley of Ousa and obtained his seventh and last victory of the war. During one of the engagements, he attacked the enemy aircraft from behind and forced it into a spin. Although the aircraft recovered, it allowed Strizhevsky to attack again from shorter range and resulted in hits on its radiator and fuel tank. Strizhevsky noticed a jet of water flowing from the machine's radiator as it began to descend. Strizhevsky attacked it two more times, wounding the pilot, but at an altitude of 1600 meters he was fired at by enemy artillery and had to break off his attack. The enemy aircraft fell near the Russian 8th Company of the 750th Infantry Regiment, which confirmed the victory for Strizhevsky.

The 9th Fighter Detachment filed a report for the battle which read: "During a patrol flight our pilot, Strizhevsky, noticed an enemy plane flying over our position away from River Onsa at Grozeshty. It was shot down after a hard battle, and it descended in the valley of Ousa, half a kilometer to the west of village Payana Ouzuluy. When going down the ravine the plane was shattered. The observer, Lieutenant Hoffman, and the pilot, Corporal Pranger, were taken prisoner. Our pilot fired 300 cartridges during the air battle, the enemy fired 450 cartridges between them; 150 cartridges were fired by the observer, and the pilot fired 300 cartridges."[2]

In July, 1917, Strizhevsky performed 57 combat missions totaling more than 90 hours flying time. During one of those missions, on July 18, he attacked an enemy aircraft over the village of Vermeshty with *Podporuchik* Loiko and *Podporuchik* Koklin. Loiko clearly observed bullets hit the cockpit of the enemy two-seater, but not before Strizhevsky was wounded with two bullets in his right leg. To make matters worse for Strizhevsky, as the smoking machine started going down, it was lost in clouds. The same heavy clouds, prevented Russian troops from seeing the battle and confirming the victory.

A review of Austro-Hungarian records indicates Brandenburg C.I 67.52 from Flik 39 was attacked and forced to land near Comanestie on July 18. Its pilot, August Novak,[3] was severely wounded and its observer, Franz Firtos, was killed. This crew might have engaged Strizhevsky that day.

Three days later, the commander of the Imperial Russian Air Service, *Palkovnik* (Colonel) Vyatcheslav Tkachev, expressed his concern about Strizhevsky's wounds and "wished him a speedy recovery and further glory through service in battle."

Strizhevsky was out of combat for some time while his wounds healed; he did not perform any combat missions the rest of July and August. By the time he was fully recovered all combat flights had ended on the Eastern Front. Further details of his life are unknown.

Despite Strizhevsky's great combat success of seven confirmed victories, his commanding officer during his service with the 9th Fighter Squadron, *Podporuchik* Ivan Loiko, never recommended him for promotion or any decorations. However, Strizhevsky's courage and success were not ignored by his allies, the Romanians.

High Royal Decree No. 131 Of January 25, 1918 read: "I Ferdinand, by the will of God and in accordance with the nation's wishes, King of Romania, grant the order—Romania's crown with swords for officer rank—to the pilot *Praporshik* Valdimir Strizhevsky of the Russian air force for his skillful fighting which brought down at least four enemy planes in our territory, among which one on the Uzul valley on June 17, 1917."

---

(2) According to Austrian Archives the plane, Brandenburg C.I 67.54 of Flik 39, was shot down. The crew was military pilot *Korporal* Adolph Pranger and observer *Leutnant* Otto Hoffmann.

(3) *Feldwebel* Augustin Novak would later become and ace with five confirmed victories to his credit.

Grigory Eduardovich Suk

Grigory Eduardovich Suk. His awards included: Soldiers Cross of Saint George, First, Second, Third, and Fourth Classes; the Romanian Order of the Crown, with Swords.

Grigory Eduardovich Suk was born to Russian and Czech parents on December 12, 1896. His uncle, Yacheslav Ivanovich Suk, was the well-known conductor of the Bolshoi Theater in Moscow. Besides the fact Suk was a nobleman and reared in the Orthodox faith, little else is known of his early life.

On August 5, 1914, immediately after the war started, Suk volunteered for the air service. He was appointed to Katchinsky Aviation School on June 9, 1915, and obtained the title of military pilot on January 25, 1916. On March 11 he was transferred to the 26th Corps Detachment and arrived at the front on March 28. His combat flying must have been outstanding because he was quickly promoted to the rank of *Podpraporshik* (Warrant Officer) on July 2 and assigned to the Moscow Military Aviation school for training on fighters. He was graduated on August 19 and appointed to the 9th Fighter Detachment.[1]

On October 27, 1916, Suk was promoted to *Praporshik* (Ensign) for distinguished service in battle. His commanding officer, *Podporuchik* (Second Lieutenant) Loiko, wrote: "Staff pilot since August 28, 1916. The pilot *Praporshik* Suk is an excellent pilot and he can brilliantly fulfill battle assignments under difficult conditions, does his work with enthusiasm. In reference to the inherent service of the detachment he is industrious and neat, but has not enough experience because he was only recently promoted to the rank of officer, and he had held no responsible position before. In business and private affairs he carries himself excellently and could be an efficient officer. He cannot be unit commander because of weak grounding in aircraft."

Suk's first successful encounter with an enemy aircraft occured on January 21, 1917, while on a patrol 3000 meters above Herzha. Within minutes he caught and attacked an enemy two-seater with his Nieuport 11 (serial 1109). Apparently damaged, the aircraft glided over enemy lines at a low altitude and then crash-landed. However, the victory was not confirmed.

On February 3, 1917, he and *Praporshik* Strizhevsky intercepted and shot down an enemy aircraft in the region of the Ousy River valley—without confirmation. On February 9 Suk had another unsuccessful interception after his machine gun jammed while firing at an enemy plane above the Shitoolion River. Finally, on February 12, while Suk was returning from a long reconnaissance flight, the engine of his Nieuport 11 failed and he forced to make a dead-stick landing at Bakey airfield. Unfortunately, Suk's inability to land the aircraft caused him to overturn and crash. As punishment, he was assigned a Morane Sauliner type H (serial 742) for several weeks.

Suk's first confirmed victory occured on March 26, 1917, while on a patrol flight 4800 meters above the Bystritsy region. Flying a Nieuport 11 (serial 1127), he saw an enemy plane below. After diving onto his opponent, Suk started firing when 300 meters away and continued until only 20 meters separated the two aircraft. The enemy plane returned fire for a short time and then began to go down, evidently damaged. While Suk turned for a second attack, he lost sight of the enemy aircraft, which had descended. Suk returned to his airfield thinking the worst, but to his surprise Russian troops confirmed the victory. Austro-Hungarian records indicate Brandenburg C.I 67.24 from Flik 40 was forced to landed in the Bystritsy region on March 26, 1917. The crew, officer pilot Kenedy and observer Duller, were slightly injured. Most likely this was the aircraft shot down by Suk.

Suk scored again on April 17, 1917, with the help of *Praporshik* Strizhevsky. Suk's subsequent report stated, "Having noticed shooting over Oneshty I flew my

---

(1) When Suk arrived at this unit on August 28, 1916, his annual salary and living allowance totaled 1512 roubles.

Henri Farman HF.20 with an unknown corps unit. Suk flew this type with the 26 Corps Detachment between January and July, 1916.

Nieuport *BeBe* (serial 1109) from Herzh to Pralea, where I noticed two enemy planes and the plane (Nieuport 21, serial 1719) of *Praporshik* Strizhevsky. I noticed his battle with the enemy flying in the lower rear; both were going down in circles. The other enemy tried to attack *Praporshik* Strizhevsky from above, but soon I attacked him and forced him away to his own position. When recharging my machine gun, I noticed the first enemy plane going straight down. I observed it till it reached 1800 meters altitude, and then I saw the enemy planes go into a spin at the altitude of 700 meters and then fall in the woods in Rakosa region." The victory was confirmed by Russian troops.[2]

On August 8, 1917, Suk obtained his third victory when he shot down Oeffag C.II 52.63 from Flik 44. The Austro-Hungarian crew, Adolf Rabel and his observer, *Oberleutnant d.R.* Franz Xaver Schlarbaum, were spotting artillery fire by radio along the route Kezdy-Vazarecheli-Herastru-Par-Lesuntas when Suk attacked. Within moments, Rabel was seriously wounded and crash-landed his plane near Romanian troops. He died soon after, but Schlarbaum was captured alive.

Suk had more inconclusive interceptions. On August 14, while flying Nieuport 21 (serial 1719) near the town of Gumora, he noticed an enemy plane, but it evaded him and quickly retreated at high speed. On August 28, while in Vickers FB.19 (serial 12), Suk again encountered an enemy plane over Gumora, but after an unsuccessful attack the enemy escaped behind its own lines.

Although these enemy aircraft were not destroyed by Suk, it is important to emphasize that the important reconnaissance missions being conducted by their crews were interrupted.

On September 4, 1917, Suk scored his fourth victory while flying 4500 meters above Radautz. A subsequent report stated, "*Praporshik* Suk flying Vicker FB. 19 (serial 12) intercepted the enemy aircraft simultaneously with *Poruchik* Loiko flying Nieuport 17 (serial 1448) over the village Yaslovets. Loiko attacked from above and Suk attacked from below. They opened fire from 150 meters and continued to fire until they closed to 20 meters. Unable to avoid combat, the enemy observer first fired at Loiko's Nieuport with his machine gun, then fired at Suk's Vickers. Loiko continued firing from a closer range. The observer fired two short bursts at Suk's Vickers, then dropped his machine gun. The enemy plane turned toward Radautz and dived away. Loiko's Nieuport experienced a jammed machine gun and he flew aside to correct it, and Suk again attacked the plane, from which the observer was shooting now with his carbine. Then the enemy plane straightened out and crashed in the village of River Auchavitsa between Radautz and the village Wolowets." Russian troops confirmed this victory for Suk and Loiko.

On September 7, 1917, Suk's aircraft was damaged by enemy artillery fire and he was forced to land. The next day, he flew a patrol with his commanding officer, Loiko. While in the region of Yaslovets village and Radautz the two Russians spotted and attacked an enemy plane from an altitude of 2700 meters. The enemy observer had started to fire on Suk's aircraft (Vickers FB.19 serial 12) during the first attack, but the enemy's machine gun apparently jammed. Suk turned into the enemy aircraft again, but his machine gun also jammed. To make matters worse for Suk, the enemy evidently noticed Suk's problem and managed to repair his gun first. With little choice, Suk was forced to withdraw and the enemy aircraft safely crossed into its own territory.

---

(2) Although Suk did not fire directly on the first enemy aircraft (eventually shot down by Strizhevsky), he prevented other enemy aircraft from intervening. The authors are of the opinion Suk allowed Strizhevsky to finish the combat successfully and therefore, according to Russian victory guidelines, shared in the destruction of the enemy aircraft.

Suk (second from left) with some unknown pilots, shows his lighter side, spring 1917.

Right: The remains of Oeffag C.II 52.63 from Flik 44. This aircraft was shot down by Suk on August 8, 1917, for his third confirmed victory.

Several days later, on September 12, at 1800 hours, three pilots from the 9th Fighter Detachment—Commander *Poruchik* Loiko (in Nieuport 17 serial 1448), *Praporshik* Suk (in Vickers FB.19 serial 12), and *Podporuchik* Sapozhnikov (in Nieuport 17 serial 1445)—were carrying out a reconnaissance in the region of Radautz. Soon after the group detected an enemy plane and attacked it simultaneously. The enemy aircraft went down trailing smoke and was forced to land near the town of Radautz. Russian troops confirmed this victory—Suk's fifth. According to Austrian Archives, a Brandenburg C.I from Flik 44 reported being attacked by at least three Russian aircraft over Radautz and forced down after the aircraft's engine was damaged. The observer, 1st Lt. Adalbert Kuneze, was uninjured; the pilot, Reserve 1st Lt. Georg Altadonna, was wounded in the neck. This crew most likely engaged the pilots of the 9th Fighter Detachment that day.

On October 14, 1917, Suk was conducting a patrol in a Spad 7 (serial 1440) above the region of Radautz when he sighted an enemy plane. Suk quickly closed the distance between the two aircraft and attacked by swooping under the enemy's tail. Then he went into a position that aimed his gun fire directly up into the bottom of the aircraft's fuselage and fired 45 cartridges at a distance of only 5–10 meters. The pilot was killed instantly and the plane was seriously damaged. It side-slipped with the motor still running and then started to tumble down. At an altitude of 1500–2000 meters it lost both wings and the remaining parts crashed at the village Slalodzy. According to eye-witnesses, the observer fell out of the plane at an altitude of 1000 meters, but his body was never found. The pilot, an Austrian sergeant, was found in the weckage and buried later that day. The plane was not identified; however, its motor was an 185 hp Austro-Daimler, serial number 18190. This was Suk's sixth confirmed victory.

The next day, Suk was patrolling in Spad 7 (serial 1440), when he noticed an enemy aircraft southeast of Radautz, but his machine gun jammed and the aircraft escaped. The gun on Spad 7 (serial 1440) plagued Suk again on October 30 during an attack on an enemy aircraft near Yaslovets. To remedy the situation, Suk switched to Spad 7 (serial 1446) on November 2, 1917, for a patrol near Suchava. Although he saw an enemy aircraft over the town and pursued it, he could not get close enough before it descended behind its lines.

Suk's luck changed on November 4, 1917, when he successfully engaged a German fighter with Spad 7 (serial 1446). After a short battle the enemy aircraft crashed in Russian lines near the village of Goura Seltche. Russian troops confirmed the machine was destroyed and the pilot killed. This was Suk's seventh confirmed victory.

Having broken his string of unsuccessful combats, Suk quickly scored again. On November 8, again flying Spad 7 (serial 1446) over village Deutch, he attacked an enemy plane returning to its lines. During Suk's third attack the enemy plane emitted heavy smoke and crashed north of the town of Radautz. Moments later, Suk was himself attacked by another enemy plane, but was forced to break off combat because his machine gun jammed.

Suk scored again two days later, on November 10, 1917, while patrolling in Spad 7 (serial 1440) at 3000 meters above Strazha. He sighted three enemy planes and attacked the closest. It escaped and descended to its own

Suk (standing to left) and an unidentified pilot stand beside the remains of Suk's sixth confirmed victory, October 14, 1917.

Below: Vickers FB.19. Suk obtained two confirmed victories in this type of aircraft.

airfield. Suk then engaged one of the remaining enemy planes in a series of six attacks. After the sixth, Suk lost sight of the enemy plane as it descended. However, according to Austrian Archives, Brandenburg C.I 269.49 from Flik 49, with pilot *Korporal* Milan Alteron and officer observer Ignaz Patsch, was forced to land after a battle with a Russian Spad. The observer was wounded in his shoulder and the pilot in his neck. The plane received 16 hits in the motor, wings, and wing struts. The pilot landed with difficulty near Radautz. This was probably the crew shot down by Suk. In any event this victory was confirmed by Russian troops—Suk's ninth and last victory of the war.

Two weeks later, Suk was killed in a flying accident. The official report stated simply "On November 28, 1917, the *Praporshik* of the 9th Fighter Detachment Suk was returning from an air fight. When he was turning about over the airfield in order to land, his plane slipped on the wing, went into a spin, fell to the ground, and he was killed."

Konstantin Konstantinovich Vakulovsky

Konstantin Konstantinovich Vakulovsky was born into nobility on October 28, 1894. As a youth he attended the Vladikavks Cadet Corps, and later entered the Nikolayevsky Engineering School. He was graduated with the rank of *Podporuchik* (2nd Lieutenant) on August 2, 1914, and was attached to the Novo-Georgievsky Fortress Air Detachment. Becoming interested in flying, he enrolled in basic aviation courses. Vakulovsky made his first flight in late 1914. Granted the title of military pilot in April 1915, he was appointed to the Novo-Georgievsky Rampart Squadron.

The fortress of Novo-Georgievsky was a symbol of Russian rule in Poland. Located down river from Warsaw, it was part of a large network of fortresses built in the late 19th centery for defense against Germany. Unfortunately, like many Russian strongholds, this fortress had been built of brick, not concrete. Its construction, designed to withstand the heavy artillery of 1880, could be easily destroyed by small field guns in 1914.

Nevertheless, the Russian high comand (*Stavka*) seemed to think the fortress would not be taken quickly, and it was supplied with 1680 artillery pieces and almost one million shells. *Stavka* was of the opinion that Novo-Georgievsk should hold for six months.

The Germans thought otherwise in the summer of 1915. As they advanced toward Warsaw in August, they quickly surrounded Novo-Georgievsk and bombarded it with heavy artillery. Most of the fortification was destroyed within weeks, and the defenders were over-powered on August 19, 1915. *Stavka* learned of this disaster only when the last of the fortress pilots took off from the besieged fortress and gave their reports.

Valkulovsky was one of the last to leave the fortress, on August 19, and for his bravery was later awarded the Order of Saint George, Fourth Class. His citation read, "To *Podporuchik*, Military Pilot of the Corps Squadron, Konstantin Vakulovsky for the fact, that on August 19, 1915, when it was very dangerous to leave the besieged Novo-Georgievsky fortress by aircraft, Vakulovsky and the patrol officer proposed to the chief of the Fortress Staff, with staff Capt. U.M. Kozmin and Lt. Anton E. Mrochkovsky,[1] to remove the fortress standards as well as Georgevsky crosses by aircraft. After they obtained permission, they vowed they would do everything possible to destroy the standards in case they would dying during an unsuccessful flight. In spite of extremely difficult weather for the flight, fierce enemy shooting at the planes, and the dangerous further flight, when because of the thick fog one had to keep the altitude of 15–20 meters at times under the enemy fire, the pilot after a 5 hour flight reached our troop positions, having delivered the sacred items of the Fortress to the front staff."

Vakulovsky and the other remaining pilots from the Novo-Georgievsky Detachment were reformed into the 33rd Corps Detachment and returned to the front October 29, 1915. Throughout the winter of 1916, Vakulovsky and his comrades performed important reconnaissance missions. Vakulovsky was rewarded with the Golden Sword of Saint George. The citation that accompanied it read, "By the Royal Order of his Highness of April 10, 1916, the Golden Sword of Saint George is bestowed on *Podporuchik* Vakulovsky, military pilot of the Corps Detachment, for his service in the rank of *Podporuchik* when flying his apparatus, he was patrolling and photographing important areas of enemy positions at the Pikstorn River down to Lake Varzgunek. He was flying and taking pictures at the altitude of 1200 meters above the enemy trenches under the active rifle and artillery fire. Especially difficult was the flight over Bushhof on February 8, 1916, being under the non-stop fire of the shells exploding next to the plane. Thanks to the great valor displayed by *Podporuchik* Vakulovsky, photography of important positions by the patrol officer was performed with great success, in spite of the fact that the apparatus was shot through in 25 places by the enemy fire, also the thrust of the wing was broken, the propeller was damaged, and the motor hood was shot through. The photographs gave important material that served as the basis in drawing up the offensive plan of action."

Vakulovsky's first recorded encounter with enemy aircraft occurred on June 27, 1916, moments after he had taken off in a captured Albatros B.I. What he later described as enemy "Fokkers" opened fire on his aircraft several times, but failed to shoot him down.[2]

On July 16, 1916, Vakulovsky was promoted to the rank of *Poruchik* (Lieutenant). Two days later, he was appointed commander of the newly formed First Fighter Detachment with the personal endorsement of Grand Duke Alexander Mihailovich.

Clearly, Vakulovsky's flying skills and courage had been noted at higher levels of command, and he wasted little time justifying the decision to place him in command of a fighter detachment. "On August 26, 1916 the pilot Vakulovsky in *Bebe*[3] attacked the enemy, which entered the battle by firing machine gun. They met at the distance of 100 meters. Our apparatus was unable to reach the same altitude as the enemy, but he forced the enemy to withdraw as he pursued the enemy to the lake Naroch firing the machine gun from below."

Vakulovsky's first victory occured soon after, on September 7, 1916. From the official report: "*Poruchik* Vakulovsky, from the First detachment, was in *Bebe*

---

(1) Anton E. Mrochkovsky would survive the First World War with one confirmed aerial victory. For more information, refer to page 385.

(2) This Albatros, serial number 400, was captured and refurbished by the Lebedev plant. The First fighter detachment used it from June 9, 1916, to January 1917.

(3) *Bebe* was the nickname of the Nieuport 11 fighter.

Morane Saulnier I No. 741. Vakulovsky used this aircraft to obtain his third victory on April 14, 1917.

(French production No.1295) attacking an enemy plane. After the second attack, the enemy apparatus heeled over on his wing, and without straightening out it went down in the direction of Lake Krakshta."

Several weeks later, on September 19, Vakulovsky was performing a reconnaissance mission near the town of Postav when an anti-aircraft shell expoded 10 meters from his Nieuport 11. Although Vakulovsky managed to land safely, he was severely shell-shocked and required several weeks to recover.

Vakulovsky returned to the front on October 25, 1916. Three days later he scored his second victory. "On October 28, 1916, the pilot *Poruchik* Vakulovsky in *Bebe* (No.1295) flew up at 0850 hours and entered into a fight with a German apparatus four times. He attacked the Albatros and chased it far into the enemy's rear until it went down to the altitude of 1500 meters. During the fourth attack the Albatros suddenly went down near Lake Vishnevsky. At the same time he himself was attacked by two enemy planes. One of them came close to Vakulovsky's aircraft and was firing explosive bullets with a machine gun. Enemy gun fire shattered his propeller and shot through the aircraft frame in five spots."

Vakulovsky was promoted to the rank of *Stabs-Kapitan* (Staff-Captain) on April 12, 1917. Two days later, he obtained his third victory while flying a Morane Saulier type I (serial 741) in the region of station Budslav (northeast of Vileyki). The Russian army confimed the victory with the report: "On April 14, 1917, a German plane was shot down in flames by Pilot *Stabs-Kapitan* Vakulovsky. The apparatus, type Schneider, motor Benz 200 hp. The enemy pilots were killed."

Vakulovsky continued his scoring on May 12, 1917, by attacking the enemy aerodrome at Kabilnichachby with *Praporshik* (Ensign) Terentjer. As Terentjer dropped bombs, Vakulovsky attacked two enemy planes that tried to intervene. The first descended almost vertically to the ground after Vakulovsky fired a complete magazine of bullets into it. The second declined combat and flew off. Although the victory was not confirmed, he was awarded the Order of St. Anne, Second Class, with Swords for the attack. Furthermore, Vakulovsky's character and combat achievements were recognized by his superiors in an official report on May 12, 1917, in which he was described as "An excellent combat pilot officer, well disciplined, good organizer, strict and demanding chief. Clearly one of our best pilots."

Vakulovsky had been fortunate to survive several years of almost constant combat, but his luck almost ran out the next month when he was shot down by ground fire while on a reconnaissance mission. The official report read: "On June 18, 1917, the commander of the First Fighter Detachment, *Stabs-Kapitan* Vakulovsky, was shot down in Baldon region by an enemy mortar that exploded under the apparatus when he was completing the photography of the third line of enemy trenches. When *Stabs-Kapitan* Vakulovsky saw that the motor stopped and the engine was leaking, he began to glide down trying to reach our positions. Over the enemy positions at the altitude of 500 meters the plane caught fire, and the pilot safely glided in the burning plane to Dalen Island, where he was under German artillery fire with the shells falling 30–40 meters away from the plane. *Stabs-Kapitan* Vakulovsky was stunned by the exploding shells, his right hand was burned up to the elbow, the mucous membrane of both his eyes was injured, his overcoat was completely burnt out. In spite of the personal injuries to his head and hand, *Stabs-Kapitan* Vakulovsky tried to save the photo camera. Although he managed to take off only one camera lens, *Stabs-Kapitan* Vakulovsky distinguished himself by displaying such glorious deeds, I consider it a great honor to thank him for his presence of mind and quick wit. Chief Commander of the Army, Infantry General Radko Dmitz. Order over the 12th Army No.570 of June 18, 1917." Soon after, Vakulovsky was awarded the Order of St. Vladimir, Fourth Class, with Swords and Bow.

Vakulovsky recovered from his wounds in early August 1917, and returned to the front soon after. On August 21, 1917, he obtained his fourth confirmed victory by shooting down an enemy plane over Riga sound (near Pleenes-Zeens, Tukkuma region).

One week later, on September 1, 1917, Vakulovsky scored his final two victories. The official report gives some idea of the heated actions he was involved in that day: "On September 1, 1917, *Stabs-Kapitan* Vakulovsky of the First Fighter Squadron had 16 air battles in one day, and two enemy planes were shot down by him. One fell in our positions in Iskul region, the second in enemy territory." Unfortunately, there is no further information about Vakulovsky after this date.

Vakulovsky's awards included Order of Saint George, Fourth Class; Golden Sword of Saint George; Order of Saint Vladimir, Fourth Class, with Swords and Ribbon; Order of Saint Anne, Second Class, with Swords; awarded two times the Order of Saint Anne, Third Class, with Swords and Ribbon; awarded three Orders of Saint Anne, Fourth Class, with inscription "For Bravery;" awarded two Orders of Saint Stanislas, Second Class, with Swords; and the Order of Saint Stanislas Third Class, with Swords and Ribbon.

Dux-built Nieuport 16 of the First Fighter Detachment, winter 1916–1917.

Vasili Ivanovich Yanchenko

Vasili Ivanovich Yanchenko. His awards included: The Order of Saint George, Fourth Class; Order of Saint Vladimir, Fourth Class, with Sword and Bow; Order of Saint Anne, Fourth Class; The Soldier's Crosses of Saint George, First, Second, Third, and Fourth Class; Romanian Order of the Star; and the Romanian Military Medal, Second Class. Original charcoal sketch by Terry Waldron.

Vasili Ivanovich Yanchenko was born on January 1, 1894, into a lower middle-class Orthodox family, native to the region of Nicholsk-Ussurisk. He received a secondary education at the Saratov Technical School, graduating as a mechanical engineer in early 1913. His interest in aviation started while still attending classes and led to his learning to fly shortly after graduation.

Yanchenko's military career started as a *Nijnichin* (Private) on November 22, 1914, after he volunteered for the Imperial Russian Air Service. On February 10, 1915, he was transferred to the St. Petersburg Polytechnical Institute for courses in general aviation. Basic pilot training followed on April 16, when he was sent to the Sevastopol Military Air School. Yanchenko completed this course by making a solo flight on the Morane Saulnier type L on September 4, 1915.

The next day he was appointed to the 12th Corps Detachment with the rank of *Starski unteroffizier* (Sergeant). He arrived at the front within days and eagerly made his first reconnaissance flight on the morning of September 15. Unfortunately, the flight had lasted only several short minutes and almost ended in disaster. While over enemy territory the motor of his Morane Saulnier L exploded, causing the fuel to catch fire. Although Yanchenko managed to land within Russian lines, he was only partly successful in fanning the flames away from the cockpit. He suffered second degree burns on his right arm and the right side of his face.

Five days later, on September 20, by order #418 of the 12th Army Corps, Yanchenko was awarded the Soldiers Cross of Saint George, Fourth Class, for "remaining calm in a life threatening situation, thereby allowing the safe return of an aircraft and crew members."

Yanchenko, undaunted by his painful injuries and through strong determination, continued to fly daily missions in the delicate Morane type Ls. Clearly, he wanted to continue flying, but more importantly he wanted to prove he had the grit to fly the more dangerous fighter types. There must have been little doubt of his potential skills, for he was quickly transferred on November 19, 1915, to the Moscow Air School for advanced pilot training on the Morane Saulnier H fighter.[1]

On January 5, 1916, Yanchenko completed his advanced pilot training and was transferred to the 3rd Corps Detachment with the rank of *Feldwebel* (Sergeant-Major). Unfortunately, he did not develop a good working relationship with his commanding officer and was temporarily demoted back to *Starski unteroffizier* (Sergeant) on January 23. He made only ten patrols between January and April of 1916.

Yanchenko requested a transfer to the newly formed 7th Fighter Detachment in early March 1916. Accepted, he was returned to the rank of *Feldwebel* and officially assigned to the unit's new location near the village of Tarnopol on April 7—only weeks before the next Russian offensive started under the command of General Brusilov.

After the offensive started, pilots from the 7th Fighter Detachment engaged in daily aerial combats. From mid-April to the end of May 1916, Yanchenko made nearly 40 combat flights.

His first victory occurred on June 25, 1916, while flying a joint mission with the unit's commander, *Praporshik* (Ensign) Ivan Orlov. The two Russians intercepted an enemy aircraft over the village of Podgaitsy. Apparently caught by surprise, the enemy crew tried to evade the Russian fighters at the last moment, but failed. Yanchenko and Orlov fired into the aircraft at point blank range; it turned over and crashed on its side near Russian troops.

The enemy was an Austro-Hungarian crew from Flik 27: *Oberleutnant* Gustav Wangler and his pilot, *Feldwebel*

---

(1) On November 29, 1915, Yanchenko was awarded the Soldiers Cross of Saint George, Third Class, by order of the 12 Army Corps #477, for activity in early November 1915.

Members of the 12th Corps Detachment, circa November 1915. Yanchenko is in back row, first on left; all others are unidentified.

Friedrich Schallinger. Both were seriously wounded and captured with the remains of their machine, Aviatik B.I 33.30. Russian troops confirmed the victory and Yanchenko was awarded the Soldier's Cross of Saint George, Second Class.

Yanchenko flew 40 combat missions between July and October 1916; however, victory number two continued to elude him. Nevertheless, his efforts were acknowledged by commanding officers. On July 8 he was conferred the rank of *Podpraporshik* (Warrant Officer); on July 21, by Order #211 of the 2nd Army Corps, he was awarded the Soldiers Cross of Saint George, First Class, for an indecisive battle with an enemy plane. Several weeks later, on August 21, by order of the 7th Army Staff, he was promoted to the rank of *Praporshik* (Ensign) for his combat merit. Yanchenko's second victory occurred on October 5, 1916. An official communiqué stated in part, *"Podporuchik* Orlov and *Praporshik* Yanchenko of the 7th Fighter Detachment took off in two Nieuport *"BeBe"* fighters at 9020 hours to pursue the enemy. Intercepting the enemy plane in the Brzezhansky direction, *Praporshik* Yanchenko attacked it by shooting bullets from the machine gun. We saw how the enemy plane started to fall down, and we saw the jet of black smoke and flames coming from the apparatus. *Podporuchik* Orlov was chasing the plane from behind. At that time our pilots were attacked by the second enemy plane, which they shot at and forced its crew to fly away to their own position."

Three days later, on October 8, by Order #1273 of the 7th Army, Yanchenko was awarded the Order of Saint Anne, Fourth Class (with inscription "For Bravery"). Two days later, October 10, by Order #1328 of the Supreme Chief Commander, he received the title of military pilot.

Orlov followed with a certificate of recommendation for Yanchenko, which stated, "*Praporshik* Yanchenko is an excellent pilot in battle just as well as in technical aspect of flight. Great education in theoretical and practical technique of aviation. He trusts only himself in the matter of plane adjustments for all the pilots of the detachment. The most suitable man for fighter aircraft. Has shown great skill in attacking enemy aircraft and will undoubtedly have much success in this area. Commander of 7th Fighter Detachment, military pilot, *Podporuchik* Orlov."

Yanchenko obtained his third victory on October 18, 1916. During his second flight of the day at 1605 hours he encountered three enemy aircraft in the region of Lipitsa-Tgurna. He engaged all three and within minutes had hit one, forcing it to withdraw beyond enemy lines. Yanchenko turned into one of the remaining enemy machines, and opened fire at close range. The enemy machine was hit, turned over, and crash-landed moments later near Russian troops.

Yanchenko finished the year with several furloughs and business trips, which greatly reduced his time at the front and his opportunities for obtaining additional

Oberleutnant Roman Schmidt of Flik 7 standing beside Brandenburg C.I 67.03 after crash-landing on the field of Austro-Hungarian Balloon Company 14, near Lesiowka, April 13, 1917. Yanchenko teamed with Donat Makeenok and Juri Gilsher to shoot Schmidt down.

victories. Nevertheless, on January 3, 1917, by Order #2028 of the Russian South-Western Front Armies, he was awarded the Order of Saint Vladimir, Fourth Class, with Swords and Bow, for an indecisive air battle that occurred on October 2, 1916.

While finishing a routine patrol several days later, Yanchenko crash-landed and destroyed a Nieuport 9 fighter (serial 285) and was slightly injured. While recuperating from his injuries, Yanchenko developed an exceptionally close friendship with fellow pilot *Praporshik* Donat Makeenok. Within a short time the two were discussing various methods for engaging enemy aircraft.

Yanchenko had recovered completely by late February 1917 and he and Makeenok had fine-tuned their tactics and were waiting for an opportunity. Soon after, on March 7, the two were flying Nieuport *BeBe* fighters at 2200 meters above the village of Svistelniki when they engaged an enemy two-seater, which was seriously damaged and started to fall. Yanchenko and Makeenok followed it to 400 meters and attacked again just over the enemy's first trench system. The enemy aircraft crash-landed just inside its territory, near Lipitza-Gura. Russian troops confirmed the victory for both pilots, Makeenok's first and Yanchenko's fourth.

On April 13, 1917, Yanchenko and Makeenok teamed up with fellow pilot *Podporuchik* Juri Gilsher to intercept two enemy aircraft reported in the region of Stanislavov at 0845 hours. Yanchenko was first to attack from out of the sun, swooping down onto the enemy machine from above and forcing its crew to descend into Makeenok's line of fire. At point blank range Makeenok easily hit the machine, which started to roll over on its wing as it fell to the west of Maydansky Buda. Moments later it crashed into a nearby wooded area, catching fire. The pilot, Sergeant Alexander Klefacs, suffered only minor injuries in the crash but his observer, Heinrich Szeliga, had been wounded by Makeenok's fire and their aircraft, Brandenburg C.I 67.04 from Flik 7, was destroyed.

The other enemy crew from Flik 7, *Oberleutnant* Roman Schmidt and his pilot, *Feldwebel* Paul Hablitschik, in Brandenburg C.I 67.03, tried to continue their mission, only to be attacked again by Yanchenko and Gilsher while over the village of Posechi. While the enemy crew desperately tried to out-maneuver Yanchenko's fighter, their machine was attacked by Gilsher, who had waited until he was only 15 meters away before firing. Bullets from Gilsher's machine gun tore into the enemy aircraft and seriously wounded Hablitschek, who, barely able to maintain control, spiraled down in a tight circle with Gilsher in close pursuit, still shooting. Moments later the enemy machine crash-landed on the field of Austro-Hungarian Balloon Company 14 near Lesiowka. Both victories were confirmed by the Russian 12th Army Corps, 8th Army South West Front, at 1525 hours.[2]

---

(2) Yanchenko, Makeenok, and Gilsher each received credit for two victories.

Nieuport 17s from the 7th Fighter Detachment, spring 1917. Yanchenko's aircraft (to right of photo) was a Dux-built Nieuport 17. An extra Madsen machine gun is mounted on the top wing and there is a black shield insignia on white background.

On April 20, 1917, Yanchenko was flying over enemy territory when his aircraft was hit by artillery fire. Although he maintained control of his Morane Saulnier type H, it was severely damaged and he was forced to crash-land inside Russian lines.[3]

During May and June, 1917, Yanchenko performed an impressive 84 patrols; however, he only obtained one additional victory. The report for June 27 stated in part "Yanchenko entered into battle with two enemy aircraft in the region of Shumlany. One of the enemy planes was shot down, but it was impossible to trace the place where he fell." The victory was Yanchenko's seventh.

On July 1, 1917, the Russian offensive under the command of General Brusilov launched Russian Armies of the Southwest Front into Galicia. The next day Yanchenko engaged in two battles. The first was indecisive and the enemy machine escaped into its own territory near Bzhezany. During the second, Yanchenko hit the enemy machine, which quickly turned over several times while in the air before crashing west of Adamuvki. Russian troops confirmed this victory for Yanchenko, his eighth.

Three days later, on July 4, the 7th Fighter Detachment was deeply saddened when its commander, *Podporuchik* Orlov, was killed in combat with two enemy fighters.

On July 6, 1917, Yanchenko in Nieuport 11 (serial 1889) was photographing enemy artillery batteries west of Bzhezany, with Makeenok following in Nieuport 11 (serial 2453). An enemy aircraft appeared and was attacked by both Russian pilots. After a short battle the enemy machine fell near the village of Lapshin. Russian troops confirmed the victory, Yanchenko's ninth.

Victory number ten followed five days later, on July 11, 1917, after Yanchenko in Nieuport 11 (serial 1889) cooperated with Makeenok during an encounter with four enemy planes. At an altitude of 2400 meters the two Russian pilots quickly isolated one enemy machine and hit it with machine gun fire. Moments later, the aircraft was surrounded in smoke and went down near Bzhezan. On July 18, Yanchenko scored, again in a Nieuport 11 (serial 1889,) by shooting down an enemy machine that turned over and went down vertically trailing smoke. Yanchenko observed it crash near the highway to the north-west of Bzhezan.

In the evening of July 20, 1917, Yanchenko, Makeenok, and Gilsher took off to intercept a large formation of enemy aircraft that appeared over their airfield. A short time later, one enemy aircraft was shot down, but Gilsher was killed in the combat.

Days later, Yanchenko described the event in a letter to Juri Gilsher's father: "Dear Vladimir Ivanovich, I participated with Juri in the battle waged against the air detachments of the enemy planes. As the participant of that battle, I eyewitnessed the heroic death of your son, and I feel responsible to give you the description of the glorious battle in which your brave son met his death and engraved upon our memory his heroic life. Almost on the eve of July 17, he single-handedly entered into the battle with the enemy two-seater and shot him down. For that brilliant deed he was awarded the Golden Sword of Saint George. Thus, he had all the battle awards. Orders of Saint George are the awards conferred to the bravest; your son having only one leg continued his selfless feat and heroic work of fighter pilot. On July 20, when the general panic began among our troops, when they were running away in disgrace and our regiments left the front and became

---

(3) Yanchenko's aircraft was destroyed and he was slightly wounded in his leg from the initial explosion.

This original oil painting by James Dietz shows Yanchenko removing Juri Gilsher's body from the remains of his crashed Nieuport on the evening of July 20, 1917.

prisoners of war without fighting, a handful of Germans started to chase our numerous troops taking the opportunity of their fear and trying to create more panic in our rear, there appeared a squadron of German planes flying over our air field to Tarnopol. This happened about 8–9 PM. Second Lieutenant Gilsher, Lieutenant Makeenok, and I flew up in our fighters. Lieutenant Makeenok moved aside to wage a battle with one of the enemy planes. Your son and I surpassed the enemy squadron near Tarnopol. We encountered 8 more enemy planes, and that squadron of then 16 planes surrounded us. It would have been disgraceful to shun the battle, Tarnopol would have been destroyed by bombs, and so we entered the battle. One of the enemy planes was shot down. When attacking the second plane your son approached it from behind, while under the machine gun fire of the enemy observer. I was above to the right, there was a distance of 50 meters between me and your son. The German was 70 meters ahead. I saw how the German opened fire and tracer bullets were clearly visible to me. They were falling along the frame of your son's plane. At that time I was attacked from above by the rest of the enemy planes. Looking up I saw about 10 planes above me, and at that time the motor of 2nd Lieutenant Gilsher's plane was torn off the frame and darted out, and the wings of the plane folded. The apparatus was partially falling apart in the air. Having several bullet holes in my plane it was not possible for me to wage battle when I saw that your son was falling down; perhaps he still needed help. Then I also went down and landed at the spot where Juri fell. That was the end. I removed his body from the wreckage, and I sent it to Tarnopol. From there it was sent to our division, there it was placed into the coffin and he was buried in solemn ceremony in the town of Bugach in Galicia. It was not possible to ship the body to Russia; because of the panic in our troops it was not possible to get the military men. The tragic, heroic death of our commanders Ivan Orlov and Juri Gilsher made very heavy impressions on our detachment and all who knew them. The air force with not forget its glorious fighters! Yours respectfully, *Praporshik* Yanchenko."

On August 5, 1917, Yanchenko with Makeenok spotted an enemy aircraft attacking a Russian reconnaissance machine trying to photograph the enemy trench system. The two Russians dove down onto the aircraft and quickly hit it with machine gun fire. The enemy crew managed to return fire and seriously wounded Makeenok before their aircraft turned over and crashed near Bzezhany.

When the Russians landed and the full extent of Makeenok's wound was revealed, he was quickly transferred to a hospital at Sevastopol. With his departure, the 7th Fighter Detachment was reduced to one "ace" pilot—Yanchenko. However, the recent loss of fellow pilots Ivan Orlov and Juri Gilsher, the stress of daily combats, and the uncertainty of the war was beginning to effect him. When not flying, Yanchenko was described a being very solemn and depressed. Obviously, the departure of Makeenok only intensified this mental state.

On September 20, 1917, Yanchenko was transferred to the 32 Corps Detachment. Three days later, on September 23, while guarding a Henri Farman F.22 conducting a reconnaissance flight, he became involved in heated battle with a enemy fighter. Yanchenko's subsequent report read: "About 1120 hours in the region of Goosyatin, an enemy plane was noticed trying to attack our Farman, I attacked it. The plane turned out to be an Albatros type D.III painted yellowish with the identification signs on the rudder and fuselage, the crosses surrounded with yellow edges, on the wings there were black crosses over the white background in the shape of a circle. After a 10 minute battle, in which the enemy displayed great piloting skill, the enemy plane suddenly went down in the region of Chebaruvka. Three other enemy planes appeared; however, they did not enter the battle and kept the distance of 150–200 meters. After the descent of the first plane they did not enter the battle and, being pursued by me, went to the rear of their position." Russian troops confirmed the victory by issuing a simple statement "In a battle to the west of Goosyatin, the pilot, *Praporshik* Yanchenko shot down the enemy plane, that fell down near Tchabaruvka."

Yanchenko obtained his 15th victory on October 5, 1917, while guarding a Henri Farman F.22 making a reconnaissance flight. The Romanian army issued this statement: "An enemy plane was noticed in the region of Zbrizh. It attempted to attack our reconnaissance plane but *Praporshik* Yanchenko attacked and shot down the enemy plane which fell at the right bank of Zbrizh (15 versts to the south of Goosyatin). The plane was an Aviatik 2-seater."

Several weeks later, on October 14, 1917, Yanchenko scored his 16th and last victory of the war. His report stated: "After seeing off Farman as far as the village Olhovets, I noticed four enemy planes that were flying in our rear positions (Gorodok). Following the enemy planes, I allowed them to reach the settlement Gordok, where I started the battle by attacking the upper single-seater 'Albatros' first. By skillful maneuvers the enemy was flying away from my firing. I was firing almost straight at the enemy; I saw how my bullets were hitting the enemy wing, but I could not straighten the pickup because of velocity loss. Being attacked by other planes at the same time, I skidded on my wing and spun. After I straightened up at the altitude of 200–300 meters over Gorodok settlement, I saw groups of planes ascending from the airfield. The enemy planes were departing at Kutkowtsy; I began to pursue them. After I surpassed one of the single-seater Albatros types over the positions at Dubrovka, I attacked the enemy several times while he was flying ahead of me on the right side. It began a steep left turn, trying to counter me, but at that time my machine gun firing hit him. The enemy skidded on the wing and, going down vertically, fell near the forest edge at Dubrovka. I landed there and found the enemy plane completely broken and the pilot officer was dead. I took his documents and sent them to the staff of the 7th Siberian Corps. The plane of the enemy turned out to be the single-seater Albatros equipped with 2 machine guns which also broke in the fall."[4]

By the end of October, 1917, Yanchenko's unit ended all hostile activity while coming under Bolshevik control. Perhaps fearing reprisals from the Soldiers Committee for his recent victories over German aviators, Yanchenko deserted the unit in November, 1917, before any action could be carried out against him.

Yanchenko went to Novocherkassk and joined the Volunteer Army under the command of Generals Denikin and Wrangel in early 1918. He was placed in command of the Second Air Squadron from August 1918 to August 1920. Several years later, Yanchenko came to the United States and for a short time worked as an engineer for Igor Sikorsky. He became an American citizen in the 1920s, and in the 1930s moved to Syracuse, New York. He remained a design engineer in Syracuse until retiring in 1952. The exact date of his death is unknown.

Yanchenko was clearly one of the most aggressive fighter pilots the Imperial Russian Air Service produced. His score of 16 confirmed aerial victories was second only to that of Alexander Kozakov.

---

(4) The Russian military issued the following report: "The enemy aircraft appears to be an Albatros C.III, having a 165 hp. motor. It was shot down in the region of Kutkovtse. The pilot of the plane and the motor were broken completely. The victory was claimed by three pilots (Grochovalsky, Pawlow, and Yanchenko) who had waged an air battle with four enemy planes."

Section 3

Aces in Foreign Service

Pilots of Foreign Service and the French Aeronautic Missions

This section is dedicated to those aces who served in a foreign land. Many of these pilots fought in both France and Russia, achieving victories in both locations. Included are Russian pilots living in France when hostilities began who offered their services to their new country. Also, there were many French pilots who became members of the French Aeronautic Missions, who performed heroically while stationed in Russia and Romania.

France had supplied aircraft and engines to Russia before the war. In addition, there were several aircraft factories and parts manufacturers established in Russia producing French designs. Not only were the Russians incapable of manufacturing all necessary equipment for aircraft production, but they needed some experienced personnel to help coordinate tactics of frontline squadrons. This was also requested of France.

The French sent three aviation support groups to the Russian and Romanian theaters of operation to help with organization and to provide experienced aviators. The first request came in January 1916, and marked the beginning of the Aeronautic Mission to Russia.

Colonel Edouard Bares, commander of the French air service, made the initial appropriations for the mission. He personally selected the aviators from those who had already distinguished themselves in aerial combat. The mission was more than just flying, it also was to guide Russia with development of its air service, including organization and technical assistance. The French were to oversee the deliveries of aircraft and supplies upon arrival at Murmansk, and the manufacturing of airframes and aero engines. At squadron level, it was the duty of the French pilots to offer not only their services but also to convey their knowledge of combat to Russian aviators.

On April 18, 1916, *Capitaine* Berger was assigned the task of accompanying the mission to Russia. He was promoted to *Chef de Battalion* (Major) with the job of overseeing the entire excursion, most importantly communicating with the Russian General Staff.

The mission was officially created on April 30 with ten pilots, ten observers, their planes, mechanics, and spares. All flying personnel had been given temporary promotions to officer rank for ease of interacting with their Russian peers. They arrived in Murmansk in May and proceeded with operations.

When they arrived, the members of the mission encountered some difficult situations. There was much disorganization and the conditions at the front were less than favorable, especially for the enlisted personnel. If this were not enough, the aviators were separated, being sent to different squadrons or other assignments. In many cases *Chef de Battalion* Berger did not know when his pilots were transferred, or to what unit.

Most of the French aviators were assigned to squadrons commanded by the Russian 8th Army in the region of Rovno, in preparation for the Brusilov Offensive in June 1916.

The fighting was intense in the air as well as on the ground. The French pilots fought bravely alongside their Russian peers. At the squadron level, there had been distrust and apprehension between the French and Russians during their first encounters, but time proved both sides to be worthy when duty called. The pilots of the mission served in bombing, fighting, and reconnaissance roles and no fewer than three perished during the summer of 1916.

In August 1916, Romania declared war on the Central Powers under an agreement made with the Allies. The terms called for Romania to invade Austria-Hungary, thus relieving pressure on the Western Front. In exchange, Romania would receive help in conquering Transylvania. The necessary supplies and materials were to be delivered through Russia. Russian officials were in accord with this decision, believing Romanian intervention would take pressure off their obligation to relieve the west, but in fact

A captured Albatros C.I, with skis applied, used by the Russian 21st Corps Detachment, late 1916. The observer is *Sous-Lieutenant* Boittiaux of the French Mission, who is ready to take off on a bombing run over Lida. Boittiaux accomplished 80 missions in four months and had earned the Order of Saint Anne. He also flew in Voisins and Farmans while serving with the 21st Detachment.

A group of aviators from Russia, Romania, and France, stationed on the Romanian Front during 1917. Seated in the front row center (directly behind the man seated on the ground), is Romanian *Capitan* Radu Irimescu, commander of *escadrila* F.5. Others unidentified, although one of the Frenchmen along side of Irimescu may be Colonel de Vergnette de la Motte.

Below: The aerodrome at Tecuci in 1917. This location was home of the Second Aviation Group of the Romanian Air Service while assigned to the Russian Fourth Army. The squadrons initially included, *escadrila* N.3, and *escadrila* F.4. Later during 1917, *escadrila* F.9 and *escadrila* N.12 were formed and assigned to the Second Group. Also, *escadrila* F.7 was transferred from headquarters command to serve at Tecuci.

the Romanian Front did little more than create an extension of the Russian Front, which had previously ended in Bukowina.

The French Military Mission to Romania included trained personnel from all branches of service. The aviation section included 42 officers and 45 NCOs, of whom 18 were pilots. Those chosen for this assignment were very capable, having proven themselves in many capacities while in France. Several became squadron commanders of the Franco-Romanian units.

Initially, there were three types of aircraft supplied to Romania; Nieuport 11s as fighters, Farmans F.40s for reconnaissance, and Breguet-Michelin BM.4s for bombing. In total, 100 aircraft were supplied.

Colonel de Vergnette de la Motte, commander of the mission, organized the entire Romanian air service into an efficient section of the army. Four groups were established, three for assignment to army groups and one directly under the control of the Romanian General Headquarters. The Second and Third Groups were assigned to Russian armies transferred to the Romanian Front. In addition, there were five aeronautical companies equipped with kite balloons for observation and artillery direction.

The French pilots provided valuable service to their fellow Romanian aviators and to the Russian and Romanian armies they served. They combined efforts during many combat missions and on one occasion a Farman F.40 of *escadrila* (Romanian squadron) F.4, of the Second Group, escorted by a Nieuport, took the commander of the Russian 4th Army, General Ragoza, over the lines to inspect the location of his own troops

Above: A Sopwith 1-1/2 Strutter, flown by *escadrille* Sop.582, during mid-July 1917, while stationed at Tchremkouf, one of the fields used by the unit during the Kerensky offensive on the southwest front. SHAA photo.

Left: The airfield at Tchorkouf was one of the locations used by the French squadrons during their service on the southwest front. The large tents are field hangars supplied by the French. SHAA photo.

opposed to the positions of the enemy. The ability to work together was further displayed by joint leadership of at least two squadrons that had both a French and Romanian commander.

Many of the French aviators distinguished themselves in combat while serving on the Romanian Front and were decorated by both Romania and Russia. Some were awarded the highest Romanian honor, the *Mihai Viteazul* III (the Order of Michael the Brave Third Class).

In November 1916, the Russian government again requested the services of French pilots. This time it asked for at least two squadrons to participate in the offensive on the southwest Russian Front in 1917. *Chef de Battalion* Berger was given the responsibility of forming these two squadrons, which he accomplished. In spite of the unfavorable reports from Russia on the difficulties within the country and the abdication of the Czar, the second Aviation Mission to Russia left France for Murmansk in March 1917.

Escadrille N.581, commanded by Lieutenant Gueydon, was a pursuit squadron equipped with Nieuport 17s and a few SPAD 7 aircraft. *Escadrille* Sop.582, commanded by *Capitaine* Balavoine, was a reconnaissance unit and used Sopwith 1-1/2 Strutters. The French had their own supply depot at Kiev which employed 20 men to distribute supplies and spare parts.

The two squadrons were placed under the command of the Russian 7th Army and participated in the Kerensky offensive of July 1917, which was directed toward Lemberg in Galicia. The pilots of N.581 had little difficulty beginning operations, but those assigned to Sop.582 encountered several problems. First, their planes did not arrive until the end of June, 1917. Second, each pilot had only received limited instruction on a Sopwith before leaving France. Also, the Sopwith was known to have a frail undercarriage. This deficiency, combined with the rough terrain, resulted in a damaged landing gear on many of the initial flights, limiting the effectiveness of Sop.582.

Despite the problems the members of the French mission fulfilled their duties and achieved several aerial victories. They remained faithful to the cause even after suffering setbacks from the retreat of the failed Kerensky offensive. They continued fighting until the end of hostilities when the new Bolshevik government agreed to an armistice with the Central Powers on December 15, 1917. Many of the French were able to leave Russia by obtaining passage to Murmansk and traveling from there to France by ship. Some remained in Russia to help the White Army fight the Bolsheviks. By February 1918, the squadrons were ordered to Moscow and disbanded. The French Aeronautical Mission to Russia had ended, but not before its members had displayed courage and dedication to duty for which many were decorated with the Order of Saint George Fourth class, or the Cross of Saint George for NCOs, the highest awards granted by Russia. Many were left behind, but their sacrifice was not forgotten.

Louis Fernand Coudouret

Formal portrait of Louis Coudouret after the war. He earned seven citations, including three in Russia along with the following awards: *Chavalier de la Legion d'Honneur, Croix de Guerre* with 5 *palmes* and two *etoiles de vermeil* (silver-gilt stars), Distinguished Conduct Medal of Great Britain, and from Russia the Order of Saint Vladimir Fourth Class, the Golden Sword of Saint George (*Georgevsky Oroogie*), and the highest award bestowed upon a junior officer, the Order of Saint George Fourth Class.

Louis Coudouret was born on May 31, 1896, in Marseilles. He volunteered for service on December 15, 1914, and was assigned to the *2eme Groupe d'Aviation* (second aviation group) with the rank of *Soldat de 2e classe* (Private second class). He was sent to Dijon and from there to Avord in April 1915, where he began his flight training. He received a promotion to *Caporal* (Corporal) on May 10, and earned his *Brevét*[1] on June 1, 1915. Two weeks later Coudouret was sent to the R.G.A.[2] where he awaited his new assignment. On July 19 he became a member of *escadrille* VB.102,[3] a squadron used exclusively for bombing. This unit was stationed at Malzeville, near Nancy, which became the nucleus for French bombardment units.

Escadrille VB.102 was part of *Groupe de Bombardment* 1 (GB.1, or First Bomb Group),[4] which consisted of three squadrons, the others being VB.101 and VB.103. The primary aircraft was the Voisin, either the type 3, also known as the LA, or the type 5, known as the LA.S,[5] both two-seater pusher. Although its maximum speed was no more than 75 miles per hour, the Voisin had a range of 300 miles and could carry 110 pounds of bombs and a forward-firing machine gun. VB.102 used a Cross of Lorraine insignia, while VB.101 and VB.103 used a five-pointed star, blue and red respectively. Three other groups, GB.2, GB.3, and GB.4, joined GB.1 at Malzeville. The French realized the need for concentrating these units for strategic bombing. The groups were located directly opposite several principal German industrial centers. These included steel factories, refineries, ammunition supply depots, and rail stations.

Coudouret acquired his first taste of combat the day after he arrived, July 20, when the squadron made a bombing run over the Conflans railway station. Seventy-one bombs were dropped from the eleven aircraft that reached the target. He also participated, in one of the 22 aircraft, in a raid on the Pechelbronn oil refineries on the morning of July 30. Despite heavy cloud cover at low altitude, the target was severely damaged. For this action, *Generale* Joffre congratulated GB.1 and GB.2 in the official army order of the day. The German forces retaliated by attacking the Malzeville plateau on August 1, but the eight aircraft dropped few bombs and caused little damage.

Within the next three months, Coudouret participated in at least ten major raids, some far behind enemy lines. Sometimes these were conducted by a few aircraft from the squadron; on other occasions a large number of planes from all the groups took part. One such raid in which Coudouret participated was the bombing of the ironworks

---

(1) The *Brevét* is the French aviation certificate given for completing the course of instruction. It was given in both a civil and military form. That granted to Coudouret was military *Brevét* number 1020.

(2) The *Reserve Generale d'Aviation* was an aviation personnel and material depot for distribution to and from frontline squadrons.

(3) French *escadrille* designation VB. (Voisin Bombardment) stood for the type of aircraft and sometimes, such as the case here, for the assignment. *Escadrille* VB.102 was previously VB.2, changing its designation on March 4,1915. All other VB. units 1 through 6 were also changed in the same manner on that date.

(4) *Groupe de Bombardment* I was formed November 23, 1914, under the command of *Commandant* de Goys de Mezeyrac. It maintained its own administration and supply, but was under the command of the *Armee* in whose sector it was posted, mainly for strategic bombing purposes.

(5) The Voisin Type 3 B2 and the Type 5 B2 were approximately the same dimensions and both were powered by Canton-Unne (Salmson) 9-cylinder radial engines of 130hp and 140hp, respectively. These airplanes were well built and held up under severe weather conditions. With engine upgrades and other modifications, the type was still in service at the armistice.

Lineup of the Voisins of *escadrille* VB.102, Malzeville, winter 1915–16. Coudouret served in this unit with distinction throughout the latter half of 1915 and early 1916, participating in many bombing raids. Photo: SHAA.

at Dillingen on August 25, when 62 aircraft from all the bombardment groups caused heavy damage that started many fires. However, daylight raids were becoming costly. Enemy fighters and anti-aircraft batteries claimed four French bombers.[6]

On September 6, 1915, 26 Voisins from GB.1, along with several aircraft from other bombardment groups, attacked targets in Saarbrucken. One Voisin from GB.1 had the distinction of launching a 58-centimeter cheddite aerial torpedo for the first time. This was the final strategic bombing mission of the year.

A week later GB.1 began tactical attacks on troop encampments and important railway centers. Coudouret participated in raids on September 13 and September 21 on the railway stations at Treves and Bensdorf, respectively. The Treves station was put out of action for three days.

On October 5, 1915, GB.1 was temporarily assigned to the *Groupe d'Armee du Centre (IIeme, IIIeme, and IVeme Armees)* to support an offensive along the Champagne Front. Stationed at Aulnay-sur-Marne, GB.1 made several attacks on the enemy's rear troop positions.

Caporal Coudouret participated throughout, taking part in three raids in five days against the railway centers in the Suippe Valley and at Bazancourt. Despite the efforts of GB.1 in holding back enemy reinforcements and supplies, the offensive was not successful. GB.1 returned to Malzeville on October 20.

On October 21, Coudouret was given a well-deserved promotion to *Sergent* (Sergeant). His first citation, awarded on October 27, read: "Very good pilot who has shown several times during long and dangerous air raids his qualities of audacity, strength, and self-control, in spite of particularly dangerous, precise and violent firing by the enemy."

By the end of 1915 the French found that daytime raids were taking too heavy a toll on the bomber units. The raid over the Suippe Valley on October 10 had proved this when six of the 17 aircraft sent from GB.1 did not return. Training for night operations began and very few missions were flown for the remainder of the year. In all, Coudouret had participated in at least 13 major raids during 1915, and most likely more which records do not reveal.

In January 1916 GB.1 provided ground support for troops at Verdun, with almost no strategic raids being flown. On February 3 all the pilots of VB.102, VB.103, and VB.112, including Coudouret, were sent to Plessis-Belleville for instruction on a new bomber, the Nieuport 14B2. Unfortunately, this aircraft turned out to be inadequate, and all three squadrons were soon re-equipped with Nieuport 11 fighters. The highly trained, specialized bomber squadrons were disbanded in order to convert their personnel to fighter pilots. *Groupe de Bombardment* 1 was also left short-handed, and the remaining squadrons had to continue to use obsolete Voisins.

On April 27, 1916, Coudouret was posted to *escadrille* N.57, stationed at Lemmes, southeast of Verdun. When he arrived, the German offensive at Verdun, which began in February, was well under way, and the squadron had already seen intense fighting. Coudouret wasted no time

---

(6) French reports list no losses for the units at Malzeville, but a German despatch from August 26 states one crashed in flames, two crash-landed with one crew being taken POW, and one shot down by a German fighter between the lines and destroyed by artillery.

Coudouret's Spad 7 in Russia during the summer of 1917 with *escadrille* N.581. Le Prieur rocket tubes are fitted for attacking enemy observation balloons. Photo: SHAA.

in displaying his ability as a fighter pilot. On May 4, 1916, while on patrol over Hermeville, he attacked an LVG two-seater and sent it crashing to the ground for his first victory. He also received his second citation which stated in part, "Pilot of exceptional audacity, enthusiasm and self-control. While assigned with escadrille VB.102, participated in remarkable bombing raids, one of them solo, deep into enemy territory and under particularly difficult conditions. Transferred to a pursuit squadron, distinguished himself from the beginning in various air attacks."

Coudouret was promoted to *Adjudant* (Warrant Officer) on May 21 for his prowess as a fighter pilot. Two months later, on July 20, he was transferred to N.112, also equipped with Nieuport fighters. *Escadrille* N.112 was one of the old GB.1 squadrons that had been converted to fighters. Coudouret stayed there for slightly more than a month before returning to his old unit on August 24, 1916. It had meanwhile been redesignated as N.102.

Escadrille N.102 had been stationed in the 2nd Armee sector near Verdun since July and remained there until January, 1917, when that area was finally secure. *Chef de Battalion* (Major) Pouderoux was the commander of the squadron throughout. By the time Coudouret joined the squadron, the German offensive at Verdun had reached its farthest advance. With the beginning of autumn, the French were ready to counter-attack, and the fighter squadrons increased offensive patrols. Lost ground was regained, with much being taken by mid-December. Throughout this difficult period, Coudouret was involved in more than 50 combats, and despite having to use an unreliable machine gun he shot down an Albatros over la Ferme du Logis, near Hermeville, on October 22, 1916. His third citation described him as "showing in all circumstances a great amount of zeal and courage."

December marked the end of the battle of Verdun. For his part, Coudouret received a commendation for the *Medaille Militaire* (Military Medal) on the 19th. Great Britain had also recognized his valor by awarding him the Distinguished Conduct Medal.

On January 17, 1917, N.102 moved to the Marne area under the command of Lieutenant Jean Derode.[7] Coudouret was not at this location for long; on February 1 he was assigned to the French Aeronautic Mission in Russia.

At the request of the Russian government, *Chef de Batillion* Berger was in charge of organizing two French squadrons to serve in Russia for the offensive of 1917. Berger personally selected individuals who had distinguished themselves in combat as accomplished aviators. Berger also felt it was necessary to promote NCO aviators to officer rank, for ease of interaction with Russian enlisted men. This affected Coudouret in two ways: he was granted a temporary promotion to *Sous-Lieutenant* on February 11, 1917, and, because of his promotion to officer rank, he was denied his *Medaille Militaire*, awarded only to NCOs. Overall it was not a bad trade.

These two squadrons sent to Russia were designated N.581 and Sop.582,[8] a pursuit unit and a reconnaissance unit respectively. Coudouret was assigned to escadrille N.581, where he was reunited with Lieutenant Lachmann, with whom he had served in *escadrille* N.57 at Verdun during 1916. In March, 1917, Coudouret, along with the other aviators and mechanics and their equipment, were on their way to Murmansk, aboard the ocean liner *Flore*.

They arrived in April and were given a warm greeting from the Russian population. The French, however, noticed the weariness and desolation on the faces of the people. By this time all were aware of the internal problems of the Russian government and the difficulties the war had caused. If the new members of the French Aeronautic Mission in Russia had any doubt of the extent of the suffering, the expressions of these men and women

---

(7) Jean Derode scored four of his seven victories while commanding *escadrille* N.102 and was given a temporary promotion to *Capitaine*. He was awarded the *Legion d'Honneur* in May 1917. He was killed in action as commander of *escadrille* Spa.99 on June 4, 1918.

(8) *Escadrille* Sop.582 was equipped with the Sopwith 1-1/2 Strutter.

Coudouret standing with his Spad 7, possibly at Robrotsche, where the Russian 19th Detachment was stationed, or at Kholotche in preparation for the Kerensky offensive.

Coudouret by the fuselage of his Spad 7, with wheel covers marked with a red and white yin-yang. There is also a name under the cockpit, but it is not discernible. The location is possibly Kamnietz-Padolsk or Volochyst.

certainly removed it.

The mission went from Murmansk to Moscow and on to Kiev before being stationed on the Galician Front at Boutchatch in May, 1917. *Escadrille* N.581 did not stay long at this location, moving north to Robrotsche, where it shared the field with the famous 19th Detachment of the First Combat Air Group under the command of *Stabs-Rotmistre* (Staff-Captain) Kazakov.

Sous-Lieutenant Coudouret and the other pilots of N.581 flew many hours of patrol, several over enemy airfields, but no aerial victories were scored. On one occasion Coudouret attacked a balloon, but his gun jammed and the balloon escaped destruction.

The squadron was stationed at Kholotche for the Kerensky offensive, which began July 1,1917, under the command of General Brusilov.[9] The Russian 7th Army, to which N.581 was attached, advanced through Kalusz and on to Galitch by July 10, with the squadron in close

support. The advance came to a halt on the 13th, and the German *Sudarmee*,[10] under the command of General Hoffman, launched a counter-offensive on July 16, aimed at the Russian 8th Army and three days later at the 11th Army. The Russian 7th Army had to retreat by July 20. *Escadrille* N.581 was ordered to fall back to Tchorkouf and from there to Gusyatin on July 23. Both N.581 and Sop.582 landed at this location. The aerodrome was poorly labeled on maps, causing aircraft to be dispersed throughout the village. Despite the confused withdrawal of the undisciplined Russian troops, N.581 managed to re-organize and head for Iarmolitse on the 24th, concluding a 100-kilometer retreat in three days.

The Russians managed to stabilize the front along the Zbrousch[11] River, allowing N.581 to remain at Iarmolitse.

---

(9) General Alexei Brusilov, commander-in-chief of the Russian forces, launched this offensive at the request of the allies to force German troops from the Western Front allowing General Robert Nivelle (C-in-C in the west) to initiate an offensive. This was to be the Third Battle of Ypres, which began on July 31, 1917.

(10) This was the combined Austro-German 'South Army' used along the Galician Front during Brusilov's offensive in 1916 and the Kerensky offensive commanded by Brusilov in 1917.

(11) Hoffman had basically eliminated the Russian forces in the south and did not press the attack any farther. This allowed the front to stabilize. In September the German 8th Army, under the command of General von Hutier, attacked in the north, the result being the collapse of the Russian 12th Army, leaving no resistance.

The Albatros C.X Coudouret forced to land near Volochyst, on November 23, 1917. This was his fourth victory and his second in Russia. The enemy crew was taken prisoner.

The unit stayed there until August 12, when it was assigned to the 3rd Army and sent south to Kamnietz-Padolsk. Throughout the July retreat and the beginning of August there were few operations, and the squadron's effectiveness was minimal due to chaotic conditions.

After having the opportunity to re-group, the unit was once again flying patrols, performing reconnaissance missions over the Dniester River and offensive patrols against enemy observation planes. The German and Austro-Hungarian units had increased reconnaissance by both airplanes and balloons. Several attacks were made on balloons and two-seaters during September. Coudouret encountered a Brandenburg and closed in, only to have his Vickers machine gun jam. While he was trying to clear it, the Austrian observer got the better of him, hitting the Spad's radiator, forcing Coudouret to land with hot water and steam gushing from the front of his airplane.

While waiting for his Spad to be repaired, he borrowed a Nieuport for a reconnaissance mission during which he was attacked by two Halberstadts. The battle became severe, dropping to an altitude of 200 meters. The German crews were determined, but Coudouret fought his way out and returned to Kamnietz-Padolsk. The Nieuport was riddled with bullets and in a state of disrepair. To make matters worse, the Germans were receiving Albatros D.V fighters to fly escorts and patrols. Coudouret encountered three Albatros D.Vs that had been strafing the troops in the front lines. He was able to force them to disperse, but was in no position to continue the fight.

Coudouret's luck began to change in October. On October 8 he and Lachmann combined to shoot down an Albatros two-seater that was probably conducting artillery spotting. It crashed in flames between the front lines at Zalec'ye. For this action Coudouret was given a citation stating: "Pilot of exceptional skill and remarkable courage, responsible many times for the success achieved by our pursuit squadron on the Russian front by persistently

Coudouret with his foes, the crew of the Albatros. They may be *Leutnant d.R.* Paul Strathmann, observer, and *Vizefeldwebel* Wilhelm Krauser, pilot of *Flieger Abteilung (Artillerie)* 232, who were listed as missing on November 23, 1917.

pursuing the enemy during many air combats."

Coudouret did not score again while the unit was stationed at Kamnietz-Padolsk. On November 15, 1917, N.581 was given orders to move to Volochyst, in the 2nd Army sector, about 50 miles north. On November 18 the

The dinner table at Volochyst, late November, early December 1917. Seated left to right, Leschi, Roy, Lauglade, unknown, Jalaguier, Louis Coudouret, unknown, and the last man, who apparetnly labeled the original photo with only '*moi*,' and did not list his name. Georges Lachmann is out of this photo, but he is seated on the left side of the table. Photo: *Museé de l'Air*.

entire group was honored when *escadrille* N.581 was cited by its former command, the 7th Army. The order stated in part, "In the course of valuable information, the French fighter squadron has delivered a series of glorious battles."

On November 23, 1917, Louis recorded his fourth victory. It began when the squadron heard the Russian anti-aircraft batteries firing at the enemy in the distance. Coudouret took off in his Spad and reached the enemy at approximately 4800 meters. He fired one burst and then a second. It was the second that hit the observer's gun, but the pilot did not give up. The German continued his attempt to evade Coudouret and even outrun the Spad. Louis got the Albatros in his sights for a third time, scoring several hits that set the machine on fire. Its pilot had to make a forced landing, causing the machine to overturn. Coudouret landed near the two Germans, who were shaken up from their mishap. He helped the wounded enemy crew to an ambulance, where they were tended to. Later in the evening they were invited to join Coudouret at the canteen at Volochyst. Their arrogance returned as the observer declared "If my machine gun had not been hit, I would have descended on you like a rabbit." Coudouret, smiling, responded, "It is unfortunate for you that that was the opposite of what happened."

The winter weather began settling in, and for the next several days there was no aerial activity. During this period Lenin had taken power in St. Petersburg and the French were anticipating a Bolshevik armistice with the Germans. The cloud cover broke on December 14, and Coudouret wasted no time in patrolling the area around Volochyst. He surprised an Albatros D.V at 2400 meters and it crashed into the front line of trenches after he had fired only eight rounds. This victory made Louis Coudouret an ace; it was also the last aerial success of N.581. The next day, December 15, the new Bolshevik government established an armistice with the Germans at Brest-Litovsk.

Shortly after, the unit moved to Loubny, near Kiev, by order of *Commandant* Bordage. Bordage also ordered Lieutenants Mayeur, Roy, and Remmert to collect all the aircraft and supplies at the depots in and around Kiev and group together with N.581. The mission needed to protect itself from whatever lay ahead. Besides the threat of civil war and the fact that many German and Austrian prisoners were roaming the countryside freely, Russian soldiers were rebelling against their officers and encouraging the French to do the same. This breakdown within the ranks did not occur with the French, but it did endanger the mission in other ways. Coudouret recalled,

"One day our quarters caught fire. The (Russian) officer rushed in followed by his men, he expended himself without consideration (for his own safety), to save our materials. He was seriously burned, and carried to an ambulance. Although he was suffering a great deal he did not open his mouth to complain. But during the night, several of his soldiers entered into his room where he was laying in bed, approached him and abruptly shot off their revolvers to the end...then they took off as fast as their legs could carry them."

The Bolsheviks had moved into the Ukraine by rail. Fighting began with Ukrainian troops, which resulted in the Bolsheviks occupying Loubny on January 25, 1918. The French could do nothing but take cover. On the 26th Coudouret took one of the aircraft and headed for Kiev to gather metal currency to offset the inflationary conditions the squadron had encountered. Unfortunately for the remainder of the group, the Bolsheviks believed the aircraft indicated that Ukrainian troops were in the vicinity. They held the French officers prisoners and threatened to destroy the aircraft and kill Coudouret when he returned from his journey. Luckily, Lachmann was able to convince the Red commander to free the officers and himself, since Coudouret never returned to Loubny.

Coudouret's plane ran out of fuel 10 miles from Kiev, forcing him to travel by whatever means he could find. He was fortunate enough to purchase an emaciated horse to continue his journey. When he reached Kiev he found an intense battle being waged between the Bolsheviks and the Ukrainians. *Commandant* Jourdan of the French mission's General Staff was killed, and many of the other French took refuge in houses within the city limits. Coudouret did the same, being forced to hide for 15 days. When the fighting quieted down, the Bolsheviks had control of Kiev. By early February, 1918, the remaining French were able to leave, although they were still sometimes threatened. Coudouret had been believed to be dead, but did rejoin N.581 after this incident. All were happy to see him, especially when he displayed the money he had acquired.

If the problems within the country were not enough for the French to bear, some of the Germans were continuing the war and began to advance into the Ukraine. It was, however, impossible for N.581 to continue to fight. They were too far from the advancing enemy, and the Bolsheviks had disassembled the machine guns of their aircraft.

The squadron was given orders on February 19 to proceed to Moscow and await further instructions. It was joined there by all the other French units and officially disbanded. Coudouret and many others waited in Moscow until March 15, when a British ship, designed for 300, carried 3000 passengers to Murmansk.

From there Coudouret waited to return to France, pondering many troubling thoughts. He worried about his homeland, since the Germans, no longer being distracted by the Russians, could put greater forces against the French and British. He thought of the Bolshevik revolution and compared it to the French revolution. He believed, "Our fathers fought to be free. Russians are fighting to no

Louis Coudouret as a member of *escadrille* Spa.103, one of the famous *les Cigognes* or 'The Storks' squadrons. He is seated next to *Capitaine* Joseph Battle who commanded Spa.103. A stork pin is above his award ribbons over the left breast pocket.

longer be free." He remembered his countrymen left behind, those who had fallen on Russian soil, buried next to their Russian comrades with whom they shared so much. Coudouret left Russia with this sentiment: "Although joyful at the thought of seeing again soon all those that are dear to us, it is not without a certain pang in our hearts that we see disappearing on the horizon the thin line of the Russian coast, boundary of that immense country that we so often flew over, defended and that the blood of so many of our comrades spilled heroically...Robinet, Poiré, Grasset, Bonnier, Moutach, Chalieux, Berné, Lignac...the graves where you rest are teeming, over there, in the middle of the immense steppes or along the furrows of the fertile plains of the Ukraine. May your names say again one day to the Russians, forgetful of their duty, this motto, that was yours, and for which you fell: 'Better to die a hundred times, than to lose Liberty.'"

He arrived in France April 1, 1918, asking to be assigned to combat duty. On May 18 his request was granted and he was posted to *escadrille* Spa.103, of the famous *Groupe de Combat* 12, commonly known as *les Cigognes* (The Storks).

A jovial *Capitaine* Louis Coudouret displaying his *Croix de Guerre* with its many palms.

Escadrille 103 had been a Voisin unit attached to GB.1 in 1915 when Coudouret was assigned to VB.102. When he arrived at Spa.103 on May 18 the unit was stationed at Hetomesnil, south of the Somme river, where it would stay, with few exceptions, for the next three months.

Coudouret wasted no time in entering combat. Three days after his arrival eight enemy aircraft attacked him and his companion, *Sergent* Robert Hoeber,[12] in the vicinity of Montdidier. They managed to escape without incident.

On May 30, 1918, Coudouret was awarded the *Legion d'Honneur* with this citation: "Pursuit pilot, model of spirit, skill and courage, shot down five enemy planes, three of them on the Russian Front."

He added to his score on June 2 when, again accompanied by *Sergent* Hoeber, they attacked an enemy fighter that crashed near Carlepont. This was Coudouret's sixth and final victory, for which he was given another citation.

On June 28 he was promoted to permanent *Sous-Lieutenant*, retroactive to March 20, 1917. He continued to serve with Spa.103, moving to the Marne area and other locations along the southern part of the front until the unit became part of the army of occupation after the Armistice. On Christmas Day of 1918, Coudouret was promoted to full lieutenant. In June of 1919, he was sent on a special mission to Peru with the 4th Regiment of Observation, a unit not associated with the air service. He completed this mission successfully, but the details are unknown. Some time after this he became a *Capitaine* in the reserves and, not losing his sense for adventure, developed the idea of flying the Atlantic Ocean.

His first attempt was in 1928, accompanied by *Capitaine* Maillou and an old friend from escadrille Spa.581, Count de Mailly-Nesle. Their airplane was overloaded, carrying 4500 liters of fuel, and was unable to gain the proper altitude. Coudouret managed to control the aircraft and hopped over trees and telegraph wires to make a hard but successful landing.

Count Mailly-Nesle provided the next aircraft, a Bernard monoplane, and by the summer of 1929, Coudouret was ready to attempt another flight. He decided the most advantageous takeoff point would be from Seville instead of Paris. As he explained his reasons, "I will take with me 4100 liters of gasoline, which should cover 6800 kilometers. If the distance between Le Bourget and New York is 6700 kilometers I don't have enough margin, so it would be safer to go from Seville to New York, which is 6000 kilometers away. I also plan to go via Halifax, 5000 kilometers from Seville, so in case of emergency I can land there."

This second attempt was never made. On July 7, 1929, while on a test flight returning to France from Spain, the Bernard developed engine trouble over Saint-Augeau, near Angouleme. In the descent, the plane hit a tree and spun into the ground. Coudouret and his two passengers, Celestino de la Cruz and Francesco Durban, both of Spain, were severely injured and taken to the Angouleme hospital. The two Spaniards survived, but Coudouret died before reaching the infirmary.

He was given a hero's sendoff, which included a souvenir booklet listing his citations and awards to remember not only his bravery but his dedicated service to his country and to Russia. *Capitaine* Louis Coudouret was laid to rest in the Grenelle cemetery in Paris on July 12, 1929.

---

(12) *Sergent* Robert Hoeber was an American and member of the Lafayette Flying Corps. It appears he and Coudouret felt confident with each other as they flew together on several occasions. Hoeber's only victory is shared with Coudouret. Hoeber earned his *Brevét* on October 20, 1917, and was posted to Spa.103 on December 19, 1917, serving with this squadron until the end of the war. He was awarded the *Croix de Guerre* with *palme*.

Victor Georgiyevitch Federov

Victor Federov in full uniform. His awards include the *Chavalier de la Legion d'Honneur*, the *Medaille Militaire*, and the *Croix de Guerre* with three *palmes* and one *etoile de vermeil*. He claimed a total of eight victories, with five being confirmed.

Victor Federov was born on November 11, 1885, in the town of Verny, in the region of Turkestan, located east of the Caspian Sea. Bordering China to the southeast, it extends to southwestern Siberia. The multi-racial population was generally poor; farming and cattle raising were the principle occupations. Federov was able to escape this area by advancing to a higher level of education, studying at the University of Kharkov[1]. He became interested in politics and joined the Social Democratic Party, which advocated ideals considered revolutionary. Because of his political views, he went to Belgium in 1908 and then to France, where his beliefs could be more freely expressed and accepted. Federov acquired a fondness for France and remained there. Since he was still in France when war broke out, he volunteered for the Foreign Legion. On August 21, 1914, *Soldat* (Private) Victor Federov became a member of the 2nd Foreign Regiment, enlisting for the duration of the war. The majority of this regiment, along with the First, was sent to Sidi-di-Abbes and Saida, in Morocco, to protect the French African colonies. This transfer was made because many legionnaires were of German and Austrian background. A few detachments stayed in France. Federov was among them, assigned to *Battalion* 'F.' This unit arrived at the front on October 24, 1914.

Federov's courage and determination were rewarded with a promotion to *Caporal* (Corporal) on November 21. He was severely wounded at Cranne on March 23, 1915. He recovered slowly, hospitalized at a temporary forward facility until April 9, when he could be moved to a Russian hospital in Paris. There he remained until May. During this time he asked for a transfer to the aviation service, since he could no longer serve in the infantry. With the help of the Russian military attaché, this request was granted.

Caporal Federov officially entered the French aviation service in May, 1915, as a chauffeur. By autumn he was sent to Buc for initial flight training and from there to d'Amberieux for advanced training, probably on Caudrons. On November 27, 1915, Federov was awarded his military pilots *Brevét*[2] and sent to the R.G.A.[3] at Dugny to await assignment.

Federov was posted to *escadrille* C.42, a Caudron unit flying the twin Le Rhône-powered type G.4, on January 21, 1916. Here he achieved a record of success in a short time, but more importantly began a lasting friendship with his *mecanicien*. As Federov stated, "I had several mechanics whom I found unsatisfactory, and then there was one introduced to me, a kid from the class of '16. That's him. Dirty, not groomed, unshaven, swimming in these large blue pants, drenched in oil, he is the one I will keep." This dilapidated figure was *Caporal* Pierre Lanero[4], his mechanic and companion for the rest of the war. Federov noted how Lanero worked with such intensity, how radiant an individual he was, and that his work was the best. By Federov's own description it seems he had the best Caudron in existence. "Now I am able to be at ease, my back does not hurt and does not vibrate. I can walk wonderfully," he exclaimed.

---

(1) At the time of his birth, the University of Kharkov was one of only nine schools of this level, with a total enrollment of only about 12,500 students from a population of 85 million. Generally the education was very high, comparable to that of Germany, and the students were extremely intelligent. Many lived in poverty, supporting themselves mostly by tutoring and translating work.
(2) This was the French pilot certificate. Federov was issued military *brevét* number 2004.
(3) The *Reserve General d'Aviation* was an aviation personnel and material depot for distribution to and from front-line squadrons.
(4) When Federov spoke of Lanero, his reference to him as a kid is due to his own age. Federov was 30 years old at the time, while Lanero was maybe 20. Federov's compassion for him was not unlike that of an older brother.

A Caudron G.4. This type was flown by Federov and Lanero during service with *escadrille* C.42 when they scored three victories during March, 1916, over Verdun. The type was equipped with two 80hp Le Rhône rotary engines, with a center nacelle for the crew. The observer sat in front to operate the machine gun. The G.4 had a top speed of 82mph and a ceiling of 14,000 feet. SHAA photo.

Federov was promoted to *Sergent* (Sergeant) on February 21, 1916, the day the German offensive at Verdun began. This was to be the site of one of the longest and bloodiest battles of the war. German General von Falkenhayn chose Verdun for this offensive because of the salient created by the Meuse river, which offered an excellent advantage for an attack. Psychologically, it was also the best location. Historically, Verdun was the entranceway into France with its system of fortresses. When this area was conquered during the Franco-Prussian War of 1870–71 it was humiliating to the French. Falkenhayn knew this and calculated they would hold it until the last man. He believed this would occupy all French resources available and deprive Britain, which Falkenhayn felt was the real force to be reckoned with, of support.

Escadrille C.42 reinforced the Verdun area in March, and on March 14 Federov, with Lanero as machine gunner, took to the skies in defense of Fort Vaux and Fort Douaumont. This was Lanero's first combat flight and would not soon be forgotten. Upon approaching Fort Vaux, Federov spotted four enemy planes below, crossing the lines. He signaled Lanero and began to descend. The crew picked out the best vantage point and attacked. Lanero began firing his machine gun, hitting his adversary. Soon the German gunner retaliated, his bullets penetrating the Caudron. Federov and Lanero ignored this and pressed on with their attack until the ammunition was exhausted. At that point, Federov saw the enemy plane pick up its nose and rise slowly, appearing to progress toward a stall. There was no time to follow its movement because other German aircraft were approaching. The only weapon at the disposal of the Caudron crew now was an infantry carbine. Fortunately, the enemy returned to their lines. Federov also turned for home, and while doing so witnessed the fall of the enemy recently encountered. When the pair landed they counted 17 holes in their aircraft. Lanero had some work to do.

Federov was constantly in the air during March, usually with Lanero. On several occasions they were outnumbered, but always attacked. One of Federov's fellow pilots complimented him, stating, "Before an operational flight he was always extremely cheerful and lively. He never complained of being tired and volunteered for patrol rounds, and flew up bright and cheerful as if he was going to a sumptuous feast." Once he entered combat, this cheerful individual became a vicious fighter. It is no wonder that within this short time he had been given the title "Air Cossack of Verdun" by his enemies. On March 26, 1916, both Federov and Lanero were cited in army orders for their air battles, especially for the victories of March 14 and March 21. It also described two separate fights on the 19th when four and three enemy aircraft were forced to retreat to their own lines. On March 22, both were nominated for the NCO award *Medaille Militaire*.

This courageous pair continued to attack the enemy consistently for almost three weeks until an encounter with three Germans almost proved fatal. This battle occurred on April 1. As Federov described it, "I am wounded. Our cause is lost. I have to save myself, but I must not let the Germans know I am caught. Meanwhile, my leg is shattered, it is impossible to operate the plane. I am making an inhuman effort not to loose consciousness. Finally I am out of the line of sight, and it is necessary to choose a place to descend. It is a hilly location, completely overgrown with woods. Finally I notice a spot free of trees. I am going straight down and suddenly see that the plain area is crisscrossed with wire fences. I have no other choice, and here with the skill I did not know I had, I landed in a place completely unimaginable. Nothing was broken and I was not shattered. Perhaps that was a miracle." Lanero was also wounded by an explosive bullet that left four fragments in his back. Both men would spend time recuperating.

The next day, April 2, 1916, Federov was awarded the *Medaille Militaire*. The citation read in part, "Energetic and courageous pilot, always ready to combat German planes." Federov believed Lanero should also receive this award, but this was not to be. It was his understanding

Victor Federov in Russian uniform, circa autumn 1916.

Victor Federov seated in the cockpit of a Morane Saulnier H. It appears his shoulderboards are that of a Russian *Podporuchik* (2nd Lieutenant), and the location may be Odessa or Sevastopol where he served as an instructor in 1917.

that the army officials thought two medals to the same squadron on the same day was too much. During his service at Verdun, Federov had claimed six German aircraft shot down, three of which were officially granted recognition. Lanero was credited with the same.

After convalescence, Federov was promoted to *Sous-Lieutenant* (2nd Lieutenant) on August 9, 1916, with these words of appreciation from *Generale* Joffre: "You have redoubled the glory covering the banners of the Verdun Army. On behalf of this Army I thank you for the service offered to France."

Next he was posted to *escadrille* N.26. This unit was stationed at Cachy, in the Somme, under the command of the 6th *Armee*. Seven squadrons were assigned to this location to form the *Groupement de Combat de la Somme*. This combined effort would give the French a greater ability to control the skies above the battlefield. Of the seven units, four would remain together to become GC.12, which included *escadrilles* N.3, N.26, N.73, N.103. This group became known as *'les Cigognes,'* the famous storks.

Federov served in N.26 for a very short time and it appears he saw little action. He longed for home and found his chance to return with the French Military Mission to Romania. As Federov wrote, "I had too much 'service' here (France); only in two weeks I have received all the awards of the French army, but I am so eager to serve Russia. I am not even afraid to die there. I have no fear to die here also, but I am a stranger to them. I can never become a Frenchman. However, in Russia I would be completely absorbed in destructive work—fight, fight, and fight Germans."

On October 10, 1916, Federov and Lanero started on their journey to Romania. This mission was assembled to help the new ally set up an air service for the Transylvanian offensive. Federov's only concern was to return to Russia eventually. He was assigned to the Franco-Romanian *escadrila* N.3, later to gain fame under the command of *Capitaine* Maurice Gond. The squadron was stationed near Bucharest during November and into December, until German and Bulgarian troops advancing from the south crossed the Danube River into the Wallachian province and closed in on the capital city.

On December 8, 1916, the unit was ordered to retreat to Tecuci, in the Moldavian province, behind the Sereth River. Federov, with five other pilots, flew to Tecuci via Ciulnita. This location was much closer to Russia and on December 19 Federov was able to transfer to the Russian air service. Salary schedules were established for incoming French personnel by the Russian high command and

The lineup of Nieuports of the 11th Corps Detachment on the Galician Front. Federov served with this unit during 1917. The Star of David, the squadron insignia, is visible on the rudder of the two planes to the right.

issued to the Field Control of Aviation and Aeronautics.[5] *Sous-Lieutenant* Federov was paid 600 roubles a month, while *Caporal* Lanero received 300. The official document stated, "When the above mentioned ranks return to France after ending their service in Russia, the remaining monthly salary due them must be paid to them in francs at the rate of exchange of two francs for one rouble."

Federov and Lanero were assigned to the training center at Odessa to instruct student pilots in flying and aerial combat. Federov did not like this position and requested a transfer to a frontline squadron. This request was granted, and he and Lanero were soon on their way to Minsk. They were assigned to the 11th Corps Detachment, one of the squadrons attached to the First Combat Air Group, under the command of *Stabs-Rotmistre* (Staff Captain) Alexander Kozakov. The unit insignia was the six-pointed Star of David in white on a black rudder. During his service at the 11th Corps Detachment Federov flew a standard Nieuport 17 with only the unit emblem as a marking.

While at the front, Lanero gained a great deal of publicity from the surrounding squadrons as a first-rate mechanic, almost reaching celebrity status. Federov was quite proud of him for this. Unfortunately, Federov did not score any victories and was ordered to report to Sevastopol, once again as an instructor.

Russia was on the eve of revolution; this upset Federov a great deal. He wrote, "I have lived in Russia at the hour of great distress, the hour of uneasiness and of a sadness unheard of." He also wrote this about his wartime companion, "And always Lanero becomes my devoted and sincere friend, finding words of encouragement and comfort."

Federov became ill and was sent to a hospital in Moscow. Lanero was able to locate the infirmary where he had been admitted, staying by his side day and night. He searched for medicine and sought other ways to comfort his friend. Federov wondered if a brother of flesh and blood would have been capable of such devotion.

After recovering, Federov came to the realization that the war was over in Russia. The internal fighting had begun. He and Lanero left Russia for France in March 1918, with other members of the mission.

They arrived in France April 10, 1918, and by May Federov was ready for front-line action. He waited at le Plessis-Belleville for an assignment throughout June until finally sent to a pursuit unit, *escadrille* Spa.89. While with this unit Federov was given a temporary promotion to *Lieutenant*, on August 9, and three days later was made a *Chevalier de la Legion d'Honneur*, with the citation: "Magnificent example of patriotism, bravery, and sense of duty. Wounded in the infantry, then transferred to the aviation service, distinguished himself by his bravery and his brilliant combats during which he shot down four enemy planes. After the campaigns of Romania and Russia, returned to the French front always being in combat a model of spirit, courage, and tenacity."

---

(5) This document was dated May 5, 1917, and was retroactive to the beginning of the individual's service. It further established the requirements for paying traveling expenses, demanded by the French army, both to Russia and when returning to France. Federov was granted 2200 roubles and Lanero 500 for arriving in Russia. Upon leaving they were to receive 775 roubles for Federov and 300 for Lanero.

The faithful *'mecano' Caporal* Pierre Lanero (center), while in Russia. He served as Federov's mechanic from January, 1916, with C.42 until October 1918, when Federov was wounded at Spa.89 and did not return to the front before the end of the war. Federov credited Lanero for most of his success.

Escadrille Spa.89 was attached to the *1er Armee* and was also part of GC.17 (*Groupe de Combat* 17) along with *escadrilles* Spa.77, Spa.91, Spa.100, and later Spa.174, under the command of *Capitaine* Joseph l'Hermite. GC.17 was in turn combined with two other groups, GC.13, and GC.20, to form *Escadre de Combat* 2, under the command of *Chef de Battalion* Phillipe Fequant. Also, by this time, the need to group even more units under one command increased. *Escadre de Combat* 2 was combined with *Escadre de Combat* 1, and some of the *Escadre de Bombardment* units to form the Division Aerienne.

The US First Army was preparing for the St. Mihiel offensive, south of Verdun along the Meuse River. Colonel William Mitchell, commander of the Air Service, US First Army, received permission from the French to have the entire Division Aerienne at his disposal for the battle. On September 7, 1918, *escadrille* Spa.89 was assigned to the US First Army. On the morning of September 12, US General John Pershing attacked the St. Mihiel salient with a main force from the south and a secondary force from the west. Within four days, the US forces had pushed forward more than 10 miles and had captured 15,000 German prisoners and 450 guns.

Near the end of the battle Federov combined with three of his squadron mates, *Adjudant* Regnier[6], *Sergent* Lasnes, and *Caporal* Havard, and also *Sergent* Stanley[7] of Spa.23, to shoot down a two-seat reconnaissance plane in the vicinity of Bar-le-Duc. This victory on September 18 was Federov's fourth. The squadron left the St. Mihiel area on September 29, moving north to the Meuse-Argonne area in support of that offensive.

This was the final offensive of the war along the southern front. It was designed to cut the rail lines by capturing the Mezieres-Sedan rail junction. The combined French and American forces pushed forward in early October. Federov became an ace during this battle when he shot down an enemy fighter over Damvillers[8] on October 9 while escorting a group of allied bombers. This was his last victory and the last for Spa.89.[9] A week later, he was wounded for a third time. A citation dated November 7, 1918, said, "Victor Federov, *Sous-Lieutenant* in the Foreign Regiment, pilot in the squadron Spa.89, courageous officer. Although in action for a period of four years, was never discouraged by fatigue or injuries. On October 16, 1918, attacked by three Fokkers and wounded during the combat, successfully brought back his bullet-riddled plane to our lines."

Federov was evacuated to a hospital, ending his wartime career. He had served France heroically, earning the highest awards. He praised Lanero for his attention to duty, his devotion, and everlasting friendship. After recovering from his wounds, Federov retired to Veroneze Street in Paris. He died on March 4, 1922, at Saint-Cloud, a few miles outside Paris. He was 36 years old, a victim of the tragedy of war.

---

(6) Emile Regnier scored all six of his victories with Spa.89. He earned his *Brevet* on September 12, 1917, and reached the rank of *Sous-Lieutenant*. He was awarded the *Croix de Guerre* with six *palmes* and one *etoile de vermeil* and one *etoile de bronze*, the *Medaille Militaire*, and the *Legion d'Honneur*. He survived the war.

(7) Alfred Holt Stanley, an American, served with Spa.23 from February 24, 1918 until the end of the war. He earned his *Brevet* on November 13, 1917, and reached the rank of *Adjudant*. He was awarded the *Medaille Militaire* and the *Croix de Guerre* with four *palmes* and two *etoiles de vermeil*.

(8) Damvilliers was located in the Argonne wood approximately 12 miles north of Verdun.

(9) Spa.89 scored nine victories during the war. Six were shared victories, and almost all were in the last five months of the war. The unit was disbanded on July 9, 1919.

Maurice Roch Gond

Maurice Roch Gond with his Nieuport 11, while serving in the Franco-Romanian *escadrila* N.3. The collar insignia denotes French aviation service, and the cloth pilot's wings are sewn on the left sleeve. The three chevrons on the lower sleeves denote the rank of *Capitaine*. His *Croix de Guerre* with star indicates a citation in regimental orders, awarded possibly for service with the 30th Dragoons or *escadrilles* N.67 or C.64. In addition, he was made a *Chevalier de la Legion d'Honneur*, and was awarded the Order of Saint George Fourth Class, Order of Saint Anne Third Class, Order of Saint Stanislau Second Class and Third Class from Russia. He also received the Order of Michael the Brave Third Class—Romania's highest award— the Romanian Star with Swords, and the Romanian War Cross. An interesting figure is applied to the fuselage of the Nieuport.

Gond was born May 31, 1884, in the small town of Joigny on the Yonne River in the province of Burgundy, about 75 miles southeast of Paris. This area, like much of the country, was agricultural. Gond's family was typically rural, with limited means that did not provide him with opportunities for higher education or social advancement. Due to the upbringing and influences of the time, he was an energetic, high-spirited individual who needed a direction to channel this vitality. He decided the best opportunity would be in military service.

Gond volunteered for service June 6, 1902, at age 18. He became a member of the 5th Infantry Regiment and went to Africa with the rank of *Soldat* (Private) as part of the army of the colonies. This was the type of job which was, politely put, less desirable. The tedious monotony of daily soldiering far from home with strange surroundings was not for those used to a high standard of living. This was, however, the beginning of a long and productive military career for Maurice Gond.

Later he was assigned to the 30th Regiment of Dragoons where his initiative was eventually rewarded with a commission. Gond became a lieutenant in October of 1912 and held that rank when the 30th Dragoons were mobilized July 30, 1914, at the beginning of the war. Late in 1914 he was given two citations for his exceptional leadership skills on scouting missions. During these early months of the war he had already shown his unflagging energy and devotion to his unit.

After more than a year of service with the 30th Dragoons, Gond transferred to the aviation service. Many cavalrymen transferred to aviation because of a greater need for aviators than cavalry. Volunteers were requested and Gond was the type to grasp an opportunity. On September 20, 1915, he entered the observers' training course, which he completed in a short time. He had already been attached to *escadrille* N.67, equipped with two-seat Nieuports. Gond was one of the first observers with N.67, which was formed on September 17, 1915, at Lyon-Bron. By the end of September, the unit was assigned to the 4th *Armee* and stationed in the Champagne sector. Gond served with N.67 throughout the winter of 1915–16 and was likely involved in many of the operations that gained the squadron its first citation. N.67 was cited in army orders on January 15, 1916, with the following statement: "It has displayed, under the leadership of *Capitaine* de Marmies, extremely remarkable active service and the most brilliant spirit during a period when the weather was very unfavorable; and it has contributed to the success of the Army's operations by the successful results of its reconnaissance, artillery spotting, photography, pursuit, and bombing, notably November 28, 1915 to December 29, 1915, and January 17, 1916, despite enemy airplanes and anti-aircraft." Although details of Gond's actual involvement in these missions is unknown, presumably he accumulated experience in the art of reconnaissance, and other two-seater duties.

In March of 1916, he was assigned to a Caudron unit, *escadrille* C.64. After only a few months with C.64, Gond was able to fulfill a great desire when he was sent to Buc for pilot training. Within a short time he was awarded

A French Caudron G.4 twin-engine bomber and reconnaissance aircraft. Gond flew this type of plane as both a pilot and observer during his service with *escadrille* C.64. This type was used in Romania also, and Gond provided escort to the units using them on several occasions. Photo: SHAA.

Brevét[1] number 3821. He returned to C.64 and flew Caudron G.4s.

In August, C.64 combined efforts with *escadrilles* C.104 (also with Caudron G.4s), F.43 (Farman F.40s), and MF.25 (Maurice Farman 11s), to conduct concentrated night bombing raids on targets in the Verdun sector. Unfortunately, details of Gond's participation in these missions are unknown. Several important targets were attacked, including munitions and supply depots, factories, and rail stations. Gond probably participated in many of these raids, otherwise he would not have been experienced enough for his next assignment as a member of the aeronautical mission to Romania. He left France in early October 1916, destined for Bucharest.

The Romanians had declared war on the Central Powers on August 27, 1916, but were clearly unprepared for war. King Ferdinand I of Romania[2] had decided neutrality could not go on, but sensed the best choice for his people would be to join the Entente. On August 16, France, Great Britain, Italy, Russia, and Romania had signed, in secret, the Treaty of Bucharest. Within the context of the agreement, the Allied powers made several military concessions to the Romanians for their promise to invade Austria-Hungary.[3] Most of the war materials and manpower were supplied by Russia and France. At the request of the Romanian government, French General Joffre assigned General Henri Berthelot, a veteran of the Western Front, to command a new detachment known as the "Military Mission of Romania." It consisted of 430 officers from all branches of service and included 74 doctors and 1500 troops. These trained personnel were in extremely short supply in the Romanian army. The aviation section consisted of 42 officers, 45 NCOs, and 162 men. Included in this total were 18 pilots, one being Maurice Gond.

On October 28, 1916, Gond and several other French pilots were at the Romanian air service headquarters when they had the opportunity to meet Romanian *Capitan* (Captain) Panait Cholet[4] who had just returned from an important reconnaissance mission. Cholet's report to Major Rujinschi pointed out the locations of enemy troop concentrations lined up behind the Danube river preparing to cross into Romania. Despite the bad news, Cholet recalled meeting the French pilots; however, Gond was the only one to make a lasting impression. Gond did not wait for introductions, but took it upon himself. He approached Cholet stating, "Flight Captain Maurice Gond, French Aeronautic Mission of Romania!" As described by Cholet, "Gond was short, and he wasn't young, but he had such piercing eyes! I was struck by his warm and reliable look."

Gond was assigned to the Franco-Romanian *escadrila* N.3 of the 2nd Aeronautic Group, equipped with Nieuport 11s, known as the *Bebe*. *Escadrila* N.3 was commanded by Romanian *Capitan* Nicolae Capsa and was stationed at Pipera, near Bucharest, as part of the capital city's protection. Throughout November 1916 the pilots of N.3 made several reconnaissance flights and escorted *escadrila* F.5 (Farman 40s) along the Danube river and the province of Dobruja. One of these reconnaissance missions was performed by Gond on November 12, when he sighted a

---

(1) The *Brevét* was the certificate awarded to pilots who had completed the aviators' course of instruction at one of the French schools. There were two types of *Brevet* certificate, one regular (civil) and one military. Gond is stated as having earned *Brevét* number 2905 on February 4, 1916, just prior to his transfer to C.64. His later flight training in July, 1916, may have been an advanced course.

(2) King Ferdinand I was born and educated in Germany. He was a member of the German royal family, the Hohenzollerns, and found it a difficult decision to side against his country of origin. Many of his ministers were for joining the Central Powers, but the King feared Austro-Hungarian manipulation.

(3) The Allies' reason for this concession was to take the pressure off the Western Front by drawing German troops to Romania. France had recently endured the destructive battles at Verdun and needed relief.

(4) Panait Cholet's father was French, his mother Romanian, and he spoke perfect French. He commanded reconnaissance units throughout the war in several locations along the front. He later became a general in the Romanian Air Service.

A Franco-Romanian Farman *esca-drila* with a mixed group of Romanian, French, and Russian crew members. Notice the different styles of uniforms. The Russian officer third from the left appears to be wearing the Order of St. George Fourth Class and the Russian fifth from the left is wearing an officer's derrick. The aircraft on the left is a Farman F.40, while the aircraft on the right is a Voisin. The two machine guns are captured Austrian Schwarzlose guns.

The Farman F.40 was used by many of the bombing and reconnaissance squadrons in Romania, especially those attached to the Second Aeronautical Group. Gond and his men often provided escort for these units. In a Farman F.40 the Russian commander of the 30th Corps conducted his own observation of his troops. Gond flew escort for that mission.

"bridge of boats" and several enemy barges and monitors along the Danube. Despite the extensive and well-executed aerial reconnaissance, the Romanian army, still ill-equipped, could not hold back German General Machensen's combined army of veteran troops from Galicia and Bulgarian units. They entered the Wallachian province November 23, 1916, forcing the Romanians to retreat to a defensive position behind the Sereth river. *Escadrila* N.3 covered for the army's withdrawal until December 8, when ordered to Ciulnita. From there it went to the town of Tecuci in the Moldavian province. Gond traveled to the new location by land since there were not enough aircraft for all the pilots of the squadron, a continuous problem.

During the first month at the new location, Gond flew mostly reconnaissance flights and offensive patrols. These missions were very important since both sides were in new positions which required both locating the enemy troops and warding off the opponent's aircraft from doing the same. There was a great amount of ground activity, but for the most part the front stabilized and N.3 remained

Gond in one of the squadron's Nieuports taking off to intercept the enemy. The Germans conducted hit and run raids on the airfield at Tecuci. On some occasions an advance call would come from headquarters, allowing the fighter pilots a few moments to become airborne before the enemy actually arrived.

Capitaine Maurice Gond (center) with several men of *escadrille* N.3 at Tecuci, late spring or early summer 1917. The members are, from left to right, Henri Manchoulas, Charles Revol-Tissot, Gond, Jacques Texier, Maurice Theron, and Francois Terry. Notice Revol-Tissot is wearing his decorations, the Third and Fourth Class Cross of Saint George.

at Tecuci until mid-September 1917. The main enemy was based at Focsani and Rimnicu-Sarat, about 20 miles away. The squadron's first success was on the morning of December 23, 1916, on a reconnaissance over Focsani, when *Sergent* (Sergeant) Jacques Texier shot down an enemy aircraft. In the afternoon Gond, with two other pilots, went to locate the wreckage. Gond's Nieuport developed engine trouble upon reaching the lines and he was forced to return to Tecuci. A short time later he spotted an enemy aircraft conducting an observation at a greater altitude. Gond pushed his motor to its limit to gain altitude as he headed for the German two-seater. The crew of this aircraft was waiting for Gond and when he closed in they exchanged bursts of machine gun fire. Gond's Lewis gun jammed after three bursts and moments later, his engine quit, forcing him to break off the fight. He had to make an emergency landing in a rough field, just inside friendly territory, that damaged his plane. He did, however, manage to disrupt the enemy's mission.

By this time Gond had shown his superiors and fellow pilots his skill and determination, for which he had earned their respect. On January 15, 1917, Nicolae Capsa was promoted to the command of the 3rd Aeronautic Group and Gond became the commander of N.3. Gond was a born leader who knew how to obtain the most from his men. He led primarily by example and made his squadron the best in the Romanian air service. Ten days after his appointment as squadron commander he was joined by Romanian *Capitan* pilot Stefen Protopopescu as joint commander of N.3. The two had a very good working relationship, both concerned for the welfare of their subordinates.

Gond flew many missions in January 1917 when weather permitted. It was bad on several occasions, but Gond always attempted a flight when an order came from headquarters. An exciting event involving Gond occurred on January 14. A German two-seater crew mistook the Tecuci airfield for their own and prepared to land. The Franco-Romanian ground crews did not pay attention at first; some thought it might have been a Spad. Just as the enemy touched down, the observer realized the mistake and signaled his pilot to take off. The pilot had already cut the engine, but was fortunate to have enough speed to start it again. He wasted no time in giving the crate full throttle. The ground crews now realized what was happening. Gond was the first to climb into a Nieuport and commence the chase, but it was to no avail. The little 80-horsepower Nieuport could not catch the more

A Nieuport 11 of *escadrille* N.3 serial number 1405, with a black cat emblem as a personal insignia. It is unknown whose usual mount this was, but many pilots flew it, including Gond. Although it was used on several missions by Gond, he did not score any victories while flying it.

powerful German machine in a high-speed chase.

February 6 was a glorious day for the squadron and one of personal gratification for Gond. Three of his men, *Adjudant* Charles Revol-Tissot, *Sergent* Jacque Texier, and *Caporal* Henri Manchoulas, were awarded the Cross of Saint George Fourth Class by the Russian Grand Duke Michailovich himself. He congratulated Gond on his excellent quality as a squadron commander. This was a high honor considering that N.3 had been operational for only a few months.

Throughout the remainder of the winter the squadron continued the usual patrols and escorts despite the lack of equipment. At one point, only one aircraft was airworthy. Due to the efficiency of the ground crews, four were available for the next day's flights, but this could not go on indefinitely. Gond stated in a report to headquarters the depressing status of the available machines. Only five of six Nieuports were flight ready. Three of these were unarmed, although Lewis guns were to be fitted soon. His main concern was ammunition, "especially tracer and incendiary bullets." With the increased enemy activity in the area, Gond also stressed the necessity of new aircraft, "so that all eight pilots can fight!"

As the winter turned to spring, activity increased and the enemy planes from Focsani, usually in pairs, conducted hit and run bombing raids consistently on the Tecuci airfield. There was very little, if any, warning of this and no time for the pilots of N.3 to get into the air for a counterattack. Gond and his men always attempted to catch the more powerful enemy machines but rarely succeeded. According to Gond's friend and fellow pilot, Romanian *Locotenent* (Lieutenant) Egon Nasta, "Gond despised these acts of cowardice and he made it a point to remember the markings on the fuselage of these enemy aircraft to make them pay at a later time."

On March 21, 1917, Gond, Texier and Manchoulas attacked a German reconnaissance plane over Birlad. Gond closed in and fired a quick burst, but once again his gun jammed. This reoccurrence of jamming was just one of the problems the squadron had to endure. Because of this, once again "Herman"—as the enemy was affectionately known—was able to escape.

Later that month Gond flew an escort for a Farman F.40 carrying the Russian general in command of the 30th Corps, who wished to inspect his troop positions in Marasesti. This was completed without incident.

Gond had his first encounter with an enemy Fokker *Eindecker* on April 13, 1917, while on morning patrol with *Adjudant* Revol-Tissot. They were patrolling an area near Focsani when they spotted the lone Fokker over the Black Forest. The two surprised the enemy, who was enjoying the morning sun and not paying attention. The German was driven away, unable to complete his mission.

Five days later Gond and Revol-Tissot were rewarded for this action. Revol-Tissot was promoted to officer rank and Gond was sited in the official army report as "an excellent pilot and remarkable commander, who through his authoritative qualities and setting personal examples, knows how to obtain maximum efficiency from his unit. In March he carried out ten air combats of extreme difficulty, where he always dominated his enemies."

On the early morning of May 1, four scout planes from N.3, including Gond, along with a flight of Russian fighters, attacked a group of seven enemy aircraft headed toward Tecuci on a bombing mission. This joint effort repelled the enemy force and only three managed to drop bombs anywhere near the airfield.

Throughout the spring N.3 performed all types of missions. Gond's men successfully carried out reconnaissance, escorts for the Farman units, offensive patrols, and most importantly, driving off the enemy bombing and reconnaissance aircraft. Their equipment was inferior to that of the enemy and, much worse, it was faulty. Gun jamming occurred much too frequently and shortages of material were excessive. Because of this, Gond visited with personnel at headquarters to request new materials. He returned with good news for the squadron; new supplies were promised.

The new equipment was badly needed and immediately put to use in the early summer of 1917, when aerial activity became intense around Marasesti, some ten miles from the Tecuci airfield. The fighting on the ground was fierce, and was said to be the "Romanian Verdun." Despite the early catastrophic losses of the Romanian army, it regrouped and fought in an organized and well-disciplined manner throughout the summer and autumn months of 1917. The Romanian general in command of the 1st Army, Eremia Grigorescu, had shown great skill in maneuvering his available troops against Mackensen's attacks, not allowing Mackensen to find a weak point that would have collapsed the entire line. This would have given the German and Austro-Hungarian armies a clear march to Jassy, where the Romanian government had relocated. Grigorescu thought very highly of Gond and congratulated him several times for his bravery and dedication to the Romanian cause, especially during this time.

Gond was extremely well-liked by the Romanians who met him, both subordinates and commanders, especially the commander of the 2nd Aeronautic Group to which N.3 was attached, Major Andrei Popovici. Gond was respected for his ability to teach. He was fair, honest and sincere, and always put the welfare of his men first. He had incredible stamina and never missed missions, a quality he was able to command from his pilots also.

On June 30, 1917, the pilots of N.3 and F.5 had assembled at the Second Aeronautic Group headquarters, where *Capitan* Cholet once again had the opportunity to meet *Capitaine* Gond. Cholet was very eager to meet the men of the well-known N.3 and commented about them: "Gond was very proud of his pilots and it was most apparent he inspired a vibrant and confident air among them."

The end of July proved successful for Gond, when he scored three victories within a fortnight. The first occurred on July 20, when he and Sergent Theron set out on a morning patrol over their own lines. They soon spotted two German reconnaissance planes headed toward Tecuci at an altitude of 16,000 feet. They each attacked one, with Gond scoring several hits on the first. The German aircraft lost altitude rapidly as the enemy crew attempted to reach their own lines with a damaged machine. *Locotenet* Egon Nasta of *escadrille* N.11 had witnessed the fight between Gond and the German when returning from a patrol. He saw the enemy aircraft descend quickly and headed toward it. Gond had veered away at this point, possibly to help Theron. Unable to find Theron, Gond dove after the damaged German. He reached the lines, were he found Nasta on the tail of the enemy, firing until he expended his ammunition. This was the finishing blow that sent the two-seater crashing to earth just over the lines.

When Gond and Nasta returned to their base, they discussed the battle and each insisted that the other was the victor. Out of respect for Gond, Nasta gave up his part of the claim, demanding the confirmation be awarded to Gond, which officially it was. Gond appreciated this gesture and the two became good friends. They met in the air on several other occasions to combine their efforts against the enemy.

On the morning of July 23, Gond flew a reconnaissance mission in the vicinity of Braila and was able to report on enemy troops advancing, which was valuable to the army. During this flight he attacked a Brandenburg C.I of Flik 29 which crashed in Romanian-

The *Mihai Viteazul* III (Order of Michael the Brave Third Class). This award was very distinguished, given for extreme bravery in the face of the enemy. It was awarded to Maurice Gond by King Ferdinand I on October 4, 1917, for his continuous service and dedication to duty from December, 1916 to September, 1917. Photo: Neal O'Connor.

held territory. The pilot, *Korporal* Kolleritsch, became a POW while the observer, *Leutnant* von Hammerlitz, perished. Gond was decorated with the *Chevalier de la Legion d'Honneur* on August 28, 1917, for this, and other actions. The citation that accompanied the award read in part, "noted for his courage during several difficult missions and in particular during certain operations that took place July 24. He already shot down five enemy planes, one of them on July 23, 1917."

The events of July 24, mentioned in the citation, were four escort missions for Farman and Caudron reconnaissance squadrons. In addition, an urgent reconnaissance was needed by army headquarters, which Gond and three of his men accomplished without incident. They returned with valuable information of enemy troop movements toward Braila. On July 29, Gond, while on patrol, attacked an enemy aircraft and shot it down near Namelousa for his fourth victory.

In August the fighting continued at an intense pace. The squadron performed 91 missions on behalf of the 2nd

Romanian Army and Russian 4th Army. During this time the pilots of N.3 were in 17 combats, including Gond's victory on August 16 when he shot down an enemy two-seater. A German reconnaissance plane had passed over Tecuci heading toward Birlad when Gond took off to pursue it. He reached the enemy about two miles from Birlad and fired several bursts. The German aircraft fell in the town of Palerma, crashing in a garden. The crew of *Leutnant* Friedrich Protzek (pilot) and *Leutnant d.R.* Hermann Steinbruck (observer, became Gond's fifth victory.[5] However, this was overshadowed when *Sergent* Texier died that evening from stomach wounds suffered in the previous day's combat. All at N.3 grieved the loss, especially Gond.

The next day King Ferdinand I visited the airfield at Tecuci to honor *Capitaine* Gond and *Sergent* Texier. Texier was award the *Virtutea Militara in aur* (Military Virtue in gold) posthumously. Gond was awarded the *Steaua Romaniei cu spade* (the Romanian Star with swords), a very high honor.

During the next week Gond and his men continued to perform their usual operations, including a night reconnaissance on August 21 from which Gond returned with valuable information on troop movements and concentrations around Marasesti. Gond completed 23 hours of combat time during August. This included a battle in which Gond, *Caporal* Manchoulas, and *Sergent* Theron fought against 13 enemy aircraft. Theron maneuvered to offer himself as a target, allowing Gond and Manchoulas a better attack position. This was the type of camaraderie displayed by Gond's men, a sign of the respect they had for him and each other.

On August 28, 1917, Gond was injured in the eye during a patrol. His condition worsened, forcing him to stop flying. His pilots were hoping for his return, but a doctor advised him to return to France for rest. Colonel Vergnette[6] granted his transfer and, although he returned to his squadron, it was only for a short stay to complete final procedures and say his good-byes. One of Gond's last accomplishments in Romania was to organize a work party to improve a landing field near Adjud. This field was closer to the front lines after the Romanian army had pushed Mackensen back at Marasesti. On September 20, 1917, Gond passed the command of N.3 to *Capitaine* Mallet and on the 24th he left for Jassy to prepare for his return to France. During this time he was awarded the Order of Saint George 4th class for his distinguished service to the

Russian 4th Army, his accomplishments in aerial combat, and his overall bravery.

Gond had performed valuable service for Romania, not only in duty but in kindness. His friendship with several Romanian pilots combined with the love of flying lifted the spirits of many. Egon Nasta stated that Gond once said to him, "To fly is to turn over the pages of the great book of the sky with fine fingers of the propeller, and piloting is a great delight for someone who devotes oneself to it." This Gond truly did.

Shortly after his departure, Gond was recommended for the *Mihai Viteazul* III (Order of Michael the Brave Third Class), an extremely high award, by Major Popovici. On October 4, 1917, Gond was given the honor in the following Royal Decree: "We confer the Great Order of *Mihai Viteazul* III on *Capitaine* Gond from the French Air Force for his efficient command of the fighter squadron N.3 which won many battles from December 1916, to August 1917."

On October 21, 1917, *escadrila* Franco-Romanian N.3 was cited in the French army orders. The following tells all: "Under the command of *Capitaine* Gond, who has demonstrated to all his pilots his valiant ardor and high sense of devotion. *Escadrila* N.3 has never ceased fighting for a year, and has been a living example to all of courage, devotion and self-sacrifice. Although provided with inferior material to that of the enemy, by their repeated attacks they have constantly affirmed their superior morale over the adversary. They have brilliantly sustained more than 100 combats, during which they forced the enemy to take flight each time, and have downed ten enemy planes."

His temporary rank of *Capitaine* was made permanent and he became the chief instructor for the Romanian student pilots at Avord. In April of 1918 he was the head flight instructor at the aviation school. After the war Gond remained in the aviation service and received several promotions. He was appointed commander of the Toulouse airbase in 1933 and became the head of the Bombardment School at Caen in 1939 with the rank of colonel.

Two of his postwar honors were the Romanian Cross of Merit with palms and induction as an Officer of the *Legion d'Honneur*. Colonel Gond retired in 1943 after a long and productive career. He died May 11, 1964, 20 days before his 80th birthday, in the Paris suburb of Asnieres. He was buried in the Forest-Gond family plot.

---

(5) Romanian Major Schipor made the report from the crash site at Palerma. The 200hp Benz motor was recovered in good condition despite the complete destruction of the airframe. Both aviators were killed and only *Leutnant* Steinbruck carried identification. Among his belongings were Romanian currency and a notebook with entries all in Spanish. The photographic equipment and the maps were destroyed and the machine gun was bent.

---

(6) Lieutenant Colonel de Vergnette de la Motte was the chief of the French Aeronautic Mission in Romania. He had an important role in reorganizing the Romanian air service before the great battles of Marasesti in the summer of 1917.

Georges Marcel Lachmann

Sous-Lieutenant Georges Marcel Lachmann before his transfer to the French Aeronautic Mission in Russia. His awards at this time consist of the *Legion d'Honneur, Medaille Militaire, Croix de Guerre* with five palms, and the Italian Order of the Crown. The collar insignia denote aviation service and the single chevron on the sleeves denote the rank of *Sous-Lieutenant*. For his service in Russia, he was awarded the Order of Saint George Fourth Class and the Order of Saint Vladimir Fourth Class.

Georges Marcel Lachmann was born in Paris on August 10, 1890. His parents were originally from the province of Alsace on the Rhine River. This area of France, along with the province of Lorraine, was taken over by the Germans after the Franco-Prussian war of 1870–71.

The Lachmanns' decision to relocate may have been to escape Prussian rule. In any case, they decided to move from rural land to the cultural and artistic center of the world, Paris. Here they had greater opportunities for social advancement, and it may be assumed they made full benefit of this. Georges was able to afford civil flight instruction, which was expensive. He obtained his civil brevet, number 1721, from the R.E.P.[1] School at Buc, on July 21, 1914.

Lachmann truly loved flying and had a strong sense of patriotism. He acquired his *brevét* prior to the war, and entered the air service on August 2, 1914. He was assigned to the 2nd Aviation Group on the same day and was issued military *brevét*, number 499, given the rank of *Sergent* (Sergeant), and assigned to *escadrille* REP.27.[2] This unit was officially formed at St. Cyr and became operational on August 30, 1914. Lachmann's first war flight was the next day, when he performed a reconnaissance mission. He served during the battle of the Marne and received his first citation describing him as "an excellent pilot who successfully conducted long reconnaissance missions in bad weather." After the battle of the Marne, REP.27 was sent to Artois. On December 20 Lachmann had a near-death experience. He was conducting an artillery spotting flight when his airplane went into a spin at 4500 feet. He managed to stabilize the craft, regaining control at 3200 feet.

In January, 1915, Lachmann was transferred to *escadrille* REP.15. This squadron was organized in 1912, one of the original 21 army units established before the war. REP.15 soon converted to Morane-Saulnier type L parasol monoplanes, changing its designation to MS.15. On March 8, while with MS.15, Lachmann was promoted to *Adjudant* (Warrant Officer). After only a few months with this unit he was sent to the R.G.A.[3] while waiting to be assigned to a pursuit squadron. His exceptional qualities as a pilot had been noticed by his superiors, resulting in this decision. Here he had the opportunity to fly all the latest types of fighters until his transfer was authorized.

On May 24, 1915, Adjudant Lachmann was assigned to *escadrille* N.57, a new unit formed on May 10 at Lyon-Bron. The squadron was stationed at Brias, northeast of Arras. The first pilots did not arrive until May 19, one being Lieutenant Espanet, a squadron mate of Lachmann in MS.15. The commanding officer, *Capitaine* Alfred Zappelli, arrived, along with Lachmann, five days later. Shortly after joining N.57, Lachmann was awarded the *Medaille Militaire* for his accomplishments with previous units, mostly important reconnaissance flights, especially one on March 27, 1915. The citation read in part, "excellent pilot who completed 200 hours of air flights over enemy territory."

On July 28, 1915, Lachmann received a temporary promotion to *Sous-lieutenant*. During this time, he

---

(1) The R.E.P. School was operated by the French aviation pioneer Robert Esnault-Pelterie. In 1908 he was honored by the Society of Civil Engineers for a thesis on radial engines, and was said to have invented the control-stick.

(2) A month after the beginning of the war two squadrons, *escadrilles* 15, and 27, were equipped with the R.E.P. type N. The R.E.P. N was a two-seat, mid-wing monoplane, with an 80 hp Gnôme motor. It was peculiar because of the red finish that was used by the R.E.P. Firm, especially for front line aircraft. Since Lachmann was very familiar with this type, it was only natural he was assigned to units supplied with this aircraft. The R.E.P. N was replaced in the spring of 1915 when it was considered unsuitable for reconnaissance and its red paint made it too visible.

(3) The *Reserve Generale d'Aviation* was an aviation personnel and material depot for distribution to and from frontline squadrons.

Lachmann in the cockpit of a R.E.P. N at the R.E.P. School in Buc. The date on the photo is July 20, 1914, most likely after a solo flight examination to complete the course of instruction. He was awarded his *Brevét* no. 1721 the following day. It was possible he preferred to be known as Marcel since the photo is signed in that manner.

demonstrated operating a machine gun by use of a cable to *Generale* Bares, the commanding officer of the French aeronautic service. This was the first successful demonstration of this procedure.

On August 13, 1915, Lachmann's services were needed elsewhere and he was sent to Italy. A unit known as the *escadrille Nieuport de Mestre*[4] was formed to defend Venice, and he was an original member. The squadron was commanded by *Capitaine* deChalleronge and consisted of only six aircraft. On November 18, 1915, Lachmann was on a mission when he was attacked by four Austrian flying boats at sea. The battle lasted for more than an hour before he drove them off. While defending Venice, Lachmann also made many reconnaissance flights over Goritzia and bombed Trieste. For these missions he was awarded the Italian Order of the Crown and his third army citation.

February of 1916 marked the beginning of the German offensive at Verdun, and *escadrille* N.57 was involved in fighting off German aircraft. On March 16 the unit was sent to Lemmes, approximately 12 miles southeast of Verdun.

With the beginning of this campaign, Lachmann requested a transfer back to his previous squadron, N.57, which was immediately granted. He arrived at Lemmes on March 24. His first victory came on July 15, 1916, when he attacked an enemy balloon over Ham and set it on fire.

On July 28 Lachmann and Lieutenant Jean Matton[5] were patrolling when they spotted an Albatros two-seater on a reconnaissance flight. Attacking the enemy, they were joined by *Marechal-des-Logis* (Sergeant of Cavalry or Artillery) Georges Flachaire[6] of N.67. The trio forced the Albatros to land inside French lines near Souilly, the enemy crew being taken prisoner. After these two victories Lachmann received his fourth citation, which read in part, "Daring pilot, dedicated, enthusiastic, eager to combat and take part in perilous missions."

On August 12 Lachmann teamed with another veteran pilot, *Adjutant* Maxime LeNoir[7] of N.23. Together they sent an enemy two-seater crashing to earth at Guiscourt; both crew members were killed.

By this time the British offensive in the Somme was well under way and had taken the pressure off the French

---

(4) This unit was also known as *l'escadrille de Venice*, which became N.92, June 1916. Later it was changed to N.392 and, on July 1, 1917, it became N.561, and subsequently SPA.561. The squadron kept this designation for the rest of the war and *Capitaine* deChalleronge was the sole commander while it was stationed on the Italian front.

(5) Jean Matton joined N.57 on July 23, 1916, and stayed only until September 25, 1916. He also served with N.77 and later with N.48, where he scored eight victories. He also commanded N.48 and obtained the rank of *Capitaine*. He was killed in action on September 10, 1917.

(6) Georges Flachaire scored all eight of his victories with N.67; this one was his second. He obtained the rank of *Sous-Lieutenant* and survived the war.

(7) Maxime LeNoir scored nine of his eleven victories with N.23. This victory shared with Lachmann was his eighth. He was very courageous, being wounded at least twice in combat. He was killed in action on October 25, 1916.

at Verdun where a trench war stalemate had developed. There were several enemy observation balloons keeping watch over French activity and Lachmann decided to make their job more difficult. On August 23 he claimed two *drachen*, one over Montfaucon and a second over Etain. Both of these victories were behind enemy lines and could not be confirmed.

In December the French launched a counter-offensive in the area of Fort Douaumont. Lachmann spotted an enemy balloon in this area at 1275 feet and attacked it, forcing the two observers to parachute from the basket.

For his achievements during the battle of Verdun, Lachmann was made a *Chevalier de la Legion d'Honneur* on January 6, 1917. The citation read in part, "Daring pilot, exceptionally motivated and eagerly seeking all kinds of missions. Received already the *Legion d'Honneur* and four citations for his numerous victories over the enemy."

On January 26, 1917, Lachmann was transferred to the French Aeronautic Mission in Russia, to become a member of *escadrille* N.581. *Escadrilles* N.581 and Sop.582 were organized at the request of the Russian government as additional units to aid in the 1917 offensive by General Brusilov. These squadrons were under the command of *Chef de Battalion* (Major) Berger. He carefully selected the aviation personnel from those who already had distinguished careers. In March 1917, Lachmann, along with several other aviators, mechanics, and their equipment, were on their way to Russia, on the ocean liner *Flore*. They arrived in Murmansk a month later and prepared to travel to Moscow and from there to Kiev. After arriving in Kiev in May, the squadrons were sent to Boutchatch to begin operations. N.581 was commanded by Lieutenant Gueydon, who was mainly in charge of operations on the ground. *Sous-Lieutenant* Lachmann was in command of the flight missions and other aerial activity.

Escadrille N.581 was surprised by an enemy bombing raid almost immediately. Lachmann ordered two of his pilots to patrol the skies around the field to prevent a recurrence. The Germans did not bother N.581 again at Boutchatch, since the squadron soon moved to the north.

On May 20, 1917, N.581 moved to Robrotsche, nine miles away, where it shared a field with the famous Russian 19th Detachment commanded by *Stabs-Rotmistre* (Staff-Captain of Cavalry) Alexander Kozakov. The group performed many flights, but scored no victories for more than a month. There were several reasons for this, including equipment failures, poor working conditions for the mechanics, and lack of enemy activity.

June 26, 1917, proved to be a disastrous day for Lachmann. An enemy observation balloon had to be destroyed before the Russian offensive. He and *Chef de Battalion* Berger decided the balloon must be attacked while it was still on the ground. To accomplish this, it was best for Lachmann to begin the mission before daylight. He and Gueydon took flight at 2AM but lost sight of each other in the fog. Lachmann set his course as best he could, heading toward what he thought was the location of the balloon. To his surprise, he found it at an altitude of 4500 feet. He immediately fired upon it. The incendiary bullets

Lachmann's Spad 7 after the crash on June 26, 1917, when due to the early morning fog, he made the mistake of destroying a Russian observation balloon thought to be German. He could not avoid the tree-covered hill directly in front of him. The result was this crash, which Lachmann was fortunate to survive.

set it on fire instantly and it crashed to the ground. Suddenly, he realized that a hill with a grove of poplar trees was directly in front of him. He did not have the time or altitude to avoid crashing into the trees. Lachmann stated later, "It's amazing I didn't die! Nothing was left of the aircraft; as for myself, after being ejected in the air like a ball, I fell on my back and received chest and facial injuries."

Lachmann had been thrown at least 60 feet. Soldiers had approached him, assuming he was dead, while Lachmann expected to be taken prisoner. Both parties were caught by surprise—Lachmann was conscious and the soldiers were Russian. He had lost his bearings in the fog and had in fact destroyed a Russian observation balloon. The Russians were able to get him medical attention quickly, giving him the best of care.

Shortly after Lachmann arrived at the hospital, the commander of the destroyed balloon visited him. The commander had just realized the attacker was not a German, and apologized for shooting at him. The two then shook hands and laughed. The Russian artillery commander stationed in that sector also visited Lachmann, declaring, "Your attack was of astonishing bravery."

On the 28th Lachmann was transferred to a hospital operated by the British. *Chef de Battalion* Berger met him there and delivered this message from a Russian general: "I was stirred by the report that I received from you, that on the 26th of June, you gave a very dangerous mission, full of risks, to Lieutenant Lachmann to destroy an enemy *drachen*, even on the ground. The atmospheric circumstances had resulted in an error of orientation which resulted in the attack on a Russian balloon at a very weak height.

A Nieuport 17 and two Spad 7s of N.581 preparing for a mission on the Galacian Front during the summer of 1917. The rear Spad with the dark-colored cowl may be Lachmann's. SHAA photo.

"I understand that Lieutenant Lachmann was very affected by this error. I beg you to please transmit to him all the esteem that I have for his valor and his bravery, that I wish him a quick recovery—assure him that mistakes of this kind, like the one of June 26, are always possible, not only in the air, but also on the ground where the conditions are even more favorable, and that those who fight in battle are excused from all such errors."

Lachmann returned to his duties before he had fully recovered from his injuries. Not only did he have several contusions, but also fractures of a finger, an arm, and a rib. He continued to lead the squadron while Lieutenant Gueydon was away temporarily, by order of *Chef de Battalion* Berger.

General Brusilov, commander-in-chief of the Russian army, launched one last attack under the order of the Provisional Government. Known as the Kerensky offensive, it began on July 1, 1917. Initial advances were made toward Lemberg with N.581 and Sop. 582 following in support of the 7th Army. The assault came to a standstill on July 16, when the Germans launched a counterattack. With the Germans advancing, N.581 and Sop.582 were ordered to retreat to Tchorkouf. *Chef de Battalion* Berger was in Kiev with Lieutenant Gueydon, attempting to resolve problems at the supply depot, so N.581 had to withdraw under Lachmann's command. Both units retired to Ezerjani on the 22nd, and on July 23 Lachmann led the retreat of N.581 to Gusyatin. The squadron was equipped with five Nieuports and two Spads, which needed to be resupplied. Lachmann commandeered the necessary fuel and oil the next day and the unit was ready to move on. It continued toward Iarmolitse on July 26 with great difficulty due to the chaotic, unorganized retreat of the ground forces. Within this four-day period the *escadrille* had fallen back 60 miles with little rest. Being forced to retreat so quickly and in such a confused manner, the *escadrilles* could no longer participate in the Galacian campaign.

During this time Lachmann was in discomfort, flying every day with the use of one arm, and being very fatigued. He had no choice but to return to Kiev for a short rest. Before his return the squadron had relocated to Kamnietz-Padolsk on August 12, 1917, resuming operations under the command of the 3rd Army Corps. Lachmann rejoined the unit at the end of August, bringing with him a new Spad from Kiev. This flight was, according to Lachmann, a difficult yet eventful experience. He was escorting the unit's supply train, which needed to stop because of overheating. Lachmann stated he had to "stop at our former landing field in Iarmolitse. I arrived in the middle of a Russian banquet where I'm asked to drink much too much vodka. The next morning, I painfully reached the squadron at Kamnietz-Padolsk after seven landings on unknown airfields and 24 hours of detention."

The field at Kamnietz-Padolsk was much more pleasant than previous locations of the squadron. Lachmann stated, "Its surroundings look like paradise to me." Although he was still not fully recovered from the injuries and the hectic retreat, Lachmann, in new surroundings with a new plane, was ready to return to action. He would soon get his chance, as a German squadron was set up opposite N.581 and aerial activity began to increase.

Lachmann wasted no time in finding a German observation balloon positioned about 20 miles away at Melnitza. On September 3, 1917, he described what happened: "I have been unable to sleep for four nights and I'm just exhausted. On September 1, as I'm cruising over the lines, I spot a *Boche*; a sausage, some 12 kilometers (7.5 miles) behind their lines. I go back to the field to pick up

Lachmann preparing for a mission. The Spad 7's cowl is dark (possibly red), and Le Prieur anti-balloon rocket tubes are attached to the inner struts. SHAA photo.

my rockets, and take off again. When I reach the lines the sausage is now at 1800 meters (5750 feet). I rush it full speed ahead, and in spite of its fast descent, manage to reach it at 500 meters (1600 feet). Out of six rockets, only one fired! I shoot at it at such close range that my wheels are no farther than one meter away from it. The sausage is on fire and the two observers jump with their parachutes. Under heavy fire from machine guns and close-range artillery, I fly over the lines at an altitude of 800 meters (2550 feet)."

Lachmann used Le Prieur anti-balloon rockets, which were often temperamental. Despite this fact, he had some success with them. The Russian military authorities were certainly impressed with his display of courage, awarding him the Order of Saint George fourth class.

His next victory occurred on September 15, when in a 20-minute fight he shot down an enemy two-seater observation plane. He described it as "a nice yellow biplane with pretty black crosses." Lachmann was able to sneak under the enemy undetected and fire more than 40 rounds. It wasn't until then the *Boche* finally became aware of Georges and began evasive maneuvers. The observer returned the fire and a dogfight ensued in which Lachmann scored several more hits. When the enemy went into a spin Lachmann was able to "cling to him like a leech, firing at him as many times as I can at an altitude of 250 meters (800 feet)." He noticed "a grayish mass shaped like a cross falling and spinning out of the aircraft; at first I thought it may be a parachute but probably not. It must be the observer, wounded or killed, ejected out of the plane during a sharp turn." The German machine crashed into the enemy front lines near the village of Chilovsti. An army report confirmed this, and also confirmed that the machine gun was found in the village of Grichard, but there was no evidence of the observer. This was Lachmann's fifth victory; he had reached ace status.

October 3 proved to be another successful day for Lachmann. He had flown patrols for six hours, attacked an enemy biplane, and sent it crashing into the front lines near Mal'Shevka. On October 8, he and Coudouret joined in shooting down an Albatros two-seater in flames between the front lines over Zalec'ye, near the Zbrousch River. On October 16, Lachmann was on patrol over the Galacian front when he attacked an enemy biplane which he forced to land behind its own lines. Later, during this same patrol, he spotted an enemy balloon over Melnitza. By the time he reached the sausage it was lowered to 950 feet, but Lachmann made a quick attack, firing only one burst of incendiary ammunition. The balloon was set on fire instantly and both observers perished. The Russians were very impressed with his action that day and cited him in the army orders.

On October 27 Lachmann tried for another enemy balloon over Cernowitz. While it was lowered to only 650 feet, Lachmann attacked at point-blank range. The observer jumped with his parachute but the balloon did not explode. Lachmann's mechanic had forgotten to load the incendiary ammunition.

The squadron was ordered to relocate north to the town of Volochyst on November 15, 1917, under the command of the 2nd Army. Here N.581 opposed enemy forces at Tarnopol. Lachmann recalled being reunited with the Belgian company of armored cars, who had taken part in the Kerensky offensive. He looked upon them admirably and commented on how valiant they were in combat.

On November 18 N.581 was cited in a report from its former command, the 7th Army. This stated, "In the course of valuable information, the French fighter squadron has delivered a series of glorious battles. This necessitates the recognition in Russia of the names of daring fighter pilots like the valiant knight of the Order of

Members of *escadrille* N.581 at Kamnietz-Padolsk November 1917, standing before the temporary hanger and the squadron's Nieuports. The closest Nieuport has been equipped with Le Prieur rockets.

Saint George, Lieutenant Lachmann, who shot down three enemy planes and burned two *drachens*."

By the end of November the weather turned bad and the unit was grounded. The Bolshevik revolution was beginning, and with this the Allied cause in the east disintegrated. Lachmann did not score again before the end of hostilities in Russia. The armistice was signed December 15, 1917, at Brest-Litovsk between the Central Powers and the new Bolshevik government. The French realized the problems of being caught in a country about to embark on total civil war, and they tried to deal with them the best they could. Lachmann commented, "Bolshevism is more damaging in the army corps that have the least discipline."

After the Russian armistice, Lachmann led N.581 to Loubny, east of Kiev. It was accompanied by the supply park under the command of Lieutenant Sers. The French, under the command of *Commandant* Bordage, tried to gather all the aircraft abandoned at the supply depots in and around Kiev. While Lieutenants Mayeur, Roy, and Remmert were attempting this, Lachmann remained in charge of the fighter detachment throughout January 1918.

On January 25, the Bolsheviks overran the town of Loubny. Lachmann had not received orders on how to proceed, so the fighter detachment did not offer any resistance. The only aerial activity by the French was a lone flight to Kiev for currency to counter the inflation experienced by the squadron while at Loubny. The Bolsheviks thought the aircraft to be from the Ukrainian forces, and accused the French of allying with them. They held Lachmann and the other French officers prisoner, confiscated their weapons, and threatened to destroy the plane when it returned. Fortunately, Lachmann was able to speak with their commander and persuade him to release the officers and return the weapons, although some of the revolvers disappeared.

The situation did not get any easier for Lachmann and his fellow Frenchmen. From January 28 to February 4 they found shelter in Kiev while the battle continued in the streets. If this were not enough, some of the Germans had rejected the thought of peace, continued the war, and advanced upon Petrograd and the Ukraine. *Escadrille* N.581 could no longer fight since the Bolsheviks had dismantled its guns.

On February 19 orders were sent from Moscow to disband the squadron and its accompanying units. *Commandant* Bordage led N.581 and the associated units to Moscow, where they were to meet the remaining French troops and await further orders. Some of the equipment was to be relinquished to the Russian authorities, while other items were to be given to the Czechoslovakian army.

Lachmann was in charge of waiting for the Czechs, but they never came. In early March, 1918, he ordered the Spads to be loaded onto the train destined for Moscow. He stayed there under the command of the military attaché, *Generale* Levergne.[8] While in Moscow, Lachmann studied Bolshevik aerial activity and helped several Russian pilots make their way to Murmansk to join other White forces.

In July 1918, Lachmann left Moscow for Murmansk by way of Petrograd, beginning a month-long adventurous and precarious journey. Others accompanied him, but on several occasions they had to split up to avoid being caught by the Bolsheviks. They regrouped after arriving at safe locations in rural areas, away from city checkpoints. This was, as Lachmann stated, "not too easy on our nerves."

Lachmann described the last segment of this exhausting trip, much of which was on foot, as follows: "My companion's feet hurt him so that he had been

---

(8) *Generale* Levergne remained head of the mission in Moscow, but the situation became dangerous for him and his constituents shortly after Lachmann's departure. Lachmann feared they would be taken prisoners by the Bolsheviks. It was later acknowledged that *Generale* Levergne and several of the other officers were evacuated to Finland, although some were held captive.

Lachmann with his Spad 7 while at Kamnietz-Padolsk. It was equipped with a single synchronized Vickers machine gun and an upper wing Lewis machine gun rarely seen on a Spad. His personal markings consisted of the dark (red) cowl and the question mark (*le point d'interrogation*), probably in red, on the fuselage sides. The Le Prieur rocket tubes have been removed. Photo: Musée de l'Air.

walking barefoot for two days, hardly able to go forward; at times he even laid down in the ditch along the road, incapable of any effort. Now I have to fend for both of us. Finally, I gave him my slippers and we arrived at last in view of Olouctz, another Bolshevik center; to make our escape possible, we had to bribe a peasant to get us through small stations and their sentries.

"Kilometer after kilometer we continued our long journey on the road to Petrozavodsk, crossing rivers and sleeping under the stars. For food we had only corned beef and a few biscuits and most of the time nothing to drink. In this part of the country the soil is very ferruginous, so once unable to control my thirst, I drank some red water from a brook, which made me even more thirsty.

"One day we hired a peasant's cart and the owner, a magnificent 80-year-old man, took us at full gallop of his two small Russian horses on a roller-coaster road with incredible curves.

"The population of this area was kind of different, not Russian or Finnish. The people there drink a lot of tea and eat an ugly dark bread that they dunk in it. They eat so much of that bread that all the women were obese and looked pregnant at first sight; even the very young girls.

"Everywhere in these poor villages there was a shortage of food. They had only a few eggs, a little bit of sour milk, and some old dark bread. Such poverty! All the people here just hate the Bolsheviks but hail the Allies.

"We have had unpleasant nights sleeping in the woods. Finally, eight days after our start, we arrive in view of Petrozavodsk. Trusting my disguise, I went first trying to get some news. Damn! The Allies have not arrived yet. They were still in Sorokka, 375 kilometers (230 miles) up north. No matter, we had to reach them and rejoin them. Some trusted friends of ours kept us in hiding so we could get some rest. I even got the nerve to visit my friend Lieutenant Foecy at the train station and had lunch with him in the wagon where he was detained and under arrest.

"My friends in town wanted to get us two fake permits and two tickets to Medvegegare, a train station located 150 kilometers (95 miles) to the north. Trusting our lucky stars, we embarked with the Bolsheviks. During the whole trip, and afraid to be betrayed by my foreign accent, I pretended to be mute and answer with gestures if asked any questions. As an aviator, I found this situation rather amusing and felt, at times, like bursting out laughing.

"On the 23rd (July), we arrived at the station, still surrounded by Red Guards, and got off the train. We managed to reach the countryside and started to walk again, but the kilometers were endless. Two days later we met an English officer, Captain Garsting, a charming and daring man, who later died heroically in Ouega. He had just left Petrograd to rejoin the Allies in the north. Several other ex-Russian officers also rejoined.

Another view of the question mark insignia on Lachmann's Spad. The Lewis machine gun has been removed from the unusual gun mount and Le Prieur rocket tubes are mounted on the struts.

"Soon afterward we came face to face with a Bolshevik commissary and several of his acolytes. He asked to see our papers and after telling him we didn't have any, we continued our route toward the north. Such cowards, they did not even dare to attack us, although only three of us were armed out of seven. Because other posts might have been warned by telegraph of our presence, we kept walking all night under a diluvial rain and intense fog. What a terrible night. There were clouds of mosquitoes also, and so far we have walked almost 37 kilometers (23 miles) with these conditions. After a few hours of rest, we started walking again with the English officer. I walked 60 kilometers (37 miles) in a 24 hour period.

"A few hours later we arrived at Sommsky channel where a dinghy took us to Sorokka. This endless trip lasted 20 days and 20 long nights. We were completely exhausted and I couldn't believe how much weight I lost.

"Three days later we arrived in Murmansk and found that the English Aviation Expedition left earlier that same day for Arkhangel, which meant my mechanic and my luggage left with along with them. Here I was, dressed in a prehistoric costume with nothing else to call my own. Luckily, an artillery unit supplied me with a superb, gaudy, khaki soldiers uniform, but anyhow I liked it."

After this Lachmann and the others rested before continuing to Arkhangel. On August 2, 1918, he arrived in Kola, a small town north of Murmansk and also the center of the Allied occupation headquarters. While at Kola, Lachmann devised a plan, based on his observations during the recent journey, which could greatly help the Allied cause and hinder the Bolsheviks. He realized that Petrozavodsk was an important center, and if held could be the area that would allow Russian sympathizers to rally with the Allies. He believed that a small force could accomplish such a task and also block the railroad south of Petrozavodsk to cut off Bolshevik reinforcements. Lachmann explained his idea to English General Menard, who agreed to the plan.

On August 7, under the command of English Captain Sheppart, with Lachmann second in command, a force of 40 men embarked from Kandalachta on a small barge named *The Satisfied* and headed toward Soumsky-Possad. This mission did not get off to a good start as Lachmann described: "Later we got stranded on a sand bar and stayed there for a day and a half. Time was going too quickly. Already three weeks had passed and the Bolsheviks were getting stronger."

Part way to their destination, Lachmann and some of the men captured a telegraph station and were able to receive all the messages from the Bolshevik commissaries in Petrozavodsk. During the next advance they were able to obtain knowledge of all Bolshevik activities. This advantage was nullified by the fact the food supply had diminished.

Meanwhile, the Allies had taken Arkhangel, which forced the retreating Bolsheviks toward Lachmann and his unit. Shortly after this, the unit arrived at Vojmosalma, still 95 miles from its destination. There they intercepted a message which made them realize they were discovered. Orders had been given to the Red Guard to cut off the only road Lachmann could use for a retreat.

Lachmann, Sheppart, and the men were surrounded, and their only choice was to fight their way out. Several of the men were killed, but Lachmann escaped and returned to Arkhangel.

In early September he reported to English Colonel Maund, commander of the Allied aviation corps, and asked to be assigned to a squadron. There were two squadrons in the area of the Dvina river, composed mainly of Russian officers whom Lachmann had helped to escape from Moscow earlier in the year. Their commander was Captain Kazakov.

Lachmann described the conditions of this area as poor. The landing fields were bad and there were no areas for emergency landings because of the heavily wooded landscape. He praised the pilots for their courage and spirit, for what they had to work with was less than acceptable. There were very few mechanics, and some recruits had little experience.

During September Lachmann flew several missions over the Dvina River in a Sopwith Strutter equipped for bombing. He and his mechanic Lecocq,[9] whom everyone knew as Coco, flew at low altitude and destroyed two Bolshevik ships. Lachmann was impressed by the terrain, which was "a desolate, deserted region, with woods and swamps." He recalled, "Quite often I think about one of these places. I had to fly over it every day, sometimes several times, to Shenkhoursk on the Dvina. It looked like an immense black hole of 45 kilometers (28 miles) in diameter that always made me think of the crater of a volcano; a crater made of mud and so big, I would have died there if my plane had fallen into it."

Winter was approaching, and with the lack of hangars, tents, and spare parts for the aircraft, it became very difficult for the squadrons to remain operational. By the beginning of November, 1918, the temperature was well below zero. Lachmann decided to return to France.

He made the journey back to Arkhangel by boat, which in itself was difficult because of the cold. Upon his arrival, he was greeted with a pleasant surprise. He had been awarded the English Military Cross for the action at Soumsky-Possad in August.

Leschi, Makozouov, and Lachmann seated at the dinner table while N.581 was stationed at Volochyst, between November 15, 1917, and December 15, 1917. Lachmann is wearing his French uniform with Russian shoulderboards with rank of a *Poruchik* (Lieutenant). Louis Coudouret and several other members of the squadron are seated around the other side of the table. Musée de l'Air photo.

Lachmann left Russia on November 7, 1918, to return to the Western Front. He had logged 126 hours of combat flight time during his service in Russia. When the Armistice was signed four days later he was still on his return to France.

Lachmann remained in the air service after the war. He served in Czechoslovakia in 1919 as commander of the aviation forces, assisting the Czechs to gain independence. For this service he was given a citation by his own country, received the Czech War Cross for bravery, and was granted the Knights class of the Order of the White Lion, given only to foreigners who helped gain Czech independence. Later he was promoted to *Commandant* and transferred to Africa to search areas for new airfields.

Lachmann's wartime awards included the Order of Saint George Fourth Class, Order of Saint Vladimir Fourth Class, *Legion d'Honneur, Medaille Militaire, Croix de Guerre* with nine palms, the English Military Cross, the Italian Order of the Crown, and the Italian War Cross.

He died on August 12, 1961, at the age of 71, in Tonnerre, a small town on the Yonne River. He was buried in the cemetery of Marolles-sous-Lignieres, in the province of Aube.

---

(9) Lecocq was Lachmann's personal mechanic. His work was excellent, but he was described by Lachmann as, "grouchy, and didn't speak much, but was liked by all the pilots." He also enjoyed flying, especially the missions over the Dvina.

Eduard M. Pulpe

A drawing of *Podporuchik* Eduard Pulpe of the 10th *Otriad* (squadron or detachment), June 1916. He was awarded the Order of Saint George Fourth Class, the *Medaille Militaire*, and the *Croix de Guerre* with four *palmes*.

The son of Latvian farmers, Eduard Pulpe[1] was born in Riga on June 22, 1880, and took an early interest in aviation. He completed his secondary education in Riga and then studied at the University of Moscow[2] graduating in 1908. He returned to Riga and became a teacher.

In 1912 he went to France to advance his education and seized the opportunity to take flight instruction. On December 19, 1913, he obtained civil *Brevét*[3] number 1571 after soloing in a Deperdussin. Still in France when war broke out, he volunteered for aviation service. Being a qualified pilot, he was readily accepted without having first to join the Foreign Legion.

Pulpe, then 34 years old, received military *Brevét* number 602 after completing an advanced course and was assigned to *escadrille* MS.23.[4] The squadron was formed during mobilization on August 4,1914, at St. Cyr and began operations in Verdun with the 2nd *Armée*. It was relocated to the Marne area for that battle in September 1914, moved to the Champagne area in early 1915 to reinforce the attacks made in February and March, and finally settled in the Somme. Pulpe arrived at MS.23 on May 1, 1915, He received a promotion on May 21 to the rank of *Sergent* (Sergeant).

In August, 1915, *escadrille* MS.23 left the Somme. After moving to various sectors of the front, the squadron returned to Verdun. On September 20 the squadron designation was changed to N.23,[5] as it began receiving swift, maneuverable Nieuports to replace the Moranes. Sometime in 1915 Pulpe was credited with two victories when he attacked eight enemy planes. Although other details are lacking, both victories were scored in the Verdun area. On October 29 he was awarded the *Medaille Militaire* with the following citation: "Voluntarily enlisted, *Sergent* with *escadrille* MS.23, pilot of exceptional courage and audacity, proved himself many times during air combats and bombardments. On September 23, 1915, when one of his comrades had failed a difficult mission he spontaneously proposed to take his place in spite of particularly dangerous conditions and accomplished it with success." Pulpe was given another citation for completing a dangerous bombing run in which he was attacked by an enemy airplane and returned with a bullet-riddled machine.

The squadron remained at Verdun where it was stationed during the German attack in February, 1916. This was a major assault to pin down the French. The location was chosen because of the salient created by the Meuse River valley.

Aerial activity became intense during late Feburary and early March. Many escorts and offensive patrols were flown. As a newly appointed *Adjudant* (Warrant Officer), Pulpe scored his third victory on March 20 north of Maucourt and east of Verdun when he attacked three German aircraft over enemy territory, succeeding in bringing one down. One of his squadron mates said, "In battle he distinguished himself by his youthful temperament and persistence," in spite of his advanced age, for a pilot, of 34. He was also known as "the pilot with a volcano in his heart."

(1) Note the German spelling of his name, Eduard instead of Edward or Edwards. It is believed this is his proper given name.
(2) The University of Moscow was one of only nine schools on this level in all of the Russian empire. They totaled only about 12,500 students in the late 19th century. Although educational standards were high, the students were usually poor and supported themselves mainly by tutoring or translation work.
(3) The *Brevét* was the French pilot's certificate, given in both civil and military form.
(4) MS.23 flew Morane-Saulnier aircraft, mostly Type 'L', and was commanded by *Capitaine* Auguste Le Reverend.
(5) The Nieuports used were not all fighter types. Besides the single seat Type 11, Type 12 two-seat aircraft were flown, as well as a few Type 10 two-seaters.

A Deperdussin TT, the type flown by Pulpe when he earned his civil *Brevét*, December 19, 1913. Powered by the 80hp Gnome, the Deperdussin had a top speed of 71mph and was used in France and Russia during the opening months of the war. Photo: SHAA.

A Morane-Saulnier L, the type used by Pulpe while assigned to *escadrille* MS.23 during 1915, before the squadron converted to Nieuports. He allegedly scored his first two victories while piloting this type of machine. Usually powered by the 80hp Le Rhône, it was capable of 72mph. The initial armament was a carbine; later these were exchanged for machine guns. Besides its use in France, the Morane saw extensive service in Russia. Photo: SHAA.

Pulpe relaxing on the tire of his Nieuport 11 *Bebe* while with the 10th Fighter Detachment stationed near Rovno, under the command of the Russian 8th Army, June–July 1916. This is possibly the aircraft used to shoot down his fifth victim in the area north of Lutsk.

On March 31, while patrolling north of Verdun, Pulpe attacked two enemy reconnaissance planes. One fled to its own lines, but Pulpe sent the second crashing to the ground near Consenvoye for his fourth victory. His third citation was issued within a short time of the two March victories. It described him as "clever and serious, calm and daring, a highly skilled pilot who carried out courageous reconnaissance that provided command with highly important information, in addition to his bringing down four enemy planes."

Pulpe received a promotion to *Sous-Lieutenant* and a new assignment in April, 1916. The French had been negotiating with the Russian military attaché in Paris, Count Ignatiev, to send aviation personnel to Russia in exchange for Russian troops to serve in France. Russia was in need of individuals experienced in all facets of military aviation, including technical assistance to industry, organizing and developing the air service, receiving and distributing French aircraft arriving at Murmansk, and serving at the front. Pulpe was one of the first selected by *Generale* Bares,[6] who promoted all selected pilots to temporary officer rank. The new French Aeronautic Mission to Russia was assembled at the R.G.A.[7] in Lyon, and was officially created on April 30, 1916. *Capitaine* Berger was promoted to *Chef de Battalion* (Major) on April 18 and was selected to lead the contingent.

The group arrived in Murmansk in May, 1916. Many of its personnel were sent to squadrons on the Galician Front to support the Brusilov offensive beginning in June. They encountered all types of circumstances; as *Sous-Lieutenant* Stribick reported, "It offered to us all occasions for continual surprise, momentary discouragements, and regrets."

Podporuchik (Lieutenant) Pulpe was assigned to the 10th Fighter Detachment stationed on the southwestern front. This unit was to support the 8th Army in its advance toward Kovel, the main objective of the Brusilov[8] offensive, which began on June 4, 1916, and gained immediate success as Russian troops advanced into Galicia. By June 10 the 8th Army had progressed beyond Lutsk, capturing many prisoners, and by early July occupied more than half the territory toward the objective. On July 1, while on patrol in the Lutsk-Kovel region, Pulpe shot down his fifth enemy aircraft to become an ace.

On the morning of August 1 Pulpe was patrolling

---

(6) *Generale* Bares was the commander of the French Aeronautic Service. He chose only those pilots who had proven themselves in combat.

(7) The *Reserve Generale d'Aviation* was an aviation personnel and material depot for distribution to and from front line units.

(8) General Brusilov was the commander of the 8th Army at the beginning of the war and was appointed commander of the southwestern front in March 1916, which included the 7th, 8th, 9th, and 11th Armies. His June 1916 offensive was a success, but came to a halt short of the main objective in September due to the lack of assistance in the north.

The schoolmaster, Eduard Pulpe.

over the Styr river when he spotted five German planes over Rogistche at a lower altitude and attacked them despite being outnumbered. Two of the enemy retreated quickly to their own lines while the other three engaged in battle to ensure their escape. Witnesses on the ground saw a remarkable display of piloting and bravery by Eduard as the combat continued for nearly an hour.[9] Eventually the Germans riddled Pulpe's machine with bullets. The Nieuport went into a spin, falling to 1000 feet, where it straightened out briefly, but the left aileron control had been destroyed and the plane plummeted to earth, crashing on the banks of the Styr. Pulpe was still conscious when help arrived. He muttered, "water," then died. He had been hit by two bullets, one in the left side of his back, causing severe internal injury. The plane was destroyed and the motor buried in the ground.

Pulpe was given another citation by the French and another *palme* to his *Croix de Guerre*. With this he was described as "A superb fighter pilot and excellent officer; an example of the highest military valor."

In an unposted letter, Pulpe wrote: "The heart's desire of each pilot is to fulfill his duty defending the Motherland. With gladness I would sacrifice my life to my native country. I do not need praise and flowers, I have only one desire—that is the victory over our everlasting enemy. I will die like anyone else. My thoughts will be always about you, my Motherland, Russia and my cradle, Latvia. I devote all my life and blood in the name of the future victory and glory."

Pulpe was awarded the Order of Saint George Fourth Class posthumously. He was laid to rest with these words from a fellow aviator of the 10th Fighter Detachment: "Pulpe was brave, modest as well as courageous, hiding his exploits rather than boasting about them."

---

(9) A report was written by the 8th Army Division's commandant, based on the eyewitness accounts. A report on the crash site was completed by members of the Commission of Investigation, confirming the cause of control loss of the aircraft.

Charles A. Revol-Tissot

Sublocotenent (2nd Lieutenant, Romanian service) Charles Revol-Tissot, seated in his Nieuport 11, while stationed at Tecuci, as a member of Franco-Romanian *escadrila* N.3. His awards include, the *Medaille Militaire, Legion d'Honneur*, Cross of Saint George Fourth Class, Medal of Saint George Fourth Class, and the Cross of Saint George Third Class. All awards were received while he held an NCO rank.

Charles Revol-Tissot was born in Paris on June 2, 1892. Little is known of his early life except that he was adventurous, continuously associated with daring activities. Luckily for Revol, Paris had become one of the leading aviation centers of the world and it offered audacious types an exciting form of recreation. He took to the air as if it were natural and, under the guidance of the Aero Club of Paris, he earned his civil *brevét* (pilot license), number 1248, on March 1, 1913. When war was declared the following year, he successfully enlisted in the French aviation service and was assigned to *escadrille* Bl.3.[1]

Escadrille Bl.3 had the distinction of being one of the first military squadrons formed in France, in July 1912. The unit was stationed at Belfort at the time of general mobilization and was equipped with only six Bleriot XI *Artillerie* aircraft and seven aviators, including *Caporal* (Corporal) Revol-Tissot. The unit's Bleriots were quite successful at photo-reconnaissance missions and target spotting for the French artillery in the battles of Alsace, Mulhouse, Schirmek, and Sarrebourg in August and September of 1914. However, these machines had also begun to show major deficiencies, especially their limited ability to carry defensive armament.

Revol clearly illustrated this fact on October 26, 1914, when he engaged in the unit's first aerial combat with *Adjudant* (Warrant Officer) Begou. Although both Frenchmen were aggressive in their attack, their only available weapon was a rifle. Unfortunately, the results were typical for the time; several shots were fired and the enemy aircraft flew away undamaged.

During the winter months of 1914–1915 the pilots of Bl.3 were busy spotting artillery for the French armies in the region of the Vailly and the plateau of Crouy. Revol took an active part in these missions and was justly noted for his service. Soon after, on March 18, 1915, the squadron's old Bleriots were replaced by Morane Saulnier L aircraft and the unit was officially redesignated MS.3.

On June 15, 1915, Revol was rewarded for his service with the *Medaille Militaire*, accompanied by this citation: "*Sergent* pilot of the Air Service; pilot of the first order, courageous to the point of rashness, very close and very sure. Demonstrated his qualities of courage on March 26, when during a reconnaissance, his plane was heavily fired upon and was hit several places by shrapnel, but he did not waver for an instant from the mission entrusted to him. He particularly distinguished himself in the cooperation of his squadron during the operations of June 5, 6, and 7."

In July 1915 *escadrille* MS.3 received its first Nieuport 10 fighter; however, it would be October, 1915, before the unit was fully equipped with the new machines.[2] At that time Revol was transferred to *escadrille* N.38, then located in the Champagne area, under the command of the French 4th Army.

When Revol arrived at *escadrille* N.38 in late October 1915, the unit's old Morane-Saulnier parasols were being replaced with Nieuport 12 two-seaters. Revol flew daily missions with these machines throughout the fall of 1915. Like other pilots, he attributed much of his success to the Nieuport's power and maneuverability, which allowed it to fly in most conditions. In fact, with the beginning of

---

(1) The French system of labeling squadrons used a prefix to identify the aircraft type used by the unit. In this case, the squadron was given the designation Bl.3 for *escadrille* 3 equipped with Bleriot aircraft. Later, this unit became the famous Spa.3, one of the *les Cigognes* (The Storks) fighter squadrons.

(2) *Escadrille* MS.3 was officially redesignated N.3 in September 1915, when almost all older aircraft were replaced with Nieuports. This changeover also took place in many other squadrons flying Morane-Saulniers.

A Bleriot XI *Artillerie* two-seat monoplane, the type Revol-Tissot flew when assigned to *escadrille* Bl.3 at the beginning of the war in France. It was in this type, accompanied by *Adjudant* Begou as observer, that he performed the first aerial combat for the squadron on October 26, 1914, attacking an enemy plane with a carbine. SHAA photo.

1916, weather conditions generally reduced flying among many of the other air units. Nevertheless, the pilots of *escadrille* N.38 conducted a significant number of reconnaissance and artillery spotting missions in their Nieuports, and supplied valuable information that contributed to the French 4th Army's victories in skirmishes at Navarin Farm in February and March, 1916.

For aerial combat the Nieuport 12 positioned the pilot in front of the observer, which allowed the observer to use a rear-mounted machine gun. Under these conditions, Revol was well prepared for engagements against enemy aircraft of 1915 design. Unfortunately, by April 1916 the enemy's new Fokker *Eindecker* was now the primary rival, and encounters were fairly frequent and costly to the French aviators. To counter this threat, in the summer of 1916 *escadrille* N.38 was re-equipped with Nieuport 11 fighters and given the task of flying escort missions for various Farman and Caudron units that were performing bombing and artillery spotting duties in the Champagne region.

During one of these missions, on July 1, 1916, Revol-Tissot teamed with *Capitaine* Colcomb (commander of N.38), *Sous-Lieutenant* Raty, *Marechal des Logis* (Cavalry Sergeant) Macquart de Terline, and *Sergent* Douchy to engage an enemy aircraft harassing a group of French bombers over Amagne-Luoguy. After a short combat, the French pilots succeeded in shooting down the enemy plane behind the lines; however, the victory was not confirmed.[3]

Five days later, on July 6, Revol operated with the same pilots to protect a group of 16 French Caudrons bombing Ham-les-Moines. Subsequent reports indicated several combats took place and that one German LVG was shot down by de Terline, with help from the other pilot. Although no report lists details, this was possibly Revol's first victory of the war.

In the later part of July, 1916, the pilots of N.38 had noticed a German Albatros two-seater routinely operating in the same sector. In fact, the enemy's route and timing were so similar they allowed the French pilots to predict the aircraft's daily return for a period of several days. This aircraft was a new, faster variant and each day it evaded the pilots of N.38. The humor of this daily event quickly faded, and on the evening of July 26 Revol agreed with fellow pilots Douchy, Burgun, and de Terline that this machine must be destroyed no matter the cost. This was especially stressed by de Terline, who stated he would not hesitate "to enter within."[4]

The four Frenchmen devised a simple plan that required them to split into pairs and dive down onto the enemy aircraft in a coordinated attack. The next day, July 27, the Albatros appeared on schedule while the four Frenchmen waited high above. Revol-Tissot and Douchy were the first pair to roll over and dive down onto the enemy aircraft, but in their eagerness their Nieuports collided, sending both into uncontrollable spins. Fortunately, both managed to straighten their falling aircraft near the ground and land safely. Meanwhile,

---

(3) Revol-Tissot flew on several occasions with these pilots when they were credited with victories, but his name is not listed as contributing toward any confirmation. It is likely he was involved and may have a claim to some kills scored while serving with N.38.

(4) Paul Joly, "Sentinels of the Champagne, *Escadrille* SPA.38," *Cross & Cockade* (US) vol.17 no.1, 1976. This term used by de Terline was a French expression for death.

Adjudant Revol-Tissot (3rd from left), with his squadron mates while serving with *escadrille* N.38 in the Champagne, September 1916. The other pilots are, from left to right, *Sergent* Georges Felix Madon, who had just arrived and had not yet scored any of his 41 victories; *Sergent* Pluvy; and to the right of Revol, *Adjudant* Gustave Douchy. Revol and Douchy were good friends, and flew many missions together. Douchy finished the war with nine victories, all scored while a member of N.38.

Burgun and de Terline had both apparently suffered from jammed machine guns and were forced into chasing the enemy aircraft with a crew that was now aware of the situation. Moments later, fearing the Albatros would escape to its own lines, de Terline rammed it with his Nieuport, killing himself and the enemy crew instantly. He remained true to his word and stopped the enemy no matter the cost.

On August 23, 1916, Revol cooperated with Douchy, Burgun, and de Fels to attack 12 enemy planes harassing French reconnaissance machines. After the battle, Douchy was officially credited with one victory; however, it was possible Revol-Tissot and the other pilots contributed to it.

Revol flew his last mission with *escadrille* N.38 on September 28, 1916, escorting a group of Caudrons on a bombing mission. Ten days later he set out for Romania as part of a support effort for that country, which had declared war on the Central Powers on August 27, 1916.

The aviation section of the French military mission (consisting of 18 pilots), arrived in Romania in mid-October 1916. *Adjudant* (Warrant Officer) Revol-Tissot was assigned to Franco-Romanian *escadrila* (Romanian squadron) N.3, stationed near Bucharest.[5] However, by the time *escadrila* N.3 reached its position the Romanian armies were in a grave situation. The German three-pronged offensive had placed its army within reach of the Romanian capital, leaving the Romanians no choice but retreat. By December 6 the Romanian army had lost nearly 350,000 troops and desperately tried to link up with Russian units to the north. To support this effort, *escadrila* N.3 was ordered to engage enemy aircraft harassing Romanian troops, but the unit's six operational aircraft had little effect because only two were equipped with machine guns.

Soon after, the pilots of *escadrila* N.3 were forced to retreat to Tecuci, to the east of the Sereth River. The squadron was reorganized approximately one week later and began flying missions in support of the Russian 4th Army. Most of the unit's flights were offensive patrols to prevent the enemy from conducting reconnaissance. Although each of the unit's aircraft were finally armed, many times they were in need of repair, leaving the operational strength of the unit at one or two machines.

Despite all the problems, Revol flew many missions during the remainder of the year and drove away enemy aircraft at least three times. One of these battles occurred on December 23, 1916, when Revol teamed with *Caporal* Manchoulas in an intense combat with two Austrian aircraft over the front lines. Apparently, both Frenchmen were headed in the direction of the Austro-German airfield at Focsani, to locate the crash site of an enemy aircraft shot down earlier that day by French aviator *Sergent* Texier. En route, the two encountered the two adversaries and started a heated battle. Within minutes both were plagued by jammed machine guns and had to call off the fight. Nonetheless, the enemy withdrew.

Revol continued to fly whenever the weather permitted and a plane was available. On January 14, 1917, he completed two missions, first driving away an enemy reconnaissance aircraft and later escorting a Farman F.40. The next day he flew three patrols, one of which was a special reconnaissance flight ordered by the Russian 4th Army, to look for German bridge emplacements. Revol began this mission at 10AM and returned in 30 minutes with the necessary information on three bridges he located. He was back in the air about an hour later when the squadron was warned of approaching enemy aircraft.

---

(5) *Escadrila* N.3 was located at Pipera, near Bucharest as a home defense unit. The squadron consisted of Romanian *Capitan* Nicolae Capsa (Commanding Officer), *Adjudant* Revol-Tissot, *Capitaine* Maurice Gond, *Caporal* Henri Manchoulas, *Sergent* Jacques Texier, *Sergent* Francois Terry, *Caporal* Maurice Theron, *Sous-Lieutenant* Victor Federov (Russian National who scored five victories during the war), and Romanian *Locotenent* Petre Macavei.

The Nieuport flown by Revol-Tissot on his last flight with Franco-Romanian *escadrila* N.3, on July 10, 1917. Shortly after takeoff his plane burst into flames and forced him to land immediately. He managed to escape the inferno, but his career at N.3 was over. He was evacuated to a rear area hospital for treatment of his wounds.

During this patrol, Revol rose above his adversary and hid in the sun. When the right moment came, he dove on the unsuspecting foe and began firing. The enemy machine was driven away and failed to complete its mission.

On February 6, Revol-Tissot, along with Manchoulas and Texier, were awarded the Soldier's Cross of Saint George Fourth Class for distinguished service to the Russian 4th Army. Later, they engaged an enemy plane, forcing it to retire to its own lines.

During a February 10 patrol Revol was denied a victory when his machine gun repeatedly failed. After Revol closed in behind an LVG, his gun jammed on the initial burst of fire. While Revol was clearing the blockage, he was attacked from above. He was able to roll his Nieuport and escape. He spotted a second reconnaissance plane and attacked it, only to have his gun repeat the earlier jam.

Four days later, while on patrol with Manchoulas and *Capitan* Protopopescu, the trio surprised an enemy machine by hiding in the sun. Manchoulas attacked first, firing the entire drum of ammunition from the Lewis gun. As he was reloading, Revol descended on the adversary like a hawk and riddled the machine with bullets. The enemy plane went into a spin and crashed south of Diochetii. Revol and Manchoulas landed near the site but found nothing except pieces of debris scattered around two dead German aviators. Russian troops who approached the wreckage cheered Revol and Manchoulas for their victory.

Revol-Tissot was granted a citation in French army orders the next day and also received the *Legion d'Honneur, Chevalier* grade. On February 19 he and Manchoulas were decorated by General Ragoza, commander of the Russian 4th Army. Both received the Soldier's Cross of Saint George Third Class and the Medal of Saint George Fourth Class, for their achievement on February 14.

During March Revol flew many missions, several with the commander of the squadron, *Capitaine* Gond. They flew several escort flights and reconnaissance missions together, including one lasting more than two hours. On March 29 Revol escorted a Farman F.40 carrying the commander of the Russian 30th Artillery Corps, who wished to inspect enemy positions. After a 35-minute patrol, Revol and the F.40 returned from a successful mission.

April 13, 1917 was a day full of excitement for Revol. At 10:30 that morning he and Gond set out on patrol. They spotted a Fokker flying peacefully along over the Black Forest. Diving on it from behind, Revol fired several shots. Just as the adversary rolled, Gond dove and attacked him. The Fokker managed an escape, but certainly was not pleased with the harassment received from the pilots of N.3.

Revol, not satisfied with merely driving away the Fokker, was in the air later that afternoon accompanied by Theron, when the pair spotted a German plane below them. Revol wasted no time attacking the enemy and unloading the entire drum of ammunition from the Lewis gun. The gunner of the enemy machine never returned a shot. Suddenly, it went into a dive and crashed about a mile behind enemy lines, north of Focsani. Revol went back that evening with a Farman F.40 equipped with a camera to photograph the site, but it was too dark. However, a Russian aeronautical observation post had witnessed the fight and confirmed the victory. The Russians must have been impressed with Revol's aerial abilities, for two days later a nearby squadron gave him a Nieuport 17 equipped with a 110hp Le Rhône which was capable of greater speed than his 80hp Nieuport 11.

For his actions on the 13th, Revol-Tissot was promoted on April 18 to the officer rank of *Sublocotenent* (2nd Lieutenant) by the Romanians. Gond was cited in the army orders of the day for his qualities as a commander, and the squadron celebrated these two accomplishments.

Throughout that spring Revol flew many patrols and escort missions without encountering any difficulties. On May 25, he joined combat with two German aircraft he had followed toward Adjud. Both enemy machines were equipped with a fixed gun for the pilot and a flexible gun for the observer. Finding himself under the fire of four guns, Revol did not back down, driving the two enemy aircraft from an altitude of 11,500 feet down to 4600 feet as they retreated across their own lines.

Two days later, Revol and Terry engaged two Fokkers in an exhausting combat. The fight was an even match and ended in a draw after all ammunition was expended. The two pairs of aircraft returned to their lines to battle another day.

Revol continued his aggressive manner into the summer months, providing support to troops involved in the heavy fighting at Marasesti. On June 30, *escadrila* N.3 was visited by Farman pilot *Capitan* Panait Cholet, who was eager to meet the members of N.3, especially those such as Revol and Manchoulas, who already had scored victories. Cholet described them as, "young and vibrant, confident of victory." Revol was further described by Romanian fighter pilot *Locotenent* Egon Nasta as, "hot-blooded!"

On the morning of July 3, 1917, Revol and Gond encountered two enemy observation planes. They attacked, but the German gunner of one machine forced Gond out of the battle with well-aimed fire that hit his engine. Although out-numbered and out-gunned, Revol continued the fight until his fuel was exhausted and he was forced to land just short of the airfield at Tecuci.

During a morning patrol on July 9 Revol was once again in a battle with two German aircraft. This time he was on patrol with Theron, who was forced to leave the battle when his engine was hit, as was Gond a few days earlier, leaving Revol to fight alone. Revol battled valiantly, but with inconclusive results. He was forced to return with an empty gun and several hits on his aircraft.

The enemy's equipment superiority was very apparent. Revol and his squadron mates had engaged in hard-fought battles in the past few weeks, but accomplished little more than preventing a few enemy reconnaissance missions. Despite the efforts of their pilots, the Allied machines were not capable of achieving air superiority.

Not only were the machines inferior to German aircraft, but they began showing signs of age. The result was experienced by Revol-Tissot on the morning of July 10, 1917, when he and *Sublocotenent* Vacas took off from the field to begin a patrol. Suddenly, while still over the field at only 600 feet, Revol's old and worn Nieuport developed a problem with the engine, causing it to catch fire. He managed to bring the plane back to the field, making an exceptional landing considering that his

Believed to be Revol-Tissot in the cockpit of a Nieuport 17.

aircraft was ablaze. With smoke emitting from the cockpit, Revol was able to get out of the machine and away from the danger of a possible explosion. He was lucky; soon the aircraft was completely engulfed in flames. He suffered some burns, cuts, and bruises, but the worst was a broken ankle suffered from the impact upon landing. He was taken to a hospital in Taganesti.

It appears he did not return to the squadron before the end of hostilities. It is unknown when or if he returned to France before November, 1918, or if he served with another unit. Nothing is known of his life after the war, except that he died July 13, 1971.

Available French sources have placed Revol-Tissot on their list of aces, with five victories, although no exact dates or details have been given. It can only be assumed that three victories were obtained in France, to be added to his two confirmed victories during his service in Romania. Whether or not confirmation of other victories exist, the fact remains that Revol-Tissot was an aggressive and courageous pilot who never backed down from a fight. For this, he was rewarded by both his native country and the Russian and Romanian allies he fought with in Moldavia.

Section 4

Distinguished Pilots of the Imperial Russian Air Service

Distinguished Pilots of the Imperial Russian Air Service

The most important functions of the airplane during World War I were aerial reconnaissance, artillery spotting, and bombing, and in no region of conflict was this so important as the Eastern Front, with its vast length and widely scattered areas of intense combat. There was a continual need to know the enemy's movements along a front that stretched approximately 900 miles, and once the enemy was located, the ability to accurately bomb its vital supply centers was of major importance. Air-to-air combat was secondary to these activities throughout the entire war. This section recognizes the courageous, accomplished aviators of the Imperial Russian Air Service who performed these critical tasks.

While performing the everyday missions necessary for keeping the army corps informed about enemy ground activity, these aircrews were frequently interrupted by enemy fighter attack or placed under a constant barrage of anti-aircraft fire, neither of which were easy on their nerves or on the poorly maintained aircraft they were flying.

Among this group are members of the *Eskadra Vozdushnykh Korablei* ("EVK" or "Squadron of Flying Ships"), a special unit organized by the Imperial Russian Air Service to fly Igor Sikorsky's giant Il'ya Muromets bombers. The crews who manned these huge four-engine aircraft usually ranged many miles behind enemy lines to conduct some of the most daring and successful long-range bombing and reconnaissance missions of the war. Besides repeatedly completing missions with success, crews of some Il'ya Muromets bombers were able to ward off multiple attacks by enemy planes, occasionally shooting them down. Among this small group is the first black aviator to shoot down an aircraft in aerial combat.

This section also includes aviators who flew the smaller reconnaissance/bombing machines. Many of their missions were undertaken as members of the Aviation Corps Detachments, the backbone of the IRAS. Carrying small bomb loads rigged with crude release mechanisms, they raided enemy positions in slow, poorly armed, outdated two-seat aircraft. Cameras were attached to the fuselage side, exposing both the equipment and observer to the harsh elements during photo-reconnaissance flights. Among these flyers are the first women aviators to serve in combat roles.

In addition to flying reconnaissance and bombing missions, some aviators in this section served in command positions and whose primary contribution was helping to organize and train the Imperial Russian Air Service. This group includes bomber commanders, squadron commanders, an Air Company leader, and one officer who progressed to Inspector of the Air Service for the Southwest Army Group and from there to commander-in-chief of the Air Service.

Finally, there are some aviators whose names have incorrectly appeared on previously published ace lists. Despite this, these men were recognized for their accomplishments and justly decorated with many awards. However, as part of our effort to correct inaccuracies, their true stories are presented for the first time.

Of the nineteen aviators whose biographies appear in this section, no fewer than five officers had earned the Order of Saint George, 4th Class and four NCOs had earned various degrees of the Soldier's Cross of Saint George, the highest awards for bravery. The sacrifices made by these individuals contributed to the success of the army units and exemplified the outstanding accomplishments of which the air service was capable, despite the fact it was under-supplied and in many instances forced to use inferior, outdated equipment. All had shown perseverance and dedication to duty and serve as examples representing the unknown aviators who performed the same painstaking duties with the same enthusiasm and courage, but whose names have been lost over time.

The standard mount of many corps units, the slow but sturdy Voisin, which was still flying when the war ended for Russia. The crews of these planes provided faithful service, demanding the most from their tired machines. Together these aviators and aircraft made commendable teams.

Ivan Mikhailovich Bagrovnikov

Ivan Bagrovnikov was born on February 5, 1893, into a prosperous, probably mercantile, family in Uglitch a Volga River town in the province of Yaroslavl about 125 miles north of Moscow.

Because of his family's prosperity and the proximity of Moscow, he was able to enter the Alexeyevsky Industrial School in Moscow. After graduation, he is believed to have returned to Uglitch; it is known he married and had two children.

He volunteered for the army at the outbreak of the war, passed the comprehensive examination for the First Cadet Corps, and entered the Alexeyevsky Military School in October, 1914. Upon graduation in February, 1915, he was commissioned as a *Praporshik* (Ensign) and appointed to the 60th Infantry Reserve Battalion.

After a short time he successfully requested a transfer to the aviation service. Bagrovnikov completed the theoretical aviation training course for officers on June 7, 1915, and the next day was assigned to the 5th Corps Detachment as an observer.

In August, 1915, after several months at the front, Bagrovnikov was approved for pilot training at Sevastopol, completed the course on February 18, 1916, and was given the title of military pilot. On April 14, after training on Voisins, he was promoted to *Podporuchik* (2nd Lieutenant) and assigned to the 9th Army Air Detachment and an observer and artillery spotter.

On August 19, 1916, he was temporarily assigned to the 8th Air Detachment, under the command of the 8th Army, to reinforce the Brusilov offensive in Galicia. The Russian 8th Army, commanded by General Kaledin, was the main force of General Brusilov's Southwest Army. Its objective was the city of Kovel, approximately 60 miles from the frontline position. By the time Bagrovnikov joined the 8th Detachment, Lutsk had been taken and nearly three-fourths of the ground toward Kovel was secured.

During his month with the 8th Detachment, Bagrovnikov flew reconnaissance missions and guided artillery fire. While on reconnaissance on August 30 he fought a lengthy battle with three Austrian machines. He fired 70 rounds of ammunition at one of them, forcing it to head for its own lines in a glide. Apparently the engine had quit after being hit by Bagrovnikov's bullets.

In September, 1916, the Brusilov offensive had come to a standstill, falling short of its objective. Bagrovnikov returned to the 9th Army Air Detachment and resumed his normal duties.

In January 1917, Bagrovnikov was temporarily in command of the 9th Army Detachment, a post that became permanent on February 27, 1917. The decision was probably upon the recommendation of the commander of the 7th Air Squadron, Military Pilot Boranov, who stated, "Acting commander of the 9th Army Squadron, *Podporuchik* Bagrovnikov is an excellent fighting pilot, decisive, calm, industrious in fulfilling battle tasks. Being an acting commander of the squadron, he maintained order and discipline. I consider him a

The standard mount of many observation units, the Voisin LA (type 3), equipped with the Salmson (Canton-Unne) 120hp water-cooled radial engine. Many were supplied to Russia by France and several were built under license by the Dux factory. There are tall box-type radiators behind the crew's compartment and two gun mounts. In front is a tripod for a forward-firing gun and the long pole that concludes at the leading edge of the upper wing to mount a machine gun for rearward fire.

A Voisin in flight, most likely at a training facility. Bagrovnikov learned to fly Voisins at the Sevastopol Aviation School in 1916, and flew this type for the remainder of the war. He earned his only victory in this type on July 20, 1917, while commanding the 9th Army Air Detachment.

worthy candidate for the squadron commander."

On July 20, 1917, while over Kozovo, Bagrovnikov was flying in a Voisin with his brother, *Praporshik* Bagrovnikov, when they spotted two enemy aircraft. They pursued the enemy, forcing one to land at Drishuv for Bagrovnikov's only victory.

Bagrovnikov has been listed as an ace in some publications, This is not so, but his daily task of artillery spotting and reconnaissance were the most important functions of the air corps. This monotonous duty was many times carried out in obsolete and worn-out aircraft, on many occasions under heavy anti-aircraft fire or attacked by enemy fighters.

In October 1917, after more than two years at the front, Bagrovnikov requested a transfer to the Sevastopol Aviation School to be an instructor. Apparently this was granted, for he was there when hostilities against the Central Powers ended two months later.

When the civil war began, Bagrovnikov joined the White army, but his fate is unknown. His known awards are the Order of Saint Stanislas Second Class with Swords and the Order of Saint Stanislas Third Class with Swords and Bow.

Jezups Stanislavovich Bashko

Jezups S. Bashko, wearing the *pogoni* (shoulderboards) of a *Stabs-Kapitan* (Staff-Captain). It has been stated he earned as many as ten awards. Those displayed are the Order of Saint George 4th Class, and the Order of Saint Vladimir 3rd Class with Crossed Swords on his left breast pocket. The badge below may possibly be the Vladimir school badge. The right breast pocket flap holds what is believed to be the Gatchina Flight School Badge. The Military Pilots Badge is below. This photo was possibly taken shortly after he received the Saint George award for the action of June 27, 1915.

"His Majesty the Emperor, on June 27 of the year 1915, most graciously deigned to confer an award on *Stabs-Kapitan*, Commander of the Il'ya Muromets *Kievski*, Military Pilot Jezups Bashko, for his excellent service fighting the enemy, when he personally carried out ten battle flights by order of the Army Staff on April 11, 22, 28, May 1, 4, 5, 27, 28, June 11 and 14,[1] of the year 1915; flying under the artillery fire, he took photographs of important fortification points and positions of the enemy; bombing was performed from the plane entrusted to him during the flights that destroyed railroads, buildings, rolling stock, and warehouses at the stations Neidenburg, Villenburg, Lovich, Yaroslav, and Przhevosk, also on June 14, an enemy train with artillery ammunition was blown up; during the flights mentioned above, he also disclosed

---
(1) All dates stated in the royal order are the old style, from the Julian calendar; thirteen days must be added to update to the current Gregorian calendar.

the location of enemy batteries and reported with precision timing important grouping and movement of enemy troops." With this official report Jezups Bashko was awarded the highest honor, the Order of Saint George Fourth Class.

When heavy aviation was introduced, it was met with mixed feelings. Many believed the four-engine Murometsy to be impractical, especially for military use. However, some supported the aircraft, realizing it had great capabilities when in the right hands. Bashko was one of those who showed the Il'ya Muromets had much to contribute to the war effort. He displayed his bravery and his belief in the aircraft by participating in many reconnaissance and bombing raids far behind enemy lines. He became a master of piloting the giant machine and was one of the best ship commanders.

Bashko was born December 27, 1889, in Dvinsk (Daugavpils, Latvia), a leading commercial center and rail junction. Little is known of his early years, other than that he was graduated from the Bialystok secondary school[2] in 1908, entered the army and was accepted to the Vladimir Military School at Saint Petersburg at age 18. After receiving a commission as a *Podporuchik* (Second Lieutenant) in the infantry, Bashko applied for flight training. In 1912 he was graduated from the Gatchina Military Flying School, located outside St. Petersburg. He made 90 recorded flights before the war, totaling more than 140 hours of time in the air.

When war was declared on August 1, 1914,[3] *Stavka* (headquarters of the supreme commander-in-chief) had already ordered ten Il'ya Murometsy for reconnaissance. *Stabs-Kapitan* Gorshov[4] was appointed to collect crew members for the Murometsy from aviation officers at the Gatchina school. After this was accomplished, Igor Sikorsky personally trained Gorshkov, who in turn trained the other six officers selected to command the Il'ya Muromets units.[5] Gorshkov became the commander of the seventh unit. Although Bashko was not one of these

---
(2) Secondary school was equivalent to high school. At the time of his birth there were approximately 500 secondary schools with about 110,000 male students. There were also about 390 schools of this type for females with 80,000 students.
(3) This is the date Germany declared war on Russia, marking the official beginning.
(4) Georgiy Georgiyevich Gorshkov was from a military family and had graduated from various cadet academies, concluding with the Officers' School of Aeronautics. He made several pre-war flights on balloons and airships before piloting airplanes. At the beginning of the war he was the deputy commander of the Gatchina Military Flying School. He commanded the EVK after the March 1917 revolution, replacing Shidlovsky. He was replaced in October 1917 by Palkovnik Pankrat'yev.
(5) At the beginning of the war, each Il'ya Muromets was to be its own combat unit and under the direct command of the army group it was assigned to. This was shortly changed with the development of the EVK.

Crew members of the IM-*Kievskiy*, *Poruchik* Bashko, *Praporshik* Andreyev, and *Kapitan* Gorshkov posing on the tail of a Muromets, at Yablonna, March 1915. With the *Kievskiy*, Gorshkov and Bashko performed the first combat mission of the EVK in February.

original commanders, he must have been thought of highly by Gorshkov, who selected Bashko as his deputy commander.

Although the first two aircraft arrived at the front in September, 1914, the rest were delayed and the results of the IM-1 and IM-2 were less than satisfactory. The entire group of Murometsy were then combined into the EVK (*Escadra Vozdushnykh Korablei*, or Squadron of Flying Ships)[6] in December, 1914. It was believed the Murometsy crews could execute their duties more advantageously as one unit. The new base was at Yablonna, located between Warsaw and the fortress of Novo-Georgievsk.

By February, 1915, the total number of Il'ya Murometsy at the front had increased to seven. They were assembled at Yablonna, along with necessary equipment and service personnel. On February 27, the Il'ya Murometsy *Kievskiy*[7] with *Poruchik* (Lieutenant) Bashko as deputy to *Kapitan* Gorshkov, performed the first mission of the EVK. Due to bad weather, the crew returned to base with no results. The next day the *Kievskiy* completed a 2-$1/2$ hour flight, bombing the enemy trenches and performing valuable reconnaissance behind the lines.

In March the crew of the *Kievskiy* began to strike fear into German personnel stationed behind the lines. Willenburg was bombed on March 9, and 10, with the railroad depot being heavily damaged. After six missions, the Russian 1st Army congratulated the crew of the *Kievskiy* for outstanding reconnaissance, photography, and especially the destruction of railroad centers. The commander of the fortress at Novo-Georgievsk expressed similar felicitations.

(6) The Il'ya Murometsy were sometimes referred to as 'ships' due to the enormous size of the planes, or because of the manner of organization. The unit was organized more like a naval squadron than an aircraft squadron.

(7) The Il'ya Muromets *Korabley Kievskiy the Second*, was an early type 'Veh,' an improvement over the type 'Beh.' It was capable of 75 mph, range 400 miles, and could reach a height of 11,500 feet. The first ship given the name *Kievskiy* was a type 'Beh' and was used as a trainer at Gatchina. It was used by Sikorsky on his famous flight from St. Petersburg to Kiev in June 1914, and was equipped with two 125hp Argus engines and two 140hp Argus engines. These same engines were used on the *Korabley Kievskiy the Second*, and most likely on the next *Kievskiy* Bashko flew, which was a later type 'Veh.' Later they were installed on the IM-13 a type 'G,' and recorded over 700 hours of flight time in approximately two years. In all there were six ships named *Kievskiy*, five used by Bashko during the war.

The EVK base photographed from the air at Yablonna in 1915. From its location about 25 miles from Warsaw, aircraft could easily reach major railway centers and other military targets in East Prussia. The large tent hangers house the Murometsy.

The Russian 1st Army headquarters had received information of German troops reinforcing the Northern Front. To confirm this, the *Kievskiy* conducted a four-hour reconnaissance on March 31, 1915,[8] over Willenburg, Neidenburg, Soldau, Lautenburg, Strassburg, Torn, and other main rail centers for troop transport. The search proved the information received by the 1st Army was false. The enemy had actually transferred units from the Northern Front in preparation for an offensive in Galicia.

During April, 1915, *Poruchik* Bashko became the commander of the *Kievskiy*. Gorshkov was promoted to *Podpolkovnik* (Lieutenant-Colonel), awarded the Order of Saint Vladimir fourth class, and soon after was given command of the Muromets detachment stationed at Lemberg. Bashko and his crew, deputy commander *Poruchik* Smirnov, artillery officer *Stabs-Kapitan* Naumov, and *Praporshik* Andreyev,[9] succeeded in bombing two rail stations on April 19 and 20. On the 19th they destroyed the center at Mlava and the bridge at Plotsk and attacked the airfield at Samnki. On the 20th the *Kievskiy* damaged the station at Soldau, hitting most of the trains parked there. On April 24, both the *Kievskiy* and the IM-3 raided

(8) Other sources list the date of this flight as March 23, 1915.
(9) This was the crew for the mission on April 20. Smirnov and Naumov did become part of the regular crew.

the city of Neidenburg. First, Bashko and his men dropped several large bombs including one of 5 *pud* (180 pounds). Then, within the hour, the IM-3 finished the job. The result was the destruction of the rail station; many fires burned through the night. The Germans tried to retaliate by bombing the base at Yablonna, but little damage resulted.

After completing several missions in May, Bashko and the crew of the *Kievskiy* were transferred to a new location as part of a special detachment in the south. The *Kievskiy* arrived on May 24, 1915, and the IM-3 arrived three days later. The two ships continued work at Lemberg and assisted the Russian 3rd Army in obtaining information on the combined German and Austro-Hungarian push in Galicia.

General Falkenhayn formed the German 11th Army, commanded by General Mackensen, to support the Austrian armies in the Carpathians. The Austro-German forces attacked between the towns of Tarnow and Gorlice after the German 10th Army created a diversion in the north. This action marked the beginning of a series of Central Power triumphs that pushed the Russians out of the Carpathians and forced them back from the Baltic regions to Galicia.

Because of the enemy advance, the two Murometsy moved from Lemberg to Lublin and then to Wlodawa,

The Il'ya Muromets *Korabley Kievskiy the First* flying over Yablonna in 1915. Bashko was deputy commander and later commander of this aircraft, which was a type 'B' or 'Veh.' It was equipped with four Argus engines; two were 125hp and two were 140hp. These were the same engines used on the machine Igor Sikorsky flew from St. Petersburg to Kiev. That plane was a type 'b' or 'Beh,' and also was named *Kievskiy*.

where operations began on June 25. The group supported the army by bombing enemy troops, rail centers, and supply depots, but mainly by reconnaissance far behind the lines. It became important to the Army to know how many reinforcements were being sent and their positions. Because of the limited range of other aircraft, the Murometsy were the only ones that could obtain this information. On June 27, 1915, Bashko and the crew of the *Kievskiy* were surveying and photographing the rear area. They also bombed the station at Przhevorsk, scoring direct hits on several munitions trains at the depot. Later it was learned that 30,000 shells had been destroyed and activity at the station was delayed for several days.

After the June 27 mission, Bashko and his artillery officer, *Stabs-Kapitan* (Staff-Captain) Naumov, were awarded the Order of Saint George fourth class, and his deputy, *Poruchik* Smirnov, was granted the *Georgevsky Oroogie* (Saint George Sword). The mechanic, Shkudov, also was awarded the Cross of Saint George. They were the first members of the EVK to be given such awards. Bashko was further honored with a promotion to *Stabs-Kapitan.*

On July 19, 1915, the *Kievskiy* embarked on a bombing run at 4AM. To carry a greater bomb load, the defensive armament was minimized. Only a Madsen light machine gun and an infantry carbine were on board. After bombing two airfields and two train stations, the crew was turning for home when three German LVG B.Is from *Feldflieger Abteilung* 21 approached. The *Kievskiy* was attacked over Shebrzheshin at an altitude of 10,400 feet while 40 *versts* (26 miles) behind enemy lines. On the first pass, enemy gunfire caused severe damage, cutting the fuel lines to the left engines, causing them to quit within minutes. The ship became difficult to control. Bashko took the controls from his deputy, *Poruchik* Smirnov, while *Stabs-Kapitan* Naumov manned the Madsen machine gun. *Poruchik* Lavrov, the mechanic, grabbed the carbine and began firing.

The enemy attacked again, causing more damage, but were repelled by the defensive fire, diving toward their home aerodrome.[10] Smirnov grabbed the controls after Bashko was wounded in the head and leg during the last attack. Lavrov attended to Bashko until he was able to take command again. When he did, Smirnov and Lavrov alternated covering the broken fuel filter for the right-side engines with their bare hands. Meanwhile, Naumov was desperately trying to clear the jammed Madsen because another enemy aircraft was approaching from the port side. Lavrov was covering the fuel filter, which left only Smirnov and the carbine to fight the lone adversary. After firing a few shots, he passed the gun to Naumov so he could relieve Lavrov, whose hands were frozen from the cold fuel. Luckily, this foe did not attack again and the *Kievskiy* continued its return flight on only two engines.

Another enemy plane attacked the *Kievskiy* when it was crossing the lines, although it quickly retreated because anti-aircraft batteries began to fire on the Il'ya Muromets, which was only at 4800 feet. The *Kievskiy* crossed the lines successfully only to have the remaining

---

(10) One enemy aircraft was seen to turn sharply entering into a 'falling leaf' maneuver. It is possible Naumov damaged this machine with the Madsen.

The *Kievskiy* after its return from the mission of March 31, 1915, over East Prussia. On this flight, the crew photographed enemy troop positions to verify information received by the Russian 1st Army. The information was proven false.

two engines quit just outside of Kholm. From 2200 feet Bashko chose a landing area and brought the ship down with a "dead stick," making a good landing considering the circumstances. This feat had not been attempted before since it was believed to be nearly impossible. The field near the village of Gorodishche was very muddy, causing an abrupt stop and damage to the airframe. If the mud had not been there, Bashko might have made a perfect landing. His wounds were treated in the nearby village, after which he was sent to a hospital in Vlodava, near the base of the Il'ya Muromets detachment.

As a result of this action, all four officers were decorated and Bashko and Lavrov were given promotions.[11]

This was the last mission for this *Kievskiy*, whose damage was too great to repair. All serviceable parts were removed and shipped to the main base in the north for use on other aircraft. The crew of the *Kievskiy* also returned to the main base of the EVK.

In July 1915, the EVK was forced to evacuate Yablonna and relocate to the east at Bialystok. After only a short stay, it fell back to Lida. The German 9th and 12th Armies had advanced into the Polish salient, taking Warsaw and the fortress of Novo-Georgievsk. The Russian 1st Army suffered many casualties and chose not to defend Brest-Litovsk, but to continue the retreat toward Pinsk in the Pripet marshes. By mid-July, the German 10th Army had captured Kovno to the north. Lida seemed the only safe place for the EVK, although this too became vulnerable.

Lida had perfect accommodations for the Murometsy, since it had been a base for balloon units and housed the airship *Astra* in a massive hangar. No important work was accomplished, although the first R-BVZ-built[12] engines began to arrive and be installed. The enemy advance forced Lida to be abandoned. On August 27, 1915, six aircraft started for Pskov, about 250 miles away. *Kapitan* Bashko was at the controls of the IM-*Kievskiy*[13] for the flight, which lasted more than five hours in bad weather and low visibility.

By the end of September, the German and Austro-Hungarian armies were firmly dug in on Russian soil. The long lines of supply had caused the troops to lose momentum and prepare for the cold winter. The Central Powers had advanced over 200 miles along some parts of the front, a great victory.

At approximately the same time, mid September 1915,

---

(11) It is possible the award Bashko received for this action was the Saint George Sword. He did earn this award at one point, although the exact date is unknown. His rank after this mission is believed to be *Kapitan* (Captain).

(12) The R-BVZ engines were Russian-manufactured engines made by the same company which produced the Il'ya Muromets. Designed by Kireyev, they were a copy of the German Argus engine with some refinements, and provided more than satisfactory results.

(13) This machine was a later type 'Veh,' with a blunt nose. It was the third *Kievskiy* and most likely used the Argus engines that were taken from the second *Kievskiy*.

The *Kievskiy* while at Yablonna, spring 1915, being inspected by Major-General Shidlovsky (bearded officer, third from right), commander of the EVK. Notice the v-shaped nose of the *Kievskiy*, the first 'Veh' model. It allowed the pilot much greater visibility.

the Second Il'ya Muromets Combat Detachment was formed. It included nine ships, one of which was the *Kievskiy*. The group left Pskov and relocated to the north at Zegewold, about 30 miles east of Riga.

The EVK detachment began conducting missions on multiple targets by several machines at once. One such raid occurred on October 18, 1915, when three ships bombed Friedrichsdorf, one raided Tukkum, and the *Kievskiy* awoke the sleeping staff of the German headquarters with its bombs.

Three days later Bashko and his crew were about 30 miles beyond the front lines, over Bausskiy, when the fuel lines froze and all the engines quit. Bashko calmly turned the ship around, putting it in a glide toward home. *Stabs-Kapitan* Naumov and *Podpraporshik* (Warrant Officer) Serednitskiy attended to the condensation problem. By forcing back pressure through the carburetors, they managed to clear some of the ice and get two engines restarted, although they ran very roughly. The *Kievskiy* crossed over the trenches at 300 feet with nearly every German rifle and machine gun firing at it. Despite the gunfire, the *Kievskiy* landed safely in a forward area, near Olai.[14] After landing the crew counted 64 bullet holes in the plane. Their troubles were not over—members of a Siberian unit approached and threatened to shoot them, believing they were German spies. Eventually this misunderstanding was cleared up.

The Second Il'ya Muromets Detachment performed nearly 25 missions while stationed at Zegewold before the year's end. Throughout 1915, the Murometsy had made approximately 100 raids, nearly 70 of them by the *Kievskiy* and ship Number Three. More than 40,000 pounds of bombs had been dropped and much photography and reconnaissance accomplished.

In December, 1915, the IM-*Korabley Kievskiy* and the IM-2 were transferred to the Galician Front to reestablish the First Il'ya Muromets Combat Detachment. After the *Kievskiy* was transferred from the First Detachment in July, the IM-3 was the only ship on the Galician Front. In November, 1915, the IM-3 went down from anti-aircraft fire.

With the beginning of 1916, Bashko and crew continued operations from Kolodziyevka, a small village outside Tarnopol. They were under the command of the Russian 7th Army, which was part of General Brusilov's Southwest Army. Brusilov was preparing an offensive for the late spring with Lemberg and Stanislau in Galicia as objectives. The army staff needed to monitor enemy troop movements and artillery positions to plan the assault. By February, 1916, the detachment was continuing to provide excellent information to the commanders and also bombing enemy railway centers.

The information obtained by Bashko, his crew, and the crew of the IM-2 ensured a successful beginning for the offensive, which began in early June. Within three weeks, the *Kievskiy* was transferred to a new base at Stankovo,

---

(14) The location that Bashko had to land on was a marshland, and although frozen must have proven difficult. To add to this demanding situation, the winter conditions had necessitated the application of a ski undercarriage. Even under such circumstances, Bashko set the giant aircraft down without mishap.

A photograph taken by the crew of the *Kievskiy* from 10,000 feet over the Przevorsk railroad station, in Galicia, on June 27, 1915. The smoke is from the explosion of a munitions train. Other trains were also damaged and the terminal was put out of action for several days. Bashko and his crew were decorated for this action.

south of Minsk, to cooperate with General Ewarth and the Western Army Group.

Bashko arrived at Stankovo on June 24, 1916, and was given command of the Third Il'ya Muromets Combat Detachment. Besides the *Kievskiy*,[15] the complement of ships included the IM-12 under *Poruchik* Gorodetsky, IM-16 under *Poruchik* Maksheyev, and IM-17 under *Stabs-Kapitan* Belyakov. The unit began operations immediately and performed the usual duties under Bashko's command.

A multiple aircraft mission was planned for September 25, 1916. On that morning, the four Murometsy from the Third Detachment and 12 single-engined planes planned to bomb the German headquarters at Boruna. This was the first attempt at a joint operation by heavy and light aircraft. The concept was good, but the execution was not. The small fighters flew from the nearby field at Myasot, while the bombers took off from Stankovo. Due to poor planning, all aircraft took off separately, causing a loss of time. The small planes used too much fuel and had to return well before the Murometsy. None of the aircraft flew together, and it appears the bombers did not rendezvous with the fighters. The *Kievskiy* was the only plane to reach and bomb the target.

With the completion of this mission, Bashko and his crew returned to Stankovo. Maksheyev and the IM-16 crew were not so lucky. While flying over Bogdanov, the IM-16 was attacked by four enemy aircraft from *Feldflieger Abteilung* 45, which were using explosive and incendiary ammunition. During the battle a fuel tank exploded, causing a raging fire. The ship went down almost instantly and crashed near Lake Krevo. The German squadron delivered a note by air stating the crew of the IM-16 were buried with full military honors. Through an intercepted message, it was discovered three German aircraft had been put out of action by the IM-16. *Poruchik* Maksheyev and his men had fought heroically. All were honored with posthumous awards of the Order of Saint George Fourth Class.

By the beginning of 1917, the Third Detachment was ordered to cease operations from Stankovo and join the main body of the EVK at the new base at Vinnitza, on the Southwestern Front, in preparation for a spring offensive in Romania. This location provided an excellent facility and more than adequate airfield.

The revolution in March and subsequent takeover by the Provisional Government at first had little effect on the EVK. It continued to be a well-maintained, self-sufficient unit. Even General Brusilov was impressed during his visit in the spring of 1917. However, with time even the

---

(15) This is the fifth *Korably Kievskiy*, which was a type G-1 and was equipped with four 140hp Argus engines. The G-1 variant first appeared December 1915, and had a maximum speed of 78 mph. These engines had been taken from the damaged IM-3 and fitted to the fourth *Kievskiy* in April 1916. It crashed during the first test flight and the engines were refitted to the G-1, which Bashko received within a short time.

The interior of the Muromets, showing the bomb racks on the left and the straps for fastening the bombs lying on the floor. Secured to the right is a Moisin-Nagant carbine. Its caliber was 7.62mm and it had a magazine of five rounds. This type of rifle and a Madsen light machine gun were the only weapons on board the *Kievskiy* when it was attacked by three enemy aircraft on July 19, 1915.

Muromets units became susceptible to the breakdown other army divisions suffered.

In April, the Third Il'ya Muromets Combat Detachment was reactivated under Bashko's command. The ships assigned to his group were the IM-17 under *Stabs-Kapitan* Belyakov, the IM-19 under *Poruchik* Grek, and the IM-4 under the command of *Poruchik* Sharov, who had recently returned from Romania. They were stationed at Buzcac, close to the Russian 7th Army headquarters on the Galician Front, where preparations were being made for a summer offensive. This operation, known as the Kerensky offensive, was Russia's last attempt at pushing Austrian troops into the Carpathian Mountains. It ended in failure, with a breakdown in the ranks causing a chaotic retreat. The Third Il'ya Muromets Detachment fell back like other units, moving from base to base. At one point, Bashko and his unit were stationed at the same location as the First Combat Air Group under the command of Alexander Kozakov. The two units accompanied each other on some missions. Bashkos' unit finally settled at

Standing in front of the blunt-nosed type 'Veh' *Kievskiy* at the Kresty Farming School, near Pskov, September 1915, are left to right, Serednitskiy (deputy commander), *Kapitan* Bashko (commander), *Poruchik* Lavrov (mechanic), and Constantin N. Finne, the EVK's senior physician. Bashko and his crew soon left this location and became members of the Second Muromets Detachment at Zegewold, east of Riga. If this machine is a *Kievskiy*, it appears to be a later model 'Veh,' because of the different nose. This aircraft was actually the third *Kievskiy* and most likely used the Argus engines salvaged from the *Kievskiy* which crashed July 19, 1915.

Strinkovtze when the front line stabilized again.

In September, Bashko and the Third Il'ya Muromets Combat Detachment returned to Stankovo, near Minsk, where it had been stationed during 1916. The non-stop flight of the *Kievskiy*[16] lasted seven and one half hours, a record at the time. Also in September, Bashko was promoted to *Palkovnik* (Colonel). Within a short time all activity stopped, as it had with the other Muromets units. The October revolution ended with the Bolsheviks gaining control and on December 15, 1917, the new Soviet government signed an armistice with the Central Powers, officially ending hostilities.

By February, 1918, Bashko's unit was the only existing Muromets detachment. Although the situation between the soldiers and officers was tense at best, everything remained intact. However, the soldiers kept close watch on the officers and did not allow them to leave the base. When German infantry units were advancing on Stankovo with no resistance, a committee of soldiers appealed to Bashko for help. He ordered the serviceable aircraft to be prepared for flight and a retreat to Bobruisk. When he walked onto the field he found the enlisted men lined up for inspection with the highest degree of discipline. They greeted him with a hearty, "Wish you health, Your Highness," as if the turbulent events within the country had not occurred.

Vinnitsa was already occupied by German forces and Bobruisk was held by Polish troops. By June Bashko was forced to move again. At 2AM on June 4, 1918, Bashko and the *Kievskiy* headed for Moscow, escaping capture from an enemy only 2.5 miles away. The night was black, with considerable cloud cover and poor visibility, compelling Bashko to fly by compass. He was exhausted, having gone many days without sleep to keep his unit together and evade capture. After five and one half hours, Bashko believed he was in the vicinity of Moscow. He was descending through a rainstorm when the left engines shut down. Unable to locate a suitable landing site and at a low altitude, he was obliged to set the *Kievskiy* down

---

(16) This was the sixth *Korabley Kievskiy*, which was a type G-2. It was the same as the G-1 except for the addition of the tail gun location. It was also equipped with four new 160hp Beardmore engines. With these powerplants, the *Kievskiy* was capable of 86 mph and reaching a ceiling of 15,000 feet. It could reach 10,000 feet in approximately 35 minutes with a duration of 4 hours and a range of 335 miles. Under favorable conditions and with no bomb load it was capable of a much greater duration and range, as proved on this flight.

Jezups Bashko seated on the porch with his dogs at an unknown location on the Galician Front, summer 1917. The dog on his left may be the one that awoke Bashko by licking his face after a crash landing on his flight to Moscow June 4, 1918. Dr. Finne and his wife are second and third from the right.

where he could. The machine crashed in the village of Yukhnovsky, more than 60 miles from Moscow. Luckily, the crew was not seriously hurt. Bashko, knocked unconscious, was revived by his pet bulldog licking his face.

Bashko was arrested and taken to Moscow by Bolshevik police, probably on suspicion of being anti-Soviet. He was not charged with any crimes against the state and was released. Because of his proven ability, he was given command of the Red forces' EVK, but the extent of his participation in the civil war is unknown. In 1921 he returned to his native Latvia, and became involved in organizing that nation's air force. Under his command, the Aviation Division became an efficient, well-disciplined organization. He also wrote textbooks on tactics and navigation, the first in Latvia. In 1926, Bashko became the chief of army aviation and remained in the Latvian air service until 1940.

His fate after 1940 is unclear. One source states he was executed by the Soviet army upon the occupation of the Baltic states in 1940 because of his actions, or rather lack of them, while commanding the Red Army EVK in the civil war. It was considered he actively evaded his duties in order to hinder the Bolshevik cause.

Another source states Bashko took an active part in the civil war, fighting for the Red Army, and was even decorated with the Soldier's Cross. In 1940 his services were put to good use by the Soviet Government. He was promoted to general and given command of an aviation regiment and subsequently an air division during World War II. He died on May 31, 1946, in the village of Jaiksha, Latvia, where he is buried.

Although many EVK officers criticized the Il'ya Muromets, Bashko never spoke against them. His actions clearly show he preferred the Murometsy over light planes. One source states he completed 81 missions with 229 combat hours. Whether or not this is true, *Palkovnik* Jezups Bashko did fly more patrols and tally more combat hours than any other Muromets commander.

Jaan M. Mahlapuu

Praporshik (Ensign) Jaan Mahlapuu, probably soon after his promotion to officer rank in 1917. The *pogoni* (shoulderboards) also indicate aviation service with the Imperial Eagle insignia and his squadron by the roman numeral XII. Mahlapuu also displays one of his NCO awards of the Cross of Saint George. He was awarded both the Third and Fourth Class.

Jaan Mahlapuu was born on November 9, 1894, in the southern Estonian town of Valga, an important rail center. He was the oldest of six children of a locomotive engineer.

Upon graduation from secondary school he became an apprentice to a locksmith and then worked as an assistant locksmith at the Valga rail yard. In July, 1915, for motives that are unclear, he left home to join the air service, leaving no word of his intention.

He enlisted as a *Nijnichin* (Private) at Pskov and was given instruction as an aviation mechanic. After some time in this capacity he was accepted for flight training and took instruction on the Deperdussin TT monoplane and some captured German machines.

In August, 1916, Mahlapuu completed training, was promoted to *Gefreiter* (Lance-Corporal) and assigned to the 12th Fighter Air Detachment at the Riga Front.

In his first month of service Mahlapuu flew five missions, three times engaging the enemy. Twice his gun jammed, but on August 25, 1916, while flying with *Praporshik* (Ensign) Garlinsky, they noticed an enemy aircraft at 7800 feet. The two Russian Nieuports, being at approximately the same altitude, approached the German machine from two angles. The adversary turned toward Garlinsky to attack, but before it could Mahlapuu opened fire on it. It went into a steep turn and dove away in the direction of its own lines. This was Mahlapuu's first combat.

During September Mahlapuu flew 13 operational patrols, at least six accompanied by Garlinsky. The most eventful took place on the afternoon of September 4, when Mahlapuu and Garlinsky were called upon to give chase to an enemy reconnaissance aircraft approaching the area. After 25 minutes, the two Nieuports caught the German crew from behind. Garlinsky was the first to open fire. Almost immediately the German pilot put his machine into a steep dive, but Mahlapuu got in a burst of machine gun fire before he made his escape.

In mid-September, Mahlapuu was promoted to *Starski Unteroffizier* (Sergeant) and awarded the Soldier's Cross of Saint George Fourth Class, for non-commissioned officers.

By the end of October Mahlapuu had earned promotion to the rank of *Feldwebel* (Sergeant-Major). His Nieuport 9[1] caused him much trouble during the month. Sometimes the engine failed and once the carburetor froze. The most annoying problem was with the machine gun. On October 22, 1916, Mahlapuu was on patrol to defend Riga against enemy observation planes when he encountered one over Ikskjul, surprising the machine with a burst from his gun. The enemy turned for home, but Mahlapuu cut off his retreat. Just as he was ready for his second attack, the machine gun jammed, allowing the German crew to return safely to their own lines.

With winter settling in, aerial activity became sporadic for the rest of the year. On a few occasions Mahlapuu, with the help of Garlinsky, managed to drive away observation planes, but he was plagued with continuous engine and machine gun difficulties. At one point he replaced the Lewis gun with an infantry Maxim but it is unknown if this solved the problem.

In the new year Mahlapuu received a different Nieuport, model 11,[2] that was smaller and more maneuverable. From this time on, he flew this type almost exclusively.

---

(1) This machine, Nieuport 9 serial number 262, was of French manufacture and was on the squadron role since April 18, 1916. He flew another Nieuport 9, serial number 173, also built in France, which had been on record since March 1916.

(2) Mahlapuu's flight records show he flew three different Nieuport 11s during his service with the 12th Fighter Detachment. Most time was recorded on serial number 1111, built by Dux in Russia; the other two were serial number 1181, also built by Dux, and serial number 1161, of French manufacture. Except on rare occasions, these three aircraft were his usual mounts for the next several months.

Mahlapuu ready for take off in his French-built Nieuport 9, most likely during late summer 1916. He flew this type on many occasions during his early service with the 12th Fighter Air Detachment, but also logged time in a Nieuport 9 in July 1917. An infantry-type Maxim machine gun is mounted on the upper wing.

On February 4, 1917, he was assigned an unusual mission. A German observation balloon had broken free and was sailing over the Gulf of Riga. When he reached Shlok, Mahlapuu spotted the balloon and headed toward it. He caught up to it about 13 miles from shore at an altitude of 7800 feet and proceeded to shoot at it. After he had emptied two clips at it, it began to descend. Mahlapuu followed it down to 3250 feet when it collapsed and fell into the sea. At that point Mahlapuu had to return to base, being low on fuel. He last saw the balloon on the surface of the water. Three days later he returned to the area to search for the balloon, but there was no trace of it.

After continuously driving away enemy reconnaissance planes from the area, he at last sent one down on February 25 for his first victory. Two weeks later, on March 11, 1917, Mahlapuu, in Nieuport 11 No. 1111, accompanied by *Praporshik* Sherebtzov flying Nieuport 11 No. 1161, took off on a patrol. As reported by their squadron commander: "Today, according to my orders, two pilots took off to attack an enemy plane, which flew from Olai towards Riga. *Praporshik* Sherebtzov inspected the Mitau road and turning toward Babit Lake, observed a large German aircraft. Sherebtzov overtook the enemy aircraft over the village of Bolderaa, attacked him from above and opened fire on him from all angles. While changing the drum on his Lewis gun, Sherebtzov descended. Meanwhile, the enemy aircraft turned to the goods station [presumably a nearby railway distribution center and supply depot] where Sherebtzov noticed a Russian fighter flying toward the enemy aircraft. After he had changed the drum and gained height, Sherebtzov saw the Russian fighter over the village of Lidak. The enemy aircraft was seen no more and at 12:20 Sherebtzov landed.

"*Feldwebel* Mahlapuu at a height of 8100 feet noticed two aircraft over Bolderaa, which were flying at the same height; the one aircraft escaping from the other. Mahlapuu began to pursue the enemy aircraft and overtook and twice attacked it over the goods station. The Albatros spun down, then turned upside down, began to spin again, and crashed near the village of Lidak. Mahlapuu landed near the German aircraft; as he was landing, one of the Germans fired at him without result. Climbing out of his fighter, Mahlapuu approached the enemy craft and in the German language asked the observer if he had been the one who had fired at him. The 18-year-old German *Leutnant* angrily admitted that he had. The German pilot was hit in the head and soon died; the young observer had a slight concussion. The crashed Albatros (type C.III, serial no. 667/16) still carried its load of three bombs. Mahlapuu awaited the arrival of the squadron orderly officer, *Stabs-Kapitan* Galyshev, and then took off to return to his aerodrome."

Grand Duke Alexander Mikhailovich sent a message of congratulations and General Klembovski, commander of the Russian 12th Army, awarded Mahlapuu the Soldier's Cross of Saint George Third Class. Soon after this he was granted a commission to officer status with the rank of *Praporshik* (Ensign).

As the climate became warmer with the coming of spring, Mahlapuu took to the air more frequently.

Mahlapuu standing in front of his German victory. The wing panel can be seen leaning against a building with the fuselage in front. This is most likely the Albatros C.III he shot down on March 11, 1917.

Sometimes he flew more than one mission a day; for instance, on May 13, he intercepted an enemy plane at 13,000 feet in the vicinity of Olai and Riga. He drove this machine away, then noticed Russian anti-aircraft fire coming from Ikskjul. He headed in that direction to attack the enemy. He approached his rival and fired the entire contents of his gun. A jam occurred after reloading, which allowed the enemy to escape. The flight lasted 1-1/2 hours. In the evening Mahlapuu was over Kekkau when he attacked an enemy artillery spotting plane. Shortly after he attacked his gun jammed, but the intrusion was enough to disrupt the enemy, not allowing the crew to adjust their army's artillery fire.

During the summer months Mahlapuu was called upon constantly to prevent enemy aircraft from observing the Russian rear area and spotting for artillery. On several occasions he attacked the enemy only to have his gun jam. Despite this common occurrence, Mahlapuu prevented the enemy from completing missions.

On July 2, 1917, Mahlapuu forced an enemy machine to go down behind its own lines. It may have landed intact and been recovered, but the outcome could not be determined, preventing confirmation of his third victory.

By the end of July Mahlapuu had flown more than 40 combat missions during the summer, totaling about 45 hours of flight time. He received a new aircraft, a Nieuport 21, serial number 1825, in late July. Although he had recently acquired it, the machine had been on record with the squadron since November, 1916. However, it was still not as old as the Nieuport 11s he had been flying.

On August 2, 1917, at 8:35PM, Mahlapuu took off to intercept an enemy airplane reported heading toward Riga. The Nieuport 21 was over his own field at 500 feet when its right wing collapsed, causing the plane to spin into the ground. The machine was demolished and Mahlapuu was killed.

Mahlapuu was the victim of faulty equipment; the old Nieuports had remained in service far too long. Many had been on the unit roster for more than a year and were worn out. As stated by a fellow pilot of the 12th Detachment, "The aircraft are kept flying only upon their 'word of honor.'"

Mahlapuu's body was returned home to Valga by rail, arriving in the station where his father worked and he had been a locksmith. He was buried in the cemetery of Saint Luke, with full military honors. His squadron companions composed a eulogy that read in part, "*Praporshik* Mahlapuu was one of the youngest and most courageous fliers in our army. There was no type of weather, wind, rain, snow, which could prevent him from flying. Mahlapuu's death is so much more tragic in that it is a direct result of the great lacks of Russian aviation."

His two confirmed victories were a great accomplishment on a front that had little activity during that time. The Russian empire had lost one of its best pilots, not to the enemy, but to faulty equipment, at the age of 22.

Above: French-built Nieuport 11, serial number 1161, most likely during early spring of 1917. Mahlapuu logged several hours of combat time in this aircraft, although on March 11, 1917, when he scored his second victory, he was flying the Dux-built Nieuport 11, serial number 1111, accompanied by *Praporshik* Sherebtzov flying serial number 1161.

Mahlapuu posing in front of one of the squadron's Nieuport 21s during the winter in early 1917. The aircraft had been refitted with skis for use on the snow-covered field. The plane is armed with only an upper-wing Lewis machine gun. Mahlapuu has received his promotion to *Praporshik* as denoted by his shoulderboard insignia, which dates the photo as being taken after his second victory on March 11, 1917.

Petr Nikolaevich Nesterov

Podporuchik Petr Nesterov, spring 1913.

Petr Nikolaevich Nesterov was born into a military family on February 27, 1887, in Nizhny Novgorod (now Gorky) Russia. He was graduated from Nizhegorodsky Cadet Corps, the local cadet school, in 1904 and was one of a number of graduates who were sent to Mikhailyevsky Artillery Academy in St. Petersburg to continue their education. Two years later the young second lieutenant was appointed to the 9th Eastern-Siberian Infantry Artillery Brigade at Vladivostok.

Soon after his arrival at Vladivostok, Nesterov was dispatched to one of the observation stations at the Vladivostok fortress aviation detachment as an balloon artillery observer. His balloon ascents made such a deep impression on him that he became obsessed with aviation and began to study the available literature with the hope of transferring to the Vladivostok aviation detachment. However, the Far East climate was bad for Nesterov's health, and by 1909 he was affected so significantly his doctors made an urgent request that he be transferred for health reasons. With the request approved, Nesterov was sent on a year-long business trip to the Caucasus. In August, 1910, Nesterov arrived at the 2nd Battery of the 21st Artillery Brigade located in Petrovsk (now Mahachkala), where he continued service.

In October, 1910, at Tiflis (now Tbilisi), Nesterov attended a flying demonstration for the first time and observed one of Russia's pioneering aviators, S.I. Utotchkin, fly a Farman biplane. He was so inspired by the event that he quickly designed his own airplane, featuring a V-tail. The control system of Nesterov's design was of interest; both halves of the tailplane could be controlled independently, and thus replaced the vertical tailplane. The tailplane could also be used as an air brake to reduce the landing run. Clearly, these ideas were well ahead of their time. Nesterov submitted this design to the aviation department of the War Ministry. However, since the design was unconventional and Nesterov had not observed any flights of a V-tailed aircraft, the project was declined.

Nesterov continued to design aircraft and in the summer of 1911 assembled and flew a glider of his own design in Nizhny Novgorod. In June, Nesterov was appointed to his previous assignment with two months leave before reporting. Taking advantage of this time, he received a medical certificate of health and succeeded in enrolling in the St. Petersburg aviation school at Gatchina.

Nesterov quickly passed ground-school portions of the curriculum and also mastered flying aircraft. On September 26, 1912, Nesterov made his first solo flight in a Farman. Two days later he passed the examination for pilot-aviator, and on October 5 he was given the title of military pilot. During October, 1912, Nesterov made 60 solo flights with a total flight time of 10 hours. In November he was sent to the aviation company at Warsaw to gain experience with newer airplanes being introduced. During his first flight at Warsaw, Nesterov tested his own method of flight by performing banked turns. This maneuver was considered dangerous and he was reprimanded by his department head, *Stabs-Kapitan* (Staff-Captain) Gorshkov.

Nesterov was graduated from the aviation school in March, 1913, awarded the Order of St. Anne, 3rd Class, and promoted to the position of aviation detachment head. In May he was appointed to the newly formed 3rd Aviation Company of Kiev, where he was temporarily placed in command of the 11th Detachment because the unit's commander was on an extended business trip.

From the start Nesterov was busy with organizational questions. His first decision was to introduce regular ground-school studies and flying, including steep turns of more than 45° bank angle and landing with the engine off. The detachment quickly became trained and battle-ready, and by the summer of 1913 it was participating together

Nesterov (second from left, with his right hand in his shirt) with pilots of the 3rd Corps Aviation Company.

with artillery in classes at Darnitsky Polygon, 10 miles from Kiev. Pilots were trained in reconnaissance and artillery spotting. To generalize the experience, Nesterov introduced proposals for close cooperation of aviation with ground troops.

Nesterov was always a good example to his subordinates; there seemed to be no end to his energy and creativity in developing military aviation. Together with Lieutenants M. Peredkov and Vyatcheslav M. Tkachev, Nesterov organized and led a group flight over the route Kiev, Oster-Kozelets, Nezhin, Kiev to teach the pilots map orientation and to find landing places in unfamiliar territory. During this flight Nesterov took a photographer to test the possibility of using movie cameras for reconnaissance. The group covered the distance of 200 miles (320 km) without casualties or damaged airplanes. However, the main accomplishment was training the pilots in cross-country flying, which would be important in combat.

On September 8, 1913,[1] while flying a Nieuport IV at Syretsk military airport, Nesterov became the first pilot in the world to complete a so-called death loop, a loop in the vertical plane. This achievement resulted in Nesterov being immediately placed under arrest for ten days for "undue risk with a machine, the property of his government." After a few days this was forgiven and Nesterov was promoted to *Stabs-Kapitan* (Staff-Captain), and on November 23, 1913, he was awarded the Russian Aero Club Gold Medal for his feat.

After his precedent-setting loop, Nesterov commented "It has been a long time since I intended to carry out this experiment with the purpose to demonstrate my theories of plane operation that are very different from the

(1) French pilot Pégoud's alleged 'first loop' was at Juvisy, France on September 1, 1913; however, this was not regarded as a true 'loop.'

generally-accepted theory. I was fearful only once—when the decision had to be made. Then I was sitting upside down, feeling superb. Before starting the experiment, I practiced a lot forcing the apparatus to take all kinds of positions in the air, making turns at 85° angle. My experiment was undertaken only when I was confident in its success. I did not want, and could not afford, risking my life, because I am father of two children, a girl and a boy, future aviators."

Late in 1913, Nesterov returned to his earlier V-tail project by modifying a Nieuport IV. Although the airplane did well in flight tests, it did not achieve the performance levels he expected. In November, Nesterov carried out flight tests of a high-intensity landing light of his design, but found it of no value in night landings because of its insufficient power.

In February, 1914, Nesterov was appointed commander of the 11th Corps Detachment. There he developed and implemented a cross-country flight training program. During March 1–5, he made a flight over the route Kiev, Odessa, Sevastopol. On 11 May he flew from Kiev to Gatchina without any special preparations, spanning 770 miles in 18 hours (eight hours in the air), with stops at Bykhovo and Vitebsk. This flight set two all-Russian records; the longest distance covered in a day and the longest flight with a passenger.

Nesterov expressed himself on flight training: "I am perfectly convinced that it is the duty of every military aviator to be able to execute looping flights and gliding flights. These exercises must certainly be included in the training program, as they will play a great part in the aero-combats. Such a combat will resemble a fight between a hawk and a crow. The aviator who is able to give his craft the mobility and flexibility of motion of the hawk will be in a better condition to seriously damage his opponent." However, the beginning of World War I

Nesterov standing along side his Nieuport IV at Kiev. On September 8, 1913 (new calendar), Nesterov used this machine to become the world's first flyer to successfully loop an aircraft in the vertical plane.

prevented completion of the training program.

The 3rd Aviation Company, to which Nesterov's detachment was attached, became part of the 3rd Army of the Southwestern Front. Nesterov's detachment was sent to Rovno, then to Dubno. On July 28, 1914, he made his first "battle flight" in a Morane Saulnier type G with the general staff observer, Junior Captain Lagarev, aboard for reconnaissance. Detachment pilots then began aerial reconnaissance and staff communication flights in support of the army.

On August 13, 1914, Nesterov received notification that he was awarded the Order of Saint Vladimir, Fourth Class for his pre-war aviation services. During a reconnaissance flight on August 25 Lieutenant Titov, Nesterov's observer, dropped two three-inch grenades over a concentration of Austro-Hungarian troops at the railroad transport unit at Rava-Russkaya. This was one of the first bombings missions carried out by Russian aviators in World War I.

During intense fighting in the Lemberg region, enemy planes frequently appeared over the Russian troops. This focused Nesterov's thoughts on how to prevent the enemy reconnaissance flights. He understood the importance of armament for air combat and offered to arm his plane with a machine gun. However, that offer was rejected. He also experimented with other armament, including hooks and knives.

By the end of August, 1914, enemy air units had intensified their reconnaissance. The crew of one Albatros was especially insistent and on August 25 this airplane even dropped a bomb on the airfield of the 11th Detachment. Apparently, after that incident Nesterov decided to destroy that enemy airplane by any means possible.

The plane reappeared the next day near the town of Zholkov. The Austrian observer was *Oberleutnant* Baron Friedrich Rosenthal, who owned several large estates occupied by the Russians. Nesterov twice attempted to intercept the Austrian Albatros without success. When

Stabs-Kapitan Nesterov, winter 1914. His awards include the Order of Saint George, Fourth Class, and the Order of Saint Vladimir, Fourth Class.

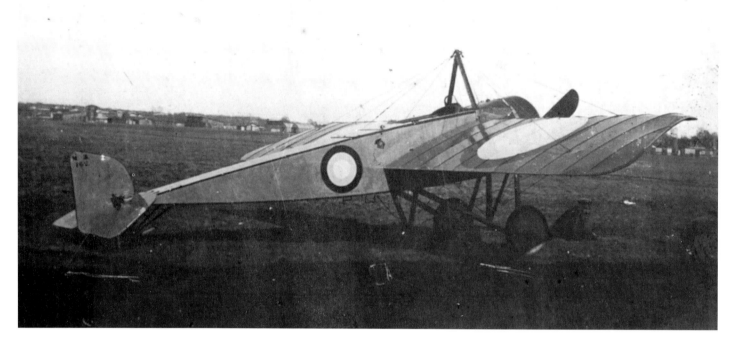

The Morane-Saulnier H #162 on which Nesterov made his five-hour flight from St. Petersburg to Moscow in July, 1914.

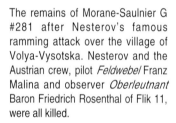

The remains of Morane-Saulnier G #281 after Nesterov's famous ramming attack over the village of Volya-Vysotska. Nesterov and the Austrian crew, pilot *Feldwebel* Franz Malina and observer *Oberleutnant* Baron Friedrich Rosenthal of Flik 11, were all killed.

Rosenthal made his third appearance that day, Nesterov was eager to meet him. Nesterov took off so quickly that he failed to fasten his seatbelt and refused to take the Browning pistol offered him by Lt. Kovanko, saying "That's all right; I shall manage without it." Flying a two-seat Morane-Saulnier G (factory number 281), Nesterov intercepted the Albatros. Quickly gaining altitude, he dived on the enemy airplane and rammed it. Nesterov's propeller cut into the wings of the Albatros; the planes were momentarily locked together, then the Albatros went down. Both occupants of the Albatros (pilot *Feldwebel* Franz Malina and observer Baron *Oberleutnant* Rosenthal) were killed. Nesterov's plane went into a spin and also crashed. However, Nesterov was observed falling out of his machine before it hit the ground. His body was found 30 to 40 feet away from the wreckage. An inspection of Nesterov's Morane-Saulnier showed the propeller was broken and pieces of the Albatros were wrapped around the propeller shaft.

This was the first ramming attack in aviation history. For his sacrifice, Nesterov was posthumously awarded the Order of Saint George, Fourth Class, by royal order of April 22, 1915: "His Imperial Highness most graciously bestowed on Junior Captain Petr Nesterov the Order of Saint George, Fourth Class, for his extremely ardent service and special effort to ram an enemy plane on his own initiative which occurred during the battle on Aug. 26, 1914, when the enemy plane was on reconnaissance mission over the town Zholkov. The enemy plane went down with two pilots near village Volya-Vysotska, and Junior Captain Nesterov died the death of a hero in that battle."

Nesterov was buried at Askold's Grave, a historic landmark in Kiev. In August, 1947, a monument was erected on the spot where he fell on Russia's Air Force Fleet day. On December 3, 1951, the town of Zholiva, Lvov province, was renamed Nesterov, and the Zholkovsky Region was renamed Nesterov Region. In 1962, by a proposal of the Central Aero Club of Russia, the F.I.A. established a challenge prize, a cup named after Nesterov, which is presented to winners of the World Aerobatic Championship.

Alexei Vasilyevich Pankrat'yev

Formal portrait of Alexei Pankrat'yev wearing the *pogoni* (shoulderboards) of a *Stabs-Kapitan* (Staff Captain). Pankrat'yev commanded the Il'ya Muromets Ship II (IM-2) from the beginning of the war until the Bolshevik revolution in 1917, when he assumed command of the EVK (*Eskadra Vozduchnykh Korablei* or Squadron of Flying Ships).

Alexei Pankrat'yev was born February 23, 1888. He began his career with the armed forces as a student at the Simbirsky Military School. Next, he was assigned to the 2nd East-Siberian Field Aeronautical Battalion and made several balloon ascents. Shortly after this he studied at the Officers Aeronautic School during 1909–1910. Upon graduation he became a member of the Brest-Litovsk Aeronautical Battalion. He continued balloon flights, but soon became interested in flying airplanes. Throughout 1911 he trained at the Gatchina flight school near St. Petersburg, and was graduated in the autumn. At that time he also conducted experiments with aeronautical radios. He remained at Gatchina as an instructor until the beginning of hostilities; one of his students was Petr Nesterov. Nothing else is known of his early life, but he became one of the best Il'ya Muromets commanders, serving in that position for most of the war.

At the outbreak of war, seven Muromets units were formed, commanded by pilots who had been instructors at Gatchina. *Poruchik* Pankrat'yev was assigned command of the second unit. Igor Sikorsky, being the only qualified pilot of the four-engined machine, gave instruction to *Kapitan* Gorshkov,[1] who then trained Pankrat'yev and the other five commanders. Each aircraft constituted an individual unit made up of the plane, four officers, 40 enlisted personnel for aircraft maintenance, and one official who was usually an engineer.

While training and organizing the Muromets units was under way, aircraft production was also undertaken. Ten of the giant planes had been ordered by *Stavka* (headquarters of the supreme commander-in-chief) before the war, but only two were nearing completion in August 1914. By mid-September the first two of these four-engined, long-range reconnaissance and bombing aircraft were ready to be transported to the front. The machines were given the number of the unit to which they were assigned, hence Pankrat'yev's plane was designated Il'ya Muromets II (IM-2). The IM-2 was a type 'Beh,' equipped with four Salmson radial engines, two of 200hp and two of 135hp. These engines proved less desirable than the Argus[2] motors, providing a top speed of only 60mph and a ceiling of about 6500 feet.

Despite this poor performance, the IM-2 started its flight to the front on September 24, 1914. Assigned to the Russian 5th Army, its destination was Dvinsk, the army's headquarters. Both the IM-1 and IM-2 were flown to the front rather than transported by rail due to the time involved in assembling the machines. Unfortunately, en route Pankrat'yev and his crew were shot at by Russian troops and also sustained engine problems, forcing the IM-2 to land at Rezhitsi. It was found that one of the Salmson engines had broken a crankshaft. With no spare parts to be found, the IM-2 was disassembled and shipped by rail to Brest-Litovsk, were it sat until February, 1915. It would be June, 1915, before Pankrat'yev and the crew of the IM-2 would see action.

Stabs-Kapitan Rudnev,[3] commander of the IM-1, felt the Il'ya Muromets was unreliable. He made several

---

(1) Georgiy Georgiyevich Gorshkov had graduated from the Officers School of Aeronautics and had made several pre-war flights in balloons and airships. He was deputy commander of the Gatchina Military Flying School when the war began. He was given the duty of selecting the seven commanders for these first Muromets groups and chose himself to command the seventh unit.
(2) Argus motors were used on the original Il'ya Muromets and provided very favorable results. Unfortunately, the Argus engines were a German product and of course were no longer available after the beginning of the war.
(3) Rudnev was a well-known aviator before the war. He was chosen as a Muromets pilot because of his experience. He preferred light aviation and spoke out against heavy aviation on many occasions. He returned to flying small aircraft shortly after his refusal to fly the IM-1.

The Il'ya Muromets II, type Б (Beh), being blessed at Korpusnoi Aerodrome near Petrograd, September, 1914, just before leaving for the front. The aircraft was equipped with four Salmson radial engines, two of 200hp and two of 135hp, giving the machine a top speed of 60 mph and a ceiling of 6500 feet. A priest and the band are present for the ceremony and a film crew is recording the occasion.

reports stating the reconnaissance missions assigned to him could not be accomplished because the aircraft was unable to reach the necessary altitude. After this he refused to fly. This attitude provoked the headquarters of the Northwest Army Group to refuse delivery of the IM-2. After these reports were submitted, *Stavka* canceled all orders placed for additional Murometsy.

When this occurred, Mikhail Shidlovsky, director of the R-BVZ factory, approached *Stavka* and personally defended the Murometsy. Despite the fact he faced the possibility of financial loss, he truly believed in heavy aviation. Part of his defense was that the large aircraft units were not properly organized. He suggested they be assembled into one unit under the control of *Stavka*. This suggestion was accepted by *Stavka*. The amazing part of this episode was that Shidlovsky received the rank of *General-Maior* (Major General) and was given command of the Murometsy unit.

The reorganization gave the Murometsy another chance to prove themselves. The IM-1 and IM-2 were transported to Yablonna, where they were joined by five other ships to form the EVK (*Eskadra Vozdushnykh Korablei* or Squadron of Flying Ships). In February, 1915 they began operations. While the two machines equipped with Argus engines[4] flew missions over East Prussia, Ship II and the other Salmson-powered Murometsy awaited installation of British Sunbeam V-8 engines. These promised better performance, but in reality were not much of an improvement. However, lack of alternative power plants forced them to be used.

---

(4) These two ships were the *Kievskiy* and the IM-3. The *Kievskiy* type 'Veh' had the engines from the original *Kievskiy* type 'Beh' flown by Sikorsky from Saint Petersburg to Kiev in June 1914, and the IM-3 had the engines taken from Rudnev's IM-1. These aircraft were both the v-nose type 'Veh.'
(5) In the case of the IM-2, the Sunbeam engines were placed on a v-nosed type 'Veh,' replacing the type 'Beh.'

Engine installation and testing of the Sunbeam-powered Murometsy[5] was not finished until June, delaying the use of the remaining aircraft. The first missions were performed late June and July, 1915, with bombing and reconnaissance flights over Lovich, Skernevitsi, Yedinorozhets, and Tsekhanno. The IM-2 along with Ship I (IM-1), commanded by *Starshi Leitenant* (Naval Lieutenant) Lavrov, Ship IV (IM-4), commanded by *Stabs-Kapitan* Datskevich, and Ship V (IM-5), commanded by *Poruchik* Alekhnovich, took part in a mission on July 17, 1915, after the Russian 1st Army ordered that several enemy troop locations be reconnoitered and bombed. The four bombers attacked along the frontlines as well as attacking enemy troop transports reinforcing the area along the Narev Front. They returned to Yablonna without damage. The mission was repeated the next day, but bad weather prevented further action.

Enemy advanced forced the Russians to retreat from the Polish salient deeper into the heart of Russia. The Germans and Austro-Hungarians had launched an offensive along the entire front, with the main attack in Galicia and secondary attacks in other areas. This forced the EVK to relocate. First the EVK fell back to Markovshizna, near Bialystok, and from there to Lida by the end of July, 1915.

No missions were flown from either of these locations, but during the stay at Lida the first of the Russian-manufactured engines arrived. A new Ship II, a blunt-nosed type 'Veh,' was fitted with 150hp R-BVZ-6, six-cylinder in-line engines that were almost direct copies of the German Benz, with several refinements. They were delivered to Lida in August. They were designed by the R-BVZ engineer Kireyev at the company's automobile factory in Riga. A graduate of a German technical school, Kireyev had worked at the Mercedes and Maybach engine-manufacturing companies before the war. He designed and produced two engines for the R-BVZ. One

The IM-2 type 'Beh,' being inspected by the Grand Duke Kirill Vladimirovich, seen from the waist up inside the gunners position. The location is the EVK base at Yablonna, May 29, 1915. A Salmson engine can be seen to the left, with its large box-type radiator.

was a copy of the Argus and the other was the Benz copy (R-BVZ-6), which produced 160hp. The first trials with the new engines proved favorable, with greater speed and altitude being obtained. Unfortunately, only a few were produced before the factory at Riga had to be relocated due to the threat of the advancing enemy. It was March, 1916, before more were manufactured and sent to the front.

Another event at Lida was the testing of the 25 *pood* (880 lb.) bomb. This bomb was only a dummy and was about six feet in length. It was carried by the IM-2 under the fuselage, at the center of gravity, by straps that were released from inside the cabin. At an altitude of 3900 feet, the IM-2 dropped the bomb. It penetrated the earth, creating a hole nearly ten feet wide.

On August 27, 1915, the EVK was forced to move again. This time the retreat was 250 miles, to the Kresty Farming School near Pskov. This location offered a decent field and several buildings for storage and workshops. The flight was difficult due to cloud cover and several pilots, including Pankrat'yev, lost their bearings. He was forced to land at Novo-Sventsyani, where he waited until he could continue to Pskov. He eventually arrived at the Kresty field without mishap.

The enemy advance halted with the approach of winter, stabilizing the front. This allowed the EVK to organize and continue operations. More aircraft were produced and delivered to Pskov, which became a training facility in addition to being the main base. In September nine of the Squadron's aircraft, including the IM-2, were transferred to Zegevold, 40 *versts* (26 miles) from Riga, to form the Second Muromets Combat Detachment.[6]

From the new base the Second Detachment conducted many raids with multiple aircraft. They wasted no time in bombing Mitava, recently occupied by the Germans. On September 30, 1915, while on a reconnaissance mission over Bausk and Mittau with ship number IV, Pankrat'yev and his crew were attacked by an enemy two-seater. The crew of the IM-2 returned the fire. Moments later, the German machine went into a quick descent and the observer was seen tugging on the back of the pilot's coat. Presumably he had been hit by bullets fired from the IM-2. Although not confirmed, this *may* have been the first aerial victory for an Il'ya Muromets crew.

The IM-2, along with the IM-5 and IM-9, made a bombing raid on Friedrichstadt on October 18, 1915. They

---

(6) All these aircraft were type 'Veh.' Those included in the roster at Zegevold were Nos. I, II, IV, V, VI, VIII, IX, X, and the *Kievskiy*. Nearly all were powered by Sunbeam motors. Only the *Kievskiy*, which was Argus powered, and Ship II with R-BVZ-6 engines, had greater performance.

Above: Pankrat'yev standing on the far left, in front of his Sunbeam-powered IM-2. His deputy commander, *Stabs-Kapitan* Sergei N. Nikolsky, is standing fifth from the left, next to the woman wearing the light-colored jacket. This machine was the early type 'Veh' with a V-nose. With the four 150 hp Sunbeam motors, performance was slightly improved over that of the Salmson engines. The top speed was 62 to 69 mph and the endurance was about 4-1/2 to 5 hours, providing a range of about 275 miles. The ceiling was improved, up to 9000 feet, but was not up to the standards of the Argus-powered Muromets. The large car-type frontal radiators created excessive drag.

Below: The V-nosed IM-2, with its Sunbeam engines. The location is possibly Yablonna, shortly after testing the new motors in June, 1915, but may also be either Bialystok or Lida in late July, 1915, after the retreat from the Polish salient. The occasion is unknown, but appears to be an inspection of some importance due to the size of the crowd gathered.

succeeded in dropping 48 1-*pud* (35 lb.) bombs which destroyed two buildings and scattered the enemy. Pankrat'yev participated in two raids in December; on both occasions he and the crew of the IM-2 launched 15 *pud* (525 lb.) of bombs, damaging the rail station at Kreitsburg and destroying an enemy army corps bakery, which left the enemy troops in that area without bread for two to three days.

At the end of 1915 the IM-2 and the IM-*Kievskiy* were transferred to the Galician Front to assist the Russian 7th Army. These two ships formed the First Muromets Combat Detachment,[7] under Pankrat'yev's command.

Both aircraft were disassembled and transported by rail to Volochyst, where they were reassembled and test flown. After testing was completed, it became apparent that the facilities at Volochyst were not suitable for the Murometsy. Pankrat'yev approached the chief of staff of the 7th Army, General Golovin, who was able to relocate the detachment to a more suitable location. The site chosen was an estate near the village of Kolodziyevka, 25 miles from Tarnopol.

(7) This was the second First Muromets Combat Detachment. The first unit given this designation was formed in May, 1915, and consisted of two ships, the IM-*Kievskiy* and the IM-3. The *Kievskiy* returned to the main force of Murometsy at Lida in July, 1915, and the IM-3 was destroyed in November, 1915, leaving no Murometsy on the Galician Front.

Officers of the EVK, including many ship commanders, at Lida, July, 1915. From left to right are mechanic Sirotin; *Starshi Leitenant* (Naval Lieutenant) G.I. Lavrov, commander IM-1; *Stabs-Kapitan* A.V. Pankrat'yev, commander IM-2; *Poruchik* G.V. Alekhnovich, Commander IM-5; *Stabs-Kapitan* Chechulin; *Poruchik* A.V. Konstenchik, deputy commander IM-5, later commander IM-10; *Poruchik* Krzhichkovskiy; *Poruchik* Lukinskiy; mechanic Kisel, official assigned to the IM-5; *Stabs-Rotmistre* A.V. Serednitskiy, later commander IM-18; Igor Sikorsky; and *Poruchik* Loiko, deputy commander IM-6. Behind them is a Sunbeam-powered Muromets.

Missions began in January 1916, with the First Detachment providing valuable reconnaissance to the 7th Army in preparation for an offensive. This work included photographing enemy troop concentrations and artillery emplacements. The method of photographing the front lines involved taking a series of pictures so each frame would overlap the last. When these photos were assembled they gave a continuous view of the enemy trench line. Processing and completing this operation sometimes was conducted on the return flight, enabling the photographs to be submitted to the army staff immediately upon landing. This was accomplished not only for the first line of defense, but also for the second and third enemy trench lines. On one occasion a special mission of this type was ordered by the army, which called for additional crew members on board the IM-2. The crew was increased by two and included extra photography equipment with no bomb load carried. During the flight the IM-2 was exposed to an unusually heavy amount of anti-aircraft fire. The crew managed to complete their mission successfully, but upon their return found much of the fabric missing from the underside of the lower wing and nearly 100 holes in the aircraft.

Pankrat'yev and his unit flew almost every day the winter weather permitted. They bombed railroad stations and troop concentrations at Yazlovets, Bugach, Monastyrzesko, Nizhniyev, Podgaytsy, Brzhezany, Rogatin, and several other locations. The IM-2 performed two bombing missions over Monastyrzesko in one day, dropping a total of 55 *pud* (1925 lb.) of bombs. Russian troops who later advanced through Monastyrzesko witnessed the vast destruction caused by the Murometsy bombing raids.

On March 30, 1916,[8] Pankrat'yev and the crew of the IM-2 were on a mission over Monastyrzesko when they were attacked by two Austro-Hungarian Brandenburg C.I aircraft of *Fliegerkompanie* (Flik) 14. *Podpraporshik* Ushakov returned their fire and succeeded in hitting one of the enemy planes. It began to fall and crashed in a forest nearby. The other machine broke off the combat. The IM-2 did sustain some damage, but the crew took the worst punishment. Deputy Commander *Poruchik* Federov was severely wounded and the mechanic, *Podpraporshik* Ushakov, was killed. The two crew members of the enemy plane suffered the same fate. The pilot, *Hauptmann* Mackensen, died from his wounds after the crash, while *Leutnant* Marek was injured, but survived.

In June the complement of planes of Pankrat'yev's unit changed. The IM-*Kievskiy* was transferred to another front to form the Third Muromets Detachment. The IM-13, under the command of *Stabs-Kapitan* Solovyev, and the IM-11, under the command of *Poruchik* Bazanov, joined

---

(8) The date of this mission is uncertain; it has been stated as both April 1 and April 7, 1916.

The Il'ya Muromets II, factory number 167. This machine was a blunt-nosed type 'Veh' and is seen here in July, 1915, being fitted with the R-BVZ-6 150hp engines. These engines increased the speed of the Il'ya Muromets to 75 mph and the ceiling to more than 9750 feet. Salmson box-type radiators have been fitted to three engines, as seen on the starboard inboard motor, while one engine was equipped with the Hazet radiator. When this aircraft was stationed in Pskov in August, 1915, the three Salmson radiators were replaced by the *Hazet* model, which not only gave better streamlining, but was also easier and simpler to install and maintain. The starboard outboard engine shows the R-BVZ logo cast into the underside of its block.

Pankrat'yev in Galicia. In July the three aircraft moved to an estate near the town of Yagelnitsa, where the detachment remained until the enemy breakthrough in the autumn of 1917 after the Kerensky offensive. The facilities at the estate were excellent; the airfield was more than adequate and the lodging was pleasurable.

The First Muromets Detachment, under Pankrat'yev's command, continued to provide effective support to General Scherbachev's 7th Army throughout the offensive.[9] Their contribution to its success was immeasurable.

The following report was submitted by the 7th Army, which bestowed upon *Stabs-Kapitan* Pankrat'yev the Order of Saint George Fourth Class: "For combat missions on May 17, 18, 19, and June 7 and 8, 1916, and related aerial reconnaissance missions in the districts of Yazlovets and Bugach. *Stabs-Kapitan* Pankrat'yev personally flew the IM-2 through intense enemy artillery fire and gave precise reports on the number and disposition of enemy batteries, as well as enemy positions on the banks of the Streltsa River. During a battle on May 18, 1916, he discovered the absence of enemy reserves in the area of Yazlovets as well as the area of Russilov, and he reported correctly on the reasons for the movement of enemy troops. This reconnaissance enabled us to take further action, which was crowned with success.

"The dropping of bombs and machine gun fire from the IM-2 brought losses to the enemy and forced them into a disorderly retreat. By means of direct hits, fires were ignited in the town of Yazlovets, which later was taken by Russian troops. He destroyed the roadbed west of the railway station at Bugach, which then had to be evacuated by the enemy. By means of accurate machine gun fire, he silenced an enemy anti-aircraft battery firing at his aircraft, and he drove off an enemy fighter that attempted to intercept his work. With the destruction of this battery, enemy fire was silenced. While on his mission he took photographs of enemy positions. These photographs were used by our troops during the battle around Yazlovets."

The deputy commander was *Stabs-Kapitan* Sergei Nikolaevich Nikolsky, who on June 7, 1916, had fought off

---

(9) This offensive, designed by General Alexei Brusilov, was launched on June 4, 1916, toward the Austrians to drive them into the Carpathian Mountains. It was also designed to reach Kovel, approximately 100 miles north of Lemberg. The 7th and 11th Armies achieved the greatest success, reaching their objectives. The operation began with success, but came to a halt by mid-September, short of reaching its goals.

The Il'ya Muromets II, at Lida, July 1915, on the occasion of testing the dummy 25-*pud* (880 lb.) bomb. From left to right in the front are R-BVZ engineer Kireyev, *Stabs-Kapitan* Nikolsky (deputy commander of the IM-2), Igor Sikorsky, and *Stabs-Kapitan* Pankrat'yev. *General-Maior* Shidlovsky, commander of the EVK, is to the right of the bomb, with long dark overcoat and white beard. The port inboard 150hp R-BVZ-6 engine has the Hazet radiator, while the starboard inboard engine and the two outboard engines still have the Salmson box-type radiator. Photo: H. Woodman.

an enemy fighter, using first a pistol and finally a Madsen machine gun, while on a mission over the Jazlowiec salient in support of advancing Russian troops. He remained with the IM-2 until given command of the IM-14 in May, 1917.

Poruchik Victor S. Federov transferred from a Voisin unit to fill in for Nikolsky during his leave in January, 1916 due to illness, remaining throughout 1916 as a member of the IM-2. Later he served on the IM-15 and was awarded the Golden Sword of Saint George for his heroic actions on May 8, 1917, when the IM-15 was attacked by three enemy fighters and shot down two of them.

Podporuchik Georgiy Vasiliyevich Pavlov was a military pilot who served on the IM-2 until September 5, 1917, when he was relieved of his position, probably because of the chaotic conditions within the EVK as well as the army.

Podpraporshik Ushakov, the mechanic of the IM-2, shot down two enemy aircraft before he was killed during combat on March 30, 1916.

These crew members played important roles on the IM-2 and were much of the reason for its success. There were many other individuals who served on the IM-2, but only for short periods.

By autumn 1916 the IM-2 was replaced with a new type G-1, fitted with the same R-BVZ-6 engines. Shortly after this Pankrat'yev and crew were transferred from the First Murometsy Detachment, leaving *Stabs-Kapitan* Solovyev (IM-13) as temporary commander. The IM-2 returned to the base at Kolodziyevka along with the IM-12, commanded by *Stabs-Kapitan* Gorodetskiy.

During an evening mission on November 8, 1916, the IM-2 and the IM-12 were attacked over Buzcac by an enemy fighter equipped with a synchronized machine gun. Despite the fact they had never encountered an aircraft with such firepower, the Murometsy crews managed to shoot down this adversary.

With the onset of winter, the main base of the EVK at Pskov was disestablished and all aircraft and personnel were transferred to Vinnitsa on the Southwestern Front. *Stavka* had made this decision in preparation for an offensive in Romania planned for early 1917. The Fourth Muromets Detachment was sent from Vinnitsa to Belograd in early 1917 to support this drive.

In March, 1917, the first revolution took place and the Provisional Government took power. Although this effected the entire country, especially the army, the EVK suffered very little at first. The only major change occurred when Shidlovsky was replaced as commander by *Palkovnik* Gorshkov.

By May, 1917, Pankrat'yev's former deputy, *Stabs-Kapitan* Nikolsky, became the commander of the First Muromets Detachment. At this time the IM-2 may have been part of the Second Detachment, commanded by *Starshi Leitenant* (Naval Lieutenant) Lavrov, which was stationed about 20 miles north of Tarnopol supporting the Russian 7th Army. Records are unclear, and it was also possible the IM-2 was stationed at Vinnitsa.

An Il'ya Muromets in flight fitted with skis for winter service. The location is possibly either Pskov or Zegevold. All the aircraft of the Second Muromets Combat Detachment, stationed at Zegevold, were fitted with skis during the winter of 1915–16. The time is most likely March, 1916, after more R-BVZ-6 engines were supplied to the front, since this machine appears to be fitted with them. Strangely, the plane seems to be the old type 'Beh' and is using a radiator similar to those used on the original *Il'ya Muromets* in July, 1914. The large tent hangers housed the aircraft and a Muromets on the field is ready for flight.

Throughout the summer of 1917, the First, Second, and Third Murometsy Detachments supported the army during the Kerensky offensive along the Galician Front. On several occasions the First Combat Air Group, under the command of Kozakov, escorted the Murometsy on missions over enemy territory.

The Kerensky offensive was a failure due to the breakdown within the ranks of the army. A chaotic retreat followed, forcing all the air units to fall back. Most of the Muromets groups withdrew to Vinnitsa. All the Muromets units remained in Vinnitsa except the Third Detachment, under the command of *Palkovnik* Bashko,

The IM-2 loaded on a flat car ready for transport. The location is possibly Zegevold, December, 1915, when Pankrat'yev and his crew were transferred to the Galician Front as part of the First Muromets Combat Detachment. Pankrat'yev is on the far left, against the flat car, while his deputy commander, *Stabs-Kapitan* Nikolsky, is second from the right with the bandaged head.

The crew of the IM-2, with the fuselage on a flat car. Left to right are, *Poruchik* Smirnov, temporarily assigned; *Stabs-Kapitan* Pankrat'yev, commander; *Stabs-Kapitan* Nikolsky, deputy commander; *Poruchik* Federov, military pilot; and *Poruchik* Pavlov, military pilot and gunner. Date and location unknown, although the aircraft is most likely a type 'Veh.'

which was relocated to an area near Minsk.

In October, *Palkovnik* Pankrat'yev was given command of the EVK after Gorshkov was relieved of this position. However, there was little left to command. The Bolsheviks had taken control of the government; civil war would soon follow. Pankrat'yev was relieved of command, handing it over to *Palkovnik* Nijhevsky, who was the EVK commander when the Soviet government formally ended hostilities with the Central Powers on December 15, 1917.

With the end of the war, the Ukrainians had taken over the EVK base in Vinnitsa. They demanded that anyone remaining must pledge loyalty to the Ukrainian government.[10] Many fled from the Ukraine to join either the White forces or the Reds. Pankrat'yev was one who joined the Bolsheviks. His intention was to create an EVK for the Soviet forces.

In early 1918, Pankrat'yev contacted the Chief

---

(10) The Ukrainian Nationalists fought for their freedom against the Bolsheviks until 1923, eventually being defeated. By then there was nothing left of the EVK base at Vinnitsa.

Right: Alexei Pankrat'yev wearing his awards. Around his neck is the Order of Saint Vladimir with Swords Third Class, below center is the Order of Saint Stanislau with Swords Second Class. The Order of Saint George Fourth Class is the first medal on the left breast pocket, next is the Order of Saint Vladimir with Swords Fourth Class, followed by the Order of Saint Anne with Swords Third Class. The addition of the swords denotes the awards were earned for combat against the enemy. The Gatchina Military Flight School Badge is on the right breast pocket with the Military Pilot's Badge below.

Pankrat'yev seated on the left, with a group of officers of the *First Aviagruppa*, commanded by *Stab-Rotmistre* Kazakov. Pankrat'yev's IM-2 was one of the Murometsy escorted by the *First Aviagruppa* during the Kerensky offensive, summer 1917.

Directorate of the Workers and Peasants Military Air Fleet (*Glavozdukhoflot*) to accomplish this. After receiving permission from the Council of People's Commissars (*Sovnarkom*), a Northern Group of the Squadron of Flying Ships was established in March, 1918. The Il'ya Murometsy used by the Red Air Fleet, totaling about 15 aircraft, were taken from the Korpusnoi Aerodrome and the R-BVZ factory. Pankrat'yev was given command of the Northern Group, remaining in that capacity until the unit was dissolved six months later.

In September, 1918, a Red EVK was established with Pankrat'yev as deputy commander.[11] It is unknown how long he remained in this position, but in 1921 he was transferred to Moscow to command the Operational Air Directorate (*Aviadarm*). In 1923 he was piloting aircraft once again. While training on a Junkers F.13 he crashed and was killed. Russia had lost one of her greatest bomber commanders.

---

(11) One source states the commander of the Red EVK was *Palkovnik* Jezups Bashko, another source states it was under the command of a man named Remezin.

Marcel Pliat

Feldwebel Marcel Pliat; his awards included the Cross of Saint George, 3rd Class and the Cross of Saint George, Fourth Class. Photo: Archives, UTC.

Marcel Pliat, half French and half black, flew as a gunner-engine mechanic on Il'ya Muromets (IM) bombers. Little is known of Pliat's early life, not even how he reached Russia. The first we know of him directly is during a notable bombing mission flown by IM-10.

On April 26, 1916, IM-10, commanded by Lt. A.M. Konstenchik, received orders to destroy the large Daudzevas railway station near Friedrichstadt. The IM-10 had bombed this target several times before, so the defenses were alerted to further attempts and many anti-aircraft guns surrounded the station. On the second bombing run of this mission, IM-10 was 2400 meters above Daudzevas and had just dropped 13 bombs, when intense anti-aircraft fire severely damaged it. Shrapnel hit *Poruchik* (Lieutenant) Konstenchik, who immediately fell from his pilot's seat and accidentally pulled the control column backward. This abruptly raised the aircraft's nose, causing it to stall and then dive steeply toward the ground. During the dive the deputy commander, military pilot *Praporshik* (Ensign) Yankovius, was able to slide into the pilot's seat and level the airplane at an altitude of 1,500 meters despite damage to three of the plane's four engines.

During the attack, *Feldwebel* (Sergeant Major) Marcel Pliat had manned the machine gunner's position on the upper gun platform. Pliat saved himself during the IM-10's abrupt 900-meter fall because he had the foresight to tie his belt to the gun platform. Pliat's right arm was broken in the fall, but he eventually made his way into the cabin and commented that "he would prefer not to fall so precipitously." He then climbed out on the wing to repair a damaged engine and remained there for half an hour performing repairs.

Lt. Konstenchik, commander of the IM-10. Photo: Archives, UTC.

An unknown gunner demonstrating the upper gun position on an Il'ya Muromets. This was Pliat's station when the IM-10 was hit by anti-aircraft fire over Daudzevas.

Below: The IM-10 after its emergency landing from the mission over Daudzevas, April 26, 1916.

Other crewmen of the IM-10 had been wounded in addition to Lieutenant Konstenchik. G.N. Shneur, the artillery officer, had suffered wounds in both hands while holding his camera, which shattered after being hit by shrapnel. Lieutenant Yankovius and volunteer engine mechanic *Feldwebel* Kasatkin attended to Konstenchik's wounds during the return flight. Despite his wounds, Konstenchik flew the badly damaged IM-10 back to the Russian aerodrome near Zegevol'd, cruising over the enemy trenches at 1,000 meters along the way, and made an emergency landing that further damaged the right wings. The wounded crew members were taken to the hospital.

The bombardment of the Daudzevas railway station was successful. The last string of bombs hit a train carrying ammunition and the station was destroyed.

For this mission Konstenchik received the Order of Saint George, Fourth Class. Yankovius received the Golden Sword of Saint George, and *Feldwebel* Pliat received the Soldier's Cross of Saint George, Third Class. In addition, Kasatkin was recommended for promotion to commissioned officer. These awards were made on October 18, 1916, by Order No. 770 of the 7th Army.

Pliat had already received the Soldier's Cross of Saint George, Fourth Class, before this event. Several historians and articles have suggested it was awarded for shooting down a German fighter, but the exact date and circumstances are unknown.

Later, the first Il'ya Muromets type G-3 with a tail gun position was received by the unit. When a new aircraft was assigned to the crew of *Poruchik* (Lieutenant) Lavrov, Marcel Pliat requested a transfer to Lavrov's crew for testing the new tail gun position. Lavrov, knowing Pliat to be brave and capable, granted the request.

On a subsequent combat mission, their plane was attacked by three German fighters. The first fighter dove at the Il'ya Muromets from a 150-meter altitude advantage and opened fire. Pliat returned fire with a Vickers machine gun from the tail gun position, surprising the fighter pilot, who turned to avoid the fire. Plait later commented "tongues of flame appeared and the German fighter disappeared below, leaving a black column of smoke." The second fighter attacked immediately, but Pliat prevented it from taking good aim. When the German fighter dived, Pliat opened fire, evidently hitting the engine. The German pilot had no time to fire and dove past the Il'ya Muromets. The deputy commander, Lt. Shokalsky, had watched the second attack and reported that the fighter was going down slowly in circles, then straightened out and landed. The third fighter abandoned the attack and flew away.

This combat brought Marcel Pliat's score as a gunner

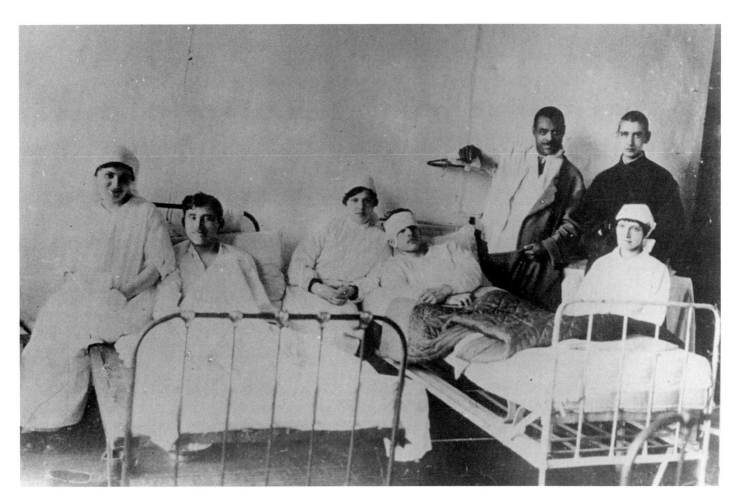

Above: Marcel Pliat standing second from right.
Below: The tail gunner's position in an Il'ya Muromets. Pliat shot down a German fighter for his second confirmed victory from such a position.

to one confirmed victory and two probables and makes him the first black aviator to shoot down an aircraft in combat.[1]

(1) Eugene Bullard, a black American flying for France, is credited with one unconfirmed and one confirmed victory in November, 1917. Bullard was the first black pilot, but the second black aviator, to shoot down an aircraft in air combat.

Boris Vasileyevich Sergievsky

Boris Sergievsky as a young infantry *Praporshik* during 1914, when he was a company commander with the 125th Kursk Infantry Regiment. By November 1917, he rose to the rank of *Stabs-Kapitan* with the 2nd Fighter Detachment and earned seven awards, which included the Order of Saint George Fourth Class, the Order of Saint Anne Third Class with swords and bow, the Order of Saint Anne Fourth Class with the inscription 'For Bravery,' the Order of Saint Stanislas Third Class with swords and bow, and for his service as an aviator the Order of Saint Vladimir Fourth Class with swords and bow, the Order of Saint Anne Second Class with swords, and the Order of Saint Stanislas Second Class with swords.

Boris Sergievsky was born in Gatchina, near Saint Petersburg, on February 20, 1888. Both of his parents' families had a tradition of military service. His maternal grandfather, had been a colonel in charge of a fortress on the Black Sea. It seems the only one not to follow family tradition was his father, who elected to be a civil engineer. In the early 1890s the Sergievsky family moved to Odessa, where his father was placed in charge of building the harbor.

Sergievsky was graduated from the Saint Paul "real school" in 1906. He excelled in his academics but managed to get into mischief; as he stated, "being first in science and last in behavior."[1] During these years he enjoyed many sporting activities, particularly athletic competition.

Sergievsky was selected from 864 applicants to enter the Polytechnic College of Kiev, scoring second highest on the entry examination. Following his father, he entered the civil engineering division of the school. During his second year some of the students organized an informal aviation club, which appealed to Sergievsky. He became acquainted with fellow student Igor Sikorsky—who as Sergievsky recalled already "had an inclination toward large planes with several engines."[2]

While still completing his studies, Sergievsky had married and had a son. In addition, he entered the army in December 1911 to fulfill his obligation of military service. After completing basic instruction he passed the officers' examination and returned to his studies.

He was assigned to the reserves in the Kiev district for the remainder of his schooling. After graduation from the Polytechnic College in 1913 he returned to the 129th Bessarabian Infantry Regiment as a *Praporshik* (Ensign), completing military training on June 12, 1913.

After this, Sergievsky attempted to transfer to the aviation service, seeing that as his only opportunity to continue flying, but in the summer of 1913 his request was turned down. He returned to the reserves in the Kiev district and was employed by the city to construct concrete bridges. He held this position until awakened in the early morning on August 7, 1914, with orders to report to the headquarters of the 125th Kursk Infantry Regiment located at Rovno.

The 125th Kursk Infantry Regiment was part of the Russian 3rd Army under the command of General Ruzski. On an early August morning, it began a march toward Galicia in Austria. Sergievsky recalled that the people from the area, perhaps many relatives, gave a departing sendoff that resembled a parade. An episode that made a lasting impression on Sergievsky was the sight of a young officer in his company having to bid farewell to his bride, whom he had married only a few days earlier. Long after the other civilians returned to the town she continued to march along side her husband. For two hours she did not let up, despite his insistence that she turn back. Eventually she collapsed from fatigue, but the soldiers could not break rank to help her. She must have felt she would never see him again, for during the first skirmish he was shot through the heart, probably the first officer of the regiment killed in action.

Sergievsky was commander of the Third Platoon of the 14th Company of his regiment. After the first day of battle he was informed he had been given command of the 14th Company, being the only officer of the company not wounded.

The 3rd Army reorganized during the next two days, since it had lost many of its officers. As Sergievsky noted,

---

[1] Sergievsky autobiographical manuscript, originally published in Russian, 1934. English translation unpublished.
[2] Ibid.

Members of the 25th Corps Detachment with one of the unit's Voisins during the summer of 1916. Sergievsky is standing fourth from the left and is displaying his Order of Saint George Fourth Class, earned for action in the infantry. It is believed that *Poruchik* Khoodjakov is seated in the forward position of the Voisin. Others unidentified.

"Three out of four Battalion Commanders were lost, and new Battalion Commanders, formerly Company Captains, had to get acquainted with their new duties."[3] The Russians advanced toward the Gnila Lipa River, where the Austrians had regrouped but again were defeated. The Russian forces took 20,000 prisoners and captured 70 guns. The Austrian 3rd Army retreated beyond Lemberg to the Wereszyca River.

During one of the final days of August, Russian 3rd Army troops were firing at an aircraft they spotted overhead without knowing its nationality. Eventually the tri-color Russian cockade was visible, but it was too late to stop the troops from shooting. The plane landed near the headquarters of Sergievsky's regiment and the pilot, *Kapitan* Petr Nesterov, abruptly marched over to the staff officers and, according to Sergievsky, "using tremendously strong language he gave a lecture to the embarrassed looking staff officers of our regiment, on what the distinction between an Austrian and a Russian plane was."[4]

On the morning of September 3, 1914, Sergievsky's battalion was ordered to march to the north toward Rava Russka, a distance of about 35 miles.

This march prevented an Austrian flanking move from the north when the Russian 3rd Army defeated the fatigued Austrian 4th Army at Rava Russka on September 5, 1914. According to Sergievsky, many thousands of prisoners were taken with very little loss of Russian personnel.[5] This loss was the beginning of an all-out retreat of the Austrian forces. By September 26, they had fallen back 100 miles and held a narrow line between the towns of Tarnow and Gorlice, extending to the Carpathian Mountains.

Sergievsky, along with his unit, marched toward the Carpathians for the next several days. When they reached the area Sergievsky recalled, "From some of the summits we were looking into Hungary."[6] In the following months Germany sent troops to reinforce the Austrian army and several offensives were launched from western Galicia and the Carpathians. All were thwarted by the Russians. Sergievsky was involved in many of these battles throughout the winter of 1914–15.

On December 9, 1914, an officer of the 164th Regiment relayed a message to Sergievsky stating that his company was needed to guard that regiment's flank from an advancing Bavarian Guard Regiment. He met the colonel of the 164th Regiment, who stated the entire army would be defeated if his unit was overrun. He merely gave Sergievsky the general direction of the advancing Germans and said, "Now do your duty as you see best."[7] When he reached the approximate area, Sergievsky

---

(3) Ibid.
(4) Ibid.
(5) Ibid.

(6) Ibid.
(7) Ibid.

noticed the German column less than a kilometer away. He positioned his company in a wooded area on the edge of a field in the pathway of the advancing enemy. The Germans were marching in column, believing they were flanking the 164th Regiment and totally unaware of what they were about to encounter. Sergievsky ordered his men not to fire until he gave the command. When the enemy was within 500 yards he gave the order to open fire and his men responded with a continuous barrage of bullets that cut through the German column from one end of the clearing to the other. The whole engagement lasted about ten minutes. When it was over, there were almost two thousand Germans lying dead in the field. Despite the victory, Sergievsky was sickened by the event. As he recalled: "In the few months of the war, my nerves were already acquainted with the horrors of war, but still on this particular day, there were actually minutes I could not stand it, and I was on the verge of a nervous breakdown."[8] The tension was broken by a message from his commander that he was recommended for a decoration for his achievement that day.

Sergievsky's unit moved south, where it was needed to help hold a strategic mountain point known simply as '384.' The location gave an excellent view for observation and both sides wanted to retain possession of it. Control of '384' changed daily, sometimes twice daily. The battalion to which Sergievsky was attached stayed in reserve, while another battalion attacked the hill and secured the location on the afternoon of December 21, 1914.

Sergievsky was awakened the next morning with instructions to attack '384' immediately, which had been retaken by an elite Hungarian regiment during the night. Shortly after this, battalion commander *Poruchik* Gladkowsky[9] entrusted the command of his unit to Sergievsky. Gladkowsky had tuberculosis and was extremely weak on this day, but he had confidence in Sergievsky's leadership. Now Sergievsky had four companies under his command and he employed three vantage points to attack the enemy at the top of '384,' holding his own company in reserve. Meanwhile, he coordinated artillery fire on the Hungarian trenches on the hill as his battalion began advancing. Upon his signal artillery fire was halted and the companies rushed the mountain top from three sides. Hand-to-hand combat ensued with bayonet and sword. Sergievsky recalled using his sword several times against the enemy, as well as his service pistol. When it was over, the remaining Hungarians, approximately 570, were taken prisoner along with 12 machine guns and four artillery pieces.

From his vantage point, Sergievsky located several Austro-Hungarian troops who had left their flank unguarded against attack. Sergievsky could not resist this temptation and ordered an advance toward this enemy position, leaving one company on '384.' He attacked the

enemy position from its flank and rear encountering little resistance. After this he ordered his men to return to hill '384.' During the night the Austrians made another attempt to retake the mountain, but were repelled by Sergievsky and his battalion.

The next day they were sent west to help in capturing another stronghold, mountain '413,' which had a steep slope facing the Russians and was well guarded by Austrian troops on both its flanks. Sergievsky realized the slopes from the enemy side were much more gradual and the mountain could be taken only if attacked from the rear. In complete silence, two of his companies crossed a shallow river by night and passed the enemy line unnoticed. At daybreak, the mountain position was easily captured. Sergievsky submitted his report to regimental Headquarters with, as he stated, "nearly 1,000 prisoners."[10]

After these exploits of bravery and command, Sergievsky was recommended for the Order of Saint George Fourth Class. A few days later, when the regiment was in reserve, Sergievsky was called to regimental headquarters. Upon arrival, his colonel read a telegram sent by the Czar bestowing this award and promoting Sergievsky to the rank of *Podporuchik* (2nd Lieutenant).[11]

On March 28, 1915, Sergievsky led an attack on an Hungarian battery in the Carpathians. Upon his unit's approach, Sergievsky remembered hearing the command for the enemy battery to fire. The next thing he knew he was on the ground with blood running down his face. He was helped to safety, but it was discovered he had a piece of shrapnel in his forehead. Later a bullet was found in his calf, but the pain from the head wound was so great he did not realize it until informed by a doctor at the field hospital. The head wound had caused temporary blindness in his left eye. Sergievsky had to be treated at a larger facility and was sent to an army hospital in the rear. Nothing could be done at this location either, and he was advised to go to the Red Cross hospital in Kiev.

The painful operation was successful. The piece of metal was removed and his optic nerve healed, restoring his sight. He remained in the hospital convalescing for six weeks before returning to duty. He was told to remain in Kiev for at least another month, but he wanted to return to the front. He joined three other officers from his regiment who had also recovered from wounds and the group returned together. When they reached the corps headquarters and asked the location of their regiment they were told, "The 125th Regiment? Well half of it is right here in this room."[12] This was an exaggeration, but was not far from the truth. The 125th Kursk Regiment started the war with 77 officers; when Sergievsky returned in May, 1915, there were only 17 still alive.

After receiving replacements, the regiment remained in reserve until the late spring, when it moved back to the front on the Gnila Lipa River. While Sergievsky was away recovering from his wounds, he did not experience the

---

(8) Ibid.

(9) Gladkowsky was diagnosed with his terminal condition before the war and was about to retire when the war broke out. He changed his decision, most likely hoping to die in battle rather than a hospital bed.

(10) Sergievsky autobiographical manuscript, 1934.

---

(11) An official listing states Segievsky's promotion to *Podporuchik* was established December 3, 1915, with seniority dating back to December 27, 1914, the time of this action.

(12) Sergievsky autobiographical manuscript, 1934.

Members of the 25th Detachment visiting with *Poruchik* Khoodjakov (laying on the cot), after he was wounded during the reconnaissance mission of an enemy rail center, June 20, 1916. Sergievsky (labeled by the number 4), accompanied Khoodjakov on this mission as observer. This crew was able to fight off two German fighters and return with valuable information, completing the mission entrusted to them.

retreat from the Carpathiansforced by an Austro-German offensive. This was the first onslaught of a drive by the Central Powers that during the spring and summer months pushed the Russians out of Poland and most of Galicia. By the end of September the flanks of the Russian armies were threatened from both north and south, and a general retreat had to be ordered.

Sergievsky remembered how disheartening the retreat was, and the effects it had on morale. He commented, "It was the first retreat since the beginning of the war that I personally experienced and it was a very unpleasant feeling. It was rather depressing on the mood and morale of everyone in the army. The strategic reasons forcing the retreat were explained to us, of course; still every step of the conquered soil that was actually bought at such a dear cost, to give it up and retreat night after night, mile after mile, without a single shot, without the slightest pursuit from the enemy, was very disappointing and very depressing."[13]

There was little activity after the retreat ended. The enemy halted to avoid over-extension of supply lines and

(13) Ibid.

to entrench for the winter. Fighting resumed in December, after frost made roads passable, but only on a small scale.

During this period Sergievsky severely injured his right ankle during a night raid on an enemy position and was incapacitated for six weeks, but remained on light duty at regimental headquarters. It was at this time that an order came through asking for volunteers to join the expanding aviation service, and Sergievsky acted upon it immediately. He had seen ground operations degenerate into the stagnation of trench warfare, and as a newly appointed *Poruchik* (Lieutenant) looked forward to being involved with aviation again. He was selected for pilot training, but was needed to serve at the front without delay. On March 15, 1916, he was sent to the 25th Corps Detachment as an officer observer and was also the squadron Adjutant for his assignment with the unit.

The 25th Detachment was equipped with Voisin LA two-seat pusher aircraft and based in the vicinity of the Pripet marshes under the command of the 3rd Army. Its main roles were reconnaissance of the enemy rear areas and artillery spotting. Sergievsky was given several orientation flights, then was ready for action. From the

Sergievsky, kneeling third from right, accompanied by members of the 2nd Fighter Detachment and nurses of the field hospital located nearby Radzivilov, where the unit was stationed. The pilots appear to be taking advantage of a moment of relaxation during the summer of 1917, a rare occasion during a time of intense enemy aerial activity.

end of April until mid-July 1916 he performed 15 missions, recording more than 26 hours in the air.

On June 6, 1916, Sergievsky, together with *Esaul* (Cossack Captain) Shevyrev, made a reconnaissance flight of more than four hours. One of his adventurous missions took place on June 20, in which he was accompanied by *Poruchik* Khoodjakov. The assignment required flying 60 miles behind the German lines to observe a rail center,[14] noting the number and type of trains, along with their intended direction determined by the way each was parked. All trains spotted en route to this station also were to be recorded, along with the direction of each.

The detachment commander would not choose a crew to fulfill this duty. He suggested drawing lots, which was done. Khoodjakov was selected as pilot and asked Sergievsky if he would undertake the mission with him. Sergievsky agreed, dispensing with the need to draw lots for an observer. Soon after the pair took off for the three-hour flight in their Voisin.

After crossing the lines they were attacked by an enemy two-seater, but Sergievsky fought off the adversary with his machine gun. The crew gathered the necessary information and started for home. On the return trip two German fighters opened fire on the Russian plane. As Sergievsky recalled, "I actually saw the covering of the wings ripped in many places by tracer bullets. The cockpit was also shot through in many places, with splinters of wood flying everywhere. I was shooting as best I could and Khoodjakov kept flying in a straight line east, not having a chance in the slow and clumsy Voisin to give a real fight.

"All of a sudden I saw Khoodjakov slump down on the stick and our plane started to fall out of control. I ceased all my shooting and reached over him to grab the controls, attempting to straighten out the plane when at the last moment he came to. The femurs of both legs were shot through completely. His right foot was shattered and he could not operate the rudder. From my position behind him, I could only partly help him operate the stick. Khoodjakov told me he would attempt to make a landing before he lost too much blood, if we could make it within a very few minutes.

"Giving full throttle to the engine and at the same time pushing the plane down, we considerably increased its speed and crossed the lines at an altitude of only a few hundred feet. All the ground fire, artillery and infantry, of the Germans in this sector was concentrated on us. Fortunately, the pilot did not suffer any additional wounds and I escaped unhurt.

"Just behind our lines I saw hospital tents with the Red Cross on top of them. Indicating them to Khoodjakov, I asked him if he could attempt to land on the little lawn in front of the tents. He did a beautiful landing, but fainted immediately after and was taken out of the cockpit unconscious."[15]

Khoodjakov was rushed into one of the tents and operated on, saving his injured leg from amputation. Sergievsky called headquarters with the information along with his location and circumstances. While waiting, he counted at least 65 bullet holes in the wings and cockpit of the Voisin. It may have been slow, but it was able to withstand a great deal of punishment.

It is believed the detachment was transferred south in the beginning of August to assist in fighting in the area opposite Lemberg. This is not confirmed, but Sergievsky has told an unusual story of what happened to *Esaul* Shevyrev during the flight to the new airfield.

Shevyrev was fearless in battle and an excellent pilot. The only drawback to his flying talent was his inability to know his location or navigate his course. During the relocation flight, the commander ordered the aircraft to fly in intervals, so as not to attract attention from the enemy. He also requested that one of the more experienced observers accompany Shevyrev, but Shevyrev refused, taking his faithful Cossack mechanic as he did on most flights.

All planes arrived safely at the new location—except the Voisin of Shevyrev. Two days later a German plane dropped a note stating Shevyrev had landed on an enemy field, which happened to be opposite the detachment's new location. He had shut off the engine and got out of the plane before he realized he was at the wrong field. Not being able to re-start the machine, Shevyrev fired his machine gun at the enemy troops approaching and even attempted to burn his plane. In their note, the Germans praised his courage and also stated he was in fine condition in a prison camp.

Sergievsky met Shevyrev in late 1918, when he was told of how a German pilot tried to fly Shevyrev's Voisin. Not knowing the trick to taking off with the aircraft, due

(14) Ibid.

(15) Ibid.

French-built Nieuport 21, serial number 2176, after a landing mishap. The pilot is unknown, but may be Sergievsky. He was known to have used this aircraft on at least one mission.

to its unusual undercarriage arrangement, the German forced the weight of the machine onto the front wheels. They collapsed, the plane dug into the ground, and the engine crushed the pilot and killed him instantly.

After serving throughout the Brusilov offensive in the summer of 1916 and into early autumn, Sergievsky was sent to flight school. He left the 25th Detachment on November 6, arriving at the Sevastopol Aviation School on November 15. He passed all the necessary training courses and in April, 1917, after receiving recognition as a military aviator, was assigned to the 2nd Fighter Detachment on June 1, 1917. It was located at Radzivilov, near Brody. The large estate offered comfortable accommodations, fully furnished. Small parties were held on occasion. Due to the convenient location, many of the officers' wives were guests, staying for several weeks at a time. Sergievsky's wife visited for two months during that summer.

When Sergievsky arrived he expected to find *Kapitan* Kruten. However, Kruten was a location near Tarnopol, where he based his command of the 2nd *Aviagruppa* (2nd Fighter Group), which included the 2nd Detachment. Sergievsky had the opportunity to meet Kruten and described him as, "a young man, extremely energetic, conscientious, and one of the best pilots I ever met in my life."[16] Sergievsky felt very fortunate to be granted assignment to this unit because of its reputation, earned mostly by Kruten's contributions.

The squadron commander was *Stabs-Kapitan* Baftalovsky, a most capable leader, with one victory scored on November 25, 1916. Baftalovsky paired himself with Sergievsky during his first combat flights to orient him. Baftalovsky attempted to give his pilots a chance of survival in the air along a sector where the level of activity was so intense. Daily flying duties seemed endless and the members of the squadron were always on alert for approaching enemy reconnaissance planes.

The squadron consisted of nine aviators, including one observer, and ten airplanes of six different types. There were five Nieuport models, of which two were reconnaissance versions, and one Morane-Saulnier. Five of the Nieuports were the type 21, and Sergievsky flew this type on many occasions.

Losses in the squadron were heavy and within the next two weeks many replacements arrived. By that time Sergievsky was already considered a veteran, having completed 13 combat patrols each averaging nearly an hour of flying time. He had began to develop his own method of attacking two-seat aircraft, which allowed a close-range shot without making an easy target of himself. He approached from head on at a slightly higher altitude. He would speed by the enemy and complete the maneuver by turning back in the direction of the hostile plane. The gunner of the machine almost always would be aiming forward, with no time to turn his gun before Sergievsky fired an initial burst. When the enemy gunner had repositioned his gun, Sergievsky then dropped below the tail of his foe to shoot once again from a clear position.

Sergievsky actually preferred to engage fighter aircraft to avoid the rear gun of two-seat aircraft. He recalled one such encounter against a German Roland D.II in an intense and lengthy battle. This may have been the combat of June 18, 1917, when Sergievsky, flying Nieuport 21, serial number 757, was driving away an enemy observation plane when attacked by its escorting fighter. As Sergievsky described the event; "His plane was faster, but my fighter could gain altitude more quickly. As we met face to face and exchanged several bursts of fire, we both decided to try for altitude advantage. Flying side by side, we were so close I could see his face and his little mustache. Being faster, the German was afraid that if he went ahead of me I would have a better chance of shooting at him from behind. He began to zigzag in order not to run too far ahead of me. Since I could not overtake him, my objective was to gain the higher altitude.

"When I finally got a few feet above him I was able to begin my attack. I fired several bursts at close range, but had to turn away to avoid a collision. I found myself below the German and it was his turn to attack. We were maneuvering in this way, each having an opportunity to fire just a few shots at the other and then attempting to

(16) Ibid.

Sergievsky, with his Dux-built Nieuport 23, while serving as temporary Detachment Commander from June 19, 1917 to September 2, 1917, when *Stabs-Kapitan* (Staff Captain) Baftalovsky was recovering from his wounds. He flew Nieuport 21s and 23s almost exclusively and developed some of his own aerial tactics during this time.

gain the advantage of altitude. Such a competition lasted for almost half an hour.

"Finally, the opportunity came for me to climb considerably higher. Seeing that he could not turn the situation to his advantage, the German headed towards his own lines to escape. That was my best opportunity. With full engine running I dove after him and he in turn started to dive to get away. Being above him I could afford to dive at a steeper angle, but he could not continue diving and still reach his own lines.

"This time I was able to empty at least a hundred cartridges from my machine gun when his engine gave out a cloud of smoke. I realized the fight was over and I should not try to kill him. It was quite sufficient for me to know that the plane was damaged or destroyed and he was going to be forced to land. It was always a rather unpleasant thought to me if I had to kill or wound anyone in aerial fighting. The main objective was to bring the plane down, if possible behind our lines so we could use it.

"His engine had stopped and he was gliding in a westerly direction. I realized he might be able to reach his own lines and reluctantly resumed firing at him. By maneuvering around the Roland, I was able to force him to change course and lower the angle of his decent. He landed in front of our first defense line of barbed wire and I turned around and flew immediately to our aerodrome, where I requisitioned an automobile and returned with several of my friends to the place at the front where I left the enemy plane."[17][18]

When Sergievsky arrived at the front he was told by those in the trenches who witnessed the battle that the enemy pilot had escaped to his own lines on foot. He had to shed his heavy flight clothing to outrun the Russian soldiers. They had to give up the chase after being fired upon, but told an amusing story about the German aviator. When he approached his own trenches, he was wearing only his socks, having taken off his entire flying suit and heavy boots to gain speed. The enemy plane was shelled by German artillery so as not to fall into Russian hands; thus Sergievsky reported his only trophies from his first victory were the German aviator's helmet, flying coat, and uniform the soldiers had recovered.

The next day *Stabs-Kapitan* Baftalovsky was seriously wounded during a combat with an enemy reconnaissance plane. He lost a lot of blood, but was somehow able to retain consciousness long enough to cross into friendly territory, where he was pulled from his overturned aircraft and taken to a field hospital. Baftalovsky and his pilots knew he would be recovering from his wounds for a

(17) Ibid.
(18) An official communiqué dated June 18, 1917, states Sergievsky fought two aircraft in the vicinity of Brody, an enemy two-seater and a fighter, which he forced to withdraw from Russian territory after several repeated attacks. It has been reported a German two-seat aircraft from *Feldflieger Abteilung* 24 went down over enemy lines, which may have been the other machine Sergievsky attacked, but this is unconfirmed. The outcome of the battle against the Roland fighter, which Sergievsky has described as his first victory, is also questionable.

long period. He appointed Sergievsky as the temporary squadron commander until he could resume his duties.

With Baftalovsky away, Sergievsky was the senior officer and the most experienced pilot in the 2nd Fighter Detachment. It became his job to lead the squadron throughout the Kerensky offensive, when the need for aerial activity was greatly increased. At the beginning of July the unit consisted of only five aviators. One of the most recent to join the unit was *Praporshik* Chudnovsky, who reported to the squadron directly from aviation school. As Sergievsky described him, "He was just twenty years old and was probably more of a child than even his age. He was most eager to take part in aerial fighting, which he thought was the most thrilling and most interesting thing in the world."[19]

Sergievsky instructed Chudnovsky to fly with him and not to engage in battle during his first flights, but only observe and learn fighting tactics. Sergievsky was protecting his new pilots just as Baftalovsky had protected him during his first days as a fledgling fighter pilot, not more than a month ago. However, Chudnovsky was too energetic and impatient. Whenever enemy planes were seen he could not wait to dive into the melee.

Sergievsky taught him the maneuver he created for attacking an enemy plane. Chudnovsky always completed the wingover turn in a position too close, nearly colliding. Sergievsky warned him of this repeatedly, but to no avail. On September 1, 1917, Chudnovsky attempted the wingover maneuver too near a German two-seater and crashed into it, cutting the fuselage in two. The wings were torn from his plane and together the aviators of both aircraft fell from 14,000 feet over German occupied territory.

A few days later, a German aircraft approached dropping a package containing Chudnovsky's belongings. Besides his wallet and family photographs, the Germans included details of his funeral. In return, they requested knowledge of two German aviators lost on approximately the same date. Instructions were given as to the time the message should be delivered. Sergievsky flew the mission himself, informing the Germans of receiving the Chudnovsky package and the fact their aviators in question were safe and had become prisoners. It is true the Germans did not fire upon Sergievsky, nor did they attempt to pursue his aircraft after it dropped the bundle.

During the summer of 1917 Sergievsky created his own method of attacking enemy observation balloons. Due to the heavy ground fire defending them, he used a deceptive tactic. Starting at 16,000 feet, he allowed the enemy anti-aircraft batteries to fire at him until one shell burst close to his aircraft. He pretended to be hit, sending his machine into a spin. The shooting stopped when the gunners believed Sergievsky's plane was damaged, allowing him to close in on the balloon. He then pulled

Praporshik (Ensign) Chudnovsky, the eager 20 year old fighter pilot. Sergievsky tried desperately to give him a chance of survival by teaching him some maneuvers and attempting to instill in him a sense of patience. Unfortunately, in his enthusiasm Chudnovsky collided with a German aircraft on September 1, 1917, and the crews of both planes perished.

out of the dive, attacked the balloon from a short distance, and escaped to the Russian lines at tree-top level.[20]

With the beginning of September came the return of *Stabs-Kapitan* Baftalovsky, who resumed his command, relieving Sergievsky of that most trying duty. Shortly after this Sergievsky was granted a two-week leave. The first place he went was Smolensk, attempting to get some alcohol stored at the supply depot. Consumption of alcoholic beverages had been forbidden since the beginning of the war, but homemade vodka was produced by anyone who could get the ingredients.

Sergievsky waited in a room to make his request to the commander of the depot. Several other officers, all of much higher rank, were waiting for the same reason. The commander asked each individual what the alcohol was for and all produced a detailed report why it was

---

(19) Sergievsky autobiographical manuscript, 1934.
(20) Sergievsky claimed to have shot down three enemy balloons using this method. There is however, no official documentation confirming these statements. Therefore, the victories mentioned above can only be considered as probables at best.

Sergievsky, third from left, while working as a test pilot for Sikorsky Aircraft Company, in Long Island, New York during 1925. Sergievsky tested all the S-series aircraft built during 1924–26. The aircraft is the S-29.

necessary for his unit. One lieutenant colonel, in charge of a veterinarian hospital, attempted to requisition 100 quarts. The commander, knowing very well the intent of this request, declared, "You must be thinking of washing your horses in alcohol, get out!" When Sergievsky approached he was greeted with the following comment, "I suppose you are going to tell me that you need alcohol for washing plane engines?" Sergievsky, realizing he had no reply except the truth, said, "Your excellency, we need the alcohol for making vodka." The commander turned to the others and said, "Now this brave young man is the only one among you who told me the truth. I am going to give him the alcohol!"[21]

Sergievsky returned from his leave to find new, inexperienced pilots had arrived to replace more losses. Besides the problems in the squadron, the front lines were beginning to collapse. Revolutionary propaganda was affecting the troops. It was only a matter of time before hostilities with the Central Powers ended and began internally.

On October 26, 1917, Sergievsky was promoted to *Stabs-Kapitan*, with seniority dating back to June 1, 1916. Other than this, cheerful moments were few. Flying was at a minimum due to supply shortages. Sergievsky completed only nine missions in the last two months of the war. One final, glorious battle for the 2nd Fighter Detachment took place on December 2, when Sergievsky and two of his comrades shot down an unsuspecting Brandenburg C.I over Smolno. It was his last victory.

On December 15, 1917, an armistice between the new Soviet government and the Central Powers was signed, ending the war for Russia. Baftalovsky's final report on Sergievsky listed his combat totals during his service with the 2nd Fighter Detachment as 98 missions with more than 100 hours of flight time. Sergievsky left the unit and returned home to Kiev to offer his services to the White army.

Together with some of his fellow officers and aviators, he was able to commandeer some of the aircraft from his old unit, flying patrols against the Bolsheviks. This continued throughout 1918, until the threat of being overrun forced his decision to leave Kiev. He and his wife fled the city, leaving behind Sergievsky's mother and son. They believed this to be the best decision, since they had no idea the dangers they would encounter in their travels. They made their way to Berlin, where Sergievsky worked for the Inter-Allied Commission for Re-evacuation of Prisoners of War, a position obtained through a White Russian representative. From there they left for England,

(21) Sergievsky autobiographical manuscript, 1934.

where he joined the RAF, serving as an instructor at the Netheravon Flying School.

In October, 1919, the White Russian army had a great need for aviators. Upon hearing this, Sergievsky and his wife returned to Russia. He was assigned as squadron leader of a unit located in Estonia, flying an R.E.8. When Estonia declared independence, its forces disarmed the Russians and confiscated the aircraft. The Sergievskys were left to fend for themselves until finally the opportunity arose to travel to Poland.

They arrived in Warsaw in 1920 and Sergievsky began organizing the air force of the White Russian 3rd Army. The Polish were also fighting the Bolsheviks and considered the White army their ally. During this period Sergievsky flew an ex-German Halberstadt two-seater, and on one occasion chauffeured the general of the 3rd Army to the front lines.

The front collapsed in late 1920, when the Poles agreed upon an armistice with the Bolsheviks. Without the Poles, the White forces could not hold against the Soviets. They had to retreat back into Poland. When they did, the Poles disarmed their former ally.

The Sergievskys were once again stranded in a foreign country, waiting for their chance to return to Russia. While in Poland, Sergievsky worked at an American YMCA helping ex-prisoners of war. By 1923, he realized there was little chance of ever returning to Russia. He decided to go to America and obtained passage for himself and his wife to New York.

His first job was as a manual laborer on the Holland tunnel, but he soon became re-acquainted with Igor Sikorsky, who was building his S-series airplanes on Long Island. For the next few years Sergievsky tested all the aircraft built there. In 1926 he flew a S-32 for the Andean National Corporation in South America. That company was building an oil pipeline and it was Sergievsky's job to fly in supplies and personnel and keep the lines of communication open.

During this time he finally established contact with his mother and son after they arrived in 1927, after almost ten years of separation. Sergievsky learned of the death of both his brothers at the hands of the Bolsheviks. He then returned to New York, once again test-piloting for Sikorsky while he acquired permission to have his mother and son join him in the United States.

In 1932 Sergievsky was employed as a pilot for the Johnson expedition, traveling throughout Africa with the two planes purchased from Sikorsky Aircraft, an S-38 and an S-39. When he returned in 1933 he flew an S-38 at the World's Fair in Chicago, giving sightseeing tours. One passenger was a 95-year-old man wearing a Confederate uniform who said he had traveled by every way possible except in an airplane. Sergievsky did not disappoint him.

During the 1930s Sergievsky met several well-known persons while piloting S-series aircraft. He flew for the Prince of Wales on a South American tour, delivered a plane to Hollywood for Howard Hughes, and flew with

Stabs-Kapitan Sergievsky in full dress uniform adorned with all his awards and decorations, including his RAF pilot wings earned after the war while serving with Britain in 1919.

Charles Lindbergh on occasion. He also tested the Clipper planes and established many world records for seaplanes and amphibians while working for Sikorsky as a test pilot.

From 1938 to 1944 Sergievsky was the vice president and test pilot of the Helicopter Corporation of America. In 1944 he served as a member of the Office of Strategic Services. After World War II he concentrated on an air charter business from New York City, flying a ten-passenger Grumman Mallard. He also was involved in many Russian-American organizations.

He died in November 1971, at age 83. His contributions to the growth of American aviation were unbounded and his service to his native land during World War I knew no limits.

He had flown for 53 years and recorded more than 9400 hours aloft both as a military and a civilian aviator. He remained a strong-willed and determined man throughout his life, mastering all obstacles. He loved people and was never reluctant to engage in conversation. He lived life his way, always in the present and never holding back anything, enjoying all that life had to give. Truly, he was an unforgettable individual.

Alexander Nikolaevich Sveshnikov

Alexander Sveshnikov seated in his Morane-Saulnier H when with the 7th Corps Air Detachment, possibly during mid-1915. The Madsen light machine gun has an unusual mount to position it at an angle to fire over the propeller arc. His *pogoni* (shoulderboard) is not completely visible, but does indicate NCO rank.

Alexander Nikolaevich Sveshnikov was born December 29, 1887, in the ancient city of Kiev in the Ukraine. His father was a prosperous entrepreneur who could afford to provide his son with a good education. He received lessons at a private school and attended a Paris university. He practiced the Russian Orthodox faith and was married before he entered military life.

Sveshnikov graduated from college in France in 1912 and received flight training before returning to Kiev later that year. In 1913 and 1914 he successfully designed, built, and flew three aircraft. The first two were single-seat monoplanes powered by a 40hp Anzani engine. Sveshnikov flew these aircraft many times, but the Sveshnikov No.3 was the most successful. Equipped with a 75hp engine, it was capable of 65mph.

When the war began Sveshnikov discontinued his design work and volunteered for service with the 3rd Air Company.[1] Due to his experience, he was immediately employed as a pilot. He officially entered that unit on October 14, 1914, as a *Nijnichin* (Private) of the Engineer Corps.

On December 30, he received his first award, the Saint George Medal Fourth Class for meritorious service. On January 4, 1915, Sveshnikov was transferred to the 7th Corps Air Detachment of the 6th Air Company. Here he served with distinction, progressing in rank at a rapid pace. He became a *Gefreiter* (Lance-Corporal) on April 21, and a *Starski Unteroffizier* (Sergeant) only two days later. On May 3, 1915, he was awarded the Soldier's Cross of Saint George, Fourth Class, for enlisted men. By the end of June Sveshnikov had earned two more awards of the Saint George Cross, the Third and Second Classes. On June 30, 1915, He was commissioned a *Praporshik* (Ensign), passing over several NCO ranks.

Although the reasons for these awards are unknown, it can be assumed his performance was outstanding. It was possible they were given for aerial reconnaissance during the Galician campaigns in the early months of the war, when the Austro-Hungarian advance was forcing the Russian army out of the Carpathian Mountains back to the Ukraine.

After serving at the front for more than a year, he received the title of Military Pilot on October 18. On December 4, 1915, Sveshnikov was given his first award as an officer, when he was given the Order of Saint Vladimir Fourth Class with Swords and Bow.

With the new year, Sveshnikov remained with the 7th Corps Air Detachment flying Morane-Saulnier H mid-wing monoplanes. In March, he received a new aircraft, a Morane-Saulnier L parasol high-wing monoplane built by Dux. This machine was an improvement over the Morane-Saulnier H and offered better visibility. He was rewarded again for distinction in battle with the Order of Saint Stanislas Third Class with Swords and Bow, on March 5, 1916.

---

[1] The 3rd Air Company was one of the first units assembled. It was stationed in Kiev and was led by the early pioneer flyer Petr Nesterov.

Sveshnikov's victory of September 22, 1917, for which he was awarded the Order of Saint George Fourth Class. The machine is a Roland D.IIa powered by a 180hp Argus engine. The aircraft landed in no-man's-land near the village of Poznanka Gnila, where it was salvaged by Russian troops.

On April 5, 1916, Sveshnikov was promoted to *Podporuchik* (Second Lieutenant) and a month later he was granted the Order of Saint Anne Third Class with Swords and Bow. He flew throughout the summer months, participating in the Brusilov offensive. It is believed the 7th Corps Air Detachment was under the command of the Russian 11th Army in the Tarnopol region.

In November, 1916, he left the 7th Detachment and went to France with several other aviators to study French aerial combat tactics and to impart them to fellow pilots upon their return. This group was attached to the famous '*Cigognes*' of *escadrille* Spa.3, learning important combat maneuvers first hand.

Sveshnikov returned to his former detachment in March, 1917, and was given command of the unit. In April the squadron's complement included Nieuport 12 two-seat aircraft that replaced the Morane-Saulniers. Sveshnikov flew this type throughout the spring and early summer until the first real fighter planes arrived.

On June 23, 1917, he received a Nieuport 23, a swift single-seater with a synchronized Vickers machine gun. With this aircraft he began to use his knowledge of aerial maneuvers learned in France. It was about this time that Sveshnikov has been reported as taking command of the Second Combat Air Group after *Kapitan* Kruten's death. He appeared to be a logical choice since the 7th Corps Detachment was attached to this unit and he had been in France with Kruten during the previous winter. It has not been confirmed if he actually held this position. At some point during the summer he was promoted to *Poruchik* (Lieutenant).

The Kerensky offensive began July 1, 1917, with the Russian 7th and 11th Armies attacking in Galicia in an attempt to reach Lemberg. The advance was halted and an Austro-German counter-offensive began by mid-July. By the end of the month the Russians had lost the last remaining territory in Galicia and Bukowina, which they had occupied before the operation began.

The 7th Corps Detachment, along with the entire Second Combat Air Group, were attached to the 11th Army during and after the retreat. Aerial activity became more intense in August after the enemy had increased its patrols. Sveshnikov was involved in a series of combats in the weeks to come.

On August 14, 1917, he forced an enemy aircraft to land near the village of Kozuvka inside Austrian-held territory. On the 22nd, while flying over Skalat, he sent a two-seater crashing into no-man's-land. A report stated that one of the enemy crew was seen running for his lines, the other was killed, and the plane was destroyed. It was Sveshnikov's first victory.

On September 6, 1917, Sveshnikov flew two patrols and was involved in three battles. At 11AM he attacked a two-seat machine, forcing it to descend quickly. He was unable to continue his pursuit when two enemy fighters approached and fired at him. He managed to escape and return to his airfield without harm. At 6PM he fought again, driving a hostile plane toward its lines.

On September 21, Sveshnikov received another new fighter. This was the powerful French Spad 7, equipped with a 150hp Hispano-Suiza engine. At mid-day he found the opportunity to use it. He located an enemy observation machine at an altitude of 9750 feet. A raging fight ensued that continued down to under 1000 feet. Suddenly, he noticed the enemy aircraft made a sharp turn. The rival crew was attempting to trick Sveshnikov into believing they were going down out of control. They straightened out just above the ground. Sveshnikov spotted this and continued his attack. The enemy escaped when Sveshnikov's machine gun jammed, and crossed the lines over Sorotsko.

The next morning Sveshnikov was once again patrolling the region of Skalat when he spotted a German fighter. He attacked it at 13,000 feet and again at 10,300 feet, where he caused much damage to his adversary. The aircraft fell to below 1500 feet before it straightened out. Sveshnikov, not to be fooled a second time, stayed right on its tail and attacked twice more until the enemy machine landed between the trenches near Poznanka Gnila. Sveshnikov's opponent quickly escaped to his own

Sveshnikov seated in his trophy. A long scar in the plywood fuselage from a bullet can be seen through the Iron Cross Insignia.

lines, but the fighter was salvaged by Russian troops in the vicinity. The battle had lasted only 15 minutes.

Sveshnikov's trophy was a Roland D.IIa, a German fighter with a 180hp Argus engine. It had been hit in the oil and fuel tanks as well as several other places in the fuselage. For this victory,[2] Sveshnikov was awarded the coveted Order of Saint George Fourth Class for bravery in battle.

Four days later, on September 26, he attacked an enemy observation balloon west of Brody. After his first pass, the balloon deflated and fell abruptly. In the official report it was described as "obviously shot down."

It was about this time that Sveshnikov was selected as a candidate to head a newly-proposed school of air combat to be established at Evpatorija. Although another was accepted, he was certainly qualified for the position. Shortly after this, it was reported, he was given a promotion to the rank of *Stabs-Kapitan* (Staff-Captain), but this has not been confirmed.

By the end of 1917, hostilities had all but ceased between the Central Powers and the Soviet government, and the Civil War in Russia was beginning. It is not known where Sveshnikov was during this period, but by June, 1918, he had made his way to Moscow. From Moscow he went to Murmansk to fight the Red Army. The journey was difficult, but he eventually arrived at his destination, possibly with the help of French Lieutenant Georges Lachmann. Lachmann had remained in Moscow, helping several Russian pilots loyal to the White forces escape Bolshevik capture. They included Alexander Kazakov.

Upon arrival in Murmansk, Sveshnikov found the area occupied by British military personnel organizing the Russian refugees. Under the command of Colonel Maund, head of the Allied aviation corps, the First Slavo-British Air Detachment was formed, with Kozakov commanding. Sveshnikov became a member of this unit and was commissioned a lieutenant by the British. He went to the front with this unit in August, reaching Obozerskaja, approximately 80 miles south of Arkhangel.

By autumn the detachment relocated to Bereznjaki, not far from its original area. Much of the surrounding terrain in this region was forest. Even the landing fields were rough, and a forced landing was every pilot's nightmare.

On December 24, 1918, Sveshnikov's aircraft developed engine trouble near Obozerskaja while he was on a reconnaissance flight and he had to set the machine down in a wooded area. He and his British observer survived the crash, but Sveshnikov was pinned under the wreckage of the airplane. The observer, who was unhurt, could not remove the debris alone and went for help to the nearby village only five miles away. It took him almost half a day to return. When help arrived, it was too late; Sveshnikov had died of hypothermia, his frozen body still trapped under the fuselage.

---

(2) This victory may not be Sveshnikov's second, but rather his first. The report of August 22 on the two-seat aircraft he shot down resembles the report of September 22, when he downed the Roland, to a great extent. It appears too much of a coincidence to be different victories and the August report is believed to be dated wrongly, with the aircraft wrongly identified as two-seat machine.

Olgerts Teteris

The ever-smiling Olgerts Teteris as a non-commissioned officer, while stationed at Pskov during July 1915. Although it is not confirmed, he is believed to have earned all four classes of the Saint George Cross for NCOs. Eventually he was commissioned with the rank of *Praporshik* (Ensign). The aircraft is a Nieuport IV monoplane he piloted while at Pskov.

Olgerts Teteris was born in the late nineteenth century in Mitau, Latvia, an important rail center about 25 miles south of Riga. He attended the Riga Polytechnic College, where he studied chemistry. Later he was employed in the office of the Education Bureau for the District of Riga.

Teteris volunteered for the air service when the war began. He was accepted immediately and sent to the Sevastopol Military Aviation School with the rank of *Nijnichin* (Private). He passed the course of instruction in July, 1915, flying Farman aircraft. Shortly thereafter, he was transferred north, to Pskov, where he was assigned to the 13th Corps Detachment and given further flight instruction on Nieuport monoplanes. These machines were obsolete, but a few remained in frontline service and for training. They were considered difficult to fly, but Teteris handled this type without mishap.

While Teteris was stationed in Pskov he met a fellow Latvian by the name of Celms. Celms, an aircraft technician, recalled one of the flights made by Teteris. Celms had gone to the Pskov air base to become acquainted with new aircraft engines and stores recently received from France. While studying some of these inside a hangar, he heard an enlisted man shout, "Come and look, someone else wants to go to Peter!" What the mechanic meant was fact that someone was going to fly a Nieuport monoplane which was emitting a smoke cloud from under its cowl as it sat on the flight line. There had been many accidents involving the little Nieuports and almost everyone felt they were too dangerous to fly. Everyone except Teteris.

The flight lasted not more than ten minutes, but it seemed endless to those on the ground. Teteris made a series of steep turns at low altitude, provoking one of the soldiers to cry out, "Call for the chaplain." However, Teteris handled the plane flawlessly and made a precise dead-stick landing. As Celms reported, "The Russians cheered so enthusiastically; as if Teteris had just flown over the ocean."[1]

Teteris walked back to the hangar, wiping the oil from his face, and Celms introduced himself. The two countrymen greeted each other and conversed for a long time, as if they had been friends forever. They discussed many subjects not related to the war, especially their intentions after it was over. Celms asked Teteris why he chose to fly the dangerous machine. Teteris replied, "to break in the disobedient airplane." Then, Teteris with a jovial laugh, said to Celms, "Would you like to fly? Come with me and I will show you how to handle this crazy machine."[2] Celms was hesitant. Teteris, with a smile, nodded, realizing Celms' reluctance.

Shortly after this Teteris went to the front with his squadron. The unit assisted the Russian armies during the great retreat in the summer of 1915. Teteris was frequently in the air keeping headquarters aware of enemy troop movements. Finally, in September, the army made a stand along the Dvina River. The 13th Detachment was stationed along the river, not far from Dvinsk. Teteris continued flying, bombing enemy locations and spotting for artillery, and by autumn he had been decorated for his bravery and service.[3]

During the winter of 1915–16 Celms' unit was transferred to the Dvinsk area near the 13th Corps. He looked forward to visiting Teteris again. The two men had much in common and enjoyed talking about their families and life in Riga. Teteris was always cheerful and enjoyed

(1) R. Celms, *The Cheerful Flyer, Olgerts Teteris,* Latvia. Magazine article, actual publication data and date unknown.
(2) Ibid.
(3) According to Celms, Teteris had earned two classes of the Saint George Cross by the end of 1915; however, this is not confirmed.

Praporshik Olgerts Teteris displaying his pilot's badge and one NCO award of the Cross of Saint George (wearing his cap tipped to his right and seated behind the man holding the tray), surrounded by his fellow members of the 13th Corps Detachment with one of the unit's Voisins. It appears the tray is filled with pastries and may be the occasion of Teteris' commission on December 2, 1916. On some of the NCOs' *pogoni* (shoulderboards), the roman numeral XIII can be seen, designating the 13th Detachment. Almost all are NCOs or enlisted men, with whom Teteris probably had greater friendships than he did with officers.

conversation. Once, however, his smile vanished when Celms described a flight in December, 1915.

Celms was a gunner accompanying his unit commander on a bomb run over the Ilukste railroad station. While returning they encountered clouds. "Suddenly, something black and roaring dashed over our machine like a black meteor," Celms said. Teteris responded, "What luck, that we did not collide." Teteris also was on his way to bomb the Ilukste station that day. Flying through the clouds to remain undetected, he came very near a collision with his friend. Fortunately, other than a brief scare, there was no damage and Teteris completed his mission.

In the spring of 1916, the 13th Detachment received Voisin pushers for reconnaissance and bombing. This machine equipped many corps units and became the standard mount throughout 1916. Teteris was sent to Sevastopol for training on the Voisin. He completed the course in three weeks and returned to the 13th Detachment before the end of May.

During the summer of 1916 Teteris had earned a notable reputation along the Northern Front and had received a promotion to senior non-commissioned officer.[4] He became known as the "shrapnel catcher" for his bold piloting and disregard for enemy anti-aircraft fire.[5] He avoided the bursts by simply flying into the smoke cloud after it went off, reasoning that no two anti-aircraft shells would explode at the same location. Even so, observers were very nervous when they had to fly with Teteris.

On August 17, 1916, Teteris was on an evening patrol with *Poruchik* (Lieutenant) Kuskov as observer. On their way to bomb an enemy rail center they encountered a hostile Fokker attacking a Morane Parasol flown by *Podporuchik* (2nd Lieutenant) Turunolayevsky of the 17th Corps Detachment. Teteris and Kuskov immediately dived on the Fokker with Kuskov firing his machine gun. The German plane turned over and went spinning into the ground. It was Teteris' first victory. For this achievement he was awarded the Soldier's Cross of Saint George Second class.[6]

In September, the general commanding the nearby army corps wished to observe the area around Dvietes

---

(4) Teteris' rank is listed only in this manner. An actual rank is not given and can be presumed as being possibly *Feldwebel* (Sergeant Major) or a *Podpraporshik* (Warrant Officer).

(5) Ironically, the name Teteris translates to English as the word *grouse*, a form of game bird. By dodging ground fire, Teteris was encountering the same dangers as the fowl itself.

(6) Some sources state the award was the Third Class and not the Second.

personally. Teteris was chosen for this important mission, selected from approximately 40 pilots stationed in the Dvinsk area. The flight was a success.

On October 21, 1916, Teteris engaged a German aircraft and the crew of the Voisin shot the enemy down for Teteris' second victory. He earned the Soldier's Cross of Saint George First Class[7] for this action and was recommended for a commission.

On November 26, 1916, Teteris and his observer, *Poruchik* Zasserman, were photographing enemy artillery placements. While returning to their base Teteris spotted a Russian plane being attacked by three German machines northwest of the Yelovka station. He headed toward the battle to help, but could not reach the area in time.

On December 2, 1916, Teteris received his commission, with the rank of *Praporshik* (Ensign). Teteris continued flying throughout the winter of 1916–17, managing to remain untouched by enemy fire. On February 28, 1917, his luck ran out.

The weather was overcast, with poor visibility and a low ceiling. In the late morning, accompanied by *Poruchik* Zasserman, Teteris started off to photograph enemy trenches in the area around Dvietes. When Teteris reached the front, enemy batteries began firing at the low-flying Voisin.

A mechanic who knew Teteris sent a letter to Celms describing the events of that day. "Teteris had been uncharacteristically gloomy" he wrote. "We saw him like that for the first time, for as you know, he usually smiled and was in high spirits."

The letter continued: "The Germans opened against them a powerful artillery fire, but Teteris flew into the very hell. He had been only 800 meters high when shrapnel hit the wing of the plane, which broke off. The machine started to fall. At first, the observer fell out and then our Teteris. Finally, the machine also hit the frozen ground with a loud noise. Since they fell between our trenches and the German trenches, it was not easy for the soldiers to pull them out. The pieces of shrapnel had not hit Teteris, and after death he looked as well as in life, only he did not smile anymore."[8][9]

His body was taken to Riga and buried there in the National Cemetery. Many thousands of people attended the funeral of their brave countryman.

---

(7) Celms, *The Cheerful Flyer, Olgerts Teteris.*

(8) Ibid.

(9) The report given by the mechanic of the 13th Detachment was almost identical to the official army report and is therefore considered accurate.

Vyatcheslav Mikhailovich Tkachev

Pod'Esaul (Cossack Staff Captain) Vyatcheslav M. Tkachev displaying his Order of Saint George 4th class for reconnaissance in August 1914. The photo was probably taken in February 1915, shortly after he received the award. He was also awarded the Golden Sword of Saint George for reconnaissance during the summer of 1916. He was honored by France with the *Croix de Guerre* and was made a *Chevalier de la Legion d'Honneur*. From Great Britain he was granted the Order of Saint Michael and the Order of Saint George.

Vyatcheslav Mikhailovich Tkachev was born in 1885, the son of a Kuban Cossack, and he grew up in a military atmosphere. The Kuban provided more than 200 units, or squadrons as they were known, of the total of 939 Cossack squadrons provided to the Russian cavalry corps, second only to the Don Cossacks' 360 units. In addition, Cossack units of artillery and Kuban infantry were part of the Russian army.

By the time Tkachev reached his early 20s he was a junior officer of the 5th Kuban Cossack Artillery Unit. During his service with this battery he acquired an interest in aviation. Due to his father's influence and prosperity, he was able to enter the Odessa School of Aviation, a private establishment and the home of the Odessa Aero Club. He was graduated from this flight school in 1911 and went on to the Sevastopol Military Aviation School in 1912. It was during these early years of his flying career that Tkachev met Petr Nesterov, who was already known for his early aviation accomplishments, and the two became friends.

Tkachev completed the course of instruction at Sevastopol and was assigned to the 11th Air Corps Detachment, part of the 3rd Air Company[1] stationed at Kiev, where he arrived in January, 1913. In August, 1913, he participated in a battle formation flight, under the command of Nesterov, which embarked from Kiev and continued over Oster and Nezhin and returned to Kiev, a distance of approximately 200 miles. According to Tkachev, this was the first military battle formation flight in history. In any case, it was a significant accomplishment for the time. Tkachev also conveyed the interesting fact that Nesterov's passenger was a photographer and had filmed the event throughout the entire route.

In October, 1913, Tkachev made a solo flight of more than 800 miles, lasting 12 hours and 27 minutes, from Kiev to Odessa and on to Ekaterinodar. Early in 1914 he participated in another battle formation with the 4th Air Detachment, also stationed at Kiev.

In March, 1914, Tkachev was given command of the 20th Corps Air Detachment, the position he held when the war began. The experience he gained from his pre-war flights proved valuable from the very onset of war. On August 25, 1914, *Pod'Esaul* (Cossack Staff Captain) Tkachev was flying reconnaissance over the Russian 4th Army sector in the vicinity of Lublin when he observed the Austro-Hungarian 1st Army advancing toward the right flank of the Russian 4th Army.

During this mission, Tkachev reportedly had to make an emergency landing to repair a fuel line broken by anti-aircraft fire. He landed near Russian troops who secured his machine until it could be repaired. The information obtained by Tkachev not only saved the 4th Army from attack but marked the beginning of a Russian advance that pushed the Austrians back for 100 miles with the loss of almost half their forces. Approximately 400,000 casualties, including 100,000 taken prisoner, were lost to the Russian forces. The Russian Army lost 250,000 of its troops.

In February, 1915, the Southwest Army Group gave Tkachev the Order of Saint George Fourth Class with the citation: "A reward is presented to the Military Pilot, *Pod'Esaul* Vyatcheslav Tkachev, for performing a courageous and decisive reconnaissance in the region of Lublin-Belzhishche-Krasnik, when he penetrated the rear and flank enemy positions in spite of very dangerous long-range enemy fire over his apparatus, that lasted the duration of the flight and damaged the apparatus. He

---

(1) According to Tkachev, this was the first Russian aviation fighting group, with several detachments assembled under one command.

fulfilled his task by discovering and defining the movement of the enemy forces with valiant presence of mind and selfless courage. He managed to obtain and deliver on time the extremely important reconnaissance report, which influenced strategic decisions that gained victory over the enemy."

Tkachev was the first aviator to be granted this honor.

After several months of commanding the 20th Detachment and flying demanding reconnaissance missions, Tkachev was exhausted and requested a leave of absence to rest. In June, 1915, a telegram was sent to the 4th Army staff from the Grand Duke Alexander Mikhailovich[2] stating, "May I request to appoint the chief of the 20th Detachment, *Esaul* (Cossack Captain) Tkachev, to serve temporarily at my disposal. I am asking this in view of his overstrained condition and my desire to save such a prominent pilot for aviation." The Grand Duke realized the value of Tkachev's experience and that he would be more valuable to Russian aviation in the long run if given time to recuperate. While serving together during the summer of 1915, the Grand Duke and Thachev developed great respect for each other, which became a strong friendship.

By August, 1915, Tkachev was back at the front with the 10th Army Air Detachment, stationed in the north in the region of the Russian 5th Army, which had pulled back east of Mitau, and the Russian 10th Army, which had withdrawn into the area between Lida and Vilna, as a result of enemy offensives.

On September 10, 1915, while on patrol over roads southwest of Mitau with his observer, *Rotmistre* (Cavalry Captain) Brshosovski, Tkachev sighted a dust cloud made by a German motor column. This was a unit taking part in General Ludendorff's northern offensive. By September 16 Russian General Mikhail Alexeyev,[3] commander of the Northwest Army Group, stopped the German advance, stabilizing the entire front along a line running north to south from Dvinsk to Czernowitz. With minor alterations, this was where the front remained until the revolution in November, 1917.

On January 5, 1916, Tkachev requested to be transferred from the 10th Army Air Detachment and assigned to the 11th Army on the Southwestern Front. This was granted by Grand Duke Alexander and Tkachev found himself flying with the 11th Army Air Detachment.

A Nieuport IV from the 20th Corps Air Detachment, commanded by Tkachev, probably in 1914. This was most likely the type of aircraft flown by Tkachev when he performed reconnaissance missions during the early months of the war, when the unit was stationed in the sector of the 4th Army during the advance into northern Galicia. Here the squadron is being visited by horse soldiers.

In April, 1916, he was informed of his appointment as squadron commander of the 11th Detachment, in which he served with distinction during the later Brusilov offensive.

On June 4, 1916, the Russian Southwest Army, under the command of General Aleksei Brusilov,[4] launched this offensive against the Austro-Hungarians in Galicia. Tkachev was involved in battles near Tarnopol, flying reconnaissance missions on June 4 and June 7 over enemy rear positions. Despite heavy anti-aircraft fire he completed the missions, returning with valuable information. During one of these flights, he was attacked by an Austrian aircraft but forced it to disengage.

Between July 2 and July 10 Tkachev made important observation flights. His surveillance, especially on July 3 over Berestechko, in the region of Lutsk, was of utmost importance. He noticed a gap between the Russian 8th and 11th Armies and an enemy force from the Austrian 4th Army preparing to flank the Russians. Because of Tkachev's observations the Russian armies were able to close the gap and surround the Austrian force, taking 30,000 prisoners and continuing the advance 20 miles beyond Lutsk.

In the beginning of August Tkachev made three flights over the Zlota Lipa and Styrpa Rivers, locating troop concentrations from the German Southern Army

---

(2) The Grand Duke was the commander of the entire Russian Air Service until the first revolution in March 1917.

(3) General Alexeyev had been given command of the Northwest Army in March 1915. He had been General Ivanov's chief of staff with the Southwest Army Group during the opening campaign in Galicia. It was Alexeyev who actually planned the operation that resulted in the capture of Przemysl and the advance into Austria. After the great retreat in 1915, Grand Duke Nicholas was relieved as supreme commander and Alexeyev was promoted to the Czar's chief of staff, virtually taking over that position. He was relieved of his command after suffering a heart attack in November, 1916. He returned in February, 1917, but was relieved of his command again by the Provisional Government in May, 1917. After the revolution in November 1917, he joined the White forces, forming an army in the south. He died of another heart attack in October, 1918.

(4) General Aleksei Brusilov had been the commander of the 8th Army at the beginning of the war, remaining in that capacity until after the retreat of 1915. It was his counter-offensive in the autumn of 1915, that stopped the Austrian advance in Galicia. General Ivanov was relieved of command of the Southwest Army Group and replaced by Brusilov in March, 1916. His theory of intense preparation and attacking with multiple assaults was similar to German principles. Unfortunately, his ideas were viewed as revolutionary by his colleagues, who preferred either a massive frontal attack against a limited area or simply to remain in a defensive position. Despite much opposition, Brusilov launched his offensive, proving his methods could be successful. The reason his plan was not a total success was lack of cooperation from other army group commanders and from the Russian high command.

Nieuport IV.

Below: Close-up of Nieuport IV fitted with skis for winter operation.

preparing for a breakthrough. Russian reinforcements were moved into position and repelled the attack. On August 14, 1916, with his observer, *Poruchik* Hrizoskoleo, he engaged an enemy two-seat aircraft in the region of Zdolbunovo and damaged it, causing the machine to land in Russian-held territory near Hotyn, for his only confirmed victory. This was probably Austrian Aviatik B.II, serial number 34.41, from Flik 5. The crew of *Zugsführer* Edmund Pirker, pilot, and *Fähnrich der Reserve* Herbert Scholz, observer, were taken prisoner.

The Brusilov offensive was an initial success, but it was stopped short of its goal by mid-September.

For his service during the summer of 1916 Tkachev was awarded the Golden Sword of Saint George, although he did not receive the honor until July, 1917. He was also put in charge of forming an aviation battle group. During September, 1916, he assembled the First Combat Air Group in the vicinity of Lutsk, consisting of about 20 planes. By combining the knowledge of his aerial tactics and those of other accomplished combat fliers, he developed a system for combat formation flying. He later compiled this information into textbook form, and it was published in January, 1917, and distributed throughout the air service. The unit was effective, driving away many enemy attempts to reconnoiter the Russian army rear positions.

The commander of the 11th Army, General Sakharov, wrote an official report on the accomplishments of Tkachev, mentioning his aerial exploits and commending his leadership ability. Besides commanding the 11th Army Detachment, Tkachev also visited other squadrons to convey his knowledge and assure their combat readiness. A telegram dated October 30, 1916, announced his appointment as temporary deputy inspector of aviation of the southwest front. It stated: "By constant inspection and directing of activities of aviation (detachment) commanders, by the Aviation Inspector (Tkachev), conformity was introduced in fighting requirements. The personal example of the Inspector of Aviation, raised the spirit in pilots and produced the feeling of competition, which was immediately displayed in a set of glorious battles, where the pilots showed their greatness of spirit and skill."

On January 2, 1917, Tkachev was informed of his promotion to *Podpolkovnik* (Lieutenant-Colonel) and he was also named inspector of aviation of the Southwest Army Group, under the command of General Brusilov. According to Tkachev, there had been no such staff position within army groups. It was created at this level due to his ability.

In February, 1917, plans were made for a new offensive. Tkachev proposed to concentrate one-third of available air detachments to support the attack. However, the March, 1917, revolution caused many changes in the army as well as in the country. This postponed any thought of a full-scale operation until the Provisional Government launched the Kerensky offensive in July, 1917.

After the March revolution, many command positions

Tkachev, with hand on prop, and *Rotmistre* V. Brshosovski, his observer standing next in line with hand in pocket, in front of a Morane-Saulnier L Parasol with other officers while assigned to the 10th Army Air Detachment. Together they spotted a German motor column advancing through Mitau on September 10, 1915, to flank the Russian 5th and 10th Armies between Dvinsk and Vilna. The information they supplied to the army staff was used to stop the German advance.

held by members of the aristocracy were reassigned to capable officers who had served under them. When General Brusilov replaced General Alexeyev as commander-in-chief of the army, Tkachev replaced Grand Duke Alexander as the commander of the air service, receiving a promotion to *General-Maior* (Major-General). His reputation as a strict, yet just, commander, and the fact he was respected by his subordinates and army commanders, no doubt played a part in this appointment.

In July, 1917, his former unit, the 20th Air Detachment, sent this telegram of congratulations to Tkachev: "The 20th Squadron is joyfully saluting with its full complement their former glorious commander for his appointment for such an important and responsible position as the Commander of Russian Aviation. From all our hearts we wish you happiness and success in your new activity. We believe that under your talented

Tkachev preparing for a mission in his Morane-Saulnier L Parasol, possibly during the summer of 1916, when he commanded the 11th Army Air Detachment assigned to the 11th Army under the command of General Sakharov. For his aerial exploits during the Brusilov offensive, June through September, 1916, he was awarded the Golden Sword of Saint George.

leadership and experience, tried and tested in battle, the Russian army, in spite of current difficult conditions, will flourish and will rank high in world aviation according to its deserts."

Tkachev set out to accomplish just that.

In the summer of 1917 he introduced a reform program for the air service. As he described it: "Knowing the weak sides of our aviation, I reorganized some arrangements and reinforced the aviation supply for the front and improved the training of flying personnel. With the purpose of raising the spirit of pilots and to perpetuate the memory of our glorious aviation heroes, I issued an order, No. 25781, with the stipulation to collect materials about the activity of the front line aviation units, to establish an aviation journal and set up a museum. Energetically, I also supported the aviation community and the First Aviation Conference in Moscow.

"In the organization department of aviation, I was giving instructions on the principles of the construction of the future air forces of our Motherland. There was stipulation to create in the future an aviation academy with two departments; to train senior commanding staff and also schooling of structural engineers for aviation."

The November revolution did not allow Tkachev to follow through with many of his plans. After Bolshevik forces had taken power, he decided to go south to join the White army. When leaving his position as commander of the air service, he sent a telegram to the Aviation Council in Petrograd, stating, "To destroy with my own hands everything that was created with my participation, with hard labor and the taking of chances, I am not capable of. As of now there is only one concern for the aviation centers and that is to save as much as possible from everything we have and to fulfill this at the present time. It is better to act as a collective and not by the private individual, and I am requesting you to set this task yourself. Now I am departing to a place where new forces, to save our Motherland, are being formed."

Tkachev explained his motives for siding with the White army: "It was neither egoistic reasons, nor political convictions, but only the feeling of patriotism that pushed me, already in 1917, to take the anti-Soviet course."

Tkachev arrived at the camp of a Guard unit, placing himself at its disposal. During the civil war, he held the position of commander-in-chief of Kuban Aviation, then minister of the interior of Kubanland, and finally the commander of Baron Wrangel's air service.

During the summer of 1920 Tkachev lead a flight of D.H.9s many times against Red cavalry at Shloba, inflicting many casualties. During one of these raids he encountered two enemy Nieuports, one flown by General Petr Mesheraup, Red air service corps commander. The two generals fought an intense, lengthy combat. Neither gained an advantage and the engagement ended in a draw. This had to be one of few occasions where opposing forces' generals battled in the air.

In November, 1920, the remaining forces under Baron Wrangel were evacuated from the Crimea. While in Constantinopol, Tkachev said to his fellow pilots, "We all

Esaul (Cossack Captain) Tkachev posing in front of his faithful mount, a Morane-Saulnier L Parasol.

have the urge to get some kind of employment in aviation. However, we should all bear in mind, we should serve only in a country that would never wage war with our Motherland and Yugoslavia is that type of country." At age 34 he left his homeland and settled in Yugoslavia.

For the next several years Tkachev worked as an editor of an aviation magazine. When World War II began and the Germans occupied Yugoslavia, he was an inspector of a gymnasium. In 1945 he decided to go back to his native land, despite the consequences. He returned to the Soviet Union and was arrested soon after by Stalin's order. He was sent to a prison to serve a 25-year sentence for his participation against the Soviet government during the civil war.

After Stalin's death, he was released in 1955, at the age of 70. He joined an industrial cooperative in Krasnodar (Ekaterinodar), binding books. It was in this town that he had made his solo flight in 1913.

During his last years he wrote his autobiography and a book titled *The Russian Eagle* about the achievements of Petr Nesterov. He died in 1965.

Peter Martinovich Tomson

Peter Martinovich Tomson. His awards included the Order of Saint George, Fourth Class; the Order of Saint Anne, Third, Class, with Sword and Ribbon; the Order of Saint Anne, Fourth Class; the Order of Saint Stanislas, Third Class, with Sword, and Ribbon; and Soldier's Cross of Saint George, Fourth Class.

Peter Martinovich Tomson was a valuable, highly-decorated pilot, who had a career typical of many Russian aviators.

Tomson was born in Estonia to a peasant family of Lutheran faith on September 4, 1891. He became interested in aviation at an early age in Russia, but traveled abroad to take flying lessons. He passed the examination for pilot in Germany on July 29, 1912, and returned to Russia soon afterward to attend classes at the Moscow aviation school. Tomson finished the school's program on November 24, 1913, and in early 1914 went to France and obtained additional experience on newer aircraft. In the spring of 1914 he passed flying exams in France for Nieuport, Etrich *Taube,* and other German and French machines.

Tomson went to Germany to take part in flying competitions, a popular sport at the time, in the early summer of 1914. In Berlin when war was declared, he was arrested and imprisoned. He managed to escape to France and enlisted in the French air service in the fall of 1914. The next year, with permission from the French War Minister, Tomson transferred to the Imperial Russian Air Service. He left France in March, 1915, arriving in Russia on April 2.

Upon his arrival in Russia, Tomson contacted the Ministry of Foreign Affairs. Based on that meeting, a report dated April 14, 1915, was submitted: "To His Imperial highness, Grand Duke Alexander Mihailovitch. The Russian pilot Tomson, who served in an aviation battalion in France, and personally met with one of our Battalion Commanders after his return to Russia, has applied to serve in the aviation detachment of the field forces. Tomson was flying Morane Saulniers in France. Permit me to ask you if Tomson might be accepted and if your answer is affirmative, what would be his mission? Faithfully yours, Commander Belyaev."

The Grand Duke responded on April 15, "I command that Tomson should undergo the test in flying. If he is also reliable in conduct and character, my request is to send him to the 2nd Air Company (Park)."

On May 7 Tomson entered Katchinsky Aviation School for a quick evaluation and was transferred to the 1st Corps Detachment as a *Nijnichin* (Private) on May 16 as an appointee pilot. On May 27 he flew his first reconnaissance mission on the Russian front. Tomson was quickly promoted; on June 11, he received the rank of *Gefreiter* (Lance-Corporal), and on June 28 the rank of *Feldwebel* (Sergeant-Major).

During late July and August of 1915 Tomson made ten reconnaissance flights in defense of Warsaw and engaged enemy aircraft on several occasions. Although he shot down no enemy aircraft, on August 9 he was awarded the Soldier's Cross of Saint George, Fourth Class, with a citation that read in part "for battle reconnaissance work against the enemy that greatly endangered his life." On August 14 Tomson was again promoted, receiving the rank of *Podpraporshik* (Warrant Officer). He continued his rapid accent, being promoted yet again on November 6, 1915, this time to the rank of *Praporshik* (Ensign) for distinguished combat service.

On November 26, during a flight from Minsk to Molodechno, Tomson was forced to make an emergency landing after the engine of his Morane Saulnier L quit at low altitude. The plane somersaulted on landing, but Tomson was not seriously injured.

The remainder of 1915 was relatively quite for Tomson. He flew few missions in December because of bad weather and was furloughed from December 26 until January 4, 1916. He resumed reconnaissance and bombing missions in early 1916 despite extremely cold temperatures. On February 4 the temperature at ground level was measured at -14° Fahrenheit. Nevertheless, Tomson flew a Morane Saulnier L that day on a two-hour patrol and dropped four bombs weighing 36 kilograms each on an enemy fortification.

Obviously, continuous flying in the extreme cold

Morane Saulnier L serial number 272. Tomson (standing in center) used this aircraft on numerous missions.

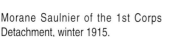

Morane Saulnier of the 1st Corps Detachment, winter 1915.

would be a physical strain on any pilot. After weeks of this activity, Tomson was stricken with pneumonia and was unable to fly from March 25, to April 2, 1916. During this period, on March 31, he was awarded the Order of Saint Anne, Fourth Class, with inscription "For Bravery."

Although Tomson was still very weak, he returned to active duty in April and continued to fly Morane Saulnier Ls and Nieuport 10s throughout the spring of 1916. In early July the 1st Corps Detachment received its first Nieuport 11 fighters. On July 28, Tomson, patrolling in a Nieuport 11, chased an enemy Albatros which appeared over the village Budslav (north of Lake Yadviol) to the village Koblyniki. Tomson shot at the Albatros, which flew away northwest losing altitude. Moments later, Tomson returned over the village Koblyniki and found himself above a German airfield on which a large flight of aircraft were being prepared for takeoff. Tomson strafed the field, causing enemy flyers who were running toward their planes to scatter. The Albatros forced down was not confirmed as a victory.

From August to September Tomson used Nieuport 10 (serial number 160) to fly 25 reconnaissance, bombing, and escort missions. On November 9 he attacked an enemy plane, but his machine gun jammed and the combat was inconclusive.

On November 10, 1916, Tomson was awarded the Order of Saint Anne, Third Class, with Swords and Bow for his activity between April and August, 1916. By November Tomson had made 108 combat flights with a total duration of nearly 176 hours. Several weeks later, he became ill again and was furloughed for poor health until year's end.

Tomson returned to the front in early January, 1917. On February 18 and 19 he fought two enemy aircraft near Smorgon and forced both of them to retreat. On February 20 he attacked two aircraft in separate engagements and forced both to crash-land in enemy territory. Although neither of these victories were confirmed, several days later, on February 24, 1917, Tomson was awarded the title of military pilot.

Tomson's first and only confirmed victory of the war occurred on March 18, 1917. The mission report stated:

Nieuport 10 (serial number 160) flown on many missions by Tomson. This photo shows pilot Lt. Vitman and observer Jr. Captain Troitsky before a reconnaissance flight from Molodechvo airfield, January, 1916.

Members of the 1st Corps Detachment conduct Sunday Mass. The detachment's aircraft (Nieuport 17s and 21s) have been positioned around a make-shift alter.

"On March 18, 1917, pilots *Praporshik* Tomson in the biplane Nieuport *Bebe* (No. 1132), and Rosenfeld in biplane Nieuport *BeBe* (No. 1033) shot down a German plane that fell in our state of siege, near our field management Zaleseye. The German aircraft broke up. The enemy flyers were killed. Tomson noticed a German plane over station Zaleseye, that was under our artillery fire, and he attacked it. The German began to move to the frontline, but Tomson began to surpass the enemy plane in pursuit. Before reaching the position the enemy turned before the wind and headed south over the village Soukrevichi. Rosenfeld's plane appeared to meet the enemy. Then the German turned against the wind and was immediately attacked by our planes. Rosenfeld was attacking from above and from the left, and Tomson attacked from below and the right side. After the first few shots the German suddenly turned and began descending to their positions. At that time Tomson fired at him all the remaining cartridges (180–200) from the distance of 10–20 meters; after that the enemy plane swayed, got into a spin and dropped like a stone in the area to the south of Zaleseye. Watching what was going on, Tomson landed near the crashed plane. In detail he inspected the wreck and the killed pilots, gave them the last honors, and returned to his airfield. The battle took place at 2100–2200 meters altitude."

Nieuport fighters of the 1st Corps detachment. The nearest two machines are Nieuport 21s (serial numbers 2239 and 1932), the farthest machine is a Nieuport 17.

On April 13, by the order of the commander of the Russian 10th Army, Tomson was awarded the Order of Saint Stanislas, Third Class, with Swords and Bow. On April 18 he was seriously injured in a crash and had to undergo medical treatment. His recovery took several months and he did not return to the detachment until August. Although still in pain, he continued to fly regularly. His efforts were noted by the commander of the Russian 10th Army, who announced that Tomson had been awarded the Order of Saint George, Fourth Class, on September 14, 1917.

After the revolution Tomson became the commander of the First Socialist Aviation Detachment. He was mentioned in Order #95 of July 25, 1919, as a pilot of the 45th Aviation Detachment (commander of the Latvian aviation group). He probably took part in the Pskov battle and the conquest of Latvia. Poor health affected him again in 1919. Developing pneumonia, he entered a Riga hospital and was in bed when German troops entered the city. Tomson was taken from the hospital with other Red Army men and brutally murdered in the street.

Pilots of the 1st Corps Detachment, 1917. Peter Tomson is standing in the last row (center); Rosenfeld is kneeling in first row (left side).

Victor Victorovich Utgoff

Victor Victorovich Utgoff. His awards included the Order of Saint George, Fourth Class; Golden Sword of Saint George; Order of Saint Vladimir, Fourth Class; Order of Saint Stanislas, Third Class; Cross of Saint George; Romanov Dynasty Medal (300 years); British Cross of Saint Michael and George; and the French Legion of Honor.

Victor Victorovich Utgoff was born into Russian nobility on 14 July, 1889, in Novoradomsk, (now Radomsko in the Polish province of Lodz). The son of an army colonel, Utgoff was reared with a healthy respect for the Russian army, in which he was expected to serve in his adult years. Surprisingly, the young Utgoff did not select the army, and in September, 1903, at the age of 13, entered the navy's Nautical Military School. Two years later he entered the Imperial Naval Academy at St. Petersburg.

On November 6, 1906, Utgoff was appointed a junior midshipman and in 1910 was promoted to midshipman, a line-officer rank indicating that he had received shipboard training in addition to his studies at the academy.

Utgoff was graduated on May 5, 1910, with the rank of *Michman*. He received the Gold Breast Badge signifying completion of his studies at the academy and was assigned to a tour of duty aboard the Black Sea Fleet cruiser *Kagul* on May 15. While he was serving on this vessel, Grand Duke Alexander, one of Russia's first major air theorists, was promoting the cause of aviation. Since, among his other titles, he carried the rank of admiral, he could wield a considerable amount of influence. Both the army and the navy had well-established balloon branches, and Alexander sought to have them expand into heavier-than-air aviation. As a result, three army and three navy officers were assigned to flight schools in France in 1910. The army purchased its first airplanes in 1911, and the navy followed suit in February, 1912, by ordering eight to ten Voisin canard amphibians from France.

In March, 1912, the commander of the Black Sea Fleet issued an order establishing an aviation branch in association with the navy's liaison services, to be based at Sevastopol. Naval officers were invited to apply for flight training, but only five did, Utgoff and Victorin Katchinsky among them.[1] On April 22, 1912, the five were assigned to a pilot's course.

In July, 1912, the five were assigned to the navy's Black Sea liaison service and attached to the school of aviation at Sevastopol. The Black Sea Fleet air organization did not come into existence as a separate entity until 1916. Until then Russian naval air groups were subordinated to the navy's Reconnaissance and Liaison Service.

Katchinsky described his brief pilot course in a letter to Victor Utgoff's son, Vadym. "It turned out that only five of us, including your father, applied. Since hydroplanes were not yet available, we were sent to a land-based flight school, the Katchinsky aerodrome, located not far from Sevastopol. The school was directed to teach us to fly without delay. I do not remember with what instructor your father learned to fly, and how. I am sure that it was much like my own experiences. Early in the morning, or late in the afternoon, we took off and circled the hangar in two or three minutes and landed. Since there might be turbulence during the middle of the day it was considered dangerous to fly then. The airplane might turn upside down which would end in catastrophe. We flew Farman 4s. After fifteen such flights, the instructor said I was ready to solo. Half an hour's flying under instruction, you well realize, is not fully sufficient. But since I was a navy officer, while the instructor was army, I said all right and took off. The takeoff, as you know, is simple, and so is flying. But the landing is more complex. I landed well, but far beyond where I should have. Afterwards, I flew for half an hour alone and then went to take my test. I had to do five figure-eights, and make a spot landing. Your father had to do the same."

---

(1) Utgoff and Katchinsky had meet at the Naval Academy. They were very close friends and, several years later, became brothers-in-law.

Victor Utgoff as a cadet at the Imperial Russian Naval Academy at St. Petersburg. Photo: Vadym Utgoff.

While in flight school the army accommodated the naval aviators with rooms made from wooden boxes in which the wings of French airplanes had been shipped. By the end of August, 1912, Utgoff and the others had all soloed on the Farman 4. In early September it was announced that all had qualified as aviators. On July 21, 1912, Utgoff passed an examination and received the title of pilot.

About the time Utgoff and the other naval officers finished their training the naval aviation section at Sevastopol received Voisin canards and single-float Curtiss Triad seaplanes. The canards had already been accepted, but Curtiss personnel were still working to get their craft to meet the Russian specifications. The contract required each plane, carrying two persons and a full tank of fuel, to climb to 1000 feet in ten minutes and cruise for one hour. Instruction of Russian naval personnel was also part of the contract. The Curtiss Triad had no instruments of any kind. The ailerons were connected to the seat, and inclining the body left or right caused the seat to move the corresponding ailerons. Air speed was determined by the position of the nose relative to the horizon, altitude by eye, and engine speed by sound.

Charles Witner, Joe Bennett, and Slim Purrington were among the Curtiss staff in Russia. They qualified all but one plane quickly. That one continually failed the altitude requirements despite modifications to decrease overall weight, increase thrust, increase wing surface area, and rev the engine to utmost power.

Witner finally offered Utgoff an opportunity to try qualifying the plane. The excited Utgoff, with his roommate (probably Katchinsky), rushed to the plane, forgetting to fuel it. Utgoff succeeded in reaching the required altitude in less than ten minutes, just before running out of fuel![2]

After all the planes were qualified, each naval pilot was checked out in one. Then, according to Katchinsky, "We (the five naval officers) flew to Katchinsky aerodrome, which was near the shore, to pay a visit to our old school. Many of the people there came down to the shore, wondering how we could fly during mid-day, when there were dangerous eddies caused by rising and falling air currents. We answered by saying that naval aviators were not frightened by eddies."

In February, 1913, Utgoff, Katchinsky, and one other unidentified naval pilot were sent to the Polytechnic

---

[2] About this time Utgoff set a Russian altitude record for seaplanes of 2800 meters.

Curtiss Triad (1911 Model E) coming ashore at Sevastopol circa 1913. Photo: Drashpil Collection, Russian Naval Museum.

Curtiss Triad (1911 Model E) at Sevastopol, early 1913. The number "3" can be seen through the thin fabric, resulting in a backwards appearance. Second from left is *Michman* Victor R. Kachinsky, third from left is *Michman* Nikolai A. Ragozin, others not identified. Photo: Drashpil Collection, Russian Naval Museum.

Institute of Emperor Peter the Great in St. Petersburg, where courses in aero-dynamics were taught. Revel Naval Air Station (about 400 miles southwest of St. Petersburg, on the Gulf of Finland), was one of the locations Utgoff visited to practice flying.

The flyers' salary at the school was a modest 120 rubles a month, although while they were actively flying this was increased by 100 rubles a month for every four hours in the air. For comparative purposes, the average wage of a skilled worker in Russia at this time was around 3.16 rubles a day. Consequently, during the winter months when flying decreased, belt-tightening was common and the flyers usually ate in the student mess, where prices were low (for example, a bowl of soup with unlimited bread cost five kopeks, one-twentieth of a ruble).

On March 4, 1913, Utgoff received the Bronze Medal celebrating 300 years of the reign of the House of Romanov, and on April 8, 1913, he was awarded the Bronze Medal celebrating the 100-year anniversary of the Fatherland War.[3]

About this time Utgoff met his future wife, Lydia Vladimirovna Offenberg, daughter of *Leitenant-General* Vladimir Christianovich Offenberg, the assistant inspector of Russian naval construction.[4]

In May, 1913, Utgoff completed the courses at the St. Petersburg school and returned to Sevastopol, where he entered the school of advanced pilotage. Some of the course requirements were learning and executing power-off loops, tailspins, the falling leaf, and tail slides. The

---

(3) The 300th Anniversary of the Rule of the Romanov House medal was instituted March 12, 1913. It was awarded to all individuals who held positions at the Imperial Court or in government service. Enlisted personnel of the army and navy who were on duty February 21, 1913, were awarded the medal.

(4) Utgoff married Lydia Offenberg on January 8, 1914.

Victor Utgoff standing next to a Curtiss Triad (1911 Model E) with fixed dual controls. The photo is dated December, 1913. The Russians used the Julian calendar, which lagged 13 days behind the Gregorian calendar used by the other Allies and the Central Powers except Turkey (until 1917). Photo: Vadym Utgoff.

tailspin was a highly dreaded event in early aviation, to be avoided at all costs. Although a few pilots got out of spins mainly by chance, there was no known standard method until the answers were worked out via research in Britain and the United States in 1916–17. So if spins were taught at the Sevastopol school in 1913, it would suggest that the Russians were far ahead in the matter at that time.

On December 12, 1913, Utgoff was promoted to *Leitenant* and ten days later was awarded the Order of Saint Stanislaus, Third Class, and attached to the Black Sea Fleet.

Just before the outbreak of war, Utgoff drafted a report describing the significance of aviation. He said the possibility of using seaplanes for reconnaissance, bombing, attacking submarines, and aerial combat was great. He also mentioned the necessity of creating special aircraft-carrying ships. Before the end of 1914 Utgoff was promoted to the rank of *Starschi Leitenant*.

In early March, 1915, Utgoff became Russia's pioneer wartime shipboard aviator, flying a Curtiss Triad launched from cruiser *Kagul* over the entrance to the Bosphorus (the strait connecting the Sea of Marmara with the Black Sea).

The Black Sea Fleet soon created a small force of seaplane carriers in early 1915. The group consisted of two converted cargo-liners, the *Imperator Nikolai I* and *Imperator Alexandr I*, and the hybrid cruiser-yacht *Almaz*. The *Imperators* were rated as *gidrokreisera* (hydro-cruisers). Later in the war a few Romanian vessels were also fitted to operate seaplanes with the fleet. Utgoff was attached to the *Imperator Nikolai I*.

The two *Imperators* carried from six to eight seaplanes each, while the smaller *Almaz* could accommodate three at most. Booms aboard the vessels placed the aircraft on the water for takeoff and recovered them upon alighting. During operations the carriers would operate 30–40 miles offshore to avoid being spotted by the enemy. There the vessel would turn broadside to the wind to create a lee through which the seaplanes would take off.

Although other problems needed to be solved, the *Almaz* and *Imperator Nikolai I* started operations in February, 1915. One problem was air-to-ship communication. At this time the Russian aircraft had no radios, so Utgoff devised a smoke signaling system. Tubes made of thin cardboard, about three inches in diameter and ten inches long, were filled with colored powder, black, red, or white. When a pilot wanted to send a signal he would toss a tube overboard. One end was attached to the plane by a line that caused the powder to pour out, creating a colored cloud. With prearranged codes, this system proved to be a reasonably efficient means of communication. Such a signal at least once warned a surface squadron of the presence of German submarines. On another occasion the color signals were used to warn Russian ships of the approach of Turkish ships from the Bosphorus.[5]

Toward the end of March, 1915, the Black Sea Fleet began a series of surface and aerial attacks on the Turkish coast. On 30 March aircraft from the *Nikolai I* bombed the Anatolian port of Zonguldak, an important coal-producing and shipping spot. During this operation Utgoff, flying through intense anti-aircraft fire, bombed and destroyed the port's power station. This had the important strategic effect of idling coal mines in the area for some time. For this feat Utgoff became the first naval

---

(5) The Boris Drashpil Collection states that Utgoff's method of air to ship communication was used at least once to warn against Turkish ships.

Above: Utgoff (in flying hat) at the controls of a Curtiss (1913 Model F) flying boat at Sevastopol, October 15, 1913. Ivan I. Stakhovsky (commander of the Black Sea air arm) is in the aircraft with Utgoff. Pluym Ochs (the Curtiss representative in St. Petersburg) is standing at the far right. A cylinder-shaped fuel tank was located on each side of the Curtiss OX, 100hp, 8 cylinder engine. Half of the foredeck folded forward, providing a boarding ramp. Photo: National Air & Space Museum, Smithsonian Institution.

Below: Utgoff (white flying hat and scarf), either landing or taking off a Curtiss (1913 Model F) flying boat, with Ivan I. Stakhovsky (commander of the Black Sea air arm), Sevastopol, October 15, 1913. Photo: Vadym Utgoff.

Black Sea naval officers and Curtiss personnel, Sevastopol, October 15, 1913. Utgoff is standing sixth from left. Ivan I. Stakhovsky (commander of the Black Sea air arm) is standing fourth from left. Others unidentified. Photo: Nation Air & Space Museum-Smithsonian Institution.

officer in the war to be awarded the Order of Saint George, Fourth Class. He was also promoted to *Kapitan 2 Ranga* and became second in command of the Black Sea Fleet aviation units.

In July, 1915, Utgoff was sent to Sevastopol to help assemble and test-fly Curtiss K (KPB) flying boats. One of the Curtiss employees with whom Utgoff worked, Pluym Ochs, was at Sevastopol for only four days before being jailed on charges of being a spy because he had been in Berlin and Vienna on business for the Curtiss company before the war. Unfortunately, his arrest seriously impeded testing the Curtiss flying boats; the Curtiss personnel had greatly depended on him because he spoke Russian.

Curtiss employees received practically no cooperation from the Russians at Sevastopol in assembly and testing of the aircraft. Several Russian officers spoke English, but only Utgoff cooperated when needed, resulting in the Curtiss staff accomplishing a great deal of work. The K boat did not operate as well as hoped so in turn most of the Russian officers became considerably annoyed with the Curtiss personnel.

The Russian navy had placed an order with Curtiss for additional flying boats in early 1915. After reviewing the situation, the navy decided it would be in its best interests to send a Russian representative to the United States. Utgoff was selected and left for the United States on August 7, 1915, with two English pounds per day as travel allowance.

Utgoff's departure was unfortunate for the Curtiss personnel in Russia, for by now Utgoff had become the main buffer between them and the other Russian officers. To quote Walter Johnson, Curtiss test pilot, "After Utgoff left for America, we lost the one friend that we had. From that time on, none of the officers showed us any courtesy or offered to help in any way that they could."

Utgoff was in the United States from October to December, 1915. During this time he either observed or participated in the flights of the first Curtiss H-7 Super America aircraft. Several records were established during the tests.[6]

Utgoff returned to Russia just as the Black Sea Fleet air organization came into existence, replacing the liaison service. He was again assigned to the hydro-cruiser *Imperator Nikolai I*.

In February, 1916, both the *Imperators* were operating off the Turkish coast. While both ships were recovering aircraft after a raid, the German submarine *U.B.7* was spotted and attacked by Russian aircraft and surface vessels. The U-boat was slightly damaged and forced to withdraw.

After Romania declared war on the Central Powers in late August, 1916, Russian ships were sent to Romanian shores. Utgoff flew many missions near the coast and saw much action as typified in his report of August 25, 1916: "Flying in the flying boat—Schetinin (Grigorovich) M.9 (serial number 114). I was with a group of six hydroplanes over the Bulgarian port of Varna. At 0510 hours I had taken off from the water with difficulty, and gaining height was moving west. Approximately 15 minutes later I reached the coast and headed toward Galatsky Bridge. To lessen the plane's weight I dropped bombs for gaining height. The observer, Non-Commissioned Officer Oskolkov, dropped one big bomb and one small bomb, hitting some red-colored building, at the same place I detected a battery of four guns, completely uncovered. From there I moved in the direction of the town. In the harbor a big steamship of khaki color was detected. I

(6) Casey, Louis S. Curtiss—*The Hammondsport Era 1907–1915*, (Crown, New York, 1981), page 216. On November 10, 1915, one record was set when a useful load of 2100 pounds was carried. It is worth mentioning that two Curtiss H-7TB aircraft were shipped to Vladivostok, Russia and moved to Sevastopol via the Trans-Siberian Railway in early 1916.

Curtiss (1913 Model F) flying boat in the foreground and a Curtiss Triad (1911 Model E) in the background, Sevastopol, circa 1913. Photo: Drashpil Collection, Russian Naval Museum.

Below: Utgoff at the controls of a Curtiss Triad Model E, Sevastopol, circa 1913. The girl is his fiancee, Lydia Offenburg. The man standing to the right of Victor Utgoff is Curtiss representative Pluym Ochs. This aircraft utilized a pivoting throw-over control wheel, which made it possible to operate the aircraft from either seat. Photo: Vadym Utgoff.

dropped on it one big and one small bomb. However, the bombs hit another, much smaller, steamship, that caught fire immediately. In the vicinity I noticed one more small ship. As soon as the bombs exploded, some hydroplanes were being lowered from that ship. I dropped one more bomb, but missed the ship. After that I went to Devino Lake, approximately 2000 meters from there, there was a white building with two chimneys; the whole thing was surrounded by a white wall. Assuming it was a plant, I dropped an incendiary bomb, but it did not explode. Right at this point, our motor had two powerful misfires which lowered our machine to 1400 meters altitude. On the return to the harbor I noticed five enemy aircraft preparing to take off. I moved in that direction with the intention of attacking them from behind. However, having noticed my machine, and understanding the disadvantage of their situation, the enemy airplanes after their take off made a sharp turn to the right and disappeared in the inland harbor. At this point our machine was attacked by anti-aircraft fire. I could see puffs of shrapnel smoke to the left and behind me. Having no more bombs and seeing no more enemy aircraft, I returned to our ship for refueling. I landed at 0645 hours and managed to break the bottom of my plane in the surge. At 0650 hours I flew up again and started pursuit of a German aircraft—pontoon Albatros. My apparatus being almost empty of fuel, I gained the height of 1000 meters fast and started an intense pursuit of one German plane, that was flying 600 meters above me. Approaching it closely, I opened machine gun fire. After firing 30 shots at the enemy aircraft, my machine gun

Above: Curtiss Triad (1911 Model E serial number "5") on board the cruiser *Kagul* in March, 1915. Photo: Harry Woodman.

Below: Curtiss Triad (serial number "5") with Utgoff at the controls. This photo shows the aircraft has been lowered from the cruiser *Kagul* and is being positioned for flight, March, 1915. Photo: Harry Woodman.

The Black Sea flyers pose with a Curtiss Triad (1911 Model E) at Sevastopol in late 1914. Back row: left of Curtiss Triad is Nikolai A. Ragozin; right side of Triad is Victor Utgoff. Middle row, left to right: Ivan I. Stakhovsky (commander of the Black Sea air arm); unidentified; Raymond F. Von Essen III; Alexander Mihailov; T.V. Kornilovich; Alexander A. Tufiaev; Boris R. Miklashevski III; N. Wiren; Konstantin M. Lamanov. Front row: A. Jouko (hand-held item censored out of photo making the round black spot); Victor Katchinsky. Photo: Vadym Utgoff.

jammed. We began to fix it and continued the pursuit for 30 minutes almost reaching Varna. However, due to lack of fuel, we had to turn back. We landed at 0735 hours and lifted onto our battle ship at 0800 hours."

In mid October, 1916, as enemy forces were nearing Constanza, the Russian navy sent a considerable force to bolster the port's defenses, including a detachment of four seaplanes designated "22/XII." The detachment arrived October 17, 1916, at Lake Singol (an inlet of the Black Sea) near Constanza, with Utgoff and Katchinsky among the pilots.

The group made several flights over Bulgarian territory. One moon-lit night Utgoff and Katchinsky, with two unidentified pilots, made a formation flight over the port of Varna, a German U-boat base. This was the first night formation flight by Russian naval aircraft during the war. There were no lights of any kind on the aircraft and there was considerable fear of a mid-air collision. In the hope of preventing this, ten-minute intervals between takeoffs were established. Utgoff and Katchinsky both reported being subjected to intense machine-gun fire from roof tops as they flew above the city and port. Post-mission reconnaissance showed the raid had caused substantial damage to the U-boat base. For this feat Utgoff and the other pilots were awarded the Golden Sword of Saint George.

On October 30, 1916, the detachment left Romania and returned to the hydro-cruisers. In late 1916, while the *Nikolai I* was operating off the Romanian coast, Utgoff made a flight near Constanza, which had fallen to the enemy. Utgoff reported he was "fired upon by some sort of spheres." Since there were no German anti-aircraft rockets in World War I, these were probably the kind of tracer-coated AA shells so often called 'flaming onions.'

In winter, it was common for ice to form in the northern areas of the Black Sea and in the Sea of Azov. Ice, when present, reduced flying boat activities at these locations. This required the effective utilization of floatplanes or land-based aircraft. In the Black Sea, it was common practice to launch aircraft from frozen lakes near the bases. Here a Farman MF is preparing to take off on ice and snow. The four men holding the plane will let go when the pilot indicates he is ready to take off. The ramp located at the bottom right corner of the photo was used to launch and retrieve flying boats when ice was not present. Photo: Drashpil Collection, Russian Naval Museum.

In March of 1917 the worsening conditions in Russia climaxed in Czar Nicholas II's abdication and the establishment of the Provisional Government headed by Alexander Kerensky. The Provisional Government lacked strong political support and exercised formal power in competition with the revolutionary Bolsheviks. Simultaneously, the discipline in the army and navy was rapidly waning as revolutionary agitators encouraged soldiers and sailors to abandon the war effort. Sailors of

Curtiss Model F flying boat number 15, next to the cruiser *Kagul* in operations off the Bosporus, March 28, 1915. Photo: Drashpil Collection, Russian Naval Museum.

Below: A Grigorovich M.5 flying boat number 38 connected to a ship's hoist, circa 1915. Photo: Drashpil Collection, Russian Naval Museum.

the Black Sea Fleet were generally supportive of the revolution. As a result, many officers were imprisoned and executed. Utgoff carried on the fight, despite having to watch not only the enemy but his own men as well.

In June, 1917, Utgoff was again attached to the seaplane carrier *Imperator Nikolai I*. By this time, many ships of the Black Sea Fleet had established their own governments, which in most cases consisted of a committee made up of sailors and officers. On the *Nikolai I* a committee would decide if a flight would be defensive or offensive. The sailors were of the opinion that if they did not attack the enemy, the enemy would reciprocate in kind.

One day in June, 1917, Utgoff was to fly over Constanza while his ship, the *Nikolai I*, was about 25 miles off the coast. Utgoff secretly loaded bombs on his Grigorovich M.9 seaplane. On the return flight, upon seeing a German submarine near the *Nikolai I*, he lined up his seaplane for a pass over the enemy vessel, while his mechanic pulled the bomb release clutch. By the time Utgoff could turn his aircraft around, the submarine was gone. Utgoff concluded the submarine must have been sunk, for it went down too quickly not to have been hit. He was wrong; the only submarine that might have been sunk by Russian naval aviation was *U.B.7* earlier in the war. At best, Utgoff may have damaged the submarine he attacked.[7]

Nevertheless, upon returning, Utgoff was summoned by the *Nikolai's* executive committee to explain his action. His gift for words saved him, but he was sent back to Sevastopol. The ship's committee had almost certainly feared the trouble he might cause. That he was not killed was probably because he was popular among the sailors and officers.

The sailors' love for Utgoff was not due to his bravery, but was because they could trust him. Utgoff loved to

(7) According to an entry in "Allied Aircraft vs. German Submarines 1916–1918," *Cross & Cockade* (USA) vol. 11, no. 4, page 293, by R.D. Layman.
Farson, Negley, *The Way Of A Transgressor*, (Harcourt Brace & Co., 1936), page 277. According to Vadym Utgoff, "The sub incident described in Farson's book matched exactly with my father's description of the event."
"Allied Aircraft vs. German Submarines 1916–1918," *Cross & Cockade* (USA) vol. 11 no. 4, 1970, page 302 by R.D. Layman. See Appendix I: Summary of U-Boats known or presumed lost due to aerial attack. *U.B.7* was lost in the Black Sea sometime in October, 1916, after sailing from the Bulgarian port of Varna. It was the same U-boat attacked by Russian aircraft and ships in February, 1916.

Black Sea flyers at Sevastopol in 1915. Those identified are: second from right, Alexander Mihailov; third from right, Ivan I. Stakhovsky; sixth from right, Utgoff; seventh from right, Alexander Tufiaev; ninth from right, Nikolai A. Ragozin. Photo: Drashpil Collection, Russian Naval Museum.

The Black Sea Aviation personnel with representatives of the Curtiss Aeroplane & Motor Co., Inc., at Sevastopol sometime between July 28, 1915, and August 2, 1915. From left to right, front-row, seated: Boris N. Luchaninov; Raymond F. Von Essen II; C. Witmer (pilot and head of the Curtiss group); Ivan I. Stakhovsky (commander of the Black Sea air arm); Victor Katchinsky (crouching); Pluym Ochs (the Curtiss represen-tative in St. Petersburg); Victor V. Utgoff; an unidentified Curtiss mechanic (either Joe Bennett or Slim Purington). Standing at rear, left to right: A. Joukov; N. Wiren; M. Lamanov; T.V. Kornilovich; Alexander A. Tufiaev; Alexander Mihailov; Nikolai A. Ragozin; a black man believed to Pluym Ochs's servant; Boris R. Miklashevski III; Boris Svietukhin. Ochs was at Sevastopol during the above-mentioned time before being jailed by the Russians, who believed him to be spying for the Germans. Photo: Drashpil Collection, Russian Naval Museum.

Curtiss flying boats on shore near Sevastopol, mid-1916. The Curtiss in the background is a 1914 Model F boat. The Curtiss in the foreground appears to be a 1913 Model F boat, differing from the 1914 model by the location of the ailerons and the addition of wing-tip extensions. On the 1914 Model F boat the ailerons were attached to the rear spar of the upper wing rather than having the characteristic interplane mounting used by Curtiss. The 1914 model also has the addition of anti-skid fins located on the top wing. Photo: Drashpil Collection, Russian Naval Museum.

A Grigorovich M.9 on the shore of the Black Sea, summer 1916.

discuss and argue. As an example of this Katchinsky wrote, "A sailor sentenced to be court-martialed was entitled to be defended by a member of the judge advocate corps, but Victor offered to defend him. He did so, so capably that the sailor was found not guilty."

While Utgoff was at Sevastopol the local government passed a series of orders placing restrictions on officers in an attempt to humiliate them and remove what little power they possessed. As a result, Utgoff had disputes with the sailors, as did many other officers.

In the summer of 1917 Utgoff and his family were sent to the United States by the Provisional Government. He was assigned to the Russian embassy in Washington, D.C. during 1917–19, serving as the assistant naval attaché for the Russian naval air arm. In November, 1917, while Utgoff was in the United States, Russia came under Bolshevik control, setting into motion a brutal civil war.

During this time three Russian naval officers came to the United States from France with several inventions, including an anti-wire-entanglement rocket and a bomb sight. Seven Russian naval officers were organized under the leadership of Utgoff to develop and promote these inventions, in which the Russian and United States governments had invested funds. However, after ten

A Curtiss K-boat at Sevastopol, circa 1916.

Czar Nicholas II inspecting the seaplane base at Sevastopol in early 1916. *Starschi Leitenant* Victor Utgoff is in a white tunic next to the man holding a rolled white document. The Czar is to the left of his son, wearing a white tunic (in dark trousers and having a dark beard). Immediately behind the Czar is his son, the Czarevitch Alexis, in a sailor's uniform. Ivan K. Grigorovich, minister of the Imperial Navy (in khaki tunic and light beard) stands to the left of the Czar. *Starschi Leitenant* Ivan I. Stakhovsky, commander of the Black Sea fleet aviation, is to the right of the Czar, between him and his son. At the left is a Grigorovich flying boat, and beyond it is the hydro-cruiser *Imperator Nikolai I*. Photo: Drashpil Collection, Russian Naval Museum.

Lieutenant-Commander Victor Utgoff in mid-1915. Photo: Vadym Utgoff.

months of unsuccessful efforts, the funds supporting this effort ran out.

The American rights were assigned to Russian naval ace Alexander deSeversky, who volunteered to continue promotional attempts. After several years deSeversky succeeded in selling the bomb sight to the U. S. Army Air Service. The money deSeversky made from the sale allowed him to develop his own company, the Seversky Aero Company, in 1922.

In late 1918, Utgoff was sent to Buffalo, New York, as a member of a commission to accept 55 Curtiss seaplanes ordered by the Russian navy. By 1920, Utgoff was prepared to return to Russia and supply the only non-Bolshevik force still in Russia, Wrangel's army in the Crimea. However, Wrangel's forces were defeated in November, 1920, leaving no authority that would let Utgoff return safely to Russia. With no choice, he decided to stay in America.

After the Russian embassy in Washington closed, Utgoff went to New York City, where he met Igor Sikorsky and became instrumental in the founding of the Sikorsky corporation. The Sikorsky factory was in a barn on Utgoff's farm (on Long Island, New York), and most of the workers were former Russian naval officers living on the farm, working for only room and board. It is safe to say that without Utgoff's energy, dedication, and resourcefulness, the Sikorsky Aircraft Corporation could not have existed.

Sikorsky and his family occupied the upper floor of Utgoff's house on Long Island and the S-29-A aircraft was built in an abandoned chicken barn on Utgoff's farm. The S-29A, a fourteen-passenger sesquiplane, was Sikorsky's first successful American design.

Up to this time Utgoff's attempts to obtain a U.S. pilot's license were fruitless because of lack of flight time in more up-to-date aircraft than those he had been flying. Consequently, he joined the aviation division of the U.S. Coast Guard at Gloucester, Massachusetts. He entered as a chief boatswain's mate. In October, 1930, he obtained a ten-day leave to practice flying on the airfield at Revere Beach near Boston.

On October 11, while returning from Boston to Revere Beach, Utgoff's airplane (an American Eagle manufactured by the American Eagle Company) spun and crashed. It was consumed by fire, killing Utgoff and the pilot of the

Photo showing the rocket system devised by Utgoff. It was to be used in assisting aircraft in takeoff, Rochester, New York, 1921. Utgoff is standing in the doorway. Photo: Vaydm Utgoff.

Igor Sikorsky standing in front of the S-29, his first aircraft built in the United States. This photo shows the S-29 being constructed on the Utgoff farm.

plane. The aircraft had dual controls, which made it impossible to determine who was flying it at the time of the crash.

One of Utgoff's sons, Vadym, remembered a conversation with his father. "Some short time before my father was killed, perhaps one or two weeks, he had been flying in that same airplane, and when he came home, he told the family that he got it into a tailspin. No matter what he did, until quite near the ground, he was unable to get it out of the tailspin."

Victor Utgoff was buried in Arlington National Cemetery in Washington with full military honors.

Several books have claimed that he was an ace with an undetermined number of victories. However, a review of his records does not support this claim. Utgoff was in several air combats during the war. His son, Vadym, remembers one occasion when he asked his father what part of an airplane he aimed at in a combat situation. His father replied "the pilot's head." One can infer from this that Utgoff might have had some success in air-to-air combat.

Victor Utgoff left a wife and four children. Mrs. Utgoff died in 1966. Of the children, the eldest, Victor, born in Sevastopol in 1915, became a U.S. naval aviator in World War II. He was killed in 1955 when he was test-piloting the prototype Martin P6M Seamaster jet flying boat. Utgoff's son Vadym, born in Russia in 1917, followed in the footsteps of his father and in 1935 was admitted to the U.S. Naval Academy. Graduating in 1939, he distinguished himself in the Pacific as the commander of the night-flying Consolidated PBYs during World War II. The other children were Valeska, born in 1928, who resides in Maine working as a nurse's aide, and Vladimir, born in 1930, who died in 1950.

Pioneer Women Pilots

At the dawn of aviation there were a few courageous, adventuresome women in a number of countries who learned to fly. Russia was no exception; at least seven Russian women learned to fly before 1915. However, the Russian women pilots exceeded their counterparts in other countries by serving in combat during World War I, thereby earning the unique distinction of being the first female combat pilots in the world.

Lydia V. Zvereva
The First Russian Woman Pilot

Lydia V. Zvereva, the first Russian aviatrix, and the first woman pilot to loop an aircraft.

Lydia V. Zvereva was the first Russian woman pilot. Born the daughter of a prominent Russian general in 1890, she was educated at the Institute for Girls of Czar Nicholas I. In 1910 she moved to St. Petersburg where she became enthusiastic about aviation. When she entered the first Russian aviation flying school at Gatchina to begin flight training on a Henri Farman pusher biplane, her girlfriends speculated that her flying attire would set the latest fashion trend. Although they thought Zvereva'a new interest would soon be forgotten, her family realized how serious she was.

Lydia wrote in her biography, "When I was a little girl, I was in ecstasy when flying up in aerostats (balloons) of Osovets Fortress. In fact, I was making models of such devices in those days when in Russia nobody performed flights yet. Only in the newspapers now and then appeared the first information about successful foreign constructions."

Her father, Vissarion Ivanovich Zverev, a hero of the Balkan War of 1877–78, supported his youngest daughter in her aspirations. Zvereva started flight school on June 18, 1911. After ten days of ground training she had her first flight in a Farman with her instructor, Vladimir Slyusarenko. Unfortunately, the flying lessons were short and had many interruptions because the school had only one training airplane. Once, before a flight, something went wrong with the Farman's engine. Her flight instructor switched the motor off and told her, "Wait here, I will bring the mechanic." After waiting a while, no one appeared, and Zvereva decided to fix the engine herself. In no time she found what was wrong, fixed it, put away the tools, and washed her hands. Zvereva was so pre-occupied that she did not notice when the mechanic arrived. They started the engine and it ran perfectly.

All training flights were postponed starting on July 21 because Zvereva's instructor took part in the St. Petersburg–Moscow flight. Unexpectedly, Slyusarenko invited Zvereva to be a passenger. "Taking off in St. Petersburg we took the direction of Moscow highway, but on our way the motor became irregular and we were forced to return. I did not take part in the second attempt because the airman Shimansky offered his engine to Slyusarenko and went as passenger himself on the same plane. The result is known—they both went down, Shimansky was killed, and I was saved at the expense of his life."

Lydia visited her teacher at the hospital in Tsarkoe Selo, where he was taken with a complicated fracture of the leg. He told her what had happened. "Thirty-five minutes after we took off the engine became irregular. While we were looking for a landing place, the engine stopped completely. We were forced to glide down. Shimansky was very nervous, and suddenly grabbed the control rod, then he grabbed me by the neck. Would it have been you instead of Shimansky, I would not be recuperating here... In spite of everything, I feel very sorry about Constantin Nikolayevich. Imagine, to pass your examination, and then three days later, you are dead!"

Zvereva obtained her Russian pilot's certificate, Number 31, on Henri Farmans on August 10, 1911. A well-known pilot, Constantin Constantinovich Artseulo, a fellow flight student, recalled later: "Zvereva carried out flights in a bold, decisive manner. I remember everybody was paying attention to her masterful piloting, including the high-altitude flights."

Later, Zvereva flew exhibitions under contract throughout western Russia, including Baku, Tiflis, and Riga, Latvia, for the next several years despite contracting pneumonia. But Zvereva had more serious thoughts; she planned her own piloting school and aviation workshops. In the fall of 1912 she started organizing them. She received great help from Fjodor Georgievich Kalep, the motor plant director. By the end of the year Zvereva had married her flight instructor, Slyusarenko. In April, 1913, they opened two aviation manufacturing plants. Lydia flew only occasionally and concentrated on helping her husband in their aircraft factories in Riga and St. Petersburg, where they built various types for the Imperial Russian Air Service.

Asked in a newspaper interview about her opinion of women in aviation, Zvereva stated, "This will be the most willing answer on my part. Women started making big progress in aviation. After me the pilot diplomas were received by sportswoman Eudocie Anatra and singer Lyubov A. Golanchikova." She then asked the interviewer not to publish her interview until receiving her autobiography to ensure accuracy. The autobiography followed in a few days. The final words were, "Thus, by opening the path to aviation for Russian women, I am inviting them to follow me to score a victory in the air by women, in this respect to have equality with men."

It was announced to the residents of Riga that Lydia Zvereva would perform a figure flight on May 19, 1914, in a Morane monoplane. The hippodrome was crowded long before flight time, and many people gathered beyond the fence. Exactly at 8PM she entered the plane, checked the motor, and took off. After reaching a height of about 800 meters, she unexpectedly switched off the motor and her Morane started diving. Moments later, the motor started rumbling again and the plane moved upward and made a loop. The crowd was quite relieved when Zvereva leveled her plane and made a beautiful spiral toward the field. The complete flight lasted about 10 minutes, and Zvereva apparently became the first woman pilot to loop an airplane.[1] For this feat she even received a card from Petr Nesterov, the world's first pilot to loop a plane.

At the beginning of the war, the workshops of Zvereva and Slyusarenko were based in St. Petersburg. There they were reorganized in a small plant, the Aviation Factory of Slyusarenko. By May, 1916, the output totaled about 80 Farmans and Moranes of different types. By that time the plant had more than 400 workers and eight office employees and specialists, an enviable proportion even today.

Zvereva fell ill of typhoid in April, 1916, and died on May 1, at the age of 26. She was buried in the St. Nicholas Cemetery of Alexander Nevski Monastery, and airplanes flew over the cemetery to honor her. Her husband, Slyusarenko, eventually left Russia; in 1962 he died of cancer in Australia.

Lydia V. Zvereva. Her girlfriends speculated that her flying attire would set the latest fashion trend. Photo via C. White.

Zvereva could not participate in the Tsarskoe Selo contest because the Aero Club demanded such a high security deposit. And at Gatchina, when her Farman was completely ready to fly, one of her "well-wishers" put iron filings into the motor. Fortunately, the flight was canceled. "I do not know who could get such an outrageous idea; could I really be competing with somebody?"

---

(1) The woman credited with first having performed a vertical loop was Miss Trehawke Davies, an Englishwoman. However, she did so as a passenger, not the pilot, of an aircraft flown by Gustav Hamel at Hendon, England.

A group of aviation enthusiasts at the Imperial All-Russian Aero Club, St. Petersburg, 1911. Third from left Lydia V. Zvereva, fourth Igor Sikorsky, sixth Nicholas Seversky.

Princess Eugenie M. Shakhovskaya
The World's First Woman Combat Pilot

Princess Eugenie M. Shakhovskaya was the second Russian woman pilot. But more importantly, she was Russia's, and the world's, first woman combat pilot. Born in 1889, she traveled extensively. While in Germany in 1911 she was impressed with German aviation and, at her own expense, learned to fly at Johannisthal, the major German flight training center in Berlin. On August 16, 1911, she obtained her pilot's certificate, German certificate number 247, flying the Wright Flyer.

When the Tripolitan War broke out between Italy and Turkey in September 1912, Princess Shakhovskaya was eager to fight at the front and applied to the Italian government for active service as a reconnaissance pilot, but her application was politely refused.

Princess Shakhovskaya continued flying and soon escaped death in a mishap. On the morning of April 24, 1913, while flying with V.M. Abramovitch as her passenger, she took off from Johannisthal aerodrome in an Aviatik. While at only 70 to 80 meters shortly after takeoff the engine failed and the plane crashed. Abramovitch, who was also a famous Russian pilot and who held the world's flight duration record at the time, was killed. Princess Shakhovskaya suffered a concussion but no other injuries.

As soon as Russia declared war on Germany in August 1914, Princess Shakhovskaya wrote to Czar Nicholas II requesting assignment to active duty as a military pilot. She told the Czar that, as sovereign of all the Russians, he could do nothing better for his armies than to allow her to serve as a military pilot for such reconnaissance and artillery spotting missions as the weather and the Germans permitted. Amused and impressed, the Czar granted her request; she was ordered to active service in November, 1914. She was given the rank of *Praporshik* (Ensign) and was posted to the First Field Air Detachment on the Northwestern Front as an artillery and reconnaissance pilot. However, it is not clear if she flew combat missions during her service with this unit.

Several historians have suggested Princess Shakhovskaya, being an attractive woman, became involved in numerous liaisons with officers in her unit. Furthermore, at an undetermined date, she was supposedly apprehended by Russian authorities and charged with giving information to the enemy. She was convicted of treason and sentenced to death by firing squad. However, before the sentence could be carried out, Czar Nicholas II intervened and granted her clemency. Her death sentence was commuted to life imprisonment in a convent.

Shakhovskaya was freed during the Bolshevik revolution and joined the Red forces. According to several sources, she became a drug addict. While under the influence of drugs, she shot one of her assistants for no apparent reason. In return, she was shot and killed by her fellow revolutionaries.

Princess Eugenie M. Shakhovskaya—the world's first woman combat pilot. Photo via C. White.

Princess Eugenie M. Shakhovskaya seated to left in a Wright Flyer. She obtained her pilot's certificate, German certificate number 247, on August 16, 1911, while flying this machine at Johannisthal, Germany. Photo via C. White.

Eudocie V. Anatra
The Third Russian Woman Pilot

Eudocie V. Anatra, the third Russian woman pilot, gained her pilot's certificate, Russian certificate number 54, on October 3, 1911. She took her flight training at the Russian Aviation Association Flying School at Gatchina, flying Henri Farmans. Little was heard about her after she completed her flight training and very little is known of her life after 1912–1913.

Princess Eugenie M. Shakhovskaya beside the Wright flyer, Johannisthal, Germany, August 1911.

Eudocie V. Anatra, the third Russian woman pilot, gained her pilot's certificate, Russian certificate number 54, on October 3, 1911.

Lyubov A. Golanchikova
The World's Second Woman Combat Pilot

The fourth Russian aviatrix, Lyubov A. Golanchikova, was also the world's second woman combat pilot. Lyubov Golanchikova was a popular actress of the time, better known by her stage name, Molly More. Golanchikova described her desire to fly as an affliction, declaring that she indeed "caught the aviation illness" after having watched an exhibition by Russian pilots Efimov, Popov, and Utochkin. She was born in 1889 and was inspired to fly when a rich Russian told her that he could "love impetuously a woman who flew!" She replied that she would learn to fly—at her risk and his expense—and he agreed. On October 9, 1911, Lyubov Golanchikova obtained her pilot's certificate, Russian certificate number 56, at the Russian Aviation Association Flying School at Gatchina. Like Lydia Zvereva and Eudocie Anatra who preceded her at this school, she learned to fly on Henri Farmans.

During a flying meet in Riga on April 19, 1912, Lyubov Golanchikova flew an exhibition. While she was attempting to land, some bystanders threw sticks at her Farman and she lost control of it. It struck a fence and she was hospitalized with minor injuries.

After her recovery, she traveled to Germany and flew with Anthony H.G. Fokker, establishing a woman's altitude record. Interestingly, this achievement is said to have induced the German government to consider the Dutch designer's aircraft seriously. In 1913 she flew with Leon Letord from Berlin-Johannisthal to Paris; she then flew exhibitions on Morane and Nieuport monoplanes.

Lyubov A. Golanchikova obtained her pilot's certificate, Russian certificate number 56, at the Russian Aviation Association Flying School at Gatchina on October 9, 1911.

When World War I broke out Golanchikova, now married to a rich merchant, returned to Russia. She turned her Voisin over to the Czarist army and temporarily gave up flying. However, she soon started test-flying aircraft built in the F.F. Terechenko factory at Chervonnoye, about 140 kilometers southwest of Kiev. Golanchikova then returned to acting part time.

She returned to flying during the Russian Revolution and joined the training squadron of the Red Air Fleet. She flew several sorties for the Reds and spent much of her time training new Red pilots. After the civil war she migrated to Germany, then eventually made her way to the United States, where she worked as a chauffeur in New York City for many years. She died there in 1961.

Helen P. Samsonova
The World's Third Woman Combat Pilot

The fifth Russian aviatrix, and the world's third woman combat pilot, was Helen P. Samsonova. Born in 1890, she raced automobiles and took third place in a race organized by the Moscow Automobile Club. She obtained her pilot's certificate, Russian certificate number 167, on August 25, 1913, at the Imperial Moscow Aviation Association Flying School. Lev Uspensky, the future writer, often watched the Farmans fly and described this "wonderful aeronautic build, which consisted of two flatnesses fastened to each other with very thin vertical struts of yellow overtempered planes, which were trans-illuminated during the flight and their undersized 'nervures' resembled the ribs in the flanks of dry-cured Caspian roach (vobla fish). The look from below gave a frightful feeling, making out a little figure sitting at the

Lyubov A. Golanchikova (standing to right) at Johannisthal aerodrome, August 1913. A unidentified German officer poses at extreme left, along with Leon Letord. The aircraft is a Morane Saulnier Monoplane.

edge of transparent sackcloth surface with legs dangling in the space filled only with invisible air that was moved forward by the wind and plane motion."

When World War I began Samsonova was a student at a medical school and immediately volunteered for service as a nurse in a military hospital. Serving in a hospital in Warsaw, she decided to volunteer to serve as an automobile chauffeur for a general in the headquarters of the 9th Army.

Soon after, Samsonova requested a transfer to an aviation unit with the general's support. Her request was approved and she was transferred into the 5th Corps Air Detachment as a reconnaissance pilot. She stayed at the front for a short time, but the unit commander, Captain G. L. Sheremetyev, was not pleased with her flying ability and she was removed.

After the first Russian Revolution, Alexander F. Kerensky, the head of the Provisional Government, quickly gave permission for women to join the army. Soon after, Samsonova enlisted in the 26th Corps Air Detachment, in which she flew as an observer on reconnaissance and artillery spotting missions. After the civil war Samsonova lived in Sukhumi, where she became a teacher of sports and physical culture. She died in 1958.

Princess Sophie A. Dolgorukaya
The World's Fourth Woman Combat Pilot

The sixth Russian aviatrix, and the world's fourth woman combat pilot, was Princess Sophie A. Dolgorukaya. Born in 1888, she was educated in France. She participated in an auto race from St. Petersburg to Kiev. She started her flight training in June, 1910, under the famous Delagrange at Chartres, France, but obtained her pilot's certificate, Russian certificate number 234, on June 5, 1914, at the Russian Aviation Association Flying School at Gatchina.

During the late stages of World War I, when Kerensky allowed women to join the army, Princess Dolgorukaya

joined the 26th Corps Air Squadron, as did Helen Samsonova. Little is known of her military flying career because she was demobilized after the civil war. Nothing is known of her later life.

Nadeshda Degtereva
The First Woman Pilot Wounded in Combat

The world's fifth woman combat pilot was Nadeshda Degtereva. Daughter of a Kiev house-proprietor, she was only 17 when she joined the air service. Apparently her belief in the righteousness of Russia's cause was stronger than most.

Historians have suggested Degtereva had a male friend who was awaiting word from military authorities on an appointment for his physical. Degtereva begged him to apply for the physical. After he passed, Degtereva took the medical certificate and, in disguise, entered the aviation park as "a 19-year-old boy." She was successful in concealing her sex, which would have disqualified her from flying duty. How she accomplished this is not known, but she is reported to have qualified as a combat pilot.

Nadeshda Degtereva was posted to the Galician Front, where she flew active combat missions as pilot of a reconnaissance plane. In the spring of 1915, during the great Battle of Galicia, she flew with her observer, a male officer, on a reconnaissance mission over enemy lines. Attacked by Austrian fighters, she and her observer defended themselves admirably. She was wounded in the arm and leg, but managed to bring her riddled aircraft back to her aerodrome and landed safely. However, because of her wounds she was hospitalized, and her true sex was discovered. For her service she was promoted to the rank of *Starski unteroffizier* (Sergeant) and awarded the Soldiers Cross of Saint George, Fourth Class.

After her recovery Degtereva was transferred to the Caucasus Front, but nothing more is known of her life or flying career.

Section 5

Famous Russian Aircraft Designers

Famous Russian Aircraft Designers' Introduction

This section includes two of the most influential designers of the Russian empire, I.I. Sikorsky and D.P. Grigorovich, whose contributions to aviation contributed greatly to the effectiveness of army and navy air units. Both were employed by private firms where they designed the majority of their aircraft, and thus their careers parallel the history of their employers and can be considered as accounts of these company's accomplishments.

Igor Ivanovich Sikorsky began developing aircraft in 1909. By 1912 his designs were winning national and international competitions. At the same time he became acquainted with M.V. Shidlovsky of the Russian Baltic Wagon Works (*Russo-Baltiisky Vagonny Zaved* or R-BVZ), who offered Sikorsky employment with the company's new aviation branch. Sikorsky designed several successful aircraft; the most successful was the Il'ya Muromets bomber. He had envisioned large multi-engined aircraft while still in college at the Kiev Polytechnic Institute, and was able to develop the concept as an employee of the R-BVZ.

Dimitry Pavlovich Grigorovich designed and built his first aircraft in 1909. After graduation from the Kiev Polytechnic Institute he was offered a position at the Shchetinin plant as head engineer and designer. He began developing flying boats for the navy in 1913, the beginning of a series of successful aircraft.

This introduction lists a few of the many prominent individuals and designers associated with the development of flight in Russia. Several others are covered in the manufacturers' section, with the company of their employment. This small selection illustrates the potential of Russian aircraft design.

Beginning of Aeronautics in Russia

Early studies of aerodynamics were conducted by Professor Mikhail V. Lomonosov, who in 1754 displayed a model of a helicopter to the Russian Academy of Sciences. This was influential on early 20th century designers; many, including Sikorsky, attempted building such machines.

Alexander F. Mozhaisky made a serious attempt at powered flight in 1884. After designing and building several flying models, he believed it was possible to produce a large aircraft capable of carrying a passenger. His monoplane, equipped with two steam engines of a total 30 horsepower, was unsuccessful, although his theories were well calculated. His failure was due to the engine's insufficient power-to-weight ratio, a factor experienced by all designers of the late 19th century.

The beginning of modern Russian aviation and the study of aeronautics can be attributed mainly to the work of Nikolai Ye. Zhukovsky. A professor of mathematics and mechanics, he studied and developed the principles of flight in the late 19th and early 20th centuries. In 1904, the Institute for Aerodynamics was established under his

leadership, educating several prominent designers of the future.

The scientist and inventor Konstantin Ye. Tsiolkovsky contributed to the development of Russian aviation with several ideas and designs. Not only did he conceive the idea of an all-metal airship, but he also designed an autopilot, that was described in his work, *A Simple Theory of Airships and Their Construction*.[1] His most unique contribution was the design of a wind tunnel built by Zhukovsky in 1902 at the Moscow Higher Technical School. This was the first of its kind in Russia and one of the first in the world.[2]

As principles of aerodynamic design became more available, many experimental aircraft began to appear. On the eve of war, approximately 200 had been designed and built. Of course, most were one-of-a-kind projects that were never mass-produced, but nonetheless contributed to the growth of Russian aeronautics. Organizations such as aero clubs were established that lead to the expansion of interest in designing, building, and flying aircraft.

Early Designers

In 1910 Nikolai V. Rebikov, an engineer for the newly formed First Russian Aerostatics Company, was put in charge of producing the company's, and Russia's, first aircraft. Two models were built, the Rossiya A and the Rossiya B, which are discussed in detail in their own chapter. Ribokov also helped design the ChUR no.1, which flew in 1912 at the Second Aeronautical Exhibition in Moscow. It was a most unusual design, incorporating a main mid-fuselage wing with a small wing above capable of changing its angle of incidence. Despite its several innovative features, the machine had flaws and was not rebuilt after Rebikov crashed it later the same year.

Yakob M. Gakkel was an electrical engineer whose interest in aviation led him to design nine aircraft between 1910 and 1912, one which was a seaplane. He was one of the founding members of the First Russian Aerostatics Company, but left the organization to continue his own work.

Gakkel continued to improve the flight characteristics with each new design. He achieved success with the type VII and VIII in 1911 and 1912, respectively, in military and civil competitions. In spite of this success, only the prototype of the VII was purchased by the war department, with no production contracts being offered. After 1912, unable to finance further aircraft construction, Gakkel turned his efforts toward design work with diesel and electric trains, where he gained much success and eventually became a professor in that field.

In 1911 Ivan I. Steglau completed the first of his three

---

(1) Shavrov, V.B., *A History of Aircraft Design in the USSR for the Period Before 1938*. Moscow, Mashinostroyeniye, 1969.

(2) Nowarra, H.J., and Duval G.R., *Russian Civil and Military Aircraft 1884–1969*. London, Fountain Press Ltd., 1971.

aircraft designs. His second machine was built in 1912 and competed in military competition. It incorporated a very innovative design for its time: the use of plywood covering for the wings, which were cantilever. Several of the components were of welded steel tube, including the X-shaped interplane struts. The aircraft was very strong and had a clean appearance. Despite its weight, its low drag gave the machine a speed of 80mph from a 100hp Argus engine. It was no wonder that during international trials Anthony Fokker studied the Steglau no.2, incorporating many of its features in his later aircraft designs. Unfortunately Steglau was not a good pilot, and he damaged his airplane several times during the competition, forcing it to be withdrawn. Due to this the machine's qualities were not realized.

Poruchik Viktor V. Dybovsky, an excellent military pilot, is best known for the design of his unique monoplane, the *Delphin*. Built in 1913, with the help of his brother Vyacheslav, the *Delphin* had a monocoque fuselage with a centrally located lower fin that acted as the tail skid. The 80hp Kalep engine was fitted inside a streamlined nose and the entire forward section was protected by a metal covering. Despite its clean appearance, it was excessively heavy and its performance was not up to expectations.

Dybovsky's other work included modifying a Nieuport IV by opening areas in the fuselage below the wing for better visibility. He also added covering to a Bleriot XI fuselage, gaining an extra 6mph. Furthermore, he designed and built an apparatus for pilots to start aircraft engines without assistance from others.

Detachment commander *Kapitan* Vladimir M. Olkhovsky designed and built a wooden monocoque fuselage. He incorporated this into developing the *Torpedo*, a two-seat monoplane for both fighter and reconnaissance work. Equipped with a 110hp Le Rhône engine, the machine responded well, but its downfall was the parasol wing being in two halves, detracting from its performance. It was tested in February, 1917, at the Odessa Flying School, where it remained as a trainer.

Throughout 1916, Olkhovsky also modified several French designs, including the Nieuport IV, Voisin LA, and the Morane-Saulnier L, improving the performance of all these machines.

Stabs-Kapitan Yevgenii R. Engels, a military pilot and graduate of a technical college, designed and built two aircraft during 1915–1916. His second, a flying boat, was the more successful. This machine, a single-seat naval fighter, was pusher-driven with a parasol wing and a wooden hull. The wing tips were angled downward, acting as floats. It was tested by Engels in December, 1916, and achieved a speed of 105mph when equipped with a 100hp Gnome engine. On December 18, 1916, during the third test flight, a spar broke, causing the plane to crash, killing Engels. The advantages of Engels flying boat were recognized when an order for 60 was placed by the war department with the Meltser Company, mainly a propeller manufacturer. Only two were produced by the end of September, both with 120hp Le Rhône engines.

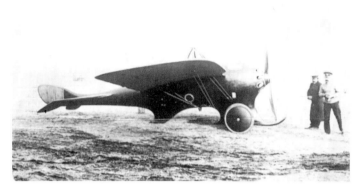

Two views of the unusual streamlined Dybovsky *Delphin*. Notice the enclosed cowling for the engine and the tailskid fin on the underside. Despite its clean appearance, the aircraft did not perform as expected.

Alexander Yu. Villish built the VM (Villish Morskoi) series of flying boats beginning in 1915. The VM-2 was a pusher-driven biplane with a wooden hull. In 1916, the Meltser Company agreed to manufacture the VM-2, but only one was produced. The VM-4 was a modified version, equipped with a 110hp Le Rhône and a device for changing the angle of incidence for the upper wing. The Lebedev firm built only a few of this type.

Villish also designed the VM-6, which could take off from land and set down on water. Several designers were approached with a request for this type of aircraft, known as the 'counter-fighter' project, by the Administration of Naval Aviation in the summer of 1917. In September, 1917, Villish produced drawings for the VM-6 single-seat monoplane along with his design of a catapult system for launching the aircraft. Construction began in late 1917, but was never finished due to the end of the war.

As mentioned earlier, due to Lomonosov's influence several others attempted to develop a helicopter, including Igor Sikorsky, V.V. Tatarinov, K.A. Antonov, and B.N. Yuriev.

Yuriev, a student of Zhukovsky, made several important steps toward the modern helicopter and received a Gold Medal at the Moscow Aeronautics Exhibition in 1912. His machine was damaged later and lack of funds forced him to discontinue his research. After the civil war, Yuriev was one of the most important individuals in the Soviet Union who contributed toward successful helicopter development.

Dimitry Pavlovich Grigorovich

Dimitry Pavovich Grigorovich, 1916.

Dimitry Pavlovich Grigorovich's first aircraft design (the G-1) was built in the city of Kiev in early 1909. His small Bleriot-type biplane utilized a 25 hp Anzani engine and framework made of bamboo. Although its fate is unknown, this project inspired the young Grigorovich and he soon attended the Kiev Polytechnic Institute. In December 1910, he graduated and moved to St. Petersburg where he continued his aviation work at the Komandantsky airfield. In addition, he became involved in journalism and published an aviation newsletter titled the *Vestnik Vozdukhoplavaniya* (Aerostatics Bulletin).

In early 1909, S.S. Shchetinin and M.A. Shcherbakov started an aircraft factory in St. Petersburg. Hearing of Grigorovich's work in 1913, Shchetinin offered him the job of plant manager (engineer/designer). At first the Shchetinin plant built French-designed Nieuport and Farman aircraft, but during the war years Grigorovich-designed flying boats became the factory's main production type.

Both Grigorovich and Shchetinin's factory started work on flying boats by accident. Apparently a damaged French-made Donnet-Leveque flying boat was brought to the factory for repair.[1] After Grigorovich studied this design and improved upon it, he designed his first flying boat, the M.1.

In the early stages of air reconnaissance, the largest problem a navy had was obtaining an airplane which could perform extended over-water flights reliably. Because engines of the time were extremely unreliable, airplanes which could take off and land on water were needed. Floatplanes and flying boats were the two designs available, the latter utilizing a boat-shaped hull that served as the aircraft's fuselage and main float.

The M.1 was the first in a series of flying boats that Grigorovich and Shchetinin developed together, but in June of 1917, Grigorovich left the Shchetinin plant and organized his own in St. Petersburg. Although he continued to design other aircraft well into the 1920s, he is probably best remembered for his work with Shchetinin during the First World War.

The Grigorovich flying boats were known also as M boats, M indicating *Morskoi* (Naval). They are presented chronologically from the M.1 to the M.24 type. Several Shchetinin-built flying boats are not discussed simply because they were designed without the aid of Grigorovich (for example the M.10).

Construction of Grigorovich Flying Boats

The Hull

The hull of a Grigorovich flying boat was designed and constructed essentially the same as a non-flying power boat. With this in mind, nautical terms are used to describe the various hull locations and shapes. The glossary includes nautical terms which may aid the reader in the descriptions given.

The Grigorovich flying boat's hull had a transition from a relatively sharp (vee-shaped) forebody to a wide flat afterbody, or planing hull. When this hull shape moved through the water at high speed, the relatively flat (planing) hull section caused the bow (front) to rise up and glide on top of the water rather than push through it. In addition, Grigorovich used a planing step on the hull bottom. At high speed this step helped to break the suction of the water on the hull, allowing an easier take-off.

The construction techniques used in building the hull of a Grigorovich flying boat remained basically the same throughout the series. The frame was assembled using exceptionally strong wood, ash being the most common. The frame was covered with plywood developed from birch or ash and joiner's glue. The thickness of the plywood varied: 3–5 mm at the sides and deck; 5–6 mm at the bottom; 10 mm at the planing step.[2] Runners were made of beech. Other small parts would use hickory, oak, birch, and mahogany.

Nearly all Grigorovich types utilized a building berth in frame construction. Five longitudinal beams served as keel and bilge with the remainder of the frame being attached by wooden brackets and screws. Several types of marine glues were used.

---

(1) Yegorov, S., *Grigorovich M-5 Flying Boat*, Modelist Konstruktor, # 9, 1985, page 78. After Captain Alexandrov (Russian naval pilot) crashed his Donnet-Leveque flying boat, he approached the Shchetinin aircraft works for the necessary repairs. This allowed Grigorovich time to study the design with the aim of developing his own flying boat.

(2) Shavrov, V.B., *Istoriya Konstruktsii Samoletov v SSSR do 1938*. [A History of Aircraft Design in the USSR for the Period Before 1938], Mashinostroyeniye, Moscow, 1969; 3d ed; 1985. page 216.

The hull's plywood covering was assembled with brass screws, white lead, and white zinc, but no glue was used. About 10,000 to 15,000 screws were used in the boat hull.[3] Most joints were covered by very thin plywood strips which were riveted into place. Some of the plywood seams and connections were covered (on the outside of the hull) with very thin copper foil strips. The foil used in the planing step was tinned.

The inside of the boat was covered with a drying oil, and the outside was covered with a colorless, oil-based varnish.

The Wings

The wings were constructed with two main spars and were wire braced. Spars and ribs were made of pine: American pine, Russian pine, and Northern pine were among the most commonly-used types. The ribs were supported with plywood plates and had voids to reduce their weight.

Wings were fabric (linen) covered and coated with a protective mixture which consisted of yachting varnish, drying oil, and methylating alcohol.

Struts used for wing and engine mounting were made of pine wood or welded steel tubes. The rudder and fin was made of either material, varying from one Grigorovich type to the next.

Normally all control cables and wire bracing were made of stringed wire, but in some cases rope was used. Turn-buckles were used on all control cables, but due to the difficulty in obtaining these a large variety was used.

(3) Ibid., page 218.

Grigorovich Colors

The hull, if not painted over, would be covered in a high gloss varnish with all metal panels painted in very pale gray. However, it was common to see the hull painted with a marine paint just below the water line. Colors used included white, light gray, and light blue.

All the flying and control surfaces were either clear-doped linen or gray, with national markings applied on both the upper and lower wings. When black or white serial numbers were applied, they would appear below the cockpit, on the sides of the hull under the lower wing, and on the outside of the wingtip floats. The rudder was usually linen or gray colored (if not made of wood), but in some cases this area was painted white with a blue Cross of Saint Andrew applied.

M.1 Flying Boat

Completed in the autumn of 1913, the Grigorovich M.1 was a single seater that closely resembled the Donnet-Leveque flying boat. The boat hull of the M.1 was shorter and its nose had a steeper downward tilt compared to the Donnet-Leveque. At the bow the keel blended into the curve of the hull. The bottom of the hull's step was hollow and the aft section of the step tilted upward greatly. The height of the step was 200 mm at the sides and 80mm at the hull center.[4] The M.1 was powered by a 50hp Gnome engine. Its wing profile and mounting location were generally the same as the Donnet-Leveque. The lower wing structure was connected to the hull by several rods made of welded steel tubes.

(4) Ibid., page 120.

Shchetinin (Grigorovich) M.2, one of the four accepted by the Imperial Russian Navy, two of which were sent to the Black Sea and two to the Baltic. The one seen here is one of the Baltic boats, Fleet Tactical Number (FTN) Sch.3; the other was FTN Sch. 2. The two Black Sea boats used the Black Sea FTN series and were numbered 29 and 30. Photo: G. Petrov.

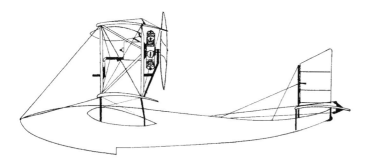

Grigorovich M.1. This drawing was based on a sketch located at the Rodina Russian Naval Museum. The M.1 was a close copy of the French Donnet-Leveque flying boat.

Grigorovich M.2 (FTN Sch. 29) used in the Black Sea, fall 1914.

Considering how closely the M.1 resembled the Donnet-Leveque design, it is not surprising the M.1 had similarly good flight characteristics. Although later modifications were made, the basic design of the M.1 stayed the same.

M.2 Flying Boat

The M.2 flying boat's hull, wing, and stabilizer area were increased considerably over the M.1 design. The beam was wide enough to accommodate two seats. The planing step was hollow and low. The aft tail section pointed at an upward tilt. A spade-shaped ski with rubber padding was fixed on hinges under the tail to improve stability in takeoff. The lower wing unit was connected to the boat hull and attached to the engine mounts by struts. Powered by a 80hp Clerget engine, the M.2 made several flights between August and September of 1914.

M.3 Flying Boat

The M.3 was a modified version of the M.2, having basically the same boat hull and a slightly changed wing structure. Although mounted with a more powerful engine (100hp Gnome Monosoupape), the M.3 did not have an improved performance. In fact, the M.3 was considered very unseaworthy. In an attempt to improve the design, the plane was test flown with its tail ski removed, but this only made its flight performance worse. A single gravity fuel tank was centrally located under the top wing. The lower wing was connected to the boat hull by a three-pronged outrigger made of welded steel tube.

M.4 Flying Boat

Built in the winter of 1914–1915, the M.4 was an altered version of the M.3. Both the airfoil and hull were modified. Although originally mounted with a spade-shaped ski (as was used on the M.3), the M.4 later had this removed. The planing step was hollow and low, and the angle of the hull's longitudinal taper was very small. One innovative design used by Dimitry Grigorovich in the M.4 design allowed the crew to alter the stabilizer's angle of incidence while in flight. The M.4 was tested at Sevastopol in the Spring of 1915. The design was considered good, and four aircraft were made.

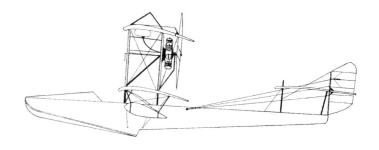

Grigorovich M.4 drawing based on a sketch at the Rodina Russian Naval Museum.

Below: Grigorovich M.2 (FTN Sch. 29) used in the Black Sea, fall 1914.

M.5 Flying Boat

Produced in the spring of 1915, the M.5 flying boat was the first Grigorovich design to enter series production. More than 100 M.5s were built for the Russian navy in an attempt to replace all foreign designs then in use. The improved boat hull, wing area, and overall layout had evolved through careful study and improvements developed from earlier Grigorovich designs.

The wing area was larger than earlier Grigorovich M boats and was mounted on top of a larger hull. The wings were connected to the nose of the hull by wire bracing in addition to cross bracing located between the wing spars. Control cables were in the open, outside the hull and wings.

The tailplane was mounted on top of the hull's upward-tilted aft section by tubular struts. The stabilizer was made of wood and supported by metal and wire bracing from underneath. The angle of incidence could be adjusted on the ground only, not in the air. The rudder and fin's framework was made from a combination of welded steel tubes and wood ribs. The hull's planing step was hollow, and its height had been reduced at the sides and axis. The chine of the planing step was fitted with wooden runners, which made land movement easier. The spade-shaped ski had been removed for good. A pressurized fuel tank was located inside the hull behind the pilot's seat. Fuel was fed to the engine by means of a hand pump.

As a combat aircraft the M.5 was powered by a 100hp Clerget engine and normally carried a crew of two. As a trainer, the M.5 utilized a 100hp Gnome-Monosoupape engine and the crew was sometimes increased to three. Surprisingly, the M.5 served as a trainer as late as 1925.

When it served in a reconnaissance role the plane could carry bombs and, in some cases, a single machine gun (Maxim type) in front of the cockpit on the right side

Grigorovich M.5 (serial number 57), being hoisted aboard the seaplane carrier *Almaz* during operations in the Black Sea, ca. 1916. The Almaz was a hybrid cruiser/yacht that operated in the Black Sea during the war. Photo: Drashpil Collection, Rodina Russian Naval Museum.

for the observer. In this role the M.5 was the first Russian-designed plane to be used on the newly converted seaplane carriers.

In early 1915 the Black Sea Fleet created a small force of seaplane carriers, consisting of two converted cargoliners, the *Imperator Nikolai I* and the *Imperator Alexandr I*,

The cockpit interior of a Grigorovich M.5. The control stick is mounted on the left side of the cockpit. The machine gun is a Maxim of 7.62 mm. The Russian letters on the right side of the photo indicate "restricted viewing for security reasons." Photo: Drashpil Collection, Rodina Russian Naval Museum.

272   THE IMPERIAL RUSSIAN AIR SERVICE

This is the prototype M.5 on the ramp at the Shchetinin (PRTV) company's establishment on Krestovsky Island (St. Peterburg), in 1915. Photo: G. Petrov.

Another view of the M.5 prototype at Krestovsky Island (St. Peterburg), in 1915. Photo: G. Petrov.

Grigorovich M.11 at Raumo in the winter 1916–17. This boat, FTN 4, was allocated to Lt. M. P. Telepnev in August 1917. Photo: Mikkola album via Y. Toivanen.

Grigorovich M.5 (serial number 32) being hoisted off either the seaplane carrier *Imperator Alexandr I* or *Imperator Nikolai I*, 1915–1916. An airman is riding a line to the aircraft, while ship's crewmen are using long poles to keep the aircraft away from the ship's sides. Photo: Drashpil Collection, Rodina Russian Naval Museum.

Grigorovich M.5 (serial number 36), equipped with a Maxim 7.62 mm machine gun. The radio antenna's circular housing can be seen with the windup crank attached. Empty bombracks are located next to the antenna housing. This flying boat had been painted with a light colored marine paint on the bottom of its hull. Photo: Drashpil Collection, Rodina Russian Naval Museum.

Profile view of a Grigorovich M.5 (serial number 47).

Grigorovich M.5 (serial number 38), mounted with an infantry-style Maxim machine gun. The circular housing is for the radio antenna. The removed panel under the gun reveals the position of the radio transmitter unit. Serial number "38" is white with black highlighting. The light-colored weight on the drum was used to help unwind the antenna when needed, Photo: Drashpil Collection, Rodina Russian Naval Museum.

Grigorovich M.5 (serial number 41), being hoisted on the seaplane carrier *Almaz*. This photo was dated 13 March 1916 by the Julian calendar, which lagged behind the Gregorian calendar by 13 days. Photo: Drashpil Collection, Rodina Russian Naval Museum.

and the hybrid cruiser-yacht *Almaz*. The *Imperators* were rated as *gidrokreisera* (hydro-cruisers). Later in the war a few Romanian vessels were also fitted to operate seaplanes with the Black Sea Fleet.

The two *Imperators* carried from six to eight seaplanes each, while the smaller *Almaz* could accommodate three at most. Cranes aboard the vessels placed the aircraft on the water for takeoff and recovered them after landing. During operations the carriers would operate 30 to 40 miles offshore to avoid being spotted by the enemy. The vessels would turn broadside to the wind to create a lee through which the seaplanes would take off.

Being easy to handle in the air and water, the M.5 design was considered very successful.

The M.5's maximum speed of 105 km/h (65.2 mph) proved to be too slow as newer enemy aircraft appeared. Attempts were made to equip the M.5 with a more powerful engine, but this only increased the weight and drag of the plane, resulting in decreased performance.

M.6, M.7, and M.8 Flying Boats

In 1915 Grigorovich started construction of a new flying boat for the Imperial Navy which was to utilize a more powerful 150hp engine. Three intermediate variants, the M.6, M.7, and M.8 were built to study and improve upon the hull structure that would be used in the final design, the M.9 flying boat. Throughout the development process the wing and tail units of the intermediate versions stayed the same.

The hull design of the first variant, the M.6, closely matched the M.5's hull, but with a very pronounced hull chine. Due to the increased weight of the engine, this design sat low in the water, which made takeoff difficult.

The M.7's hull was further altered. The angle of the step was increased and the planning step raised to make takeoff easier. The M.7 had a heavy takeoff, but handled satisfactorily in the air.

The M.8's hull was again altered to have its planing step increased to approximately 150 mm.[5] The hull had a moderate chine and the rear of the hull rose up at a steep angle. Although the M.8 was considered unsuccessful (it was unable to lift out of the water), Grigorovich's study of it and the other variants led to the M.9 flying boat.

---

(5) Shavrov, V.B., *A History of Aircraft Design in the USSR for the Period Before 1938*, Mashinostroyeniye, Moscow, 1969; 3d ed; 1985. page 220.

M.9 Flying Boat

The M.9 was the most successful of all the flying boats designed by Grigorovich. Its qualities in both seaworthiness and flying performance caused the M.9 to be built in greater numbers than any other Grigorovich type (a total of 500). The M.9 was used in both the Black Sea and in the Baltic Sea. At least 32 naval flying stations were equipped with the type.[6] Like the M.5, the M.9 was used on the seaplane carriers of both fleets.

Just as the first M.9 finished flight trials in January of 1916, the M.9 was put into production. Initially there were two types of hulls. The first had a hollow bottom at the planing step (similar to the M.5) and the lateral breadth of the planing step was shaped like an elongated triangular plywood box. The second version (made in the largest numbers) featured a narrow board along the bottom of the planing step which added to the breadth. Both hull types had shallow keels. Although the majority of the M.9s produced were powered by a 150hp Salmson engine, several other engines were used: 140hp and 160hp Salmson; 220hp Renault; and the 140hp Hispano Suiza.

The M.9 could achieve a maximum speed of only 110 km/h (68.3 mph) due to the high drag produced by the Salmson engine, two radiators, carburetor, air scoop, oil tank, controls and bracing wires, which were all exposed to the air stream. Although several improvements were introduced over time, the fundamental design stayed the same.

Like most Russian aircraft, the M.9 served in a reconnaissance role, patrolling and bombing targets. The M.9 was a three seater, but almost always carried a crew of two.

Although not built for air-to-air combat, due to the numbers made and its use throughout the navy, it is not surprising that the M.9 was involved in aerial combats. Many Russian naval pilots achieved victories in these planes, with two reaching ace status.

The first German submarine loss possibly caused by aerial attack may be attributed to a Grigorovich. This was *UB-7*, which disappeared in the Black Sea and may have been the submarine reportedly bombed by a Grigorovich in October, 1916.[7] *U.B.7* had been attacked earlier off the Turkish coast by Grigorovich flying boats returning to their carriers. It was slightly damaged and forced to withdraw.[8]

The M.9 was armed with a single machine gun mounted on a pivoting arm in the forward cockpit. The armament was based on weapon availability, and included the following types: Maxim; Lewis; Vickers; and Hotchkiss. Sometimes an Oerlikon cannon was used. Several pilots tried to change this situation by arranging an additional gun for rear defense. However, for the most part, only the single forward-mounted gun was used. In addition to a gun, the Grigorovich flying boats could be equipped to carry several small bombs on each side of the hull.

A closeup of a M.9 (serial number 4). The M.9 could achieve a maximum speed of only 110 km/h (68.3 mph) due to the drag produced by the Salmson engine, two radiators, carburetor, air scoop, oil tank, controls, and bracing wires, which were all exposed to the air stream as clearly shown in this photo.

---

(6) Nowarra, H.J., *Marine Aircraft of the 1914–1918 War*, Harleyford publications, England, 1966, page 138.

(7) Layman, R.D., *Allied Aircraft vs German Submarines 1916–1918*, Cross & Cockade (USA), vol 11 # 4, 1970, page 302. See appendix 1: summary of U-boats known or presumed lost due to aerial attack.

(8) The U.B.7 was attacked and damaged off the Turkish coast by Grigorovich flying boats operating from both the *Imperator* hydro-cruisers. However, the aircraft used in this attack may have been the Grigorovich M.5 type, not the M.9.

Grigorovich M.9 shown at Oranienburg in 1920. Photo: G. Petrov.

Above: The M.9's strut-mounted fuel tanks are located on each side of the main wing and the long radiator assemblies are located on each side of the engine. This aircraft is shown on the wooden docks at Oranienbaum (near St. Petersburg), 1920. Photo: G. Petrov.

Above: Grigorovich M.9 on the wooden quay at the Air Detachment base at Raumo in Finland in 1917.

Right: Grigorovich M.9 (serial number 102), at Revel Air Station, located on the Baltic Sea, 1916. Naval Pilot *Leitenant* Nikolai A. Ragozin is shown wearing the white-colored hat. He shot down a German fighter on December 20, 1916, while flying a M.9 (his only aerial victory of the war). Photo: Drashpil Collection, Rodina Russian Naval Museum.

M.9 flying boats on the deck of the river aircraft carrier barge *Kommuna*, 1919. The *Kommuna* was equipped to carry up to nine Grigorovich M.9 flying boats for the Bolshevik Volga River flotilla throughout the Russian Civil War.

Although in need of repair, this M.9 offers a unique view of the Bolshevik's red star located on the top wing.

A mechanic examining a 150hp Salmson engine of a M.9 at Mariehamn (Aland Islands) in 1917. Photo: Alands Museum via H. Woodman.

M.11 Flying Boat

The M.11 was built in the summer of 1916 to meet the navy's need for a small fighter. This single bay biplane was smaller than other flying boats and appeared in both single- and two-seater versions.

The two-seater had a tandem cockpit with the pilot in the rear seat, and was the first M.11 version built and flown. Badly underpowered by its 100hp Gnome engine, the M.11's two-seater flight tests demonstrated an overall poor performance. As a result, only a small number of two-seaters were ordered. However, these were delivered with 110hp Le Rhône engines, which had become the standard for all M.11s, both single- and two-seaters. The observer/gunner had a machine gun mounted on a pivoting arm that allowed movement from side to side.

Although sent to the front for combat, the M.11 two seaters served only as trainers.

The single-seater M.11 utilized one fixed machine gun faired over on the deck in front of the pilot. For the first time in the Grigorovich series, armor plating was added: a steel disc (4–5 mm thick) was mounted in the cowl to protect the engine; a plate (6 mm thick) was mounted in front of the pilot's seat, a steel windscreen replaced the one normally used; and the rims on the leading edge of each wing strut were also protected by armor (2–3 mm thick).[9] One version even utilized a small periscope which allowed its pilot to remain under cover.[10] All the M.11s were fitted with a pusher propeller and had their engines enclosed in a cylindrical nacelle.

Most of the Grigorovich flying boats could be fitted with skis in winter, but the M.11 appears to have been the model on which the concept was developed by Alexander Seversky (a navy ace). The use of aircraft skis was not unique. Glenn Curtiss had used skis on flying boats prior to Grigorovich, and in Russia, Igor Sikorsky had also used skis on his giant aircraft, the *Il'ya Muromets*. It was Seversky's mounting design that was innovative, being the first to allow a Grigorovich flying boat to use skis. Although the ski system lacked shock absorbers and created a considerable amount of drag, the use of skis prevented damage to the boat hull and allowed smoother landings.[11] In addition, the ski system now allowed Grigorovich flying boats to take off on snow or ice.

The mounting design called for flanged steel tubes

(9) Op. cit., page 229.
(10) Ibid., page 224.
(11) Grigorovich flying boats were able to, and in fact occasionally did, land on snow and ice without the aid of skis.

Above: Grigorovich M.11 (two-seater) at the officers winter training school at Baku, early 1917. Photo: G. Petrov.

Grigorovich M.11 single-seater at Revel air station. The cylindrical nacelle enclosed the engine's fuel tank. Photo: Drashpil Collection, Rodina Russian Naval Museum.

(legs) to be placed in one of two locations: the bottom of the hull just in front of the planing step; or attached to the sides of the hull, just below the planing step. A steel tube axle was inserted through the two main tubes and the skis were attached to the axle. A smaller ski was also attached to the tail.

On the M.11 the angle of chine and keel of the boat hull was small and the bottom of the planing step was fitted with a strip. The upper wing had a slightly larger chord and span than the lower wing. In addition, the upper wing had a sweep of five degrees and was slightly staggered. Ailerons were located on the top wing and protruded past the wing's trailing edge. The wire-braced (cable type) wings had airfoils that differed between top and bottom wing and were stable between three and eleven degrees of incidence. The tail fin was on top of the horizontal stabilizer which was spaced above the hull. However, when the M.11 was mounted on skis, the tail fin would have its surface extended below the surface of the horizontal stabilizer.

The Imperial Russian Navy ordered 100 planes in 1916, but only 75 were produced. The M.11 was used operationally in both the Black Sea and the Baltic Sea. Navy pilots liked the armor protection of the M.11, but compared to the other Grigorovich types it was difficult to control and not very seaworthy. The hull sat deep in the water, making takeoffs and landings difficult. Several pilots introduced modifications in an attempt to improve their plane's performance. One Black Sea pilot added a spring to his rudder pedals to balance the rudder's moment. Another pilot changed his M.11 by altering the span and cord of the upper and lower wings. Nevertheless, the usual M.11 remained in production.

M.12 Flying Boat

The next Grigorovich design was the M.12 flying boat. Developed in late 1916, this machine was basically a M.11 variant. The main wings were the same on both types. The main difference was the shape of the hull's nose and the tail unit area. Both types could obtain a maximum speed of 92 mph, but the M.12 had a higher rate of climb than the M.11. A 110hp Le Rhône was the standard engine on the M.12. Built in several small batches for the Black Sea and Baltic Sea fleets, the M.12 was in service until 1922.

M.15 Flying Boat

Built in mid 1916, the M.15 was simply a smaller version of the M.9 powered by a 150hp Hispano Suiza engine. The reduced size and weight made the M.15 a successful hydroplane. However, the M.15 did not replace the M.9, which was still in production. Of about 80 aircraft ordered, most were utilized as trainers in both the Black Sea and Baltic Sea. The M.15 carried a crew of two in a combat role, but could accommodate three as a trainer.

Above: Grigorovich M.15 mounted on skis, winter 1916.

Below: Grigorovich M.12, spring 1917. Photo: Drashpil Collection, Rodina Russian Naval Museum.

Grigorovich M.15 powered by a 150 hp Hispano-Suiza engine.

M.16 Floatplane

Not a flying boat, this floatplane was designed by Grigorovich after the navy requested a reconnaissance plane for winter conditions using a 150hp Salmson engine. Produced in late 1916, the M.16 was a three-bay biplane mounted on two flat-bottomed main floats and a smaller tail float. A nacelle carried the crew of two, and the plane's airframe matched that of the Farman (16, 20, 22) designs. The wings were similar to the M.9 flying boat, but larger. Utilizing a pusher propeller, the M.16 weighed and performed the same as the M.9 flying boat.[12]

_____
(12) Op. cit., page 226.

Above: Lewis gun mounted in the forward section of an M.15 Photo: Drashpil Collection, Rodina Russian Naval Museum.

Below: This photograph was taken on 17 March, 1917, and shows a Grigorovich M.16 landing on the ice at Mariehamn. Having flown from Abo, the crew brought the news of the abdication of the Czar and the formation of the Provisional Government in Russia. Photo: Alands Museum via H. Woodman.

Left: M.16 (serial number 11), winter 1917.

M.17, M.18, M.19, M.20, and M.24 Flying Boats

It appears friction developed between Shchetinin and Grigorovich at this point and in June of 1917 Grigorovich left the Shchetinin plant and organized his own company in St. Petersburg. Each of the next five designs he introduced was a variant of an earlier Grigorovich type.

The M.17 flying boat was basically the same design as the M.15. Power was provided by a 150hp Hispano-Suiza engine, but at least one used a 130 hp Clerget engine. The exact number produced is unknown, but was probably small. Several were still in use in the Black Sea as late as 1922.

The M.18 flying boat was developed concurrently with the M.17 and differed only by the fact it used a 200hp Hispano-Suiza engine.

The M.19 flying boat was a modified version of the M.9 which incorporated several features of the M.15.

Although production was started in mid 1918, it stopped shortly afterwards. On the few aircraft made, the standard engine was a 160hp Salmson.

The M.20 was was very similar to the M.5, which was still in production. The M.20 was powered by a 120hp Le Rhône engine. Produced in small numbers, this flying boat served the Bolshevik forces during the Russian Civil War.

The final flying boat in this series was the M.24. Known as the Commune, this type was built at the Krasniy-Lyotchik Works in St. Petersburg in 1924. The M.24 was a modified version of the M.9, but with a 220hp Renault engine. Although the exact number produced is unknown, this type served with the Bolshevik forces until 1926.

Grigorovich M.20 used by the Bolshevik forces during the Russian Civil War.

Grigorovich Flying Boat Data

Designer: Grigorovich, Dimitry Pavlovich Manufacturer: Shchetinin Plant

Model:	M.1	M.2	M.3	M.5	M.6	M.7	M.8
Year:	1913	1914	1914	1915	1915	1915	1915
Engine(s) type:	50 hp Gnome	80 hp Clerget	100 hp Gnome	100 hp Gnome	150 hp Sunbeam	150 hp Sunbeam	150 hp Sunbeam
Length, m:	7.8	8.0	8.0	8.6	9.0	9.0	9.0
Wing Span, m:	9.0	13.68	13.68	13.62	16.0	16.0	16.0
Wing Area, m^2:	18.0	33.5	33.5	37.9	54.8	54.8	54.8
Wt. empty, kg:	420	—	—	660	—	—	—
Wt. fuel/oil, kg:	—	—	—	140	—	—	—
Wt. load, kg:	200	200	—	300	—	—	—
Wt. flying, kg:	620	870	870	960	—	—	—
Wingload, kg/m^2:	—	26.0	26.0	25.3	—	—	—
Powerload, kg/hp:	12.4	10.9	8.7	9.6	—	—	—
Speed, km/h:	—	—	—	105	—	94.4	—

Model:	M.9	M.11	M.12	M.15	M.16	M.20
Year:	1915	1916	1916	1916	1916	1917
Engine(s) type:	150 hp Salmson	100 hp Gnome	110 hp LeRhône	150 hp Hisso	150 hp Salmson	120 hp Le Rhône
Length, m:	9.0	7.6	7.6	8.4	8.6	8.2
Wing Span, m:	16.0	8.75	8.75	11.9	18.0	13.62
Wing Area, m^2:	54.8	26.0	26.0	44.0	61.8	37.9
Wt. empty, kg:	1060	665	620	840	1100	660
Wt. fuel/oil, kg:	220	90	106	184	185	124
Wt. load, kg:	550	250	250	480	350	300
Wt. flying, kg:	1610	915	870	1320	1450	960
Wingload, kg/m^2:	29.4	35.0	—	29.5	23.5	25.3
Powerload, kg/hp:	10.7	9.1	18.0	9.45	9.7	7.1
Speed, km/h:	110	140	140	125	110	115

Notes:
1. The M.1 was a close copy of the Leveque flying boat.
2. the M.5 used a 130 hp Clerget engine for combat roles. A total of 105 M.5s were built.
3. Only a few M.7s were built.
4. The M.8 was never able to take off from the water.
5. The M.11 was the first in the series to have armor plating.

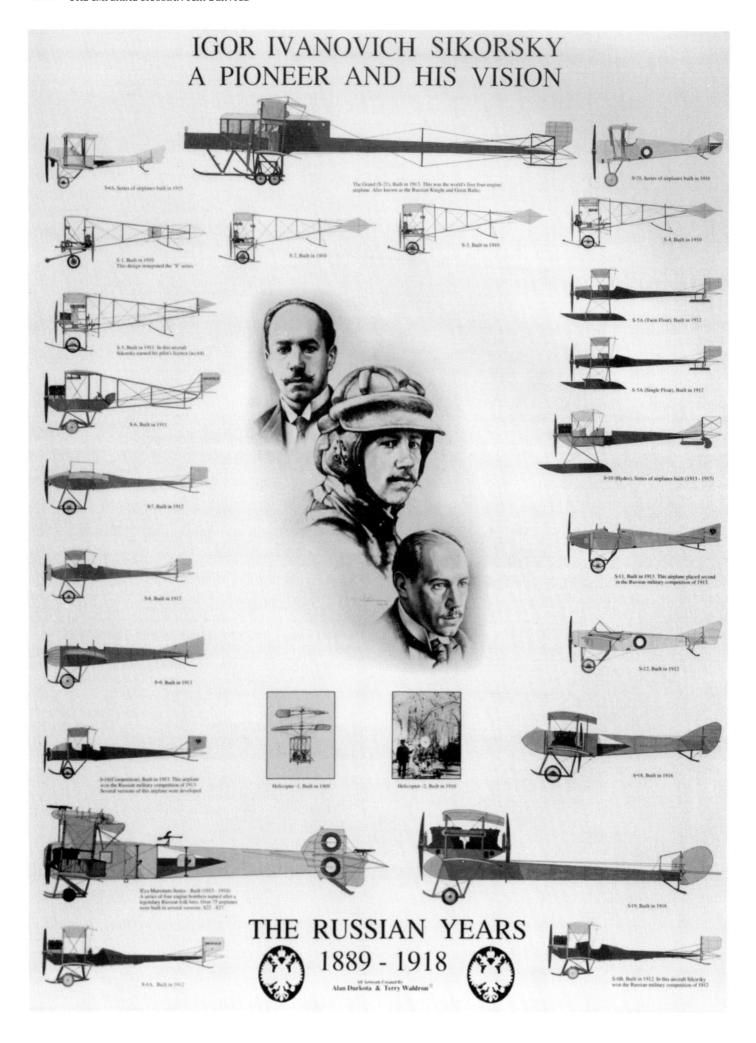

Igor Ivanovich Sikorsky

Igor Ivanovich Sikorsky.

Igor Ivanovich Sikorsky was born in the city of Kiev on May 25, 1889. His father, Ivan A. Sikorsky, was a prominent professor who had pursued an academic career and conducted pioneering research in the field of psychiatry. The elder Sikorsky earned a considerable reputation and wealth as a lecturer and writer in both Russia and Western Europe. Through the father's encouragement, the Sikorsky home was filled with numerous books, lively conversation, and an atmosphere that encouraged intellectual curiosity.

To a considerable degree, Igor Sikorsky's interest in aviation can be linked to his boyhood fascination with the writings of Jules Verne, the imaginative French novelist of the nineteenth century. Igor Sikorsky's mother would read such novels to him. He would later write how he was especially intrigued with Verne's book *Clipper of the Clouds*, which described an aircraft capable of vertical flight. This imaginative flying machine stimulated the young Sikorsky to dream about building a helicopter, a dream that would have an lasting place in his long career.

The same year the Wright brothers flew at Kitty Hawk, Igor Sikorsky entered the Imperial Russian Naval Academy at St. Petersburg. He spent three years there and completed his studies in 1906. A naval career was less appealing for him than practical engineering. Consequently, he resigned from the naval academy in 1906, and after a brief stay in Paris, entered the Polytechnic Institute of Kiev to study electrical engineering.

While Igor Sikorsky was on vacation with his father in Berchtesgarden, Germany, in 1908, the Wright brothers made their historic visit to Europe to demonstrate their flying machine. Sikorsky read the local newspaper accounts of Wilbur Wright's demonstrations in Paris, as well as the achievements of Count von Zeppelin's early airships. Then 19 years old, Igor Sikorsky decided to enter the field of aviation. In December of that year, Igor's sister, Olga, offered him the required money to finance his first helicopter. In January 1909, he went to Paris to obtain the necessary materials to build a flying machine. He visited aerodromes and met famed aviators Ferdinand Ferber and Louis Bleriot.

Sikorsky returned to Kiev in May 1909, with an Anzani 25-horsepower engine, the type recommended by Bleriot, "The most dependable among the mainly undependable engines." That same engine was used by Bleriot in his epic flight across the English channel in July of that year. Sikorsky was building his first flying machine when he heard the news of Bleriot's historic achievement.

Following is a brief review of the early aircraft designed and built by Igor Sikorsky while in Russia (1909–1917). Aircraft are listed by Igor Sikorsky's own catalogue numbering system ("S" number). The numerical sequence, however, does not reflect the actual order in which the aircraft were built.

Helicopter No. 1

Sikorsky started construction of his first flying machine, helicopter number one (H-1), in the summer of 1909. The airframe consisted of a rectangular wire-braced wooden cage without landing gear. Power was provided by a 25hp Anzani engine, which was installed at the base of the frame. The transmission (belt-driven wooden pulleys) drove the co-axial shafts made of steel tubing. The shaft held two twin-blade rotors. The upper-most rotor had a diameter of 15.09 feet; the lower rotor's diameter was 16.4 feet. The rotor blades were made of steel tube and covered with linen; they were wire braced to the shaft.

The H-1 was completed in July 1909, and Sikorsky started testing at that time. The rotor blade angle of attack was made adjustable by wire cables (via turnbuckle adjustments). Igor Sikorsky had planned to add control surfaces directly below the rotors to tilt the helicopter in the direction of flight by rotor downwash acting on the control surface; however, this system was not installed since he was mainly interested in obtaining lift. The helicopter was repeatedly ground-tested and maximum rotor speed eventually stabilized at 160 RPM. After two

Above: Helicopter No. 1. constructed in the spring of 1909. Power was provided by an Anzani 25hp engine. Photo: Archives, United Technologies Corporation.

Below: A sketch of Sikorsky's first helicopter, the H-1.

months of intensive testing and at least one close call (at maximum RPM, the machine nearly turned over on him), Sikorsky discontinued further work. He concluded the machine could generate an estimated 350 pounds of thrust. However, the total weight of the helicopter was over 450 pounds. By October, Sikorsky disassembled the H-1 and concluded, "This machine was a failure to the extent that it could not fly, but in other respects, it was a very important and necessary stepping stone."

Helicopter No. 2

In February 1910, Sikorsky began construction of helicopter No. 2 (H-2). The H-2 had two three-bladed rotors that were situated on top of a small fuselage cage made of steel tube and wire braced. The blades were constructed with spars and ribs and were wire braced to the shaft. Power was provided by a 25hp Anzani engine. Like the first machine, this helicopter seems to have had collective pitch control only; no provision had been made for horizontal flight controls.

Igor Sikorsky with his Helicopter No. 2. at Kiev in the spring of 1910. This helicopter was also powered with an Anzani 25hp engine. Photo: Archives, United Technologies Corporation.

Testing took place during April and early May of 1910. About mid-May Sikorsky concluded that the 400-pound machine was incapable of flying with a person on board. As a result, Sikorsky "temporarily postponed" further helicopter research as his first fixed-wing design, the S-1, was rapidly nearing completion. The H-2 was exhibited at the First Kiev aeronautics show in June of 1910, and disassembled soon afterwards.

Sikorsky S-1

In early 1910 a group of students at the Kiev Polytechnical Institute formed a small society to build aircraft. The prime organizer was Igor Sikorsky, who was instrumental in building two hangars on a field in Kurenevka, a suburb of Kiev. The next two aircraft were the collective efforts of F.I. Bylinkin, V.V. Iordan, and Igor Sikorsky. Since the first two aircraft were "jointly designed," it was decided to call them the B.I.S.-1 and

Igor Sikorsky seated in his first airplane design, the S-1, a pusher biplane. This design inaugurated his "S" series in 1910. Photo: Archives, United Technologies Corporation.

A profile view of the S-1 shows the machine's ailerons were attached to main wing struts. Badly under-powered with a 15hp Anzani engine, this aircraft was incapable of flight. Photo: Archives, United Technologies Corporation.

B.I.S.-2, with initials in alphabetical order. The B.I.S. designation was dropped in a few months, with the third design carrying an "S."

The S-1 was a two-bay biplane powered by a 15hp Anzani engine and mounted with a pusher propeller. The pilot's seat was situated on the leading edge of the lower wing. Ailerons were attached to the center of the rear struts. Control of the elevator was carried out by means of a handle located on the right side of the pilot's seat, and control of the ailerons by means of a handle on the left side.

The S-1 was completed in April 1910, and all three designers learned to taxi in it. Unfortunately, the S-1 did not fly because the engine power was insufficient. After an estimated three weeks of testing, the S-1 was rebuilt into the S-2.

Sikorsky S-2

The S-2 (B.I.S. No. 2) was completed in the summer of 1910. Power was provided by a 25hp Anzani engine mounted in a tractor configuration. Ailerons were attached to the trailing edge of the lower wing and were operated by means of a control lever on the right side of the pilot. The undercarriage was supplied with an anti-nose-over strut.

On June 3, 1910, Sikorsky made his first flight in the S-2. He took off from a pasture field about two miles from Kiev. "Having never before been in the air, even as a passenger, I had to learn quickly the necessary movements which were familiar in imagination but not yet in reality."

The flight lasted 12 seconds and covered a straight-line distance of about 200 yards; the peak altitude was five feet.

On July 3, 1910, Sikorsky piloted the S-2 for its longest flight, a distance of 1,900 feet and 42 seconds airborne. The next day Sikorsky attempted a circuit of the field. He passed over the airfield fence at some 80 feet altitude, and was caught in a down draft. The S-2 crashed and was totally wrecked; the pilot was bruised but uninjured. Sikorsky later stated, "During its whole career, the S-2 spent some eight minutes in the air. Yet these few minutes in the air represented almost the only reliable source of practical information with respect to design, construction, and piloting that were at my disposal." The S-2 was the third all-Russian-designed aircraft to fly in 1910.

Sikorsky S-3

Undaunted, Sikorsky began designing the S-3 in July 1910. This aircraft was very similar to the S-2 but was powered by a 40hp Anzani engine, and had ailerons located on both wings. In late November 1910, Sikorsky began flight testing the S-3 with a series of straight-line flights, lasting 30–40 seconds each, during which altitudes of 40 feet were reached. Sikorsky then decided to try a circuit of the field on December 13, 1910. The S-3 climbed well and had reached some 100 feet altitude as it crossed the airfield boundary. However, as he started a gentle turn, the engine began to lose power. Sikorsky made an emergency landing on a frozen pond, the ice broke under the impact, and the S-3 was badly damaged. The whole flying career of the S-3 lasted a little over a week and consisted of thirteen flights of a total duration of about seven minutes. The S-3 was scrapped and much of the hardware was eventually used in the S-4.

Above: The S-3 was completed in late November 1910. Similar in design to the S-2, it was powered by a 40hp Anzani engine. Sikorsky's total flying time in the S-3 was 7 minutes, the total "life" of the machine just over one week. Photo: Archives, United Technologies Corporation.

Left: The S-2 made its first flight on June 3, 1910. It's longest flight (42 seconds airborne), was made on July 3, and covered a distance of 1,900 feet. Photo: Archives, United Technologies Corporation.

Sikorsky S-4

The S-4 was basically a rebuilt S-3, but with an increased wing area and a 50hp Anzani engine. Little information is available on the perfor-mance of this machine; however, most sources seem to agree that it was not overly successful. The S-4 was exhibited at the Aeronautical show in Kharkov during the spring of 1911, and retired as the S-5 began to show its potential.

Right: The S-4 was completed in November 1910 and crashed in December 1910. Rebuilt, it was shown at an aeronautical exhibition in Kharkov, Russia, in the spring of 1911. Photo: Archives, United Technologies Corporation.

Sikorsky S-5

Designed concurrently with the S-4, the S-5 was completed in April 1911, and quickly dominated Sikorsky's attention. On May 17, Sikorsky made what he called his first "real flight," lasting four minutes during which he took off, completed a circuit of the airfield, and landed where he had started. Sikorsky would simply state, "The two and a half years of hard work had finally resulted in success."

The S-5 utilized a control wheel instead of a control handle, and for the first time a Sikorsky aircraft had a second seat added. By June 14, Sikorsky was confident enough to carry passengers. On August 18, 1911, Sikorsky received his F.A.I. Pilots License (number 64) on the S-5 and established four all-Russian records; altitude of 1,640 feet, distance of 52.8 miles, duration of 52 minutes, and a ground speed of 77.6 mph. In September, he was invited to participate in the Army maneuvers in Fasova, some 35 miles from Kiev. The 35 mile trip in the S-5 marked Sikorsky's first cross-country flight. The performance of the S-5 was so impressive that it led to Sikorsky's first meeting with Czar Nicholas II, who was attending the exercise.

In October Sikorsky earned his first money with a series of exhibition flights at a country fair at the town of Beleya Tzerkov, near Kiev. On his last flight the 50 h.p. Argus engine quit immediately after takeoff. His low altitude (150 feet) did not allow any maneuvering, and Sikorsky was forced to make an emergency landing. The S-5 was demolished and Sikorsky was badly bruised.

Igor Sikorsky's pilot license, number 64, issued on August 18, 1911 (old style). The Imperial Russian Aero Club, as an affiliate of the International Federation of Aeronautics (*Fédération Aéronautique Internationale*—FAI), supervised the licensing of aviators in Russia. The photograph shows Sikorsky at the controls of his S-5. Photo: Archives, United Technologies Corporation.

The S-5 was completed in late April 1911. On May 17, 1911, Sikorsky made what he called his first "real flight" lasting four minutes, during which he took off, completed a circuit of the field, and landed where he had taken off. Photo: Archives, United Technologies Corporation.

Upon examining the engine to determine why it stopped, the body of a mosquito was found lodged in the carburetor jet, effectively choking off the fuel to the engine. It was this crash that started Igor Sikorsky thinking of a multi-engined aircraft capable of continuing flight after the failure of an engine.

Below: Igor Sikorsky standing in front of the S-5. The power provided by the machine's 50hp Argus engine allowed Sikorsky to record a series of altitude, speed, and distance records. Photo: Archives, United Technologies Corporation.

Sikorsky S-6

While testing the S-5 in August 1911, Sikorsky began construction of the S-6 and completed it in November. The fuselage was in the form of a pod or gondola with a tail boom. The boom was made of four cross-braced steel rods which swept aft to the tail. The machine built to seat three, a forward cockpit for two side-by-side passengers and an aft cockpit for the pilot. To reduce drag the fuel tank had a streamlined shape and was attached efficiently to the upper wing. In addition, the wheel spokes were covered with an aluminum disc. The radiator was made of long aluminum pipe, with the end pressed into the collectors and fixed lengthwise to the upper booms of the tail framework. Power was provided by a 100hp Argus engine.

The S-6 had a long takeoff run, fairly high landing speed, and handled very sluggishly in the air. After some study, Sikorsky decided the S-6 had too much drag, primarily caused by the tail boom and radiator. It was grounded in December and then completely rebuilt as the S-6A.

Sikorsky standing beside the S-6 at Kiev in December 1911. Photo: Archives, United Technologies Corporation.

The S-6 at Kiev in December 1911. This machine was completely rebuilt as the S-6A in early 1912. Photo: Archives, United Technologies Corporation.

Sikorsky S-6A

Although the two aircraft looked nothing alike, the S-6A was basically a redesigned S-6. The most important design change was the elimination of the tail boom, which was replaced with a fuselage covered with thin plywood (0.125 inches thick). To reduce drag, the radiator was placed underneath the fuselage, the wing struts were streamlined, and the lower-wing ailerons were removed.

On its first test flights in early March, the S-6A's performance exceeded the most optimistic predictions. Takeoff and landing runs were shorter, and rate of climb was improved with significantly higher payloads. Depending on fuel load and number of passengers aboard, speed ranged from 68 to 75 mph while carrying loads of up to 1,000 pounds. On March 14, Sikorsky established a new world's speed record with 2 passengers (3 men on board) when he attained a speed of 65.8 mph.

In April 1912, the S-6A was shown at the Moscow Aeronautical Exhibition, winning Sikorsky top prize—the "Great Golden Medal" for achievement in aviation.

The Russian Baltic Railroad Car Factory (R-BVZ)

With the success of the S-6A, Sikorsky received numerous offers of employment In the spring of 1912, he completed negotiations with the Russian Baltic Railroad Car Factory (*Russko-Baltiisky Vagonny Zaved* or R-BVZ), and entered what many consider the second phase of his aviation career.

The company obtained exclusive design rights for the S-6A and any subsequent designs for a period of five years. Sikorsky received the position of "designer and chief engineer of the company's aircraft factory," salary, royalties, and the right to build not less than one experimental airplane every year. He would later write, "Looking backward at that time, I realized to what a considerable extent this success was due to the support and encouragement which I always received from members of my family. I must also mention the fine cooperation and honest, hard work that was always done by the small group of men who worked with me during the three years. The six men who formed my permanent staff."

In late spring, 1912, Sikorsky shipped the S-6A by train to St. Petersburg. There he and his staff of six men went to work in a factory rented by the R-BVZ. At his new job Sikorsky immediately started to design new aircraft for the Russian War Department's International Aircraft Competition.

The redesigned S-6A was ready to fly in March, 1912. In April, the S-6A was shown at the Moscow Aeronautical Exhibition, winning Igor Sikorsky the top prize, the "Great Golden Medal."

Below: The S-6A shown at the Moscow Aeronautical Exhibition, April 1912. Photo: Archives, United Technologies Corporation.

Sikorsky S-6B

In layout, dimensions, and structure the S-6B was only slightly different from the S-6A. The most noticeable difference was the half-round fairing on the top of the fuselage which separated the two cockpits. The landing gear had two axles and supported four wheels. Powered

by a 100hp Argus engine, the S-6B obtained a top speed of 70.4 mph with a load of 721 pounds. With the S-6B, Sikorsky made his first night flight from the Komandantsky Airfield.

Sikorsky finished the S-6B in July 1912. He entered it in the Russian Military's International Aviation Competition of 1912, and won first place—a prize of 30,000 Rubles. Sikorsky split the prize money with the R-BVZ administration. His share enabled him to repay his family and, it is said, to purchase his first automobile.

The S-6B was completed in July, 1912. Sikorsky won the Russian Military Competition with this machine in late September 1912. Photo: Archives, United Technologies Corporation.

Igor Sikorsky made his first night flight using the S-6B.

The S-6B's two fuel tanks were mounted on the inner wing struts. Anti-skid fins are located on both outer wing struts. Power was provided by a 100hp Argus II engine. Photo: Archives, United Technologies Corporation.

Sikorsky S-7

The S-7 was completed in July 1912, and utilized many parts from the S-6A. This two-seater monoplane was powered by a 70hp Gnome engine and sat two people side-by-side. Built mainly for the Russian Military's International Aviation Competition of 1912, it participated in the event until its undercarriage collapsed during a plowed field take-off trial. Subsequently repaired, it was used as a trainer during the summer of 1913 and eventually sold to the Bulgarian army on the eve of World War I. Nothing further is known of this aircraft.

Igor Sikorsky's first monoplane, the S-7, was completed in July, 1912. Photo: Archives, United Technologies Corporation.

The S-7 was powered by a 70hp Gnome-Le Rhône engine. Photo: Archives, United Technologies Corporation.

Sikorsky S-8 (*Malyutka*—Baby)

Also known as the "Baby" because of its small size, the S-8 was developed as a training biplane with side-by-side seating arrangement. The forward fuselage consisted of an ash frame, covered with 0.25 inch thick plywood that was attached by screws and joiner's glue, and the rear fuselage was wire braced and fabric covered. The top deck of the fuselage had a broad half-round streamlined failing located behind the seats. The lower wings were left uncovered from the wing root to the first wing ribs to provide better visibility in flight. The wing structure was similar to that of the S-6A, with triple struts having inclined braces.

This machine used a 50hp Gnome engine and obtained a top speed of 50 mph. With the S-8, Sikorsky made a night flight on September 17, 1912, which lasted 1.5 hours, and during which he attained an altitude of 4,921 feet. He landed back at the Komandantsky aerodrome with the aid of bonfires lit by his ground crew. The S-8 was used for training purposes until it was scrapped in late 1912.

The S-8 *Malyutka* or Baby was built in late July 1912. Power was provided by a 50hp Gnome engine.

Sikorsky S-9 (*Kruglyi*—Round)

Built in the spring of 1913, the S-9, or "Round" was interesting as it represented the first monocoque fuselage constructed in Russia. The S-9 was a wire-braced, mid-wing monoplane with a circular fuselage made of pine and ash and covered with plywood. Designed as a three-seater, the S-9 had the pilot's seat located forward of the twin passenger cockpit. Completed in the spring of 1913, it turned out to be a failure. Its 100hp Gnome engine was insufficient for the overweight machine (2,200 pounds). Although a more powerful Gnome Monosoupape engine was installed, the S-9 could only attain a top speed of 62 mph. Test flights were eventually discontinued and the machine was scrapped in the fall of 1913.

The S-9 *Kruglyi* or Round was built in late March, 1913, and was the first monocoque fuselage constructed in Russia.

Although the S-9 was a sophisticated design, the total weight was heavier than predicted (2,200 pounds), and as a result the flight characteristics were disappointing.

A 100hp Gnome Monosoupape engine was installed in the S-9, but it reached speeds of only 62 mph. Photo: Archives, United Technologies Corporation.

The Imperial Russian Navy

During mid-summer 1912, Sikorsky's activities at the R-BVZ attracted the attention of senior Russian naval authorities, who were investigating the use of aircraft in the reconnaissance role. Upon their request, and with the approval of the R-BVZ, Igor Sikorsky served in the capacity of an engineer with the Russian Navy's Aviation Section, Combined Services, Baltic Fleet.

The air reconnaissance service was given the general assignment of off-shore sea observation within defined areas. But when moving from theory to practice, the Imperial Russian Navy came across problems as yet unsolved. The navy's largest problem was to obtain airplanes which met operational requirements. Due to the need for extended flights over water with extremely unreliable engines, airplanes which could take-off and land on water were needed.

Sikorsky felt he could design a floatplane which would meet the navy's needs, but due to his workload preparing for the First Russian Military International Aircraft Competition held in 1912, his early navy prototypes seem to have been non-innovative variants of his earlier landplanes.

Sikorsky S-5A Twin-Float Seaplane

Although the S-5A was completed in December 1912 (after the S-8), its initial construction had been started with the S-6B in mid-summer. As a result, the S-5A was a close copy of the Sikorsky S-6A landplane, but with a slightly smaller wing. The plane was fitted with two main floats and a small tail "cylinder" float. The fuselage width remained constant throughout its length, but its depth reduced greatly at the tail, which resulted in a very fragile appearance. In reality the plywood-covered (and wire-braced) fuselage actually resulted in a far more durable structure than was first thought. The aircraft was flight-tested by Gleb V. Alechnovich (a R-BVZ test pilot), in the harbor of St. Petersburg. Badly under-powered by its 60hp Gnome engine, the S-5A was not accepted by the navy and remained as a trainer at the R-BVZ factory. It is presumed this machine was converted to a landplane configuration and probably scrapped by the end of 1913.

The S-5A twin-float seaplane being tested at St. Petersburg, early 1913.

Sikorsky S-5A Single-Float Seaplane

Built just after the twin-float version, this modified S-5A utilized a single main float of the same design as the two float version. However, its single float was twice as wide to provide the displacement achieved by the multi-float scheme. The small tail "cylinder" float remained and wing-tip floats were also fitted. Power was provided by a 80hp Gnome engine, which helped the aircraft fly better than the Russian navy's Curtiss and Farman floatplanes then in use.

The wings of the S-5A (single float) floatplane were of unequal length, with ailerons on the upper wing only. Constructed of wood and fabric covered, both wings were rectangular, with slightly rounded tips. Anti-skid vertical fins were located on each side of the fuselage and were connected to the wing's wooden struts. The tail surfaces were of light steel tubing covered with fabric. Rudder and elevator controls were of the normal cable-pulley type.

This machine was accepted by the Imperial Navy's Baltic Fleet sometime in early 1913, and put into service at Revel Air Station as a reconnaissance machine in September 1914.

Sikorsky S-10 Airplanes

Under this designation (S-10), about 16 similar airplanes were manufactured. They were essentially production versions of the S-6B from which they varied slightly. All of these aircraft were eventually fitted with floats and served with the navy's Baltic Fleet as trainers or reconnaissance machines until the end of 1915.

The S-5A twin-float seaplane was completed in December, 1912.

The S-5A single-float seaplane at St. Petersburg, winter 1912–13.

Sikorsky S-10 (1913 Competition Version)

This aircraft was the first in the series and was built especially for the Russian Military's International Aircraft Competition of 1913. The S-10 was basically a S-6B Sikorsky aircraft which had its structure modified somewhat in response to the contest requirements. The two seats (pilot and co-pilot) were arranged side-by-side, which allowed the pivoting control wheel to swing to either position during flight. Although the S-10's upper wing was increased in comparison to the S-6B aircraft, its outer wing panels could be folded for easier storage. As with the S-6B aircraft, the S-10 was initially powered with a 100hp Argus engine, but prior to the contest the Argus was replaced with a 80hp Gnome engine.

Although not as fast or maneuverable as the Sikorsky S-6A or S-6B aircraft, the S-10 achieved top honors by taking first prize at the competition. On 25 September 1913, the S-10 established a new Russian record when Gleb V. Alekhnovich flew a distance of 310 miles in 5 hours.

Above Right: The S-10 (1913 Competition) was powered by a 100hp Gnome-Monosoupape engine.

After war was declared the S-10 (competition version) was converted to a floatplane due to its similarity to the production S-10 floatplane series. The S-10 was re-equipped with a 100hp Gnome engine to increase its power. In addition, the S-10's wing span was reduced to 13.7 meters (one bay was removed), which had become the standard for all S-10 floatplanes at that time. This aircraft was sent to the Baltic Fleet to serve as a trainer.

The S-10 (1913 Competition version). In this aircraft, Sikorsky won first prize in the Russian Military Competition of 1913.

A crowd gathered near the winning aircraft—the S-10 Competition, during the Russian Military Competition of 1913. Igor Sikorsky is standing 7th from left; V.S. Panasiuk, his mechanic, is standing to the left of Sikorsky.

Sikorsky S-10 A

This aircraft was developed simultaneously with the S-10 competition version (mid-summer, 1913). Power was supplied by a 125hp Anzani engine (derated to 100hp). Its wing span was set at 13.7 meters, which was shorter than the competition S-10's wing span at the time of development, but the S-10A's wing span would become the standard for all S-10 floatplanes. The biggest difference was the S-10A's tandem cockpit seating arrangement, which had also become a standard for all future S-10s. Due to the more powerful engine and decreased wing span, this version had a higher speed and rate of climb than the competition S-10, but its overall performance was not sufficient to have had a chance of winning the Military Competition of 1913. Nonetheless, this machine did establish a Russian altitude record of 3,420 meters (11,221 feet) with G.V. Alekhnovich at the controls. With the outbreak of war in 1914, the S-10A was mounted on floats and had its engine changed to a 100hp Gnome-Monosoupape. The S-10A floatplane was assigned to the Imperial Russian Navy's Baltic Fleet.

Sikorsky S-10 B

Developed in mid-summer 1913, this aircraft utilized a tandem cockpit arrangement (the instructor in the rear seat). Power was provided by a 100hp Argus engine. At one point the wing span was extended from a triple to a quadruple-bay configuration. It is believed the S-10B had also been converted to a floatplane and assigned to the Baltic Fleet in 1914 as a trainer.

Sikorsky S-10 (*Gidro*—Hydro) Series

After completion of the three prototypes (S-10, S-10A, and S-10B), the designation S-10 Hydro refers to the production S-10 floatplanes built in several small orders for the Imperial Russian Navy's Baltic Fleet from the summer of 1913 to mid-1915. About sixteen S-10 floatplanes were made and powered by either a 100hp

The R-BVZ factory at St. Petersburg, 1913. Several types of aircraft can be seen in this photograph. The S-10B is shown in the foreground with the upper wing's outer bay folded down.

Above: An S-10 floatplane at the R-BVZ factory in St. Petersburg. Photo: NASM.

An S-10 at Revel Naval Air Station, located in the Baltic Sea, 1915. The S-10's two fuel tanks are mounted on the inner wing struts. Anti-skid fins are located on both outer wings struts. The 100hp Argus engine was secured by additional struts that connected to the engines mount and float's undercarriage. Photo: Drashpil Collection, Russian Naval Museum.

An S-10 aircraft equipped with an Argus 100hp engine and the tubular radiator system located on the fuselage, Revel Air Station, winter 1915. One of the wing strut-mounted fuel tanks is shown in the upper left corner of the photo. Photo: Drashpil Collection, Russian Naval Museum.

Monosoupape or Argus engine. The S-10 floatplanes had some similarities to the S-5A twin-float plane. However, the cockpits were moved slightly to the rear and the fuselage fairing was deeper. The fuselage structure was entirely of wood except for the metal upper decking covering the pilot and observer. For strength, additional struts were used to connect the floats with the engine mounts. The tail assembly consisted of a tubular steel frame covered in fabric and controlled by cables that ran through the interior of the fuselage. The wings were of wood construction and covered in fabric, with only the top wing having ailerons. Gravity-fed fuel tanks were connected to wing struts located on each side of the fuselage. The wings were extremely thin to maximize efficiency while minimizing drag. The S-10 powered with an Argus engine had tubular radiators installed on each side of the fuselage. All S-10 hydros had two main wooden floats, shaped like those used on the S-5A, but larger. The same was true of the cylinder-shaped tail float. Located just behind the tail float, a long metal post extended from the rudder down into the water. On the end of the post a large water rudder was connected to improve steering while taxying.

The S-10's long, fragile-looking rear fuselage was somewhat prone to breaking in a rough water landing. As a result, the navy pilots were not too enthusiastic about flying them. On 15 December 1913, naval aviator I.I. Kulnyev was flying over the Baltic town of Libau when his S-10 was accidentally rolled inverted at an altitude of 120 feet. Kulnyev was able to recover control of the plane and landed safely.

Close-up of the tubular radiator system used on a S-10 floatplane equipped with a 100hp Argus engine. Photo: Drashpil Collection, Russian Naval Museum.

S-10 at Revel Air Station, winter 1915. Russian cockades were applied to both the upper and lower wings. In this photo one of the lower wing cockades can be seen. Photo: Drashpil Collection, Russian Naval Museum.

An S-10 entering the water, Revel Air Station, winter 1915. Photo: Drashpil Collection, Russian Naval Museum.

Right: An S-10 in a hangar at Revel Air Station, 1915. The tail float and water rudder are both clearly visible. Photo: Drashpil Collection, Russian Naval Museum.

Below: Two Sikorsky S-10 floatplanes (foreground) and two Grigorovich flying boats on the beach at Revel Air Station, 1915. Photo: Drashpil Collection, Russian Naval Museum.

Sikorsky S-11 (*Polukruglyi*—Half Round)

The S-11 was a wire-braced, mid-wing monoplane built specifically for the Russian Military International Aviation Competition of 1913. The S-11 was powered by a 100hp Gnome Monosoupape engine and obtained a top speed of 63 mph. For the competition, ailerons in the wings were controlled by a pushrod inside the wing. However, after that event the ailerons were replaced by a warping control which was significantly lighter. The landing gear was made of steel tube with wood supports. The S-11 was marketed as a reconnaissance aircraft and its layout provided side-by-side seating with controls on the left side only. Although the S-11 finished second in the competition, it remained a prototype while the smaller S-12 went into production.

The S-11 *Polukruglyi* or Half-Round was completed in the summer of 1913, and finished second in the Russian military competition of that year.

Sikorsky S-12

The S-12 was a lighter version of the S-11, and was built as a trainer with a smaller 80hp Gnome engine. In September 1913, Russian pilot G.V. Yankovsky looped the prototype, making it the first all-Russian-designed aircraft to perform this maneuver. The S-12 was successful and at least 12 examples were built with 80hp Le Rhône engines. Most examples of the S-12 survived the war and served in Soviet air units, one example until 1922.

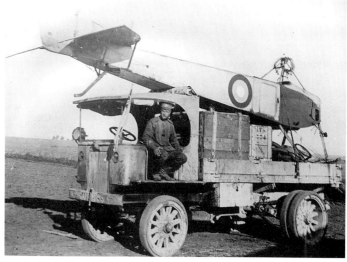

Above: An S-12 being transported to a repair depot, 1915. Photo: Archives, United Technologies Corporation.

Left: The S-12 series was started in the summer of 1913. About twelve machines were built, most using 80hp Le Rhône engines.

Above: An S-12 at the front, early 1914. Cockades can be seen on the wing. Photo: Archives, United Technologies Corporation.

A crew preparing an S-12 for a reconnaissance mission, 1915. Photo: Archives, United Technologies Corporation.

Sikorsky S-13 and S-14

Both machines were started in the fall of 1914; however, due to the critical shortages of engines and other materials, both projects were scrapped in the early part of the war. Technical data are unavailable, but both machines were most likely single-seat biplane fighters.

Sikorsky S-15

Besides a brief mention in one technical book, very little information is available on this machine. It is believed to have been a light naval bombing plane with twin floats and a 125hp Argus engine. It is likely this machine was a S-10 floatplane with several small modifications.

Sikorsky S-16

The S-16 was a small, two-seat reconnaissance and escort aircraft designed to operate with the giant Il'ya Muromets bombers being sent to the front. The first machine was completed on February 6, 1915, and fitted with a 110hp Le Rhône engine. Some 34 S-16s were built and there were five variants with differing dimensions and engines.

The S-16 was the first Sikorsky fighter to be equipped with a synchronized machine gun firing through the propeller. The synchronization was prone to malfunctions, and pilots usually re-installed the gun on the center of the top wing or in an aft-firing position.

Structural modifications from batch to batch included curved fin and rudder, coupled ailerons on both upper and lower wings, and ailerons on upper wing only. At least one S-16 was mounted on twin floats. During winter operations the wheels were replaced by skis. The S-16s

The S-16 was the first Sikorsky fighter to be equipped with a synchronized machine gun firing through the propeller.

were well liked by the crews who flew them. Many remained in service throughout the war and several aircraft were operational with the Soviet air units until 1924.

Sikorsky S-17

Two S-17 prototypes were built in the winter of 1916 and sent to the front for evaluation. Although technical data in unavailable, some sources suggest the machine was very similar to the S-16. The S-17 was heavily armored and powered by a 150hp Sunbeam engine. One machine crashed in early 1917 and the fate of the second is unknown.

The S-16 series was started in February, 1915. During winter operations, the wheels were removed and skis were mounted. Photo: Archives, United Technologies Corporation.

Wooden frame of a Sikorsky S-16cep under construction at the R-BVZ factory. The fuel tank can be seen under the seat.

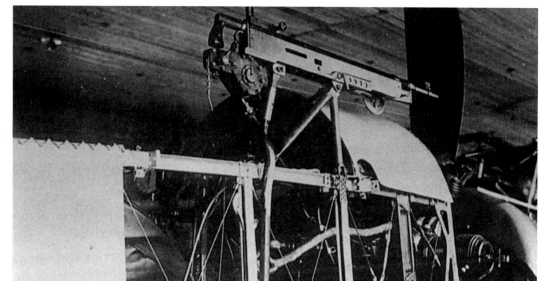

Sikorsky S-16cep equipped with a Colt machine gun.

Sikorsky S-16 (serial no. 155) equipped with skis.

Sikorsky S-18

The S-18 was a large, twin-engined biplane completed in May 1917. The fuselage was armor-plated around the cockpits and the remainder was a mix of wood and fabric construction. Designed for a crew of two, a gunner-observer was positioned in the nose and a pilot in a separate cockpit. The lower nose of the fuselage was glazed to allow a clear field of view. Two 150hp Sunbeam engines drove pusher propellers and were water-cooled by radiators placed in front of the engines. The ultimate fate of the S-18 is unknown.

Sikorsky S-19 (Twin Tail)

Completed in late 1916, the S-19 was a twin-tail-boom biplane, with the lower wings set on top of the boom. The booms extended slightly forward of the lower wing and provided a cockpit position, one for the pilot and the other for the forward-firing gunner. Between the two booms and above the center section of the lower wing, two water-cooled 150hp Sunbeam engines were mounted back to back, the front engine drove a tractor propeller while the rear engine drove a pusher. Two large fuel tanks were mounted on struts between the wings. One source

The S-18 prototype during assembly, late winter 1917. This aircraft was equipped with two 150hp Sunbeam engines mounted in a pusher configuration. The engines were water-cooled by large automobile radiators placed in front. Photo: Archives, United Technologies Corporation.

The S-18's gunner-observer position was located in the nose of the fuselage. The lower portion was covered with glass to allow a clear field of view. Photo: Archives, United Technologies Corporation.

suggests this machine was designed as heavy ground-attack aircraft. Very little technical data exists on the S-19. The one prototype built proved disappointing. The aircraft was probably scrapped in early 1917.

Below: Several sources have hinted the S-19 was intended to be a heavy ground-attack aircraft. Photo: Archives, United Technologies Corporation.

Above: The S-19 "Twin Tail" was completed in late 1916.

Sikorsky S-20

The S-20 was a single-seat fighter biplane fitted with a 100hp Gnome Monosoupape engine. Completed in September 1916, this machine closely resembled the Nieuport fighter being built under license in Russia. All available data claim the performance of the S-20 equaled the best fighters then operational on the eastern front. At least five machine were built and powered by a slightly larger 120hp Le Rhône engine.

There is evidence that suggests the Russian army liked the S-20. However, the license-built Nieuports were favored so that Igor Sikorsky and the R-BVZ plant would concentrate on production of the improved Il'ya Muromets bombers.

The S-20 series was started in September of 1916. It was fitted with a 100hp Gnome-Monosoupape. Available documentation claims that the performance of the S-20 matched the best fighters then operational on the Eastern Front. Photo: Archives, United Technologies Corporation.

An S-20 shown at the front in late 1916. Directly behind the S-20 is a large portable cloth hangar; extending out is the nose of an Il'ya Muromets bomber (type "V").

Although the S-20 was successful, production was terminated so Sikorsky could concentrate on production of the Il'ya Muromets bombers.

The Sikorsky Grand (S-21)

During construction of the S-5A single-float plane, Sikorsky expressed his ideas about a large multi-engined flying ship to Mikhail Vladimirovich Shidlovsky, the chairman of the R-BVZ. Shidlovsky accepted the proposed project with enthusiasm and gave Sikorsky approval to start work on the design. On 30 August 1912, actual construction began on what became known as the *Bol'shoi Bal'tisky* (The Great Baltic), more commonly known as "The Grand." It was the first successful four-engined airplane in the world and marked a milestone in aeronautical design and history.

For its day, the Grand was gigantic, with a wing span of 88 feet and a fuselage length of 65 feet. The design of the Grand was very innovative. The airplane had a large landing gear consisting of two skids and four sets of four wheels— 16 in all! The fuselage was plywood covered to increase rigidity. The wing incorporated a high aspect ratio, long and narrow with minimum drag. An observation balcony at the nose of the Grand was positioned forward of an enclosed cabin with large windows. A narrow folding door provided access to the open balcony during flight. Two control wheels and seats in the cockpit gave the pilot and copilot an excellent field of vision. Behind the cockpit

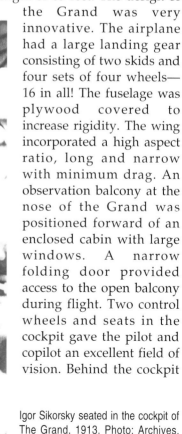

Igor Sikorsky seated in the cockpit of The Grand, 1913. Photo: Archives, United Technologies Corporation.

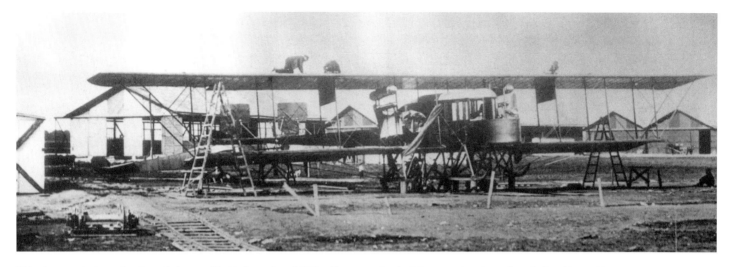

This photograph shows the Grand being modified in the spring of 1913 with a second pair of Argus engines in tandem. At first this machine was called the *Bolshoi Baltiiskiy* (Great Baltic), later it was given the official name *Russkiy Vityaz* (Russian Knight), but it soon acquired the popular name "The Grand." Photo: Archives, United Technologies Corporation.

was a passenger cabin equipped with a folding table, wicker chairs, lights powered by wind-driven generators, and a glass floor bulkhead for viewing the ground below. Behind the passenger cabin was a miniature coat closet and even a toilet. In many ways the Grand embodied a fanciful imagination worthy of Jules Verne. Sikorsky wrote, "Imagination had obviously entered into this fuselage design. It was like something out of Jules Verne, though not so impractical."

As work progressed on the plane, according to Sikorsky, "The opinion outside the factory was mostly skeptical. During my night work, besides current problems, I often spent a certain amount of time studying criticisms. Some could be disposed of easily; others sometimes necessitated serious thought. As a rule," Sikorsky continued, "I avoided arguments on this subject.

Czar Nicholas II confers with Igor Sikorsky in the front balcony of the Grand at Czarskoe Selo in the summer of 1913. Photo: Archives, United Technologies Corporation.

Igor Sikorsky (under The Grand), Czar Nicholas II (standing to the right of Sikorsky), and Russian army officers pose with the Grand at Czarskoe Selo in the summer of 1913.

Below: The Grand rests on blocks for repairs at St. Petersburg in 1913. Photo: Archives, United Technologies Corporation.

This photograph shows the Grand's porthole-shaped windows located in the rear of the enclosed cabin. Photo: Archives, United Technologies Corporation.

I usually replied in a vague and general way, explaining my confidence in the final success of the large plane."

In February 1913 the Grand was taken to the Komandantsky aerodrome to prepare for testing. Originally equipped with two 100hp Argus engines, it made its first successful flights on March 2. The Grand's low power provided only marginal performance. However, Sikorsky was satisfied, considering he proved the aircraft could successfully fly.

Following the initial test flights, the aircraft was grounded while two additional 100hp Argus engines were installed as pushers behind the two tractor engines. The first flight of the four-engined (tractor-pusher) configuration was made on May 13, 1913, with Igor

The Grand pictured in 1913 in its final configuration with four Argus 100hp engines mounted on the leading edge of the lower wing.

The Grand in flight, 1913.

Sikorsky as pilot in command. The historic flight took place at 10 PM during a typical "White Night" in Northern Russia, and lasted ten minutes.

In June 1913, the two pusher-mounted engines were moved to the leading edge of the lower wing and placed in a four-abreast configuration. In this, its final configuration, the Grand was renamed the *Russkiy Vityaz* (The Russian Knight). This version first flew on July 23, when Sikorsky conducted a "cross-country" trip to an Army airfield at Czarskoe Selo, some 25 miles south of St. Petersburg. Sikorsky successfully landed the machine in view of a large crowd that included Czar Nicholas II, who later inspected the machine. Less than two weeks later, on August 2, the Grand made what was then considered its most spectacular flight—a two-hour ride with eight people on board.

The life span of the Grand was just over four months and ended on September 11, 1913. During the Russian Military International Aircraft Competition, a Meller No.2 airplane lost its engine while in flight. The falling engine landed on the Grand's left wing and damaged it severely. After this freak accident the aircraft was not rebuilt because the structure was weakened beyond repair. In the end the Grand had logged 58 flights, with an estimated 40 total flying hours.

Sikorsky Il'ya Muromets (The Prototype: S-22A)

Following the destruction of the Grand, Sikorsky shifted his attention to the next giant flying machine, the S-22A. Although loosely based on the Grand's design, Sikorsky's plans called for a larger and more comfortable machine that would incorporate all that he had learned from his previous designs. This aircraft carried the R-BVZ Serial No. 107, and was completed in late October 1913.

Unlike the Grand, the S-22A did not have a large front balcony and its nose section was entirely glazed. The cabin area was larger and introduced several innovative features, including a separate state room for passengers, a bed room, and even a toilet. A small handrailed platform

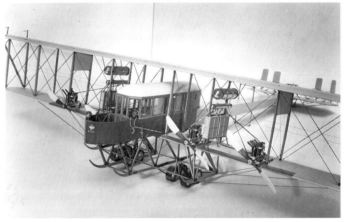

A model of the Grand. Photo: Archives, United Technologies Corporation.

was added to the front section of the fuselage and was equipped with a searchlight. Part of the engine exhaust pipes passed through the cabin to provide heat during cold winter flying. Electricity was provided by a wind-driven generator which could power internal and external lights. Most important, mechanics could reach the four 100hp Argus engines in flight by climbing through openings in the fuselage and walking along the lower wing.

The fuselage was constructed of wood and covered with fabric (except at the nose, where plywood was used instead). The cockpit had dual flight controls. The main wings varied in span and chord. Only the upper wing had ailerons, which projected beyond the wings trailing edge. Anti-skid vertical fins were positioned on wing struts, with their location varying at times. A strange addition was a smaller auxiliary wing located in the middle of the fuselage intended to increase lift. The middle wing was connected to a set of cabane struts located above the platform. The stabilizer was of exceptional span and chord, with considerable curvature.

The first flight of the S-22A was made on December 11, 1913, and almost ended in disaster. Apparently, the combination of the main wings and the middle auxiliary wing created lift too far aft, causing the plane to stall at a very low altitude. The S-22A crashed just inside the

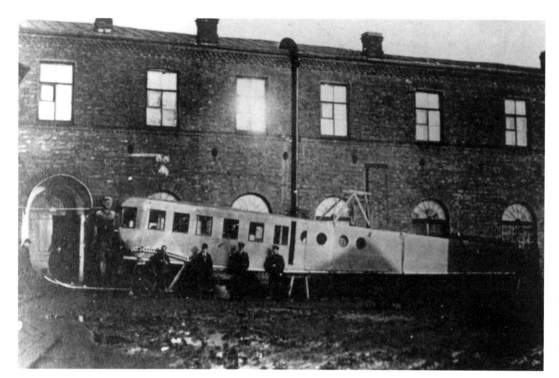

The original Il'ya Muromets No.1 shown under construction at the R-BVZ factory at St. Petersburg, 1913. The amidships cabane structure used for the rear wing can be seen above The last window. The first Il'ya Muromets was numbered 107 by the R-BVZ. Photo: NASM.

The Il'ya Muromets at Korpusnoi Aerodrome, near St. Petersburg, in February 1914. Two passengers can be seen on the top of the fuselage. Photo: NASM.

Komandantsky airfield and impacted on its left wing. Although there were no serious injuries to the crew, the left wing panels and landing gear were destroyed.

The aircraft was repaired in early January 1914, and in the process the middle auxiliary wing was removed, leaving the mid-fuselage cabane structure to serve as a railing for the platform below it. Sikorsky resumed testing and an immediate improvement was noted in the handing qualities. A number of impressive flights were carried out during the winter of 1914. On February 12, Sikorsky flew sixteen passengers to an altitude of 1,000 feet. Soon afterwards he carried eight passengers to an altitude of 3,000 feet, and conducted a two-hour sightseeing trip over St. Petersburg. Perhaps the most impressive demonstrations were the in-flight simulated engine repair or spark plug changes. Surprisingly, a number of

The first Il'ya Muromets shown after its fourth modification, early 1914. The handrailed balcony in the front of the fuselage was intended for in-flight observation. Photo: NASM.

The interior of the Il'ya Muromets offered unique comforts in the early days of flying. Photo: Archives, United Technologies Corporation.

Above: Igor Sikorsky (center) stands with a group of friends in front of the Il'ya Muromets in March 1914. It was in this machine that Sikorsky made his epic flight from St. Petersburg to Kiev in the summer of 1914.
Below: The Il'ya Muromets experimental middle wing can be seen in this photograph. Photo: Archives, United Technologies Corporation.

photographs showing members of the crew wing-walking out to a dead engine have survived to this day. Some time between February and March of 1914, the S-22A was formally named the "*Il'ya Muromets*" after a legendary Russian Knight. Sikorsky wrote, "While there was obviously a round open for further refinement in almost every respect, the *Il'ya Muromets* was a serviceable transport aircraft ready for practical use."

In April 1914, The Imperial Russian Navy ordered a float-equipped version of the *Il'ya Muromets* for immediate evaluation as a long-range reconnaissance aircraft. To save time, the R-BVZ proposed the prototype S-22A be re-engineered and mounted on floats. The navy accepted the proposal and the aircraft was converted in late May.

The plane was equipped with floats constructed of wood and connected to the plane by flexible rubber shock absorbers which kept the plane's movements smooth even in rough water. In addition, the two inboard Argus engines were replaced by two Salmson (Canton-Unné) 2-M-7 water-cooled radial engines of 200hp each. The two outboard Argus engines were raised high over the lower wing and mounted on steel trestles.

The *Il'ya Muromets* was accepted by the navy and tested at Libau Naval Station, located on the island of Oesel in the Baltic Sea. This aircraft was put under the command of a naval pilot, *Leitenant* G.I. Lavrov, who made several test flights with excellent results. Unfortunately, on the first day of the Baltic Fleet's mobilization the aircraft was destroyed after a flight from Libau. A combination of engine trouble (possibly two engine failures) and strong head winds forced the plane to land at Tserel (located on the shore of the Baltic Sea). Although only slightly damaged in the landing, the crew mistook approaching surface ships to be German, and burned the aircraft to prevent its capture. The ships turned out to be Russian, but this was discovered too late to save the Imperial Navy's only Il'ya Muromets.

The original Il'ya Muromets modified with a float undercarriage. Shown at Libau Naval Air Station, Baltic Sea, July 1914. Igor Sikorsky can be seen standing on a float at the left of the photograph. This plane was mounted with two Salmson (Canon-Unne) 2-M-7 water-cooled 200hp engines and two 115hp Argus engines. Photo: Archives, United Technologies Corporation.

Above: Il'ya Muromets No. 107 being lowered into the water at Libau Naval Air base, July 1914. A cylindrical fuel tank can be seen above each engine. Photo: NASM.

Il'ya Muromets No. 107 at Libau, July 1914. The hand railing used for the mid-fuselage platforms can be seen above the circular windows. Located on the undercarriage, just above the floats, are flexible rubber shock absorbers. One of the Salmson engine radiator systems can be seen on each side of the inboard engine, just below the cylindrical gas tank. Photo: Drashpil Collection, Russian Naval Museum.

Il'ya Muromets at Libau, July 1914. Photo: Drashpil Collection, Russian Naval Museum.

Sikorsky Il'ya Muromets S-22B

The second Il'ya Muromets aircraft was completed in April 1914, and carried the R-BVZ Serial No. 128 (factory airframe number 128). As the second prototype, it was more commonly referred to as the S-22B.

The S-22B showed considerable improvement over the S-22A. The second prototype was reduced in size; fuselage length was 62 feet and wing span was 101 feet. Power was supplied by more powerful engines, two 140hp Argus engines inboard, and two 125hp Argus engines outboard. The overall weight was reduced by less plywood and the use of more fabric covering.

In an effort to stimulate a production contract, Sikorsky continued his demonstration flights. In mid-May he flew members of parliament on a long flight. On June 4, he carried ten passengers to an altitude of 6,500 feet for a one and one half hour flight over the St. Petersburg countryside. The next day, June 5, Sikorsky established a new world's record, carrying five passengers a distance of 400 miles.

The Il'ya Muromets had performed well. However, Sikorsky decided to make a truly spectacular demonstration of the capabilities of his design; he started preparing for a cross-country flight from St. Petersburg to Kiev and back again (800 miles each way).

With extra fuel stored in the cabin, the flight started one hour after midnight on the early morning of June 29, 1914. The crew consisted of Igor Sikorsky as pilot, and three others; naval officer George Lavrov, army officer Christopher Prussis, and Sikorsky's long-time mechanic, Vladimir Panasiuk, who dined on sandwiches and fruit at a cloth-covered table, an event Igor Sikorsky believed was "The first time that meals were properly served on board a plane while in the air."

After a dramatic flight, which included an engine fire, an emergency landing, and one planned mid-point fuel

An Il'ya Muromets (type B) equipped with Salmson engines at the front. Photo: Archives, United Technologies Corporation.

An Il'ya Muromets (type B) equipped with four Argus engines shown in flight, late 1914. Photo: Archives, United Technologies Corporation.

An Il'ya Muromets (type B) fitted with a 37mm Hotchkiss cannon and Argus engines. Igor Sikorsky is seventh from left. General M.V. Shidlovskiy (fourth from left) and Russian War Minister V.A. Sukhomlinov (fifth from the left) are also pictured. Photo: Archives, United Technologies Corporation.

stop, the S-22B landed in Kiev, two days and 13 hours flying time later. On July 11, the return flight started. The next day, with one mid-point re-fueling stop and 13.5 hours flying time, the S-22B landed safely back at St. Petersburg. The aircraft was renamed the Il'ya Muromets *"Korablei Kievskiy"* (Ship of Kiev) to honor the achievement. The name *"Kievskiy"* would later be given to five successive Il'ya Muromets variants built between 1915 and 1917.

After the start of the war, this machine, along with another "B" (R-BVZ No. 135) was delivered to the Imperial Russian Army on August 31, 1914. Another five "B" versions were built and powered by four Salmson engines (200hp inboard and 135hp outboard). These aircraft (R-BVZ No. 136—139) were all assigned to the Squadron of Flying Ships in December 1914.

An Il'ya Muromets (type B) at St. Petersburg in the fall of 1914. Captain G.G. Gorshkov is visible in the cockpit. An elaborate decoration—the Imperial Russian coat of arms—has been added to the front of this machine. Photo: NASM.

Profile of a type B, winter 1915. Photo: Archives, United Technologies Corporation.

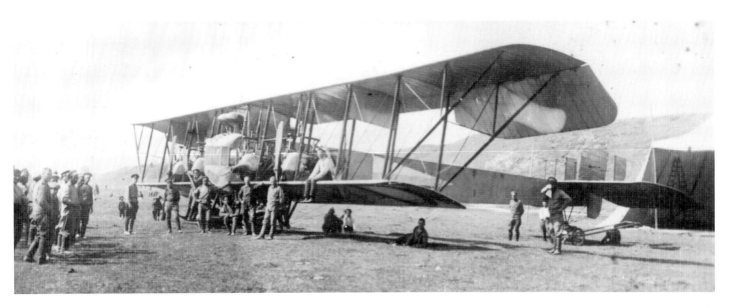

The Il'ya Muromets *"Kievskiy"* at Yablonna, near Warsaw, in 1915. Photo: Archives, United Technologies Corporation.

The *Kievskiy's* glazed flooring, illustrated in this photograph, gave the ship's pilot a great advantage in navigating.

Grand Duke Alexander Mikhailovich (second from right), was appointed by Nicholas II to head Russian military aviation in World War One. The grand duke is pictured here inspecting the Il'ya Muromets (ship No.1) at Yablonna in 1915. To the left of the grand duke is General M. V. Shidlovskiy, commander of the EVK. Photo: Archives, United Technologies Corporation.

Sikorsky Il'ya Muromets S-23 "V"

While the first "B" version Il'ya Muromets aircraft were delivered, Sikorsky led his R-BVZ design/manufacturing team through a unprecedented effort to redesign the basic passenger-carrying Il'ya Muromets into a bomber. With a round-the-clock effort, the first prototype aircraft was completed in less than two months and first flew in December 1914.

Designated the "V," this machine was smaller and much lighter (nearly 2,000 pounds) than the "B" version. The fuselage was slimmer and the nose became sharper. Extra windows were added to improve the pilot's view. The fuel tanks, mounted above each engine of the "B" versions, were replaced with two large tanks mounted on top of the fuselage and partly hidden below the upper wing.

By the spring of 1915, the shortages of aviation engines became critical in Russia. Although the Russian government had placed orders with the British and French, these countries were slow in delivering since they were also short of engines. The Russians carefully salvaged engines from crashed or worn out aircraft and reinstalled them in newer machines. This helps explain the great variety of engines among the Il'ya Muromets variants.

An estimated thirty-two "V" aircraft were built and powered by Argus, Sunbeam, and R.B.Z.6 engines. Several sources suggest the following variants:
- Twenty two "V"s powered by four 150hp Sunbeam engines.
- Four "V"s powered by four 150hp RBZ-6 engines (copies of Argus engines).
- One "V" powered by four 140hp Argus engines.
- One "V" powered by two 140hp and two 125hp Argus engines. This machine (R-BVZ No. 143), was the second Il'ya Muromets to carry the name "*Kievskiy*."

In addition, four twin-engined "V"s were built as trainers:
- Two "V"s powered by two 200hp Salmson engines.
- Two "V"s powered by two 225hp Sunbeam engines.

Right: A type V equipped with four 150hp Sunbeam engines. The Cyrillic letter Б (Beh) is pronounced like the English letter *B* and denotes a type "B" aircraft. The Cyrillic letter В (Veh) is pronounced like the English letter *V* and denotes a type "V" aircraft.

Below: An Il'ya Muromets (type V), shows two of its four Argus engines. The flat glassed nose of the V type distinguished it from the earlier type B and *Kievskiy* models. Photo: Archives, United Technologies Corporation.

Above: Il'ya Muromets type V (serial no. 19), summer 1915. The Russian letter B (shown on the rudder) is pronounced as "Veh." Thus this type is referred to as a type "Veh."

Right: Il'ya Muromets type V (serial no. 21), 1915. This machine is equipped with four 150hp R-BVZ engines.

Below: An Il'ya Muromets type V (ship No. 6), equipped with two Salmson engines, was used as a trainer. This particular machine was destroyed in a training flight at Yablonna in February 1915. Photo: NASM.

Sikorsky Il'ya Muromets S-24 (G-1)

The first G-1 (R-BVZ No. 183) was completed in December 1915. It carried a crew of six and was powered by four Sunbeam 150hp engines. As with the "V" series, the types of engines varied. The second G-1 (R-BVZ No. 187) was powered by four 125hp Argus engines, and the third G-1 (R-BVZ No. 190) was powered by four 140hp Argus engines. The fourth machine (R-BVZ No. unknown) used four 160hp Sunbeams. Several partially completed G-1's were modified into later G-2, G-3, and G-4 configurations.

Sikorsky Il'ya Muromets S-25 Series (G-2, G-3, G-4)

The first G-2 was built in the winter of 1916, then production shifted to the G-3 and G-4. However, several additional G-2s were built by early 1918, for a total of eight G-2 aircraft. The first G-2 also carried the name *"Kievskiy."*

For self defense, the first G-2 had a large rectangular fuel tank on top of the fuselage, with a small gap through which a machine gunner could stand, with his head and shoulders above the upper wing. Once in this position the

The Il'ya Muromets type G-2s were the first type equipped with a rear machine-gun position. Photo: Archives, United Technologies Corporation.

An Il'ya Muromets type G-3 with a combination of Renault (outboard) and R-BVZ (inboard) engines. Photo: Archives, United Technologies Corporation.

French officers (first, third, and fourth from left) take a close look at a type G-3. Photo: Archives, United Technologies Corporation.

gunner usually had two machine guns (one forward-firing and one aft-firing). Two additional machine gun stations were positioned immediately aft of the wings where hatches on each side of the fuselage were located. Perhaps the most innovative gunner's position on the G-2 was the tail-gunner's. To reach this position in flight, the crewman rode a small railed cart though the fuselage to the tail section.

The first G-2 was equipped with four 160hp Beardmore engines; however, the seven production machines were powered with either RBZ-6 or Renault engines. The production machines also replaced the single rectangular fuel tank with two long torpedo-shaped tanks arranged in a side-by-side configuration. All the G-2 aircraft survived through the Russian Civil War and eventually were converted to passenger-carrying airliners. The last machine was scrapped in 1924.

The first G-3 was completed in early 1916, followed by four additional G-3s in 1916–1917, and three more during the Russian Revolution.

A Il'ya Muromets type G-3 displays a Russian pennant and several cockades. Photo: Archives, United Technologies Corporation.

The G-3s were powered by two 220hp Renault engines (inboard), and two 150hp R-BVZ-6 engines (outboard). Two large rudders were mounted near the outboard tips of the stabilizer. Two fixed fins, one above and one below the tail, were added for stability. Defensive positions included a large waist-gunner's opening on each side of the fuselage, an aft belly hatch for fire below, and a slightly enlarged tail-gunner's position. Armament consisted of six machine guns and an average bomb load of 400 pounds. Although the first two machines in the series had fuel tanks mounted between the upper wing and fuselage top, other G-3s had two large cylindrical tanks mounted on the top wing center-section.

The last version in the series, the G-4, like the G-3, was powered by two Renault and two R-BVZ-6 engines. The prototype was completed and tested in July 1917. Although this "G" version probably performed best of all, it was built in very small numbers (perhaps only four) because of the civil disorders prior to the October Revolution.

Sikorsky Il'ya Muromets (S-26 "D-1" and "D-2")

The D-1 and D-2 prototype aircraft were built in late 1915, during a production break between the G-1 and G-2 variants. The D-1 was smaller than the other Il'ya Muromets and powered by four 150hp Sunbeams in a tractor-pusher configuration on each side of the fuselage. The second prototype (D-2), was slightly longer and had its four Sunbeam engines mounted conventionally.

The major innovation of the S-26 was its structural design; the forward fuselage and center wing panels, with engine mounts, were designed as a single unit. Engines, outer wing panels, and the aft fuselage were attached to the center "core" of this structure. The eight-foot-high forward cabin was completely glass-paneled (floor to ceiling). The aircraft had a three-man crew; pilot, navigator/bombardier, and mechanic/gunner.

The D-1 was first flown in January 1916, but due to poor performance it was scrapped soon afterwards. The D-2 was tested in February 1916 and flew satisfactorily. This machine was sent to the front; however, further "D" production plans were canceled in favor of the "G" version aircraft.

Sikorsky Il'ya Muromets (S-27 "E" Series)

The "E" prototype was completed at the end of 1916, and powered by four 220hp Renault engines. With a wing span of 102 feet and a gross weight at take-off of 15,5000 pounds, the S-27 was the biggest and heaviest version of the Il'ya Muromets series.

The prototype E did not have a tail-gun; however, at a midships position, it had a retractable, aft-facing belly-gun position. The nose had additional glass panels added for better visibility. With a crew of eight and armed with five machine guns, the S-27 prototype was sent to the front in early 1917.

Between February and March 1917, the prototype "E" was joined by two production "E" models, identified as aircraft "E-1" and "E-2." This machine had some changes that included a tail gunner's position, armament increased to eight machine guns, and a crew of eight; two pilots, one mechanic, and five gunners.

At least five more "E" versions built during 1917 were tested and stored at the R-BVZ's facilities at Komandantsky Aircraft. Later, these "E" machines would become part of the Soviet Air Force.

An Il'ya Muromets type D (D.I.M.) at Pskov in the summer of 1916. This four-engine version had French-made Renault engines mounted in tandem on each side. Photo: Archives, United Technologies Corporation.

An Il'ya Muromets type E at Pskov in the summer of 1916. Photo: Archives, United Technologies Corporation.

Sikorsky Aircraft Data

Model:	S-1	S-2	S-3	S-4	S-5	S-6	S-6A
Year:	1910	1910	1910	1910	1911	1911	1912
Engine(s) type:	15hp Anzani	25hp Anzani	35hp Anzani	50hp Anzani	50hp Argus	100hp Argus	100hp Argus
Length, m:	8	8	8	8	8.5	8.8	9.2
Wing Span, m: top/bottom	8	8	8	8	12/9	11.8	14.5/11.7
Wing Area, m^2:	24	24	24	24	33	35.4	39
Wt. empty, kg:	180	190	220	260	320	650	650
Wt. fuel/oil, kg:	10	10	20	30	40	60	60
Wt. load, kg:	70	70	90	100	120	340	450
Wt. flying, kg:	250	260	310	360	440	990	1100
Wingload, kg/m^2:	10.4	10.8	13	12.9	13.3	24	23
Powerload, kg/hp:	16	10.2	8.9	7.2	8.8	8.5	9
Speed, km/h:	—	—	—	—	—	—	—

Model:	S-6B	S-7	S-8	S-9	S-5A (twin float)	S-5A (single float)	S-10 (competition)
Year:	1912	1912	1912	1913	1912	1912	1913
Engine(s) type:	100hp Argus	70hp Gnome	50hp Gnome	100hp Gnome[1]	60hp Gnome	80hp Gnome	80hp Gnome
Length, m:	8.5	8.2	7.5	—	8	8	8
Wing Span, m: top/bottom	14.9/10.9	10	12/8	12	12/8.5	12/8.5	16.9/12
Wing Area, m^2:	37.5	20	27	30	30	30	46
Wt. empty, kg:	590	449	—	690	—	—	567
Wt. fuel/oil, kg:	—	—	—	—	—	—	—
Wt. load, kg:	327	327	—	300	—	—	444
Wt. flying, kg:	917	776	—	990	—	—	1011
Wingload, kg/m^2:	10.4	10.8	13	12.9	—	—	22
Powerload, kg/hp:	16	10.2	8.9	7.2	—	—	12.7
Speed, km/h:	—	—	—	—	—	—	99

Notes:
1. Gnome Monosaupape.
2. 80hp Gnome or 60hp Kalep.
3. S22 #107 is the prototype *Il'ya Mouromets*.
4. S22 #128 is the *Kievsky*.

Sikorsky Aircraft Data

Model:	S-10A	S-10B	S-10 Hydro	S-11	S-12	S-15	S-16
Year:	1913	1913	1913–1915	1913	1913	1913	1915
Engine(s) type:	125hp Anzani	100hp Gnome[1]	100hp Argus	100hp Gnome	80hp Gnome	125hp Argus	80hp Gnome[2]
Length, m:	—	—	—	7.6	—	—	5
Wing Span, m: top/bottom	13.7/8.8	13.7/8.8	13.7/8.8	11.6	—	—	8
Wing Area, m²:	35.5	35.5	35.5	26	19.7	—	25.3
Wt. empty, kg:	—	565	700	578	419	—	407
Wt. fuel/oil, kg:	120	160	—	—	72	—	96
Wt. load, kg:	—	310	380	427	262	—	270
Wt. flying, kg:	—	875	1080	1005	681	—	676
Wingload, kg/m²:	—	10.8	13	38.6	34.5	—	26.7
Powerload, kg/hp:	—	8.7	10.8	10	8.5	—	8.5
Speed, km/h:	—	—	—	102	—	—	120

Model:	S-17	S-18	S-19	S-20	S-21 (1st Grand)	S-21 (2nd Grand)	S-21 (3rd Grand)
Year:	1916	1916	1916	1916	1913	1913	1913
Engine(s) type:	150hp Sunbeam	150hp Sunbeam x2	150hp Sunbeam x2	120hp LeRhône	100hp Argus x2	100hp Argus x4 (2 push/2 trac.)	100hp Argus x4 (tractor)
Length, m:	—	—	17.1	7.6	20	20	20
Wing Span, m: top/bottom	13.8	16.5/15.3	28	11.6	27/20	27/20	27/20
Wing Area, m²:	43.5	58	—	26.0	120	120	120
Wt. empty, kg:	845	1485	—	395	3000	3400	3500
Wt. fuel/oil, kg:	160	380	—	65	150	250	250
Wt. load, kg:	342	600	—	175	400	600	700
Wt. flying, kg:	1190	2100	—	570	3400	4000	4200
Wingload, kg/m²:	26.7	36.2	—	33.5	28.5	33	35
Powerload, kg/hp:	8.5	7	—	10	18	11	11.5
Speed, km/h:	—	—	115	190	80	90	90

Model:	S-22 (#107)[3]	S-22 (#128)[4]	S-22B (#135)	S-22B (#136–9)	S-23V (#143)	S-23V (#151)	S-23V (#159)
Year:	1913	1914	1914	1914	1914	1914	1915
Engine(s) type:	100hp Argus x4	125hp Argus x2 140hp Argus x2	130hp Argus x4	200hp Salmson x2 135hp Salmson x2	140hp Argus x2 125hp Argus x2	140hp Argus x4	150hp Sunbeam x4
Length, m:	22	19	19	19	17.1	17.1	17.5
Wing Span, m: top/bottom	32/22	30.95/22.45	30.95/22.45	30.95/22.45	29.8/21	29.8/21	29.8/21
Wing Area, m²:	182	150	150	150	125	125	125
Wt. empty, kg:	2800	3040	3100	3600	2900	2950	3150
Wt. fuel/oil, kg:	384	700	700	700	550	550	600
Wt. load, kg:	1300	1610	1500	1200	1500	1500	1450
Wt. flying, kg:	5100	4650	4600	4800	4400	4450	4600
Wingload, kg/m²:	28	31	30.7	32	35.3	35.5	36.8
Powerload, kg/hp:	13.8	8.6	8.3	7.2	8.1	8.3	7.7
Speed, km/h:	95	100	105	96	125	120	110

Model:	S-23V (#167)	S-24G-1	S-25G-2	S-25G-3	S-26D-1	S-26D-2	S-27E
Year:	1915	1916	1916	1916	1916	1916	1917
Engine(s) type:	150hp R-BVZ x4	160hp Sunbeam x4	160hp Beardmore x4	220hp Renault x2 150hp R-BVZ x2	150hp Sunbeam x4	150hp Sunbeam x4	220hp Renault x4
Length, m:	27.5	17.1	17.1	17.1	15.5	17	18.8
Wing Span, m: top/bottom	29.8/21	30.87/22	30.87/22	30.87/22	24.9/17.6	29.7/29.7	34.5/26.6
Wing Area, m²:	125	148	159.6	159.6	132	148	220
Wt. empty, kg:	3500	3800	3800	3800	3150	3800	5000
Wt. fuel/oil, kg:	600	650	686	656	690	540	920
Wt. load, kg:	1500	1560	1700	1500	1250	1400	2460
Wt. flying, kg:	5000	5400	5500	5300	4400	5200	7460
Wingload, kg/m²:	40	36.5	34.5	33.2	33.2	35.5	34.2
Powerload, kg/hp:	8.3	8.4	8.6	7.1	7.3	8.5	8.5
Speed, km/h:	120	135	137	120	120	110	130

Igor Sikorsky After Russia

By Sergei Sikorsky

Following the October 1917 Bolshevik Revolution, Russia began to slide deeper and deeper into anarchy. A number of Sikorsky's friends fell victim to sabotage or were simply murdered by the Red Terror 'hit squads,' often for no other crime than wearing the uniform of an Imperial Russian Air Service officer. Such was the fate of Colonel Gorshkoff, under whose command the first combat mission of a Mouromets had been flown over German territory on February 15, 1915.

As indications mounted that Igor Sikorsky himself was targeted by the Red Terror hit squads, he decided to leave Russia and offer his services to the Allies who were still waging the war against Germany. In March, 1918, he left Murmansk aboard a small British steamer, never to return.

In Paris he was welcomed by the technical section of the French air force and immediately commissioned to design a large bomber using two Liberty engines. During the summer of 1918, the French requested the aircraft be redesigned to use four Hispano-Suiza engines. In the fall, an order for five prototypes was placed with a French aircraft factory. However, in November of 1918, Germany surrendered to the Allies and World War I was over. The bomber project was canceled.

After some deliberation, Igor Sikorsky came to the conclusion that it would be difficult to find aviation work in France because of the general post-war disarmament. In his words, "The United States seemed to me to be the only place which offered a real opportunity in what was then a rather precarious profession."

On March 30, 1919, he arrived in New York with very little money and no friends or business contacts, but with the conviction that aviation would play an important role in the development of the United States.

The following years were very difficult for Igor Sikorsky. What little money he had brought with him from Europe was soon gone. A few promising starts proved to be dead ends. To survive, he began teaching mathematics and astronomy to Russian refugees in a school in New York, augmenting his modest salary by lecturing on a variety of subjects, including his aviation achievements in pre-revolutionary Russia. With time, enough people came forward with offers of small sums of money or promises to work for free on weekends. Thus, on March 5, 1923, "Sikorsky Aero Engineering Corporation" was born. The starting capitol was just under $1,000 in cash and some $2,000 in the form of rather questionable promises and notes.

Working on a farm near Roosevelt Field, Long Island, Igor Sikorsky and his small group of mostly White Russian refugees built his first American aircraft, the S-29A. As the aircraft was being assembled during the summer of 1923, the group was visited by the great Russian-born pianist and composer, Sergei Rachmaninoff, who donated $5,000 to the struggling company. With this generous support, an old hangar was rented on Roosevelt Field, and the S-29A ("A" for America) was completed

there over the winter and into the spring of 1924. The first test flight, on May 4, 1924, ended in a crash-landing due to engines which lacked sufficient power. In a great act of faith by his supporters, additional funds were contributed, the aircraft repaired, and more powerful 400hp Liberty engines installed. The second flight, on September 25, 1924, was a complete success.

The S-29A weighed 12,000 pounds fully-loaded and carried 14 passengers in a roomy cabin in (then) great comfort at a cruising speed of some 100 mph (miles per hour). Almost immediately, the S-29 began to earn desperately-needed money for the company. One of the first 'charters' flown by Igor Sikorsky was to transport two grand pianos from Roosevelt Field to Washington DC. The flight earned the company $500 and much valuable publicity. The S-29A continued to earn money for Sikorsky for the next two years, and was then sold to a colorful racing pilot, Roscoe Turner, who barnstormed across the United States with it for a variety of clients. In 1928 Turner sold it to Howard Hughes, who rebuilt it to look like a World War I German Gotha bomber and had it crashed in his epic aviation film *Hells Angels*.

Years later, the writer had a chance to discuss the S-29 with Roscoe Turner himself. He made the comment that, when Igor Sikorsky "checked him out" on the S-29, he (Turner) was very much impressed with Igor Sikorsky's talents as an instructor on this "heavy" aircraft. In fact, Turner ventured the opinion that when Sikorsky trained him on the S-29, that Turner was being checked out by the man who had more flight-test time on heavy, multi-engined aircraft than anyone else in the world. In retrospect, if one added the total flying hours logged by Sikorsky as a test pilot of the Il'ya Mouromets production aircraft and the time logged while training the squadron pilots of the Mouromets units, he could very well have had more heavy multi-engine time by 1926 than any other active pilot.

Through the mid-1920s, Sikorsky Aero Engineering Corporation struggled to survive by building small lots of airplanes for oil exploration companies, private customers, and the like. An additional source of income was to re-wing the Curtiss JN-4, better known as the "Jennie." Igor Sikorsky's talented assistant, Michael Gluhareff, designed a new wing which vastly improved the performance of the old biplane by making it into a much-improved high-wing monoplane with much more benign stall characteristics. At least one of the Sikorsky-wing Jennies was still flying in the late 1930s. In 1926, construction started on another large, twin-engined transport airplane, the S-35, which was to replace the workhorse S-29A.

The project began to interest a French ace of WWI, Captain Rene Fonck, who was hoping to win the Orteig Prize for the first airplane to fly non-stop from New York to Paris. With great difficulty, the half-completed S-35 was redesigned and rebuilt into a significantly larger, three-engined airplane with a 3,600 mile range. Fonck's hope to beat the other entrants to the prize drove him to attempt the flight with too little practice and not enough preparation. In the early morning of September 21, 1926, the S-35 crashed on takeoff, killing two of the four-man crew. Fonck and his co-pilot survived.

Somehow the struggling company survived the disaster and began work on the concept of a twin-engined, passenger-carrying amphibian, designated the S-38. It was to prove to be the right ship at the right time.

In the spring of 1927, Charles Lindbergh won the Orteig Prize with his brilliant solo flight from New York to Paris. The interest and enthusiasm in the flight made America instantly air-minded, and airlines began to spring up overnight. Igor Sikorsky somehow felt the time was right, and accelerated development of the S-38. As the design matured during the fall of 1927, a great gamble was taken by Sikorsky by borrowing enough money to order ten sets of engines, propellers, wheels, and raw material, and start the construction of ten aircraft even before the first one had flown!

The S-38 prototype first flew in late May, 1928. Its performance was superior to any amphibian then flying anywhere in the world. Powered by two P&W (Pratt & Whitney) 420hp "Wasps," it carried ten people at a top speed of 130 mph, cruised at 100 mph, could climb with full load at 1,000 fpm (feet per minute), and, most importantly, could continue in level flight at full load on one engine. The first series was sold out quickly, most going to the U.S. Navy and Pan American Airways. A second series of ten were started and sold from the production line. Sikorsky found itself with more orders than they could produce in their Long Island facilities.

In 1929, an S-38 was used by Colonel Lindbergh to inaugurate air mail service between the United States and the Panama Canal. Sikorsky re-capitalized with $5,000,000 as Sikorsky Aviation Corporation, built a new plant in Stratford, Connecticut, and later that same year became a subsidiary of United Aircraft in a remarkably benign take-over that netted the original investors roughly $2 for every $1 invested in 1923. It may even be said the S-38 and the fusion with United Aircraft allowed Sikorsky Aircraft to survive the Great Depression, the growth and gradual demise of the flying boat era, and the slow, difficult birth of the modern helicopter.

The S-38 was used by literally dozens of airlines, military services, and private individuals and was flown all around the world. Between 1928 and the early 1930s, some 110 were built.

In 1930, Pan American gave Sikorsky a contract to build what was to be the biggest airplane yet built in the United States. The S-40, when completed in 1931, carried 40 passengers in great comfort over distances of 500 miles at cruise speeds of 115 mph. In October, 1931, the first of these airliners flew to Washington where it was christened "American Clipper" by President Hoover's wife. It was to become the first of a long line of Pan American Clippers. The American Clipper departed from Miami on its maiden voyage on November 19, 1931, piloted by Pan American's chief pilot Basil Rowe, with Charles Lindbergh and Igor Sikorsky as his co-pilots. Three were built for Pan Am, flew without incident for millions of miles during the 1930s, were used as navigation trainers during WWII, and eventually retired and scrapped in 1946 and 1947.

The next Sikorsky airliner was the S-41, a larger

version of the S-38. Built in limited number, it was eclipsed by the S-42. This new aircraft was basically conceived by Sikorsky, Lindbergh, and Basil Rowe during their November, 1931 inaugural flight of the S-40. Basically, the challenge was to build a true trans-oceanic airliner, capable of carrying enough fuel to fly non-stop 2,500 miles against a 30 mph headwind at a cruising speed of 150 mph.

The S-42, which first flew in 1934, broke with existing tradition by doubling the wing-loading from 15 to 30 pounds per square foot, twice what was then considered the maximum allowable for commercial, passenger-carrying aircraft. Powered by four P&W 750hp engines, the first commercial installation of the radically-new variable-pitch propellers designed by Hamilton Standard, the S-42 also featured a high-aspect ratio wing with an advanced, three-quarter-span flap which aided takeoff and provided a conservative, 65 mph landing speed. This new technology gave a top speed of 188 mph, cruise speed of 160 mph, a range of 1,200 miles with a payload of 7,000 pounds, and a range of 3,000 miles if payload was reduced to 1,500 pounds. Shortly after its first test flights were completed, it was used to establish a series of new world records with put the United States into the lead as far as total records were concerned; holding 17 to France's 16 in the summer of 1934. Ten of there Clippers were delivered to Pan Am, which pioneered scheduled air service across both the Atlantic and Pacific Oceans with the aircraft.

The last of the big Sikorsky flying boats was the VS-44 "Excalibur" series, which were delivered to American Export Airlines in 1941 and 1942. The airline operated three of them for the U.S. Navy during WWII. Their cruising speed of 180 mph and range of 4,900 miles matched or exceeded most of the commercial land planes then operational.

However, as the war stimulated the construction of more and more airports, the era of the large flying boat was clearly coming to an end. It is possible that Igor Sikorsky could see the shift as the land planes grew faster and longer-ranged. At any rate, and whatever the reasons, from 1935 onward, his private engineering sketch books begin to show a growing interest in the helicopter. In this context, it is interesting to note that his first helicopter patent application dates back to 1931. His 1935 patent drawings clearly show his interest in the single lifting-rotor and small tail rotor.

In late 1938, with flying boat production orders steadily declining, Sikorsky Aircraft was in trouble. It was then that Igor Sikorsky approached the management of United Aircraft with the unique proposal that it was time to develop a helicopter. In a series of meetings with the management of United, Sikorsky was able to get permission to start the project. The VS-300, as the new machine was designated, was basically designed in the spring of 1939, built during the summer, and made its first brief lift-off on September 14, 1939. It was a strange-looking machine, with an open tubular structure, pilot seated in the open nose, and no windshield or other protection.

Igor Sikorsky himself remarked that "It was a

wonderful chance to relive one's life all over again…to design a new flying machine without knowing how…to build it without really knowing how…and then to climb into the machine and try to test-fly it without having ever flown a helicopter!"

From September 1939, the following three years were spent in a remarkable program to solve all the problems of a totally-unknown machine. The helicopter (and Igor Sikorsky) survived a number of minor crashes and near crashes while some 200 major and minor redesigns and modifications were tested and evaluated.

However, by the summer of 1942, Sikorsky the engineer and Sikorsky the experimental test pilot had finally developed the world's first successful single-rotor helicopter. This configuration, once thought impossible, was perfected by the determination and tenacity of its designer and is now the preferred helicopter configuration.

The little VS-300 continued flying through late 1943. As the larger R-4 series of helicopters entered production, it hosted a small but select number of test pilots, military and civilian, who investigated the new world of vertical flight. Included in that small group was Lindbergh, then a consultant for United Aircraft, who flew the VS-300 a number of times in 1942 and 1943. The VS-300 was flown for the last time, by Sikorsky, on October 7, 1943, and then handed over to Henry Ford's Dearborn Museum.

The further development of the helicopter is perhaps too well known to repeat here. It is sufficient to note that the civil and military helicopter has created a change in the way we work, wage war, or even take vacations. It has expanded many industries, such as the off-shore oil industry, literally allowing humanity to live and work in areas that would have been unreachable, or unthinkable, a short 50 years ago.

However, perhaps the greatest source of satisfaction to Igor Sikorsky in his final years was the knowledge that the helicopter had amply fulfilled his prediction, made to United Aircraft in 1939, "…that the helicopter will become a unique instrument for the saving of human lives."

To date, it is conservatively estimated that well over a million human lives have been saved by the helicopter, a proud record for a machine barely 50 years old.

Igor Sikorsky was born at a time when most people considered heavier-than-air flight an impossible dream. He lived to see man walk on the moon. His talents as a visionary, as an engineer, and as an exceptional test pilot, helped make those impossible dreams come true.

Igor Sikorsky hangs from one of the first experimental air rescue hoists during tests to develop life-saving techniques. The hoist is fitted to an HNS-1, the navy version of the R-4. One of Sikorsky's strongest beliefs was that the helicopter was destined to be a rescue vehicle. Photo: Archives, United Technologies Corporation.

Section 6

Russian Aircraft Manufacturers

Russian Manufacturers' Introduction

This section includes three of the five major aircraft manufacturing companies, Anatra, Dux, and Lebedev, that contributed to the growth and development of the IRAS. Each is described from its beginning until the end of 1917.[1] Included are descriptions of all known aircraft types produced by each firm and, whenever possible, the quantity built.

The bulk of the contributions from the other two influential manufacturers are covered in the designer's section. They are the Russo-Baltic Railroad Car Company (*Russko-Baltiisky Vagonny Zaved* or R-BVZ), which employed Igor Sikorsky, and the First Russian Joint Stock Aeronautical Company, S.S. Shchetinin and M.A. Shcherbakov, which employed D.P. Grigorovich. Short descriptions of these company's activities are provided to supplement the information in the designer chapters.

The R-BVZ organized an aviation division in Riga in 1910 and transferred the facility to Petrograd in 1912 after only ten aircraft had been built during the two-year period. Approximately 92 planes of foreign design were produced for the army before the war. The firm delivered about 220 machines throughout the war and also built 64 aircraft engines. The plant occupied an area of 3,690 square yards and had more than 500 employees.

The Shchetinin and Shcherbakov firm was founded in 1909 and built several French designs, including the Bleriot XI, Farman IV, and Nieuport IV. By October 1913 the plant had produced 103 aircraft. It also carried out the first static testing of aircraft wing strength on the Nieuport IV.

Throughout the war the firm primarily constructed flying boats and floatplanes. By the end of 1917 the Shchetinin facility had delivered 1340 aircraft, 1030 of which were seaplanes for the navy. The plant occupied 14,640 square yards and employed more than 1700 workers. A testing facility was built in 1916 in the Caucasus, where weather conditions during the winter months were more favorable than in St. Petersburg. A large manufacturing facility was being prepared in Yaroslavl to produce orders placed for landplanes, including 180 SPAD 7 fighters. Unfortunately, this facility never began operations. The factory in St. Petersburg burnt down in June 1921 due to unknown causes.

Secondary Aircraft Manufacturers

There were several other contributors to the IRAS supply of aircraft. These companies, although small, are worthy of mention. All are described in this section of the manufacturers introduction. Those included are the V.V. Slyusarenko Aircraft Company, the Aviation Plant of F.E.

---

(1) Some of the manufacturing facilities continued to produce aircraft into 1918 but were controlled by Soviet rule. The company's procedures and production records during the Civil War have not been included.

Moska, the First Crimean Aviation Plant of V.F. Adamenko, and the Workshop of F.F. Tereshchenko.

There were several smaller firms and organizations that produced a few aircraft. In addition, there were many other individuals who built one-of-a-kind aircraft or modified aircraft which saw service. These are too numerous to mention. They built about 589 aircraft, although most were not accepted by the military.

V.V. Slyusarenko Aviation Company

This firm was founded in 1913 by sport pilot Vladimir Victorovich Slyusarenko and his wife, Lydia Vissarionovna Zvereva, the first woman pilot in Russia. It started as a repair facility and flying school in Riga, and soon received its first military contract for ten Farman XVI aircraft. This order was completed by the summer of 1914.

When the war began, the plant was moved to Petrograd, where it continued to build French aircraft under license. By the end of August, 1916, Slyusarenko had delivered 40 aircraft—25 Morane-Saulnier L and 15 Farman XXbis machines.

At that time the plant expanded, occupying an area of 14,110 square yards and employing 460 workers. In 1917 contracts were awarded for 20 Lebed 12s, 45 Morane-Saulnier Gs and 28 Hs, 20 Farman IVs, and 4 Farman XVIs. Most of these were completed and delivered.

Several experimental aircraft were built and tested by Slyusarenko, although most were unsuccessful. One model, a modified Farman XVI, was accepted. It was built as a single-seater with reduced wing span and one less bay in the wing. Powered by an 80hp Gnome, it had a speed of 80 mph.

During the war Slyusarenko produced 138 aircraft, of which 134 were accepted and delivered. However, by the end of 1917 the firm encountered the devastating economic effects of the revolution, and it closed in 1918.

Aviation Plant of F.E. Moska

Francesco Evgistovich Moska was an Italian pilot and designer who came to Russia and worked for the Dux firm in 1912–13. He then worked in Bezobrazov's workshop, helping to design and build a triplane. When the war began, Moska started his own company in Moscow and obtained a contract for 75 Farman IV machines.

He also designed and built his own aircraft. With the help of his assistant, Bystritsky, the Moska MB and MBbis were developed. Both were parasol monoplanes incorporating folding wings and tail assembly for ease of transportation.

The MB was a two-seat aircraft equipped with a 50hp Gnome, while the MBbis was a single-seater with a Le Rhône or Clerget engine of greater power. The MBbis was sometimes fitted with an unsynchronized Colt or Lewis

The Moska MBbis. Approximately 50 of these single-seat monoplane fighters were ordered and built during 1916 and 1917. Equipped with a 80hp Le Rhône, the machine was reported to have good flying characteristics but was outdated when it reached the front. Its usual armament was a Colt machine gun firing forward, with deflector plates on the propeller for protection instead of a synchronization gear. Its most unique feature was its folding wings and tail to facilitate transportation.

machine gun and its propeller was equipped with deflector plates for protection.

Both models passed military tests and were accepted. Only 12 of the MB type were produced and about 50 of the MBbis were built, many of which were used during the civil war.

The plant occupied 8,370 square yards and employed 324 workers in 1917. It produced a total of 140 aircraft, but records show only 64 were accepted by the end of the war.

The First Crimean Aviation Plant of V.F. Adamenko

This company, founded by V.F. Adamenko in 1913 in the Crimea, was a small facility that manufactured spare parts and repaired damaged aircraft. During 1915–17 the 186 employees produced 40 copies of Farman trainers for the Sevastopol Aviation School, all of which were accepted.

The Workshop of F.F. Tereshchenko

Fedor Fedorovich Tereshchenko became involved with aviation in 1909 when he built an aircraft similar to a Bleriot XI. A wealthy factory owner in Kiev, he was able to furnish a complete aviation workshop. He built this facility at his estate at Chervonny, about 90 miles outside Kiev.

Twenty Farman XVIs were constructed and delivered along with 12 other aircraft of French design. Tereshchenko also repaired many damaged aircraft. He created a mobile repair train able to go directly to the front where aircraft could be refurbished without having to be transported to a rear area facility. This train included portable hangars, which he developed. They were actually large tents where repair work could be completed away from the elements.

He experimented in designing aircraft with others, including V.P. Grigoryev, S.S. Zimbinsky, and A. dePischoff. DePischoff was an Austro-French pilot and designer who coordinated his efforts with Tereshchenko to develop the Tereshchenko No. 5, No. 5bis, and No. 6, all single-seat, high-wing monoplanes. The type 5 and 5bis used 50 and 80hp Gnome engines respectively, while the type 6 used a 60hp Le Rhône. Reportedly, all versions flew well, although none went into production.

Component Manufacturers

Other important contributors to the IRAS were companies that built engines, propellers, and electrical and mechanical components.

The Gnome and Le Rhône Company of Moscow was founded in 1913. The facility occupied an area of 3,265 square yards and employed 435 workers. It produced 641 rotary engines during the war.

The Salmson Company of Moscow commenced operations in 1915 and built 228 radial engines through March of 1917.

The 'Motor' Company of Moscow occupied a 13,555-square-yard facility and employed 330 workers. It had been operating since 1898, and expanded to building aero engines in 1915. The firm built only four engines in 1917, but probably produced other aircraft components.

The Joint-Stock Carriage-Autocar Company of P. Ilyin, founded in 1908 in Moscow, began building aero engines in 1916. The firm occupied 7,080 square yards and had 371 employees. It manufactured 20 engines, most in 1917.

The Airscrew Plant of A. Zassa and Y. Lansky, in St. Petersburg, began production in 1915. Occupying 9,800 square yards of space, its 117 employees produced 1132 propellers.

Two Nieuport fighters undergoing repair in a typical workshop. F.F. Tereshchenko developed a similar type of repair center on his estate in Chervonny where he repaired many aircraft for frontline units. He also organized a repair service train that traveled to the front area to fix damaged airplanes without having to ship them back to the factories.

The F. Meltser Plant of St. Petersburg was founded in 1885 as a furniture manufacturer and entered the aviation industry in 1916. At that time the firm occupied 5,980 square yards and employed about 575 workers. During the war Meltser's main production was propellers, of which 2,663 were made. The company also produced four aircraft. One VM-2 flying boat designed by A.Vu. Villish was built in late 1916 and used as a trainer at Baku. One VM-5 flying boat was built, and two flying boats designed by Ye.R. Engels were delivered in the late summer of 1917 from an order for 60. The machines were equipped with 120hp Le Rhône engines and had good performance.

The Duflou and Constantinovich (Deka) Company of Aleksandrovsk was a large facility that employed 454 workers and had built the scout class airship *Kobtchik*. It also supplied winches, tents, and other balloon service products. In addition, the plant began building experimental aero engines by copying the German Mercedes, one which was installed in a Lebed aircraft. It is believed that many electrical components were manufactured for aircraft.

Aircraft Production

Russian production of aircraft, although much lower than other major allied nations, was considerably higher than the estimated total of foreign-built aircraft imported. Approximately 6,242 aircraft were built in Russia before and during the war. Of this total, about 600 to 700 were produced before the war. Of the remaining 5,500 to 5,600, 1,100 were navy seaplanes, 280 were experimental, and 200 were built by military organizations. The rest were manufactured by privately owned companies. In addition to these, according to Russian sources, approximately 1,800 were imported from the allies.[2][3]

Engine production is where Russia fell far behind. Russian industry had very limited tooling for such precision manufacturing. Most engine production was nothing more than assembling French engine parts, with only simple machining procedures. Most of the production was carried out by the Russian-based Gnome and Rhône Company and the Salmson Company. During September, 1917, approximately 600 completed airframes were awaiting engines. Only 90 received Russian-built power plants and 230 received imported engines, leaving

(2) Several imported aircraft remained crated in storage facilities behind the lines and were still there when the Bolshevik revolution forced Russia out of the war. These aircraft have been counted in the final tally. It has been estimated that only 600 reached the front, about 400 of those being Voisins, the rest mostly Nieuports.

(3) Shavrov, *History of Aircraft Design in the USSR*, Moscow, 1969.

This may be a repair facility or small workshop. Several Russian aircraft manufacturers were nothing more than this type of operation. Of interest are the wooden working diagram of the 7-cylinder engine, probably a 70hp Gnome, and the two personnel, one navy and one army.

A Salmson radial engine mounted on a stand for testing. The Salmson Company of Moscow built 228 such engines from 1915 to March 1917.

almost half of the new planes sitting in storage facilities. Total engine production reached only 1,511, while approximately 4,000 engines were imported from France.[4]

(4) The majority of imported engines were from France. Although several were from England, the United States, and even some acquired from Germany before the war, these numbers were small.

The Rossiya B
Russia's First Production Aircraft

Nikolas P. Seversky standing in the cockpit of his Rossiya B near Saint Petersburg, winter 1911. A true sportsman pilot, he flew in winter despite extreme cold and snow. The aircraft's wheels indicate the snow's depth.

Although ballooning dominated Russian aeronautics in the late Nineteenth Century, there already existed a growing interest in building a heavier-than-air flying machine. With the achievements of the Wright brothers in 1903, the study of aircraft theory became the primary concern of aeronautics in Russia. Within several years, organized clubs had formed throughout the country to study airplane designs and construction techniques. Several such clubs published periodicals based on information received from a large European community of aviation enthusiasts. By 1909 the Imperial All-Russian Aero Club's magazine, *Aeronautics*, had emerged as one of most authoritative periodicals devoted to flight.

After Louis Bleriot's historic flight across the English Channel in 1909, the Russian government acquired a keen interest in airplane development. To Grand Duke Alexander (considered Russia's first major air theorist), the military implications of Bleriot's flight were immediately evident. He argued for building of military air groups, forming of special commissions to study aeronautics, and flight training for military officers. In addition, the Duke hoped to broaden public awareness. To achieve this, he used flying clubs as a means to promote aviation throughout Russia. The Imperial All-Russian Aero Club in particular enjoyed the patronage of Duke Alexander and other key figures from the military services and the government. Because of their influence, the Russian government provided funds to purchase airplanes for testing.

In 1910, members from the Imperial All-Russian Aero Club formed an organization known as the First Russian Aerostatics Company, located at the Shchetinin Works in St. Petersburg. The company's main purpose was to design and construct a Russian aircraft. Technical data had been assembled on various foreign designs, but the primary inspiration was a set of Bleriot airplane photographs acquired from a correspondent in France. The company's non-innovative design was built and designated the Rossiya B. With Matievich Mazievich (a Russian military officer who had pilot training in France) at the controls, the Rossiya B completed its first successful flight on 26 August, 1910.

Although the Rossiya B was not the first Russian-designed and built aircraft to fly, it was the first to be mass-produced (exact quantity unknown). Of the several Russian aircraft designs completed earlier, the Kudashev

Russian-made Bleriot XI near St. Petersburg, summer 1912. Russia's first aviation factory, the Shchetinin Works, built both Bleriots and Rossiya-designed aircraft.

Model 1 was the first to fly, on 23 May, 1910. The Shchetinin Works in St. Petersburg would build both Bleriot and Rossiya B aircraft in 1910, in addition to the Rossiya A (a biplane version of the Rossiya B) which appeared in the same year.

The Rossiya monoplane had a wooden box girder fuselage, braced by wire, with only the forward section covered with fabric. The wooden struts of the landing gear supported steel tubing, on which spring shock absorbers were connected to each wheel by a Y-shaped strut. The two-section wing was secured to the fuselage by bracing wires attached to the upper cabane strut and the landing gear axle. The wing's front spar was rigid; the rear spar was flexible, allowing lateral control by warping of the trailing edges through movement of wires secured to the wings and attached to both the cabane pulley and a mount beneath the fuselage. The stabilizer was below the fuselage and could be adjusted for varying incidence. The rudder was mounted to the fuselage by hinges and moved by cables attached to the control wheel. Power was supplied by an Anzani three-cylinder air-cooled engine that developed about 25 hp.

It is not surprising that the Rossiya B and the Bleriot XI had many similar traits. In fact, they differed in only a few respects. The Rossiya B substituted a skid for the Bleriot-type swiveling tailwheel. The Bleriot tailwheel aggravated a pronounced ground-looping tendency. It was believed the skid would give the Rossiya B better directional control on landings and takeoffs, and would in addition serve as a brake in case of difficult landings. Other known differences between the two included size and placement of landing gear struts, wingspan, and fuselage length.

The first Rossiya B was sold to Nikolas G. Prokoffiev Seversky, considered one of Russian's first pioneer sportsman pilots, who owned his own aircraft in 1909 (non-Russian made).[1] Some sources have falsely credited Seversky as the first Russian to own his own aircraft. In Seversky's defense it can be said the Rossiya B he purchased would be his second aircraft, making him the first private owner of the first production aircraft designed and built in Russia.

The Rossiya B served Seversky well on local hops for two years before being retired to ground duty. Factors contributing to its grounding were increased weight, through absorption of moisture; power loss through engine wear; and, possibly, minor changes in the structure due to maintenance. It was still going strong as of 1917, however, as a grass-cutter[2] for student training. Considering that most students would have subjected the aircraft to hard usage as a training tool, this clearly demonstrated the strength of its construction.

Nikolas' son, Alexander de Seversky, was mechanically inclined and developed an early interest in his father's aircraft.[3] While working on them he gathered information which would greatly influence his later life. Facts have indicated that Alexander used his father's Rossiya B as a 'grass-cutter.' This might explain why, several years later at the military aviation school in Gatchina, he required dual instruction in a Gnome-powered Farman 4 totaling only 6 minutes 28 seconds before he was pronounced ready to solo.

The following data are from Shavrov, Vadim Borisovich:

Model: Rossiya B, tractor monoplane	
Designer: Rebikov, Nikolai Vasilyevich	
Manufacturer: First Russian Aerostatics Company	
Year: 1910	Span: 7.5 m
Engine: 25 hp Anzani	Wing area: 14 sq m
Length: 7.5 m	Fuel/oil: 25 kg
Empty weight: 230 kg	Flying weight: 330 kg
Weight load: 100 kg	Speed: approximately 70 km/h
Wing Loading: 23.6 kg/sq. m	Power Loading: 13.2 kg/hp

Model: Rossiya A, pusher biplane	
Designer: Rebikov, Nikolai Vasilyevich	
Manufacturer: First Russian Aerostatics Company	
Year: 1910	Span: 10.5 m/7.0 m
Engine: 50 hp Gnome	Wing area: 38 sq m
Length: approximately 12.0 m	Fuel/oil: 30 kg
Empty weight: 440 kg	Flying weight: 620 kg
Weight load: 180 kg	Speed: approximately 70 km/h
Wing Loading: 16.3 kg/sq. m	Power Loading: 12.4 kg/hp

---

(1) During World War I Nikolas G. Prokoffiev Seversky served as a pilot with the EVK.

(2) 'Grass-cutter' refers to a powered, non-flying aircraft which student pilots used to develop taxiing skills.

(3) Alexander Seversky later became an ace with six confirmed victories.

Anatra Factory

The Anatra Aircraft Company was founded in 1913 by Artur Antonovich Anatra, a businessman and banker in Odessa. In 1912 Anatra had offered to build aircraft for the war department in reply to requests for such services. On June 23, 1913, he received an order for five Farman IV aircraft and began production from the workshops at the Odessa Aero Club. This first batch of airplanes were delivered in November and subsequent orders were placed for production of French types. The other French models built between 1913 and 1917 included not only Farmans, but also the Nieuport type 11, Voisin pushers, and Morane-Saulnier parasols.

In 1915 the firm began to create its own types. French designer Elisée Alfred DesCamps[1] produced several models during his employment at Anatra, including the Anade, Anasal, and the Anadis. Other designers at Anatra were V.N. Khioni and A.K. Mikhalkevich, who together constructed the Anadva, a twin-engine, twin-boom aircraft. The plant also built a modification of the Voisin, designated as the V.I. (Voisin Ivanov), after its designer, *Podporuchik* Petr Ivanov.

In 1915 a second plant was opened in Simferopol. It produced modified Voisin LAS, Farman type IV and type VII, and Nieuport 17bis aircraft. These machines were delivered to the Sevastopol Military Aviation School.

Throughout the war the Anatra company built 1056 military aircraft at the Odessa plant and 50 in Simferopol. By the end of hostilities two aircraft a day were being produced. At Odessa the firm had 1684 employees and occupied an area of 1,356,000 square yards, including the airfield. At Simferopol there were approximately 735 employees and the facility covered 215,280 square yards.

Both locations remained open after the war and were eventually reorganized under Soviet rule. They were both closed by the end of 1922.

Anade

Also known as the Anatra D, the Anade was developed during the summer of 1915 as an advanced two-seat reconnaissance biplane to supply the corps squadrons with aircraft that would replace the slow and obsolete types still in service.

The Anade had a fuselage that was linen-covered in the rear and plywood-covered from the cockpit forward. The fuel tank was constructed in three sections; in case of puncture not all fuel would be lost. The cowling was aluminum and came in two designs. The first was known as the "short nose," while the second, the "long nose," had

---

(1) DesCamps is usually referred to as Dekan, the translated spelling of his name in Russian.

The Anatra Anade, with cockades displayed in 12 positions, standard practice of the Anatra Company. This machine has the early 'short-nose' design covering the 100hp Gnome rotary engine. The aircraft carries no armament and appears to have a small tail unit. This may possibly be a prototype, which proved unsatisfactory. After increasing the size of the tail and other modifications, the type was more stable. The wheel covers are aluminum.

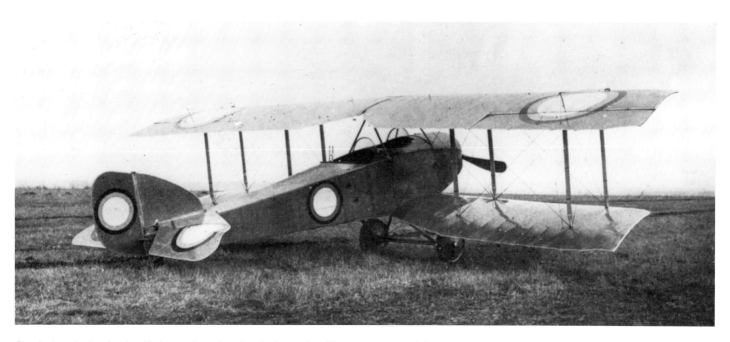

Standard production Anade with the usual number of cockades applied. The rear gun mount is in place and large windscreens have been fitted. The aileron control cables are externally mounted, with pulley assemblies attached to the leading edge of the upper wing. The machine performed well, but was unfortunately plagued with poor wing spar construction, causing several fatal accidents and resulting distrust of Anatra machines. Despite this defect, 170 Anades were built.

circular cooling cutouts similar to the style used later on the Anasal. Both versions were powered by 100hp Gnome-Monosoupape rotary engines.

The wings were linen covered, with wooden struts employed in the two-bay construction. Ailerons were applied only to the upper wing. Cabane and tail struts were steel tubing, as was the undercarriage, which was V-shaped and streamlined.

The armament included a flexible machine gun, usually a Colt or a Maxim, for the observer, and on later machines a Maxim, synchronized with a DesCamps interrupter gear, for the pilot. About 60 lb. of bombs could also be carried.

On January 1, 1916, the first test of the Anade took place. It was unstable and several changes were made, primarily to the wings. Both the sweep and the angle of incidence were increased and the complete wing assembly was moved back along the fuselage. The upper wing had its span reduced and the ailerons were enlarged by increasing their chord. Another modification was the addition of 15 lb. of ballast mounted to the forward outboard wing strut on the starboard bottom wing. Other improvements included moving the pilot and observer seats forward and increasing the tail surface by 50 per cent.

After several more trials, the problems were solved. Soon afterward the aircraft entered production. The first machine was accepted on May 29, 1916. These aircraft proved to be stable and in the right hands were capable of aerobatics, as displayed by *Stabs-Kapitan* Makarov when he performed loops in the Anade on two occasions in the spring of 1917. However, in August 1916, while testing an Anade, *Sous-Lieutenant* Bonnier, of the French mission, perished in a crash, apparently not from a stability problem but from poor quality of material and construction. Upon inspection, a broken cable was found that caused a loss of control. Lack of wood for wing spars

An Anade after landing on its nose. This view shows the shape of the wings and the plywood forward fuselage and linen rear half. The square between the rear undercarriage legs is a removable panel.

also created construction problems. Spars were built in two sections, with nothing more than a short overlapping joint glued and wrapped with fabric. In July 1917, *Sous-Lieutenant* Jean Robinet, a member of the French mission, and his passenger were killed during a test flight when a spar of this construction failed, causing a crash. Incidents such as this became common among corps squadrons, creating distrust of Anatra machines.

A trainer, with duel controls and a modified landing gear to prevent nose-overs, was one of the 170 machines built during 1916–1917. It has been reported that the final modification was the removal of the starboard wing strut ballast in August 1917. However, photographic evidence does not show use of such ballast at any time.

An Anade captured by the Austrians on the Galician Front in 1916. This machine is fitted with the 'long-nose' cowl with cooling cutouts. The number '5' on the rudder is most likely a squadron identification number.

Starboard view of the Anade number '5,' displaying its only armament, a Maxim machine gun mounted in the rear cockpit for the observer. This view shows to good advantage the plywood and linen areas of the fuselage and the control cables, especially the aileron lines and fittings along the upper wing.

Anakle

The Anakle or Anakler, was identical to the Anade except for a change of engines. This machine was given a 110hp Clerget rotary and a slightly modified cowl. Production of this type was limited and may possibly be included in the total of Anade production. The Anakle was about 3 mph faster than the Anade.

Voisin Ivanov

In 1916 *Podporuchik* Petr Ivanov of the 26th Corps Detachment modified a Voisin LAS while stationed at the 6th *Aviapark*. It became known as the Voisin Ivanov or V.I. Modifications consisted of streamlining the nacelle and adding a third steel tube spar in the wings. Ivanov also streamlined the wing struts. In addition, the fuel tank was

The Anakle or Anakler had an airframe that was identical to the Anade. The only change was the 110hp Clerget rotary engine and the horseshoe cowl. The separation between the two upper wing panels is evident. Also seen is a gun sight, indicating a machine gun was installed for the pilot. The Anakle was about 3 mph faster than the Anade, but only a few were built.

built to prevent total leakage in case of puncture, and was protected from engine fire by an aluminum firewall.

The machine was tested in April 1916 with good results. It proved to be faster than the Voisin LAS by 12 mph while equipped with the same power plant. Shortly after this an order was placed with Anatra for 125 units. The V.I. received mixed reviews at the front. It has been reported that production models lacked stability, and many serious accidents occurred. Approximately 100 aircraft were built and the model was still in service in 1917.

Anasal

The Anatra DS Anasal was very similar in style and shape to the Anade with one major change; the installation of the 150hp water-cooled Salmson Canton-Unne radial engine. The cowling covered all but the top cylinder heads that protruded from cutouts. Radiators have been reported as being installed in two locations, either box-type mounted on the fuselage sides or at the leading edge of the upper wing, which appears to be more popular. The fuselage construction was changed, being entirely plywood. Two guns, one fixed for the pilot and one flexible for the observer, became standard equipment. When fitted with a special airscrew designed by Grigorashvili, the speed of the Anasal was increased by 4mph.

The initial test flight took place on August 7, 1916, with an order being placed in early 1917. In service the Anasal was comparable in performance to enemy aircraft of similar type. However, reports were filed declaring the difficulty of handling the machine. Pilots had to maintain total concentration while holding level flight, never relaxing, or risk loss of control of the aircraft. Attempts to correct this problem were made throughout production, but apparently with little effect. While testing an Anasal on May 8, 1917, *Sous-Lieutenant* Marcel Bloch,[2] of the French mission, was seriously injured in a crash, the

(2) Marcel Bloch was a member of the French mission assigned to escadrille N.581. Shortly after his arrival he was temporarily transferred to the Anatra firm as a test pilot. After the accident he remained in Russia recuperating until he was well enough to return to France. He had previously scored five victories, all balloons, with *escadrille* N.62. In addition to being highly decorated by his own country, he received the Order of Saint George Fourth Class and the Order of Saint Anne Fourth Class from Russia.

Standard production Anasal equipped with a 150hp Salmson radial engine. This machine was similar in shape to the Anade, but was slightly larger. It was capable of 90 mph and had a ceiling of 14,100 feet. Despite problems with stability, it was favorably received at the front compared with other available designs. About 70 were manufactured during 1917.

An Anasal in Czechoslovakian service in 1920, with markings and colors of that country. The radiator is mounted on the upper wing leading edge and the exhaust pipe protrudes from the cowl. Streamlined wood interplane struts and steel tube undercarriage struts are evident.

reasons for which are unknown, but were most likely due to either lack of stability or poor construction, a problem which plagued most Anatra aircraft.

Approximately 70 units were produced before the end of hostilities. The Anasal was later used by the Austrians and eventually the Czechs in the postwar period.

Anatra DSS

The Anatra DSS or Anasal SS, was slightly larger than the Anasal. It was equipped with the 160hp Salmson engine, giving the machine a speed about 4mph faster than the Anasal. The DSS was produced in small numbers in February, 1917.

Anamon

Also named the Anatra DM, this machine was a single-seat monoplane with a plywood monocoque fuselage. Equipped with a 100hp Gnome, it had good speed of 102 mph during initial trials in June 1916. This was later reduced due to the added weight of a machine gun. The machine gun was not synchronized, but equipped with deflector plates as previously used on French Moranes.

An attempt was made to create better visibility for the pilot with cutouts in the trailing edge of the wing at its root. Unfortunately, test pilots reported the seat was too low and visibility was poor. It resembled a Deperdussin, gave no advantages over Moranes or Nieuports, and failed to gain acceptance during trial flights. After a crash of this machine the project was discontinued.

Anatra DE

This three-engine bomber was designed to carry a crew of four, three machine guns, and a bomb load of 880 lb. One 140hp Salmson was mounted to the nose and two 80hp Le Rhône rotaries driving pusher airscrews were mounted to nacelles between the wings. Each nacelle was fitted with a flexible machine gun.

The idea of how this aircraft was to be utilized was innovative. The bomber was to complete its journey to the target using all three engines and return with only the Salmson operating. This technique was to give the machine a duration of 3.5 hours.

The plane was tested on July 6, 1916, despite its actual weight being about 700 lb. more than expected. It is not believed that performance met expectations since the aircraft was not repaired after sustaining damage during landing. It was reported that modification was necessary, but apparently no further work was accomplished and the type DE was abandoned.

Anadis

This aircraft closely resembled the Anasal with some major changes, the most important of which was the installation of a 150hp Hispano-Suiza engine. This resulted in a redesign of the fuselage to a monocoque plywood type, giving a very streamlined appearance. The machine was a single-seat fighter although it was the size of two-seat types.

The Anadis was tested during November 1916, performing favorably. Speed was 95 mph and maneuverability was good. It gave better performance than the

The Anadis single-seat fighter with a monocoque fuselage. The engine of this aircraft was a 150hp Hispano-Suiza. The machine was lighter than the Anasal and its performance was better. This photo was taken in November, 1917, prior to *Stabs-Kapitan* Makarov (seen wearing flight outfit) starting a long distance journey to visit the allied fronts. This trip was to include stops at Salonika, Rome, Marseilles, and eventually Paris. He had to make an emergency landing at Jassy, Romania, when engine failure forced him to abort his mission.

Anasal and weighted 265 lb. less.

Testing did not resume until October, 1917, when *Stabs-Kapitan* Makarov requested permission to complete a flight to France via the route Salonika, Rome, Marseilles, and Paris, for the purposes of observing allied aviation practices. The Anadis was the perfect machine for such a flight because it could carry fuel for 14 hours flight. Makarov began his journey in November; but engine trouble forced him to land at Jassy, Romania.

Despite its general acceptance, it appears this was the only Anadis built.

Anadva type VKh

Sometimes referred to as the Dvukhvostka, the Anadva was a biplane bomber with twin engines. Its most unusual feature was the twin booms, which were actually two Anade fuselages, both with complete tail units. The pilot's cockpit was in the port boom while the observer was located in the starboard boom. The long-span wings were of three-bay construction. Only the upper wing had ailerons; they also incorporated a gunner's station. It was fitted with a device attached to both outer forward interplane struts to correct stability if power was lost from either engine. Tests proved they did not function as planned. Originally the crew of the plane was three, but later it was designed to hold six.

The aircraft incorporated the construction techniques of A.K. Mikhalkevich, which involved the use of a series of templates to calculate measurements and angles. In July, 1916, the Gnome-powered Anadva was test flown.[3] It was found to need some refinements, so a second machine was built: the Anadva-Salmson.

Anadva-Salmson

The Anadva-Salmson was developed from the type VKh and was fitted with two 140hp Salmson engines. The booms were changed to Anasal fuselages and the wings were increased in span. The aircraft made trial flights in May, 1917, and was reported to have good qualities as a light bomber.

The EVK wished to use the Anadva-Salmson to supplement its Il'ya Murometsy. An order was placed in November 1917 for 50 units, but due to the revolution it was never fulfilled.

The table on the next page provides the specifications and performance figures for the ten known Anatra models.[4]

---

(3) In the summer of 1917 the VKh was converted into a seaplane by the addition of floats. It was damaged upon landing after a test flight in August 1917.

(4) Shavrov, V. B., *A History of Aircraft Design in the USSR for the Period Before 1938*, Mashinostroyeniye, Moscow, 1969.

Anatra Aircraft Data

Specification	Anade	Anakle	Anasal	Anasal SS	Anamon	Anatra DE	Anadis	AnadvaVKh	Anadva-S.	V.I.
Year Built	1915	1916	1916	1917	1916	1916	1916	1916	1917	1916
Max. Speed, km/h	130	135	144	153	158	160	153	—	140	125
Time to 1000m, min.	7.0	—	5.5	6.7	—	8.0	7.5	—	7.6	8.4
Time to 3000m, min.	26	—	24	—	22	—	37	—	34	47
Svc. Ceiling, m	4000	4000	4300	4400	4500	—	3750	—	4000	3500
Flt. Duration, Hrs.	3.5	3.5	3.5	3.0	2.5	—	14.0	3.0	—	—
Takeoff Run, m	60	60	75	75	150	—	90	—	60	90
Landing Run, m	90	90	70	70	150	—	55	—	60	80
Engines, number	1	1	1	1	1	1	1	2	2	1
type	G-M	Clerget	Salmson	Salmson	G-M	Salmson	Hisso	G-M	Salmson	Salmson
Power, hp	100	110	150	160	100	140 & 2 Le Rhône 80	150	100	140	150
Length, m	7.7	7.7	8.1	8.95	6.34	9.0	7.75	7.7	8.1	9.5
Span, m (U/L)	11.5/10.3	11.5/10.3	11.4	12.3	8.6	16.0	11.4	19.0	19.1	14.7/12.5
Wing Area, m^2	35.0	35.0	37.0	35.0	14.0	50.0	37.0	62.0	62.0	39.0
Empty Wt., kg	515	—	814	808	360	1527	665	—	1280	852
Fuel Wt., kg	90	90	130	130	70	447	380	160	180	130
Oil Wt., kg	25	25	23	23	20	total	35	45	30	23
Payload, kg	350	350	350	350	175	820	500	600	650	350
Gross Wt., kg	865	—	1164	1160	535	2347	1165	—	1930	1202
Wing Load, kg/m^2	24.7	—	31.5	33.0	38.3	47.0	31.5	—	31.2	30.8
Power, kg/hp	8.6	—	7.7	7.2	5.3	7.8	7.7	—	6.9	8.0

Notes:
1. Anadva-S. is Anadva-Salmson.
2. G-M is Gnome Monosoupape.
3. Hisso is Hispano-Suiza.
4. V.I. is Voisin Ivanov.

Dux Factory

The Dux factory showing the assembly line for building Farman aircraft. The Dux facility occupied 59,800 square yards and employed more than 2400 workers by the end of the war.

The Dux Company (*Aktsionyernoye Obshchestvo Vozdukhoplavania*)[1] was founded in 1894 in Moscow and built bicycles and motorcycles of low horsepower. In 1910 the firm changed over to manufacturing aircraft and airships under the control of Y.A. Meller. In its first year the firm built only six airplanes, but raised that number to 543 during 1917.

The company produced mostly French models under license but also experimented with its own designs. Engineer V.V. Bortashevich controlled production of the first aircraft types: Nieuport IV, Bleriot XI, and Farman IV and VII. Other designers who began work with Dux, including N.N. Polikarpov and F.E. Moska, later went on to distinguished careers. Moska eventually opened his own manufacturing facility during the war, producing several aircraft. A Dux branch in St. Petersburg was stocked with spare parts and equipped as a repair facility.

The Dux plant occupied an area of 59,800 square yards. By 1914 it employed about 1025 workers and produced 10–12 machines per month. By 1917 the firm had grown to more than 2400 employees and was completing nearly two aircraft a day using assembly line procedures. During the period 1910–1917 the Dux plant built 1733 airplanes, of which 1569 were accepted for military use, including approximately 150 before the war.

The designs of the Dux engineers are discussed first, followed by license-built French aircraft. Some of the Dux models were modified French types built as prototypes, or at the most a limited production run. Other French designs were slightly modified for production by Dux but are considered to be the original designs. Several of these types were produced in numbers.

(1) This name was used after the firm converted to aircraft manufacturing. Dux is from *Vozdukhoplavania*, which translates as aeronautics.

Dux Designs

Monoplane 'Dux'

Equipped with a 70hp Gnome rotary engine, this machine was virtually a copy of the Nieuport IV. It was built for the 1912 military competition, where it achieved a maximum speed of 65 mph. This version had an additional seat for a third occupant. Only a few were built.

Biplane 'Dux'

This aircraft was a modification of the standard Farman IV. It incorporated several design changes, including an increased wingspan and a modified vertical tailplane. It was built for the 1912 military competition, finishing second. However, the improvements made by Dux were not recognized by the War Department and orders for the original French design were continued.

Dux Bleriot XI

Dux built at least two versions of the Bleriot XI, including this trainer, equipped with a 50hp Gnome. It was larger than the original French design and only a small number were manufactured.

Dux Farman VII

This model was also known as the Farman IX Dux. Its nacelle, which distinguished it from French type VIIs, had a plywood fairing covering the crew seats. The fairing tapered to a point at the nose. Powered by a 70hp Gnome, performance was somewhat better than the French original and several were produced. In some cases the front elevator was removed.

Meller I

The Meller no.1 was named after the company's owner and designed by F.E. Moska. It was made from parts of several of the French aircraft being manufactured at the Dux plant.

The machine was a parasol monoplane, pusher-driven by a 100hp Gnome engine. The wing was taken from a Nieuport IV, as was the undercarriage. The nacelle was from a Farman XV and the horizontal section of the tail was from a Farman XVI. A steel tube framework was used to connect the components of the aircraft, but its structure was too complex in its attempt to avoid the propeller. The plane did not have any exceptional qualities and only one was produced.

Meller II

The second design in the Meller series of three aircraft resembled the Farman XVI. Also a pusher machine, its tail booms were exclusively a Dux design. A folding wing design was incorporated for easy storage.

The aircraft was flown during the Russian Military International Aircraft Competitionon when its 100hp Gnome broke away from the airframe. The pilot was able to glide to a safe landing, but the engine fell through the wing of Sikorsky's *Grand*, causing irreparable damage.

The second in a series of three aircraft named after the owner of the Dux factory, the Meller no.2, which was developed from a Farman design. However, the tail boom assembly was a Dux design. While at St. Petersburg in 1913, this 100hp Gnome engine fell off this aircraft during a flight on September 11 and fell through the wing of Sikorsky's *Grand*, causing irreparable damage.

Meller III

This 1913 monoplane was powered by a Salmson 80hp water-cooled engine turning twin airscrews driven by chains attached to steel tubes on each wing. Some of the basic principals of the Nieuport IV were incorporated, but with modifications, such as the use of ailerons instead of wing warping. Tail components taken from the Farman XVI were also evident. Again, this machine was unsuccessful.

Dux No. 2

This aircraft was a pusher design powered by a 80hp Gnome mounted along the rear spar of the parasol monoplane wing. A triangular boom continued to the tail unit from the nacelle to allow the prop to clear the components of the machine. Once again, this aircraft used parts from a Nieuport IV and a Farman XVI. Due to construction deficiencies, it did not compete in the 1913 trials and further development was not attempted until 1915.

The Dux no.2 was pusher-driven by an 80hp Gnome engine. It had poor performance and suffered from construction problems. In 1915 an attempt was made to improve the no.2 with an increase in horsepower and wing and undercarriage modifications. However, the machine was not improved and the project was canceled.

Dux Military

This machine was an attempt to improve the Dux No. 2 by using the wing from a Morane Parasol and a Gnome engine of greater horsepower. Since the original machine was very low to the ground, a redesigned undercarriage was developed. Despite these changes, the aircraft had poor characteristics and the project was discontinued.

Twin-engine Dux

Equipped with two 80hp Le Rhônes driving pusher airscrews, this machine was intended to replace the Farman XXX. Each engine had an enclosed nacelle with cutouts for cooling. The fuel tanks were inside the nacelles with a bulkhead separating them from the engines. The estimated speed was 87 mph. The fuselage was a standard fabric-covered box type with a gunner's cockpit in front of the pilot. The upper wing was larger than the lower wing in both span and chord. The interplane struts and engine mounting struts were wood.

The design was considered satisfactory, but work was stopped for unknown reasons in 1917 and the aircraft was never completed.

French Designs

Many French designs were built under license in significant numbers at the Dux plant. A description of all known machines produced follows. In some cases, production numbers cannot be determined.

Nieuport IV

The Dux-built Nieuport IV was the standard production model. Equipped with a 70hp Gnome engine, it was used as a reconnaissance aircraft from 1912 through 1915, when it was relegated to training duty. Petr Nesterov performed his famous first loop in one of these machines in September, 1913.

Dux-built Nieuport IV mid-wing monoplane equipped with a 70hp Gnome engine. The Dux name can be seen on the rudder. About 300 were manufactured in Russia and served as reconnaissance and training machines.

A mid-wing monoplane, the Nieuport IV was mainly a single-seat machine, but could have a rear seat installed behind the pilot. It had a peculiar control system, incorporating foot pedals to operate the warping of the wing while a lever on the side of the cockpit controlled the tail surfaces. One wooden anti-nose-over device was mounted between the wheels of the landing gear to help prevent landing accidents. A few machines built at Dux were fitted with a 100hp Gnome. In total, about 300 Nieuport IV variants were produced in Russia, many built at the Dux plant.

Bleriot XIbis

The XIbis model had a 50hp Gnome and was sometimes referred to as the "racing Bleriot" as opposed to the "training Bleriot" equipped with a 25hp Anzani engine. Dux began to produce these machines in the summer of 1911. They varied in wing size and were fitted with a slightly different undercarriage than the Anzani-powered aircraft. Other than that, they were virtually identical to the 1909–10 training models.

Farman IV

The Farman IV was the first of many Farman models to serve and be built in Russia.[2] It was probably the most widely produced aircraft in Russia before and during the war. Almost all Farmans were constructed to a standard design. All were pusher, two-seat biplanes with a triangular boom assembly joined at the tail. Many used rotary or radial engines. All models up to the type XXII had four wheels, set in pairs, on the landing gear. When nacelles were introduced they were of similar shape for several types. Generally, they were all simple and easy to maintain and repair, which was a key reason for their popularity.

The Farman IV was built as a trainer with many modifications by many companies throughout its service

A Nieuport IV after a heavy landing; apparently the anti-noseover device did not work this time. The view does show to good advantage the outline of the aircraft. The cockades have a thin white ring between the red and blue rings and outside the red outer ring. This was a common feature of all Dux-built machines.

---

(2) The Farman III was the first model to be used in Russia, although it was imported from France and most likely not built in Russia.

The Farman IV was the standard trainer in Russia. During its service life many modifications were made to the basic type IV, including the addition of an airfoil rib and fabric covering on both sides of the wings instead of only on the upper surface. The ailerons drooped when the plane was at rest because they operated downward only. The airflow held them horizontal during flight. The 50hp Gnome can be seen attached to the rear of the lower wing. The typical Farman four-wheel undercarriage is prominent with its runners to help prevent nose-over accidents. Many of this type were manufactured by Dux.

life. Most commonly equipped with a 50hp Gnome, it was a three-bay biplane. The original French design was a simple wood structure with wings and tailplane covered by fabric on one side only, with simple ribs of a non-airfoil shape. It had an elevator in the front attached to long booms and completely open seating for the pilot and passengers. Ailerons operated downward only and hung down while the plane was on the ground.

The Farman IV was easy to build and maintain and was inexpensive to produce, making it an affordable trainer. Dux made several modifications to it. The span of the front elevator was larger and the undercarriage runners were lengthened. The wings were improved by incorporating an airfoil shape in the wing ribs and by covering both sides of the wings with fabric. Many were constructed by Dux, but the exact number is unknown.

Farman VII

This machine was very similar to the type IV. It was powered by a 50hp Gnome engine and retained the frontal elevator. The wing design was different, being of two-bays, with the lower wing of shorter span than the upper. As with the type IV, the type VII was used as a trainer. Manufacturing involvement by Dux is unknown, but the company probably produced several examples.

The Farman VII. This machine differed from the Farman IV in having a shorter bottom wing with two-bays. This model is similar to the type built by Dux which had a nacelle for the crew. Dux produced this model, but the number is unknown. Photo: SHAA.

Farman IX

The Dux Farman IX was the first in the series to incorporate an enclosed cockpit for the crew. This nacelle also enclosed the fuel tank. Dux originally modified a Farman VII, which was designated a Dux type IX.

Farman XV

The Farman XV was the forerunner of the next three widely-produced models that followed. It incorporated a two-seat nacelle to house the crew. It used many of the construction techniques and most of the materials of earlier Farmans, yet was stronger. Like all early Farmans it was a pusher equipped with a Gnome engine of either 80hp or 100hp. Dux built 18 of these machines, which were a three-bay design with a longer wingspan than the original French version.

Farman XVI

This model was similar to the Farman XV, but with refined wings. The span was shorter, with only two bays of struts, although the upper wing was of much greater length and chord than the lower wing. Several engine types were installed, but the Gnome rotary was usually fitted.

Early in the war the machine was used for reconnaissance, but later it was relegated to training duties. About 300 were produced in Russia, several by Dux.

Farman XX

This model was an improved Farman XVI, strengthened and simplified for ease of maintenance. It was employed as a reconnaissance and training machine. Some were built with dual controls for training. Other than a few refinements, it was virtually identical to the Farman XVI and was powered by the same engine types. The number produced by Dux is unknown, but about 200 were built in Russia.

Farman XXII and Farman XXIIbis

These aircraft were also pushers, with the same wing design as previous models. The main difference was an improved undercarriage of curved steel tube struts instead of a series of N-shaped braces. The type XXIIbis was identical to the XXII except for an uprated engine, a 100hp Gnome. The aircraft was used for reconnaissance and later became a trainer. Several were built, but the exact number is unknown.

Dux-built Farman XXII. The Farman XXII had a strengthened under-carriage of curved steel tube. A reconnaissance machine, it was equipped with a 80hp Gnome engine. The XXIIbis model was fitted with a 100hp Gnome and had greater performance. Both types were built by Dux.

The Farman XX was virtually the type XVI with minor refinements. It initially performed reconnaissance duties and later was employed as a trainer. About 200 were built in Russia, many by Dux. Photo: SHAA.

The Farman XXII was popular as a reconnaissance aircraft and later as a training machine. Equipped with an 80hp Gnome, it was one of the first widely-manufactured Farmans to be built with a nacelle for the crew. Of the 300 produced in Russia, many were built by Dux. Photo: SHAA.

Farman XXVII

The type XXVII was a three-bay biplane with wings of equal span and chord. It was similar to earlier models except for the use of a 150hp Salmson radial engine. It had a four-wheel undercarriage, with two wheels forward, under the nose, and two main wheels under the wing. It was a two-seat observation aircraft and the pilot sat in front. The observer was equipped with a machine gun attached to a curved bracket in order to fire over the pilot. Dux built 50 of these machines during 1916.

Farman XXX and Farman XXXbis

The Farman XXX reconnaissance machine had its nacelle raised above the lower wing. It was built in two versions, with either a blunt nose or a pointed nose, housing the two crew members. The blunt-nosed version positioned the observer in front, while the pointed-nosed type placed the pilot forward. The machine gun mounting for the pointed-nosed XXX was the same as that for the type XXVII. The blunt-nosed type used a ring mount that was connected to the gunner's seat as a complete assembly, allowing both gun and gunner to pivot together.

The wings were of two-bay construction, with the upper wing of greater span than the lower. Ailerons were fitted to the upper wing only. The engine was usually a 150hp Salmson radial, but several were built with 130hp and 140hp Salmsons. The undercarriage was low to the ground and was a strong design using only two wheels.

The type XXXbis had the upgraded 160hp Salmson engine and also introduced twin exhaust pipes positioned upward, replacing the short individual pipes on every cylinder seen on earlier models. In total, Dux built about 400 type XXX variants.

The Farman XXVII showing its large wingspan and three-bay construction. Notice the change of the undercarriage to a Voisin style with two forward wheels. This aircraft was an improvement over previous Farmans, having better performance. The 150hp Salmson radial replaced the lower-power rotaries of previous models. A two-seat observation plane, it was equipped with a machine gun for the observer. Dux built 50 of the type XXVII models.

The Dux-built, blunt-nosed Farman XXX. Clearly evident are its raised nacelle and short landing gear. This version placed the pilot in the rear and the observer/gunner in the forward position to operate the machine gun from the pivoting mount attached to the nose.

A Dux-built, blunt-nosed Farman XXX parked in an tent-type hangar at a forward location. Shown to good advantage are the radiators and the attachment of the boom struts and wire bracing fittings.

Also built by Dux, this Farman XXX is the pointed-nose type with the pilot seated in front. Because of their long duration of four hours, these machines played an important role as reconnaissance machines for the corps detachments. Eventually a type XXXbis was introduced with a 160hp Salmson. Dux built about 400 Farman XXX variants.

Voisin L

Like the Farmans, all Voisin designs built by Dux were pusher reconnaissance aircraft. All incorporated a steel tube framework with linen-covered wings and flying surfaces. Wood was used for ribs and plywood for the nacelle. They were sturdy and stable in the air, although slow and not maneuverable. Their structure was simple, making this aircraft fairly easy to build and repair. About 400 of all types were built in Russia by all companies.

The Voisin L was the first of this series. It was powered by a 130hp Salmson engine with two large box-type radiators mounted behind the crew in the shape of an inverted V. The nacelle protruded forward from the lower wing and had an unusual undercarriage of four-wheel design, with two at the nose and two under the wing. The wings were of equal span and chord, with ailerons fitted to the upper wing only, and non-streamlined wooden interplane struts.

The pilot was seated in front of the observer, who also operated the machine gun if the aircraft was so equipped. Swiveling gun mountings were in two locations. A forward gun was attached to a bracket raised above the pilot's head. A second mount was behind the observer on a V-shaped bracket that concluded at the leading edge of the upper wing; from this position the gunner could fire rearward. In all cases he had to stand to fire the guns. Voisins could also carry small bomb loads of approximately 400 lb. attached by a variety of racks.

Voisin LA, LAS, LBS

All these versions are similar and became very important to aviation corps detachments throughout the war, performing the majority of reconnaissance missions and bombing raids. They were larger than the Voisin L and used engines of higher horsepower. The LA was powered by the 140hp Salmson, while the LAS and LBS used the 150hp Salmson and occasionally the 160hp Salmson on the latter. The LA had the same non-streamlined struts as the L, while the LAS and LBS changed to streamlined struts. The LBS had a longer wingspan than the LA and LAS. Other than these minor differences, all appeared similar and had similar performance. Dux built only a small number of LBSs; no reliable production numbers are known.

Cannon-Voisin

A few of this model Voisin were sent from France. One was built by Dux, with a modified nacelle to install the Colt 1.5-inch gun in the nose. The machine differed from French versions, being modified by Dux designer

Another important aircraft used by the corps detachments was the Voisin L series. This Dux-built Voisin LA shows the two boxed radiators for the Salmson engine. Although no machine guns are fitted, both mounting brackets are in place, one over the pilot and one at the leading edge of the upper wing. If the two guns were installed, the observer could fire forward and behind his aircraft. Unfortunately, he had to do this while standing. The Dux roundel is evident as well as the information table stenciled on the nose. It reads "Maximum load 350 kilograms."

V.S. Denisov. It was powered by a 225hp Salmson engine and was finished in November, 1915. It passed flight tests and served at the front in a corps unit.

Nieuport 9

Other than the Nieuport IV monoplane of 1912, all Nieuports used during the war were single-bay, V-strut sesquiplanes with a single-spar lower wing. Most were single-seat aircraft, although some were two-seaters. All were powered by rotary engines of different makes and horsepower ratings. The fuselage was a box, wire-braced and linen-covered, with aluminum panels and cowling around the engine area, including a triangular fairing at the rear of the cowl. All main components were of wood except the tail, which was welded steel tube.

Russian-built Nieuports are easily differentiated from their French counterparts by color. The dope used by Dux and other Russian manufacturers was gray, giving a much darker appearance than the French aluminum coloring. Also, the lumber used for the struts was a lighter color than that seen on French machines, clearly showing the use of a different kind of wood.

The Nieuport 9 was strictly a Russian designation; it was a Nieuport 10 airframe with the front cockpit (observer's seat) faired over with a panel. A headrest was added behind the cockpit, which was not on the Nieuport 10. A machine gun was installed on the upper wing to fire over the arc of the propeller. The Nieuport 9 was usually equipped with a 80hp Le Rhône engine, but approximately 20 were built with a 100hp Gnome. The Gnome-powered aircraft had five circular cutouts in the cowl for added cooling.

Production of the Nieuport 9 and 10, like other Nieuport variants, cannot be determined with precision, although it is known that about 700 were built.[3]

Nieuport 10 and 10bis

The Nieuport 10 had the same airframe as the Nieuport 9, but was a two-seat reconnaissance aircraft with the observer in the forward cockpit. The standard powerplant was the 80hp Le Rhône. The 10bis had a shorter wing span and was sometimes equipped with a 100hp Gnome, having the same cooling holes in the cowl as that of the Nieuport 9. Dux also built a 10bis with a 110hp Le Rhône engine during 1917.

Nieuport 11

This machine, known as the *Bebe*, was smaller than previous models although similar in appearance. The 11 was built strictly as a fighter. It was usually fitted with a 80hp Le Rhône and a machine gun on the upper wing.

Nieuport 16

The type 16 was almost identical to the Nieuport 11. The engine was the 110hp Le Rhône and it retained the horseshoe cowl of previous models. The airframe had a headrest for the pilot, while the Nieuport 11 did not. With greater horsepower it had better performance than the 11.

Nieuport 17

The Nieuport 17 was the first of the series known as the 15-meter Nieuports[4] built solely as single-seat fighters. Larger than the 11 and 16, it also used the 110hp Le Rhône engine, but with a circular, closed cowl. Armament consisted of either one or two machine guns.

---

(3) This total includes all Nieuports, considered to be fighters, built by all Russian manufacturers, not just those machines built by Dux.

(4) The wing areas of the types 17, 21, 23, and 24bis were all approximately 15 square meters.

The Dux Nieuport 9 single seater. This aircraft was a single-seat variant of the Nieuport 10 powered by a 80hp Le Rhône and had a headrest for the pilot. It also has a fuel tank mounted on the upper wing. As with most Nieuports manufactured at the Dux plant, this machine has the roundels applied in 14 positions, including both surfaces of the horizontal stabilizer. Gray dope was applied, making Dux-built Nieuports appear darker than the aluminum-painted French-built aircraft.

Another Dux-built Nieuport 9. This machine is fitted with a Colt gun on the upper wing to fire above the propeller arc. The cowl with five circular cutouts indicates it is also one of approximately 20 built with a 100hp Gnome engine. The under-wing roundels are shown to good advantage.

Right: The Nieuport 16 was based on the Nieuport 11. Changes included a headrest and, more important, the engine. A 110hp Le Rhône replaced the 80hp Le Rhône of the Nieuport 11, improving performance. An aluminum panel fairs the rear edge of the cowl to the fuselage. The Colt machine gun appears to be fitted to a mount made in the field, and the pilot has mounted a rear-view mirror in the upper wing cutout.

Below: This Dux-built Nieuport 16 is fitted with skis for winter service. The Dux roundels and the distinction between the gray-doped fabric and the aluminum cowl are shown to advantage.

Nieuports nearing completion inside the Dux factory. By mid-1917 Dux was producing two machines a day.

Dux Nieuports which appear finished and ready for delivery. This building, obviously not the factory, is most likely a storage facility to house the completed airplanes until shipment.

Either a synchronized gun mounted on the fuselage could be installed or a gun fitted on the upper wing to fire above the propeller. In some cases, both guns were fitted. These machines had good performance and remained in service from late 1916 until the end of the war in December, 1917.

Nieuport 21

The same size as the Nieuport 17, the Nieuport 21 was equipped with a Le Rhône of only 80hp. Although performance was somewhat less than the 17, the machine handled very well and was enjoyable to fly.

Nieuport 23

The Nieuport 23 was almost two feet longer than the previous two models, and was fitted with the new 120hp Le Rhône, which gave better climb and a little more speed. The only other external difference was the machine gun mounting, which was offset to the starboard side of the fuselage. Many of these machines in service were Dux-built.

Nieuport 24bis

This model was the same length as the Nieuport 23 with a longer wing span. It also incorporated a new tail design commonly seen on later French versions, the Nieuport 27 and 28. Performance was good, somewhat better than the 23. Very few were built before the war's end.

Morane-Saulnier G

The type G was developed before the war and was used as a two-seat observation aircraft. The cockpit was a single opening for both crew members with limited space—in fact, one large cushion over the fuel tank formed both seats. A mid-wing monoplane, it offered poor downward visibility during reconnaissance missions. The fuselage was a simple wire-braced box structure with fabric covering. The tail had no fixed horizontal or vertical stabilizers. The standard power plant was the 80hp Gnome. The aircraft was transferred from frontline service to training duties by the end of 1915. Small batches were built in Russia, several by Dux.

A Morane-Saulnier G seen at the Gatchina flight school after a rough landing. This angle offers a good view of the wing shape and box-style fuselage as well as the small cockpit. These machines were used as both observation and training aircraft.

Morane-Saulnier L

The fuselage of the type L was almost the same as that of the type G. The L was also a monoplane, but the wing was mounted above the fuselage in a parasol arrangement. A two-seat reconnaissance plane, it offered a better downward view for the observer. A cutout in the wing was provided for spotting enemy aircraft from above.

Wing-warping was used instead of ailerons, and the aircraft displayed good flight qualities and performed well throughout the early years of the war. It was fitted with either the 80hp Gnome or the 80hp Le Rhône. During its development a vertical stabilizer was added. Machine guns were sometimes mounted for the observer and also for the pilot. The forward gun was first mounted on top of the wing and later on the fuselage deck, with either deflector plates on the propeller or a synchronizer.

Dux built 400 of these machines.

Additional Morane-Saulnier Models

Described as the Morane-Monocoque, this machine was smaller than the G model, yet similar to it except for the fuselage. It was experimental and was fitted with a 120hp Le Rhône engine. Only one was built by Dux.

The Morane-Saulnier N was nearly identical to the Monocoque. Powered by an 80hp Le Rhône, one aircraft of this version was started at Dux, but it was never finished.

One aircraft designated as the Morane-Biplane was built by Dux in 1917. This machine had an N-type fuselage and was a single-bay biplane equipped with a 110hp Le Rhône and two synchronized Vickers machine guns.

Spad 7

The SPAD 7 was one of the best fighters employed in Russia during the war. A single-seat, two-bay biplane, the SPAD 7 offered very good performance and flying characteristics. The 150hp Hispano-Suiza engine was fully cowled and fitted with a circular radiator. The synchronized Vickers machine gun was mounted in front of the pilot slightly to starboard of the centerline. Nearly 100 of these machines were built at the Dux plant by the end of 1917.

Tellier Flying Boat

A French design, the Tellier flying boat was a two-bay biplane with a pusher-mounted 200hp Hispano-Suiza. It was a three-seat aircraft equipped with one machine gun. It was to be manufactured by Dux during the latter half of 1917, but due to the lack of engines no aircraft were completed. A construction and testing facility was built on the Black Sea coast, where Dux produced 20 sets of wings and hulls.

Data for Dux-built machines are given in the tables on the next two pages.

A Morane-Saulnier L with skis for winter use. The wings are marked with Dux-style roundels and the fuselage with French markings. The cowl does not have the MS logo, so it may be a repaired aircraft using parts of different machines. Dux repaired several aircraft at its facility in Petrograd; this could be one. The Morane-Saulnier L was fitted with either an 80hp Le Rhône or, as the aircraft shown, an 80hp Gnome. Early in the war it was a popular reconnaissance aircraft, and Dux built 400.

Dux-Built Aircraft Data

Specification	Meller I	Meller II	Meller III	Dux No.2	Dux Military	Bleriot XIbis	Bleriot XI Dux	Farman IV	Farman VII	Farman IX
Year Built	1913	1913	1913	1913	1915	1910	1912	1910	1911	1911
Max. Speed, km/h	—	—	—	—	—	95	90	65	86	90
Landing Spd, km/h	—	—	—	—	—	—	—	60	60	60
Time to 1000m, min.	—	—	—	—	—	—	—	—	—	—
Time to 3000m, min.	—	—	—	—	—	—	—	—	—	—
Svc. Ceiling, m	—	—	—	—	—	—	—	—	—	—
Flt. Duration, Hrs.	—	—	—	—	—	—	—	—	—	—
Engines, number	1	1	1	1	1	1	1	1	1	1
type	G-M	G-M	Salmson	Gnome	G-M	Gnome	Gnome	Gnome	Gnome	Gnome
Power, hp	100	100	80	80	100	50	50	50	50	70
Length, m	9.4	8.1	10.5	7.6	7.6	7.75	7.2	12.5	9.0	8.0
Span, m (U/L)	12.1	13.7	12.4	12.3	11.2	8.9	8.9	10.5	12.0/7.0	12.0/7.0
Wing Area, m²	22.5	35.0	30.0	22.5	18.0	14.5	20.9	41.0	31.0	28.0
Empty Wt., kg	440	460	—	—	420	240	295	400	345	260
Fuel Wt., kg	95	100	—	—	130	—	—	30	75	75
Oil Wt., kg	25	total	—	—	total	total	35	total	total	total
Payload, kg	280	250	—	—	280	130	145	180	255	225
Gross Wt., kg	720	710	—	—	700	370	440	580	600	485
Wing Load, kg/m²	32.0	20.3	—	—	39.0	25.0	21.0	14.0	19.4	17.3
Power, kg/hp	7.2	7.1	—	—	7.0	7.4	8.8	11.6	12.0	7.0

Specification	Farman XV	Farman XVI	Farman XX	Farman XXII	Farman XXIIbis	Farman XXVII	Farman XXX	Voisin L	Voisin LA	Voisin LAS
Year Built	1912	1913	1913	1913	1913	1916	1916	1914	1914	1915
Max. Speed, km/h	96	90	95	90	118	132	136	100	100	105
Landing Spd, km/h	60	60	55	55	60	60	60	70	70	70
Time to 1000m, min.	—	20	20	—	8.5	7.5	5.0	13	12	11
Time to 2000m, min.	—	55	55	—	23	20	13	28	26	23
Time to 3000m, min.	—	—	—	—	—	34	24	—	—	55
Svc. Ceiling, m	—	2500	2500	—	3000	4500	4500	2800	2800	3000
Flt. Duration, Hrs.	—	2.5	3.5	3.5	—	4.0	4.0	4.0	4.0	4.0
Range, km	—	220	315	300	—	520	540	—	—	—
Engines, number	1	1	1	1	1	1	1	1	1	1
type	G-M	Gnome	Gnome	Gnome	G-M	Salmson	Salmson	Salmson	Salmson	Salmson
Power, hp	100	80	80	80	100	150	150	130	140	150
Length, m	9.92	8.06	8.06	8.09	8.9	9.22	8.65	9.5	9.5	9.5
Span, m (U/L)	17.75/ 11.42	13.77/ 7.58	13.77/ 7.58	15.0/ 7.58	15.0/ 7.3	16.15/ 16.15	15.81/ 9.2	13.51/ 13.51	14.74/ 12.54	14.74/ 12.54
Wing Area, m²	52.28	35.0	35.0	41.0	40.24	60.6	60.0	39.0	42.0	42.0
Empty Wt., kg	544	410	416	430	525	700	830	820	345	260
Fuel Wt., kg	94	70	82	82	98	160	160	140	140	140
Oil Wt., kg	30	total	27	27	31	24	24	25	26	26
Payload, kg	320	240	259	250	320	350	350	300	350	350
Gross Wt., kg	864	650	675	680	845	1050	1180	1120	1250	1250
Wing Load, kg/m²	16.5	18.4	19.1	16.5	21.0	17.3	23.6	28.8	29.8	29.8
Power, kg/hp	8.6	8.1	8.4	8.5	8.4	7.0	7.9	8.6	8.9	8.3

Notes:
1. In oil weight row, 'Total' means total weight of fuel and oil combined.
2. G-M is Gnome-Monosoupape.

358 THE IMPERIAL RUSSIAN AIR SERVICE

Specification	Voisin LBS	Voisin w cannon	Nieuport IV Dux	Nieuport 9	Nieuport 10	Nieuport 10bis	Nieuport 10bis	Nieuport 10 Dux	Nieuport 11	Nieuport 16
Year Built	1915	1915	1912	1915	1915	1916	1916	1917	1916	1916
Max. Speed, km/h	105	120	104	138	138	135	138	145	152	165
Landing Spd, km/h	68	70	—	—	—	—	—	—	—	—
Time to 1000m, min.	10	9	15	6	6	7	5.5	3.5	4	2.8
Time to 2000m, min.	22	20	—	13	13	20	13	8	10	6.4
Time to 3000m, min.	40	36	—	28	28	34	24	15	19	10
Time to 4000m, min.	—	—	—	—	—	—	44	15	33	16.5
Svc. Ceiling, m	3500	4000	2000	3800	3800	3600	4200	4800	4500	4800
Flt. Duration, Hrs.	4.0	2.8	3.0	2.0	2.0	2.0	2.0	2.0	2.0	2.0
Range, km	—	220	—	—	—	—	—	—	—	—
Engines, number	1	1	1	1	1	1	1	1	1	1
type	Salmson	Salmson	Gnome	Le Rhône	Le Rhône	Le Rhône	G-M	Le Rhône	Le Rhône	Le Rhône
Power, hp	160	225	70	80	80	80	100	110	80	110
Length, m	9.5	11.0	8.0	7.1	7.1	7.1	7.1	7.1	5.6	5.6
Span, m (U/L)	15.7/14.5	18.8/16.0	12.3	9.0	9.0	8.2	8.2	8.2	7.5	7.5
Wing Area, m²	47.0	63.0	22.5	17.6	17.6	17.6	17.6	17.6	13.5	13.5
Empty Wt., kg	975	1315	422	430	430	430	455	435	350	375
Fuel Wt., kg	140	150	64	45	45	45	60	64	45	45
Oil Wt., kg	26	30	26	12	12	12	20	22	12	12
Payload, kg	350	550	238	175	250	175	175	175	175	175
Gross Wt., kg	1325	1865	660	605	680	605	630	610	525	550
Wing Load, kg/m²	28.2	29.6	29.3	34.4	38.6	34.4	35.8	34.7	38.9	39.6
Power, kg/hp	8.3	8.3	9.4	7.6	8.5	7.6	6.3	5.6	6.6	4.9

Specification	Nieuport 17	Nieuport 21	Nieuport 23	Nieuport 24bis	Morane Saul. G	Morane Saul. L	Morane Saul. N	Morane Biplane	Spad 7	Tellier
Year Built	1916	1916	1917	1917	1912	1914	1916	1916	1916	1916
Max. Speed, km/h	164	150	168	171	115	127	—	160	185/195	125
Time to 1000m, min.	3.2	4	2.7	2.7	10	6	—	4.5	2.5	13
Time to 2000m, min.	6.8	8.7	5.8	5.7	25	15	—	9.5	5.5	27
Time to 3000m, min.	11.5	15.7	9.7	9.4	—	33	—	16	9	—
Time to 4000m, min.	19.5	25.6	15	14.4	—	—	—	—	—	—
Time to 5000m, min.	35	46	23	21.5	—	—	—	—	—	—
Svc. Ceiling, m	5300	5250	6500	6800	2600	3500	—	5700	6000	3500
Flt. Duration, Hrs.	2.0	2.0	1.7	1.7	2.5	2.6	—	2.0	2.0	4.0
Engines, number	1	1	1	1	1	1	1	1	1	1
type	Le Rhône	Le Rhône	Le Rhône	Le Rhône	Gnome	Le Rhône	Le Rhône	Le Rhône	Hisso	Hisso
Power, hp	110	80	120	120	80	80	80	110	140/150	200
Length, m	5.8	5.8	6.4	6.4	6.7	6.8	5.8	7.1	6.1	—
Span, m (U/L)	8.02/7.76	8.02/7.76	8.03/7.76	8.16/7.76	10.2	11.2	8.1	—	7.8	—
Wing Area, m²	14.7	14.7	14.7	15.0	16.0	18.0	11.0	23.0	18.0	41.0
Empty Wt., kg	375	370	355	375	350	395	400	440	545	1134
Fuel Wt., kg	65	55	67	67	89	91	—	65	100	237
Oil Wt., kg	total	total	total	total	19	33	—	total	total	20
Payload, kg	185	175	192	192	275	275	175	185	250	595
Gross Wt., kg	560	545	547	567	625	670	575	625	795	1729
Wing Load, kg/m²	38.0	37.0	37.0	38.0	39.0	37.2	52.1	27.2	43.0	42.0
Power, kg/hp	5.1	6.8	4.6	4.7	7.8	8.4	7.2	5.7	5.2	8.9

Notes:
1. In oil weight row, 'Total' means total weight of fuel and oil combined.
2. G-M is Gnome-Monosoupape.
3. Hisso is Hispano-Suiza.

Lebedev Factory

Vladimir Alexandrovich Lebedev, founder of the Lebedev Aeronautics Company, seated on the far right, with several of his colleagues.

The V.A. Lebedev Joint-Stock Aeronautics Company (*Aktzionernoe Obschestvo Vozdukhoplavania V. A. Lebedeva*) was founded by Vladimir Alexandrovich Lebedev in April, 1914, in St. Petersburg adjacent to the Komandantsky airfield. Lebedev had already been involved in aviation for five years, both as a pilot and as a designer/manufacturer.

In 1909 he built a sailplane, and shortly afterward received his flight training in France at the Farman school. When Lebedev returned to Russia with a Farman F-IV, he began to teach others the art of piloting and also gave rides in his machine. On May 28, 1911, Lebedev recorded a flight with four passengers in his Farman, an outstanding accomplishment for that time. In 1912 he opened a workshop that produced French-designed propellers and Deperdussin parts.

In September, 1913, he developed and constructed an aviation train consisting of horse-drawn wagons for servicing an aviation detachment by carrying its aircraft and necessary supplies. Nieuport IV machines, along with fuel, oil, and spare parts were successfully carried along the trial route from St. Petersburg to Levashko, Tolkov, and back to St. Petersburg without incident. He also experimented with painting aircraft a 'defensive color' (most likely gray) which, as reported by U. S. attaché Lieutenant Sherman Miles, "was scarcely visible even at a comparatively small height."

The company began producing small batches of French-designed aircraft before the war and throughout the first months of hostilities. From late 1914 to the end of 1917 the firm developed its own designs named *Lebed* (Swan) in a series numbered 1 through 24 (designated by roman numerals).[1] However, many of these were based on captured machines that had been sent to the factory for evaluation.

The firm expanded to include two other facilities for aircraft production, at Yaroslavl and Taganrog, but these accomplished very little. A plant in Penza was established for manufacturing propellers. The firm also experimented with several large multi-engined aircraft. By the end of the war, Lebedev had produced 700 aircraft, of which 674 were delivered. The production rate had increased to one airplane a day and the company's facility occupied a total area of 136,100 square yards and employed 1156 workers.

In November 1914, Lieutenant Miles had the opportunity to interview Lebedev, who had already built 73 machines for the Russian Air Service. Miles asked him several questions on different aspects of Russian military aviation. In some instances, his replies were vague due to censorship, and Miles was not allowed to view the factory.[2] However, in some cases Lebedev answered in a very informative manner. He commented that the service life of airframes and rotary engines was only two months and that of an inline engine six months. He believed wireless transmitting apparatus was not efficient for use in an airplane because of its limited range, although he expressed the need for applying armor to aircraft. In his opinion, protection of the pilot was of vital importance, stating, "I have seen an aero with 30 bullet holes, both rifle and shrapnel and not much the worse for it, while in another case a single bullet brought down the aero by killing the pilot. We have learned that aeros must be armored."[3]

Lebedev noted that Russian troops fired upon their own aircraft, a problem occurring in other allied as well as enemy armies. Lastly, he was asked his opinion of the efficiency of the German and Russian air service performance and its relationship to training procedures. He replied that the German service appeared to be well trained, especially in the area of artillery spotting, which led him to believe the Germans must have practiced to a great extent during peacetime. On the other hand, Lebedev felt the Russian army lacked aeronautical training declaring, "We have several hundred pilots, but not more than 10 per cent to 15 per cent of them have proved efficient during the war. And even if a man is an excellent pilot, it is the greatest mistake to suppose that he can observe. He may fly wherever you like, but he will not see anything worth reporting. Nor does it follow that a carefully trained general staff officer can observe from an aero if he has not had practice. It is a different point of

---

(1) The use of the numbering system was not always adhered to; in many cases designs were given names without numbers and sometimes numbers were skipped.

(2) Although secrecy was of great importance to the Russians, Miles may not have been granted the privilege of viewing the Lebedev facility due to the firm starting production of the experimental Svyatogor twin-engine bomber, believed to have great promise at that time.

(3) There is, however, no evidence of armor plate used on any Lebed aircraft. This may be due to a lack of material, or, more likely, excessive weight.

view, which entirely upsets the eye. An observer must constantly fly, preferably with his own pilot, in time of peace, and thus get the necessary training. Then there is the higher command. Generals who do not know the aeronautical service from having used it in time of peace cannot judge of its capabilities, and either demand impossible tasks, or miss opportunities. This also can only be remedied by constant peacetime training."

Early Production of French Designs

The first machines produced at the Lebedev plant in early 1914 were Deperdussin type D monoplanes with 80hp Gnome engines. This two-seater was capable of 66 mph and was used in reconnaissance and photographic roles at the beginning of hostilities. It featured a cut-out in the bottom of the fuselage for better downward view. Lebedev built 63 of these machines for the Russian army and some were still in service in 1917. Two machines were modified by the addition of floats and issued to the Russian navy in 1915.

By July, 1914, the company had began production of a second type, the Voisin pusher biplane (L series). This machine, equipped with a 130hp Salmson nine-cylinder, water-cooled radial engine, was a strong yet slow machine. Its main framework, including the wings, was constructed from steel tube. Top speed was only about 65 mph, with a ceiling of 9200 feet, but the machine had a duration of four hours, making it useful for reconnaissance. The Voisin LA and LAS became the workhorses of the army corps detachments for most of the war.

Between late 1914 and 1916, the plant produced 34 Franco-British Aviation FBA type C flying boats for the Russian navy. These boats were equipped with a 130hp Clerget and were capable of 68 mph with a range of 186 miles.

During 1915 the firm built a small batch of 30 Morane-Saulnier type L aircraft delivered to the army for use in reconnaissance. It has also been reported that some Farman XXX and Nieuport aircraft were built by Lebedev.

Lebed I–VI

There is no definite information on the first six Lebed designs. If any aircraft were so numbered, it was most likely they were captured machines that were repaired with some modifications and produced as one of a kind or, at the very least, built in small numbers. It is possible some of the French-designed machines were labeled by the factory with these lower numbers.

Lebed 7

In late 1914 and 1915 Lebedev produced copies of the Sopwith Tabloid. This single-seat scout was designated as the Lebed 7. It incorporated equal-span and equal-chord wings of single-bay construction and wing warping as did the original Tabloid. It saw service as a patrol and reconnaissance aircraft during the first year of the war. Equipped with an 80hp Gnome engine, it was capable of nearly 90 mph, a very good speed for the time. It could climb to 1200 feet in a minute. Photographic evidence does not show any armament; apparently no fixed guns were installed. Records show Lebed 7s were on strength with the 21st Corps Detachment from 1914 until the winter of 1915–16. Production records do not exist, but a very limited number were built.

Port side rear view of a Lebed 7 serving with a corps detachment, showing to good advantage the Sopwith Tabloid wing style. Also visible is the characteristic Lebed windscreen. It appears the cockades have been applied only to the wings.

A factory photo of the Lebed 7. The factory work number can be easily seen on the components of the tail. The L_758, with the model number centered, was the standard Lebedev stenciling method used to label the machines. It can be seen on most of the detachable panels of the aircraft. This is a factory number only and it appears no further serial numbering system was used or applied.

Left: Front view of the Lebed 7, revealing its likeness to the Tabloid. The cowl with similar cutouts partially encloses the 80hp Gnome rotary. This machine was on strength with the 21st Corps Detachment, November 1914. The pilot on the left is Felix Vernitsky, who was killed in action on October 14, 1915, in Galicia.

Members of the 21st Corps Detachment preparing for a mission in late 1914. The Lebed 7 carries the markings of the squadron on the tail, aircraft 1, and on the fuselage with Roman numerals XXI. The Lebed work number is above that, just aft of the cockpit. The squadron's Farman is also ready for flight.

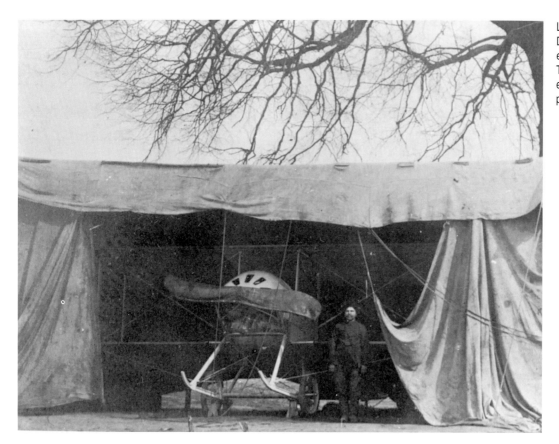

Lebed 7 belonging to the 21st Detachment being protected from the elements during the winter of 1915. The cowl has unusual cutouts for extra airflow and the propeller has a protective cover.

Lebed 8

Two examples of a two-bay experimental model of the Lebed 7 were produced and designated Lebed 8. The upper wing incorporated ailerons. Span was longer, but was equal for both wings. The chord appears to be the same as on the single-bay machine. The wing tips were squared off instead of the usual angled back style. Of interest was the use of a large windscreen, a trademark of the Lebedev firm. Performance of the Lebed 8 is unknown and it appears no further development was attempted.

Lebed 9

The Lebed 9 was an experimental single-seat scout powered by an 80hp Gnome or Le Rhône rotary engine. A single-bay biplane, it employed ailerons on the upper wing. All struts were wood and the fuselage was fabric covered with the top and bottom being rounded. The forward deck around the cockpit was wooden and featured a headrest for the pilot. The cowl panels were gray metal. Performance was stated as being unsatisfactory and only the prototype was built.

The experimental Lebed 8 was a modified Lebed 7. It retained the fuselage of the Lebed 7 but had a completely different wing design. Two sets of struts were incorporated with ailerons added, eliminating the original wing warping controls. An experimental gray color was applied overall and cockades have been applied in ten positions. Only two were built, with no further development taking place.

The experimental Lebed 9 single-seat aircraft on the Komandantsky airfield. The only marking applied is the Lebed work number on the vertical stabilizer, giving the model number IX. The headrest is of interest, but was not used on other models. This machine proved unsatisfactory and no other units were produced.

Lebed 10

The Lebed 10 was a two-seat experimental biplane with a long, two-bay wing. It incorporated ailerons on both upper and lower wings and the actuating cable was externally mounted, traveling through pulleys installed at the leading edge of the wings which are clearly visible in photographs. Wing struts were of wood while landing gear and cabane supports were of steel tube, a standard construction method on most Lebeds. Similar in style to the Lebed 9, the fuselage maintained the fabric covering and the round shape of the top and bottom areas. This model did away with the headrest and featured only a half cowl exposing most of its 80hp Le Rhône engine. The forward metal surfaces featured large access panels for servicing, similar to the Nieuport style. It was underpowered and not suitable for reconnaissance work; consequently only a few were built.

The Lebed 10 seen outside the factory. The exposed 80hp Le Rhône engine and two-bay wing construction can be seen to good advantage. This airplane was intended as a patrol and reconnaissance machine, but it proved to be under-powered and very few were built.

Lebed 11

In the summer of 1915 the Lebedev company was given a sample of an Albatros B model two-seat machine, equipped with a 150hp Benz engine. Russian authorities, believing it good practice to copy such proven designs, requested Lebedev to manufacture a similar type. Since producing copies of existing foreign types saved time and money in development, it was not long before Lebedev engineer Leopold Mikhailovich Shkulnik and his assistant, Ribokov, developed the Lebed 11. This machine was produced in small numbers, approximately ten being manufactured, with little standardization. Wing span, length, and especially engines varied between aircraft. Most had captured and overhauled engines, but at least one had a nine-cylinder, 130hp Salmson Canton-Unne. There were six different wing designs, incorporating both two-bay and three-bay configurations, which ranged in span from 42.6 feet to 47.5 feet. These machines were the forerunner of the Lebed 12.

In addition to producing Lebed series copies of Albatros models, Lebedev was in charge of repairing captured German and Austrian types, including Albatros, Rumplers, and Aviatiks. Through this work Lebedev managed to acquire several enemy engine types and their associated parts, such as radiators. The Lebedev firm salvaged the captured radiators and incorporated them on Lebed aircraft. This type of cooling system was a series of rectangular, side-mounted units of German design, originally produced by the firm Haegle and Zweigle, simply known as H-Z, or 'Ha Zet' as pronounced in German. The *Hazet* radiator was copied and manufactured in Russia for use on aircraft with inline and radial engines and was very popular.

Further modified Albatros models were experimented with using the 150hp British Sunbeam V-8, including a floatplane design.

Right: A close-up of the nose of the machine below, showing a good view of the Hiero engine, the *Hazet* radiators, and the metal inspection panels on the plywood fuselage.

A Lebed 11 equipped with an Austrian Hiero engine. The resemblance to early Albatros B and C models is evident. This Lebed XI incorporates angular aileron washout, usually associated with the Lebed 12. It employs the *Hazet* radiator units and is fitted with the characteristic large windscreen and a Shkulnik gun mount.

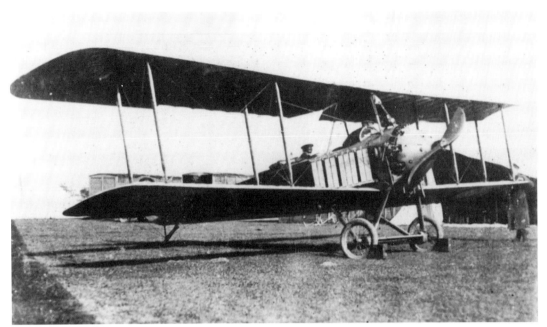

A Lebed 11 or 12 with a Salmson Canton-Unne radial engine installed. The aircraft has the raised deck on the fuselage behind the gunner more common to the 12, but the upper wing cutout is similar to an Albatros and the ailerons do not have the angular washout. These charac-teristics were usually not associated with the type 12. It is also possible this machine used components from captured aircraft.

Lebed-Morskoi LM-1

In the spring of 1916 the LM-1 (Lebed Naval type 1) was completed. It was a three-bay Albatros floatplane copy, similar to the Albatros B.II except for use of a Sunbeam V-8 engine. By 1917 the Russian navy needed a two-seat tractor aircraft with a flexible gun for defending the rear. An order was placed on June 27, 1917, for 175 units. It was intended to power these with the 220hp Renault, but due to shortages of engines of more than 200hp this did not take place. Only two were produced at Taganrog by the end of hostilities, both powered by 200hp Hispano Suiza engines.

Deperdussin Sport

The Deperdussin Sport was an experimental aircraft built in the beginning of 1916 and was a development of the French 1914 model. A monoplane, it retained a similar style of wing warping, with braces attached to the fuselage ahead of the cockpit. The elevators also maintained the same shape as earlier Deperdussin types, but the rudder was the rounded style, a common Lebedev feature. The biggest design change was the monocoque plywood fuselage, giving the machine a flying barrel appearance. This machine was equipped with a 100hp Gnome rotary engine and displayed the typical Lebed windscreen. The cockpit was a single large opening, giving the appearance of being a two-seat machine, although this has been disputed. If the aircraft carried two crewmen, it allowed for ease of communication. The Sport had a top speed of 112 mph and was to have a synchronized machine gun. For unknown reasons, this model was not accepted, the gun was never mounted, and production did not occur past the prototype.

The Lebed-Morskoi LM-1, floatplane version of an Albatros B.II copy. The aircraft featured three-bay construction and was virtually identical to the Albatros except for the power plant, which was a British 150hp Sunbeam V-8.

The Lebed Deperdussin Sport built in 1916. The type retained several Deperdussin features, including the undercarriage supports and the wire bracing brackets forward of the cockpit. Much of the tail and wings were similar in design to the original. The large cockpit opening, the plywood monocoque fuselage, and the Lebed-style windscreen are evident.

Front view of the Lebed Deperdussin Sport displaying the circular cowl around the 100hp Gnome rotary engine. At 112 mph the aircraft had excellent speed, and it was to be equipped with a synchronized, forward-firing machine gun. Unfortunately, the machine was not ordered and no further development occurred.

Lebed 12

The prototype Lebed 12 was built in the autumn of 1915 and was ready for testing in January, 1916. This model displayed the Albatros-style wings, yet incorporated the angular washout in the ailerons as used on LVG C.II aircraft. Control horns appear to be used only on the type 12 and are not evident in photographs of other Lebed models. The fuselage was plywood covered and was of rectangular box construction, giving it great strength. This structure was also easy to build, but it added more weight to the airframe than a linen-covered fuselage. Aluminum panels were used in the forward areas covering the engine, which caused drag and gave the machine a bulky appearance. The aircraft maintained the Albatros B.I-style empennage, which was a welded steel tube frame. It had wood interplane struts and streamlined steel tube for the cabane and undercarriage.

Lebed 12 engines were all Salmson Canton-Unne nine-cylinder, water-cooled radials of 130 through 160hp, most being 150hp. Nearly all were supplied with *Hazet* style radiators. The fuel tank was located under the pilot's seat and in some cases was covered by a protective rubber insulator, designed by *Stabs-Kapitan* (Staff-Captain) Grigorov. The observer's cockpit had a raised plywood deck with an unusual cutout, possibly for positioning the

Believed to be a Lebed 12, this may possibly be a late Lebed 11 equipped with a Salmson radial and a Shkulnik gun mount. The fuselage raised deck area and angular aileron washout are prominent. The machine gun is an American Colt.

Left: A Lebed 12, displaying roundels in only six positions, making use of the pennant emblem on the fuselage sides. The typical Lebed work number stencils (L12457) are shown to good advantage on most of the airframe panels. The small circular disk in the center of the rudder cockade is believed to be a factory emblem and can be seen, in many instances, applied to the rudder on other machines.

Below: L12457 shown from the front, revealing the Salmson radial engine and metal supports, after having its aluminum cowl panels removed. The use of natural doped linen is evident as the upper wing cockade and internal wing structure are clearly visible.

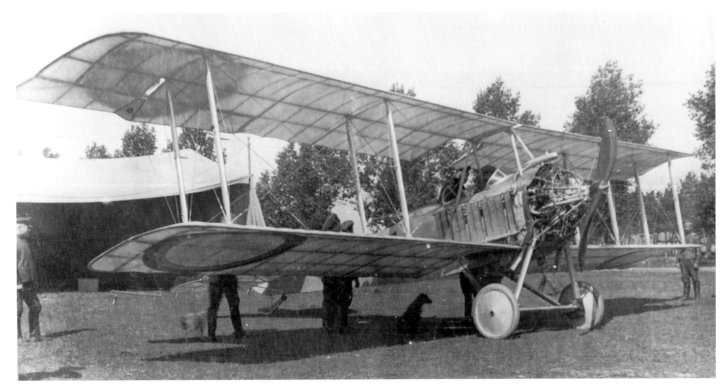

Above: The same Lebed 12 as the previous photo with cowl panels re-applied. The circular factory emblem, as carried on the rudder, can be seen in the center of all the wooden wing struts. The work number may also be stenciled below this.

Left: In this view of a Bolshevik Lebed 12, the angular washout of the port aileron is easily visible. The Shkulnik gun mount can be seen as well as a tank applied above the engine, possibly for oil. The machine appears to be over-painted in a dark color.

This Bolshevik Lebed 12 is preparing for a mission during a winter operation. The aircraft has been refitted with skis and appears to have been repainted overall.

Close-up of the nose of a Lebed 12, giving an excellent view of the forward panels around the engine and on the fuselage. Also visible are the streamlined steel tubing struts of the undercarriage and cabane. The *Hazet* radiator is shown to good advantage and the Shkulnik gun mount can be seen. Of interest is the upper wing cutout. Its angular shape is not standard for the type 12, and may be due to replacement wings used in repairing the machine.

gun for downward fire. From this location an American Colt, the only standard weapon supplied with the aircraft, set on a mount developed by Shkulnik. This device proved difficult to operate in combat and an improved substitute, designed by Leonid Dementyevich Kolpakov, replaced it. This was a more flexible ring type, which also allowed the gun to be raised and lowered. In April, 1917, Kolpakov improved his design by incorporating a gunner's seat and gun attached to a bar which pivoted together as one unit, allowing greater mobility and ease of use; however, very few were installed in Lebeds. In late 1916 some Lebed 12s had a bomb rack, developed by Kolpakov, mounted on the lower fuselage center section.

The wing span for the Lebed 12 is estimated as 43 feet 1.7 inches for the upper wing and 39 feet 4.4 inches for the lower. The chord was equal for both wings at 5 feet 8.88 inches. The length of the machine was 25 feet 9.4 inches, and the height was 10 feet 7.9 inches. Equipped with the 150hp Salmson, it was capable of 83 mph. The machine climbed to 3280 feet (1000 meters) in 10 minutes, and to 8200 feet (2500 meters) in 35 minutes. Its ceiling was 11,500 feet. Empty it weighted 1905 lb. and fully loaded 2678 lb. It had a duration of about three hours and could carry a bomb load of approximately 200 lb.

On January 10, 1916, *Poruchik* Sleptzov test flew the prototype Lebed 12, work number 325. He made two 15-

A close-up of the gunner's area of the Lebed 12. This view clearly displays the raised plywood deck, with the unusual cutout located center/rear of this panel. The purpose of this is unknown, but may possibly be a gun rest or extend through the fuselage for firing directly below. The gun mount is the improved Kolpakov type, allowing the gun to be raised or lowered. The large Lebedev windscreens are most prominent.

minute flights in the aircraft, which was powered with a 130hp Salmson engine. He concluded that the machine handled favorably compared with the Albatros. On July 2, 1916, the central military board ordered 225 Lebed 12s for army air corps detachments. The machine began to replace the Voisin as the standard corps unit aircraft, but suffered many problems. The exhaust pipes of the Salmson were positioned downward, causing the airflow to route the exhaust fumes into the rear cockpit, so the observer could either be asphyxiated or stand up and be frozen in the open air. From the pilot's viewpoint it was difficult to pull out of a dive and on occasion the Lebed 12 would catch fire in the air. While considered better than the Voisins, the Lebeds were not as popular as the Farman XXX or the Anatra Anasal. It has been estimated that 218 Lebed 12 aircraft were manufactured. In addition to these, it has been estimated that 30 were produced of other variants, similar to the Lebed 12. It has been reported that 171 repair kits were produced and issued for servicing the aircraft at the front.

Lebed 12bis

In 1917, a modification was made to the Lebed 12. This was designated the Lebed 12bis, and had the same airframe as the Lebed 12 with a different engine. A 150hp Hispano-Suiza was installed, reducing the size of the cowling that had been necessary to mount the Salmson. This V-8 motor changed the appearance, but did little for performance. Only two were built, with the second reported as being fitted with a different engine.

Lebed 13

The Lebed 13 was a modification of the Lebed 12 using the Salmson 150hp engine. It was capable of 93 mph and was scheduled to be manufactured in March, 1916. However, no records of production have been found.

Lebed 14

The Lebed 14 or *Grand* was the company's first attempt at building a multi-engined bomber. The project began in 1915, and the design had great promise. Powered by two 150hp Salmson radials, it was expected to be capable of nearly 87 mph and carry a load of 1985 lb. The wings were of three-bay design, fabric covered, with the upper wing span greater than the lower. The engines were mounted in standard fashion between the wings on a series of braces and drove tractor propellers. There were metal cowlings forward and aft of the engines for streamlining.

The fuselage was a plywood, monocoque style. The use of plywood included the tail unit and the nose. A forward gunner's compartment was in the nose with an area for an observer/photographer below that. Farther back were the pilot's cockpit and a rear gunner's position. The aircraft was designed to carry three machine guns.

Construction of the Lebed 14 progressed slowly and it was not finished before the end of hostilities.

The Lebed 14, also known as the *Grand*, under construction at the factory. This was the company's first attempt at a multi-engined aircraft. The machine had a monocoque plywood fuselage and carried a crew of four, including two gunners and a photographer. Equipped with two Salmson radial engines, the project showed great promise. Unfortunately, progress was slow and the airplane was never finished.

The model number of this Lebed is unknown. The work order number is visible on the trailing edge of the starboard wing panel and reveals the typical Lebed marking system, but is not discernible. It appears to be a later design, above 12 and below 20. Of interest are the tall side-mounted radiators of the type usually seen on Voisins. The upper wing is in two sections, as with other Lebeds, but it separates over the port cabane. Straps can be seen connecting the two sections. Also, the pilot's cockpit is in the rear; the control wheel is just visible. The engine appears to be a six-cylinder inline, possibly a Hiero.

Lebed 15

Very little is known of this model, except it has been stated the machine was to be equipped with a 220hp Renault engine. This was more than likely another modification of the Lebed 12 or an Albatros copy. Production was set to begin in March, 1916, but due to engine shortages was not undertaken. It is unknown if a prototype was even built.

Lebed 16

The Lebed 16 was another twin-engine biplane project that appears to have been inspired by the German AEG G-series. It was designed for reconnaissance and was equipped with two 80hp Le Rhône rotary engines mounted on the top of the lower wing secured by V-shaped struts, which were attached to the underside of the upper wing. Streamlined metal cowls protected the engines. As with the Lebed 14, the Lebed 16 had a plywood fuselage and an upper wing of greater span than the lower. The pilot sat between the observer stationed in the nose and the mechanic in the rear. Both these areas were equipped with a machine gun, giving good protection from front and rear attacks.

The aircraft was tested in the beginning of 1917 with favorable results. For unknown reasons the project was discontinued and no further aircraft were produced.

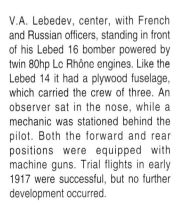

V.A. Lebedev, center, with French and Russian officers, standing in front of his Lebed 16 bomber powered by twin 80hp Le Rhône engines. Like the Lebed 14 it had a plywood fuselage, which carried the crew of three. An observer sat in the nose, while a mechanic was stationed behind the pilot. Both the forward and rear positions were equipped with machine guns. Trial flights in early 1917 were successful, but no further development occurred.

The port side of the Lebed 17. The fuselage side can be seen faired-out to meet the engine cowl, giving better streamlining than the Lebed 12. This model retained the raised plywood deck around the gunner's cockpit, but from that point the fuselage is linen-covered. Just visible in this view are the two triangular cutouts in the upper wing above the cockpit allowing an improved view for the pilot. Another feature of the Lebed 17 was the addition of a forward-firing gun for the pilot. Unfortunately, this aircraft is not fitted with its armament and does not show the location of this weapon. The large windscreens are still utilized and the rear gun mount appears to be a Kolpakov type.

Lebed 17

The Lebed 17, although similar to the Lebed 12, was an improvement in many respects. This model still used the Salmson radial engine, but had the fuselage modified by a rounded plywood panel for better streamlining. Only the forward section was wood, with the rear of the fuselage being linen covered to save weight. The *Hazet* style radiators were replaced by a more efficient design of two small tubular units attached to the front cabane struts. The metal cowling was also improved to reduce drag.

The Lebed 17 was a single-bay biplane with ailerons in the upper wing only. The upper wing incorporated two triangular celluloid cutouts and the lower wing had curved cutouts at the inboard trailing edge location, both of which allowed for greater pilot visibility. Interestingly, the Lebed 17 reverted to using externally mounted aileron control cables as seen on earlier Lebed models. The aircraft increased its firepower by adding a forward-firing, synchronized machine gun while maintaining the rear gun and the standard raised deck area with unusual cutout, presumably for downward firing.

The Lebed 17 was tested in August, 1917, with very good results. Unfortunately, it came too near the end of the war and only a few were produced.

Top view of the Lebed 17. Evident are the single-bay construction of the wings, ailerons in the upper wing only, and the externally-mounted aileron cables and pulleys at the leading edge of the wing. The pilot's field of vision was increased by the addition of celluloid panels in the upper wing and the large rounded cutouts at the inboard, trailing edge of the lower wing. Also visible is the rectangular cutout in the raised deck behind the gunner's cockpit. The plane is finished in natural linen and clear varnished plywood, with roundels applied in ten positions. The Lebed 17 was test flown in August 1917 with good results, but due to the end of hostilities only a few were produced.

Lebed 18

Little is known of this type other than it was a copy of a German design and was to be powered by an Italian 230hp Fiat engine. In January, 1917, the Lebed company stated it would produce 300 units, but not one was manufactured.

Lebed 21

This two-seat reconnaissance monoplane was equipped with the typical Lebedev power plant, the 150hp Salmson. Its flying characteristics have been described as poor, and the only available data are rate of climb: 20 minutes to 6500 feet. Seven were manufactured, the first being delivered on September 12, 1917.

Lebed 24

The Lebed 24 was another modified Albatros design and was to incorporate either the 200hp Hispano-Suisa or the 230hp Fiat engine. An order was placed for 200 units in 1917, but due to engine delivery problems and shortages the order was never filled.

Sopwith 1-1/2 Strutter

An order was placed for 260 Sopwith 1-1/2 Strutter aircraft with 130hp Clerget engines, to be manufactured at either the Taganrog or Yaroslav facilities. Only five were built in 1917.

Additional Lebed Designs

A few experimental models were produced, apparently without a series number designation. The reason for this is unknown, as well as the reason for a break in the numerical sequence. The following list is undoubtedly incomplete, but gives a good representation of types developed by Lebedev.

It has been reported a small amount of Sunbeam-powered, three-bay Albatros two-seat aircraft were delivered to the army in late 1916. These were simply the LM-1 in landplane form and may have evolved from that project. The capacity in which they were employed is unknown, but the type was obsolete and presumably was used as a trainer.

Supposedly, a pusher machine was designed in April, 1916. Other than it was intended to equip it with either a Salmson or a Renault engine, nothing is known of this aircraft.

An experimental Albatros-type biplane with a 101hp Duflou and Constantinovich engine was built in 1916, but no other information is available on this machine.

Another Albatros-style airplane was built in late 1916 with a 100hp Fiat engine installed. The top speed was only 59 mph and rate of climb was 25 minutes to an altitude of 3250 feet. Despite this very poor performance, three examples were produced and accepted.

Experimental Designs by Others Developed at the Lebedev Plant

At least four additional aircraft were built at the Petrograd facility which were the ideas of other inventors.

The first was the Kolpakov K-1, developed by L.D. Kolpakov-Miroshnichenko. Because of his help and guidance at the Lebedev plant with the designs of several armament devices, he was able to work on his own experimental aircraft. This two-seat biplane was powered by a 100hp Austro-Daimler engine. A unique feature of was the ability to change the wing angle of incidence. A mechanical assembly allowed for the angle to be changed 7 degrees. Its purpose was to achieve a greater angle of attack for a quick takeoff, and while in flight revert the wings back to a normal position for cruising. The machine was tested in 1916, but lost power and crashed immediately after lifting off the ground. The wings were damaged and the project was not pursued.

The second machine was the "Svyatogor," designed by Vasili Andrianovich Slesarev and built at the Lebedev facility, with production beginning in December, 1914. This giant three-bay biplane had a span of 118 feet and length of 69 feet. It was powered by two 220hp Renault engines inside the fuselage. The two airscrews, located about mid-wing of the large aircraft, were driven by a belt-type transmission. An unusual feature of this machine was its Voisin-style landing gear. Two large wooden wheels of 6.5-foot diameter were located under the lower wing, while the front wheels (also wooden) were directly under the nose. They were not small either, being about five feet in diameter. Expectations of this giant were far beyond any conceivable reality. The machine's excessive weight was too much for 440hp. At the end of 1916, during a taxiing trial, a wheel was caught in a ditch and damaged part of the fuselage and a propeller. Eventually the project was abandoned and the plane was left at the edge of the field, never having left the ground.

The third aircraft was designed by naval pilot *Leitenant* (Naval Lieutenant) Georgy Anatolyevich Fride. The machine, the Fride Morskoi Parasol, was built and test-flown in 1916. It was an original idea incorporating the wing of a Morane-Saulnier parasol. The hull had two sets of fins, known as hydrovanes, attached to the underside both fore and aft to help with lifting the plane from the water. The initial flight was unsuccessful with no further production taking place.

The fourth aircraft was a flying boat designed by Alexander Yustusovich Villish. This two-seat pusher biplane, known as the VM-4, was powered by a 110hp Le Rhône. This aircraft, like Kolpakov's, also incorporated a wing capable of changing the angle of incidence while in flight. However, it was discovered that the plane performed well without it and the device was not used. Only a few examples were built; these were used as trainers at the Baku flight school.

Where known, data on Lebedev-built aircraft are included in the text.

Section 7

Colors and Markings

Colors and Markings

As every World War I aviation enthusiast knows, the exact color schemes and markings of a particular aircraft are of paramount importance and obtained with difficulty. Whereas contemporary aircraft have been amply documented in official manuals and color film, World War I aircraft colors and markings are sparsely documented and imprecise—with the exception of the few surviving museum examples scattered around the world. To obtain this information, one must rely on the testimony of wartime aviators, memoirs, rare combat art, fabric swatches, intelligence bulletins, and aircraft reports. Even then, the precise color values can only be approximated. At best, one can develop an intuitive "feel" for the "color values" inherent in a black and white photograph.

Color Schemes Applied to Aircraft Used in The Imperial Russian Air Service

The Russians did not adopt complex camouflage schemes for their aircraft, and only a small number of machines displayed unit or individual markings. The lack of an advanced paints and finishes industry in Russia was a key contributor, but in truth, the idea of aircraft concealment was of little concern to the Russians and remained a low priority throughout the entire war. The color schemes applied to aircraft used by the Imperial Russian Air Service can be divided into four distinct types.

Type A: Plain Finish (Clear Dope)

Most of the pre-war machines built in Russia and imported from France left their respective factories in one of the early linen schemes or in a clear-doped finish overall. For the model builder, it is safe to assume this finish was applied on many aircraft throughout the entire war.

Plain-finished aircraft were delivered with unpainted linen, metal, and wood surfaces. Plain linen describes the color obtained from bleached linen that has been covered with clear dope. With time, the changes to the dope color yielded a wide spectrum of colors ranging from pale cream, yellow to grayish-yellow, and depending on the final coating a light-brown color. For many Russian-built aircraft, the known finish was several coats of clear acetone-based dope for tightening the fabric which was then covered by a further coat of a spirit and oil-based varnish. This gave the fabric an overall dirty yellow to light-brown color which was streaky according to some photographs.

Plain wood refers to unpainted wood that has only been varnished. The color range is quite broad according to the type of wood and varnish used, and less so, changes due to aging. Plain metal indicates metal parts covered with clear protective varnish, but not painted.

Type B: Protective Covering—Single Opaque Scheme

In the winter of 1915 the first opaque schemes were applied to Russian aircraft and those obtained from France. The objective of the protective covering medium was to protect clear-doped, unbleached linen fabric from the sun's harmful ultra-violet rays; otherwise it was often necessary to recover an entire airframe after only a matter of a few months of active service in Russia's harsh climate. These schemes were based on a single color, and it should be noted that, if the pigmented dope was a sprayed-on finish, it had to be a varnish enamel because the Russians and French did not develop a cellulose-acetate that could be sprayed. Known single opaque schemes are:
1. Earth Tone: A small number of French-built Nieuport type 10s and 16s were delivered with fabric finished in a khaki, olive, or reddish-brown with traces of aluminum powder in suspension.
2. Aluminum: Some of the first aircraft used by the Russians with an aluminum scheme were the French-built Voisin LA and Nieuport type 17. The color extended to all fabric-covered surfaces, wheel covers, and certain struts. The overall aluminum-doped scheme was also applied to French-built Nieuport 21s and 23s.
3. Yellowish-Gray: In addition to some Nieuport fighters having this color as an underside finish, all Spad A-2 and Spad 7 aircraft supplied to Russia in 1916–17 were finished in an overall yellowish-gray scheme. The metal panels were painted to closely match the fabric color.
4. Pale Gray: Russian manufacturers, notably Dux, began applying an overall finish of pale gray to various aircraft in the spring of 1915, and this continued throughout the war. French-built Farmans and Voisins, as well as a small number of Curtiss type "F" flying boats, were delivered to Russia in a pale gray that closely matched the Russian gray color.

Type C: Protective Covering—Camouflage Scheme

Only a small number of aircraft used by Russia in World War I were finished with a true camouflage scheme, and in almost cases these were French-built machines supplied to Russia in 1916–17.

Early 1916 saw the introduction of camouflage patterns on French aircraft and it was initially adopted on both Nieuport 11 and 16 types. Thus far a definitive set of patterns and representative color matches are unknown, but from the four samples obtained it seems likely that the chosen varnish enamels of drab greens and browns were sprayed over the upper-surfaces of the aircraft, leaving the under-surfaces in their base color (typically clear dope or pale yellow). When these dark colors were applied, narrow borders of a contrasting light color were often left on flying and control surfaces to provide an outline appearance. The majority of French-built Nieuports painted in this manner had their upper wing roundels painted over. Although these were reinstated in many cases, the new roundels rarely matched the colors or dimensions of original factory-applied roundels.

Type D: Naval Water-Proofing

In early 1916 the Schetinin factory began applying water-proofing yacht enamel to the hulls of Grigorovich M.5 flying boats. For the M.5s and the later M.9s, the paint was applied to the underside of the hull and along the sides, up to and including the chine edges. The colors were generally white, pale gray, or light sky blue. Later this enamel was extended up the hull sides marking the normal water line. Only two Grigorovich flying boats (M.15s tactical nos. 1 and 5) were known to have been painted in an overall pale gray color. To what extent the Russians used rubberized fabric on seaplanes is unknown, but it is safe to assume this fabric was used. The Curtiss company is reported to have used this material on flying boats built for Russia, and reports suggest the color was either pale gray or light brown.

National Markings

Aeronautic ensigns were usually attached to the support cables of gray-colored kite balloons in the early part of the war, and in some cases the ensign was painted directly on the side of the balloon itself. The aeronautic ensign displayed a white flag having the upper left corner finished in blue. The small blue field was in turn segmented by crisscrossing vertical, horizontal, and diagonal white bands. The diagonal white bands held thinner red bands. The flag also displayed a winged black naval anchor in the lower right corner.

The Naval Cross of St. Andrew was normally flown as an ensign from the stern of Russian warships. Although this emblem was applied to many naval aircraft, it was generally discontinued in 1916. The design displayed a light blue cross against a white field.

The Russian national flag of rectangular shape was split into three equal horizontal bands with white on top, blue in the center, and red on the bottom. This national marking appeared on various Russian aircraft, but notably the first two Sikorsky Il'ya Muromets bombers prepared for war (both were adorned with national flags on each side of the fuselage).

The Russian pennants of triangular shape with stripes of white on top, blue center, and red on the bottom appeared on the fuselages of various Russian aircraft throughout the war and were more common than the national flag. A second form of pennant, and perhaps the most attractive, differed by having a small segment of orange at the base of the white strip. Applied on the orange segment was an Imperial Russian double-headed eagle in black. The orange and black thus represent the colors of the Order of St. George. A third pennant has been suggested in documentation, wherein the Imperial Russian double-headed eagle was replaced with the solid black image of St. George on horseback slaying the dragon. Unfortunately, the authors have yet to see photographs or original illustrations of this design.

Russian roundels with a large white center and blue and red outer rings were carried on most Russian aircraft in proportions similar to the French roundel. Nevertheless, many variations in proportions were applied throughout the war. Perhaps the only Russian manufacturer to maintain some level of consistency was the Dux factory, which bordered the red ring on the roundel with two narrow rings of white. To further distinguish its Nieuports, in many cases Dux applied a remarkable number of Russian roundels—14 in all (roundels in six positions on upper and lower surfaces of the wings, roundels in six positions on the tailplane and elevators, and two roundels on the fuselage sides). Although the Anatra and Lebedev aircraft manufacturing companies generally applied standard roundels on their machines (white centers with blue, then red outer rings), the proportions likely changed from time to time. Unlike Russian-built aircraft, French-built machines maintained consistent roundel positions and proportions for aircraft supplied to Russia, but additional roundels applied at aircraft parks or field units rarely matched the originals in color, proportion, or size.

Most French machines built specifically for Russia arrived with rudders finished with stripes of colors that matched the national colors of white leading edge, blue center, and red trailing edge. Likewise, many machines built for French service and later sold to Russia had rudders finished in the standard French sequence of blue leading edge, white center, and red trailing edge.

Table of Fabrics Examined

Methuen notations are given for known fabric samples. Pantone® (a printing color standard) equivalents are given in brackets. Actual colors varied from aircraft to aircraft based on weathering, paint batches, etcetera.

Color Subject	Methuen	Pantone®
Roundel Red:		
Russian Applied	10C8	(187C)
French Applied	10C–D8	(1805C)
Roundel Blue:		
Russian Applied	22C–D8	(300C–301C)
French Applied	22–23D4, 23C–D8	(3015C)
St. Andrew Blue:	21B–C8	(285C)
St. George Orange:	6B–C8	(138C–1385C)
Clear-Doped Linen:		
Pale Cream:	2–3A3–4, 3B7,	(127C, 110C, 155C,
	4A3, 4C3	4525C)
Yellowish-gray:	4B2–3	(4545C)
Light Brown:	5C3	(467C)
Il'ya Muromets:	6–7D5–6	(4645C–465C)
Single Opaque Scheme:		
Solid Earth Tone:		
Khaki:	4D5	(5835C–5845C)
Olive:	2–3E6, 29F8	(582C–5743C)
Reddish-Brown:	8E–F4	(4705C–4695C)
Aluminum:		
Yellow:	5C–D8, 5E4	(130C–131C)
Pale Gray:		
Dux:	20C–D1	(428C–422C)
Curtiss:	20D1	(422C)

Camouflage Scheme Examples:
a) Green/Reddish Brown   26E2–3/8E–F4   (5763C–5773C/4705C–4695C)
b) Green/Brown   29E5/3D4–5   (5747C–5757C/5835C)
c) Green/Khaki   26E2*/4D5*   (5703C/5835C–5845C)
d) Green/Brown   26E2*/8F8*   (5763C/4975C)
e) Green/Brown   26E3-2*/3D4–5*(5763C–5773C/5835C)

* Had traces of aluminum powder in suspension to protect fabric from the sun's ultra-violet rays. However, it did not give a bright, silvery, metallic-type finish.

Serial Number System for Aircraft Used in the Imperial Russian Air Service

Aircraft manufactured in Russia, unlike those of other belligerent countries, were rarely identified by a standard serial number system. Generally, if any number system was displayed it reflected those applied by a foreign manufacturer before delivery to Russia, or those applied by the Russian army or navy unit to which the machine had been assigned. A large variety of number sequences were used by various formations and in some cases, such as the EVK, a number series was used which was exclusive to that unit.

From 1915, aircraft manufactured by Lebedev, Dux, and Anatra started to arrive with their factory or airframe number painted in small characters on various locations, such as the nose, wings, or tail unit.

Likewise, from mid-1915, Il'ya Muromets (IMs) started to arrive from the R-BVZ factory with the factory airframe number painted in small characters on the metal nose, just under the wing leading edge. In addition, the IMs had their own production series number. This consisted of an Cyrillic letter (initial) indicating the type, for example B (Veh) followed by a number, such as 24, which indicated that the IM was of the type Veh and was the 24th IM built. This serial was in dark paint (most likely black) and appeared on the nose as a prefix to the factory number.

Naval aircraft used by both the Baltic Fleet and Black Sea Fleet were assigned a tactical number. The tactical number is a term denoting 'Fleet Number.' Up to October 1916 the numbers were re-allocated to new machines from existing machines that were scrapped or lost. However, this re-allocation of used numbers seems to have stopped with the delivery of Grigorovich M.11s in October 1916.

For example, the original tactical numbers 2–26 were allocated to the Curtiss floatplanes and flying boats in the Black Sea Fleet purchased before 1916. However, the same numbers were then re-allocated to new M.11s received in October, 1916. In addition to the tactical numbers, many aircraft used in the Baltic Fleet also had a prefix of Cyrillic letters to denoted the aircraft type. This unique combination of letters and number was used as a telegraphic code.

Aircraft Type	English Prefix	Cyrillic Prefix
Anri (Henri) Farman	AF	(А∞)
Maurice Farman	MF	(М∞)
Sikorsky S-10	S	(С)
FBA Flying Boat	FBA	(∞bA)
Schetinin M.2*	Sch-2	(Щ-2)
Schetinin M.9*	SchS	(ЩС)
Schetinin M.15*	SchI	(ЩИ)
Nieuport (Landplane)	NR	(НР)

* Grigorovich Flying Boat

Morane Saulnier type I of the 4th Corps Detachment, circa winter 1915. The large tricolor pennant appeared on each side of the fuselage.

COLORS AND MARKINGS 379

Voisin LA (serial B.241), flown by Ensign A. Pantrat'yev, whose name appeared in Cyrillic letters on the side of the nacelle. This aircraft was shot down by *Ltn.* Thiele of *Fl. Abt.* 35 on May 21, 1916.

Left: Nieuport 12 displaying French roundels on each wing panel and red stars on the fuselage and wheel covers. This aircraft crashed on its own field, circa 1916.

Nieuport 11, pilot and unit unknown. This machine is decorated with a black cat centered in a white circle.

Left: Nieuport 17, pilot and unit unknown. The aircraft's rudder was decorated with a white witch's head on black background.

Below: Nieuport 17 lying on its back after a bad landing, unit and pilot unknown. The fuselage is decorated with a black bat, white skull, and crossed wooden propeller and sword.

Bottom: Nieuport 17 of the 19th Corps Detachment. Cyrillic letters denote 'BOB.' The pennant of orange and black denotes the orange and black colors for the Order of Saint George. The white skull on black rudder was a unit marking.

COLORS AND MARKINGS 381

Above and left: Nieuport 21 with Russian pilot Kibanov. Each side of the fuselage displayed a different image of a horse's head. The top deck was decorated with crossed riding crops and a horse shoe for good luck. Kibanov was shot down near Minsk on October 11, 1917.

Left and below: Nieuport 21 of the 7th Fighter Detachment flown by Grochowalski. The rudder had a black shield which displayed the Order of Saint George, Fourth Class. Grochowalski survived the war with one victory and later became a key figure in the establishment of the Polish Air Force during 1919–20.

Below: Nieuport 21 captured by Bolsheviks on the railway station at Kazandshik, circa 1917–18. The fuselage displays the Imperial Russian double-headed eagle. the rudder a serial number "1."

Russian Ensign Alexander Riaboff standing beside his Nieuport 17. His personal marking was the detailed image of Il'ya Muromets flying on an eagle's back which appeared on the rudder.

Dux-built Nieuport 17 with roundels in 14 positions. The unit and date are unknown; however, the red star that appears on the rudder roundel indicates the civil war period. The unusual serpent markings run the length of the fuselage.

Nieuport 10 lying on its back after a bad landing. The fuselage sides display in Cyrillic letters the name of the pilot—Anton I. Mrochkovsky.

384 THE IMPERIAL RUSSIAN AIR SERVICE

Paragraph numbers are keyed to the color illustrations. Roundel types mentioned in the descriptions are shown at the end of the color section on page 440.

1. *Cossacks and Scouts,* an original painting by aviation artist James Dietz, depicts a mounted column of Caucasian-Terek Cossacks entering the airfield of the 19th Corps Detachment, circa winter 1917. Air units often provided information to Cossack units to better coordinate reconnaissance of forward areas.

2. The Deperdussin TT and similar Deperdussin aircraft were French designs imported before the war. They served from the beginning months of hostilities into early 1915. By that time they became outdated for frontline service and were regulated to training duties. This example was in type A, plain finish. It had natural metal cowl panels and landing gear struts. All fabric surfaces were clear-doped linen. The forward cockpit was fitted with a gun ring supporting a Madsen machine gun. Roundels appeared on the upper and lower surface of the wing and on each side of the rudder (all type B).

3. The Voisin L series aircraft were the workhorses of the IRAS. They served in many of the corps detachments for reconnaissance and light bombing throughout the war. This type LA, a French-built machine, was finished in a single opaque finish—aluminum dope overall. The struts and rear wheel covers were natural metal. The gun mount was fitted with a Colt machine gun. Roundels appeared on the wings and elevator in eight positions (type D), and on each side of the nacelle (type B). Although not present on this machine, it was common for roundels to also appear on the vertical stabilizer.

4. Henri Farman type HF.20. Most of the Farman aircraft types, whether received from France or license-built in Russia, were in type A, plain finish. In many instances the nacelle was finished in a solid opaque color, usually gray. This Farman HF.20 represents a typical machine with pale gray nacelle and clear-doped linen wings and tail unit. All struts were natural wood. Roundels appeared on wings in four positions and on the rudder (all type B).

5. Morane Saulnier type G (serial number 281) flown by Petr Nesterov during his famous ramming attack. It was finished overall in clear-doped linen with cowling, forward fuselage plywood panels, and all struts finished in black. Roundels appeared on wing upper and lower surface (type D). The Cyrillic letters *M* (em) and *Г* (geh) on the rudder denote an MS type G aircraft. Source: photograph page 204.

6. Morane Saulnier type G (serial number 316) flown by Alexander Kozakov with his unique anchor system. It was finished overall in clear-doped linen with cowling, forward fuselage plywood panels, and all struts finished in black. Roundels appeared on upper and lower wing surfaces and on each side of fuselage (all type D). The Cyrillic letters *M* (em) and *Г* (geh) on the rudder denote an MS type G aircraft.

7. Morane Saulnier type H flown by Nikolai Kokorin to obtain his second victory. It was finished overall in clear-doped linen with cowling, forward fuselage plywood panels, and all struts finished in black. Roundels appeared on the upper and lower wing surfaces and on the outer surfaces of the wheel covers (all type D). The fuselage and all flying surfaces were bordered in black. The Colt-Browning machine gun was equipped with a belt container and deflector box and mounted to the center cabane strut to allow firing above the propeller arc. The Cyrillic letters *M* (em) and *Ж* (zheh) on the rudder denote an MS type H aircraft. Source: photograph page 56.

8. Morane Saulnier type H flown by Alexander Sveshnikov while with the 7th Corps Detachment. It was finished overall in clear-doped linen with cowling, forward fuselage plywood panels, and all struts finished in black. Roundels appeared on the upper and lower wing surfaces (type D) and on each side of the fuselage (type F). The Madsen machine gun was mounted to the center cabane strut. The Cyrillic letters *M* (em) and *Ж* (zheh) on the rudder denote an MS type H aircraft. Source: photograph page 228.

9. Morane Saulnier type L flown by Vyatcheslav Tkachev while with the 11th Army Detachment. It was finished overall in clear-doped linen with cowling, forward fuselage plywood decking, wheel covers, and all struts finished in black. Roundels appeared on the upper and lower wing surfaces (type D). The number of bombs carried and the attachment system varied considerably; this MS L utilized simple hooks to hold bombs to the edge of the front cockpit. The bombs were manually released. Source: photograph page 238.

10. Morane Saulnier type L flown by Peter Tomson while with the 1st Corps Detachment, winter 1916. It was finished overall in clear-doped linen with cowling, forward fuselage plywood decking, and all struts finished in black. Roundels appeared on the upper and lower surface of the wing (type D). The factory serial number of this machine was 272. The detachment's identification number 3 appeared on both sides of the fuselage and rudder.

11. Morane Saulnier type L flown by Vasili Yanchenko while with the 12th Corps Detachment, fall 1915. It was finished overall in clear-doped linen with cowling, forward fuselage plywood decking, and all struts finished in black. Roundels appeared on the upper and lower surface of the wing (type G), on each side of the fuselage (type D), and on the outer wheel covers (type B).

12. Morane Saulnier type I fitted with skis and attached to the 4th Corps Detachment, winter 1915–16. This MS I had its wings and tail surfaces finished in clear-doped linen; metal panels and cowling were painted black. Roundels were applied on upper and lower wing surfaces and on the rudder (all type F). The fabric section of the fuselage was doped white and a large Russian pennant was painted on both sides. The top decking in front of the cockpit was built up to accommodate a Maxim machine gun and a windscreen through which the gun passed. Source: photographs on pages 13 and 378.

13. Morane Saulnier type I flown by Ivan Smirnov to obtain two victories while with the 19th Corps Detachment. It was finished overall in clear-doped linen with metal panels and cowling painted a dark green. Roundels were applied on upper and lower wing surfaces (type D). The rudder and vertical fin were black and the white skull and cross-bones were applied to both sides. This particular machine was equipped with a Maxim machine gun. Although the spinner was reportedly removed, the source photographs on pages 117 and 118 do not support this.

14. Morane Saulnier type I (serial number 741) flown by Konstantin Vakulovsky to obtain his third victory while with the 1st Fighter Detachment. It was finished overall in clear-doped linen with metal panels, cowling, and wheel covers painted red. Roundels were applied on upper and lower wing surfaces (type D). The vertical fin was finished in white with a dark border that matches the stitch line on the fuselage. Source: photograph page 132.

15. Morane Saulnier type N assigned to the Gatchina Aviation School, circa 1917. It was finished overall in clear-doped linen with metal panels, cowling, wheel covers, and struts painted red. Roundels applied on upper and lower wing surfaces (type D). The propeller was fitted with deflector plates.

16. Morane Saulnier type P of the 19th Corps Detachment, circa 1917. It was finished overall in clear-doped linen with metal panels, cowling, wheel covers, and struts painted pale gray. Roundels were applied on upper and lower wing surfaces (type D). The rudder and vertical fin were black and a white skull was applied to both sides. The observer's gun ring was fitted with a Madsen machine gun. This aircraft appears in the background of source photograph on page 118.

17. Morane Saulnier type P (serial number 526) of an unknown unit, circa 1917. It was finished overall in clear-doped linen with metal panels, cowling, wheel covers, and struts painted red. Roundels were applied on upper and lower wing surfaces (type D), and on both sides of fuselage (type B). The observer's gun ring was fitted with a Lewis machine gun. Source: photograph page 12.

18. The Morane Saulnier logo appeared in either a flat black or plain metal finish and was applied on each side of the cowling or center front of cowling.

19. The Morane Saulnier top views indicate typical positions of roundels.

20. Nieuport type 4G as flown by Petr Nesterov on September 5, 1913, when he became the first aviator to successfully loop an aircraft in the vertical plane. It has natural metal cowl panels and landing gear struts. All fabric surfaces were clear-doped linen. Both sides of the rudder displayed the aircraft's only markings—black Roman numerals for the 11th Corps Detachment and the unit aircraft number 1. Source: photograph page 203.

21. Nieuport type 4G as flown by Vyatcheslav Tkachev, circa fall 1914. It has natural metal cowl panels and landing gear struts. All fabric surfaces were clear-doped linen. A black Roman numeral for the 20th Corps detachment appeared on both sides of the fuselage. The unit's aircraft number 2 appeared in black on each side of the rudder. Source: photograph page 235.

22. Nieuport type 10 (serial number 222) as flown by Alexander Kozakov to obtain two victories while with the 19th Corps Detachment. All fabric surfaces were clear-doped linen. Cowl panels, side fuselage plates, cabane struts, and landing gear struts were natural aluminum. An upper decking plate of natural aluminum was attached over the forward cockpit to support the Maxim machine gun at a 24° angle. The front of the top wing has a small V-shaped cutout to provide the needed clearance for the gun muzzle. Roundels were applied to the wings in six positions (type D). The imperial double-headed eagle crest appeared on the front of the cowling. Source: photographs pages 59, 60, and 61.

23. Nieuport type 10 as flown by Anton E. Mrochkovsky. All fabric surfaces were clear-doped linen. Cowl panels, side fuselage plates, cabane struts, and landing gear struts were natural aluminum. Roundels were applied to the wings in six positions (type D) and to each side of the fuselage (type B). During the winter of 1916 skis were installed replacing the wheels. The inscription on the fuselage reads, "War Pilot Lieutenant Mrochkovsky." Source: photograph page 383.

Archival sources have revealed that two individuals named Anton E. Mrochkovsky served with the IRAS during World War I. Which pilot used this aircraft is unknown.

The first Anton E. Mrochkovsky was Russian, born August 18, 1882. He entered the military in 1902 and transferred to the air service in 1912. He was assigned to the 11th Corps Detachment before the war and was the unit's commander in 1915. He obtained the rank of *Kapitan* (Captain) and was the Deputy-Commander of the 3rd Corps Detachment in 1917. He received the following awards: Golden Sword of Saint George; Order of Saint Vladimir, Fourth Class, with Swords and Bow; Order of Saint Anne, Third Class, with Swords and Bow; Order of Saint Anne, Fourth Class, with inscription "For Bravery"; Order of Saint Stanislas, Second Class, with Swords and Bow; and Order of Saint Stanislas, Third Class.

The second Anton E. Mrochkovsky was Polish, born May 29, 1896. He entered military service in 1914 and became a military pilot in the summer of 1915. He served with the 24th Corps Detachment and the 7th Army Detachment. He obtained one victory in 1915. He played an important role in forming of the Polish Air Force during 1919–20, and later commanded the 19th Polish Eskadra (Squadron). He earned at least the Order of Saint Anne, Fourth Class.

24. Nieuport type 10 as flown by pilots of the 19th Corps Detachment. All fabric surfaces were clear-doped linen. Cowl panels, side fuselage plates, cabane struts, and landing gear struts were natural aluminum. Roundels were applied to the wings in six positions (type D) and on each side of the fuselage (type B). White skull and cross-

bones have been applied to both sides of the black rudder. This Nieuport is a typical example of the many type 10s used by pilots Argeyev, Smirnov, Leman, and Lipsky. Source: photographs page 63.

A second Nieuport type 10 used by Alexander Kozakov utilized the alternate skull and cross-bones in solid black applied to both sides of a solid white rudder. All fabric surfaces were clear-doped linen, and cowl panels, side fuselage plates, cabane struts, and landing gear struts were plain aluminum. Roundels were applied to wings in six positions (type D). Source: photograph page 65.

Several Nieuport type 10s used by the 19th Corps Detachment had fuselage and upper wing surfaces finished in a single opaque finish—solid earth tone overall—with the under-surface of wings and tailplane in plain linen. They had natural aluminum cowl panels, side fuselage plates, cabane struts, and landing gear struts. Roundels appeared on under-surfaces of upper and lower wings only (type B). The rudders on those aircraft were black and the unit's distinctive white skull and cross-bones (as depicted on this profile) were applied to both sides. Source: photograph page 117.

A third Nieuport type 10 used by Alexander Kozakov was also finished in the single opaque scheme and utilized a skull and cross-bones that match the shape as depicted on this profile; however, his aircraft's rudder was solid white and the skull and cross-bones design was solid black. Source: photograph page 117.

25. Dux-built Nieuport type 9 used by the Baltic Sea Fleet, circa 1917. All fabric surfaces were finished in a single opaque finish—pale gray overall. Cowl panels, side fuselage plates, cabane struts, and landing gear struts were natural aluminum. Roundels appeared in 14 positions (type E). A small Cross of St. Andrew appears directly below the cockpit. The tactical fleet number *36* appears in black on both sides of the fuselage. Source: photograph page 31.

26. Nieuport type 9 (serial number 262) flown by Jaan Mahlapuu while with 12th Fighter Detachment, circa summer 1916. All fabric surfaces were clear-doped linen. Cowl panels, side fuselage plates, cabane struts, and landing gear struts were natural aluminum. Roundels were applied to wings in six positions (type D). The Maxim machine gun was mounted to the top wing and positioned to fire above the propeller arc. Source: photograph page 198.

27. Nieuport type 12 (serial number 1043) flown by Shiukov while with the 3rd Corps Detachment. This machine had fuselage and upper wing surfaces finished in a two-tone camouflage scheme—solid bands of drab greens and browns overall. Under surface of wings and tailplane were plain linen. The edges of wings and tailplane had a narrow outline border of light blue. Cowl panels, side fuselage plates, cabane struts, and landing gear struts were natural aluminum. The top wing center section was covered in clear cellulose. Roundels appeared on under-surfaces of upper and lower wings only (type B). This machine was equipped with a Lewis machine gun.

Source: photograph on page 15.

28. Nieuport type 11 flown by Jacques Texier while with Franco-Romanian *Escadrila* N.3. All fabric surfaces were clear-doped linen. Edges of all flying surfaces and fuselage had a narrow outline border of light blue. Cowl panels, side fuselage plates, cabane struts, and landing gear struts were natural aluminum. French roundels were applied to the wings in six positions. Texier's personal marking was a brown cat walking in grass, surrounded by a light blue rectangular outline. This unique marking appeared on the port (left) side of the fuselage; however, it is unknown if it was repeated on the starboard side. Texier was awarded the Russian Soldier's Cross of Saint George, Fourth Class, and the Romanian *Virtutea Militara in aur* (Military Virtue in gold). He died on August 16, 1917, from wounds received in combat.

29. Nieuport type 11 flown by Henri Manchoulas while with Franco-Romanian *Escadrila* N.3. All fabric surfaces were clear-doped linen. Cowl panels, side fuselage plates, cabane struts, and landing gear struts were natural aluminum. French roundels were applied to the wings in six positions. Manchoulas' Nieuport sported a green four-leafed clover on both sides of the fuselage for a personal marking. He was credited with one victory on June 25, 1917, and was awarded the Russian Solder's Cross of Saint George, Fourth and Third Classes, as well as the Saint George Medal, Fourth Class.

30. Nieuport type 11 (serial number 1232) flown Juri Gilsher while with the 7th Fighter Detachment, circa June 1917. This machine had fuselage and upper wing surfaces finished in a two-tone camouflage scheme—solid bands of drab greens and browns overall. Under surfaces of wings and tailplane were in plain linen. The edges of wings and tailplane had a narrow outline border of light blue. Cowl panels, side fuselage plates, cabane struts, and landing gear struts were natural aluminum. Roundels appeared on under-surfaces of upper and lower wings only (type D). Source: photograph page 53.

Russian pilots Kruten, Mahlapuu, and Pulpe each flew French-built Nieuport type 11s finished in this exact scheme while in Russia. The serial number for Kruten's machine was 1137 and for Mahlapuu's 1161. Source: photographs pages 74 and 176.

31. Nieuport type 11—unknown unit or pilot. All fabric surfaces were clear-doped linen. Cowl panels, side fuselage plates, cabane struts, and landing gear struts were natural aluminum. Roundels were applied to the wings in six positions (type B). The black cat inside a black circle appeared on both sides of the fuselage and closely resembled unit markings applied to aircraft of French *Escadrille* N.87. Presumably its design was influenced by a French pilot serving in Russia or a Russian aviator who had returned from France. Source: photograph page 379.

32. Nieuport type 11 flown Maurice Gond while with Franco-Romanian *Escadrila* N.3. This machine had fuselage and upper wing surfaces finished in a two tone camouflage scheme—solid bands of drab greens and browns overall. Under surfaces of wings and tailplane in

plain linen. Edges of wings and tailplane had a narrow outline border of light blue. Cowl panels, side fuselage plates, cabane struts, and landing gear struts were natural aluminum. French roundels appeared on under-surfaces of upper and lower wings only. Gond's personal emblem was an archer, was most likely in a light blue color that closely match the wing border color. Source: photograph page 161.

33. Nieuport type 16 as used by the 11th Corps Detachment, summer 1916. This machine had fuselage and upper wing surfaces finished in a single opaque finish—earth tone overall. Under surface of wings and tailplane in plain linen. Cowl panels, cabane struts, and landing gear struts were natural aluminum. Roundels appeared on the wings in six positions (type B). The unit's distinctive markings—black rudder with a white six pointed star—was applied to both sides.

Several Nieuport type 16s finished in this scheme were used by the 19th Corps detachment, the white rudder being decorated with black skull and cross bones.

34. Dux-built Nieuport type 16 used by Second Combat Air Group, circa summer 1916. All fabric surfaces were finished in a single opaque finish—pale gray overall. Cowl panels, cabane struts, and landing gear struts were natural aluminum. Roundels appeared in 14 positions (type E). A thin black band wrapped around the fuselage sides and top decking.

35. Nieuport type 17 (serial number 2232) flown by Yevgraph Kruten to obtain three victories. Finished in a single opaque finish—aluminum doped fabric and plain aluminum panels overall. Roundels appeared on the wings in six positions (type D). Kruten's personal marking—the black image of a medieval knight—appeared on both sides of the fuselage. It most likely represented the legendary Russian warrior Il'ya Muromets. Source: photograph page 78.

36. Nieuport type 17 flown by Victor Federov while with the 11th Corps Detachment, circa spring 1917. Finished in a single opaque finish—aluminum doped fabric and plain aluminum panels overall. Roundels appeared on the wings in six positions (type D). The black rudder was decorated on both sides with a white six-pointed star. Source: photograph page 156.

37. Nieuport type 17, unknown unit and pilot, circa spring 1917. Finished in a single opaque finish—aluminum doped fabric and plain aluminum panels overall. Roundels appeared on the wings in six positions (type D). The black rudder was decorated on both sides with a witch head. The lower cowling of this machine was cut down. The standard Vickers armament was supplemented with a Lewis machine gun. Source: photograph page 380.

38. Nieuport type 17 as flown by pilots of the 19th Corps Detachment. Finished in a single opaque finish—aluminum doped fabric and plain aluminum panels overall. The lower cowling of this machine was cut down. Both sides of the fuselage bear the Cyrillic letters 'Bob.' in black and white and a pennant in orange and black stripes

representing the colors of the Order of Saint George. The outer wheel covers were decorated in a white and black yin-yang design. Roundels appeared on the wings in six positions (type D). The white rudder was decorated on both sides with a black skull and cross bones. *Bob* translates to *Bean;* however, the significance of the word is unknown. Source: photograph page 380.

39. Dux-built Nieuport type 17 flown by Vasili Yanchenko while with the 7th Fighter Detachment. All fabric surfaces were finished in a single opaque finish—pale gray overall. Cowl panels, cabane struts, and landing gear struts were natural aluminum. Roundels appeared in 12 positions (type E). Yanchenko's personal marking—a solid black shield—appeared on both sides of the rudder. The standard Vickers armament was supplemented with a Lewis machine gun. Source: photograph page 137.

40. Dux-built Nieuport type 17 flown by Boris Sergievsky while with the 2nd Fighter Detachment. All fabric surfaces were finished in a single opaque finish—pale gray overall. Cowl panels, cabane struts, and landing gear struts were natural aluminum. Roundels appeared in 14 positions (type E). Supplementary flying wires were added between wing-strut and landing gear. Source: photograph page 224.

41. Nieuport type 17 flown by Alexander Kozakov while with the 19th Corps Detachment. Finished in a single opaque finish—aluminum doped fabric and plain aluminum panels overall. Roundels appeared on the wings in six positions (type D). The white rudder was decorated on both sides with a black skull and cross bones.

Kozakov's second Nieuport 17 was a Dux-built machine. That machine was finished in a single opaque finish—pale gray overall. Cowl panels, cabane struts, and landing gear struts were natural aluminum. Roundels appeared in 14 positions (type E). Black skull and cross bones on white rudder. Source: photograph for both aircraft page 65.

42. Nieuport type 17 unit and pilot unknown. All fabric surfaces were finished in a single opaque finish—pale gray overall. Cowl panels, cabane struts, and landing gear struts were natural aluminum. Roundels appeared on the wings in six positions (type D) and on the rudder (type B). This aircraft sported a unusual marking, a black bat with white skull holding criss-crossing propeller and sword. Source: photograph page 380.

43. Nieuport type 17 as flown by Donat Makeenok while with the 7th Fighter Detachment. Finished in a single opaque finish—aluminum doped fabric and plain aluminum panels overall. Roundels appeared on the wings in six positions (type D). A black shield displaying an image of a white snowy owl appeared on each side of the rudder. At least the port (left) side of the fuselage was decorated with an image of a woman holding a sword and standing behind an unfurled flag. The flag's red color illustrated in the close-up image is speculative. Source: photograph page 89.

388 THE IMPERIAL RUSSIAN AIR SERVICE

44. Dux-built Nieuport type 21 used by the Russian naval air station at Tserel on Oesel island in the Baltic. All fabric surfaces were finished in a single opaque finish—pale gray overall. Cowl panels, cabane struts, and landing gear struts were natural aluminum. Roundels appeared in 14 positions (type E). A small Cross of St. Andrew and a red tactical number 3 appeared on the port (left) side of the fuselage; however, it is unknown if either image was repeated on the starboard side. This aircraft was part of a sub-flight of four machines and was assigned to Ensign Leonidovich Yakovlev. However, it is believed others pilots in the unit flew this machine, including Alexander Seversky. Source: photograph page 107.

45. Nieuport type 21 (serial number 1514) flown by Ivan Smirnov to obtain two victories. This machine had fuselage and upper wing surfaces finished in a two tone camouflage scheme—solid bands of drab greens and browns overall. Under surfaces of wings and tailplane were in plain linen, and the edges of wings and tailplane had a narrow outline border of light blue. Cowl panels, cabane struts, and landing gear struts were natural aluminum. This machine was equipped with a Madsen machine gun having an ammo belt which extended from the fuselage. Roundels appeared on the under surfaces of upper wing and lower wing only (type D). Source: photograph page 117.

46. Nieuport type 21 (serial number 4572) flown by Yevgraph Kruten. It was finished in a single opaque finish—aluminum doped fabric and plain aluminum panels overall. Roundels appeared on the wings in six positions (type D). Kruten's personal marking was an image of a medieval knight which appeared on both sides of the fuselage. The Colt-Browning machine gun was equipped with a belt container and deflector box. Source: photograph page 75.

Russian pilots Loiko, Suk, Strizhevsky, and Pishvanov all flew French-built Nieuport 21s which sported a single opaque finish—aluminum doped fabric and plain aluminum panels overall. These aircraft each had roundels that appeared on the wings in six positions (type D). All were equipped with Lewis machine guns. Serial numbers were on rudders as follows: Loiko (1127, 1902); Suk (1719); Strizhevsky (1719); and Pishvanov (4191). Information has suggested no personal marking were applied to these machines.

47. Nieuport type 21 (serial number 1825) flown by Jaan Mahlapuu while with the 12th Fighter Detachment. It was finished in a single opaque finish—aluminum doped fabric and plain metal panels overall. Roundels appeared on the wings in six positions (type D). A large Russian pennant appeared on each side of the fuselage.

48. Nieuport type 23 flown by Tadeusz Grochowalski while with the 7th Fighter Detachment, spring 1917. It was finished in a single opaque finish—aluminum doped fabric and plain metal panels overall. Roundels appeared on the wings in six positions (type D). Both sides of the rudder were decorated with a black shield outlined in light gray and having the image of the Order of Saint

George. Source: photographs page 382.

Grochowalski was Polish, born September 20, 1888. He served as an observer with the 8th Army Detachment in the summer of 1916, and became a military pilot soon after. He obtained one victory on October 19, 1917, and was presented the following awards: Order of Saint Vladimir, Fourth Class, with Sword and Bow; Order of Saint Anne, Third Class, with Sword and Bow; Order of Saint Anne, Fourth Class, with inscription "For Bravery"; Order of Saint Stanislas, Third Class, With Sword and Bow; and Order of Saint Stanislas, Second Class, with Sword and Bow. Grochowalski played an important role in the Polish Air Force during 1919–20, serving as commander of the 1st Polish *Eskadra* (Squadron).

49. Nieuport type 23 flown by Russian pilot Kibanov who was shot down and killed near Minsk on December 1917 . It was finished in a single opaque finish—aluminum doped fabric and plain metal panels overall. French roundels appeared on wings—six positions. The port (left) side of fuselage was decorated with the image of a horse's head and riding crop. The slightly different image of the horse's head and riding crop shown in close-up decorated the starboard side of the fuselage. The top decking was decorated with a narrow red band, black horse shoe, and criss-crossing riding crops. Supplementary flying wires were added between wing-struts and landing gear. Source: photographs page 381.

50. Spad G.1 (serial number 97). Unknown unit and pilot. It was finished in a single opaque finish—yellowish-gray doped fabric with all metal and plywood panels painted to closely match the fabric color. Roundels appeared on the wings in four positions and the fuselage in two positions (all type D). The large curved machine gun mounting system normally seen on Spad A.2s was removed, and three Colt machine guns with ammunition belts have been placed inside the nacelle. The plywood sides of the nacelle have been replaced with curved metal plates having cutouts to allow a single Colt machine gun to extend out in a forward firing position on each side. The third Colt extended through an opening more centrally located on the nacelle. The Spad manufacturer's logo appears on the front of the nacelle. Source: photographs page 20.

51. Spad A.2 flown by Russian pilots Huber and Bashinsky to obtain the only known victory in a Spad A.2. It was finished in a single opaque finish—yellowish-gray doped fabric with all metal and plywood panels painted to closely match the fabric color. Outer wheel covers were finished in red. Roundels appeared in 10 positions (type D). This machine was equipped with a Madsen machine gun. The 19th Corps Detachment unit insignia of white skull and cross bones was applied to both sides of the black rudder. Source: photograph page 63. Records indicate this particular Spad A.2 went through several modifications. The photograph on page 63 shows a Maxim machine gun mounted to the nacelle and the large curved support system was removed. It is not known if this Maxim gun mount system was used for the victory on September 6, 1916.

Russian pilots Argeyev, Leman, Lipsky, and Smirnov were all recorded as flying Spad A.2s with this unit. A second Spad A.2 with the 19th Corps had similar markings. Source: photograph page 118.

52. Spad A.2 (serial number 79). Unknown unit and pilot. It was finished in a single opaque finish—yellowish-gray doped fabric with all metal and plywood panels painted to closely match the fabric color. This machine was equipped with skis for use in snow. Roundels appeared on the wings in four positions and on the fuselage in two positions (all type D). This machine was equipped with a Lewis machine gun.

53. Spad 7 flown by Ivan Smirnov to obtain six victories while with the 19th Corps Detachment. It was finished in a single opaque finish—yellowish-gray doped fabric with all metal panels painted to closely match the fabric color. Roundels appeared on the wings in four positions (type F). The black rudder was decorated on both sides with white skull and cross bones. Source: photograph page 119.

54. Spad 7 flow by Louis Coudouret to obtain three victories while with *Escadrille* N.581. It was finished in a single opaque finish—yellowish-gray doped fabric with all metal panels painted to closely match the fabric color. French roundels appeared on the wings in four positions. The outer wheel covers were decorated with a red and white yin-yang pattern. The port (left) side of the fuselage displayed a small name; however, it is not legible in reference photographs. Source: photographs pages 147 and 148.

55. Spad 7 flown by George Lachmann to obtain five victories while with *Escadrille* N.581. It was finished in a single opaque finish—yellowish-gray doped fabric with all metal panels painted to closely match the fabric color. French roundels appeared on the wings in four positions. A red question mark appeared on both sides of the fuselage and a narrow red band was applied the cowling. This machine's armament was supplemented with a Lewis machine gun and Le Prieur rockets. Lachmann used Le Prieur rockets to obtain his fourth victory on September 1, 1917. Source: photographs pages 169, 171, 172.

56. Spad 7 flown by Alexander Kozakov and Cossack pilot Shangin while with the 19th Corps Detachment. It was finished in a single opaque finish—yellowish-gray doped fabric with all metal panels painted to closely match the fabric color. Roundels appeared on the wings in four positions (type F). Alternating bands of red-blue-red appeared on the cowling. Both sides of the white rudder were decorated with a black skull and cross bones. Source: photograph page 68.

57. Spad 7 (serial number 1471). Unknown unit and pilot. It was finished in a single opaque finish—yellowish-gray doped fabric with all metal panels painted to closely match the fabric color. Roundels appeared on the wings in four positions and on the rudder in two positions (all type F). A thin narrow band of red wrapped around the fuselage and both sides of the vertical fin was decorated with white, blue, and red bands. Source: photograph page 21.

Russian pilots Strizhevsky, and Suk each flew French-built Spad 7s which sported a single opaque finish—yellowish-gray doped fabric with all metal panels painted to closely match the fabric color. These aircraft each had roundels that appeared on the wings in four positions (type D or type F). The rudder had horizontal stripes of white, blue and red (red to rear). The serial numbers on rudders were: Strizhevsky (1446); and Suk (1446, 1440). Information has suggested no personal marking were applied to these machines.

58. Lebed 7 from the 21st Corps Detachment, circa winter 1915. It has natural metal cowl panels and clear-varnished wood struts and undercarriage. All fabric surfaces were clear-doped linen. Roundels were applied in 10 positions (all type F). The manufacturer's name and type—Lebedev VII, appears in Cyrillic letter on each side of the fuselage as well as the Roman numerals for the 21st Corps. The detachment's aircraft identification number "1" appeared on both sides of the vertical fin. Source: photograph page 361.

59. Lebed 8. Lebedev began applying opaque paint as part of an early study of camouflage schemes in1915. The Lebed 8 was perhaps the first Lebed type finished in a single opaque finish—solid pale gray overall—but it retained clear-varnished wood struts and undercarriage. The Lebed 8 had a longer wingspan than the type 7 and incorporated ailerons in the upper wing. Roundels were applied in 10 positions (all type F). Source: photograph page 362.

60. All Lebed 11s were finished in a scheme of natural metal panels and struts, clear-doped linen, and varnished wooden fuselage panels. On occasion struts were wooden. Only a few type 11s were built and their dimensions vary, but these were the forerunners of the type 12. On this machine roundels were applied to wings and rudder in six positions (type F). Although not shown, the observer's gun ring could accommodate a single machine gun. Source: photograph page 364.

61. Almost all Lebed 12s were finished in a scheme of natural metal panels and struts, clear-doped linen, and varnished wooden fuselage panels. On occasion struts were wooden. Several aircraft were painted in a single solid opaque scheme. In this case, the aircraft's fuselage was varnished plywood, fabric surfaces were clear-doped linen, and all metal panels and struts were left natural colors. Roundels have been applied in six positions (type F). A triangular Russian pennant appeared each side of the fuselage. The Kolpakov gun mount has a Colt machine gun attached. Source: photograph page 367.

62. Most of the Anatra D (Anade) aircraft were finished in a scheme of clear-doped linen and varnished wooden fuselage panels and wing struts. The metal panels, cabane struts and landing gear were either natural or painted pale gray. This machine was decorated with roundels in 12 positions (type D). Although not shown, an observer's gun ring was often attached to the rear cockpit and could accommodate a single machine gun. Source: photograph page 338.

63. Most of the Anatra DS (Anasal) aircraft were finished in a scheme of clear-doped linen and varnished wooden fuselage panels and struts. The metal panels and landing gear were either natural or painted pale gray. This machine was in service in the Czechoslovakian air force during 1918. The Czechoslovakian roundels, virtually identical to Russian, appeared in eight positions (type B). The fuselage was marked with an Austro-Hungarian serial number. Source: photograph page 342.

64. Grigorovich M.5s (tactical numbers 36 and 38) flown by Victor Utgoff while attached to the Hydro-Cruiser *Imperator Nikolai I*. Most M.5s were finished in a scheme of clear-doped linen and varnished wooden boat hull and struts. Usually the bottom surface of the boat hull and all metal fittings were painted with marine paint in pale gray, white, or light blue. Both of these aircraft sport roundels in four positions (type B) and undersides of pale gray. Each carried white tactical numbers having a gray outline on the boat hull. Machine 36 was equipped with a Maxim machine gun. Source: photographs pages 252 and 274.

65. Grigorovich M.9 (tactical number 161), Baltic Sea Fleet, circa 1916. Most M.9s were finished in a scheme of clear-doped linen and varnished wooden boat hull and struts. Usually the bottom surface of the boat hull and sides up to the water line were painted with a marine paint. In many cases metal parts were painted pale gray. This aircraft had roundels in four positions (type D). The tactical number appeared in black on each side. Source: photograph page 105.

Pilots Safonov, Seversky, and Utgoff all flew M.9s which sported the scheme described above. Serial numbers on hull sides were: Safonov (18, 19); Seversky (50); Utgoff (114).

66. Grigorovich M.15 (tactical number 1), flown by Mikhail Safonov while with the Baltic Sea Fleet, circa 1917. Most M.15s were finished in a scheme of clear-doped linen and varnished wooden fuselage and struts. Usually the bottom surface of the boat hull and sides up to the water line were painted with a marine paint. In many cases metal parts were painted pale gray. This machine was one of only two M.15s painted pale gray overall (tactical numbers 1 and 5). Roundels appeared in four positions (type B). Tactical number *1* appeared on each side of the hull. Source: photographs pages 100 and 107.

Safonov and Seversky each flew M.15s which sported the scheme of clear-doped linen and varnished wooden fuselage and struts. Marine paint was applied to the bottom surface of the boat hull and the sides up to the water line. Roundels appeared in four positions (type B). Serial numbers appeared on each side of hull as follows: Safonov (2); Seversky (9).

67. FBA or Franco British Aviation (tactical number 48), Baltic Sea Fleet, circa fall 1915. Most FBAs were finished in a scheme of clear-doped linen and varnished wooden fuselage and struts. Metal parts were painted pale gray. Roundels appeared in four positions (type F). The white rudder has the Cross of Saint Andrew applied to both sides. A small triangular pennant of blue, white, and red

appears on the port (left) side of the nose. FBA No.48 appeared in black on each side of the hull. Source: photograph page 29.

Alexander Seversky was shot down in FBA No. 7 which sported a similar scheme. It is unknown if any personal marking were applied to that aircraft.

68. Curtiss Triad type E (tactical number 5) flown by Victor Utgoff and launched from the cruiser *Kagul*, circa March 1915. Most Triads were finished in a scheme of clear-doped linen and varnished wooden float and struts. Metal parts were painted pale gray. The black tactical number *5* appeared on the outer surface of each vertical fin. Source: photograph page 250.

69. Curtiss (1913 F-Boat) flown by Victor Utgoff while attached to the Hydro Cruiser *Almaz*. All fabric surfaces and metal parts were painted pale gray. The wooden boat hull and struts were stained and varnished. The Curtiss logo appeared on each side of the vertical tail unit. Roundels appeared in four positions (type B). Tactical numbers appeared in black on vertical wing fins and wing tip floats. In some cases these tactical numbers were white.

70. Curtiss (1914 F-Boat) flown by Victorin Kachinsky while attached to the Hydro Cruiser *Imperator Nikolai I*. All fabric surfaces were plain linen and metal parts were painted pale gray. The wooden boat hull and struts were stained and varnished. The Curtiss logo appeared on each side of the vertical fin. Roundels appeared in four positions (type B). Tactical numbers appeared in black on rudder and wing tip floats. In some cases these tactical numbers were white. The small emblem—a Cross of Saint Andrew with red and white tail pennants—indicated this aircraft was flown by Detachment Commander Kachinsky. The Black Sea Fleet used this design with four different color combinations. The other three displayed tail pennants of both white, both red, and one white (on top) and red (bottom).

71. Maurice Farman type M.F.11 flown by Mikhail Safonov, circa March 1916. It was finished pale gray overall. Under sides of the nacelle, wing struts, and tail boom were varnished wood. Rudders were white with the Cross of Saint Andrew on each outer surface. Roundels were applied in four position (type B). Tactical number *31* appeared in black on each side of the nacelle, as well as a prefix of Cyrillic letters *M* (em) and *F* (ef) to denote an Maurice Farman aircraft. Many Maurice Farman aircraft appeared in plain linen finish.

72. Sikorsky S-5A single-float seaplane, circa September 1914. It was finished in plain linen overall with all wood surfaces stained and varnished. Metal surfaces were painted pale gray. Source: photograph page 297.

73. Sikorsky S-10 Hydro (tactical number 3), circa winter 1915. It was finished in plain linen overall with all wood surfaces stained and varnished. Metal surfaces were painted pale gray. Roundels appeared in four positions (type B). The rudder was white with a Cross of Saint Andrew applied to both sides. Tactical number *3* appeared in black on each side of the fuselage, as well as a Cyrillic

letter prefix *C* (S) to denote an Sikorsky aircraft. Source: photographs pages 299, 300, and 301.

74. Sikorsky S.6A, circa April 1912. This aircraft was shown at the 1912 Moscow Aeronautical Exhibition, winning Sikorsky top prize—the "Great Golden Medal"— for achievement in aviation. It was finished in plain linen overall with all wood surfaces stained and varnished. Metal surfaces were painted pale gray. Sikorsky's name appeared on each side of the rudder in Cyrillic letters, as well as the aircraft designation *6ª*.

75. Sikorsky S.6B, circa July 1912. This aircraft was entered in the Russian military's International Aviation Competition of 1912 and won first place—a prize of 30,000 Rubles. It was finished in plain linen overall with all wood surfaces stained and varnished. Metal surfaces were painted pale gray.

76. Sikorsky S.10 Competition version, circa fall 1913. This machine was entered in the Russian military's International Competition of 1913 and won first place. After war was declared this machine was converted to a float plane and served with the Baltic Sea Fleet. It was finished with natural metal surfaces and plain linen overall. All wood surfaces were stained and varnished. The R-BVZ company logo—a Russian double-headed eagle surrounded by the R-BVZ name—appeared on each side of the rudder in black.

77. Sikorsky S.11, circa fall 1913. This machine was entered in the Russian military's International Competition of 1913 and won second place. It was finished with plain linen overall and varnished wooden side plates and landing gear struts. All metal surfaces were finished in pale gray. The R-BVZ company logo—a Russian double-headed eagle surrounded by the R-BVZ name—appeared on each side of the rudder in black.

78. Sikorsky S.12, circa fall 1913. At least 12 examples were built and served as trainers with the Russian army during World War I. This example was finished with plain linen overall and varnished wooden landing gear struts. All metal surfaces were finished in pale gray. Roundels appeared in six positions (type D).

79. Sikorsky S.16 (R-BVZ factory number 155). This was the second prototype in the S-16 series. The ailerons located on the upper and lower wings were the most distinguishing factor from the S-16 cep series aircraft. At one point this machine was fitted with skis for operation in snow. This aircraft was finished with plain linen overall and varnished wooden landing gear supports and wing struts. All metal surfaces were left natural. Roundels appeared in four positions (type F).

80. (a & b). Sikorsky S.16 cep, circa 1916. The two profiles illustrate typical examples of the S-16 cep series. Both were finished with plain linen overall and varnished wooden landing gear supports and wing struts. All metal surfaces were left natural. Roundels appeared in four positions (type F). Each side of the fuselage is decorated with a triangular Russian pennant. The top aircraft was equipped with a synchronization system that allowed one machine gun to be mounted on either side of the fuselage, in this case a Colt. The other illustration shows a S-16 cep equipped with skis ands a Lewis machine gun.

81. Sikorsky S.16 cep (serial number 201) flown by Juri Gilsher while with the 7th Fighter Detachment, circa May 1916. It was finished with plain linen overall and varnished wooden landing gear supports and wing struts. All metal surfaces were left natural. Roundels appeared in four positions (type F). Each side of the fuselage and rudder were decorated with a triangular Russian pennant. This machine was equipped with a synchronization system that allowed a single Maxim machine gun to be fitted to the port (left) side of the fuselage.

82. Sikorsky S.20, circa fall 1916. At least five examples were built and served as frontline fighters with the Russian army during World War I. This example was finished with plain linen overall and varnished wooden landing gear supports and wing struts. All metal surfaces were left natural. In some cases the upper wing cutouts were covered with cellulose. Roundels appeared in six positions (type D). Each side of the rudder was decorated with a triangular Russian pennant. Although not shown, this type was usually equipped with a synchronization system that allowed one machine gun to be mounted on either side of the fuselage. However, in many cases the system was prone to malfunctions, so the gun was repositioned on the top wing.

83. The Sikorsky Grand (S-21 or *Russian Knight*) was the world's first four-engine aircraft. Finished with plain linen overall and natural metal surfaces. The plywood fuselage and other wood surfaces were all stained and varnished. The top of the cabin was painted white.

84. Sikorsky Il'ya Muromets type B (S-22 ship), circa winter 1915–1916. Almost all of the Il'ya Muromets bombers were finished in a varnished linen that gave an overall light brown scheme. Wooden struts were varnished and metal plates were left in natural color. Russian pennants were applied to each side of the fuselage and roundels were in four positions on the wings (type D).

85. Sikorsky Il'ya Muromets type G.3 (S-25 series), circa winter 1916–17. Only five G-3s were built before the Russian revolution. Four of the machines were finished in a varnished linen that gave a overall light brown scheme. However, information has suggested the fifth aircraft was painted pale gray overall as this profile illustrates. Wooden struts were varnished. Russian pennants were applied to each side of the fuselage. Roundels were applied in 12 positions as follows: wings—four; outer surfaces of rudders—four; and vertical tail unit—four. This aircraft was equipped with Lewis, Madsen, and Colt machine guns.

86. Il'ya Muromets type V (S-23 series—ship number 2). Except for a single G.3 finished in pale gray, almost all Il'ya Muromets bombers were finished in a varnished linen that gave a overall light brown scheme. Wooden struts were varnished and metal plates were left in natural color or painted pale gray. Russian pennants were applied

to each side of the fuselage and roundels were applied in four positions on the wings (type D). The black Cyrillic letter *B* (ve) appeared on each outer rudder as a prefix to the aircraft's factory number.

87. Uniform #1 by Terry Waldron (left side): Alexander Seversky in full black leather flying suit. Heavy wool leggings were normally worn under the leather boots to absorb moisture. A cloth liner was normally worn under the leather flying helmet and appeared in a variety of colors and fabrics. The liner provided flaps that wrapped around the neck. Russian naval aviators had to endure high winds and freezing weather in the Baltic and Black Sea. In winter months the freezing water temperature would reduce a person's survival time to minutes if immersed. Combining wool and leather for protective clothing was necessary to reduce the aviators' exposure to moisture. *Pogoni* that indicated the aviator's rank were worn on the shoulders of his jacket.

88. Uniform #2 by Terry Waldron (center): Yevgraph Kruten in a summer flying uniform. Apparently influenced by French attire, Kruten's wool tunic was navy blue in color; however, many tunics of similar design appeared in khaki color. *Pogoni* that indicated his rank were worn on the shoulders of his tunic. The pants were black with red piping running down each side. The cap was navy blue in color and had a black leather brim. These caps also appeared in khaki with red piping. Although speculative, Kruten, a cavalry officer, was reported to have worn his riding spurs in flight. He is shown with spurs, holding a riding crop, and displaying the Order of Saint George, 4th Class.

89. Uniform #3 by Terry Waldron. A naval aviator in the Black Sea Fleet in full brown leather flying suit. The boots were rubberized to prevent moisture leak through. The life preserver of heavy cloth appeared in a variety of colors and sported a wrap-around waist strap. A light colored cotton head cover was usually worn under the leather flying helmet, but during warmer weather conditions the leather helmet was worn by itself with goggles. *Pogoni* indicating the aviator's rank were worn on the shoulders of his jacket.

90. Uniform #4 by Terry Waldron. Juri Gilsher wearing a black leather jacket with dark colored plush wool collar. *Pogoni* that indicated his rank were worn on the shoulders

of his jacket. His pants were navy blue in color. He wore black leather boots with knee high wool leggings of light gray. He wore a black peak cap with red and yellow piping and a Russian cockade in front center.

91. Uniform #5 by Terry Waldron. Alexander Riaboff wearing a heavy winter coat made from black bear fur. He also wore black leather boots and a khaki cap with black leather brim and red piping. The center of the cap displays a Russian cockade.

92. Uniform #6 by Terry Waldron shows an aviator wearing a heavy winter wool trench coat. These coats appeared in a large variety of fabrics and colors. This particular coat was tan wool and had a plush white wool collar. The aviator wore black leather boots and a khaki cap with black leather brim and red piping. The center of the cap displays a Russian cockade. *Pogoni* indicating the aviator's rank were worn on the shoulders of his coat.

93. *Flowers* is an original painting by aviation artist James Dietz. The scene depicts Vasili Yanchenko holding his fallen comrade, Juri Gilsher, who died in the famous air battle of 20 July, 1917, after his Nieuport broke-up in mid air and crashed. Ironically, Juri Gilsher had obtained his fifth victory only moments before his death.

94. *Yevgraph Nikoliavich Kruten* is an original painting by aviation artist James Dietz depicting the Russian ace standing next to his trusted mount—a French-built Nieuport type 17 fighter. Kruten's Nieuports 17 and 21 each displayed a medieval knight which probably represented the legendary Russian warrior Il'ya Muromets. Like Il'ya, Kruten, as a warrior, embodied the ideals of heroism and courage, a defender of Russia against its enemies.

95. Awards page 1.

96. Awards page 2.

97. Various types of Russian roundels keyed to aircraft profiles in the color section. Right column, top to bottom: Aeronautic Ensign, Russian national flag, Cross of Saint Andrew, Russian pennant, Russian pennant with Imperial Russian double-headed eagle.

1. *Cossacks and Scouts* by James Dietz

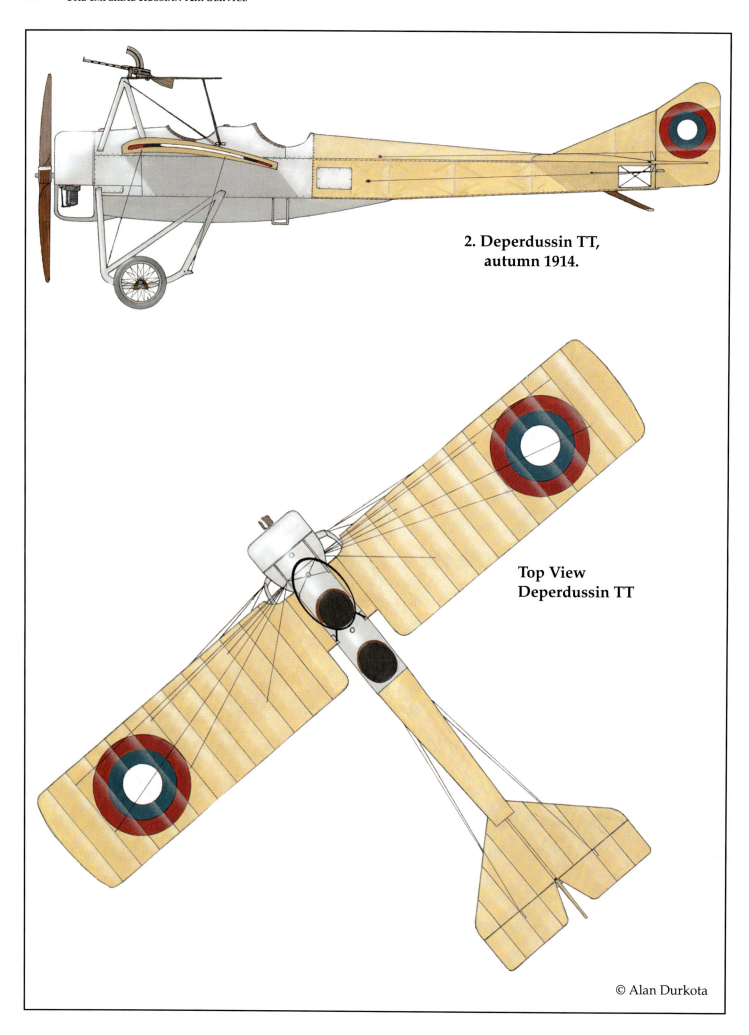

2. Deperdussin TT, autumn 1914.

Top View Deperdussin TT

© Alan Durkota

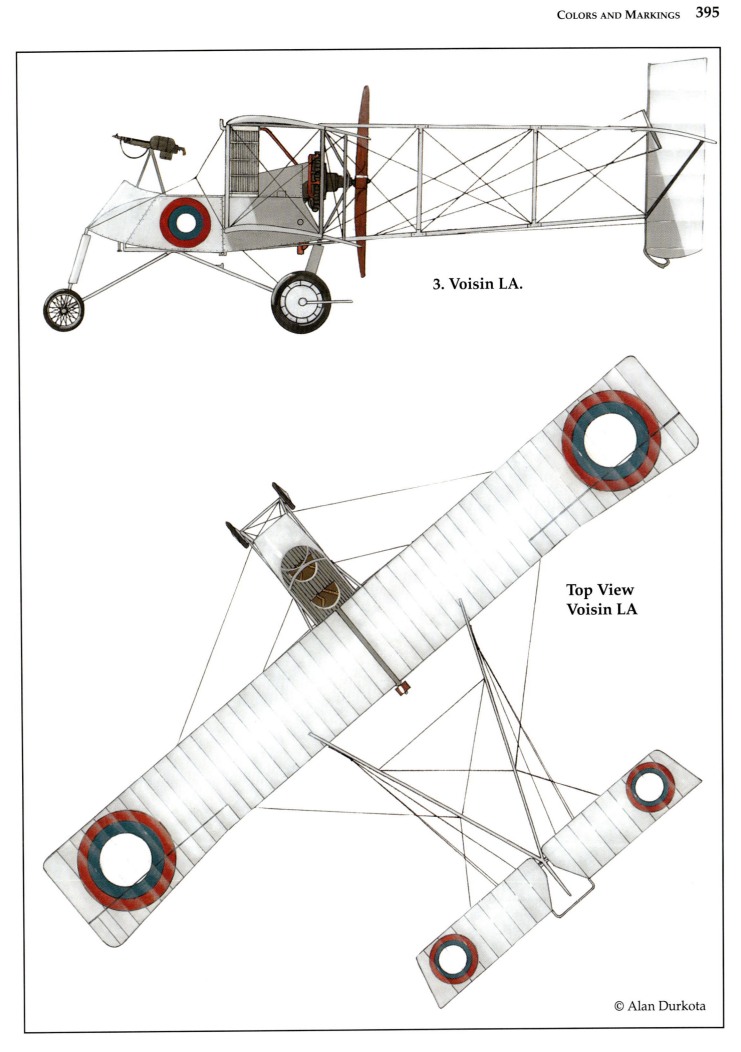

3. Voisin LA.

Top View Voisin LA

© Alan Durkota

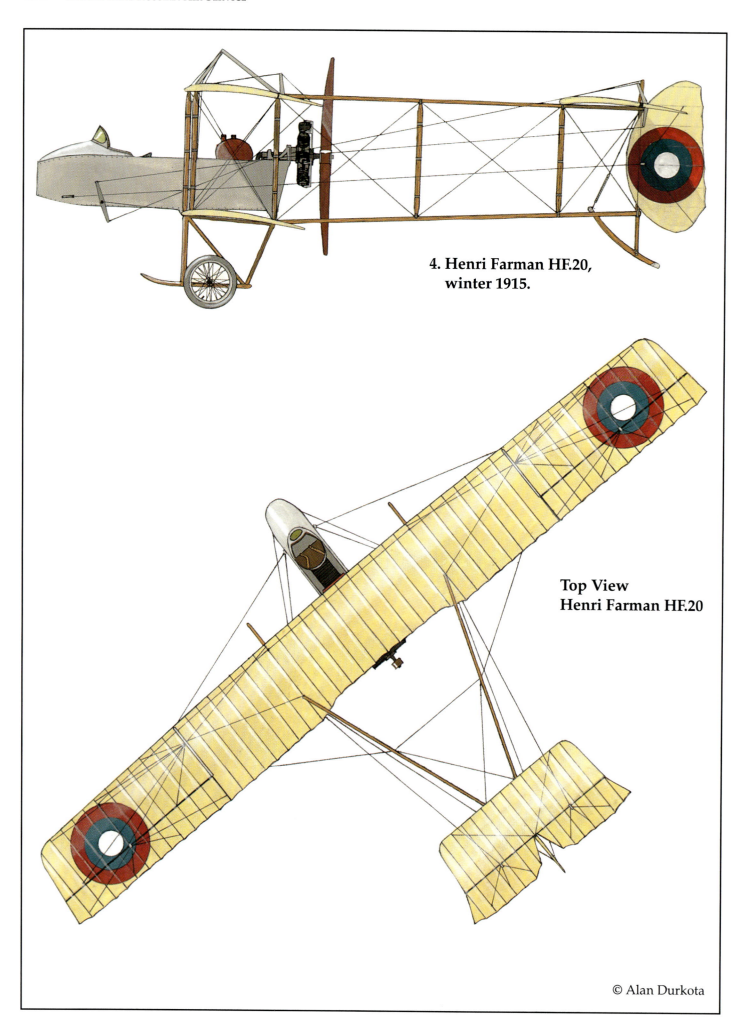

4. Henri Farman HF.20, winter 1915.

Top View
Henri Farman HF.20

© Alan Durkota

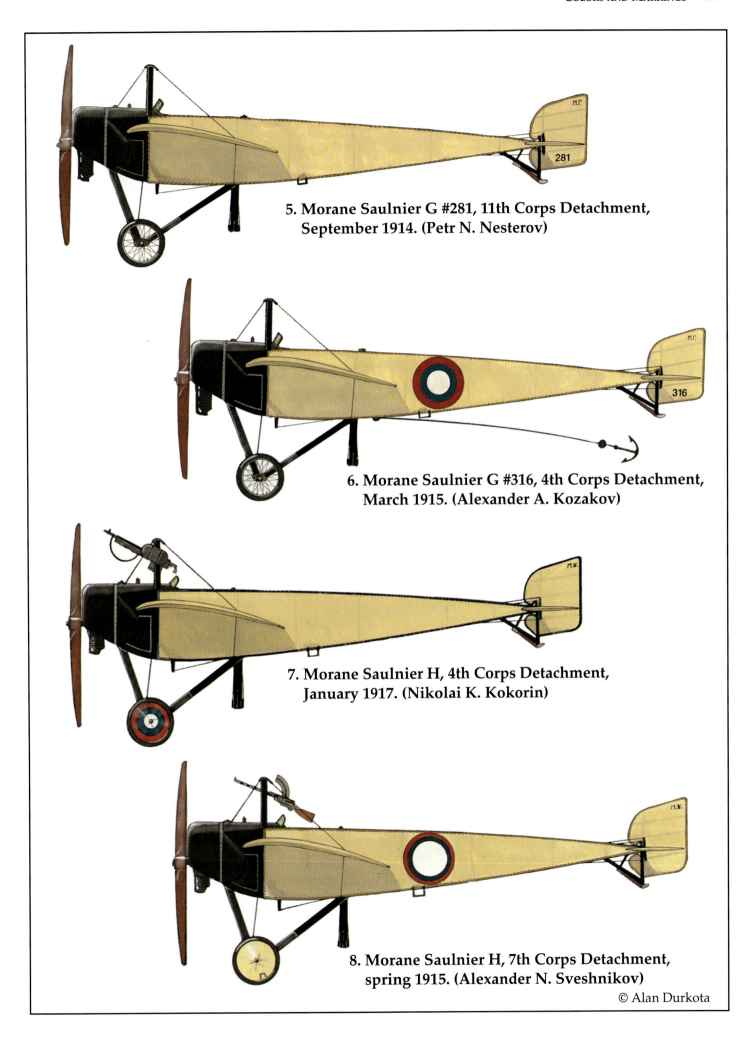

5. Morane Saulnier G #281, 11th Corps Detachment, September 1914. (Petr N. Nesterov)

6. Morane Saulnier G #316, 4th Corps Detachment, March 1915. (Alexander A. Kozakov)

7. Morane Saulnier H, 4th Corps Detachment, January 1917. (Nikolai K. Kokorin)

8. Morane Saulnier H, 7th Corps Detachment, spring 1915. (Alexander N. Sveshnikov)

© Alan Durkota

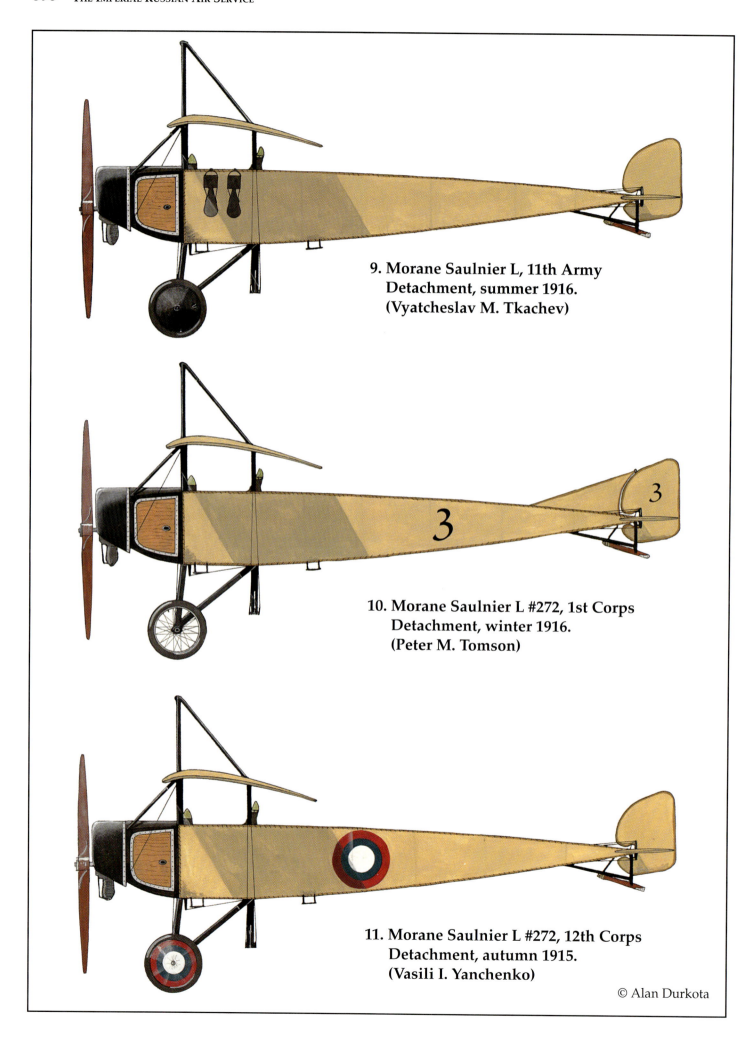

9. Morane Saulnier L, 11th Army Detachment, summer 1916. (Vyatcheslav M. Tkachev)

10. Morane Saulnier L #272, 1st Corps Detachment, winter 1916. (Peter M. Tomson)

11. Morane Saulnier L #272, 12th Corps Detachment, autumn 1915. (Vasili I. Yanchenko)

© Alan Durkota

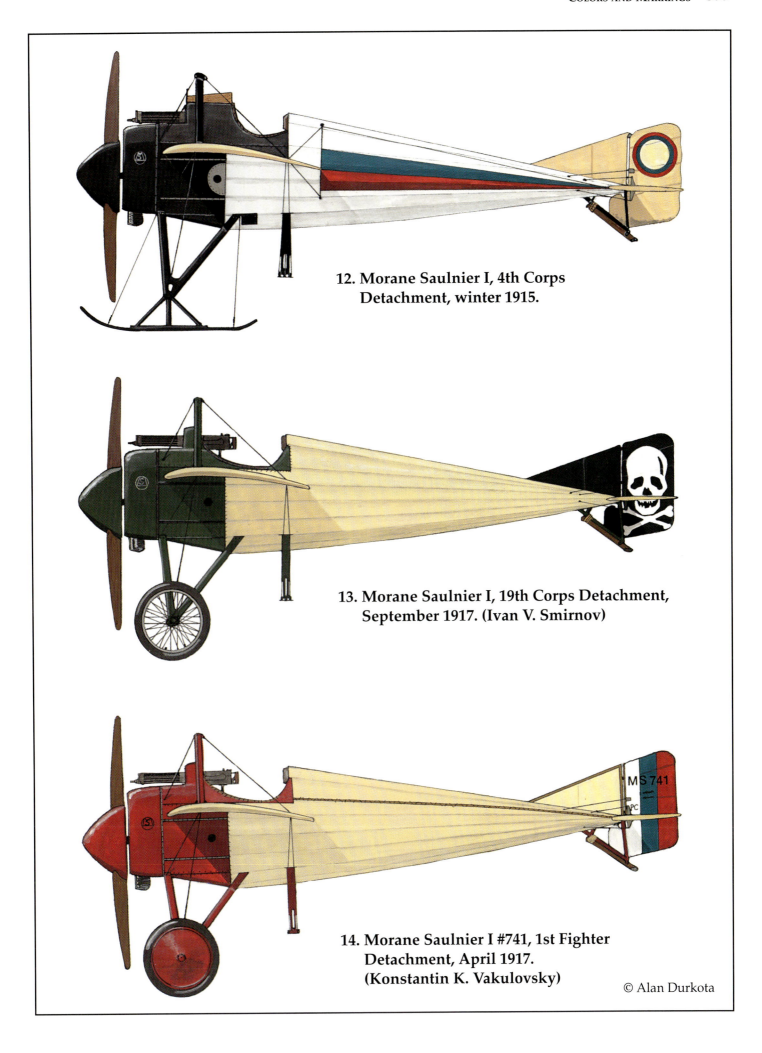

12. Morane Saulnier I, 4th Corps Detachment, winter 1915.

13. Morane Saulnier I, 19th Corps Detachment, September 1917. (Ivan V. Smirnov)

14. Morane Saulnier I #741, 1st Fighter Detachment, April 1917. (Konstantin K. Vakulovsky)

© Alan Durkota

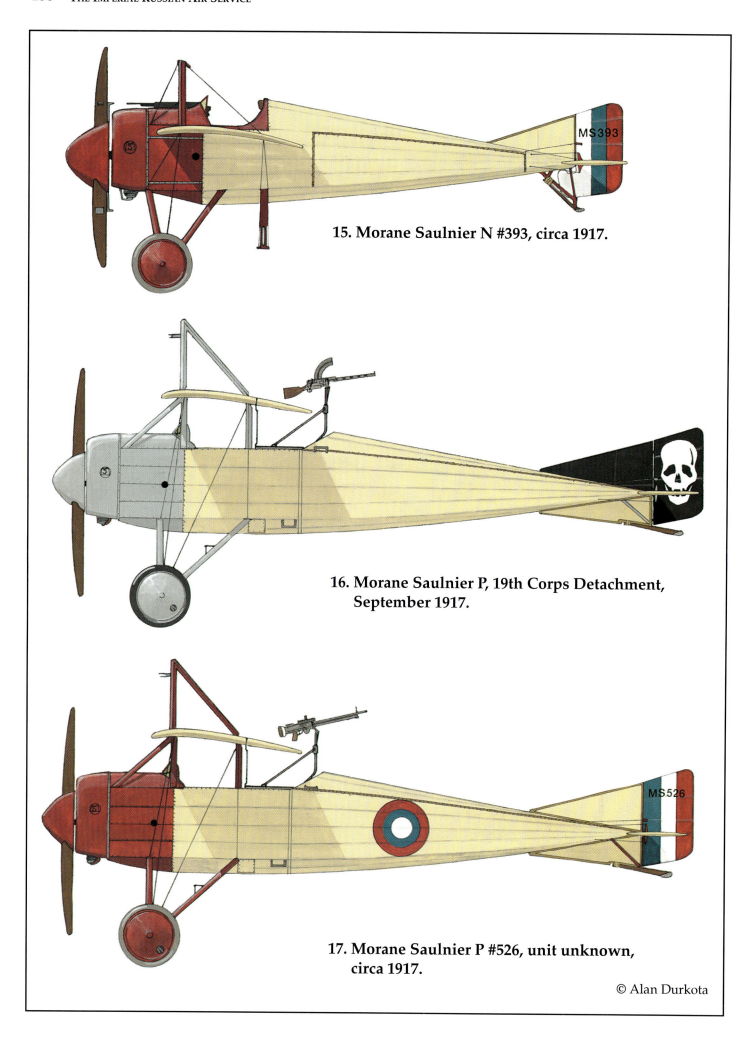

15. Morane Saulnier N #393, circa 1917.

16. Morane Saulnier P, 19th Corps Detachment, September 1917.

17. Morane Saulnier P #526, unit unknown, circa 1917.

© Alan Durkota

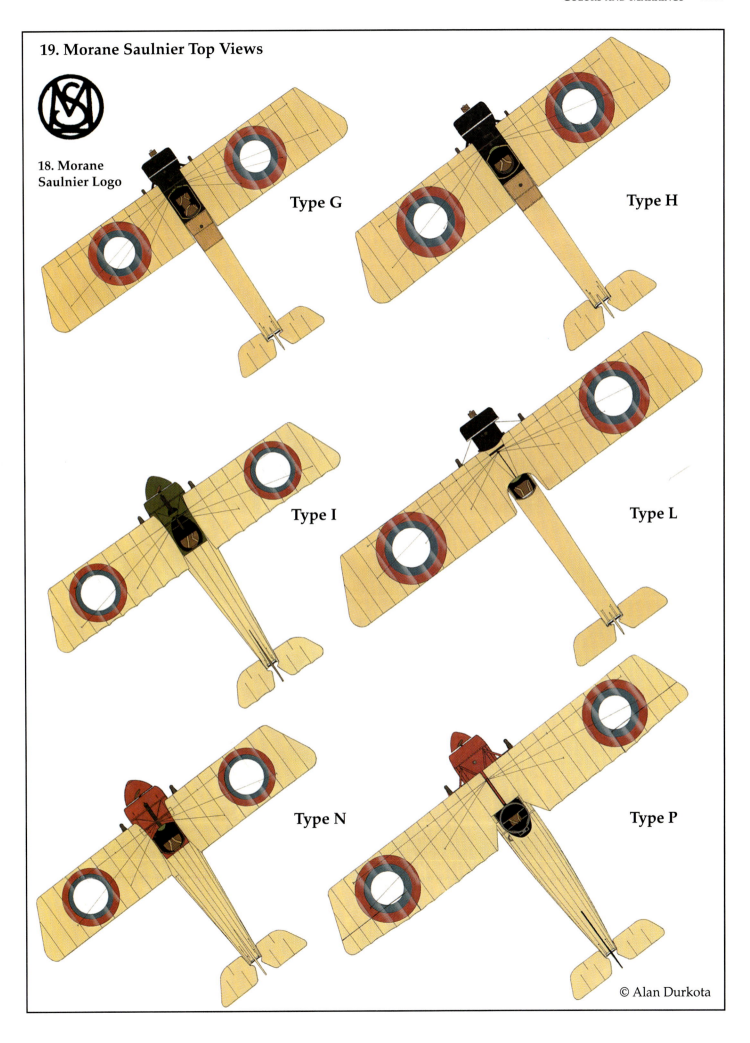

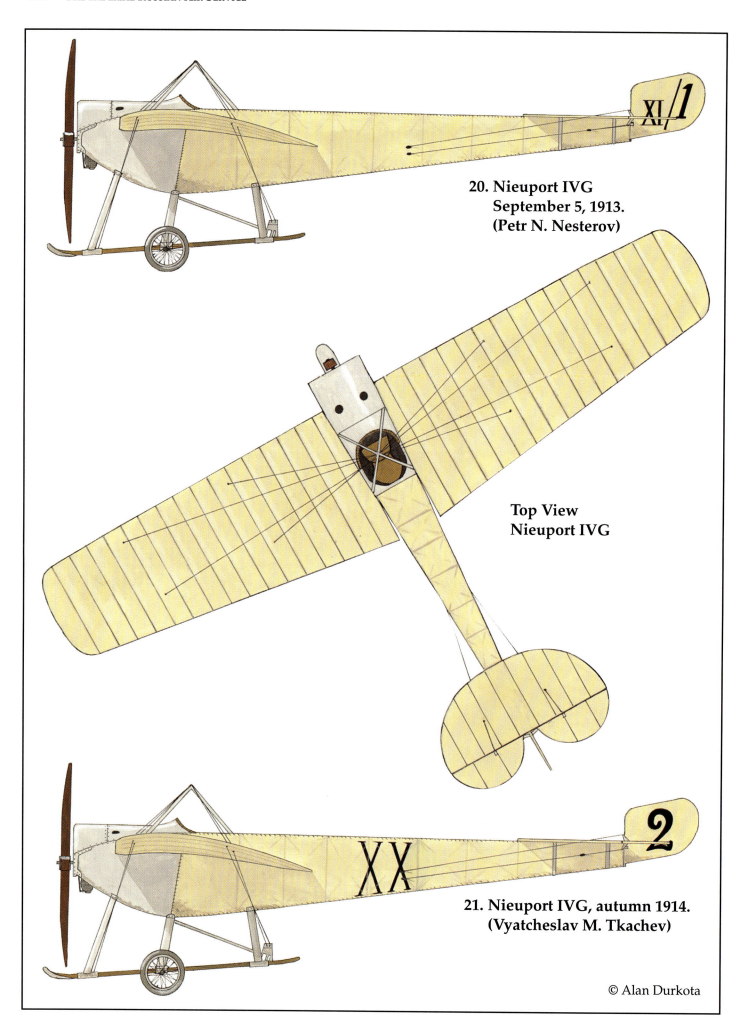

20. Nieuport IVG September 5, 1913. (Petr N. Nesterov)

Top View Nieuport IVG

21. Nieuport IVG, autumn 1914. (Vyatcheslav M. Tkachev)

© Alan Durkota

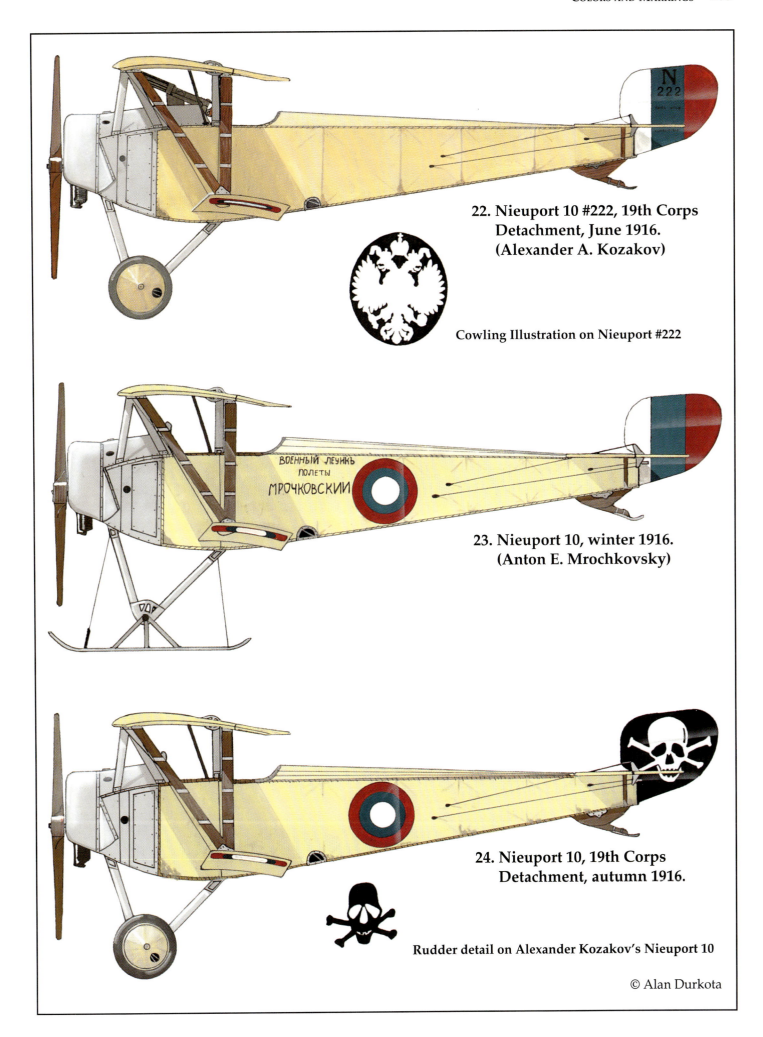

22. Nieuport 10 #222, 19th Corps Detachment, June 1916. (Alexander A. Kozakov)

Cowling Illustration on Nieuport #222

23. Nieuport 10, winter 1916. (Anton E. Mrochkovsky)

24. Nieuport 10, 19th Corps Detachment, autumn 1916.

Rudder detail on Alexander Kozakov's Nieuport 10

© Alan Durkota

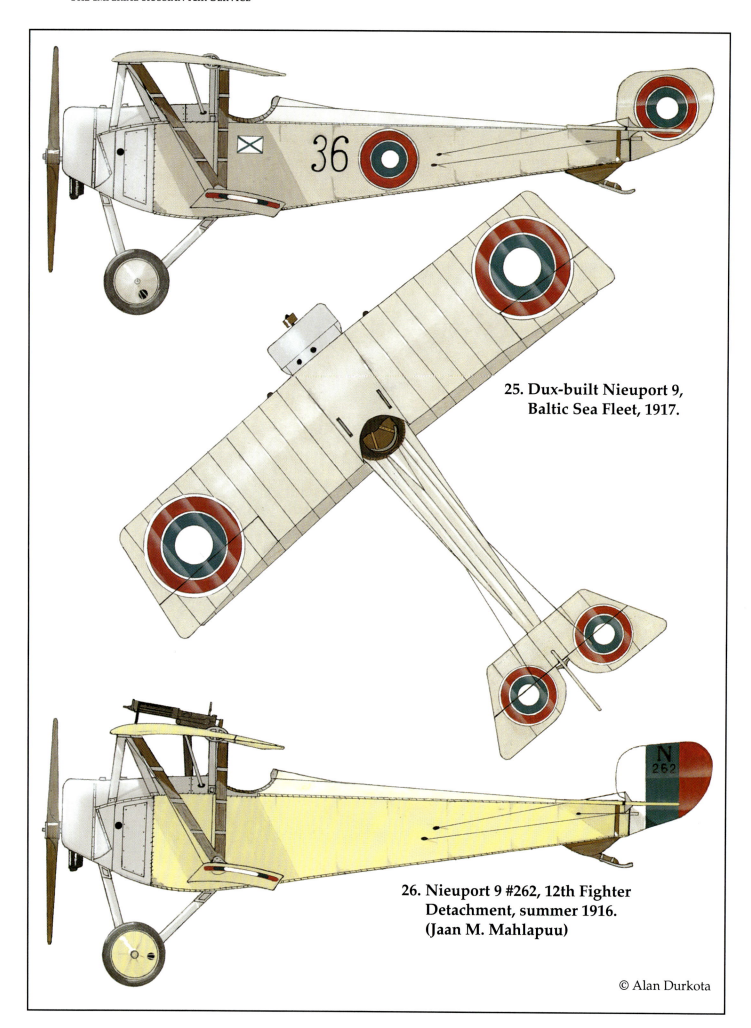

25. Dux-built Nieuport 9, Baltic Sea Fleet, 1917.

26. Nieuport 9 #262, 12th Fighter Detachment, summer 1916. (Jaan M. Mahlapuu)

© Alan Durkota

COLORS AND MARKINGS 405

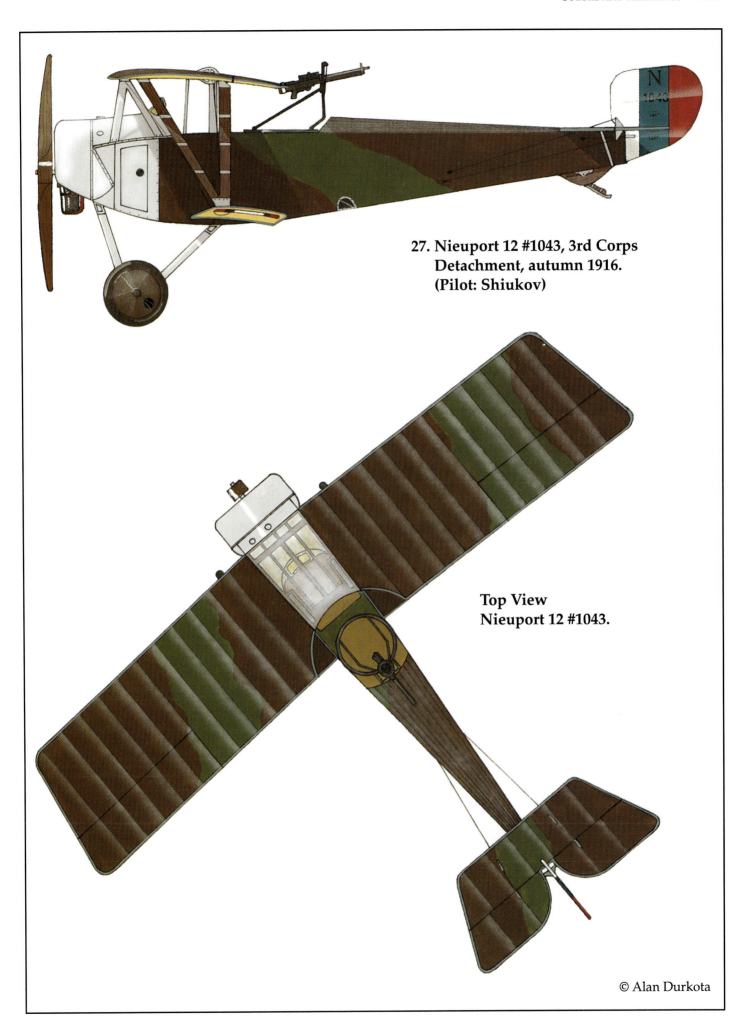

27. Nieuport 12 #1043, 3rd Corps Detachment, autumn 1916. (Pilot: Shiukov)

Top View Nieuport 12 #1043.

© Alan Durkota

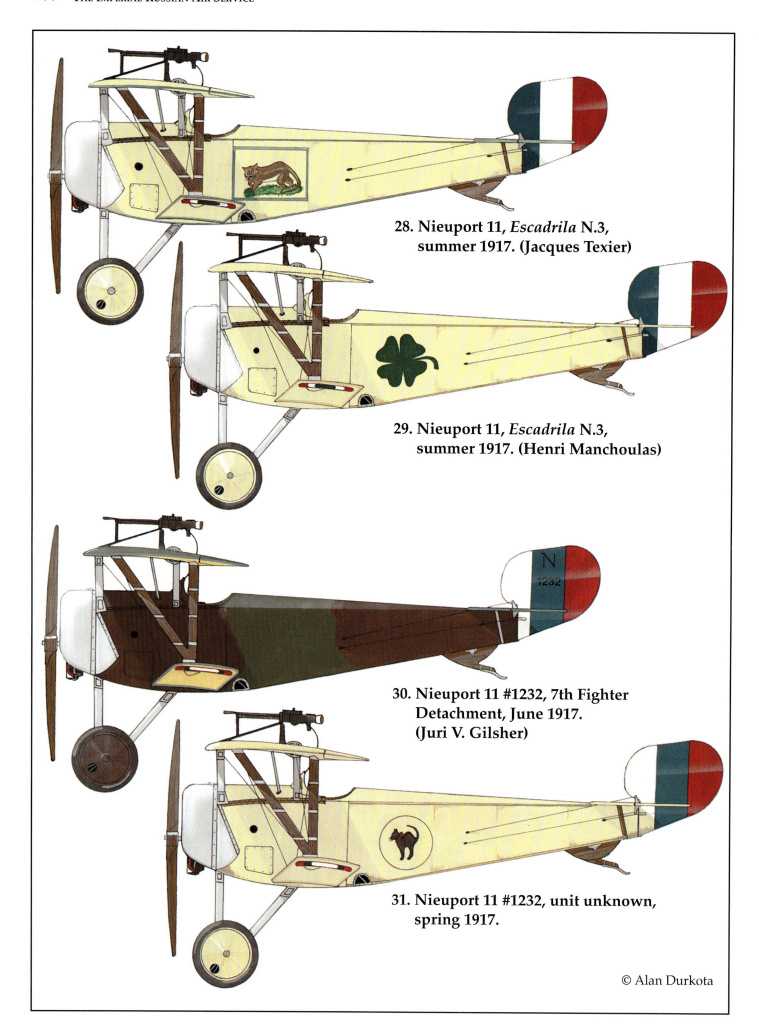

28. Nieuport 11, *Escadrila* N.3, summer 1917. (Jacques Texier)

29. Nieuport 11, *Escadrila* N.3, summer 1917. (Henri Manchoulas)

30. Nieuport 11 #1232, 7th Fighter Detachment, June 1917. (Juri V. Gilsher)

31. Nieuport 11 #1232, unit unknown, spring 1917.

© Alan Durkota

Colors and Markings 407

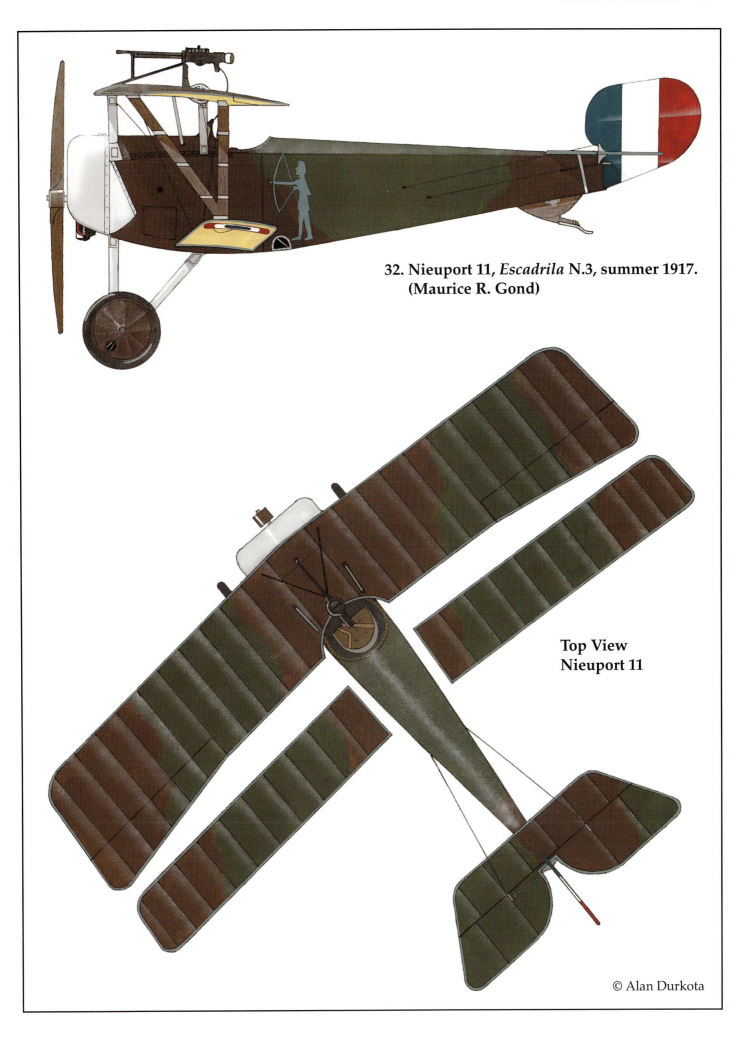

32. Nieuport 11, *Escadrila* N.3, summer 1917.
(Maurice R. Gond)

**Top View
Nieuport 11**

© Alan Durkota

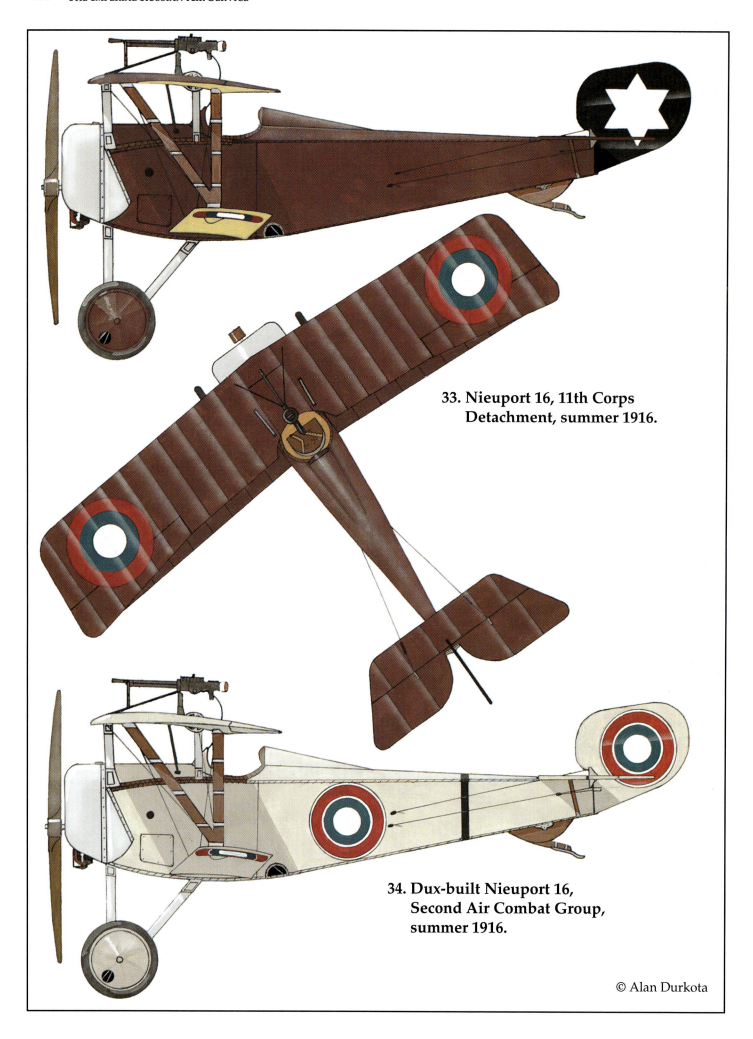

33. Nieuport 16, 11th Corps Detachment, summer 1916.

34. Dux-built Nieuport 16, Second Air Combat Group, summer 1916.

© Alan Durkota

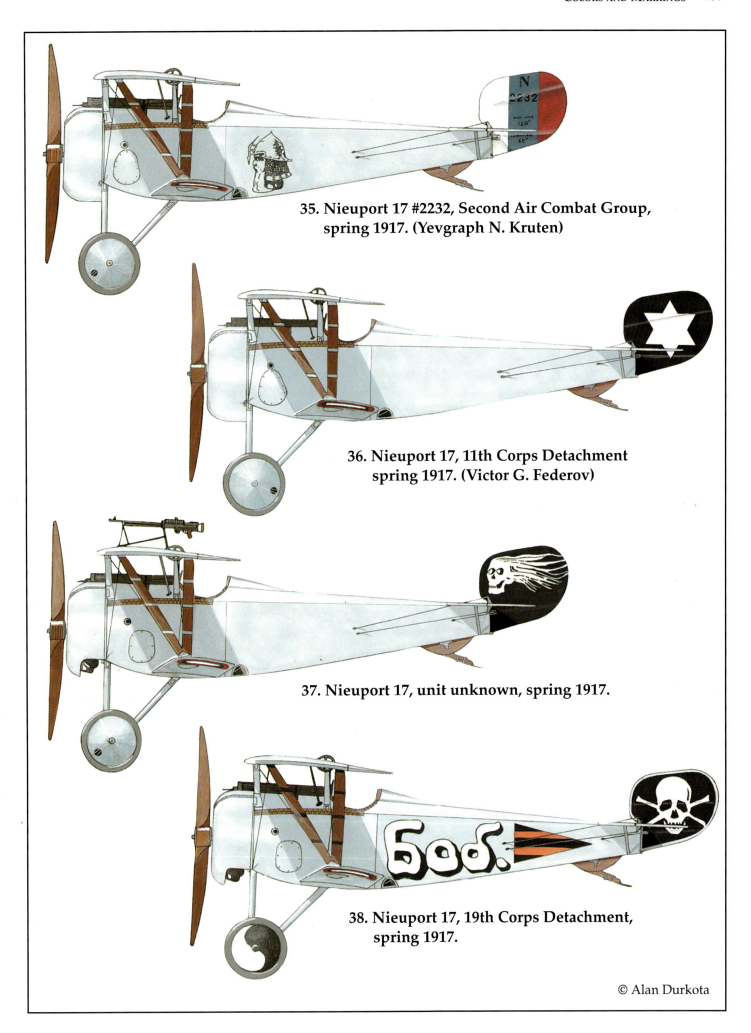

35. Nieuport 17 #2232, Second Air Combat Group, spring 1917. (Yevgraph N. Kruten)

36. Nieuport 17, 11th Corps Detachment spring 1917. (Victor G. Federov)

37. Nieuport 17, unit unknown, spring 1917.

38. Nieuport 17, 19th Corps Detachment, spring 1917.

© Alan Durkota

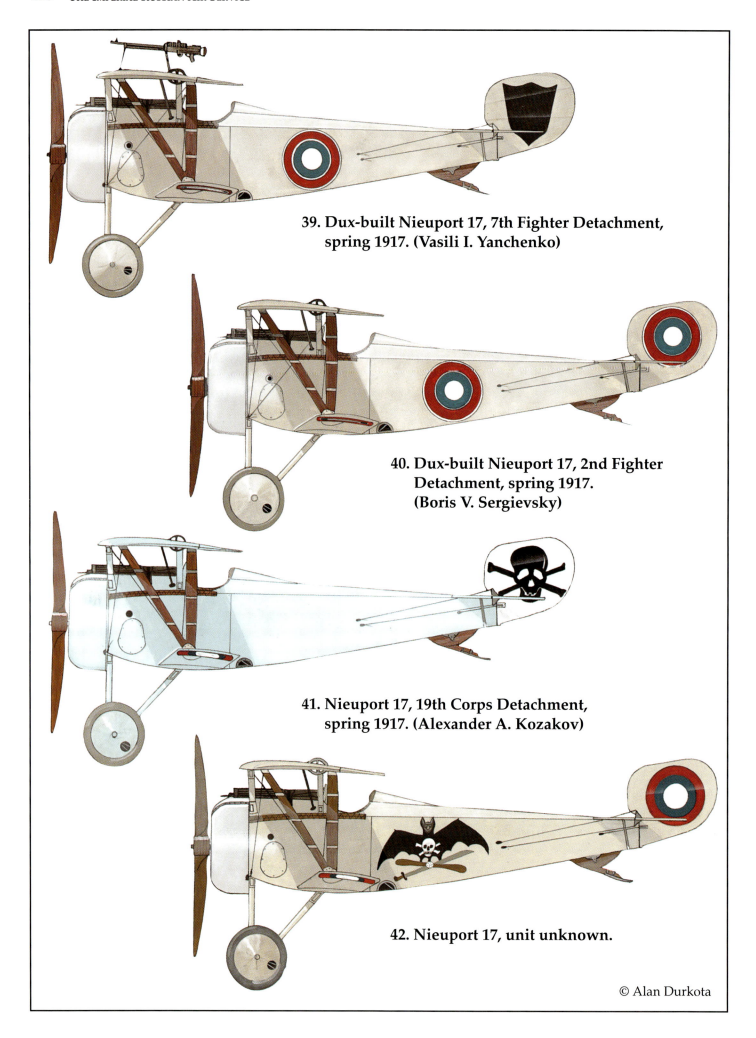

39. Dux-built Nieuport 17, 7th Fighter Detachment, spring 1917. (Vasili I. Yanchenko)

40. Dux-built Nieuport 17, 2nd Fighter Detachment, spring 1917. (Boris V. Sergievsky)

41. Nieuport 17, 19th Corps Detachment, spring 1917. (Alexander A. Kozakov)

42. Nieuport 17, unit unknown.

© Alan Durkota

COLORS AND MARKINGS **411**

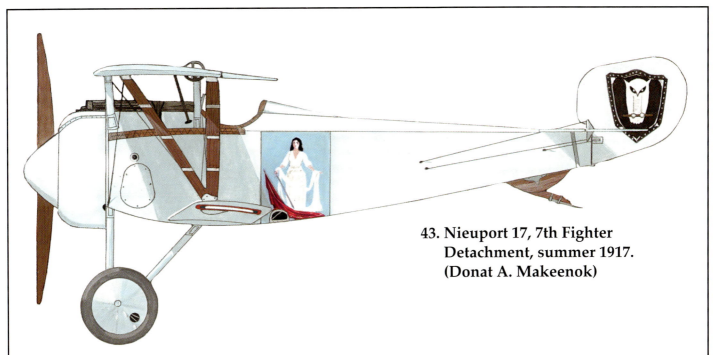

43. Nieuport 17, 7th Fighter Detachment, summer 1917. (Donat A. Makeenok)

Enlargement of personal insignia.

Terry Waldron and
Alan Durkota
© Alan Durkota

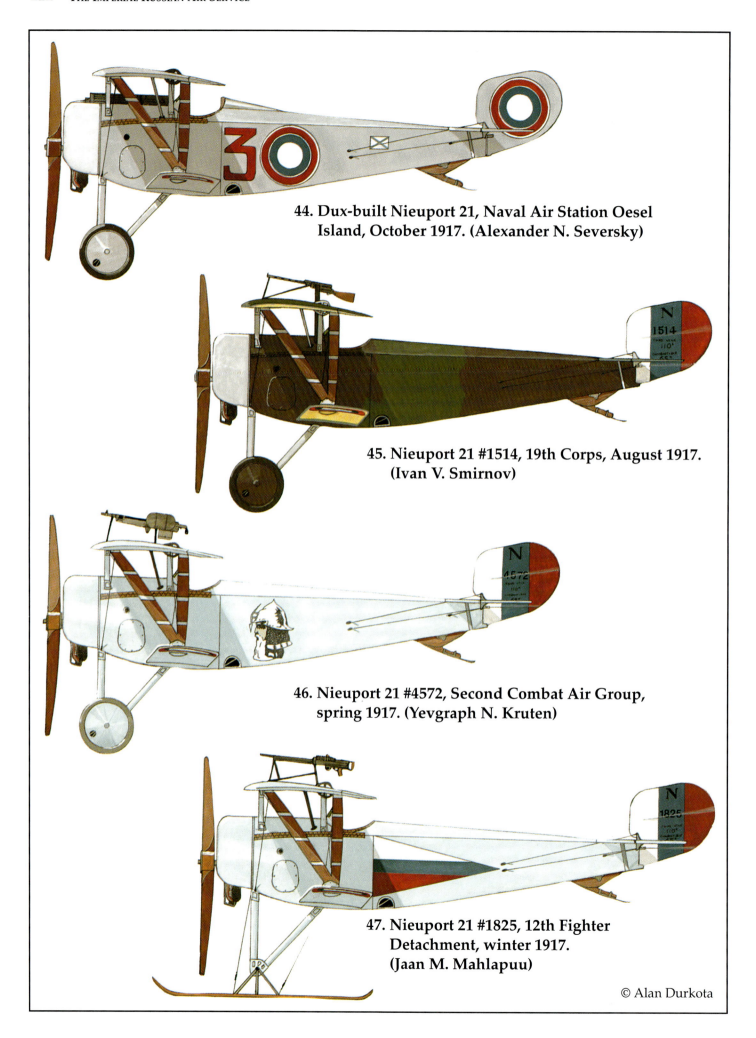

44. Dux-built Nieuport 21, Naval Air Station Oesel Island, October 1917. (Alexander N. Seversky)

45. Nieuport 21 #1514, 19th Corps, August 1917. (Ivan V. Smirnov)

46. Nieuport 21 #4572, Second Combat Air Group, spring 1917. (Yevgraph N. Kruten)

47. Nieuport 21 #1825, 12th Fighter Detachment, winter 1917. (Jaan M. Mahlapuu)

© Alan Durkota

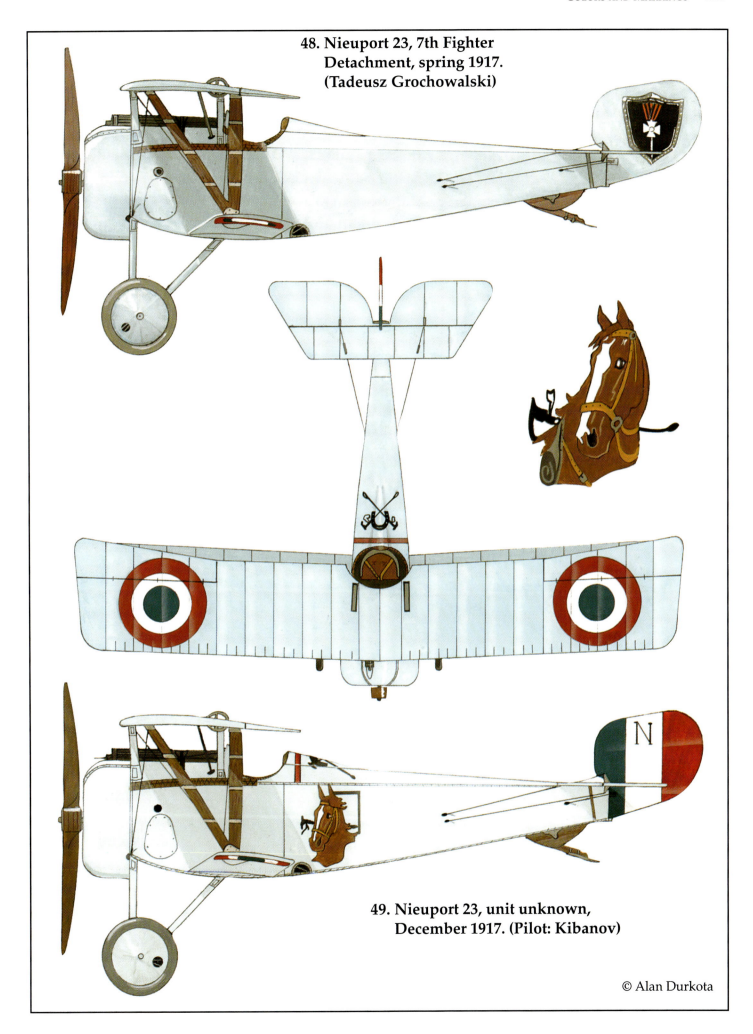

48. Nieuport 23, 7th Fighter Detachment, spring 1917. (Tadeusz Grochowalski)

49. Nieuport 23, unit unknown, December 1917. (Pilot: Kibanov)

© Alan Durkota

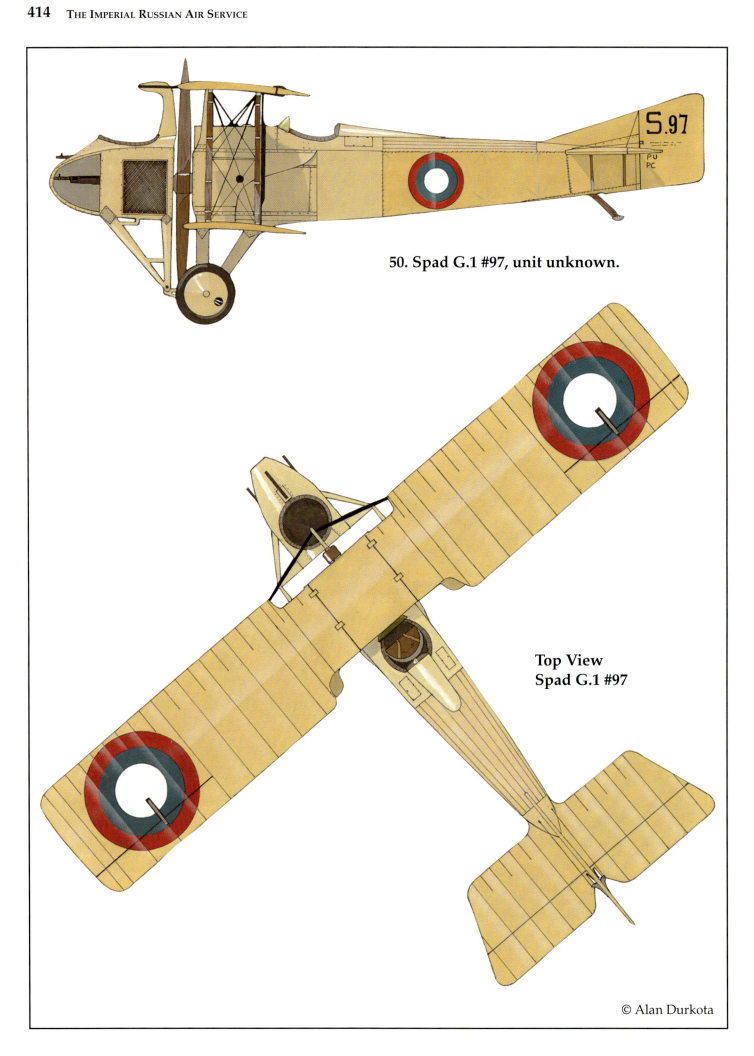

50. Spad G.1 #97, unit unknown.

Top View
Spad G.1 #97

© Alan Durkota

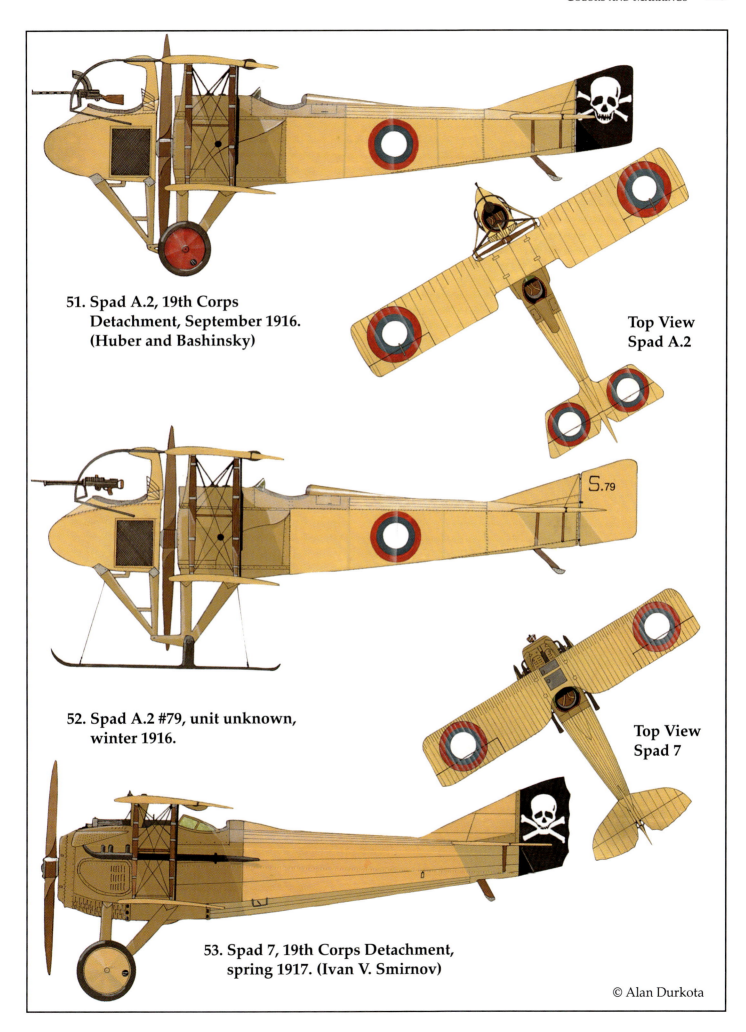

51. Spad A.2, 19th Corps Detachment, September 1916. (Huber and Bashinsky)

Top View Spad A.2

52. Spad A.2 #79, unit unknown, winter 1916.

Top View Spad 7

53. Spad 7, 19th Corps Detachment, spring 1917. (Ivan V. Smirnov)

© Alan Durkota

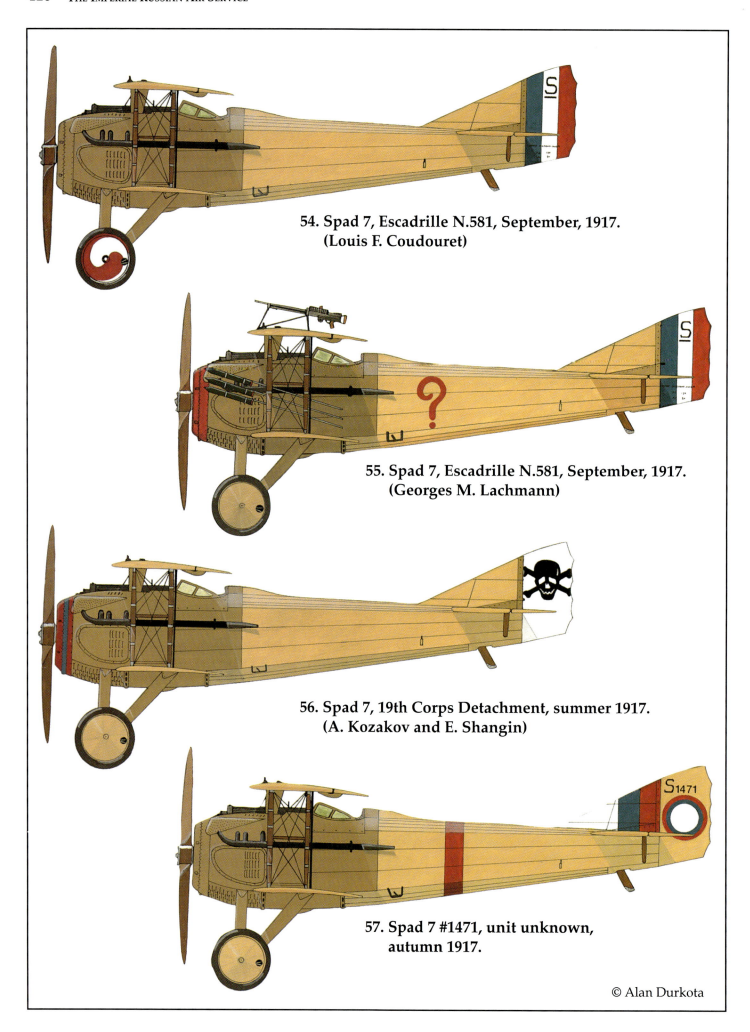

54. Spad 7, Escadrille N.581, September, 1917. (Louis F. Coudouret)

55. Spad 7, Escadrille N.581, September, 1917. (Georges M. Lachmann)

56. Spad 7, 19th Corps Detachment, summer 1917. (A. Kozakov and E. Shangin)

57. Spad 7 #1471, unit unknown, autumn 1917.

© Alan Durkota

Colors and Markings 417

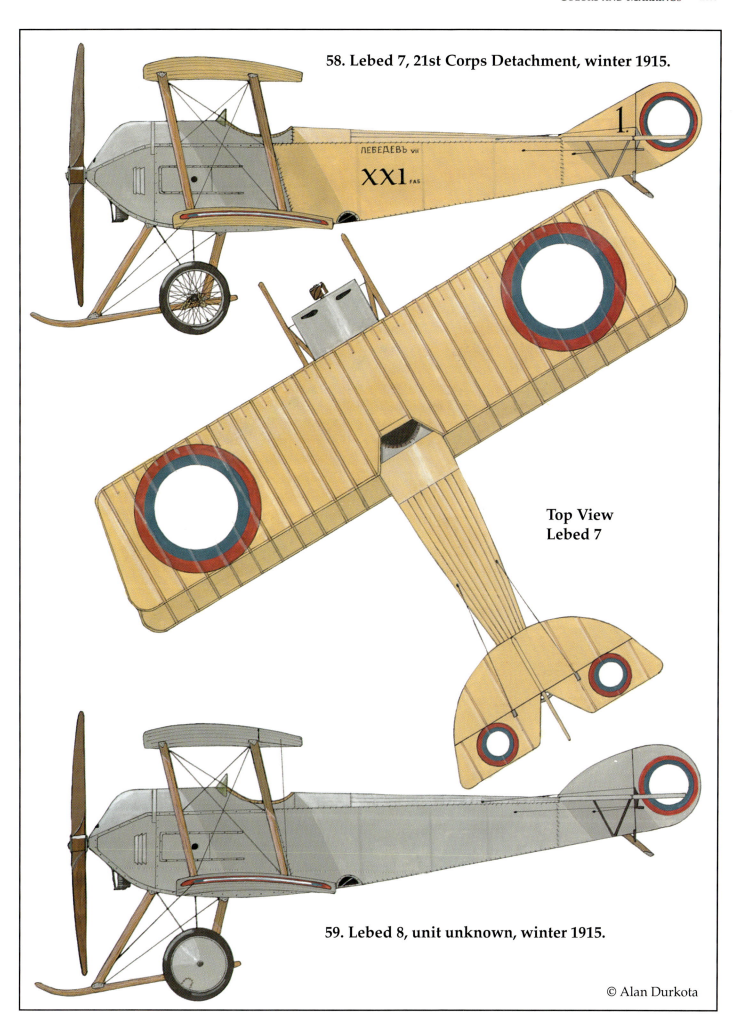

58. Lebed 7, 21st Corps Detachment, winter 1915.

Top View
Lebed 7

59. Lebed 8, unit unknown, winter 1915.

© Alan Durkota

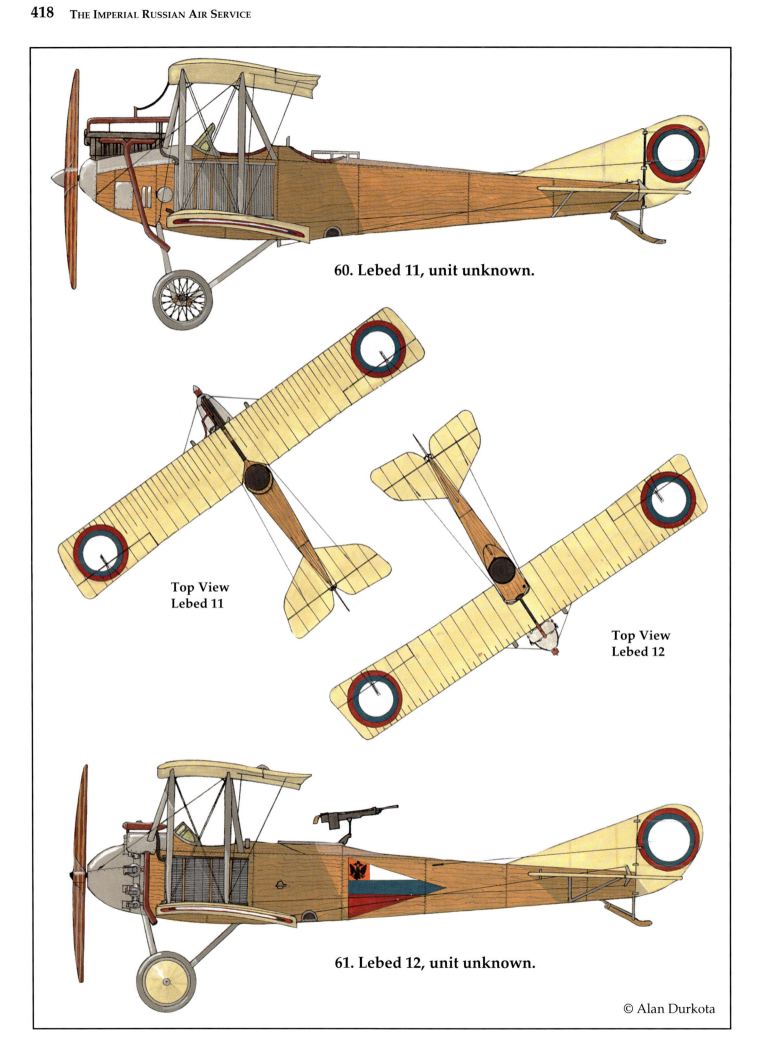

60. Lebed 11, unit unknown.

Top View Lebed 11

Top View Lebed 12

61. Lebed 12, unit unknown.

© Alan Durkota

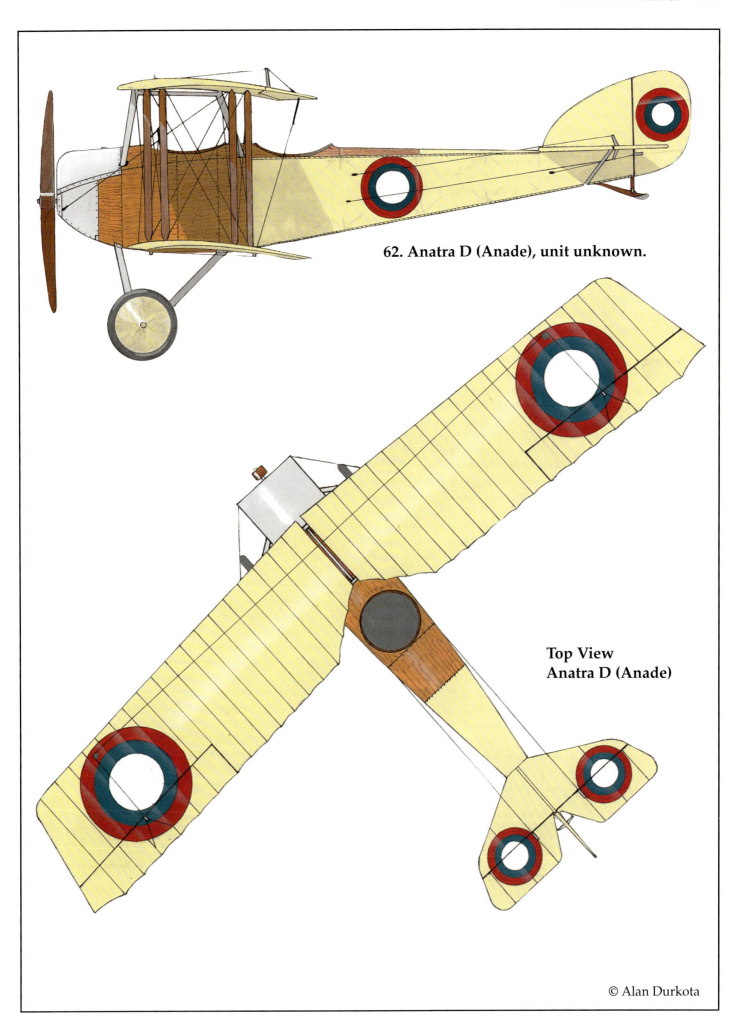

62. Anatra D (Anade), unit unknown.

Top View
Anatra D (Anade)

© Alan Durkota

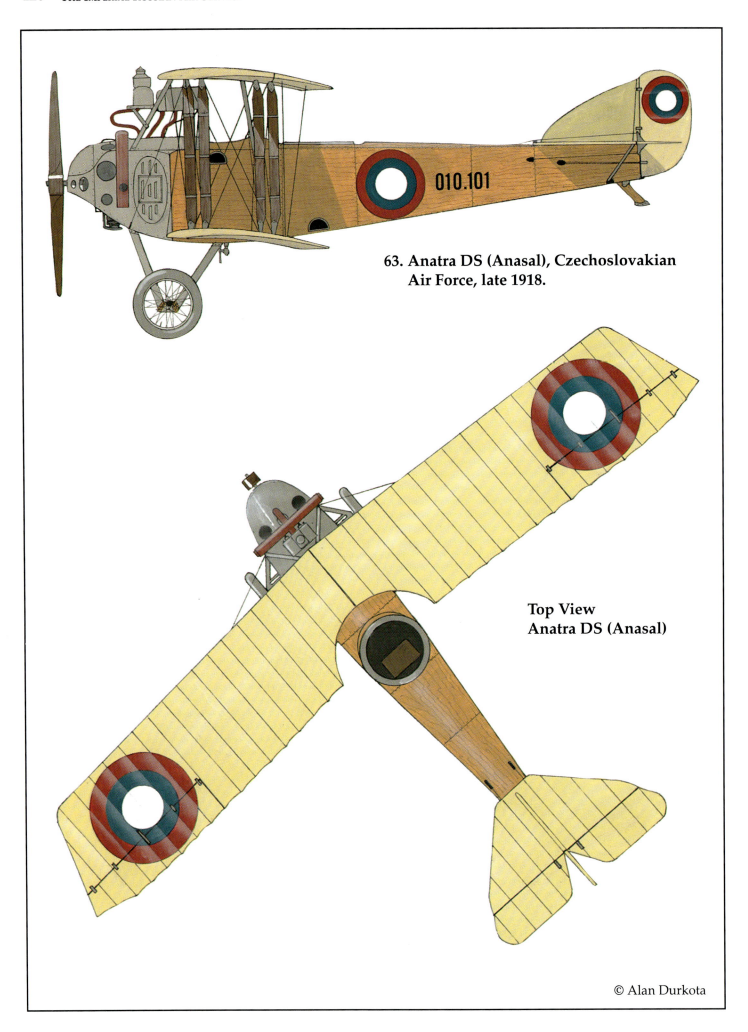

63. Anatra DS (Anasal), Czechoslovakian Air Force, late 1918.

Top View
Anatra DS (Anasal)

© Alan Durkota

COLORS AND MARKINGS 421

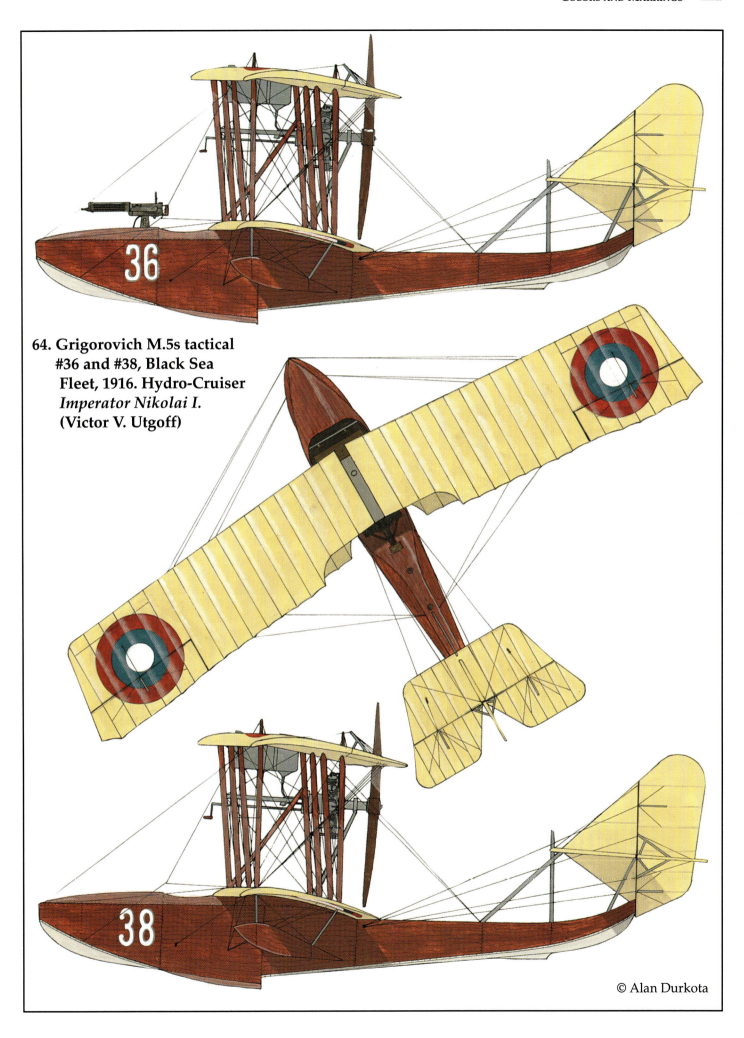

64. Grigorovich M.5s tactical #36 and #38, Black Sea Fleet, 1916. Hydro-Cruiser *Imperator Nikolai I.* (Victor V. Utgoff)

© Alan Durkota

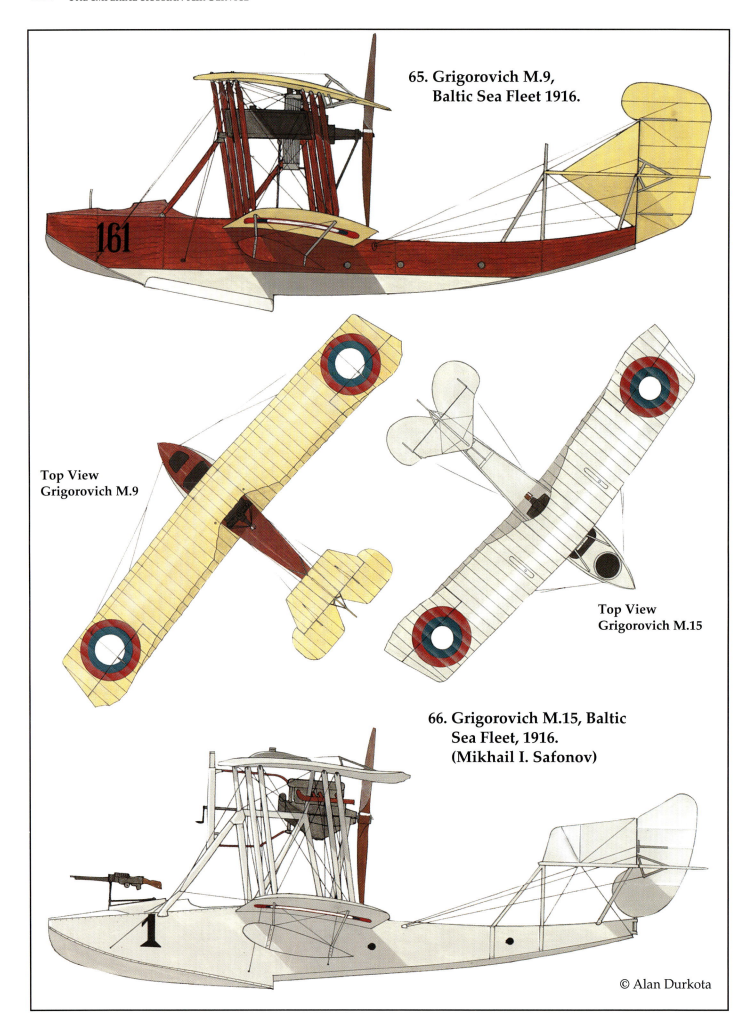
65. Grigorovich M.9, Baltic Sea Fleet 1916.

Top View Grigorovich M.9

Top View Grigorovich M.15

66. Grigorovich M.15, Baltic Sea Fleet, 1916. (Mikhail I. Safonov)

© Alan Durkota

COLORS AND MARKINGS 423

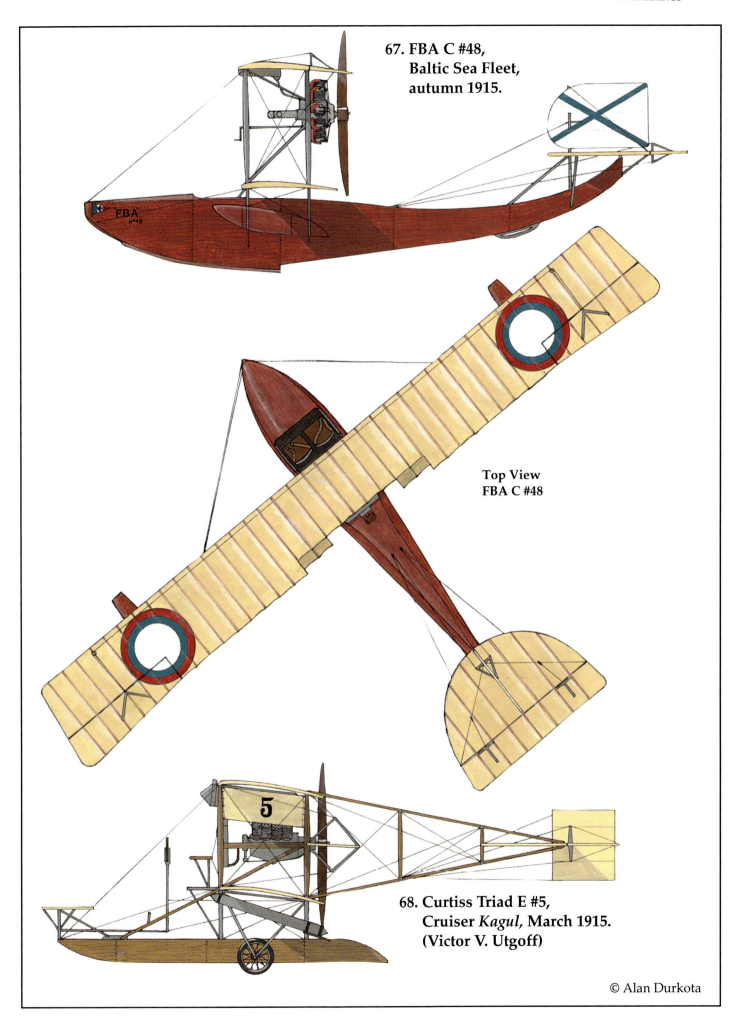

67. FBA C #48, Baltic Sea Fleet, autumn 1915.

Top View FBA C #48

68. Curtiss Triad E #5, Cruiser *Kagul*, March 1915. (Victor V. Utgoff)

© Alan Durkota

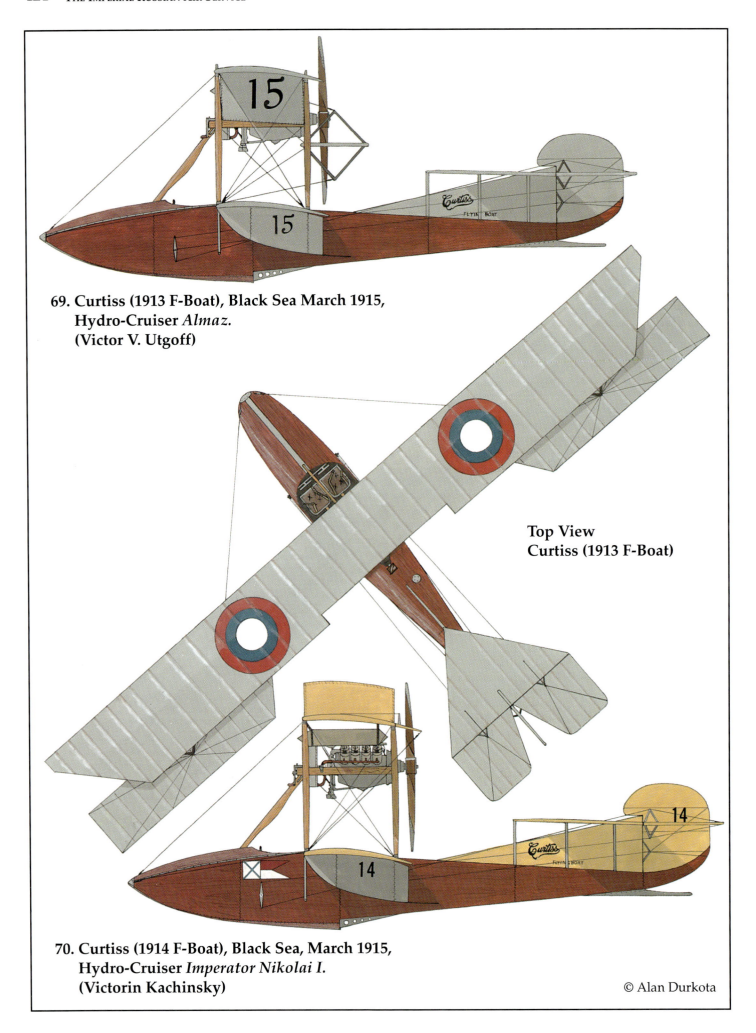

69. Curtiss (1913 F-Boat), Black Sea March 1915, Hydro-Cruiser *Almaz*. (Victor V. Utgoff)

Top View Curtiss (1913 F-Boat)

70. Curtiss (1914 F-Boat), Black Sea, March 1915, Hydro-Cruiser *Imperator Nikolai I*. (Victorin Kachinsky)

© Alan Durkota

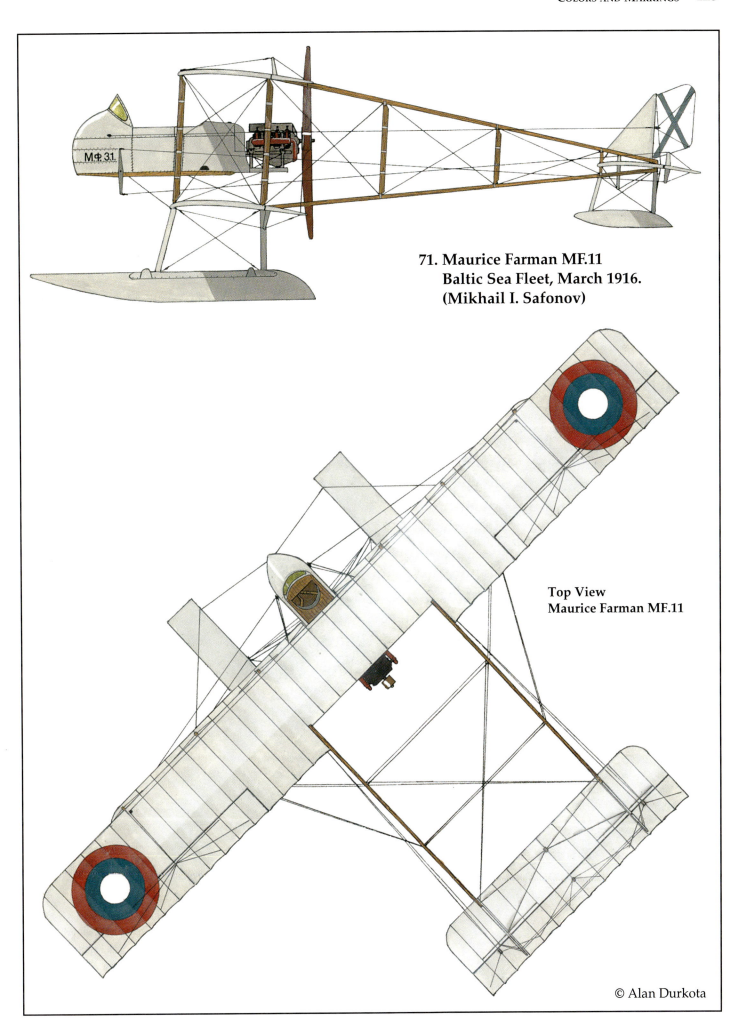

71. Maurice Farman MF.11
Baltic Sea Fleet, March 1916.
(Mikhail I. Safonov)

Top View
Maurice Farman MF.11

© Alan Durkota

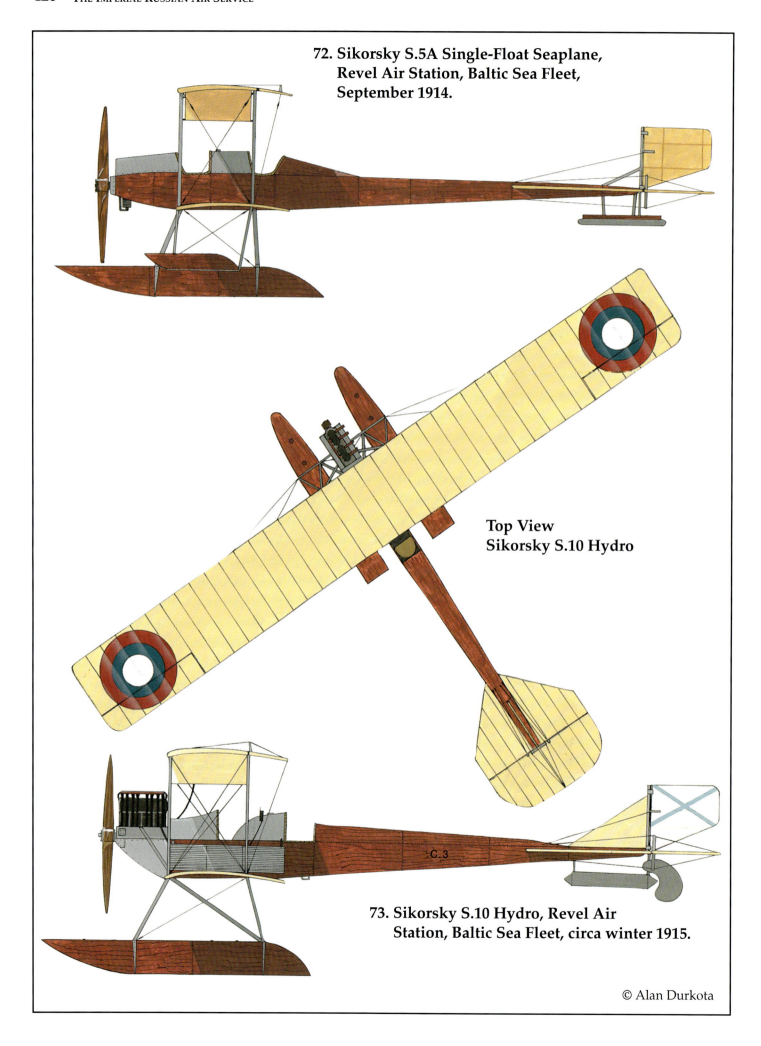

72. Sikorsky S.5A Single-Float Seaplane, Revel Air Station, Baltic Sea Fleet, September 1914.

Top View Sikorsky S.10 Hydro

73. Sikorsky S.10 Hydro, Revel Air Station, Baltic Sea Fleet, circa winter 1915.

© Alan Durkota

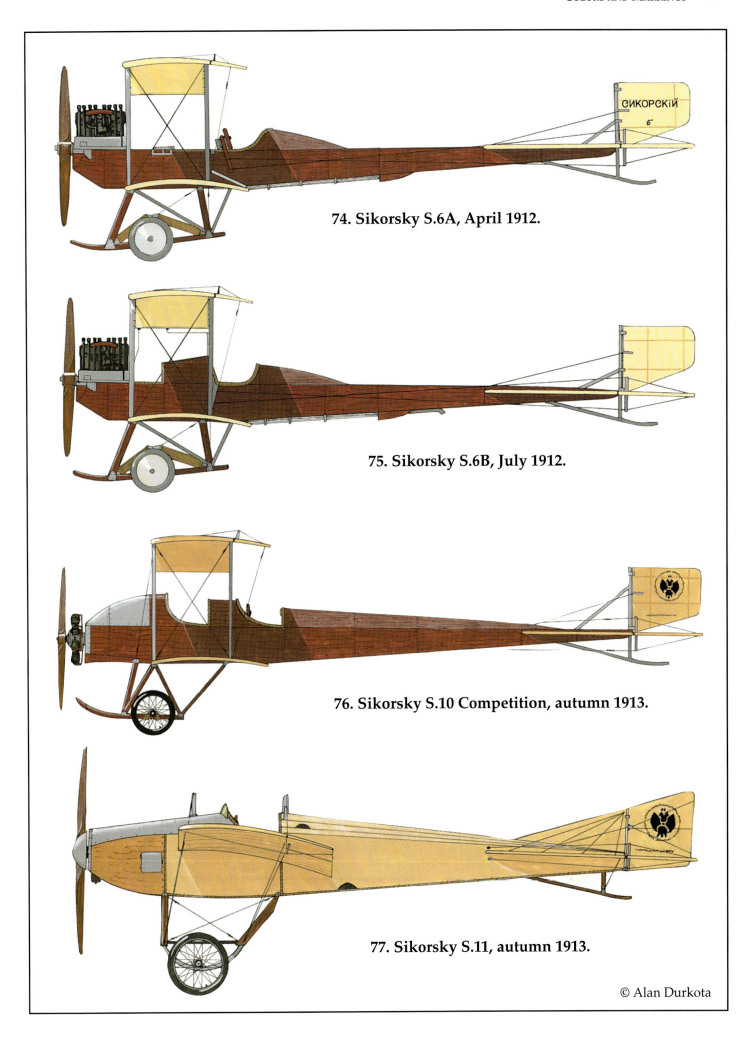

74. Sikorsky S.6A, April 1912.

75. Sikorsky S.6B, July 1912.

76. Sikorsky S.10 Competition, autumn 1913.

77. Sikorsky S.11, autumn 1913.

© Alan Durkota

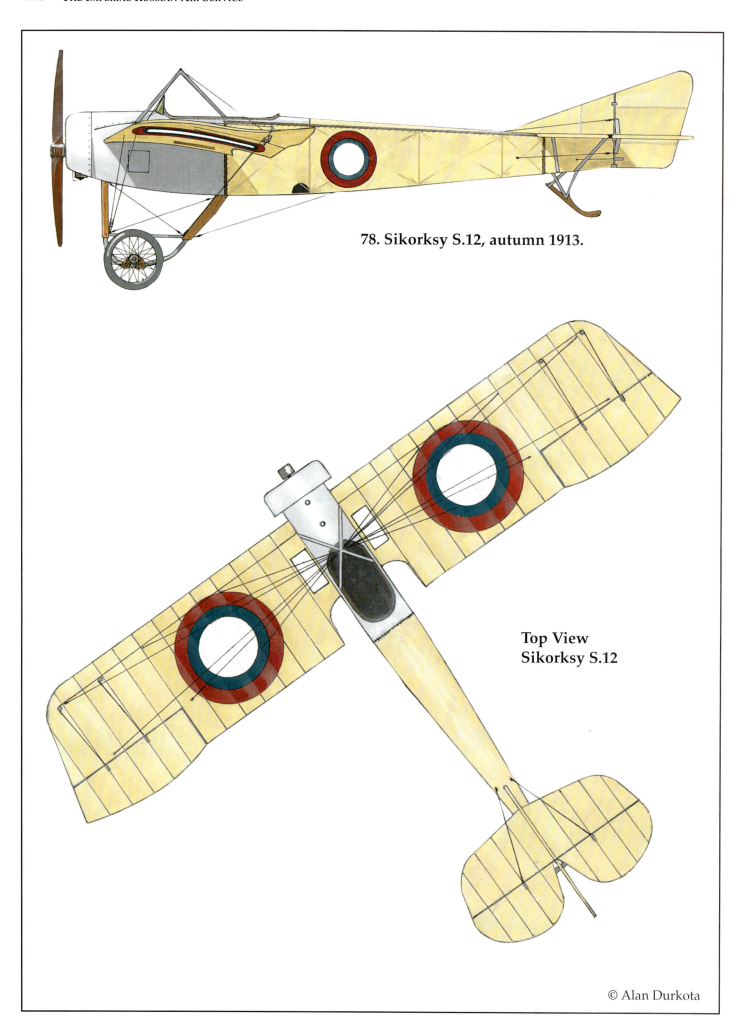

78. Sikorksy S.12, autumn 1913.

Top View
Sikorksy S.12

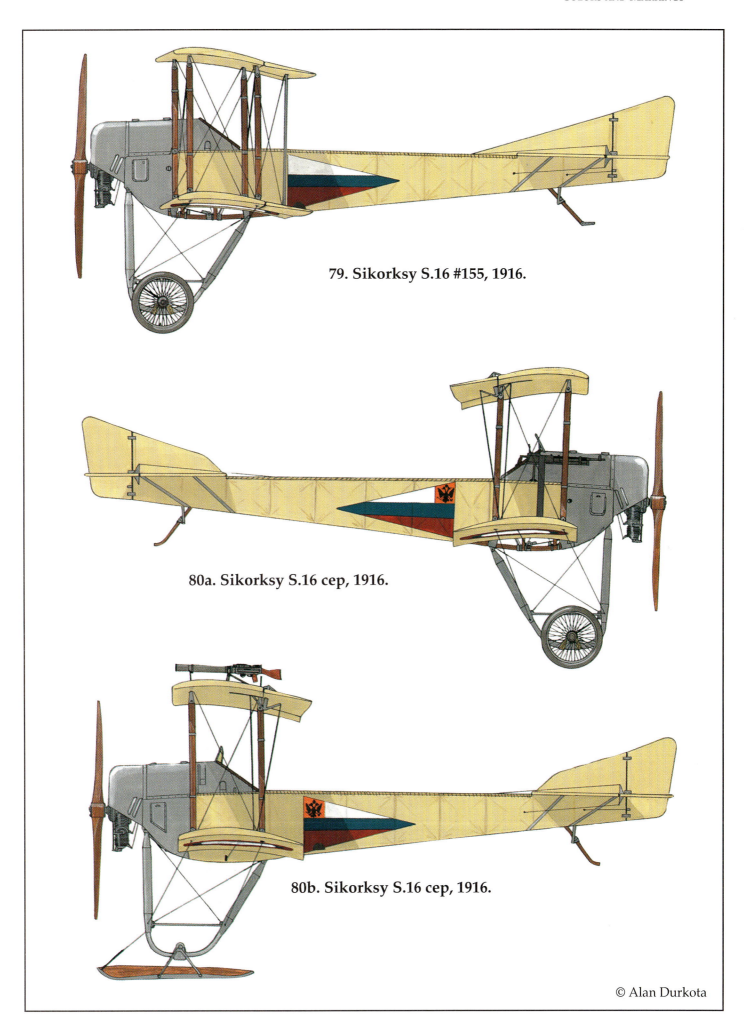

79. Sikorksy S.16 #155, 1916.

80a. Sikorksy S.16 сер, 1916.

80b. Sikorksy S.16 сер, 1916.

© Alan Durkota

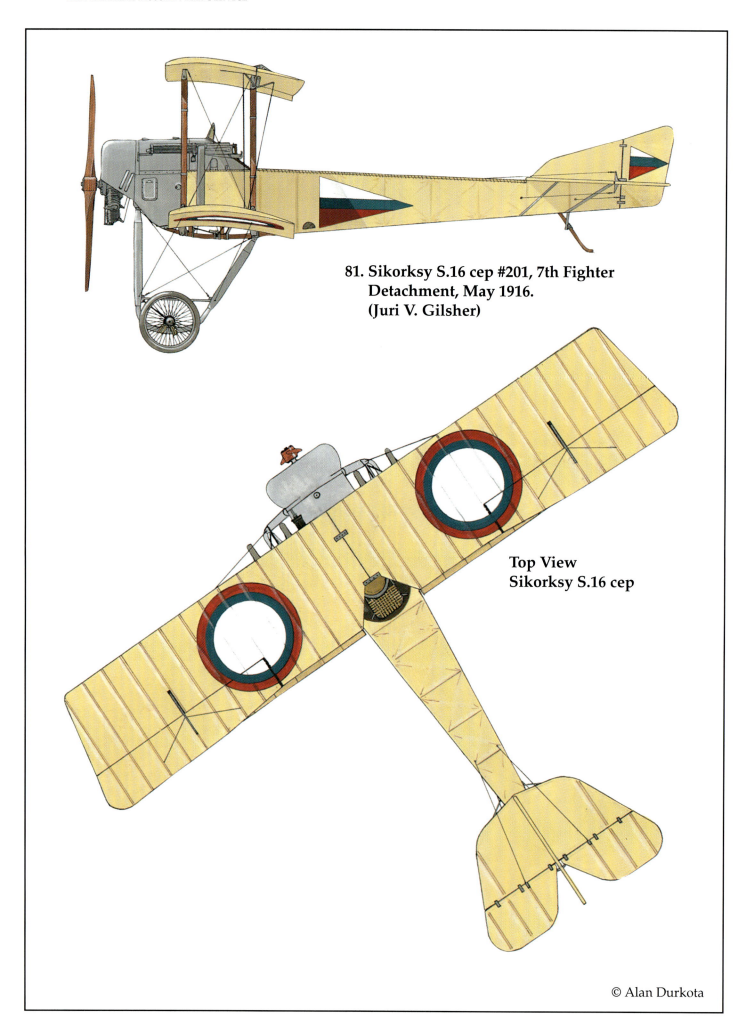

81. Sikorksy S.16 cep #201, 7th Fighter Detachment, May 1916. (Juri V. Gilsher)

Top View
Sikorksy S.16 cep

© Alan Durkota

Colors and Markings 431

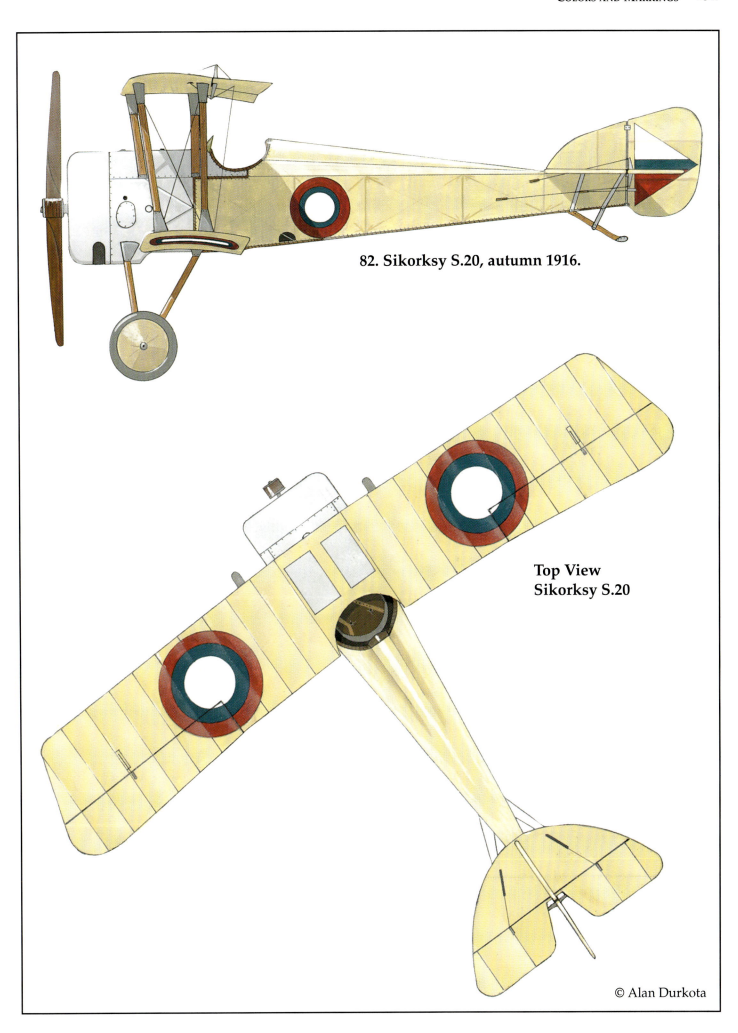

82. Sikorksy S.20, autumn 1916.

**Top View
Sikorksy S.20**

© Alan Durkota

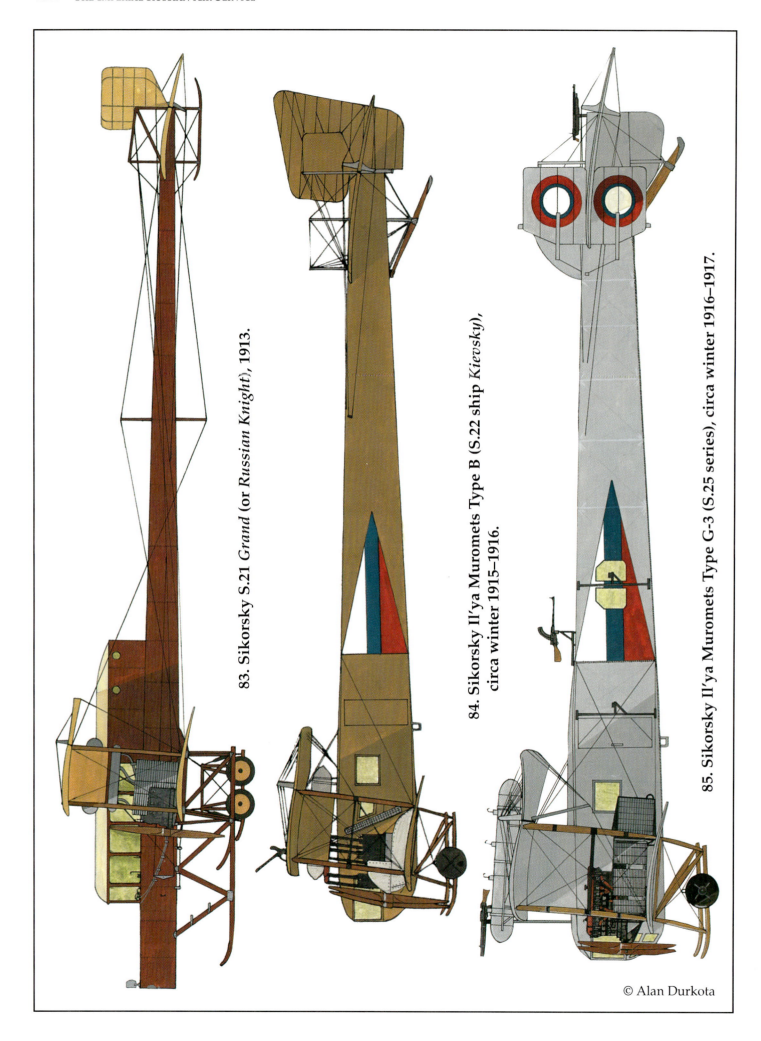

83. Sikorsky S.21 *Grand* (or *Russian Knight*), 1913.

84. Sikorsky Il'ya Muromets Type B (S.22 ship *Kievsky*), circa winter 1915–1916.

85. Sikorsky Il'ya Muromets Type G-3 (S.25 series), circa winter 1916–1917.

© Alan Durkota

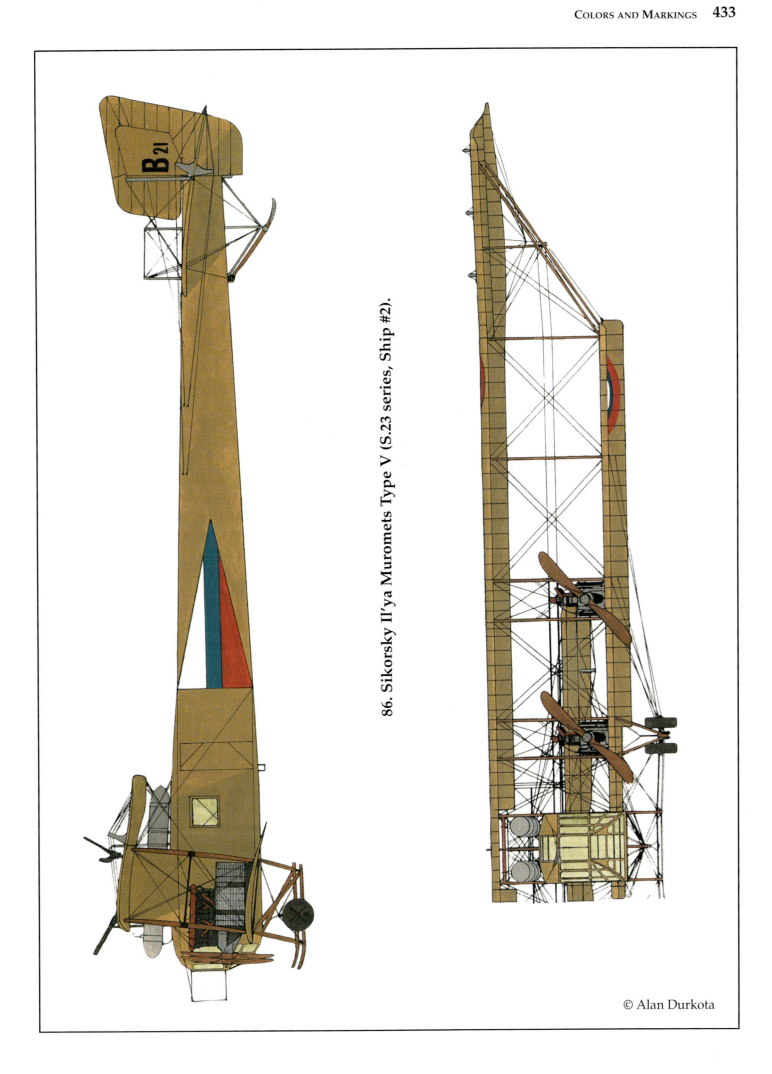

86. Sikorsky Il'ya Muromets Type V (S.23 series, Ship #2).

© Alan Durkota

434 The Imperial Russian Air Service

87. Alexander Seversky.

88. Yevgraph Kruten.

89. Naval Aviator, Black Sea Fleet.

Terry Waldron

Colors and Markings

90. Juri V. Gilsher.

91. Alexander Riaboff.

92. Army Aviator in Winter Coat.

Terry Waldron

93. *Flowers* by James Dietz.

94. *Yevgraph Nikoliavich Kruten* by James Dietz.

Order of St. George Fourth Class, Obverse

Order of St. George Fourth Class, Reverse

Cross of St. George First Class, Obverse

Cross of St. George First Class, Reverse

Cross of St. George First Class, Non-Christain, Reverse

St. George Medal First Class, Obverse

Colors and Markings 439

Order of St. Vladimir Third Class with Swords

Order of St. Vladimir Third Class with Swords, Reverse

Order of St. Anne Second Class with Swords

Order of St. Anne Second Class with Swords, Reverse

Order of St. Stanislas Second Class with Swords

Order of St. Stanislas Second Class, Reverse

440 THE IMPERIAL RUSSIAN AIR SERVICE

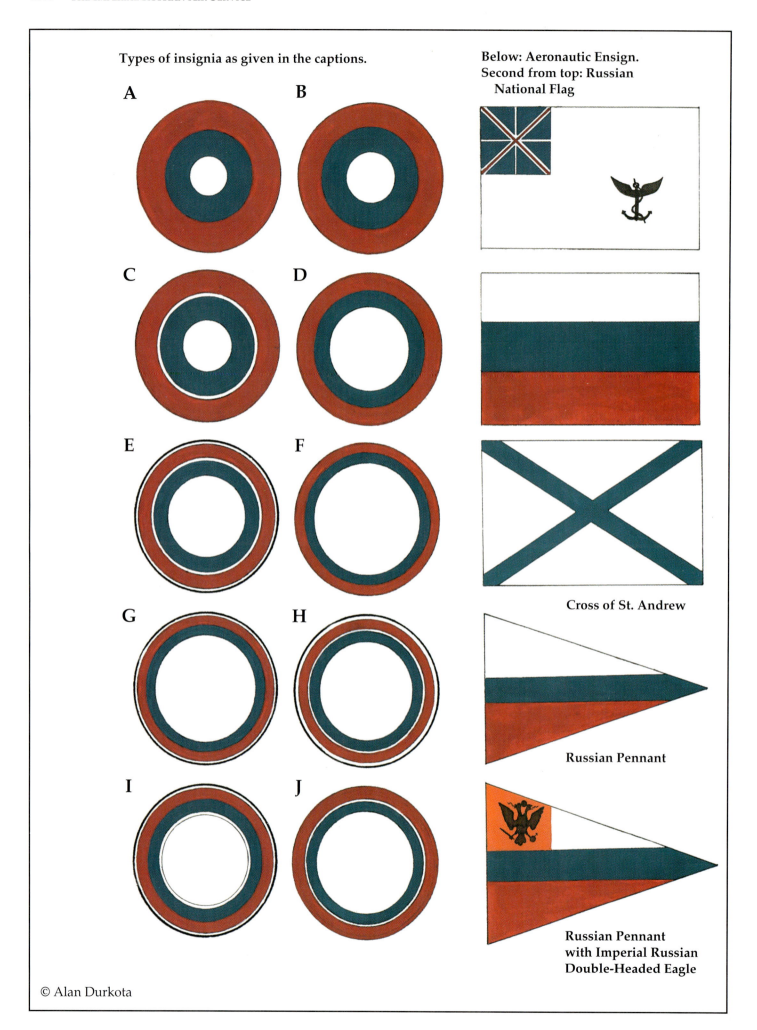

Types of insignia as given in the captions.

Below: Aeronautic Ensign.
Second from top: Russian National Flag

Cross of St. Andrew

Russian Pennant

Russian Pennant with Imperial Russian Double-Headed Eagle

© Alan Durkota

Section 8

Appendices

Appendix 1—The Aeronautical Corps

During the nineteenth century ballooning was becoming a popular form of entertainment and an adventurous sport in many countries around the world, including Russia. This interest inspired the first Russian aviation magazine, entitled *Vozdukhoplavatel* ('The Balloonist'), to be published in 1880. The balloon's use as a military weapon was first considered in 1869, when Dmitriy Miliutin, war minister to Czar Alexander II, established a committee to study the science of aeronautics for that specific purpose. In 1885 a balloonist school was built for the Russian army at Volkov field outside Saint Petersburg. This marked the beginning of the Russian army balloon corps and military aviation.

One balloon battalion was formed and used during the Russo-Japanese War of 1904–05; it proved successful in observing enemy activities. This led Russian military authorities to propose that more balloon units be established. In 1906 it was decided to form ten field aeronautical battalions. Within the next year three battalions and a training facility were established; in addition, several units were assigned to fortifications. By the end of 1912 the Russian army had 13 aeronautical companies equipped with captive balloons. However, airships were another story.

Airships of the Imperial Russian Balloon Corps

Other countries in Europe had a number of guided aerostats, as they were commonly called, in their arsenals, and with the threat of war in the Balkans, Russian authorities felt such craft should be acquired for military use. In 1909 the Russian army still had no airships and only a few had been built in Russia, as one-of-a-kind experiments.

In the 1880s the inventor O.S. Kostovich built an airship named *Rossiya* (Russia). It employed keel-girder construction and was not very successful. However, Kostovich also built the 80-horsepower engine used on the ship, that at the time was quite an accomplishment. In 1892 Konstantin E. Tsiolkovsky published an article on the construction of corrugated metal airships. The article was widely accepted throughout Europe and he was regarded highly in the Russian aviation community by his peers, including Professor Nikolai Zhukovsky. Shortly before the war he requested a grant from the government to build such a ship, but was refused. The designer Danilewsky built two ships in 1897–98 which were propelled by a bicycle transmission operating flapping wings. They lifted off the ground, but were not practical and were of no military value.

In September 1908 the Army Airship Works in Saint Petersburg built an experimental ship called the *Outchebny*, designed by *Kapitan* A.N. Shabski. It was of girderless construction, was equipped with a 50 hp Vivinus engine, and had a gas volume of 1800m³ (1800 cubic meters). Capable of only 23 miles per hour and carrying a crew of two, it became an army trainer, serving in that role for several years.[1]

In June 1909 the Russian army ordered its first craft from the Army Airship Works. The ship was named the *Krechet* and was developed by the Lebaudy brothers from a French design. It was of keel-girder construction and equipped with two 100 hp Panhard-Levassor engines giving a speed of 31 mph. The *Krechet* was finished 11 months later and made its maiden flight on July 30, 1910. After being accepted, it was assigned to the 9th Aeronautical Company in Riga.

For the next three years the Russian government purchased several airships from Germany and France of the Parcival, Zodiac, and Astra designs, and also several from Russian manufacturers. By the beginning of 1914 Russia had obtained a sizable airship armada, the fourth largest in the world and ahead of Britain, Austria, and Japan. The army had six airships of cruiser classification and nine small field scout craft.

Airships were classified into four types, based on size by internal gas capacity measured in cubic meters. The largest classification were the line-ships, with capacities of more than 10,000 m³. The next series were first-class cruisers, with a volume of greater than 7500m³ up to 10,000m³. After this were the second-class cruisers with volumes of between 5000m³ and 7500m³. Finally there were the small field scouts, with volumes of less than 5000m³.

The Russian army did not have any airships of the line-ship class, which were comparable to the German Z-class (Zeppelin class). It was not until February 1915 that the airship *Gigant*, with a volume of 18,000m³, was ready for testing.

The remaining three classes are listed in the following table,[2] specifying the data of the 15 airships in service.

This was the status of the Russian army airship fleet in January 1914, and it was practically unchanged six months later when hostilities began. The army had envisioned twice as many airships, hoping to have an equal number of large and field craft. An effort was made to expand airship territorial coverage by building several new airship sheds throughout European Russia. These totalled less than 28, of which at least four were built in 1914. The largest shed was 545 feet long and 157 feet wide.

---

(1) The *Outchebny*, also spelled *Uchebny*, was stated as being originally equipped with an 8 hp automobile engine, which was possible. It is likely the craft's engine was upgraded to the 50 hp unit at a later date.

(2) This table is compiled from specific data listed in the following sources; d'Orcy, Ladislau, *Airships of the World*, Century Co. 1917; Official US military reports from Lieutenant Sherman Miles, Military Attaché, Petrograd, 1913–1914; and Duz, P.D., *The history of aeronautics and aviation in the USSR for the period 1914–1918*, Moscow, 1944.

The Four First-Class Cruisers

Airship Name or Type	Size—Length x Beam (m)	Volume m³, Construction	Engine(s) and hp	Speed, Service Ceiling, Duration	Station and Balloon Co.	Notes
Parsival No. 14 *Burevestnik* (Storm Petrel)		10,000 non-rigid		47 mph 6500 feet	Berditchev, 4th Balloon Company	German-built 1913, crew 7–10
Astra No.13		9800 non-rigid	2 x 170	39 mph 8125 feet	Lida, 3rd Balloon Company	French-built 1913, crew 8–12
Clement-Bayard No.17 (Condor)		9600	2 x 130	34 mph 9750 feet	Brest, 2nd Balloon Company	French-built 1913, crew 7–10
Albatros		8000 non-rigid, car-girder type	2 x 150 Koerting engines	38 mph 6500 feet	Salizi-Gatchina, 12th Balloon Company	Izhorskii Co. 1913, crew 8–12, payload 3200kg

The Two Second-Class Cruisers

Airship Name or Type	Size—Length x Beam (m)	Volume m³, Construction	Engine(s) and hp	Speed, Service Ceiling, Duration	Station and Balloon Co.	Notes
Grif		6700	2 x 110		Berditchev	Parsival type
Krechet	70 x 14	5680 semi-rigid, keel-girder type	2 x 100 Panhard-Levassor engines	31 mph	Riga, 9th Balloon Company	Army Airship Works, 1910

The Nine Field Scout Airships

Airship Name or Type	Size—Length x Beam (m)	Volume m³, Construction	Engine(s) and hp	Speed, Service Ceiling, Duration	Station and Balloon Co.	Notes
Lebed (Swan)		3800	70		St. Petersburg	
Clement-Bayard No.1, possibly the *Berkut* (Golden Eagle)		2140 (conflicting report states 3500)	100	22 mph 6500 feet 10-hours	Brest, 2nd Balloon Company	French-built 1910, crew 5–8
Yastreb (Hawk)	50 x 13	2500	70 Dansette-Gillet engine	29 mph 5850 feet 6-hours	Salizi-Gatchina, 12th Balloon Company	Dux Co. 1910, crew 4
Sokol (Falcon)	50 x 10	2500 non-rigid, car-girder type	80 DeDion-Bouton engine	34 mph		Izhorskii Co. 1911
Golub (Dove)	46 x 9.5	2270 non-rigid, car-girder type	75 Koerting engine	31 mph 3250 feet 4-hours	Lida, 3rd Balloon Company	Izhorskii Co. 1911, crew 4
Kobtchik (Merlin)	48 x 9.5	2150 car-girder type	2 x 45	31 mph		Duflou and Constantinovitch, 1912 modified Zodiac plan
Tchaika (Seagull)		2140	60		Brest	Zodiac Co. design
Korshoun (Vulture)		2140	60		Far East	Zodiac Co. design
Mikst (Mushroom)						

Sheds were located in Berditchev, Brest-Litovsk, Dvinsk and St. Petersburg.[3]

[3] Another source states there were also large sheds in Grodno, Kovno, and Belostok.

The main airship manufacturers in Russia were the Izhorskii Works in St. Petersburg, the Army Airship Works in St. Petersburg, the Dux Company in Moscow, and the Russo-Baltic Wagon Works (R-BVZ) in Riga. Some of the chief designers were *Palkovnik* (Colonel) B.V. Golubov and D.S. Sukhorzhevskii, who were employed by Izhorskii. In 1911 they jointly designed the *Golub*, which was used for several reconnaissance and bombing trials; a searchlight was even added for experimental night missions. In 1913 this pair built the *Albatros*, which proved successful during the opening months of the war.

Kapitan A.M. Shabski not only developed the *Outchebny* for the Army Airship Works, but also designed the *Yastreb*, built by the Dux Company. After that, he helped General A.M. Kovanko build the *Gigant*[4] for the R-BVZ. The R-BVZ began the project in December, 1912, and was expected to deliver the airship in April, 1914.

The *Gigant* was to be of semi-rigid construction and approximately 350 feet long. It was to have four engines with a total horsepower of at least 600 and be capable of 40 mph minimum, reach an altitude of 11,500 feet, and carry enough fuel and oil for a 20-hour non-stop flight.

Completion was delayed until February, 1915, when the 18,000m^3 airship was ready for a trial flight. Unfortunately, during its maiden voyage the engines shifted, causing the *Gigant* to buckle. This in turn caused one of the airscrews to hit a bracing line and the craft collapsed, falling in a nearby forest. The damage was extensive, but not impossible to repair. The factory rebuilt the *Gigant* and it was ready for another test in October, 1915. However, the high command refused to supply the necessary hydrogen. The gas, in short supply, was of

---

(4) There are conflicting reports on the actual statistics for *Gigant* (Giant). It is listed as being 262 feet with two 160 hp engines and a volume of 13,000m^3; also 444 feet with four 215 hp engines and a volume of 20,000m^3; and finally 492 feet with a volume of 30,000m^3. The minimum requirements were stated as 344 feet with four 150 hp engines and a volume of 18,000m^3. It can be assumed the manufacturer held the dirigible reasonably close to these requirements.

Below: The personnel of the 4th Siberian Aeronautical Company, circa 1912. This was one of the first balloon units assembled in the Russian army.

An army balloon leaving the ground. Training flights such as these were conducted in the late nineteenth century from Volkov Field, the location of the army balloon school founded in 1885. This was the beginning of Russian military aviation.

Appendix 1—The Aeronautical Corps 445

The *Outchebny* airship; built in 1908, it was designed by *Kapitan* A.N. Shabski. It was originally powered by an 8 hp motor, but is reported to have a 50 hp motor and attain a speed of 23mph. It was used as a trainer by the army for several years.

Right: The *Krechet* was the first airship ordered by the army and accepted into service. It was built in St. Petersburg from a French design and first flew on July 30, 1910. Soon after, it was assigned to the 9th Aeronautical Company stationed in Riga.

Below: Drawings of the *Krechet* showing starboard side and bottom views with dimensions. The vast bracing wires and control surfaces, as well as the crew's compartment and location of the twin airscrews, can be seen to good advantage.

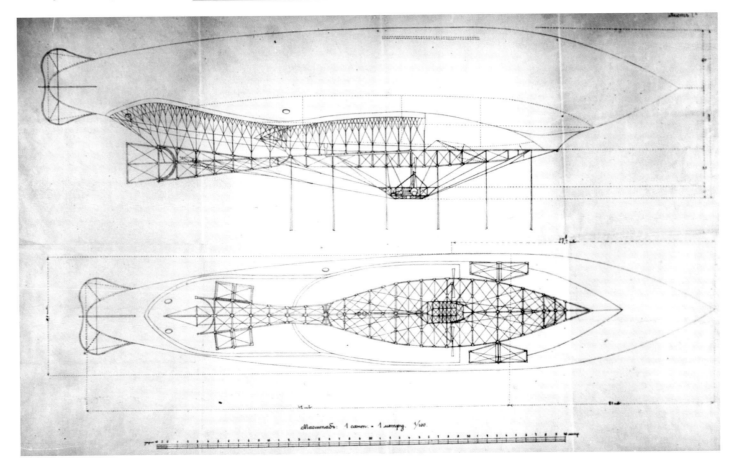

The field scout *Golub* (Dove), designed by B.V. Golubov and D.S. Sukhorzhevskii, was built at the Izhorskii Works in 1911. While serving with the 3rd Aeronautical Company, its main role was performing reconnaissance and bombing trials. Later, a searchlight was added for experimenting with night maneuvers.

greater importance to the captive balloon units. The amount required to fill the *Gigant* would service eight aeronautical companies for a month. By the end of 1915, airships were viewed as being excessively vulnerable to enemy ground fire and aircraft. The authorities therefore believed it was wasteful to use the gas supply on this experimental airship. By the middle of 1916 the *Gigant* was disassembled and its parts recycled for use on smaller balloons and aircraft.

In the summer of 1914 the Izhorskii Company began planning an airship larger than the *Gigant*. The two designers, Golubov and Sukhorzhevskii, headed the project, which the war department encouraged. The *Aerial Cruiser*, as it was named, was required to have a volume of 25,000m³ and a minimum speed of 52mph when equipped with two 250 hp engines. It was to have a range of 185 miles, reach an altitude of 8200 feet, and carry a one-ton bomb load for a 15 to 20 hour flight. The *Aerial Cruiser* was to be 426 feet long, with a height of 92 feet. The ship was nearly ready for a trial flight in the early summer of 1916, but, due to a shortage of hydrogen, testing was postponed indefinitely.

The only other attempt at providing a line-ship for the army was purchase of one from France. A 20,000m³ guided craft was ordered from the Clement-Bayard firm, but due to delays and loss of interest was never delivered.

Airship crews consisted of a commander, a deputy commander, observers, machine-gunners, mechanics, and a radio operator. Equipment included one to three machine guns with ammunition and spare parts, a radio set, photographic apparatus, and bombs.

Wartime operations soon exposed the airships' inadequacies. Most of the small field scouts were outdated in August 1914. They were too slow and flew at low altitudes, rendering them vulnerable to enemy artillery fire. There were also at least ten different types of craft, requiring mechanical knowledge of every type and a vast spare parts inventory. The cruisers were the most effective, but even they became obsolete by the summer of 1915.

Wartime successes were few, but there were some. Airships still had a considerably greater range than airplanes during the opening months of the war. The 2nd Aeronautical Company, stationed at the fortress of Brest-Litovsk, had good success using the *Condor* and the *Berkut*. Although specific dates and details are not known, the *Condor* did report valuable information on enemy troop movements to army headquarters via radio. The two ships were used to bomb German ammunition depots, rail centers, and, on one occasion, frontline troops during the spring of 1915, which caused enough damage (or resentment) that the enemy retaliated by raiding the fortress at Brest-Litovsk for several days and bombing the airship hangars. Due to the increase of enemy aerial activity, combined with the airships' lack of mobility, the ships of the 2nd Aeronautical Company could not defend themselves and both were destroyed during the summer of 1915.

While stationed at Lida with the 3rd Aeronautical Company the *Astra* successfully bombed the enemy rail center at Lyck in early 1915, destroying both troop and ammunition cars. It remained in service until the end of the war, but was not reported as being used after mid-1915.

Appendix 1—The Aeronautical Corps 447

The *Lebed* (Swan) was the largest of the field scouts at 3800 cubic meters. It was stationed in St. Petersburg, but nothing is known of its service record. It flies the Aeronautical Corps flag.

Right: The *Astra XIII* was a French-built dirigible of 9800 cubic meter volume. It was a twin-engine, first class cruiser, capable of 39mph. During the war it served with the 3rd Aeronautical Company and saw action over the Polish Salient and East Prussia in early 1915.

Below: The *Albatros* entered service in 1913, and was assigned to the 12th Aeronautical Company stationed at Salizi, near St. Petersburg. A first-class cruiser, it was equipped with twin engines and could carry a bomb load of 3200kg. It was used on several raids along the Northern Front in 1914 and early 1915, and has the distinction of being the only Russian-built airship to participate in combat. It was lost during a raid when it encountered bad weather.

Airship *Dux* built by the Dux factory.

The *Albatros*, assigned to the 12th Aeronautical Company, made many raids over the Baltic Sea and against German forces on the northern front before it was destroyed during inclement weather. Available evidence shows the *Albatros* to be the only Russian-built airship to fly combat missions; the others were French-built.

During the great retreat in the summer of 1915 the Russians lost two important facilities. The mill at Sosnovitsa, where hydrogen was stored, was lost, and the base of the 2nd Aeronautical Company was destroyed. These setbacks, along with the fact that airships were becoming almost impossible to defend in the air, forced the Russian high command to decide not to accept any more of the craft. In fact, not one was accepted after hostilities began. Airships were phased out of service and by the autumn of 1915, only captive balloons remained in service with the aeronautical companies.

Kite Balloons of the Imperial Russian Balloon Corps

The kite balloon, or stationary aerostat, sailed in the air much like a kite, suspended from lines attached to the winch on the ground. The observers perched in the basket had a difficult assignment, with the wind buffeting the balloon and under constant threat of attack by enemy aircraft or artillery. The work of the balloon observers was of utmost importance, especially in directing artillery fire.

In August 1914, the Aeronautical Corps had 46 kite balloons and 37 motor-driven winches. This seemed adequate, but failure to increase production of the materials and equipment required by the balloon corps greatly hampered efficiency. Long supply lines caused delays in receiving material, and when equipment was delivered it was often faulty and difficult to operate. However, when these problems were overcome the balloon observers provided excellent information to their infantry corps and artillery batteries.

The balloons were Parcival-type designs similar to the German *drachen*. They were 84 feet long and had a capacity of 750m^3.[5] The design was little more than a cylindrical shape with rounded ends, giving the appearance of a sausage. A smaller-diameter lobe was attached to the underside of the body along the rear half of the centerline, curving up around the rear to act as a rudder. This section was not filled with gas; it was open at the front and filled with air when the balloon was aloft, providing stability. As the war progressed, the balloons increased in size, first to 850m^3 and later to 1000m^3. Balloons of larger capacity were able to lift two observers to a greater height for a longer time. A balloon could maintain its ability to lift its crew to a maximum altitude of 800 to 1000 meters for a period of less than two weeks before it would begin to show signs of deterioration. To counter this, a special material was used for the envelope. In November 1916, First Lieutenant Francis Riggs, the military attaché of the U.S. embassy, reported the material as "of light gray colored silk."[6] It was actually rubberized cotton cloth, providing strength and protection from exposure to the elements. Riggs also found the balloon difficult to see clearly, perhaps because his view was from below with the sky as background.

An improved type of kite balloon, called the Caquot after its designer, was developed in France. A few of these balloons were purchased, but not until 1917. They provided greater stability and could reach a higher altitude; unfortunately, not enough were in service in the Russian Balloon Corps.

---

(5) Duz, op. cit.
(6) Official report on Russian observation balloons, by U. S. First Lieutenant E. Francis Riggs, military attaché to Russia, dated November 20, 1916.

A typical Parcival-style observation balloon with two-man crew, displaying the Aeronautical Corps flag as identification. This photo was taken early in the war during the summer of 1914.

The winches were almost all horse drawn, with very few being transported by truck. The winches sustained much abuse and needed replacement after a year of service. Many of the early horse-drawn units were made by Dublou and Constantinovich, but were of poor quality and functioned poorly. They were difficult to transport because of their 1.5-ton weight. Their engines developed only 30 horsepower, which required manpower to help lower the balloon. Three groups of 15 enlisted men were attached to a harness device and pulled simultaneously like plow horses. The engine overheated easily and then failed to operate. Not until 1917 was a winch produced that had a reliable engine of 45 hp fitted to the chassis of a 1.5-ton truck and was capable of lowering a balloon at the rate of about 200 feet per minute. This winch was easy to operate and had vastly improved mobility, allowing a balloon to be moved while it was airborne. The Russian balloon crews were grateful for this luxury item, although they lagged behind other nations that were already using truck-driven winches of greater power.[7]

The aerostats were filled with hydrogen produced chemically. Two gas-generating devices were in use. The first, obtained from France before the war, employed the 'Oxylite' system to produce gas by an alkali-silicon reaction using silicol, caustic soda, and water. It could produce 300m³ of hydrogen per hour and was operated by a crew of 10 to 15. Most were horse-drawn, although some were mounted on trucks. These machines were very heavy and difficult to transport.

The other system, of Russian design, incorporated an alkali-aluminum mixture. It became the main type in service. The unit was mounted on eight two-wheeled carts divided into two sections, with a crew of 60 to operate it. Each section had two generators, one cooler, and one pump and produced 100m³ of gas per hour. However, this was in short supply as only one factory in Russia manufactured it. During 1914 there were only 22 hydrogen-producing systems in service, and many more were required. There was also a limited amount of gas produced at the caustic soda factories near St. Petersburg and delivered to the front in large pipes, but this was not enough to solve the problem.[8]

Not only were the systems in short supply, but the chemicals, especially silicol and aluminum, were hard to find. To obtain them the Russians had to rely on their allies, but, like other essential items, they came slowly over long supply routes. Requirements for the first year and a half were set at 3500 tons of silicol, 13,265 tons of aluminum, and 70,000 tons of caustic soda. Russian production, even supplemented by imports, could not supply these quantities, which in reality were underestimated—especially the amount of aluminum.[9]

The balloon corps suffered many problems. A very limited number of private concerns were involved in manufacturing the necessary materials. Chemicals for

(7) Duz, op. cit.

(8) Ibid.
(9) Ibid.

This balloon is being tended on the ground by unit personnel, who are possibly anchoring it after a mission. This view shows to good advantage the limp fabric of the small lobe attached to the underside of the aerostat. This piece was not filled with gas, but would inflate with wind while aloft to provide stability.

A Russian field aeronautical unit launching a balloon. Horse-drawn supply wagons can be seen to the left. This photo was submitted by U. S. Lieutenant Francis Riggs with his report on Russian observation balloons in November 1916, when he was the military attaché stationed in St. Petersburg.

providing hydrogen were not properly distributed. There were no distinct supply depots established in forward areas for the aeronautical units. There were no motor vehicles designed for transporting such materials, only horse-drawn wagons, and the distance over which supplies had to be transported was huge, taking much time. All these difficulties contributed to balloon corps inefficiency. Unfortunately, these problems were never solved.

The complement of each aeronautical company was originally two, later increased to three, balloon units, known as observation posts or stations.[10] Each post had two captive balloons, one of which was held in reserve. Each company was maintained by 60 to 100 enlisted men. Each had an auxiliary detachment in charge of supply and communications with the infantry or artillery corps in the sector.

There were two types of aeronautical companies, field units and fortress units, which were under the direct command of their assigned corps headquarters or fortress commander. Since greater emphasis was placed on providing fortresses with aeronautical companies, only two field companies were able to conduct operations when the war began. It was therefore decided to disband the Battalion of Officers Balloon School and form three new aeronautical companies and a reserve balloon battalion, although not all were designated as field units.[11]

At first, companies engaged only in reconnaissance. It soon became apparent there was a need for artillery spotting, and some observation posts were placed under

---

(10) Due to gas shortages, each post was allotted only 4000m^3 of hydrogen per year. Fortunately, a filled aerostat could continue operating for a month with only an additional 50 cubic meters of gas per day.

(11) Duz, op. cit.

A crew beginning to send a balloon aloft. The equipment includes horse-drawn wagons, which carried the heavy gas-producing machines and winches throughout most of the war.

the command of artillery divisions by corps commanders. Observation for artillery spotting could be done for up to 5.5 miles under normal conditions, and sometimes up to nearly 9 miles. Balloons could perform this duty more efficiently than airplanes, due to their ability to maintain constant communication with the ground and remain in the same location throughout an operation.

The balloon observer had maps, telephones and related communication equipment, a carbine, and an assortment of powerful telescopes. Theoretically, every ascent lasted approximately two hours, but this could change according to circumstances. Lieutenant Riggs reported "From my own observation, it would seem that one or two 'sausages' in a sector remain in the air at critical points during daylight. The full number take to the air only during an action. I watched a group of 'sausages' during an action and each one came down to the ground about every hour." He was also told by a Russian officer on the Southwest Front that each battery of artillery was assigned an observation post of an aeronautical company. Riggs correctly believed this statement was exaggerated. However, on one occasion he did witness six balloons attached to two army corps and believed there to be more balloon units on both flanks of these corps.[12]

The 14th Aeronautical Company was one of the three units created from the disbanded Battalion of Officers

(12) Riggs report, op. cit.

Balloon School and was assigned to the Ivangorod fortress, beginning operations mid-September 1914. It maintained continuous service throughout the autumn months of 1914. An original member of the unit, *Praporshik* (Ensign) N.I. Shabashev, described his experiences and the group's operations. First, he and the other observers had to become familiar with the fort and the surrounding area. Next, they learned to recognize enemy positions and detect troop movements. Finally, they were trained to direct artillery fire. Throughout the remainder of September the winds blew at 40 to 50 mph, creating turbulence which made it difficult to complete a mission. Enemy artillery fire was also encountered, which interrupted procedures. Operating under conditions such as these, balloonists had to be in excellent physical condition as well as mentally alert.

Despite poor weather, Shabashev and the 14th Company continued observation in October. They located enemy batteries, trench embankments, and camps in rear areas revealed by campfires. Russian artillery shelled enemy battery emplacements while the 14th Company observers corrected the fire. This saved the railroad bridge over the Vistula River, an important Russian supply line. They directly helped defeat an approaching German column by directing fire on it. Later, they detected the retreat of the enemy troops.

At the end of October the fortress commander wrote

An observation balloon secured in a wooded area, guarded by a sentry from an aeronautical post. This view shows to good advantage the observer's basket, the rope attachments to the envelope, and the deflated lobe on the rear of the balloon which was filled by wind upon ascent, not by gas.

Above and below: Two views of a typical field company hard at work, tending to the balloons, preparing them for another day's work. The balloons are left uncovered and exposed to the elements. This led to deterioration, requiring the use of a rubberized fabric for the envelope.

of the importance of the work of the 14th company, stating it was, "valiant and useful."[13] Many times rain and fog, combined with smoke from fires, lowered visibility, making the job very difficult.

After the retreat during the summer of 1915, many of the fortresses were overrun, reducing the need for this type of balloon company. The need for field companies, however, increased. By the end of 1915 the fortress units were transformed into field companies, increasing their number to 25. At that point each army received at least two or three aeronautical companies. The front had stabilized and trench warfare became the norm, creating the need for more observation and artillery spotting. By the spring of 1916 the Germans brought more of their balloons to the east and many artillery duels commenced.

One such took place on April 29, 1916, between an enemy balloon directing artillery on the balloon of the Russian 2nd Observation Post of the 12th Aeronautical Company. The unit was stationed near Dvinsk along the Northern Front, and its 2nd Observation Post was located near the village of Katenevka when an important reconnaissance mission was ordered to locate enemy batteries and observe the frontline trenches and rear areas. The official report stated: "For nearly 19 hours the enemy fired from heavy artillery at the aerostat, which was manned by *Stabs-Kapitan* Boshenyatov and *Praporshik* Anoshchenko[14] as observers. The enemy carried out ranging with extreme rapidity; shells bursting in close proximity to the aerostat winch. Hence, the commander of the 12th Company (*Podpolkovnik* Prince Baratov), undertook a maneuver of taking the winch together with the raised aerostat out of fire. In the beginning the winch

---

(13) Shabashev, N., *Privyaznoe Vozdukhoplavanie 1914–1917* (Captive Ballooning During 1914–1917), Moscow, 1921.

(14) Anoshchenko served as an observer with the 12th Aeronautical Company throughout 1916. After the reorganization of balloon units, he was promoted to commander of the 5th Aeronautical Detachment.

Appendix 1—The Aeronautical Corps 453

This view appears to be an entire aeronautical company, with nine balloons anchored at rest. This unit may be in reserve awaiting assignment. Once again, all balloons are left uncovered. Later, large tents were issued for use as hangars.

There were either two or three observation posts to each aeronautical company. This view shows a standard post securing its balloons within a small clearing in a wooded area.

Another view of an observation post securing its balloon after a mission. A canvas barrier has been installed for what appears as a wind barrier for added protection.

Praporshik (Ensign) N.I. Shabashev in the basket of his balloon, about to ascend. Shabashev served with the 14th Aeronautical Company at the beginning of the war when the unit was stationed at the Ivangorod Fortress, and made several successful observations.

(weighing more than 200 *pud* [7060 lb.]) was carried by lower ranks, and when local conditions permitted, horses were harnessed.

"Firing, which was spotted evidently from an enemy captive aerostat, was so accurate that as soon as the winch was withdrawn, its location was immediately showered with shells. Shelling prolonged for 1.5 hours; the enemy fired 144 shells total.

"When the aerostat was under fire, as it offered a big target (nearly 12 *sajens* [84 ft.] in length), the enemy was observed from the aerostat basket. The heavy battery firing shells was accurately determined; a report on its location, caliber, and number of guns was sent to the Headquarters of the 23rd Army Corps, to the Inspector of the Artillery of the 29th Army Corps, and to the Chief of Heavy Artillery on the left bank of the Dvina River. At the same time, location of trenches of the second line were also detected. Reconnaissance conducted in this connection was the basis of further reconnaissance in the enemy's rear.

"Thanks to successful maneuvering of the winch with the aerostat in the sky, the task of reconnaissance was carried out without loss of personnel, despite obvious danger threatening the lives of observers as well as the lives of the entire team who selflessly took the aerostat out of range of the shelling."(15)

At the start of 1917 aeronautical companies were reorganized into army and corps balloon detachments and assigned to balloon divisions in a similar structure to that of aircraft units. Aeronautical supply depots were introduced to service the divisions. Four depots were formed, one designated to each front; the Northwest, West, Southwest, and Romanian. Unfortunately, they were too far from the fighting to help relieve the supply problem.

By the autumn of 1917 there were 88 detachments, 59 corps and 29 army, equipped with almost 200 balloons and 28,000 enlisted personnel serving in 14 divisions.(16) All detachments included three observation posts. There were two fortress detachments still in service, one at Revel and one at Sveaborg, making a grand total of 90 aeronautical detachments. Despite the growth of the balloon corps, the Russian army did not possess enough balloons to cover the vast front. Army headquarters had requested one detachment for each infantry division, but this was impossible due to shortages of material and trained observers.

Use of parachutes came into practice for balloonists to jump from the basket when being attacked by enemy aircraft. If the balloon was hit by incendiary bullets the highly flammable hydrogen would ignite, disintegrating the craft within 20 seconds. This left the observer little time to react and escape the same fate. Early in the war only a few units were equipped with the parachute design known as *zhukmes*. These were of French design and set in a case tied to the observer's basket. They were considered unreliable and balloonists preferred not to use them.

G.E. Kotelnikov developed a pack parachute in late 1916 and some were manufactured by Treugol'nik in St. Petersburg. This chute was packed in a metal case and involved too many steps for the observer and required several spring-loaded mechanical operations, any of which could malfunction. Each post was given only one of these chutes, even though two observers usually performed each mission.

One method used to assure the parachute would not tangle was to suspend it loosely from the side of the basket while it was still attached to the observer. With the

---

(15) Duz, op. cit., from a report taken from, Anoshchenko, N. D. *Samolety ili Aerostaty* (Airplanes and Aerostats), Moscow, 1924.
(16) Duz, op. cit.

Above and below: Two views of an aeronautical company in 1915 manually transporting a balloon across an open field. A sudden gust of wind that has lifted the back of the balloon with the ground crew, hanging onto the tie-down lines, suspended in the air. The practice of moving an ascended balloon did not evolve until the introduction of the truck-driven winch in 1917.

A captive balloon aloft during the cold winter months. The observer's job was made even more difficult than normal by the elements, requiring that balloon crewmen be in good physical condition.

parachute already in a semi-opened position, it could catch the wind more easily and would be less apt to fail. One disadvantage of this method was that any large gust of wind could lift the occupant out of the basket. This happened to balloon observer Mishchkoit of the 6th Balloon detachment on January 25, 1917. He landed safely, but the initial shock must have been frightening.

Another attempt was made at modifying the Kotelnikov parachute by balloon observer *Podporuchik* N. D. Anoshchenko. He developed a system of suspending the parachute shroud in a cloth case hanging from the side of the balloon, thus eliminating both the possibility of a tangle and of being caught by a strong wind. Many successful tests were conducted by Anoshchenko's detachment in early 1917. Later, Kotelnikov did away with the metal container, substituting a more modern soft pack. In May 1917, this was tested by the 28th Corps Aeronautical Detachment with excellent results.

Despite the favorable outcome of this test, the Kotelnikov units were not issued in quantity. The *zhukmes* replaced them, even after a failure during testing in February, 1917. In May, 1917, Anoshchenko tested the *zhukmes* himself and his conclusions assured other Russian observers that the device was acceptable. Other balloon detachment commanders confirmed Anoshchenko's report and the demand for *zhukmes* increased. By summer 1917, an order was placed with the Treugol'nik Company for 100 units.[17]

During 1917, even after several positive tests at detachment level, parachute operations continued to be tragic. Out of 62 jumps made in combat conditions, 5 with Kotelnikov and 57 with *zhukmes*, 17 resulted in death, a 27% fatality rate.[18]

One further attempt was made by a balloon division to develop its own prototype, which was considered very modern in design. It was tested by the 20th Aeronautical Detachment with good results. Unfortunately, nothing was done to further develop this product, or to manufacture the improved Kotelnikov unit.

Although balloon units had difficulties, they managed to perform their duties. Many units excelled at directing artillery and surveillance of enemy positions and maneuvers. In most instances, army corps and balloon units stationed in the same area became very familiar with each other's activities. This produced positive results until

---

(17) Ibid. The Treugol'nik Company did not have silk to make parachutes; eventually they were purchased from France.
(18) Ibid.

Above: The 9th Aeronautical Company lofting a balloon, spring 1916. This open field appears to have unfavorable wind conditions, as the balloon's tail lobe has immediately filled with air and the side flaps are also extended. The horse-drawn carts are of interest and seem to be carrying the alkali-aluminum type hydrogen-producing apparatus.

A kite balloon aloft with *Praporshik* (Ensign) N.D. Anoshchenko as one of the observers. He served with the 12th Aeronautical Company during 1916, and was involved in an artillery duel with a German *drachen* which lasted 19 hours. Eventually he was able to direct his own artillery to silence the enemy battery. In 1917 Anoshchenko was promoted to *Poruchik* (1st Lieutenant) and given command of the 5th Aeronautical Detachment.

the unit was transferred, resulting in each having to become familiar with another unit. Command centers along the front constantly repeated this procedure, unaware of the consequences of these actions. Fortunately, in early 1917, aeronautical detachments were permanently assigned to infantry corps. However, this was not so for artillery units, which needed the greatest amount of coordination with a balloon unit.

Although a number of balloons were destroyed by enemy airplanes,[19] Russian balloon detachments brought down their share of attackers. When these attacks increased, the aeronautical detachments were issued machine guns and a few artillery pieces. In addition, the observers had an 11-shot Winchester rifle in the basket. It

---
(19) Available sources state a total of 54 were destroyed, six in 1916 and 48 in 1917, seven of these while on the ground.

Appendix 1—The Aeronautical Corps 457

An enemy plane photographed from a Russian balloon. Incendiary ammunition fired from such aircraft would explode the balloon's hydrogen, destroying the craft within 20 seconds. To escape death observers had to depend on parachutes, but these were unreliable. In 1917, 27% of all parachute jumps from balloons resulted in fatalities.

A balloon aloft as viewed by ground gunners charged with defending it against hostile aircraft. Without their protection the balloons, whose observers were armed only with rifles, were virtually defenseless and easy targets.

Below: A gun crew, possibly attached to an aeronautical detachment as protection against enemy aircraft. The observer on the right with field glasses apparently has spotted something approaching.

was of little use but gave the crew some reassurance.

Throughout the final year of the war 15 enemy aircraft were shot down by aeronautical units. Shabashev's unit, the 14th Company, shot down the first on September 23, 1916, sending a hostile aircraft into a wire entanglement in front of the enemy trenches.

In 1917 three detachments were credited with two victories each. The 9th Corps achieved this feat first, scoring their second triumph on July 6. The enemy aircraft crashed near the flamed balloon, with both enemy crewmen wounded by machine-gun fire. The 4th Army Aeronautical Detachment captured two planes in two days, bringing them down on August 7 and 8, without loss of the balloon.

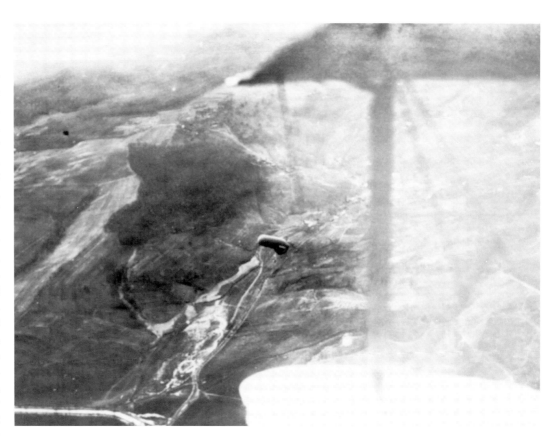

A Russian kite balloon photographed from an Austrian aircraft of *Fliegerkompanie* (Flik) 14 during 1917. The Austrian crew may have been sent to destroy the balloon. Forty-eight Russian balloons were destroyed during 1917 by enemy attacks, but sometimes Russian gunners of the aeronautical detachments were victorious.

The 1st Army Balloon Detachment scored in quick succession, bringing down two enemy machines in a little more than two hours. On September 7, 1917, at 11:30, the first attack came and was driven off from the fire below; as the observer of the 1st unit, Gubarev, reported, the plane crashed between the lines. At 1:45 a second enemy plane was hit and captured with little damage near Berestechko, where its crew was taken prisoner.

The last recorded victory of a balloon unit was on September 29, 1917, when the 11th Army Aeronautical Detachment hit the engine of an Austrian plane with machine-gun fire, causing it to glide to a landing in the vicinity of Brody. The enemy crew did not succeed in destroying the balloon, but managed to burn their Brandenburg C.I. The machine, serial number 69.96, was flown by *Zugsführer* Bela Fejes, pilot, and *Leutnant* Paul Mayer, observer, of Flik 14. They were put in the custody of the 2nd Fighter Detachment at Radzivilov until sent to a prison camp.

Leutnant (2nd Lieutenant) Paul Mayer, observer, and *Zugsführer* (Sergeant) Bela Fejes, pilot, of *Fliegerkompanie* (Flik) 14, were shot down and taken prisoners after failing to destroy a kite balloon. The 11th Army Aeronautical Detachment shot down their Brandenburg C.I, serial number 69.96, on September 29, 1917, in the vicinity of Brody. It was the last recorded victory during the war for a balloon detachment. The Austrian crew succeeded in burning their plane before it could be captured intact. They are seen here at Radzivilov as guests of the 2nd Fighter Detachment.

Imperial Russian Orders, Medals, Badges, and Decorations Awarded to Aviators in World War One

For most of the young army and navy officers of Imperial Russia, receipt of an award or special badge was the height of ambition—understandable in a generation schooled in self-discipline and sense of duty and knowing no other way of life. Decorations represented and symbolized a successful professional career, and to obtain such symbols no risk was too great and no chance too dangerous to take.

"A man won't sell you his life,
but he'll give it to you for a piece of colored ribbon."
Old Soldier's Saying

The military historian who understands the statutes of an award and the circumstances in which it was obtained may better perceive the man. The photographic researcher who can identify various awards may be aided in determining a photograph's date and gain other clues to information. This appendix will cover all the major Imperial Russian awards that a pilot or observer could have obtained.

Order of Saint George

For an officer in Imperial Russia, the highest decoration was the Order of Saint George. It was the supreme tribute and carried great prestige. It was given for exceptional heroism, often on a single occasion but at times for superior performance in a series of engagements. Statutes were issued emphasizing that neither past service, nor rank, nor wounds received in battle were to influence the recommendation for the award. The order, like all the higher military orders of Imperial Russia, was also bestowed on men in important commands, and also given to those of royalty. During World War I, several notable foreigners also were awarded the order.

All Russian rulers, with the exception of Emperor Paul I, were made Knights of the Order of Saint George. It was Emperor Alexander I who greatly increased the prestige of the order by refusing to decorate himself with it until he fulfilled all the conditions for the award. It was not until 13 December, 1805, after his successful campaign against Napoleon, that he accepted the order, and then permitting himself to wear only the fourth, or lowest, class.

The order was founded on 26 November, 1769, by Empress Catherine II to reward her officers for deeds of exceptional bravery. Although the award was issued in four classes (first being the highest), the first and second class could be bestowed only on the personal decree of the emperor and the third and fourth upon close examination and approval by a group of Saint George Knights known as the Georgevsky Council located in St. Petersburg. An exception was made during wartime, when a commanding general could bestow the fourth class in the field if the recommendation had the approval of at least seven Knights of the order.

In 1913 the statutes of the order were revised. Various books list some of the more important regulations; the following list is taken from data at the Rodina Russian Museum and Library.

1. The Order of Saint George had to be worn by the recipient at all times (either ribbon or actual medal would suffice).
2. The recipient had to work his way through the classes, i.e., no matter how brave the act, he started with the fourth (lowest) class. If the officer received a higher class, the insignia of all those lower class were worn along with the highest.
3. The third class could be awarded only to staff officers and senior officers or their equivalent. This statute made the fourth class the highest Russian award a non-senior officer (i.e. *Kapitan* (Captain) or lower) could receive during the First World War.
4. An officer had to be recommended by a senior officer within two months of the act of courage. If the senior officer misrepresented the facts in any way he could be court-martialled.
5. Approval of the third and fourth class had to be authorized by a Saint George Council consisting of at least seven members attached to the officer's army corps, but preferably from different branches of the service. If seven members could not be assembled, the recommendation was forwarded to the permanent Saint George Council in St. Petersburg.
6. The first and second classes could be awarded only at the pleasure of the emperor.
7. Recipients of the award were guaranteed a promotion in rank after a specific time—for junior officers, one year; for senior lieutenants and junior captains, three years; for staff officers (Lt. Colonels and Colonels), one year; and for senior officers, four years.
8. An officer who received the order in any class could not be forced to retire during periods of military reduction.
9. Names of the knights were engraved on plaques in the Saint George room of the Kremlin Palace in Moscow, and plaques were installed at all educational establishments from which the officer graduated. Recipients of the order were eligible for a pension, but the numbers were limited, so an officer sometimes had to wait for a vacancy. The fourth class award allowed 372 pensions of 150 rubles per year. For comparative purposes, the average wage of a skilled worker in Russia at this time was approximately 3.16 rubles a day.

The ribbon of the Order of Saint George, Fourth Class, was orange and black, divided vertically into five equal stripes. The edge and center stripes were black and the two dividing ones were orange. The ribbon's colors denote "Through Darkness to Light," with the black representing darkness and the orange light or life. The motto of the order is "For Military Merit and Valor."

The badge was a white-enameled cross pattee edged with gold, having in its center a pink or red-enameled circular plaque on which was depicted Saint George on horseback slaying a dragon. The reverse was similar, except for the central plague, which was black-enameled with the cipher of the saint in gold. Sometimes the color of this plague varied. The fourth class badge was 35 mm in diameter. It was worn on the left breast.

There was only one variation made in the design of the cross—when the award was made to non-Christians. The representation of Saint George slaying a dragon was then replaced by the Imperial Russian double-headed eagle.

A slightly lesser award connected with the Order of Saint George was known as the *Georgevsky Oroogie* (Golden Sword of Saint George). This sword had a small white-enamel Order of Saint George badge set in the end surface of the hilt with a black and orange ribbon attached.

This award was for officers only and was presented for deeds not coming within the statutes of the Saint George Order and for which no cross could be given. It must be stressed, however, that the Golden Sword of Saint George was given for outstanding acts of bravery, and considered by all Russian officers as second only to the Order of Saint George.

In addition to the officer's order and sword, there was an award for non-commissioned officers and enlisted men for extreme bravery in the face of the enemy. It was called either the Saint George Cross or Cross of Saint George, and was founded by Emperor Alexander I on 13 February, 1807, and divided into four classes by Emperor Alexander II on 19 February, 1856. To receive this decoration, the individual had to be recommended by his immediate superior officer within one month, with a statement of the reasons for his recommendation. The recipient was automatically promoted to the next highest rank. Other benefits were that decorated enlisted men could not receive corporal punishment and upon retirement paid no taxes. By statutes of 1913, those decorated received additional payment from the date of the heroic deed as follows:

First class: 120 roubles per year,
Second class: 96 roubles per year,
Third class: 60 roubles per year,
Fourth class: 36 roubles per year.

Upon retirement these amounts were continued over and above the pension. Holders of the cross could not be reduced in rank or have their decoration taken away without benefit of a court-martial.

Although the exact number of crosses issued during 1914–1917 cannot be ascertained, one source indicates it was awarded more than 200,000 times.

The ribbon for all four classes of the Saint George Cross was the same as the order for the officers (orange and black).

The badge (all classes) portrayed Saint George killing a dragon. The back ("reverse") had the class as well as the official number of the award. The badge for all four classes had a diameter of 32 mm. The first class award was gold, suspended from a ribbon with a bow. Second class was

The front ("obverse") (above) and back ("reverse") (below) of the Order of Saint George, Fourth Class. This particular badge clearly shows the representation of Saint George on horseback slaying a dragon.

gold suspended from a ribbon without a bow. Third class was silver suspended from a ribbon with a bow, and fourth class silver suspended from a ribbon without a bow. It should be noted that toward the end of World War I precious metals were in short supply, so first and second

Above: The obverse side of the NCOs Cross of Saint George. This particular badge is the first class cross with bowed ribbon. All classes awarded to Christians show a mounted figure of Saint George slaying a dragon.

Above: The reverse side of a NCOs Cross of Saint George. The left and right arms of the cross were stamped with the number of the award. The lower arm was stamped with the number of the class and the Russian cipher for "class." This particular award is a second class award and badge number 82-095.

class crosses were made of bronze while third and fourth class were of white metal. As with the Order of Saint George, when this award was made to non-Christians the figure of Saint George was replaced by the Imperial Russian eagle.

In 1913, Emperor Nicholas II instituted four awards called the Saint George Medal.[1] These were awarded to men whose deeds did not merit a cross. Similar to the cross there were two in gold and two in silver, and they were also divided into four classes (with and without a bow as described above for the Saint George Cross). The front ("obverse") side shows the head of Emperor Nicholas II and the reverse bears the inscription "For Valor."

Order of Saint Vladimir

Saint Vladimir, after whom the order was named, was the first Christian ruler of Russia. The order was instituted by Empress Catherine II ("Catherine the Great") on 22 September, 1782, to commemorate the 25th year of her reign. The award came in four classes and was originally presented to any individual who served the state with honor. For a military officer, its award initially required the following:

1. Twenty-five years in the army.
2. Naval officers who had made at least 18 deep sea voyages (ocean tour of duty) and had participated in at least one battle.
3. Naval officers with 20 deep sea voyages without having participated in battle.
4. Chaplains with 25 years service who had participated in at least one battle.

It must be stressed, however, that the order was not given only for long tenure, but for outstanding merit as well. The order was awarded with swords for military valor or achievement. Statutes of this award gave the recipient in any class the right of hereditary nobility. The first class of the order was very rarely awarded. It carried extensive privileges and rights, and the recipient ranked among the fourth class of officials at the Imperial court.

The Saint Vladimir ribbon was of three equal vertical stripes, two of black and one of red in the center. The badge was gold-rimmed, red-enameled cross. Just inside the gold rim was a narrow black-enameled band and a second gold-rimmed band. The center medallion was of black enamel and portrayed the Imperial Russian mantle (emblem of authority) with the cipher (initials) of the saint in the center. The mantle was surmounted by the Imperial Russian crown. On the reverse was the date of the order's founding. In some cases, an inscription on the back indicated which military rank or civil position the recipient held. If awarded to an army or navy officer with crossed swords, they appeared between the arms of the cross. If an army or navy officer had received a lower class of Saint Vladimir with crossed swords and then received a higher class without swords, the swords were placed above the badge of the higher class.

(1) This award was given to both officers and NCOs by the Provisional Government of Russia in 1917.

The award came in the following four classes:

First class—50mm badge, worn suspended from a sash, diagonally across the chest.

Second class—50 mm badge, worn at the neck.

Third class—45 mm badge, worn at the neck.

Fourth class—35 mm badge, worn on the left breast directly after the Order of Saint George Fourth Class, in the order precedence (i.e., it would be to the left, from the wearer's perspective).

This award also appeared as an eight-pointed silver and gold star, and in this form was presented to higher-ranking officers or officials and carried the motto "Kindness, Honor, Glory."

When awarded to non-Christians, the cipher and cross were, as usual, replaced by the Imperial Russian eagle.

Order of Saint Anne

On 14 February, 1735, Duke Charles Frederick of Schleswig-Holstein founded the Order of Saint Anne in memory of his wife, Anna Petrovna, daughter of Peter the Great. When their son, Peter III (the future emperor of Russia), went to Russia in 1742, Duke Charles began conferring the order upon Russians. On 15 April, 1797, Russian Emperor Paul I established the order as purely Russian and divided it into four classes.

Recipients of the first class received hereditary nobility while those of the lower classes received personal nobility. Membership in the nobility carried tremendous honor and privileges, and naturally this order was greatly prized.

The personal basis for receiving this award was primarily a long and distinguished career in the civil service and for valor or distinguished service in the military. When awarded for military bravery it was given with swords.

The ribbon colors for the order were red, edged with a narrow yellow stripe on each side.

The badge was the same in appearance for the first three classes, the distinction between classes being made in size and in manner of wearing. It had a red-enameled gold cross pattee, with gold shaped filigree (decorations) between the arms of the cross. In the center was a circular medallion of white enamel bearing the figure of Saint Anne with mountains in colored enamel in the background. This medallion too was circled by a gold

The obverse (above) and reverse (below) of the Order of Saint Vladimir. This particular badge is the Third Class award with swords.

The obverse side of the Order of Saint Anne with Swords, Second Class. The second-class badge had a long ribbon allowing it to be worn from the neck. The third-class badge was worn at the left breast.

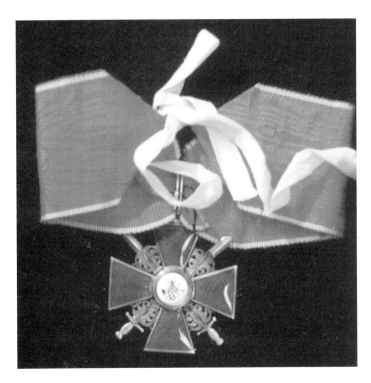

The reverse side of the Order of Saint Anne with Swords, Second Class. The medal clearly shows a series of interwoven 'A's.

The Order of Saint Anne, Fourth Class. This award was worn around the hilt of the officer's dress sword.

band. On the reverse, the medallion showed a series of intertwined letter 'A's in blue on a white enamel background.

The fourth class badge was a smaller, circular-shaped medal with the Saint Anne ribbon, worn from the hilt of the recipient's sword. The center of the medallion had a red enamel cross surmounted with an Imperial Russian crown. When the fourth class was awarded with swords, they appeared in the medallion above the crown.

The classes were:

First class—50 mm to 58 mm badge, worn from a sash, diagonally across the chest.

Second class—44 mm to 50 mm badge, worn from the neck.

Third class—30 mm to 36 mm badge, worn on the left breast.

Fourth class—30 mm to 36 mm badge, worn on the hilt of sword.

As with the Order of Saint Vladimir, the Order of Saint Anne also had an eight-pointed star for senior officers and officials. This star had a center plaque with the first letter of the motto AMANTIBUS, JUSTITIAM, PIETATEM, FIDEM, "To those who love Justice, Piety, and Faith" surrounding a red enameled cross.

Some Saint Anne awards had dark cherry-colored glass instead of enamel, which resulted in a black appearance. These are sometimes referred to as "Black Annes."

When awarded to non-Christians, the insignia of Saint Anne on the badge and cross on the star were replaced by the Imperial Russian eagle.

Order of Saint Stanislas

Saint Stanislas was a Roman Catholic prelate canonized in 1253. The order was founded 7 May, 1765, by Stanislas August Poniatowsky, the independent king of Poland. Like other Polish orders, it passed through various phases before it finally became a Russian order and, even then, its statutes were subsequently altered and revised several times. Emperor Nicholas I incorporated the order in 1831, and from that date until 1917 the emperor was its grand master.

The order was awarded to individuals who exemplified "Christian virtues," or for distinguished civil or military service. The first class carried the right of hereditary nobility. The award was given with swords for military bravery.

The ribbon was red with two white vertical stripes. The badge was the same in appearance in all three classes, except in size and manner of wearing, and consisted of a red-enameled Maltese cross, each of whose eight points was tipped with a gold ball. Between the arms of the cross, were a gold double-headed Imperial Russian eagle. The center medallion was white-enameled and portrayed in red the monogram of Saint Stanislas surrounded by a green and gold laurel wreath. The points of the cross were connected by a gold arc. Like the Order of Saint Anne, some Saint Stanislas awards had dark cherry-colored glass instead of enamel. The classes were:

The obverse side of the Order of Saint Stanislas, Second Class. Like the Order of Saint Anne, some Saint Stanislas awards were made with a dark cherry-colored glass instead of being enameled, resulting in a black enamel appearance.

The reverse side of the Order of Saint Stanislas badge.

First class—63 mm badge, worn suspended from a sash, diagonally across the chest.
Second class—44 mm to 47 mm badge, worn from the neck.
Third class—37 mm badge, worn on the breast.

The order could also be given in the form of an eight-pointed silver star, for senior officers and officials, and carried the motto *"Praemiando Incitat"* meaning, "Encouraged by Reward."

When awarded to non-Christians the initials on both the star and the badge were replaced by the Imperial Russian eagle.

Aviation Badges

The Russian government clearly understood the potential of military aeronautics well before World War I. Balloon units had been formed by both the army and navy in the late 19th century and some of these saw limited use during the Russo-Japanese War of 1904–5.

Officers of these units sported one of the world's first aviation insignia; a balloonist's badge awarded to graduates of the Aeronautical Training Grounds and the Military Electro-Technical School. It was a wreath-shaped badge of oxidized silver topped by an Imperial Russian eagle holding crossed axes.[2]

After the advent of heavier-than-air flight, aviation schools were founded in 1910. Among the first were the Sevastopol Aeronautical School, the Gatchina Aviation School, and the Officers School of Aviation. Other such schools were established to meet the needs of World War I, including the Military School of Air Observers, founded in 1916. Pilot or observer graduates of an army aviation school were allowed to wear a black colored badge on their *pogoni* (shoulder boards).[3] The badge consisted of crossed twin-bladed propellers and sword surmounted by a double-headed eagle. In addition, each graduate of an aviation school was allowed to wear the school's pilot or observers breast badge of oxidized silver upon being given the title of military aviator. Officer pilots and observers who did not graduate from a military school were not allowed to wear an aviation school breast badge, but were still allowed to wear the eagle badges on their *pogoni*.

For noncommissioned officers and lower ranking pilots and observers, their *pogoni* were decorated with a yellow metal badge of a winged propeller known as an *utka* (duck).

For non-commissioned meteorologists, photographers, and doctors, the soldier's "duck" was stenciled on the *pogoni* with yellow paint. However, any pilot or observer could change his "duck" to a black eagle after being promoted to the first officer's rank.

Russia's naval aviators did not wear the black eagle badge on their shoulder boards, for it could be confused with the black eagles worn by officers of the rank of admiral. Only non-naval aviation personal attached to naval duties could wear the black eagles. Naval pilots' and observers' breast badges differed from army badges, and consisted of a badge of oxidized silver showed a winged Imperial Russian crest surmounted by an anchor. The naval observer's breast badge was similar to the naval pilot's, but with the anchor replaced with a vertical telescope.

(2) Some sources indicate this badge was also awarded to some of Russia's first aviators while the newer school badges (Sevastopol and Gatchina school badges) were being designed.
(3) The black eagle badge worn on the shoulder boards also appeared in silver.

Appendix 2—Awards 465

The army officer's pilot badge was made of oxidized silver, composed of a circular wreath upon which are crossed swords. This is topped by a set of wings on which is the Imperial Russian shield with crown. Several aviation schools issued this badge, with small differences in the size of the shield, swords, and crown. Note the sword length is different for the two pilot badges.

Above: The navy officer's pilot badge was made of oxidized silver and showed a winged Imperial Russian crest surmounted by an anchor. The navy observer's badge was also made of oxidized silver and similar to the navy pilot's badge as shown, but the anchor was replaced with a vertical telescope.

Above left: The observers' school was established in 1916, with graduating officers receiving this badge. It is similar to the army pilot's badge, but on the center shield is written the monogram of Emperor Nicholas II. In addition, below the crossed swords is a vertical telescope.

Left: For graduates who studied consecutively at the Aeronautical Training Grounds and the Military Electro-Technical School an aeronautical badge was established on 24 February, 1896. The wreath-shaped badge was of oxidized silver topped by an Imperial Russian eagle holding crossed axes. Superimposed on the wreath is a gold anchor with wings. Balloonists and later airship crew members were among the first Russian aviators to receive this badge, making it one of Russia's first balloonist badges. Although some sources indicate other badges may have been designed for balloon and airship training, these designs are not known to the authors.

Other Shoulder Board Badge Markings For Aviation Personal

On paper, officers in the Imperial Russian Air Services had four types of dress uniforms: full dress; duty dress; work dress; and flying uniform. In practice, however, most officer flyers continued to wear the uniforms of the units from which they had come, with the addition of the black metal eagle badges on their shoulder boards and one of the following three additional markings:

1. The permanent complement of the aviation companies had shoulder boards marked with the company's number in Arabic numerals, with a propeller and wings stenciled on the boards.
2. The corps detachment had markings of the corps staff with propeller and wings.
3. In the field detachments and those of special assignment, Arabic numerals, according to detachment number and the letters "ПΩ" or "O.C." with the propeller and wings. The officers' markings were of gold and the pilots' eagles were of oxidized silver. All others had gold eagles, with the lower ranks' markings being stenciled on with yellow paint.

The double-headed Imperial Russian eagle badge worn on the shoulder boards of officer pilots and observers.

This photo shows different *pogoni* with the black and sometimes silver-colored eagle badge. The badges at the top of the photo are, from left to right: army pilot's badge; navy pilot's badge; army observer's badge.

Appendix 3: Combat Victory Lists of Aces and Selected Pilots

Pavel Victorovitch Argeyev (d'Argueeff)

Victory	Date	Squadron	Aircraft Flown	Place	Enemy Aircraft	Enemy Crew	Confirmation	Comments
1	10/1/17	19	Nieuport		Albatros two-seater.	*Feldwebel* pilot (wounded, POW), obs. killed.	Squadron reports.	CO of 19th, wounded in battle. Awarded Order St. Vladimir, Fourth Class.
N/C	8/4/17	19	Nieuport	Mitau, over German lines (in AM).	German single-seater.	Pilot escaped.	None.	
2	21/4/17	19	Nieuport	Behind Russian lines (in PM).	German two-seater.		Squadron reports, Army reports.	Awarded Golden Sword of St. George.
3	6/5/17	19	Nieuport	Brezezany (0945 hrs).	Brandenburg C.I 26.51 of Flik 1; destroyed on ground by artillery.	Pisch (pilot), Morelli (obs.)	Army reports.	With Kozakov, Zabrov, and Leman.
4	17/5/17	19	Nieuport	Jakobstadt, Northern Front.	LVG two-seater of Fl. Abt. (A)242.	*Ltn.* Witgen and *Ltn.* Bode both wounded & POW.	Army reports.	With Kozakov.
5	8/6/17	19	Nieuport	Podgartze, near Kozova.	Brandenburg C.I 63.75 of Flik 25.	*Korp.* Kimmel (pilot) and *Oblt.* Paylay (obs.) POW.	Army reports.	With Kozakov, awarded St. Anne Fourth Class.
6	20/6/17	19	Nieuport	Tsmenitzi near Nejnokov.	Rumpler C.I 4739/16 of Fl. Abt. 24; group of 2 shot down.	*Korp.* Bolweg (pilot) and *Ltn.* Deter (obs.) wounded, POW.	Army reports.	With Kozakov.
7	1/6/18	SPA. 124	Spad 13	Entre Puisieux Beaumont, France.	LVG two-seater.		Resumé 1.300	Wounded in arm.
8	13/6/18	SPA. 124	Spad 13	France.	Rumpler two-seater.		Resumé 22.586	
9	14/6/18	SPA. 124	Spad 13	France.	Two-seater.		Resumé 18.776	
10	26/6/18	SPA. 124	Spad 13	France.	Two-seater.		Resumé 2.664	Wounded in groin and foot.
11	27/9/18	SPA. 124	Spad 13	North Cernay, France.	Fokker D.VII.		Resumé 39.367	
12	28/9/18	SPA. 124	Spad 13	Manre (Meaux) Sechault, France (1010 hrs).	Two-seater.		Resumé 40.778	
13	28/9/18	SPA. 124	Spad 13	Sechault Laval, France (1520 hrs).	Two-seater.		Resumé 40.778	

Pavel Victorovitch Argeyev (d'Argueeff) (continued)

Victory	Date	Squadron	Aircraft Flown	Place	Enemy Aircraft	Enemy Crew	Confirmation	Comments
N/C	5/10/18	SPA. 124	Spad 13	NE Autry, France (1125 hrs).	Two-seater.		None	
14	5/10/18	SPA. 124	Spad 13	Orfeuil, France (1815 hrs).	Two-seater.		Resumé 14.434	
15	30/10/18	SPA. 124	Spad 13	East of Quatre, Champs, France.	Two-seater.		Resumé 6.943	

Louis Coudouret

Victory	Date	Squadron	Aircraft Flown	Place	Enemy Aircraft	Enemy Crew	Confirmation	Comments
1	4/5/16	N.57	Nieuport 11	d'Hermaville, France.	LVG two-seater.		Resumé 2.650.	
2	22/10/16	N.102	Nieuport	le Ferme du Logis, France.	Albatros two-seater.		Squadron reports, Army reports.	
3	8/10/17	N.581	Spad 7	Zalec'ye, Russia.	Albatros two-seater.	Both KIA.	Russian Army report #254.	With Lt. Lachmann.
4	23/11/17	N.581	Spad 7	Volochyst, Russia.	Albatros C.X of Fl.Abt. (A)232.	Ltn. d.R. Paul Strathmann (obs.) and Vzfw. Wilhelm Krauser (pilot) both POW.	Russian Army report #254.	
5	14/12/17	N.581	Spad 7	Volochyst, Russia.	Albatros D.V.		Russian Army.	
6	2/6/18	Spa.103 (Cigognes)	Spad 13	Carlepont, France.	Single-seater.		Resumé 9.576.	With Sgt. Hoeber.

Victor Georgiyevitch Federov

Victory	Date	Squadron	Aircraft Flown	Place	Enemy Aircraft	Enemy Crew	Confirmation	Comments
1	14/3/16	C.42	Caudron G.4	Charny (Verdun) France.			Resumé 9.936.	Awarded Croix de Guerre and Military Medal. With Lanero.
2	21/3/16	C.42	Caudron G.4	Douaumont (Verdun) France.	Two-seater.	Both POW.	Resumé 14.500.	With Lanero.
3	30/3/16	C.42	Caudron G.4	Moranville (Verdun) France.	Two-seater.		Army reports, squadron reports.	With Lanero.
4	18/9/18	Spa.89	Spad 13	Belrupt, France.	Two-seater.		Resumé 23.082.	
5	9/10/18	Spa.89	Spad 13	Damvillers, France.	Fighter.		Resumé 20.11.	

Juri Vladimirovich Gilsher

Victory	Date	Squadron	Aircraft Flown	Place	Enemy Aircraft	Enemy Crew	Confirmation	Comments
1	13/4/17	7	Nieuport 21 serial no. 1872	Galicia near villages Bogorodchany and Posetch.	Brandenburg C.I 67.03 of Flik 7.	*Feldwebel* Paul Hablitschek (pilot) and *Oblt.* Roman Schmidt (obs.).	12th Army Corps/8th Army South/Western Front.	Shared with Makeenok and Yanchenko; Russian aircraft shot down in this battle.
2	13/4/17	7	Nieuport 21 serial no. 1872	Galicia near villages Bogorodchany and Stanislau.	Brandenburg C.I 67.04 of Flik 7.	*Ltn.* Heinrich Szeliga (obs.) and Klefac (pilot) wounded.	12th Army Corps/8th Army South/Western Front.	Shared with Makeenok and Yanchenko; same flight of four Russian aircraft.
3	15/5/17	7	Nieuport 21 serial no. 1872	Boshovze, Galicia; crashed near village Boushuv.	Oeffag C.III 52.52 of Flik 11; destroyed on ground by artillery.	Pius Moosbrugger (pilot) wounded, 1Lt. Julius Hochenegg (obs.) killed.	Russian artillery reports.	Received Order of St. George Fourth Class.
4	17/7/17	7	Nieuport 11 serial no. 1679	Brzezav region SW of Posuchov village.	Enemy aircraft destroyed on ground by artillery.		Russian artillery reports.	Received the Golden Sword of St. George.
5	20/7/17	7	Nieuport 21 serial no. 2451	Tarnopol.	Enemy aircraft forced down from group of 8. Second group of 10 enemy aircraft in support.		Russian reports.	Shared with Yanchenko. Gilsher was killed in this battle.

Maurice Roch Gond

Victory	Date	Squadron	Aircraft Flown	Place	Enemy Aircraft	Enemy Crew	Confirmation	Comments
1								
2	20/7/17	N.3	Nieuport 11	Tecuci, Romania.	Two-seater.		Army and squadron reports.	With Lt. Egon Nasta, N.11.
3	23/7/17	N.3	Nieuport 11	Scanzeia.	Brandenburg C.I 69.58 of Flik 29.	*Korp.* Kolleritsch (pilot) POW, *Ltn.* Von Hammerlitz (obs.) KIA.	Squadron reports, Russian 4th Army.	Decorated with the *Chevalier de la Legion d'Honneur*.
4	29/7/17	N.3	Nieuport 11	Namelousa.			Squadron reports, Russian 4th Army.	Citation with award for Michael the Brave Third Class.
5	16/8/17	N.3	Nieuport 11	Palerma.	German two-seater.	*Ltn.* Friedrich Protzek (pilot), *Ltn. d.R.* Hermann Steinbruck (obs.), both KIA.	Romanian Army report, (file 1175, Romanian archives).	

Nikolai Kirillovich Kokorin

Victory	Date	Squadron	Aircraft Flown	Place	Enemy Aircraft	Enemy Crew	Confirmation	Comments
1	25/11/16	4	Nieuport 10	Rozitze/Kolmichalin over Russian Territory.	German aircraft, shot down.	Both POW.	Russian Army.	Golden Sword of Saint George.
2	2/1/17	4	Morane Saulnier Type H	Voulka-Porskia near Luzk.	Two-seater shot down, crashed on landing.	Unknown.	Squadron reports.	Order of Saint George Fourth Class.
3	14/4/17	4	Nieuport	Uvse Village.	German Albatros, nosed over on landing.	Both POW.	Russian Army.	With Zomblevich.
4	24/5/17	4	Nieuport 21	Braejan area, Shabalin Village.	Brandenburg C.I 64.62 of Flik 11.	Knotis (pilot) and *Oblt.* Franz Fasching (obs.) both wounded.	Squadron reports.	
5	26/5/17	4	Nieuport 21	Northwest of Kosovo.	Brandenburg C.I 64.51 of Flik 9 shot down in flames.	Lager Anton (pilot) and Willibolt Patzelt (obs.)† both killed.	Army reports.	With Zomblevich.

Alexander Alexandrovich Kozakov

Victory	Date	Squadron	Aircraft Flown	Place	Enemy Aircraft	Enemy Crew	Confirmation	Comments
1	31/3/15	4th Corps	Morane Saulnier type G s/n 316.	Near Guzov-Volja, Bank of Visla.	Albatros two-seater.	Both killed.	Squadron reports. Russian Army.	Rammed enemy with undercarriage. Awarded Golden Sword of St. George.
2	27/6/16	19th	Nieuport 10 s/n 222.	Lake Drisvjaty over front lines, 1600 hrs.	Albatros two-seater.		Squadron reports.	
3	29/7/16	19th	Nieuport 10 s/n 222.	Dvinsk, south of Drisvjaty, 1500 hours.	Albatros C.III in group of 12 aircraft.	Both killed.	Army Order 696.	
4	6/9/16	19th	Nieuport 11	Kovel.	Two-seater, Fl. Abt. 46.	*Ltn.* Mueller (pilot) POW. *Ltn.* Bergen (obs.) POW.	Squadron/Army records.	Enemy landed at Kozakov's airfield.
N/C	8/9/16	19th	Nieuport 11	Kovertsy-Rozchishe.			None.	
5	21/12/16	19th	Nieuport 11	Lutsk, south of Zabocol village, 1500 hours.	Brandenburg C.I 27.14; group of 3 a/c, Flik 10.	Sgt. Johann Kolbe (pilot) killed, *Ltn.* Franz Weigl (obs.) wounded, POW.	Squadron records, Army records	Awarded Order of St. George, Fourth Class.
6	6/5/17	19th	Nieuport 11	Brezezany, 0945 hours.	Brandenburg C.I 26.51 of Flik 1, landed in fog.	*Zgfr.* Pracny (pilot) & *Ltn.* Ferstel (obs.), POW.	Squadron/Army records.	Shared with Argeyev, Leman, and Zhabrov.
7	10/5/17	19th	Nieuport 11	Sarniki village.	Fokker shot down from group of 3.		Squadron/Army records.	Shared with pilots Leman & Polyakov.
8	17/5/17	19th	Nieuport 11	Podgaitsy.	LVG two-seater, Fl.Ab. (A) 242.	*Ltn.* Witgen & *Ltn.* Bode, both wounded & POW.	Squadron/Army records.	Shared with Argeyev.

Alexander Alexandrovich Kozakov (continued)

Victory	Date	Squadron	Aircraft Flown	Place	Enemy Aircraft	Enemy Crew	Confirmation	Comments
9	8/6/17	19th	Nieuport 17	West of Kozov, 0800 hours.	Brandenburg C.I 63.75 of Flik 25.	*Korp.* Kimmel (pilot) & *Oblt.* Paylay (obs.) POW.	Squadron/Army records.	Shared with Argeyev.
10	25/5/17	19th	Nieuport 17	West of Konjukhi Village.	EA from group of 2.		Squadron records.	
11	20/6/17	19th	Nieuport 17	Attacked near Mikulintsev, forced to land at Podgaitsy.	Rumpler C.I 4739/16 of Fl. Abt. 24, 0900 hours.	*Korp.* Bolweg (pilot) & *Oblt.* Deter (obs.), both wounded and POW.	Squadron/Army records.	Shared with Argeyev.
12	27/6/17	19th	Nieuport 17	Near Stavetyn, fell @ Lipizadoluo, 1700 hours.	German aircraft.		Squadron/Army records.	
13	27/6/17	19th	Nieuport 17	Stavetyn, near Nejnolov, 2100 hours.	Rumpler of Fl. Abt. 29.	Both POW.	Squadron/Army records.	Shared with Leman; Kozakov wounded.
14	27/7/17	19th	Nieuport 17	Village Obertyn.	Brandenburg C.I 26.27 of Flik 20.	Pracny (pilot), Ferstol (obs.)	Squadron/Army records.	Shared with Shangin.
15	2/8/17	19th	Nieuport 17	Dolinyany Village.	Brandenburg C.I 64.67 of Flik 26.	*Korp.* Tratan Varza (pilot) killed, *Ltn.* Franz Slavik (obs.) wounded, POW.	Squadron/Army records.	Shared with Shangin.
16	8/8/17	19th	Nieuport 17	Village Ivane-Pusto.	Aircraft crash-landed.	Maushalter (killed) Freinzel (missing).	Squadron/Army records	Shared with Shangin, Kozakov wounded in leg.
N/C	24/8/17	19th	Nieuport 17	Gusyatin.	Forced to land.		None.	With Smirnov.
17	29/8/17	19th	Nieuport 17	Village Lapkovtsy, 1100 hours.	Albatros C.III of Fl. Abt 24	*Ltn.* Hans Kaushalter (pilot) killed, *Ltn.* Freinzel (obs.) killed.	Squadron/Army records.	
N/C	7/9/17	19th	Nieuport 17	Gusyatin.	Forced to land.		None.	With other pilots.
18	11/9/17	19th	Nieuport 17	Near Gusyatin @ 1600 hours.	Brandenburg C.I 269.18 of Flik 18.	*Korp.* Fritz Weber (pilot) *Oblt.* Theodor Fishcher (obs.), both POW.	Squadron/Army records.	Kozakov picked up both POWs in his car.
19	23/9/17	19th	Nieuport 17	South of Gusyatin.	Brandenburg C.I 269.26 of Flik 36.	Rudolph Simacek (pilot), Leo Onciul (obs.)	Squadron/Army records.	With Shirinkin, pilot from 7th Fighter Detachment.
20	26/10/17	19th	Nieuport 17	Scalat Region.	German aircraft.		7th Army SW Front.	Shared with Smirnov.

Yevgraph Nikolaevich Kruten

Victory	Date	Squadron	Aircraft Flown	Place	Enemy Aircraft	Enemy Crew	Confirmation	Comments
1	6/3/15	2nd	Voisin LA Serial No. 42	Region of Sohachen / Ravka.			Squadron reports.	Awarded Order of St. Anne Fourth Class.
2	11/8/16	2nd	Nieuport 11 Serial No. 1137	Near Village Svoyatichi.	Albatros C.III Serial No. 422, captured.	POW.	Squadron and Army records.	
3	14/8/16	2nd	Nieuport 11 Serial No. 1137	Near Nesvich.	Rumpler Serial No. 615, captured.	Both POW.	Squadron and Army records.	
4	Feb. 1917	N.3	Spad 7	France.	German aircraft.		Squadron records.	Awarded French *Croix de Guerre* with Palm.
5	31/5/17	2nd	Nieuport 17 Serial No. 2232	Tarnopol NE of Brezezany.	Brandenburg C.I 69.78.	Killed.	Squadron records and Army record #3746.	
6	5/6/17	2nd	Nieuport 17 Serial No. 2232	Tarnopol.	Two-seater.	Gunner killed.	Squadron records.	
7	6/6/17	2nd	Nieuport 17 Serial No. 2232	Tarnopol.	Brandenburg C.I 64.55 of Flik 18.	*Ltn.d.R.* Willibald Patzelt (p.) &*Korp.* Anton Lager (obs.).	Squadron records and Army record #3746.	

Georges Marcel Lachmann

Victory	Date	Squadron	Aircraft Flown	Place	Enemy Aircraft	Enemy Crew	Confirmation	Comments
1	15/7/16	N.57	Nieuport	Environs de Ham, France.	Observation balloon.	Observer jumped to safety.	Resume 11.151.	
2	28/7/16	N.57	Nieuport	Pres de Souilly, France.	German Albatros two-seater.	POW.	Resume 20.978.	With *Lt.* Matton and *Mdl.* Flachaire, N.67.
3	12/8/16	N.57	Nieuport	Guiscourt, France.	German two-seater.	Both crew jumped, killed.	Resume 9.371.	With *Adj.* Maxime Lenoir of N.23.
N/C	23/8/16	N.57	Nieuport	Montfaucon, France.	Observation balloon.		None.	
N/C	23/8/16	N.57	Nieuport	Etain, France.	Observation balloon.		None.	
*	26/6/17	N.581	Spad 7	Russia.	Russian observation balloon.		Russian troops.	Crashed into hillside.
4	1/9/17	N.581	Spad 7 with Le Prieur rockets	Near Melnitza, Galicia.	Observation balloon.	Both jumped to safety.	Squadron reports.	Awarded Order St. George Fourth Class.
5	15/9/17	N.581	Spad 7	Chilovsti Galicia.	Two-seater.	Both KIA.	Squadron and Army reports.	
6	3/10/17	N.581	Spad 7	Mal'Shevka.	Brandenburg C.I 169.14 of Flik 40.	*Feldwebel* Tompa (pilot', *Ltn.* Lipthay (obs.).	Squadron and Army reports.	
7	8/10/17	N.581	Spad 7	Zalecye, near Zbrousch River, Galicia.	Albatros two-seater.	Both KIA.	Squadron reports, Army Report #254.	With Coudouret.
8	16/10/17	N.581	Spad 7	Melnitza, Galicia.	Observation balloon.	Both observers killed.	Squadron and Army reports.	

Ernst K. Leman

Victory	Date	Squadron	Aircraft Flown	Place	Enemy Aircraft	Enemy Crew	Confirmation	Comments
1	6/5/17	19th	Nieuport	Shebalin Village.	Brandenburg C.I 26.51 of Flik 1.	Pisch (pilot), Morelli (obs.).	Army reports.	With Kozakov, Argeyev, and Zhabrov.
2	10/5/17	19th	Nieuport	Sarniki.	Fokker type.		Army reports.	With Kozakov and Polyakov.
3	27/6/17	19th	Nieuport	Tsmenitzi.	Enemy two-seater.		Army reports.	With Kozakov, awarded Order St. Anne Fourth Class.
4	17/8/17	19th	Nieuport				Squadron reports.	
5	26/9/17	19th	Nieuport	Near Gusiatina.	Enemy two-seater.		Army report #253.	With Krisanov who was also shot down.

Ivan Alexandrovitch Loiko

Victory	Date	Squadron	Aircraft Flown	Place	Enemy Aircraft	Enemy Crew	Confirmation	Comments
1	26/10/16	9th	Nieuport 11 serial no. 1109	Mamalyga Station.			Russian troops.	With two other pilots.
2	27/12/16	9th	Nieuport 11 serial no. 1109	Oneshty.	Brandenburg two-seater.		Russian troops.	
N/C	11/5/17	9th	Morane Saulnier H serial no. 732	Sooshitsy Villey.			None.	With Strizhevsky.
N/C	18/7/17	9th	Nieuport 17 serial no. 1445	Vermeshty Village.	Two-seater.		None.	With Strizhevsky and Karklin.
3	4/9/17	9th	Nieuport 17 serial no. 1448	Auchavita Village near Radautz.	Two-seater.		Russian troops.	With Suk.
4	6/9/17	9th	Nieuport 17 serial no. 1448	Teodoreshty Village.	Two-seater.		Russian troops, 29th Army.	With Karklin. Awarded Order of St. Vladimir, Fourth Class.
N/C	7/9/17	9th	Nieuport 17 serial no. 1448	Raduatz.	Two-seater.		None.	
N/C	8/9/17	9th	Nieuport 17 serial no. 1448	Unter-Gorodniki.	Two-seater.		None.	With Suk.
5	12/9/17	9th	Nieuport 17 serial no. 1448	Raduatz.	Brandenburg C.I of Flik 44.	*Oblt. d.R.* George Altadonna (pilot) and *Oblt.* Albert Kunezelo (obs.).	Russian troops.	With Suk. Awarded Order of St. George, Fourth Class.
6	3/10/17	9th	Nieuport 23 serial no. 5045	Yaslovets.				With Sapozhnikov.

Donat Aduiovich Makeenok

Victory	Date	Squadron	Aircraft Flown	Place	Enemy Aircraft	Enemy Crew	Confirmation	Comments
1	7/3/17	7th	Nieuport 21 serial no. 2453	Lipitza-Guru, near Svistelniki.			Russian troops.	With Yanchenko.
2	13/4/17	7th	Nieuport 21 serial no. 2453	Bogorodchany.	Brandenburg C.I 67.03, Flik 7.	*Fw.* Paul Hablitschek (pilot), *Oblt.* Roman Schmidt (obs.).	12th Army Corps/8th Army Southwestern Front.	Shared with Gilsher and Yanchenko.
3	13/4/17	7th	Nieuport 21 serial no. 2453	Bogorodchany.	Brandenburg C.I 67.04, Flik 7.	*Ltn.* Heinrich Szeliga (obs.) and Klefac (pilot) wounded.	12th Army Corps/8th Army Southwestern Front.	Shared with Gilsher and Yanchenko.
4	16/4/17	7th	Nieuport 21 serial no. 2453	Yamritsa Kozeyarki.			Russian troops.	
N/C	27/4/17	7th	Nieuport 21 serial no. 2453	Kosjarko.			None.	
5	29/6/17	7th	Nieuport 21 serial no. 2453	Potootory Station.			Russian troops.	
6	6/7/17	7th	Nieuport 17	Near Brzezhany.			Russian troops.	With Yanchenko.
7	11/7/17	7th	Nieuport 17	Brzezhany.			Russian troops.	With Yanchenko.
8	5/8/17	7th	Nieuport 17	Brzezhany.			Russian troops.	With Yanchenko.

Ivan Alexsandrovich Orlov

Victory	Date	Squadron	Aircraft Flown	Place	Enemy Aircraft	Enemy Crew	Confirmation	Comments
1	8/6/16	7th	Nieuport 11	Petlikovze, Russia.	Lloyd C.II 42.21 of Flik 9.	Walter Schmidt (obs.) killed, Karl Rumiha (pilot) wounded.	A/H reports, Russian army.	
2	25/6/16	7th	Nieuport 11	Podgaitsy Village, Russia.	Aviatik B.III 33.30 of Flik 27.	*Zgfhr.* F. Schallinger (pilot), *Fähnrich d.R.* G. Wangler (obs.), both wounded and POW.	Squadron reports, army reports.	With Yanchenko.
3	4/10/16	7th	Nieuport 11	Zlota-Lipca, Russia.	Two-seater.	Both POW.	Army reports.	With Yanchenko.
4	24/1/17	Spa	Spad 7	France.			Army reports.	
5	21/5/17	7th	Nieuport 17	Near Prysup, Russia.	Albatros two-seater of Fl.Abt. (A)242.	Both POW.	Army reports.	

Alexander Mikhailovich Pishvanov

Victory	Date	Squadron	Aircraft Flown	Place	Enemy Aircraft	Enemy Crew	Confirmation	Comments
1	21/3/17	10th	Nieuport 21 serial no. 1890	Near Galatz.			Russian troops.	
2	28/3/17	10th	Nieuport 21 serial no. 1890	South of Galatz; landed near Beldoneschi.	Aviatik.		Romanian army.	Awarded Order St. Anne, Fourth Class.
N/C	15/4/17	10th	Nieuport 21 serial no. 1890	Near Galatz.			None.	
3	26/6/17	10th	Nieuport 21 serial no. 1890	Near Galatz.			Russian troops.	Awarded Order St. Stanislas, Third Class.
4	4/7/17	10th	Nieuport 21 serial no. 1890	Endependance, Romania.	Brandenburg C.I 68.54.	*Oblt.* Rupert Terk (pilot), *Oblt.* Josef Brunner (obs.), both escaped.	Squadron reports, Austro-Hungarian records.	Awarded Order St. Vladimir, Fourth Class.
5	7/7/17	10th	Nieuport 21 serial no. 1890	Latinul Village, Romania.		Escaped.	Artillery reports, squadron reports.	Aircraft destroyed by Russian artillery; awarded Order St. George, Fourth Class.

Eduard Martynovich Pulpe

Victory	Date	Squadron	Aircraft Flown	Place	Enemy Aircraft	Enemy Crew	Confirmation	Comments
1	1915	M.S.23	Morane Saulnier type L	Verdun, France.	German aircraft.		Army reports, squadron reports.	Exact date unknown.
2	1915	M.S.23	Morane Saulnier type L	Verdun, France.	German aircraft.		Army reports, squadron reports	Exact date unknown. (Victories #1 and #2 scored in same battle against 8 aircraft.)
3	20/3/16	N.23	Nieuport (10, 11, or 12)	North or Maucourt, France.	German aircraft over German lines. Fight against 3 aircraft.		Resumé #13.839.	
4	31/3/16	N.23	Nieuport (10, 11, or 12)	Consenvoye, France.	German aircraft over German lines. Fight against 3 aircraft.		Resumé #2.---.	
5	1/7/16	10th	Nieuport 11	Kovel, Russia.	Enemy aircraft.		Army reports, squadron reports	

Charles A. Revol-Tissot

Victory	Date	Squadron	Aircraft Flown	Place	Enemy Aircraft	Enemy Crew	Confirmation	Comments
1, 2, 3				France.	German aircraft.			Details unknown, presumably in France before transfer to Romania.
4	14/2/17	N.3	Nieuport 11	South of Diochetii, Romania.	German two-seater.		Russian army reports.	With *Caporal* Manchoulas.
5	13/4/17	N.3	Nieuport 11	North of Focsani, Romania.	Two-seater.		Russian aeronautical post reports.	

Mikhail Ivanovich Safonov

Victory	Date	Squadron	Aircraft Flown	Place	Enemy Aircraft	Enemy Crew	Confirmation	Comments
1	9/9/16	Glagol	M-9 #29	Gulf of Riga.	German seaplane.		Naval reports.	Awarded Order St. Anne, Fourth Class.
2	14/7/17	Glagol	M-15	Gulf of Riga, near Domesness.	German aircraft.		Naval reports.	
3	7/9/17	Glagol	Nieuport fighter NR-1	Arensburg.	German two-seater.		Naval reports.	
4	16/11/17	Glagol	Nieuport fighter NR-1	Moon Island.	German aircraft.		Naval reports.	
5	17/11/17	Glagol	Nieuport fighter NR-1	Moon Island.	German twin-engine bomber.		Naval reports.	

Alexander Nikolaivich Prokoffiev de Seversky

Victory	Date	Squadron	Aircraft Flown	Place	Enemy Aircraft	Enemy Crew	Confirmation	Comments
1	4/7/16	2nd Baltic	Grigorovitch Type 9	Gulf of Riga.	German fighter.		Naval reports.	
2	13/8/16	2nd Baltic	Grigorovitch Type 9	Over German base, Lake Angern.	German seaplane.		Squadron reports.	
3	13/8/16	2nd Baltic	Grigorovitch Type 9	Over German base, Lake Angern.	German seaplane.		Squadron reports.	
4	13/8/16	2nd Baltic	Grigorovitch Type 9	Over German base, Lake Angern.	German seaplane.		Squadron reports.	Awarded Golden Sword of St. George.
5	10/10/17	2nd Baltic	Nieuport 21	Zerel Island, Gulf of Riga.	German fighter.		Naval reports.	
6	10/10/17	2nd Baltic	Nieuport 21	Zerel Island, Gulf of Riga.	German two-seater.		Naval reports.	

Ivan Vasilievich Smirnov

Victory	Date	Squadron	Aircraft Flown	Place	Enemy Aircraft	Enemy Crew	Confirmation	Comments
1	2/1/17	19	Nieuport 10	Galicia-Lutsk.	Aviatik C-type C2775/16.	Both killed.	Russian troops.	Smirnov promoted to Sergeant. Shared with Pentko.
2	2/5/17	19	Morane Saulnier Type I	Galicia, near Gnilche west of Zavaluv.	German Albatros from Fl.Abt. 220.	Herman Laden (pilot), both POW.	3rd Caucasian Corps.	Awarded St. George Cross 2nd Class.
3	16/8/17	19	Nieuport 21 #1514		Enemy aircraft.		Squadron reports.	
4	23/8/17	19	Nieuport 21 #1514	Galicia-Gusyatin Ludvipol.	German two-seater.	A. Heft (pilot), both POW.	Russian troops.	Shared with Lt. Huber.
5	8/9/17	19	Morane Saulnier Type I	Galicia-Gusyatin area at 2000 hours.	Enemy two-seater.		Infantry reports, Russian reports.	
6	24/9/17	19	Spad 7	Region of Balin and Prilip.	German two-seater of Fl.Abt. 240(A), captured.	*Uffz.* Hermann Utsch (pilot), *Ltn.* Paul Thierfelder (obs.) killed.	Squadron reports. Captured aircraft.	
7	24/10/17	19	Spad 7	Kowel.	German aircraft.	*Gefr.* Helmut Tehsenvity (pilot) killed.	Squadron reports, Infantry report.	
8	10/11/17	19	Spad 7	Gusyatin, south of Zielona.	Brandenburg C.I 269.08 of Flik 9.	Pilot killed.	Squadron records, Infantry Order 4332.	Shot down by Lipsky with Smirnov.
9	10/11/17	19	Spad 7	Village of Zelyonaya, behind Russian lines.	Brandenburg C.I 269.68 of Flik 9.	*Korp.* Josef Ryba (pilot), *Ltn.d.R.* Josef Barcal (obs.), both killed.	Squadron records, Infantry Order 4332.	Shared with Lipsky.
10	23/11/17	19	Spad 7	Letovo, north of Zelenaya.	Lloyd C.V 46.22 of Flik 18.	Both killed.	Squadron records.	
11	26/11/17	19	Spad 7	Scalat region.	Enemy aircraft.		7th Army reports, South-West Front.	Shared with Kozakov.

Vladimir Ivanovich Strizhevsky

Victory	Date	Squadron	Aircraft Flown	Place	Enemy Aircraft	Enemy Crew	Confirmation	Comments
1	7/3/17	9th	Nieuport 21 serial no. 1719	Region of Herzh.			Russian troops.	
2	11/4/17	9th	Spad 7 serial no. 1446	Town of Siret.	German LVG two-seater.	Killed.	Romanian and Russian troops.	
N/C	16/4/17	9th	Spad 7 serial no. 1446		Brandenburg D.I.		None.	
3	17/4/17	9th	Nieuport 17 serial no. 1448	Rakoas Woods.			Russian troops.	With Suk.
4	23/4/17	9th	Nieuport 17 serial no. 1448	Near Siret and Guru-Hunrsrului.	German LVG two-seater.	POW.	Romanian and Russian troops.	
N/C	11/5/17	9th	Nieuport 17 serial no. 1448	Bogda-Neshti.			None.	
5	17/5/17	9th	Spad 7 serial no. 1446	Bacau.	Brandenburg D.I.		Romanian and Russian troops.	
6	17/6/17	9th	Spad 7 serial no. 1446	Uzul Valley.	German Fokker E-type.		Romanian and Russian troops.	
7	18/6/17	9th	Nieuport 17 serial no. 1448	Region of Okna.	Brandenburg C.I 67.54 of Flik 39.	*Ltn.* Otto Hoffman (obs.) and *Korp.* Adolph Pranzer (pilot) POW.	Romanian and Russian troops.	
N/C	18/7/17	9th	Nieuport 17 serial no. 1448	Vermeshty.				With Loiko. Strizhevsky wounded.

Grigori Eduardovitch Suk

Victory	Date	Squadron	Aircraft Flown	Place	Enemy Aircraft	Enemy Crew	Confirmation	Comments
1	26/3/17	9th	Nieuport 11 serial no. 1127	Nezdy-Vozargal.	Brandenburg C.I 67.24 of Flik 40.	*Korp.* Kenedy (pilot) and *Ltn.* Duller (obs.).	Russian troops.	
2	17/4/17	9th	Nieuport 11 serial no. 1109	Region of Rakosa.	Two-seater.		Russian troops.	With Strizhevsky.
3	8/8/17	9th	Nieuport 21 serial no. 1719	Romania, Okno region.	Oeffag C.II 52.63 of Flik 44.	*Zugsf.* Adolf Rabel (pilot) killed, *Oblt.* Franz Xaver-Schlarbaum (obs.) wounded, POW.	Russian troops.	
4	4/9/17	9th	Vickers F.B.19 serial no. 12	Vermeshty Village.	Two-seater.		Russian troops.	Shared with Loiko.
N/C	8/9/17	9th	Vickers F.B.19 serial no. 12	Town of Seret.	Two-seater.		None.	With Loiko.
5	12/9/17	9th	Vickers F.B.19 serial no. 12	Romania, Arbora near Radautz, 1800 hrs.	Two-seater from Flik 44.	*Oblt.d.R.* George Altadonna (pilot) wounded, *Oblt.* Albert Kuneze (obs.).	Russian troops.	Shared with Loiko and Sapozhnikov.
6	14/10/17	9th	Spad 7 serial no. 1440	Romania, SE of Radautz.	Two-seater.	Crew killed (pilot killed in crash, observer fell out of plane).	Fell on Russian troops.	
7	4/11/17	9th	Spad 7 serial no. 1446	Village Goura-Seltche.	Fighter.	Killed.	Russian troops.	
8	8/11/17	9th	Spad 7 serial no. 1446	Romania, North of Radautz.			Russian troops.	
9	10/11/17	9th	Spad 7 serial no. 1440	Romania, near Radautz.	Brandenburg C.I 269.49 of Flik 49.	*Korp.* Milan Alteron (pilot) and *Oblt.* Ignaz Patsch (obs.) both wounded.	Delayed confirmation, Russian troops.	

Konstantin Konstantinovitch Vakulovsky

Victory	Date	Squadron	Aircraft Flown	Place	Enemy Aircraft	Enemy Crew	Confirmation	Comments
1	7/9/16	1st	Nieuport 11 serial no. 1295	Lake Kwakshta.	Enemy aircraft.		Squadron and Army reports.	
2	28/10/16	1st	Nieuport 11 serial no. 1295	Lake Vishnevsky.	Enemy Albatros.		Squadron reports.	
3	14/4/17	1st	Morane Saulnier type I serial no. 741	Northeast of Budslav Village.	Enemy two-seater.	Both killed.	Squadron and Army reports.	
4	21/8/17	1st	Nieuport 17 serial no. 1450	Riga Sound, Tukkuma Region.	Enemy fighter.		Squadron and Army reports.	
5	1/9/17	1st	Nieuport 23 serial no. 3747	Iskul Region.	Enemy aircraft.		Squadron and Army reports.	
6	1/9/17	1st	Nieuport 23 serial no. 3747	Iskul Region.	Enemy aircraft.		Squadron and Army reports.	

Vasili Ivanovich Yanchenko

Victory	Date	Squadron	Aircraft Flown	Place	Enemy Aircraft	Enemy Crew	Confirmation	Comments
1	25/6/16	7th	Nieuport 11	Podgaitsy Village.	Aviatik B.III 30.30 of Flik 27.	*Zgfhr.* F. Schallinger (pilot), *Fähnrich d.R.* G. Wangler (obs.), both wounded, POW.	Army/squadron reports.	Shared with Orlov.
2	4/10/16	7th	Nieuport 11	Zlota-Lipa, Brzezhany Region.	Two-seater.	Both POW.	Army/squadron reports.	Shared with Orlov.
3	18/10/16	7th	Nieuport 11		Aircraft from group of 3.		Army/squadron reports.	
4	7/3/17	7th	Nieuport 11	Svistelniki, landed west of Lipitza.			Army/squadron reports.	Shared with Makeenok.
5	13/4/17	7th	Morane Saulnier Type H	Bogorodchani, Galicia.	Brandenburg C.I 67.03 of Flik 7.	*Fw.* Paul Hablitschek (pilot), *Oblt.* Roman Schmidt (obs.)	Army/squadron reports.	Shared with Gilsher and Makeenok.
6	13/4/17	7th	Morane Saulnier Type H	Bogorodchani, Galicia.	Brandenburg C.I 67.04 of Flik 7.	Kelfac (pilot) wounded, *Ltn.* Heinrich Szelica (obs.)	Army/squadron reports.	Shared with Gilsher and Makeenok.
7	27/6/17	7th	Nieuport 17	Shumlany.			Army/squadron reports.	
8	2/7/17	7th	Nieuport 11 serial no. 1889	Near Krasne, landed near Brzezhany.	Brandenburg C.I 27.44 of Flik 14.	*Flusz.* Stefin Hegedus (pilot), *Ltn.* Fritz Steiner (obs.)	Army/squadron reports.	
9	6/7/17	7th	Nieuport 11 serial no. 1889	North of Brzezhany.	Aircraft from group of 4.		Army/squadron reports.	Shared with Makeenok.
10	11/7/17	7th	Nieuport 11 serial no. 1889	Brzezhany.			Army/squadron reports.	Shared with Makeenok.
11	18/7/17	7th	Nieuport 11 serial no. 1889	Brzezhany.			Army/squadron reports.	
12	20/7/17	7th	Nieuport 11 serial no. 1889	Tarnopol.	German aircraft.		Army Order #11158.	Shared with Gilsher who was killed in battle.
13	5/8/17	7th	Nieuport 11	Brzezhany.			Russian troops.	Shared with Makeenok.
14	23/9/17	7th	Nieuport 11	Gusyatin, Romania.	Albatros D.III.		Army/squadron reports.	
15	8/10/17	32nd	Nieuport 21	Zbrizh Region.	Aviatik two-seater.		Army Order 254/Squadron reports.	
16	14/10/17	32nd	Nieuport 21	Gorodok/Jaslowec (@ 1630 hours).	Albatros D.III 53.20 of Flik 30.	*Feldwebel* Obeslo killed.	Army Order 254.	

Ivan Mikhailovich Bagrovnikov

Victory	Date	Squadron	Aircraft Flown	Place	Enemy Aircraft	Enemy Crew	Confirmation	Comments
1	20/7/17	9th	Voisin	North of Kozovo @ 2030 hours.	Aircraft forced to land.		Squadron reports.	With brother, *Praporshik* Bagrovnikov.

Jezups S. Bashko and Crew of *Kievsky I* (M.V. Smirnov, A.A. Naumov, A.M. Lavrov)

Victory	Date	Squadron	Aircraft Flown	Place	Enemy Aircraft	Enemy Crew	Confirmation	Comments
N/C	19/7/15	1st	IM *Kievsky I*	Szedrzeszuw.	Two-seater of Fl.Abt. 21.		Squadron reports.	*Kievsky I* crash-landed inside Russian lines after being attacked 3 times.

Jaan M. Mahlapuu

Victory	Date	Squadron	Aircraft Flown	Place	Enemy Aircraft	Enemy Crew	Confirmation	Comments
1	25/2/17	12th	Nieuport 11				12th Army report.	
2	11/3/17	12th	Nieuport 11 serial no. 1111	Over Lidak.	Albatros C.III 667/16.		12th Army reports #79 and #570.	Awarded Cross of St. George Third Class.
N/C	2/7/17	12th	Nieuport 11		Aircraft forced to land behind enemy lines.			

Petr Nikolayevich Nesterov

Victory	Date	Squadron	Aircraft Flown	Place	Enemy Aircraft	Enemy Crew	Confirmation	Comments
1	7/9/14	3rd	Morane Saulnier G serial no. 281	Near Zholkov.	Austrian two-seater.	*Oblt.* Baron Friedrich von Rosenthal (obs.) and *Feldwebel* Franz Malina (pilot), both KIA.	Army report.	Rammed enemy aircraft, KIA.

Aleksei V. Pankrat'yev and Crew of IM-2 (S.N. Nicolsky, V.S. Federov, *Podporuchik* Pavlov, *Podpraporshik* Ushakov)

Victory	Date	Squadron	Aircraft Flown	Place	Enemy Aircraft	Enemy Crew	Confirmation	Comments
N/C	30/9/15	2nd	IM #2	Bausk/Mittau.	Albatros two-seater.			With IM-4. Ushakov was the gunner who sent EA down out of control.
1	30/3/16	2nd	IM #2	Monasterzisko.	Brandenburg C.I of Flik 14.	*Hptm.* Mackensen (obs.) killed, *Ltn.* Marek (pilot) POW.	Army reports, squadron Reports.	Ushakov shot down the plane. He was killed and Federov was wounded.
2	8/11/16	1st	IM #2	Buzcac.	Fighter shot down.		Squadron reports.	With IM #12.

Additional Victories By Victor S. Federov and Crew After A.V. Pankrat'yev Was Transferred

Victory	Date	Squadron	Aircraft Flown	Place	Enemy Aircraft	Enemy Crew	Confirmation	Comments
1	8/5/17		IM #15	Near Meshishchuv.	Fokker crashed in enemy trenches.		Seen by IM #15 Crew.	C.O. Capt. Klemborskiy, Dep. C.O. Lt. Demichev-Ivanov, Arty. Off. Capt. Ivanovskiy,
2	8/5/17		IM #15	Near Meshishchuv.	Fokker crashed in Russian Lines.		Reports of units near 41st Army Corps HQ.	Pilot Staff-Capt. V.S. Federov, Mech. Sgt.-Major Golubets.

Marcel Pliat

Victory	Date	Squadron	Aircraft Flown	Place	Enemy Aircraft	Enemy Crew	Confirmation	Comments
1	Early 1916	EVK	IM-10		EA shot down.		EVK reports.	Awarded Soldier's Cross of St. George Fourth Class.
2	Spring 1916	EVK	IM Type G-3		EA shot down, forced to land.		EVK report filed by Lt. Lavrov and Lt. Shokalsky.	
N/C	Spring 1916	EVK	IM Type G-3		EA damaged, smoking.		EVK report filed by Lt. Lavrov and Lt. Shokalsky.	

Boris Vasilevitch Sergievsky

Victory	Date	Squadron	Aircraft Flown	Place	Enemy Aircraft	Enemy Crew	Confirmation	Comments
N/C	18/6/17	2nd	Nieuport	Buczacz, Galicia.	Two-seater from FLAbt. 24 forced to land behind enemy lines.			
1	18/6/17	2nd	Nieuport	Galicia.	Roland fighter forced to land in no-man's-land.	Escaped to own lines.	Army reports.	
2	7/9/14	2nd	Nieuport	Smolno, Galicia.	Brandenburg C.I 269.17 of Flik 3, destroyed by artillery after landing.		Artillery reports.	With pilots Ingaunis and Snegirev.

Alexander Nikolayevich Sveshnikov

Victory	Date	Squadron	Aircraft Flown	Place	Enemy Aircraft	Enemy Crew	Confirmation	Comments
N/C	14/8/17	7th	Nieuport 23	Austrian territory near Kozuvka.	EA forced to land.			
1	22/9/17	7th	Spad 7	Trenches near Poznanka.	Roland D.IIa	Pilot escaped to own lines.	Aircraft recovered by Russian troops.	
2	26/9/17	7th	Spad 7	West of Brody.	Observation balloon.		Army report.	

Olgerts Teteris

Victory	Date	Squadron	Aircraft Flown	Place	Enemy Aircraft	Enemy Crew	Confirmation	Comments
1	17/8/16	13th	Voisin		German aircraft.		Army reports.	With *Poruchik* Kuskov (obs.)
2	21/10/16	13th	Voisin		German aircraft.		Army reports.	

Vyatcheslav Mikhailovich Tkachev

Victory	Date	Squadron	Aircraft Flown	Place	Enemy Aircraft	Enemy Crew	Confirmation	Comments
1	14/8/16	11th	Morane Saulnier L	Near Hotyn in Zdolbunovo.	Aviatik B.II 34.41 of Flik 5	*Zügfuhrer* Edmund Pirker (pilot), *Fähnrich d.R.* Herbert Scholz (obs.)	Army report.	With *Poruchik* Hrizoskoleo (obs.)

Peter (Edward) Martinovitch Tomson

Victory	Date	Squadron	Aircraft Flown	Place	Enemy Aircraft	Enemy Crew	Confirmation	Comments
N/C	28/7/16	1st	Nieuport	Kobyluck.	Albatros.		None.	
N/C	18/2/17	1st	Nieuport	Smorgon.			None.	
N/C	19/2/17	1st	Nieuport	Smorgon.			None.	
N/C	10/3/17	1st	Nieuport	Smorgon.			None.	
1	18/3/17	1st	Nieuport 11 Serial No. 1132	Southwest of Smorgon, crashed near Zalesie.	German two-seater from Fl.Abt. 25.	Robert Steinmetz (pilot) *Ltn.* Kurt Poelchau (obs.) both killed.	Army/squadron reports.	Shared with Rosenfeld.

Appendix 4: Aircraft Flown by Pilots

Argeyev (d'Argueff)
Nieuport 11 (French built, serial no. unknown, while in France)
Nieuport 17 (serial no. unknown)
Spad 7 (French built, serial no. unknown)
Spad 13 (French built, serial no. unknown, while in France)

Bagrovnikov
Voisin LA (serial no. unknown)

Bashko
Il'ya Mouromets (R-BVZ built, Kievskiy-2 through -6)

Coudouret
Nieuport 11 (French built, serial no. unknown, while in France)
Nieuport 14 (French built, serial no. unknown, while in France)
Nieuport 17 (French built, serial no. unknown)
Spad 7 (French built, serial no. unknown)
Spad 13 (French built, serial no. unknown, while in France)
Voisin LA (French built, serial no. unknown, while in France)

Fedorov
Caudron G.4 (French built, serial no. unknown, while in France)
Nieuport 11 (French built, serial no. unknown, while in Romania)
Nieuport 17 (serial no. unknown)
Spad 13 (French built, serial no. unknown, while in France)

Gilsher
Nieuport 11 (Dux built, serial nos. 1679, 2451)
Nieuport 11 (French built, serial no. 1232)
Nieuport 21 (French built, serial no. 1872)
Sikorsky S-16 (serial no. 201)

Gond
Caudron G.4 (French built, serial no. unknown, while in France)
Nieuport 11 (French built, serial nos. 1419, 1644)
Nieuport 12 (French built, serial no. unknown, while in France)
Nieuport 17 (French built, serial no. unknown)

Kokorin
Henri Farman F.22 (serial no. unknown)
Morane Saulnier H (serial no. unknown)
Morane Saulnier L (serial no. unknown)
Nieuport 10 (serial no. unknown)
Nieuport 21 (serial no. unknown)
Spad A.2 (serial no. unknown)

Kozakov
Morane Saulnier G (serial nos. 316)
Morane Saulnier L (serial nos. 522, 526, 529)
Nieuport 4 (French built, serial no. unknown)
Nieuport 9 (serial no. unknown)
Nieuport 10 (French built, serial no. 222)
Nieuport 17 (serial no. unknown)
Spad 7 (French built, serial no. unknown)

Kruten
Nieuport 10 (French built, serial no. 704)
Nieuport 11 (French built, serial no. 1137)
Nieuport 17 (French built, serial no. 2232)
Nieuport 21 (French built, serial no. 4572)
Spad 7 (French built, serial no. unknown, while in France)
Vickers FB.19 (British built, serial no. 539)
Voisin LA (serial nos. 42, 256)

Lachmann
Nieuport 11 (French built, serial no. unknown, while in France
and Italy)
Nieuport 17 (French built, serial no. unknown)
REP 'N' (French built, serial no. unknown, while in France)
Spad 7 (French built, serial no. unknown)

Leman
Nieuport 10 (serial no. unknown)
Nieuport 11 (serial no. unknown)
Nieuport 16 (serial no. unknown)
Nieuport 17 (serial no. unknown)
Spad A.2 (serial no. unknown)

Loiko
Morane Saulnier H (serial no. 732)
Nieuport 10 (serial no. unknown)
Nieuport 11 (serial no. 1109)
Nieuport 17 (French built, serial nos. 1445, 1448, 1902)
Nieuport 21 (French built, serial nos. 1127, 1902)
Nieuport 23 (serial no. 5045)
Voisin LA (serial no. unknown)

Mahlapuu
Nieuport 9 (serial nos. 173, 262)
Nieuport 11 (Dux built, serial nos. 1111, 1181)
Nieuport 11 (French built, serial no. 1161)
Nieuport 21 (French built, serial no. 1825)

Makeenok
Morane Saulnier L (serial no. unknown)
Nieuport 4 (serial no. unknown)
Nieuport 17 (serial no. unknown)
Nieuport 21 (serial no. 2453)

Nesterov
Morane Saulnier G (serial nos. 162, 281)
Nieuport 4 (serial no. 41A)

Orlov
Moska-2 (serial no. 7)
Nieuport 10 (Lebed built, serial unknown)
Nieuport 10 (French built, serial no. 702)
Nieuport 11 (French built, serial nos. 1514, 1679)
Spad 7 (French built, serial no. unknown, while in France)
Voisin LA (Anatra built, serial no. 366)

Pankrat'yev
Il'ya Mouromets (R-BVZ built, Ship #2) Type 'Beh,' 'Veh,' and 'G-1'

Pishvanov
Nieuport 10 (French built, serial no. 709)
Nieuport 11 (serial no. 846)
Nieuport 17 (serial no. 1890)
Nieuport 21 (serial no. 4191)
Nieuport 27 (serial no. 2749)

Plait
Il'ya Mouromets (R-BVZ built, Ship #10)

Pulpe
Morane Saulnier L (French built, serial no. unknown, while in
France)
Nieuport 11 (French built, serial no. unknown)

Revol-Tissot
Bleriot 'Artillerie' 2-seater (French built, serial no. unknown, while in France)
Nieuport 11 (French built, serial no. unknown, while in Romania)
Nieuport 12 (French built, serial no. unknown, while in France)
Nieuport 17 (French built, serial no. unknown, while in Romania)

Safonov
Grigorovich M.9 (Sch S-18, Sch S-29)
Grigorovich M.15 (SchI-1, SchI-2)
Maurice Farman MF.11 Floatplane (naval serial no. 31)
Nieuport 21 (Dux built, Naval serial nos. 1, 2, 4, 5)

Sergievsky
Nieuport 21 (Dux built, serial no. unknown)
Nieuport 21 (French built, serial no. 2176)
Voisin LA (serial no. unknown)

Seversky
FBA Type C #7
Grigorovich M.9 (Sch S-50)
Grigorovich M.11
Grigorovich M.15 (SchI-9)
Nieuport 21 (Dux built, Naval serial nos. 3, 6, 7, 8)

Smirnov
Deperdussin TT (tactical no. 2)
Morane Saulnier I (serial no. unknown)
Morane Saulnier L (serial no. unknown)
Nieuport 10 (French built, serial no. 1514)
Nieuport 21 (French built, serial no. 1514)
Spad A.2 (French built, serial no. unknown)
Spad 7 (French built, serial no. unknown)

Strizhevsky
Morane Saulnier L (serial no. unknown)
Nieuport 11 (Dux built, serial no. 1016)
Nieuport 17 (Dux built, serial no. 1448)
Nieuport 21 (French built, serial no. 1719)
Spad 7 (French built, serial no. 1446)

Suk
Henri Farman F.22 (serial no. unknown)
Morane Saulnier H (serial no. 742)
Nieuport 10 (Dux built, serial no. 714)
Nieuport 11 (French built, serial nos. 1109, 1127, 1719)
Nieuport 17 (serial nos. 1442, 1445, 1448)
Nieuport 21 (French built, serial no. 1719)
Spad 7 (French built, serial nos. 1440, 1446)
Vickers FB.19 (British built, serial no. 12)

Sveshnikov
Morane Saulnier H (serial no. unknown)
Morane Saulnier L (Dux built, serial no. 493)
Morane Saulnier L (French built, serial no. 551)
Nieuport 12 (French built, serial no. 1051)
Nieuport 21 (French built, serial no. 2588)
Spad 7 (French built, serial no. 1500)

Teteris
Voisin LA (serial no. unknown)

Tkachev
Morane Saulnier L (serial no. unknown)
Nieuport 4 (serial no. 48A)

Tomson
Morane Saulnier L (serial no. 272)
Nieuport 10 (serial no. 160)
Nieuport 11 (French built, serial no. 1132)
Rumpler (captured German, serial number 419)

Utgoff
Curtiss Triad (Curtiss built, Naval serial nos. 3, 4, 5, 6)
Curtiss F-boat (Curtiss built, serial no. 15)
Curtiss K-KPB (Curtiss built, serial no. unknown)
FBA Type C (Russian built, serial no. unknown)
Grigorovich M.5 (serial nos. 36, 38)
Grigorovich M.9 (serial no. 114)
Henri Farman HF.20 Floatplane (serial no. unknown)
Maurice Farman MF.11 Floatplane (serial no. unknown)

Vakulovsky
Albatros (captured German, serial no. 269)
Morane Saulnier I (serial no. 741)
Morane Saulnier L (serial no. unknown)
Nieuport 4 (serial no. unknown)
Nieuport 11 (French built, serial nos. 1295)
Nieuport 17 (Dux built, serial nos. 1450)
Nieuport 23 (French built, serial nos. 3747, 3757)

Yanchenko
Morane Saulnier H (serial no. unknown)
Nieuport 9 (serial no. 285)
Nieuport 11 (serial no. 1889)
Nieuport 17 (serial no. unknown)
Nieuport 23 (serial no. unknown)

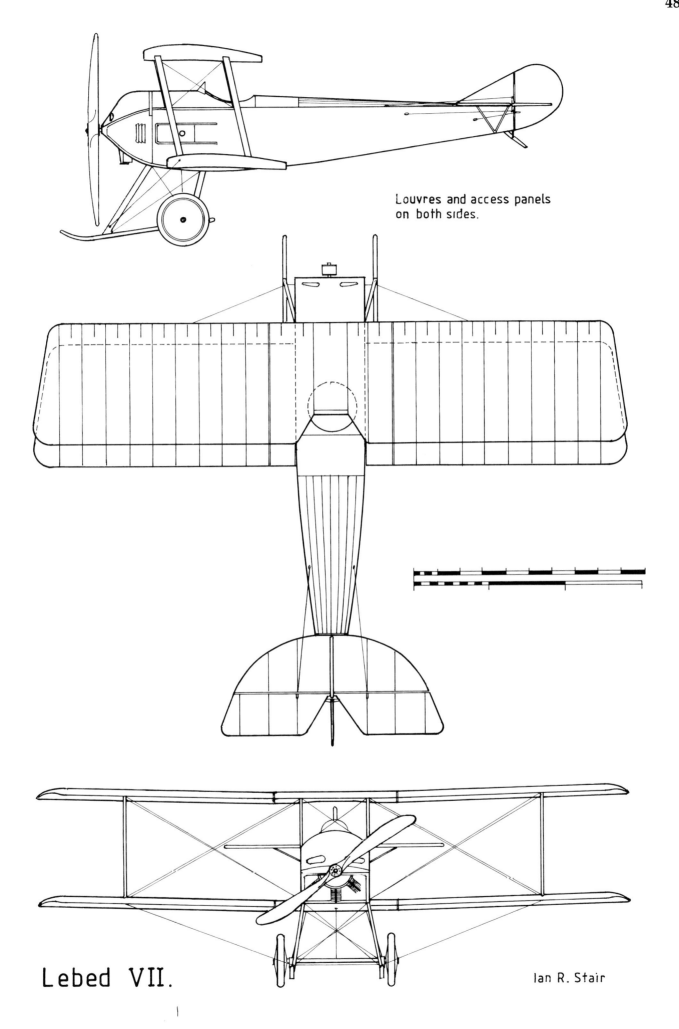

Louvres and access panels on both sides.

Lebed VII. Ian R. Stair

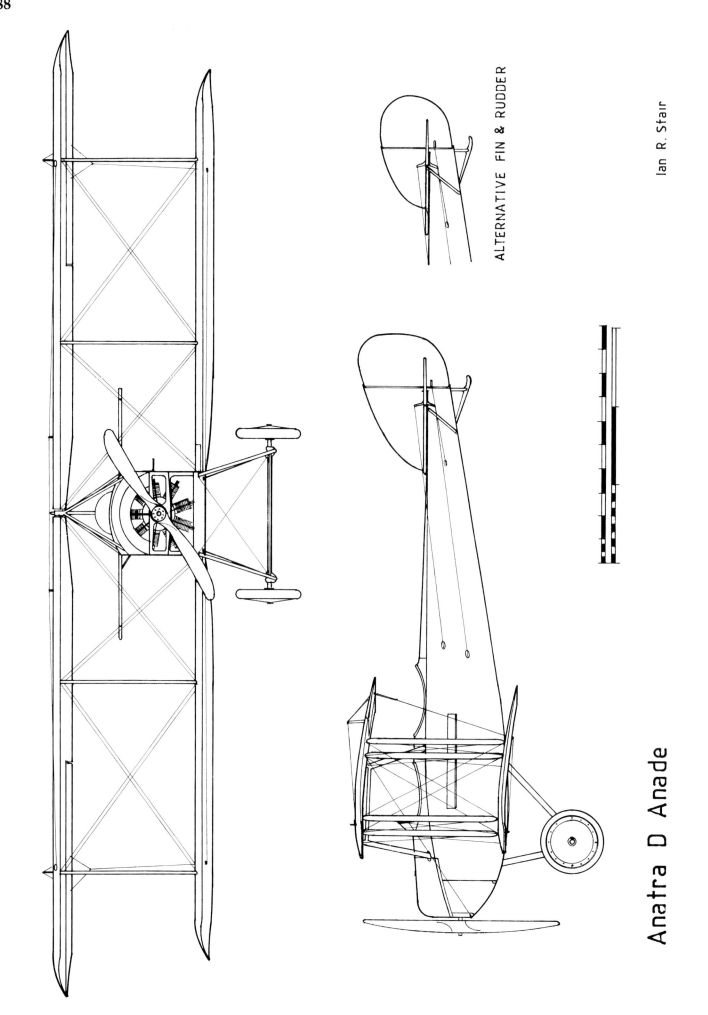

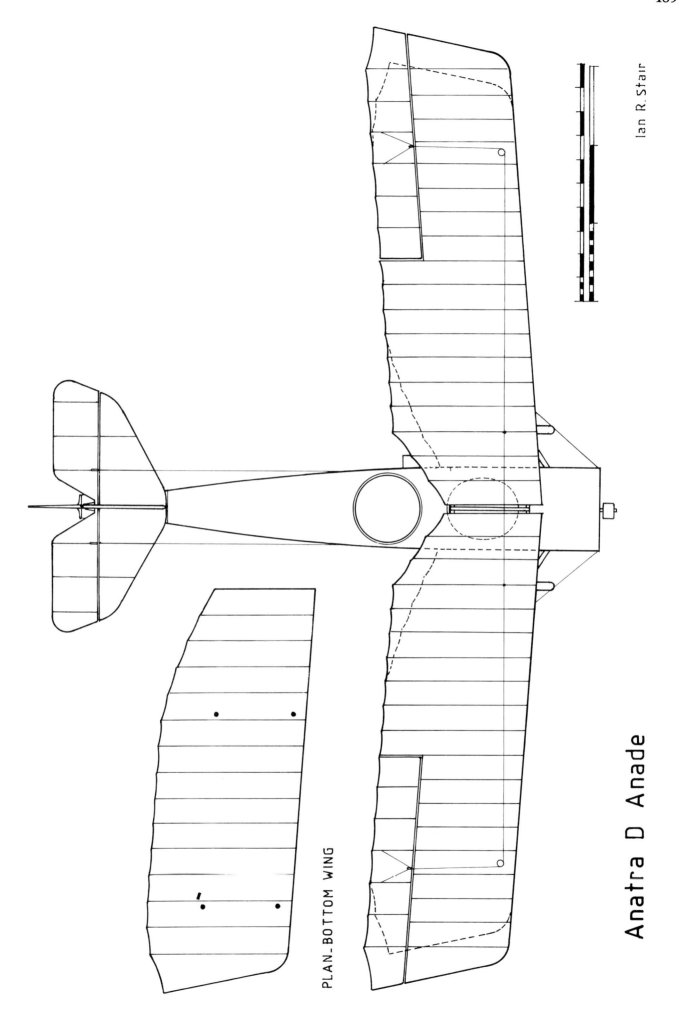

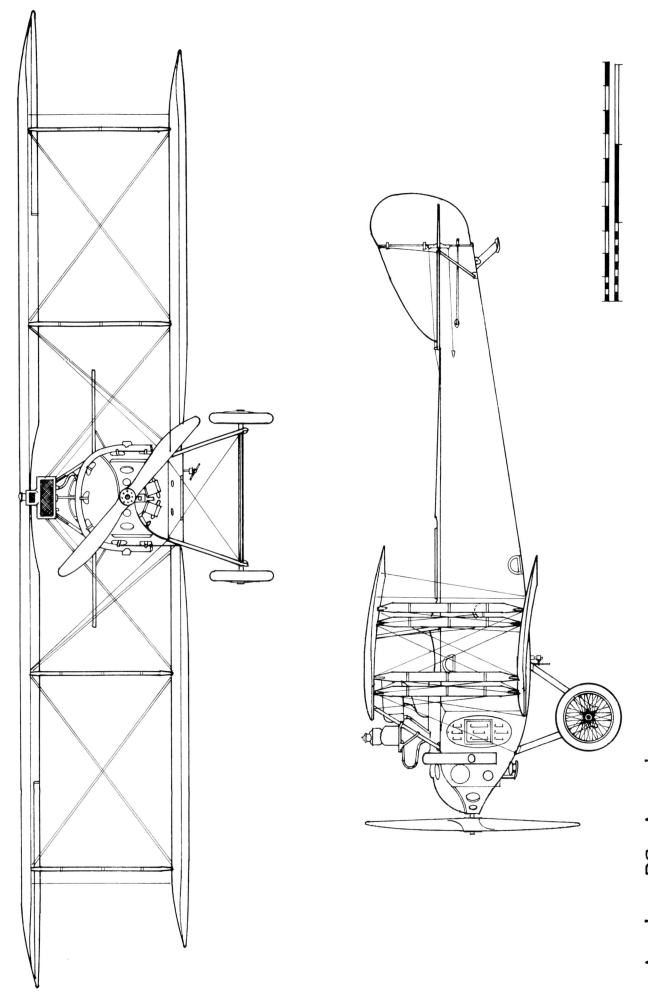

Anatra DS Anasal.

Ian R. Stair.

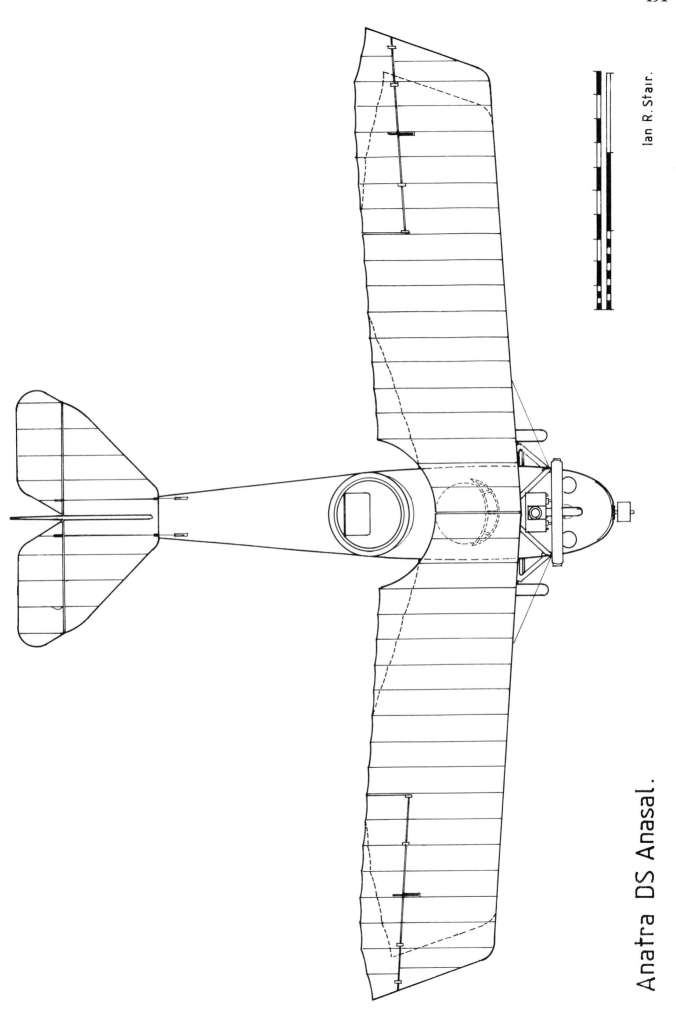

Anatra DS Anasal.

Ian R. Stair.

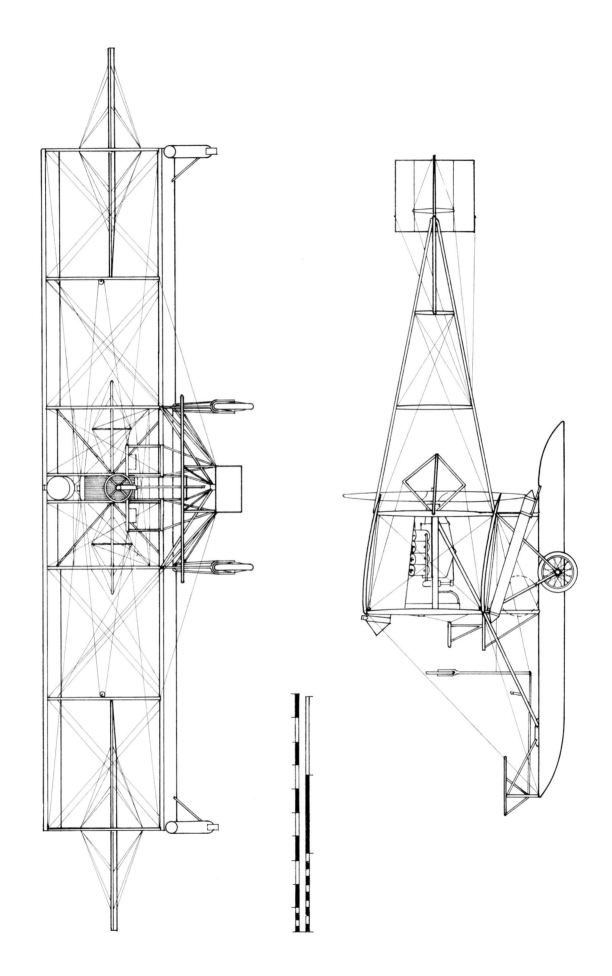

Curtiss Triad

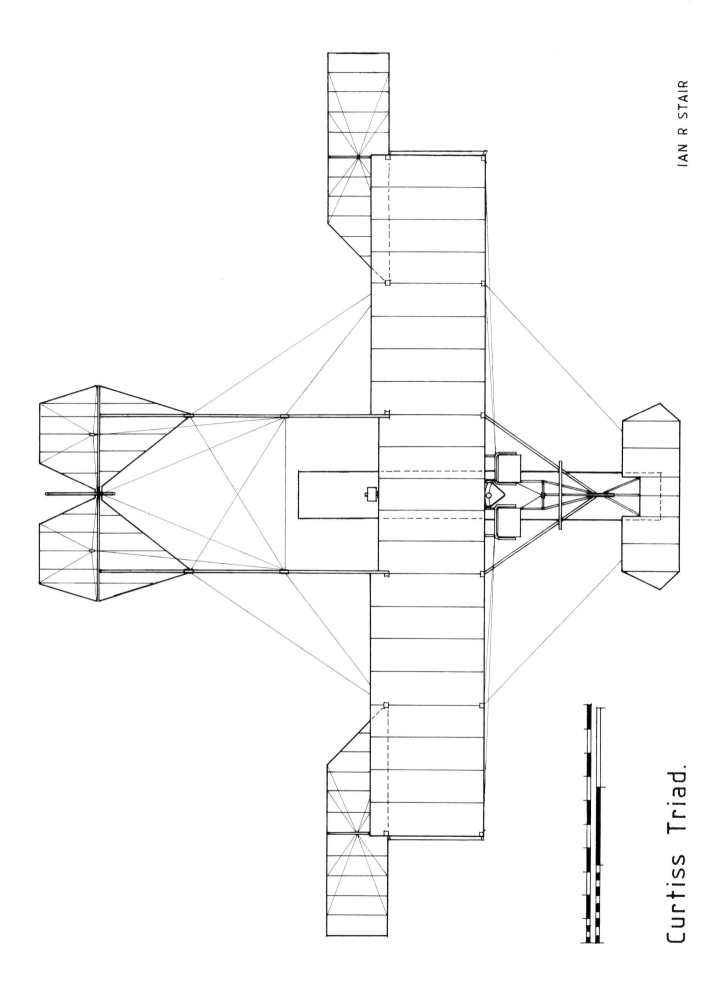

Curtiss Triad.

494

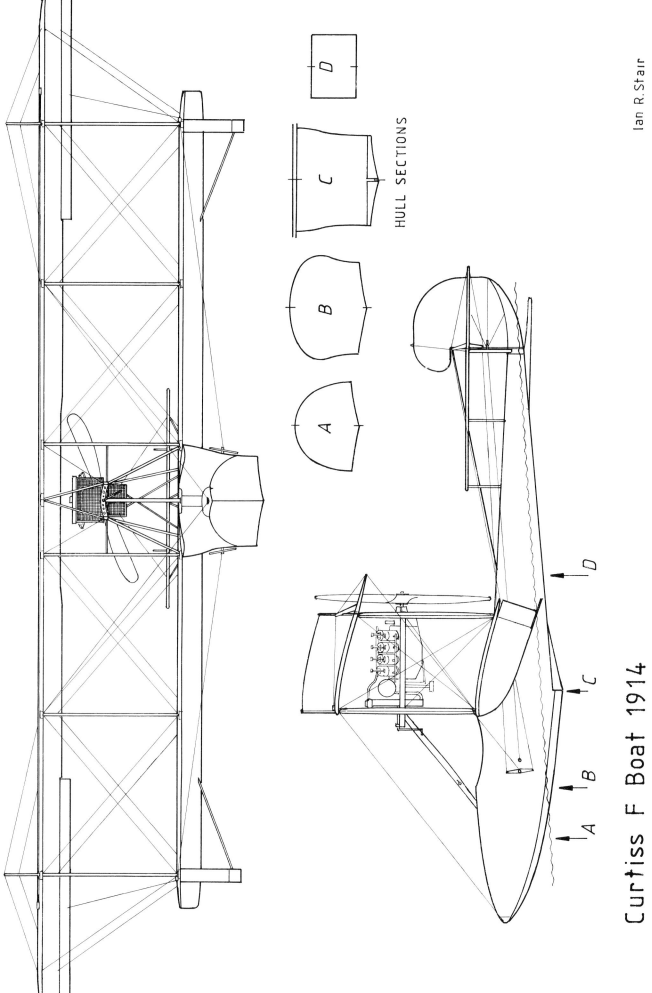

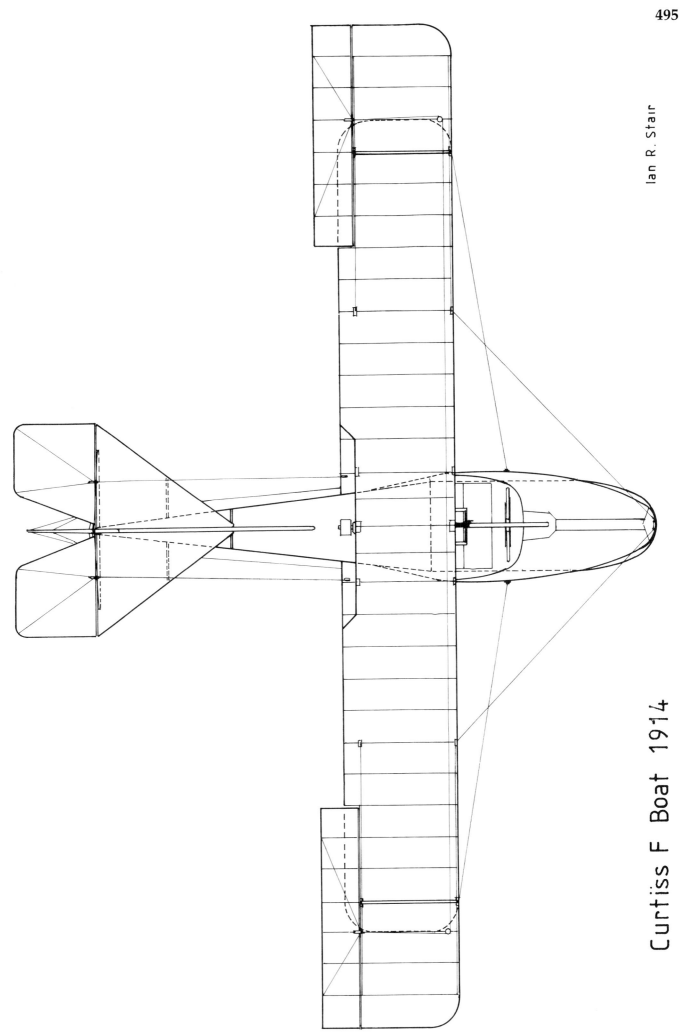

Curtiss F Boat 1914

Ian R. Stair

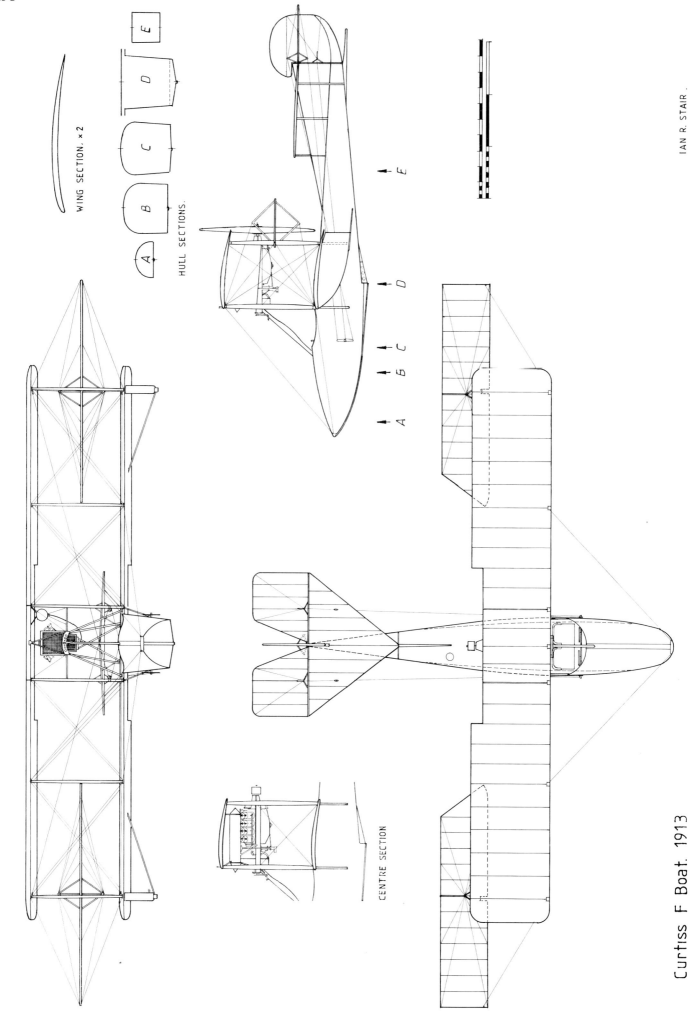

Curtiss F Boat. 1913

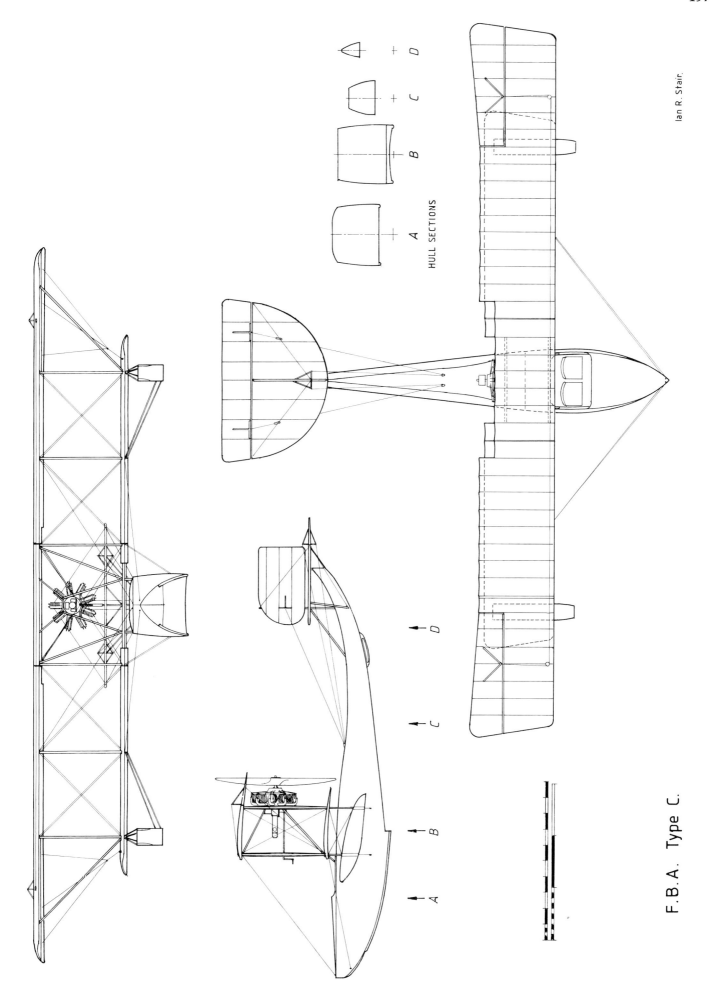

F.B.A. Type C.

There was much variation in detail particularly
in cockpit and rudder shape.

Ian R. Stair

Deperdussin TT.

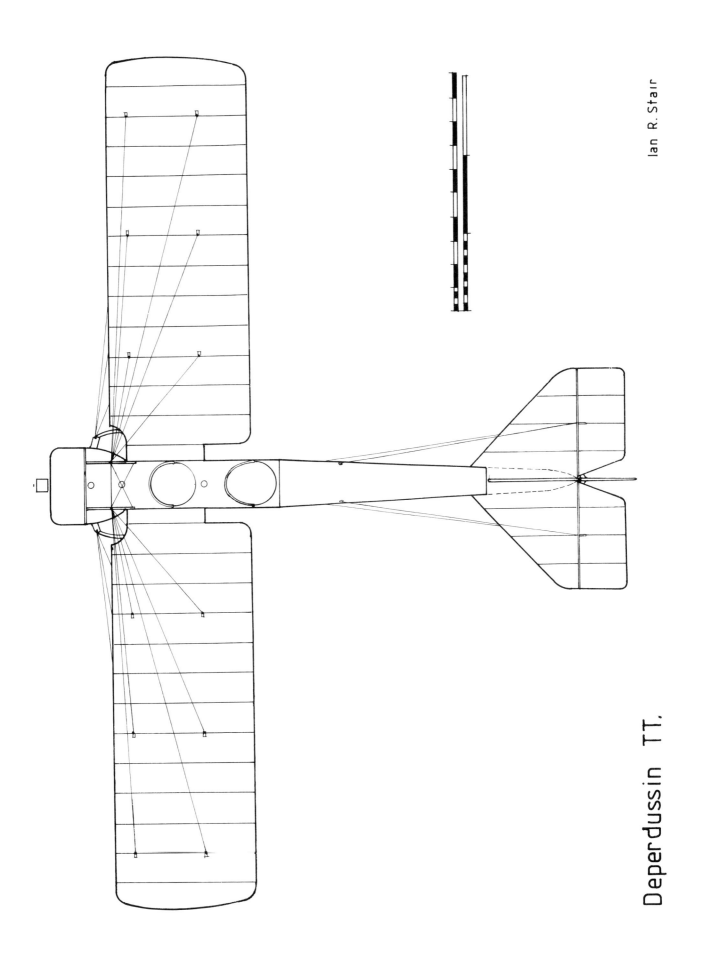

Deperdussin TT.

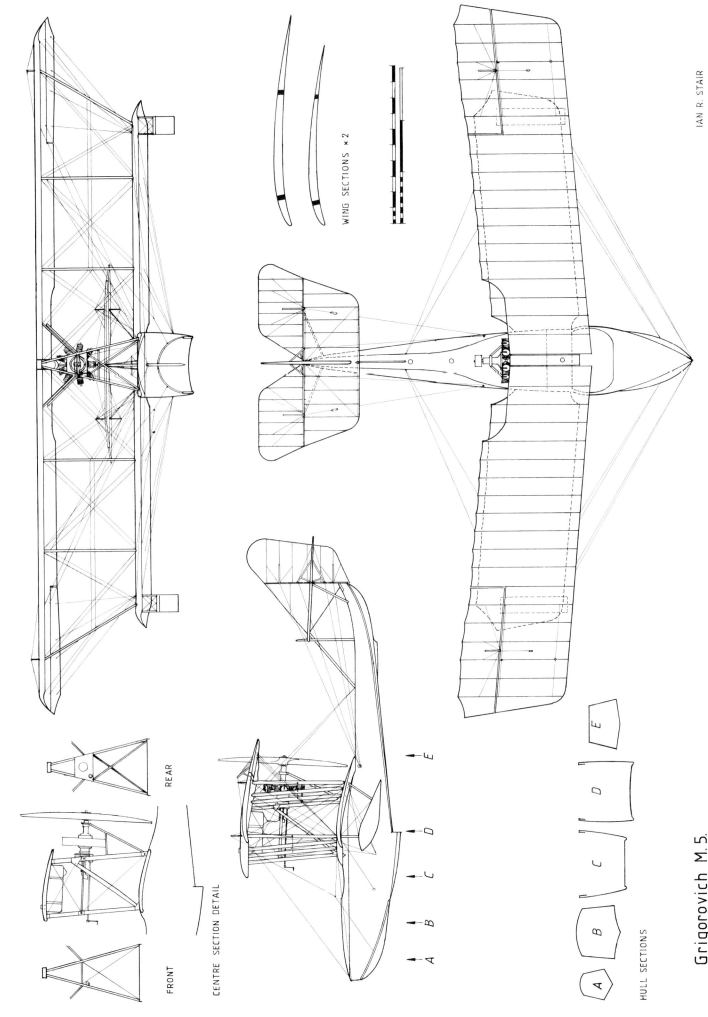

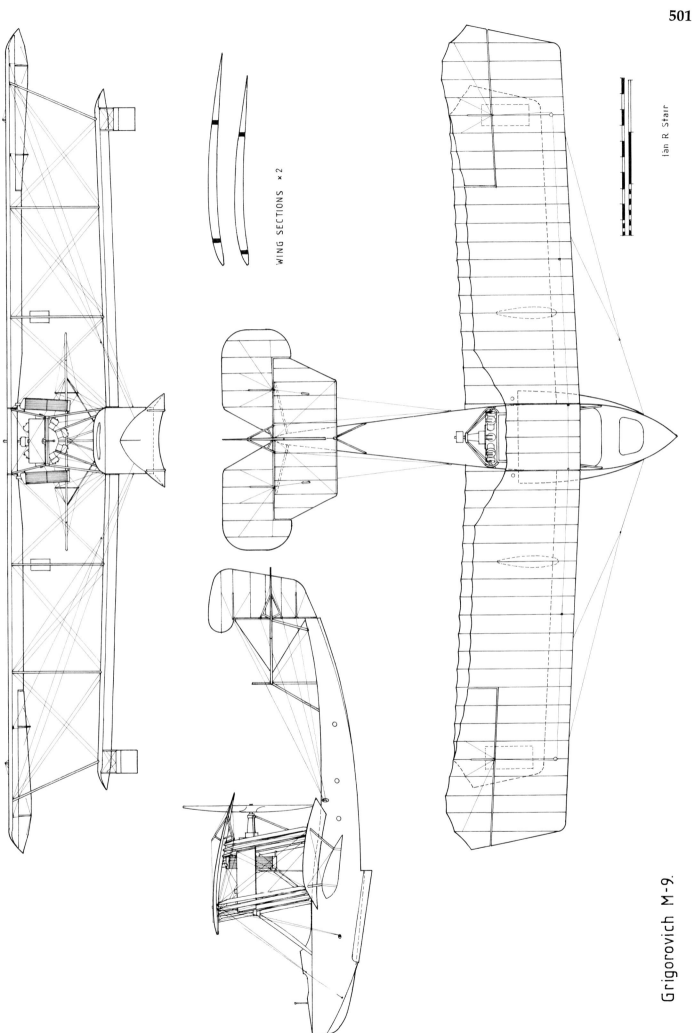

Grigorovich M-9.

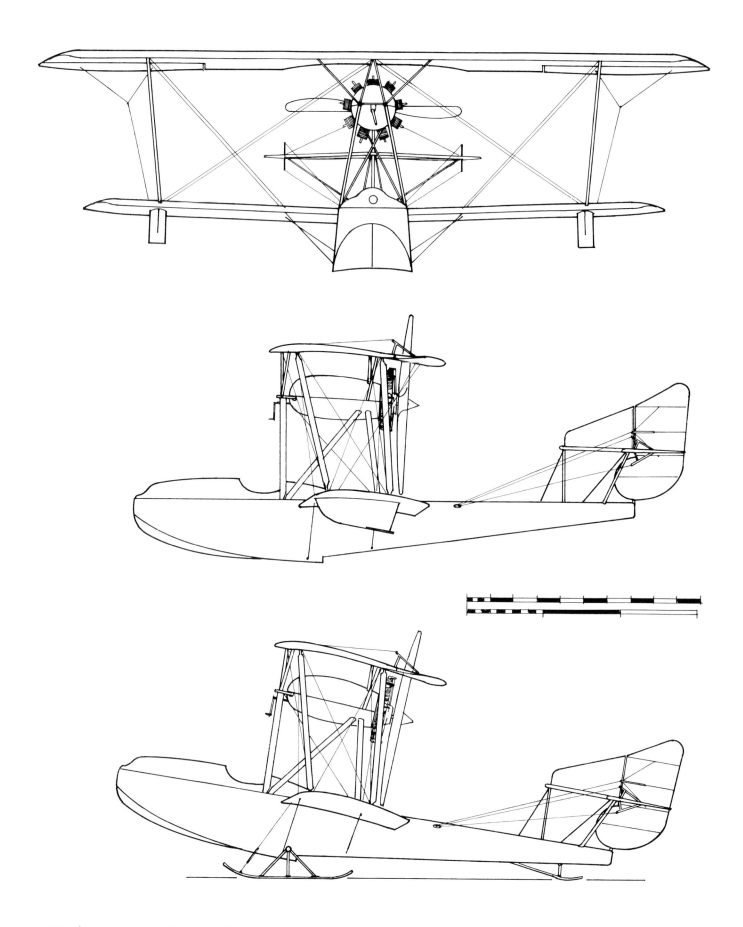

Grigorovich M.11.
Single seater.

DRAWN FROM LIMITED INFORMATION BY IAN R. STAIR.

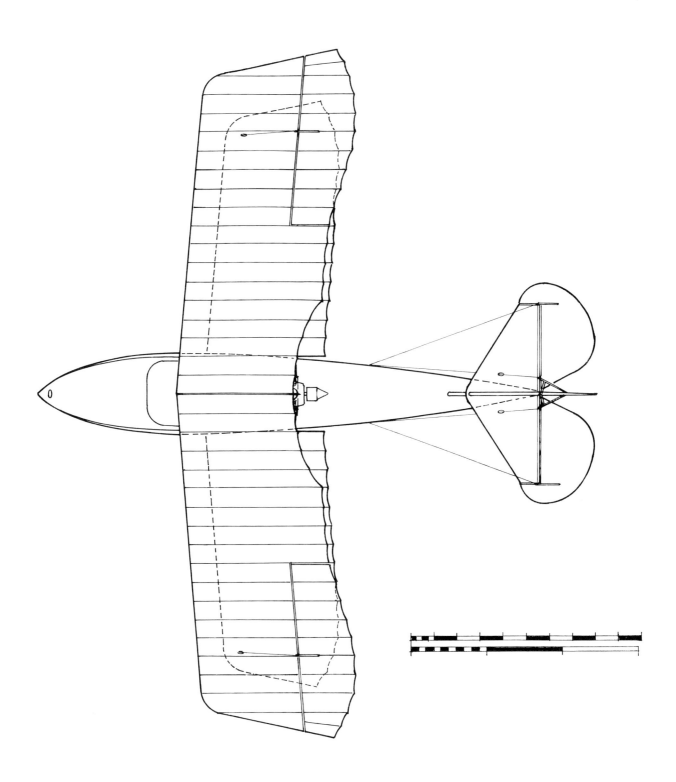

Grigorovich M.11.
Single seater

DRAWN FROM LIMITED INFORMATION
BY IAN R. STAIR

Grigorovich M-15

Ian R. Stair.

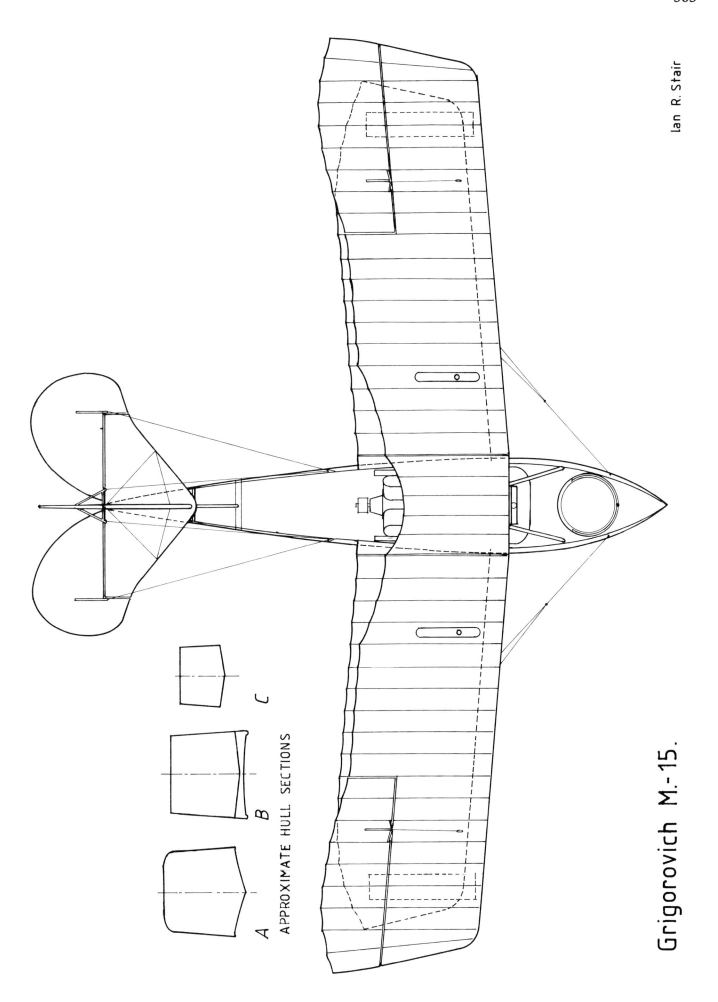

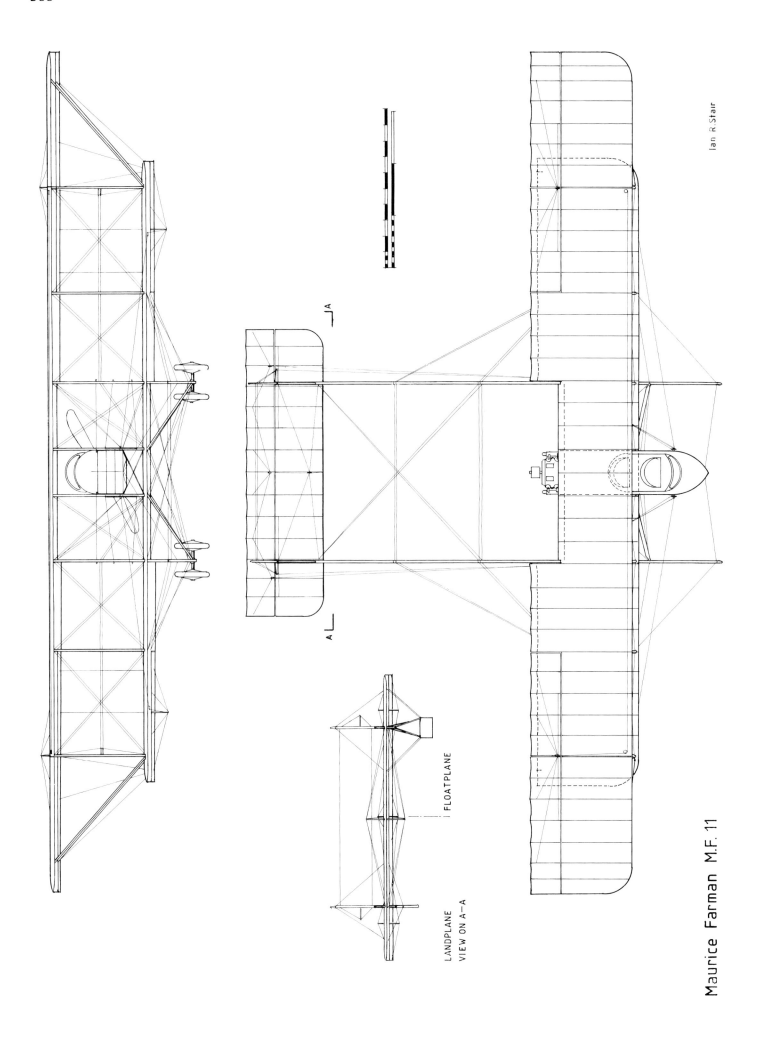

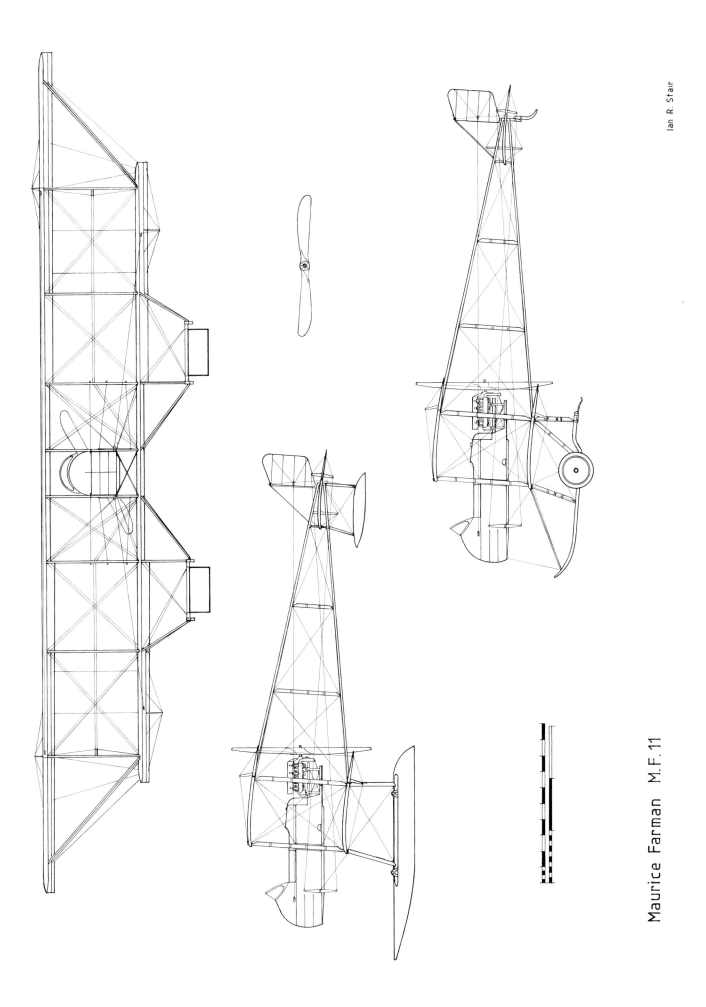

Maurice Farman M.F.11

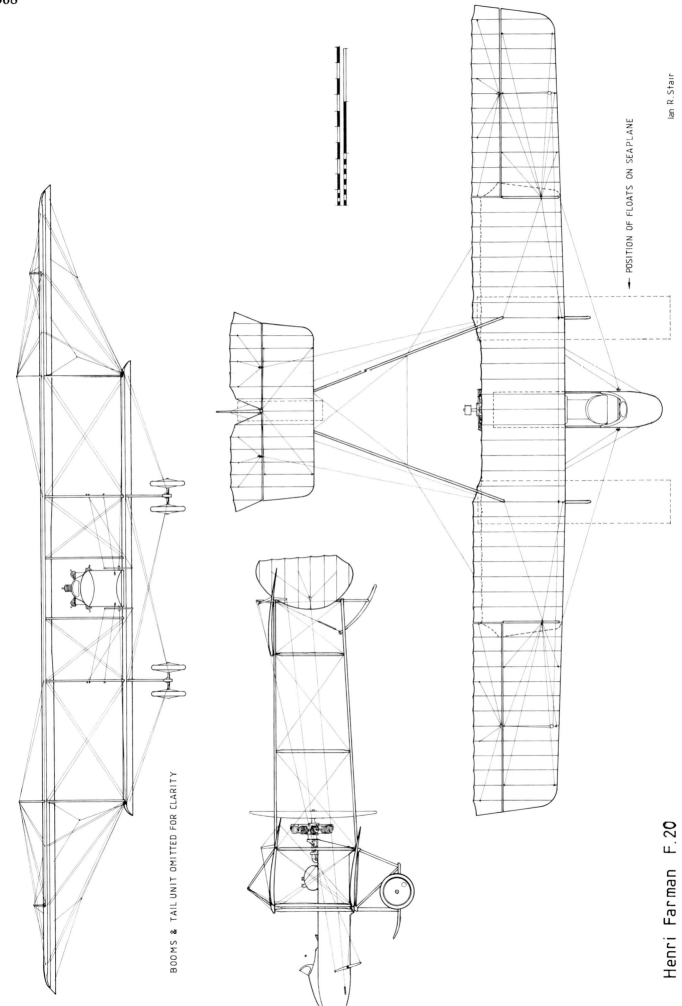

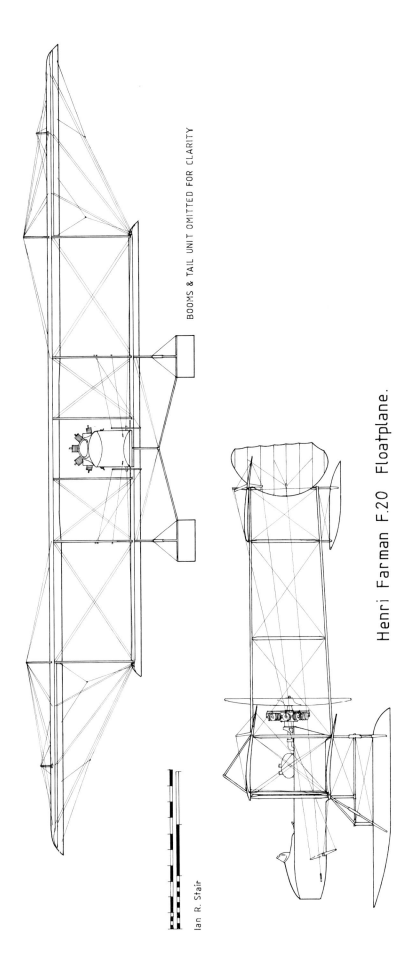

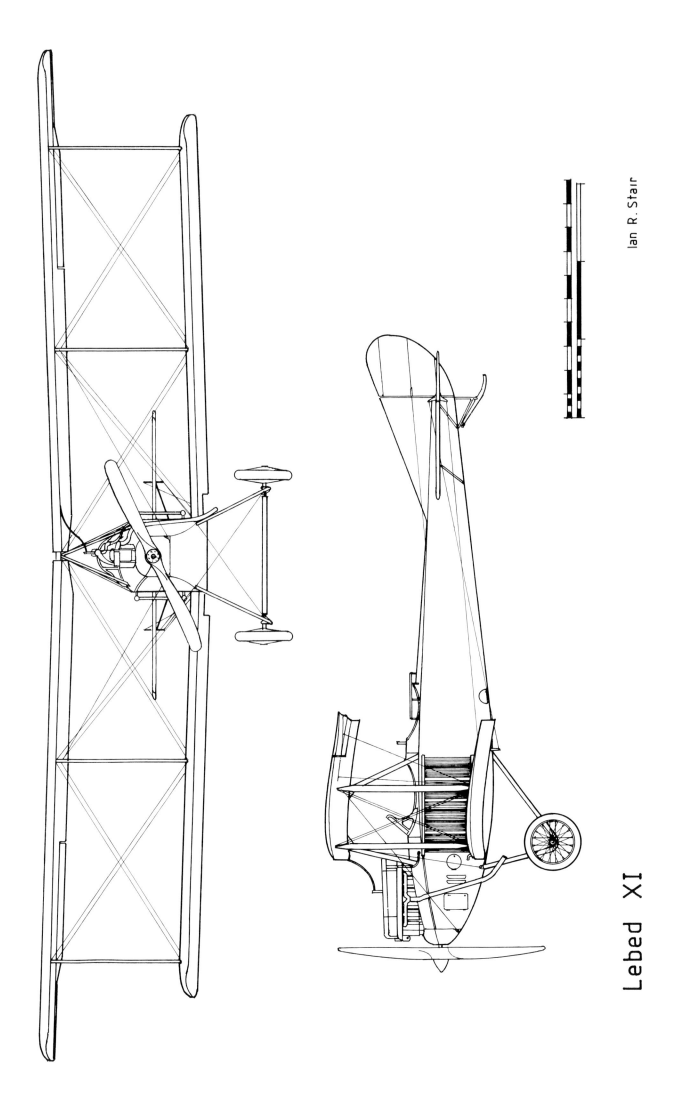

Lebed XI

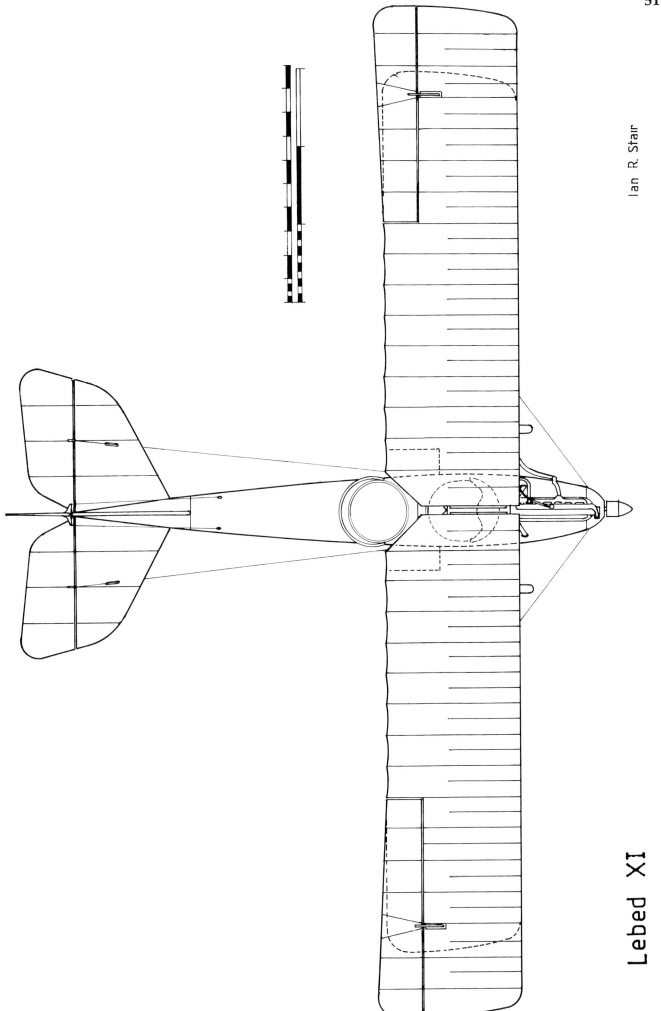

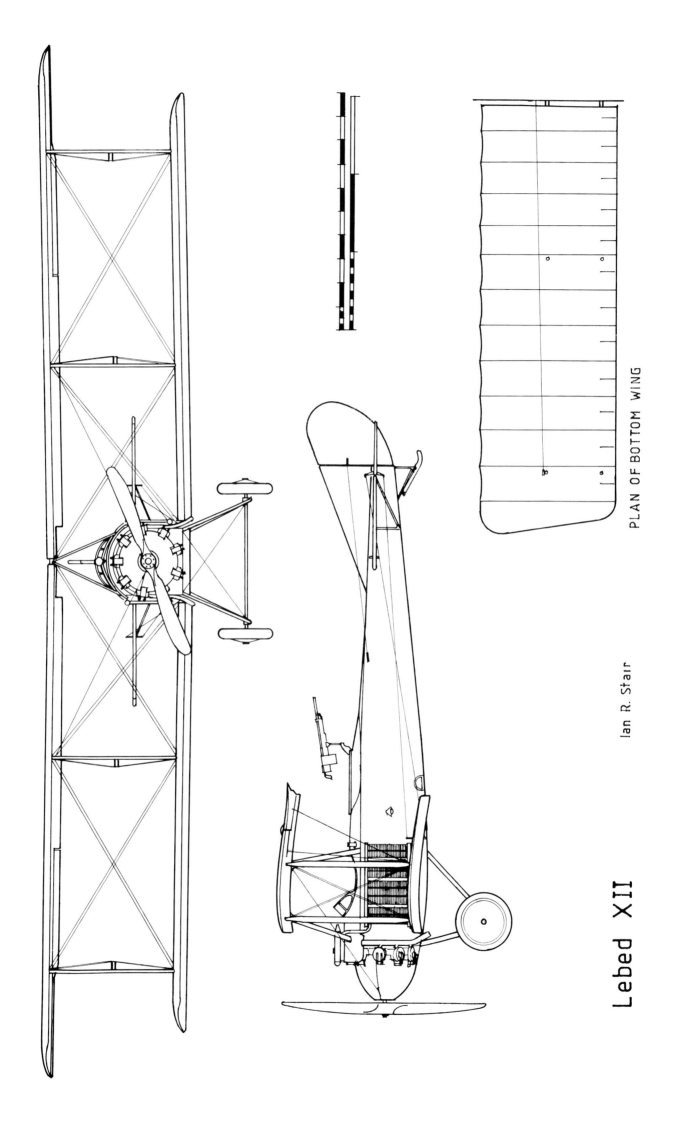

PLAN OF BOTTOM WING

Ian R. Stair

Lebed XII

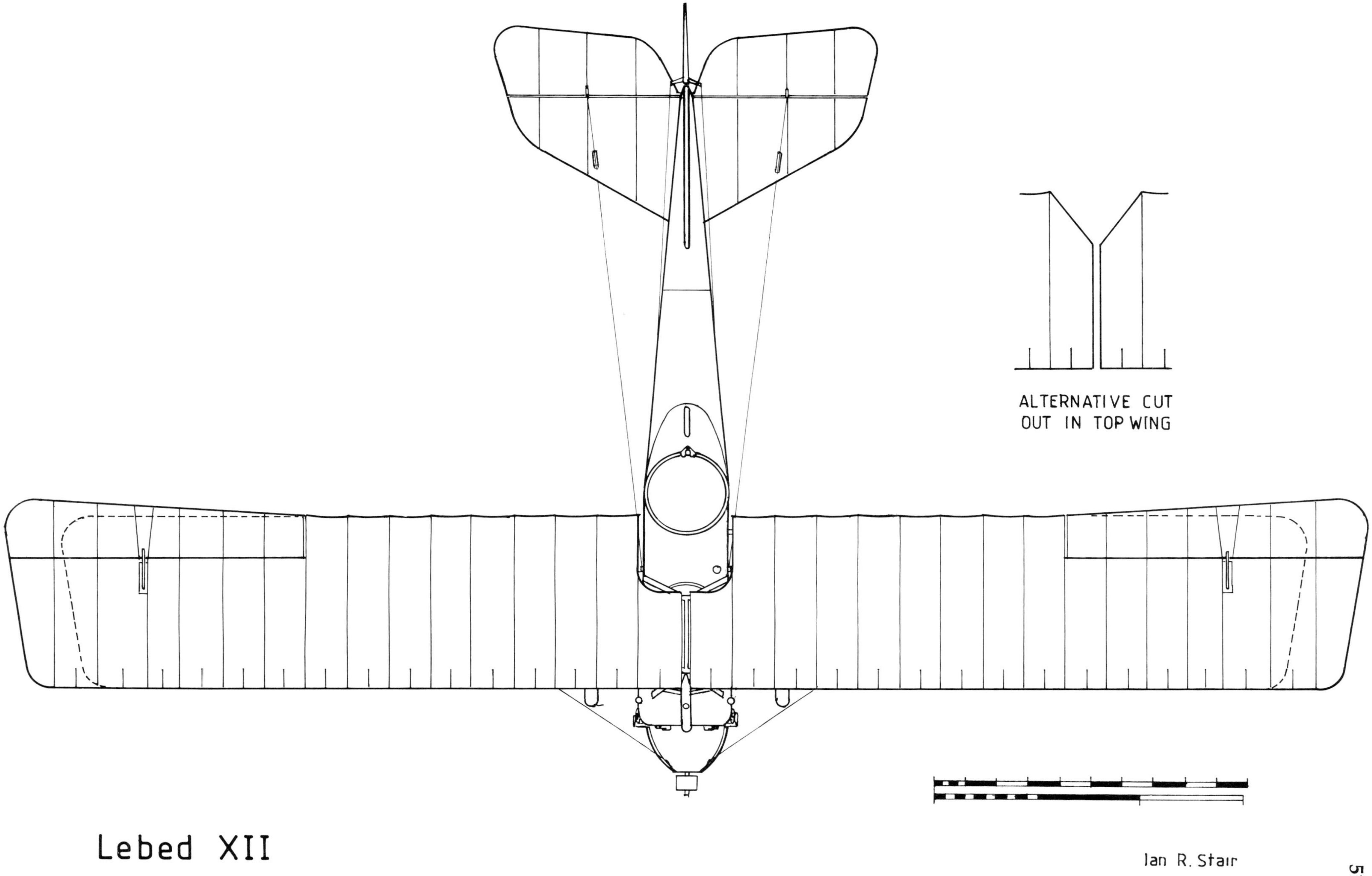

ALTERNATIVE CUT
OUT IN TOP WING

Ian R. Stair

Lebed XII

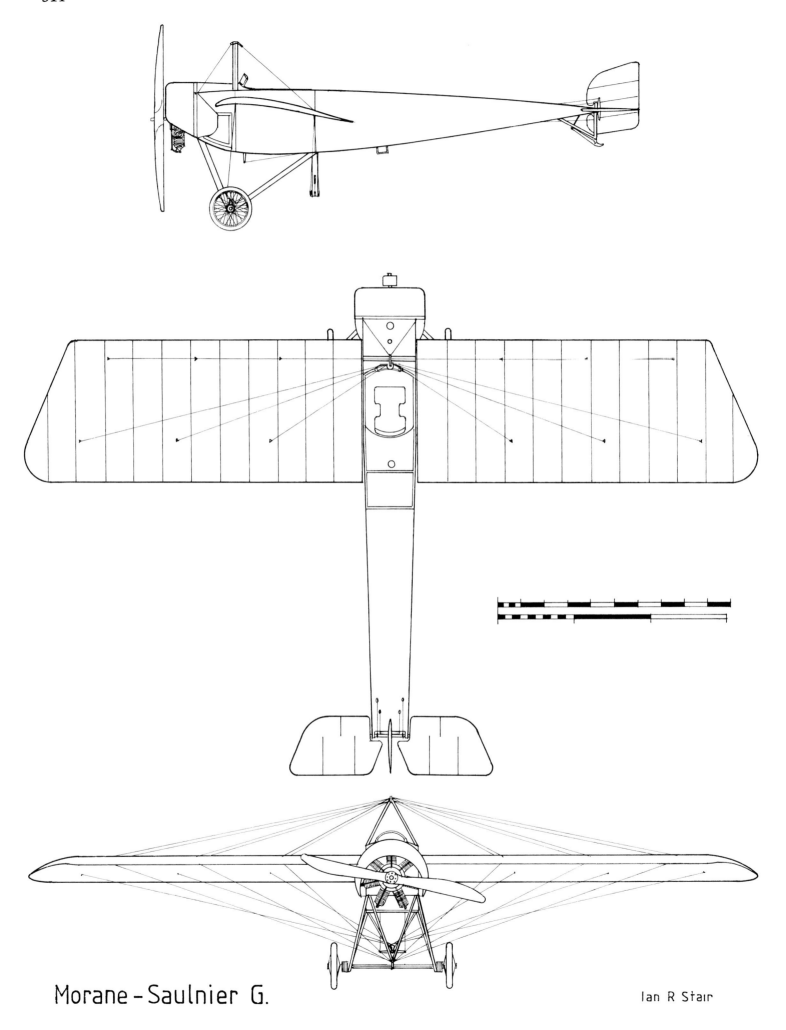

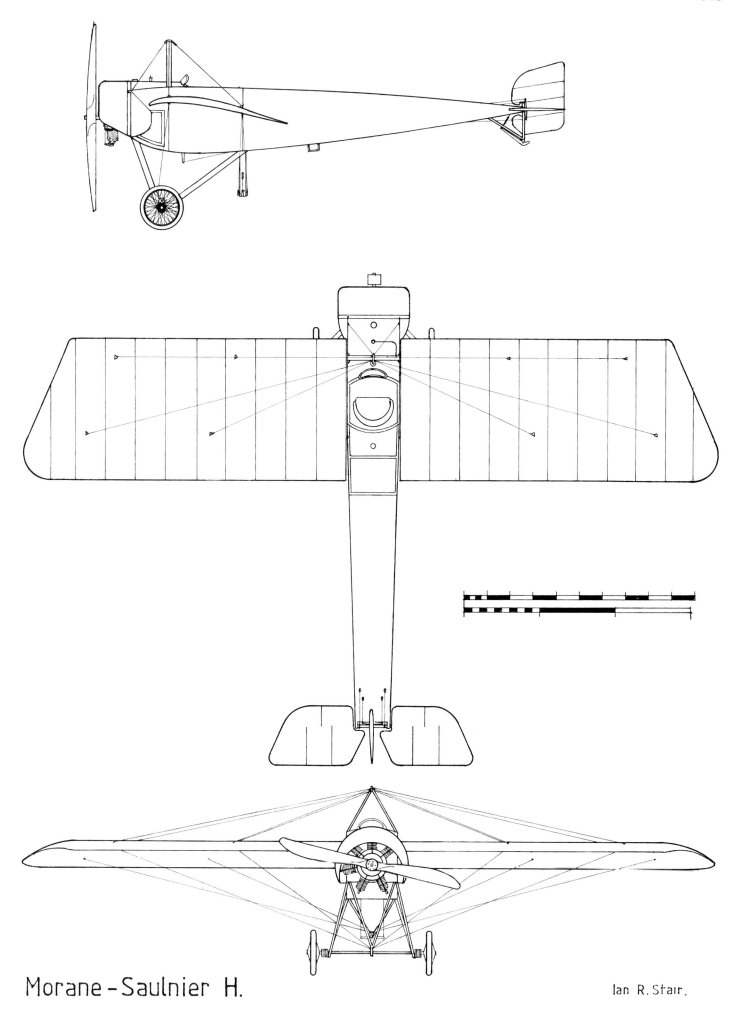

Morane-Saulnier H.

Ian R. Stair.

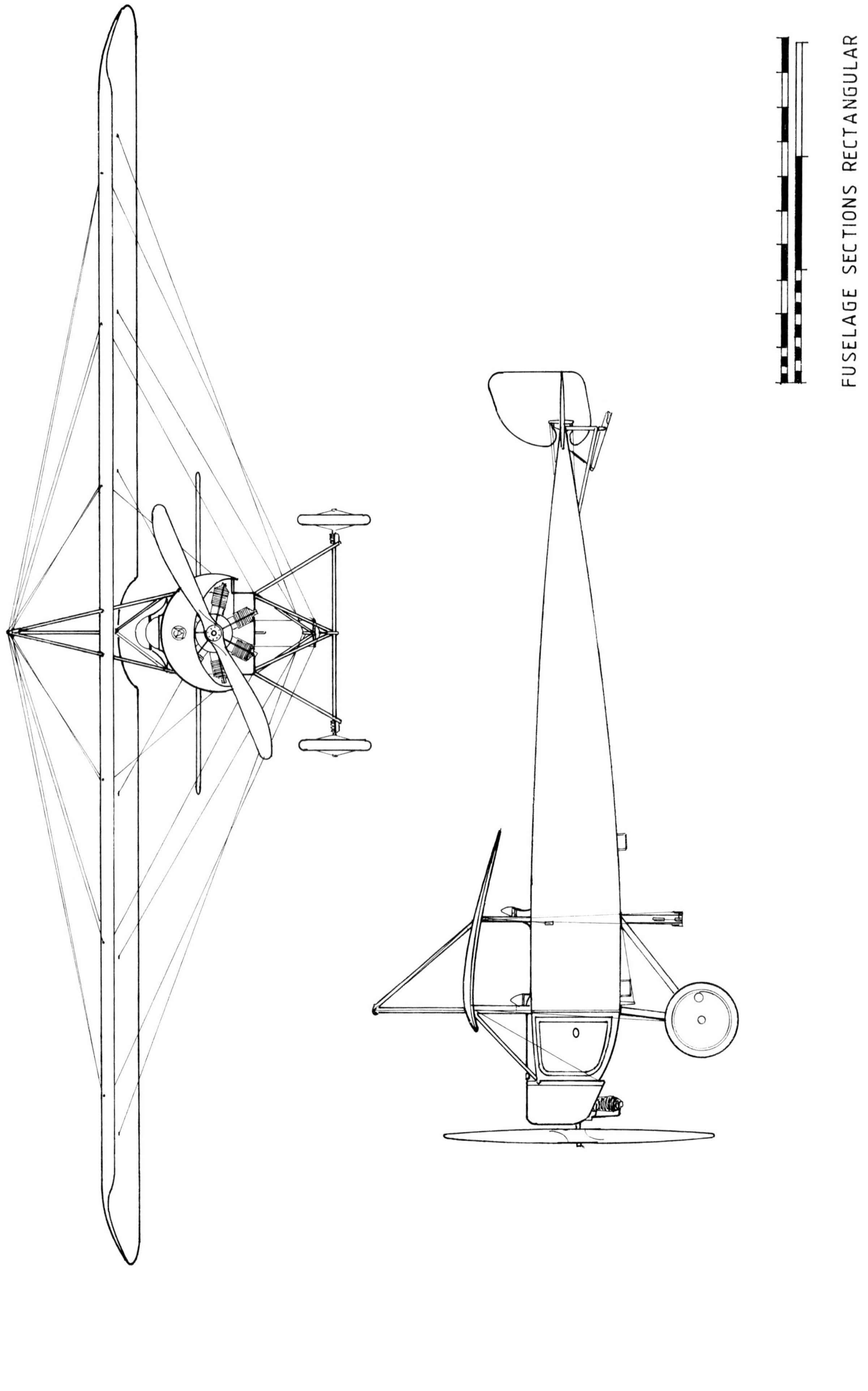

FUSELAGE SECTIONS RECTANGULAR

Ian R Stair.

Morane-Saulnier Type L

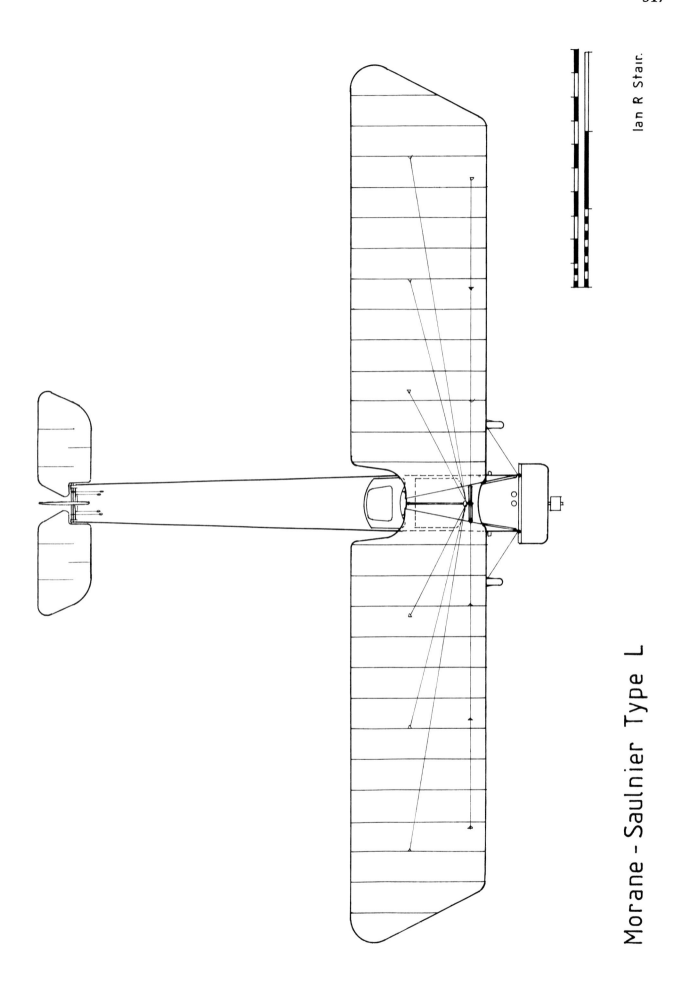

Morane-Saulnier Type L

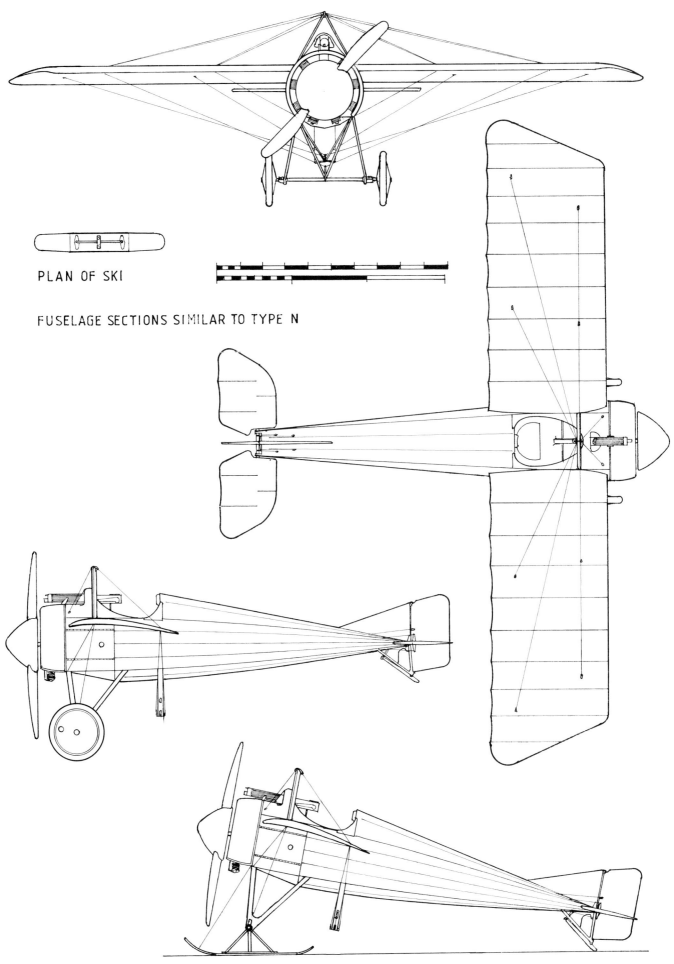

Morane-Saulnier Type I. Ian R. Stair

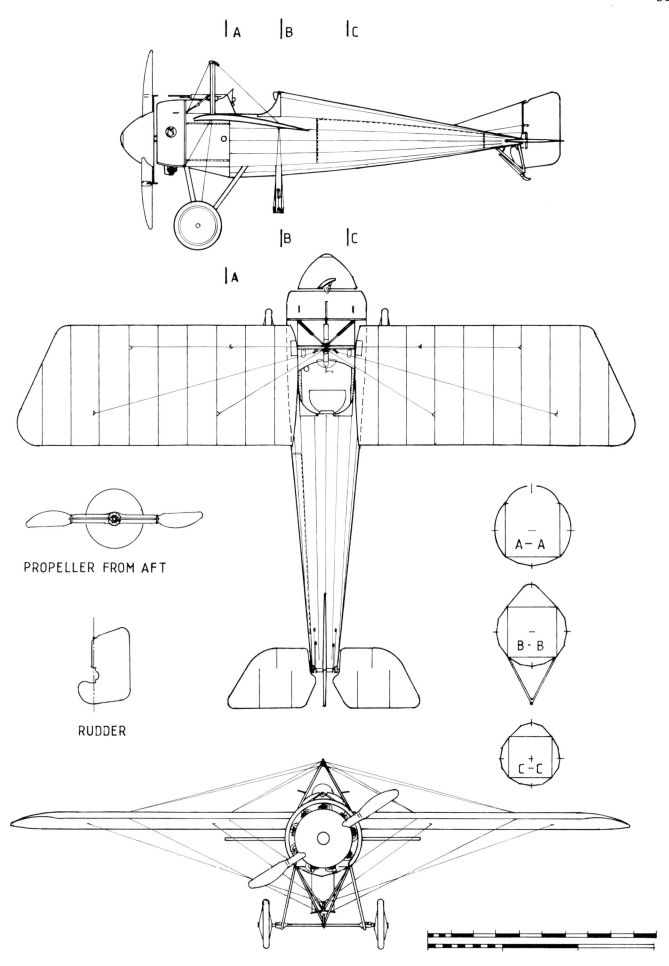

Morane-Saulnier Type N.

Ian R. Stair

520

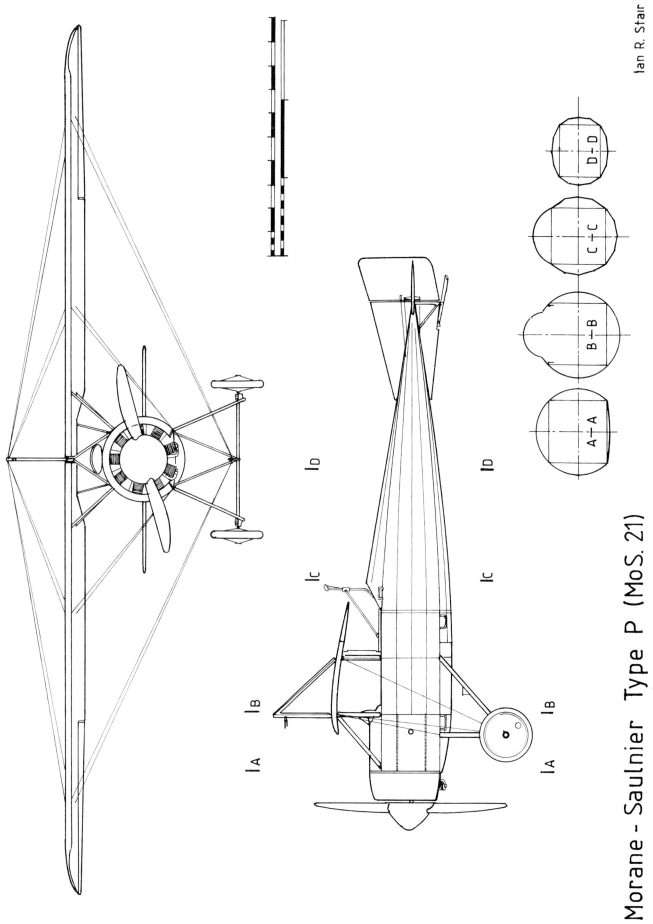

Morane-Saulnier Type P (MoS. 21)

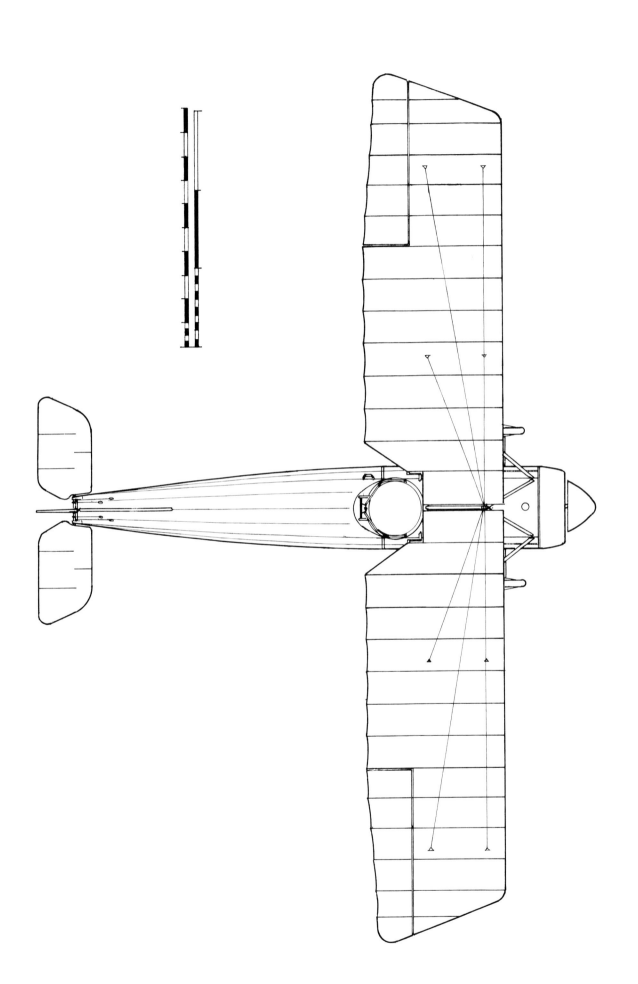

Morane-Saulnier Type P (MoS. 21)

Ian R. Stair

Nieuport 6M.

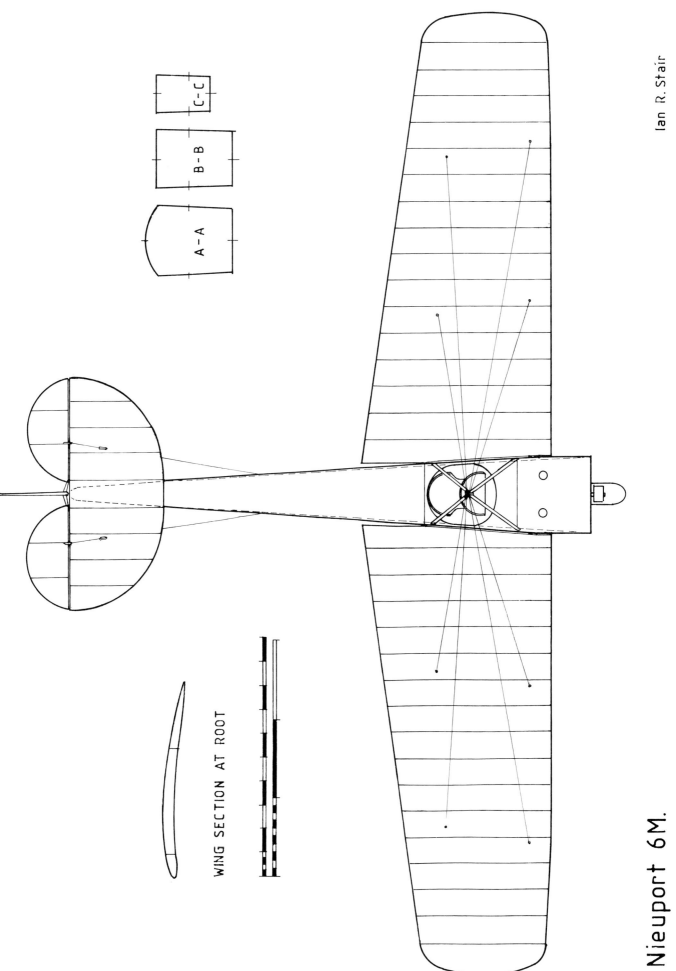

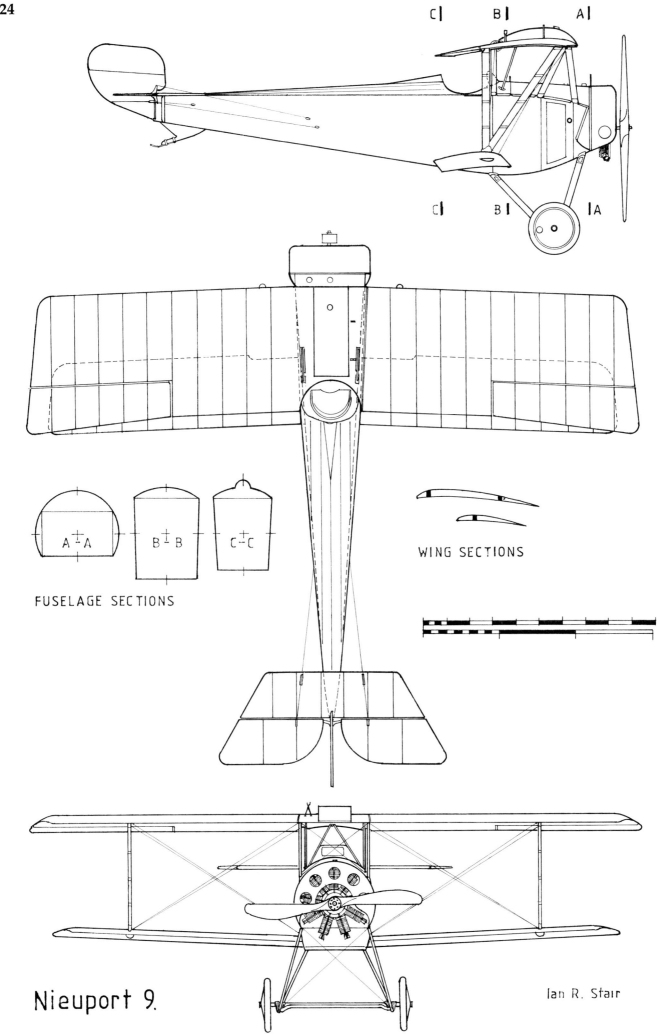

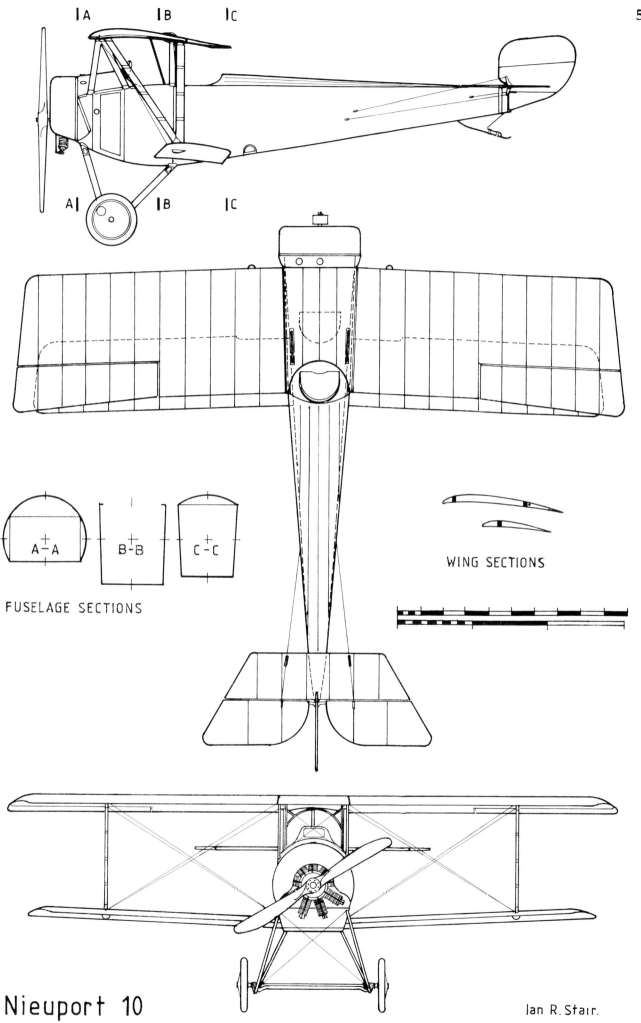

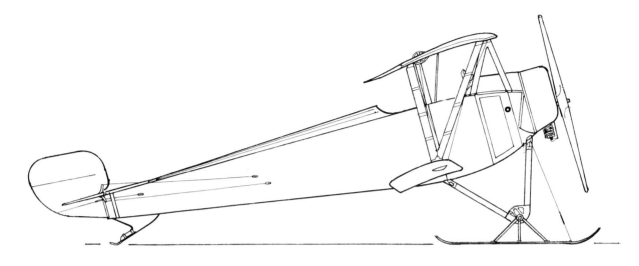

Nieuport 10

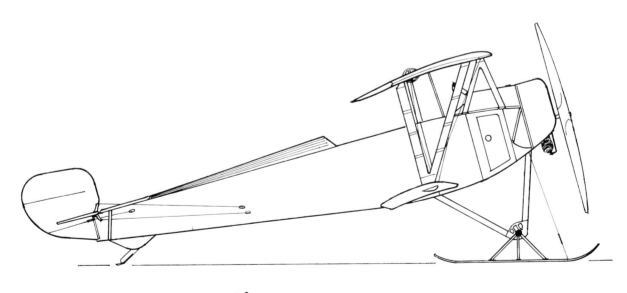

Nieuport 12

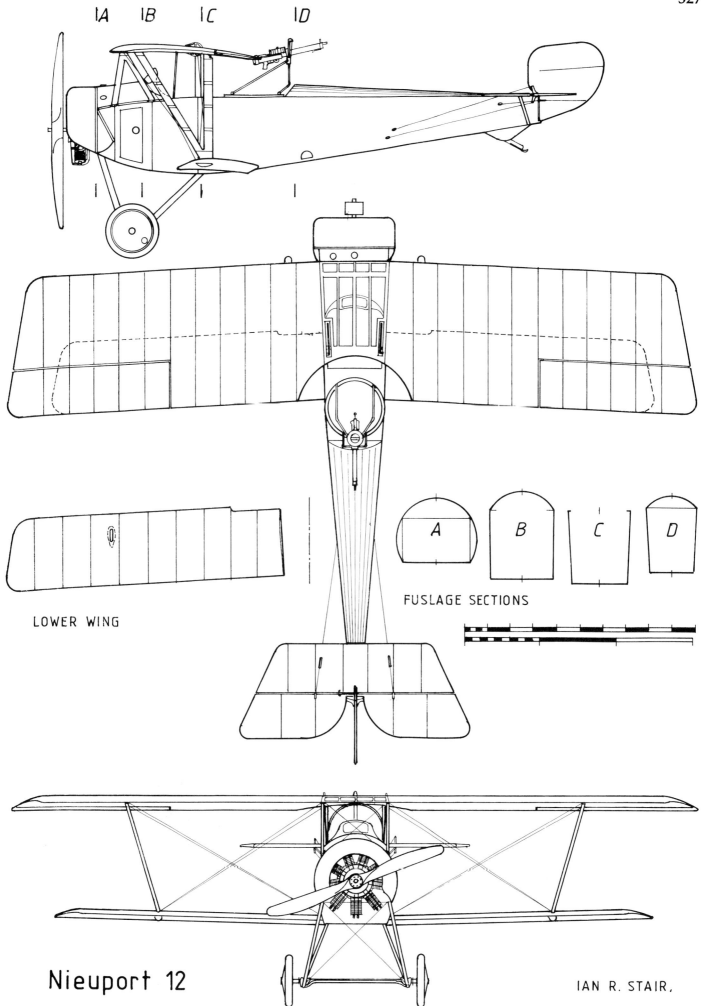

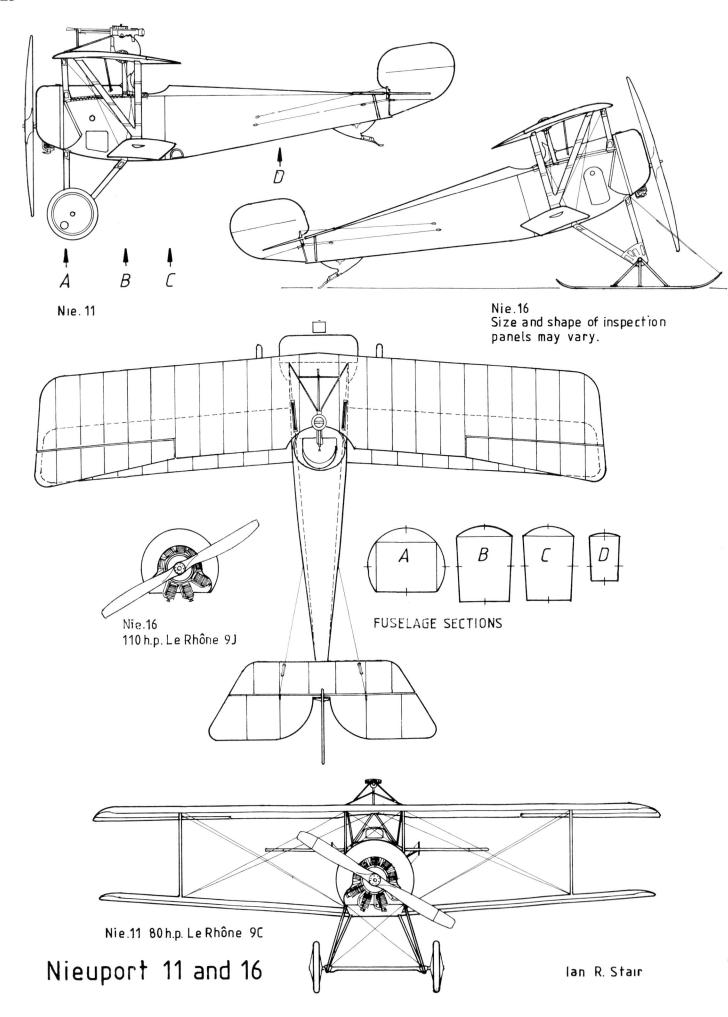

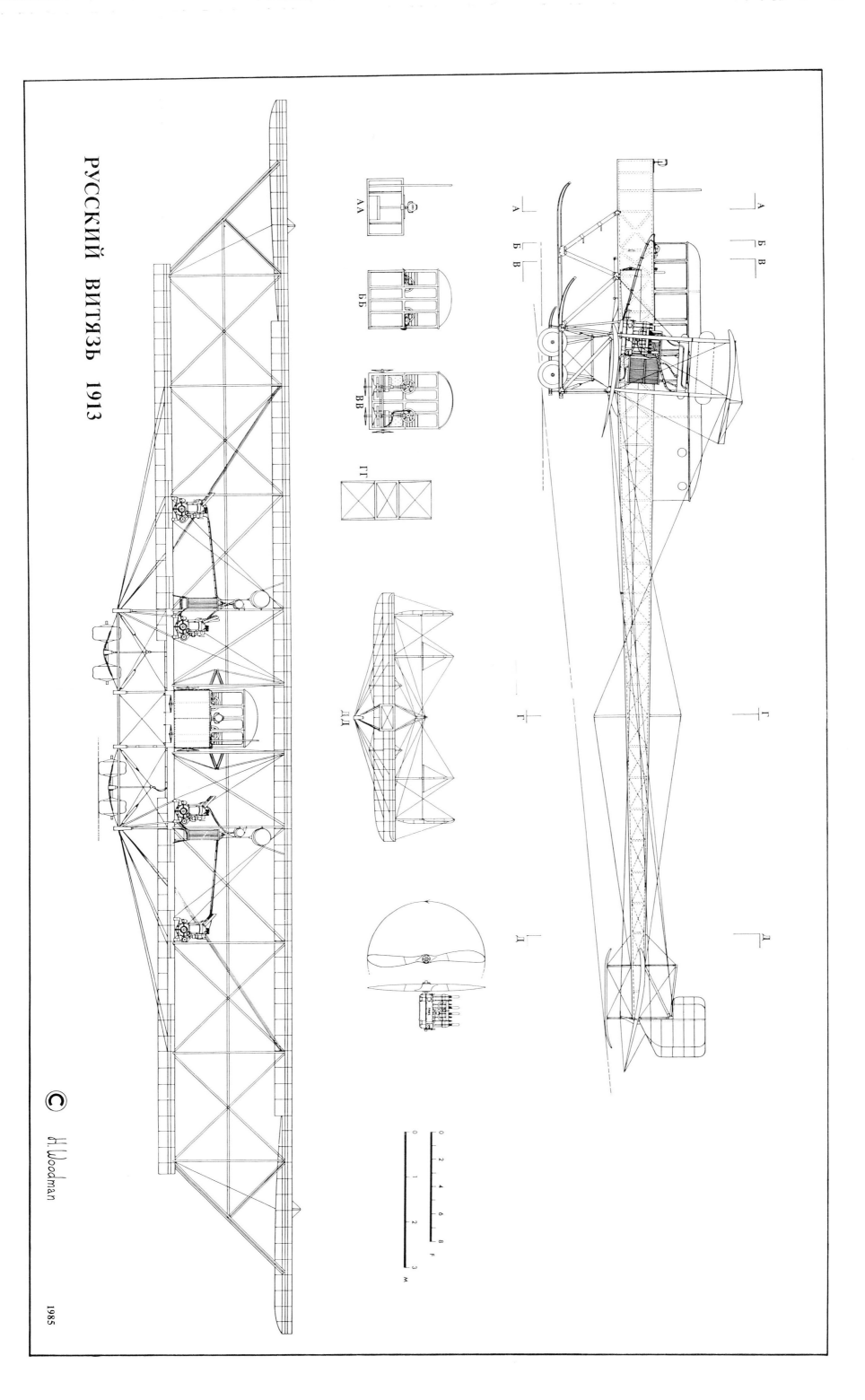

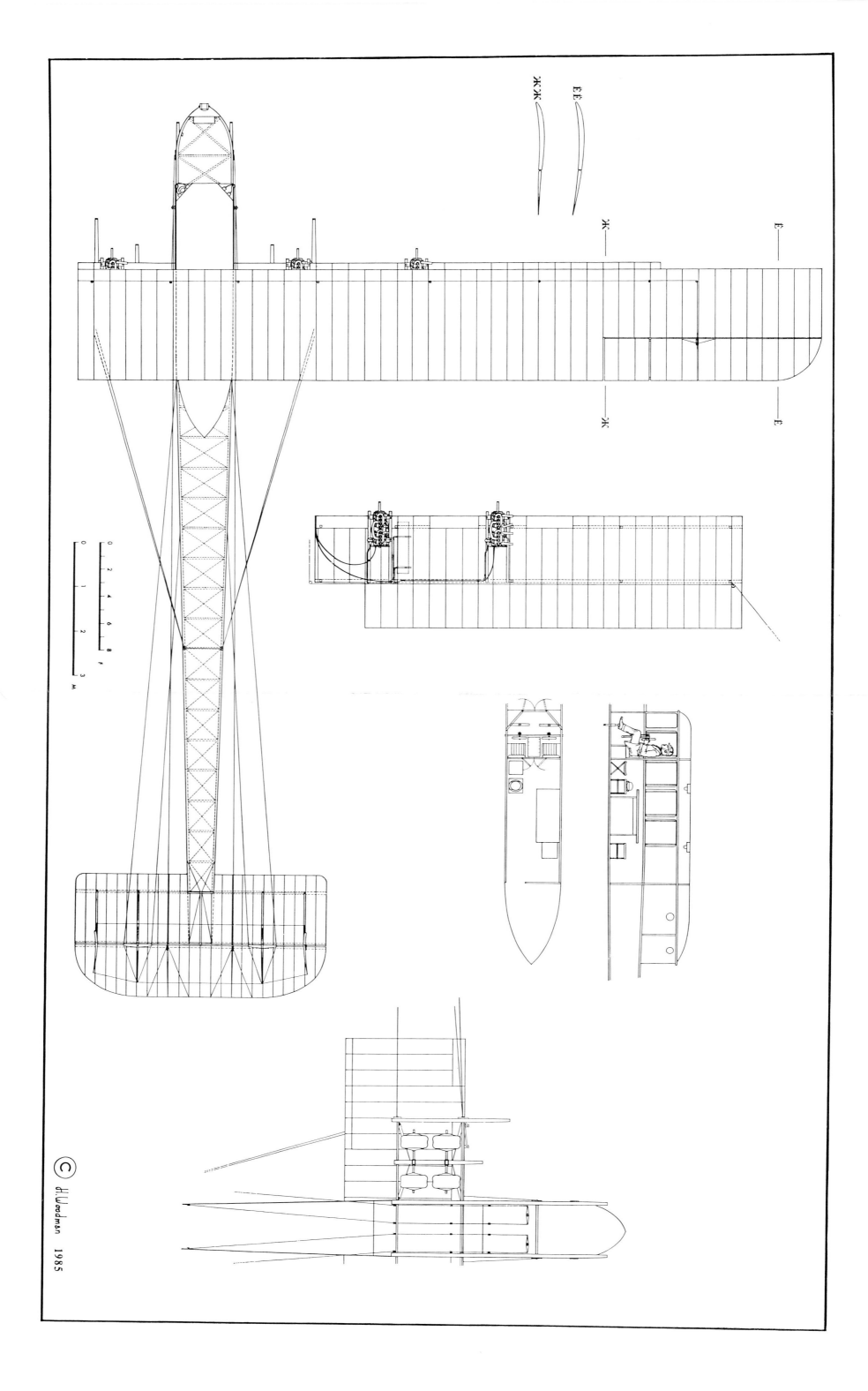

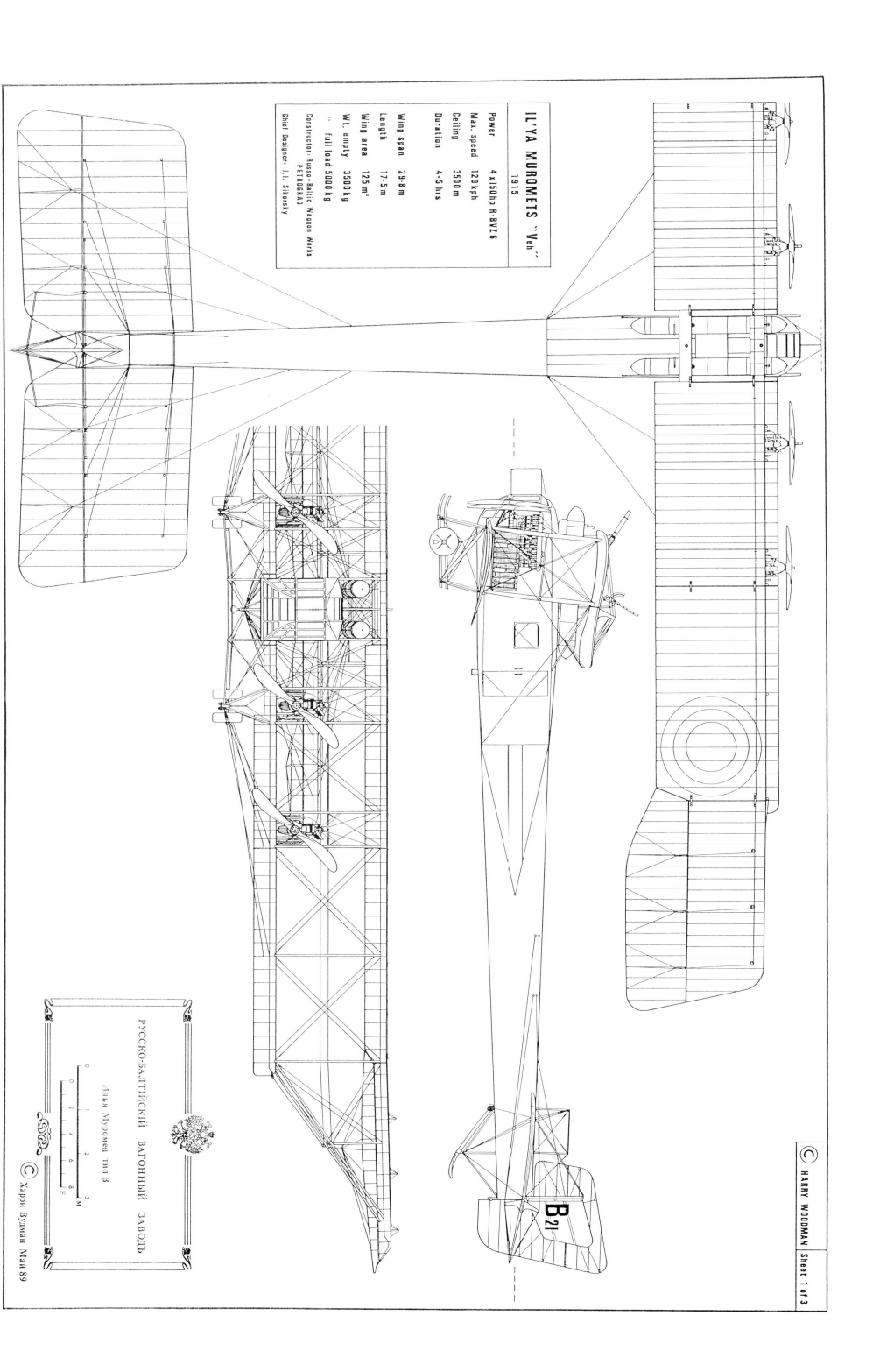

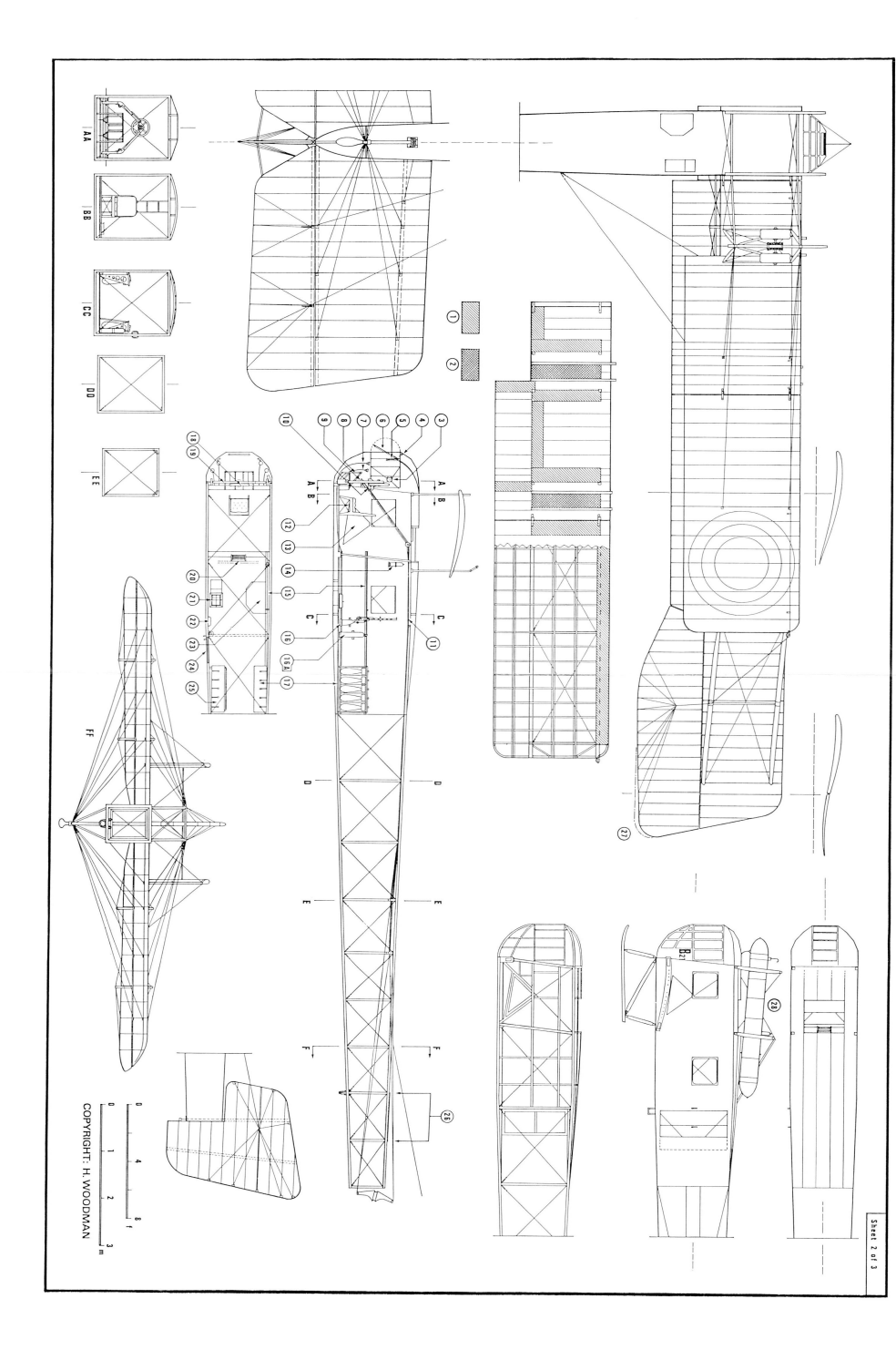

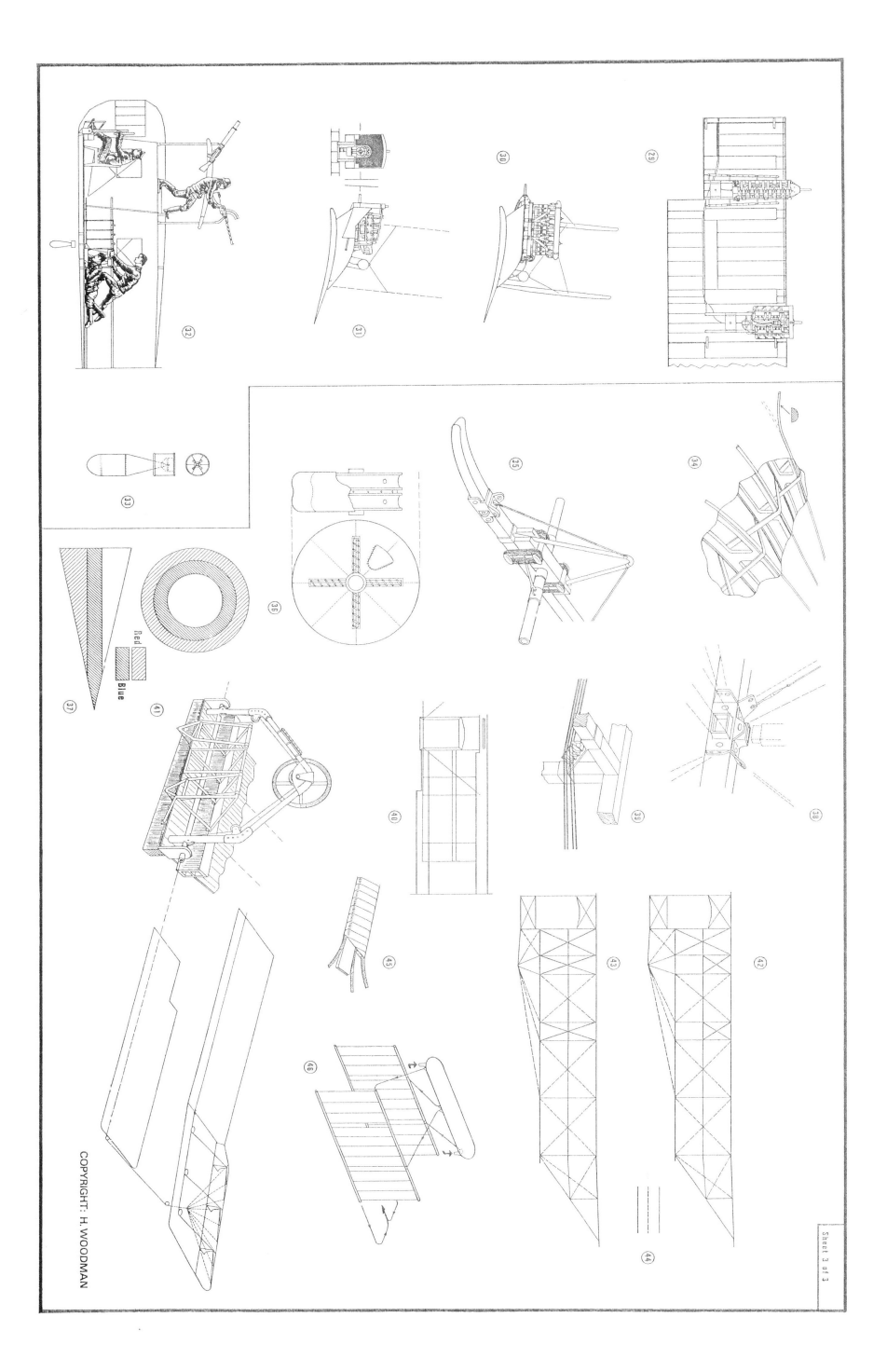

Key to Harry Woodman's Il'ya Muromets Drawings:

1. Plywood foot panels.
2. Aluminum sheet.
3. Altimeter (barometric type).
4. Bank indicator (ball in glass tube).
5. Fuel indicator gauge (one each side).
6. Front windscreen (which pivoted on centerline).
7. Tachometer (rev. counter); two each side.
8. Rudder pedal frame.
9. Point at which elevator cables enter semi-circular structure. Full details of subsequent run of cables to 'Deperdussin' type frame not yet ascertained, so this detail is omitted.
10. Engine switches, four mounted on plate, starboard side, position varied.
11. Run of elevator cables from tail through channel member, then to engines along the horizontal struts between inner interplane struts.
12. Wooden pilot's seat, wire braced and fixed to floor. No seat belt seen on any photograph.
13. Starboard access panel to enable crew member (usually mechanic if carried) to leave fuselage and climb out on to wings to repair or service engines or subdue fires. There was a similar panel on the port side.
14. Fire extinguisher at usual position on starboard side.
15. Upper bomb rack rail (wooden) along starboard side. Second rail below.
16. Rack for Madsen machine gun or rifle. Position varied, it was sometimes situated further aft, on port side.
16A. Compressed air cylinder used for starting Sunbeam engines after forced landing. Enough air carried to start one or possibly two motors only. The position of this cylinder varied, on one machine it was clamped to rear of pilot's seat. It is seen here on port side.
17. Rack, or 'cassette,' carrying 5 x 2 pud (70lb. or 32 kg) HE bombs of Oranovsky pattern. The rack could be fitted with a support of tubular steel enabling them to be carried free-standing as on port side (see 25).
18. Wheel for aileron control.
19. 'Deperdussin'-type frame for aileron and elevator control.
20. Metal ladder to upper observation position and gun post.
21. Bomb sight (Sikorsky pattern).
22. Stand for machine gun or rifle (port).
23. Hatch cover or bomb bay, also used to take vertical photographs. Hatch cover was presumably lifted out but may have been hinged on one side.
24. Sliding door on port side only on this model. Door was a slim wooden framework covered in plywood and slid between split vertical members and double bracing wires. Handles were fitted on both sides.
25. Bomb rack with support frame to allow free-standing storage. When carrier on side rails was empty it was lifted off and a full rack hooked on to rails. (See side view at CC.)

26. The upper surface here was covered with plywood under fabric to provide support for men adjusting tail bracing or while assembling tailplane.
27. Dotted line shows true shape of aileron tip without wash-out.
28. Plan and side view of cabin area of fuselage. Note upper hatch with wooden plank firestep and position of fuel tanks. Actual position of fuel pipes from tanks into fuselage not known but photographs suggest that they connect with a pump fitted to top cross bracing member, then to engines along the horizontal struts between inner interplane struts.
Upper shape of cabin was formed by fabric over light stringers. The lower drawing shows the basic wooden structure of cabin area. Behind the metal framed, aluminum and reinforced glass of the nose area, the cabin was lined with 3mm plywood with a fabric outer skin. The floor was of 10mm plywood and extended only as far as the fuselage former behind the door.
29. View of starboard lower wing inner section (shown in vertical projection). The left engine is in its career, with Hazet engine as fitted to Ship II later in its career, with Hazet radiators (note angle). The right engine shows appearance of original 150hp Sunbeam as fitted when Ship II was built. The run of the tachometer cables (actually, Bowden type) is shown over the rear spar. The line near leading edge shows position of compressed air tubes to Sunbeam engines when fitted.
30. Side view of inner R-BVZ-6 engine showing position of oil tank and its supports. Note anti-vibration cables from tanks to interplane struts. Similar cables were fitted to the water expansion tanks over engines.
31. Appearance of Sunbeam motor (outboard) when fitted. The engine mounts were wooden framed and plywood covered. Metal facings were attached under engine bedding lugs.
32. Sketch of cabin showing crew positions in flight. The normal crew for the IM type B (Veh) was four but could vary according to mission. A mechanic could be included as well as a photographer and special observers on occasions. The sketch depicts Ship II while assigned to the 1st *Otryad* (First Muromets Combat Detachment) based at Kolodziyevka (near Tarnopol) in Galicia, Spring 1916. In May of 1916, the crew were as shown, pilot and Commander, *Stabs-Kapitan* A. V. Pankrat'yev; at the upper gun position is *Podporuchik* G. V. Pavlov, who was an assistant pilot; at the bomb sight on the floor is the Deputy Commander, *Stabs-Kapitan* S. N. Nikolsky acting as artillery officer; operating the bomb carrier is *Poruchik* K. Smirnov, assistant artillery officer.
33. 25 pud (410kg—904lb.) HE bomb, one of several developed by a team under Professor N. Ye. Zhukhovsky at the Moscow Technical High School in

1915. It was suspended under the center of gravity of the Il'ya Muromets by a strap and cable release inside fuselage.
34. Scrap view of intermeshing strapping of ribs to strengthen structure. A common form of support during early years of airplane construction.
35. Scrap view of undercarriage member reconstructed from a technical description and a study of photographs. The inverted 'V' was a metal tube supported by cables which prevented the skid from bowing upwards during landing pressures.
36. Structure of double wheel. There were two separate rims joined by a circular flange. The outer cover was of leather stitched like a football(soccer ball) case. It is presumed that the wheels with deflated tires then inflated through rim valves and valve flaps. The case was closed with substantial lacing as shown.
37. Roundel and fuselage pennant.
38. Scrap view of standardized metal fitting for fuselage assembly. Note that the side, top and bottom wires were all doubled while the interior transverse wires were single.
39. Scrap view of diagonal fitting with pulleys through which elevator cables passed.
40. Rear view showing position of the two drag wires on both sides.
41. Scrap view of 'Deperdussin'-type frame with wheel control for ailerons. The frame moved fore and aft for elevator control, however, exact method of transmission is not yet known. The strip on the right arm of the frame held finger-push switches to enable the commander to make light signals to his crew. The rudder pedal frame is also shown but the exact run of the cables from the pedal bottoms to the rear is not yet known.
42. Diagrammatic view of bracing wires attached to leading spars.
43. Ditto for rear spars.
44. Key to wiring diagrams: The thin line indicates single wires, the middle dotted line double wires, while the thick line represents triple wiring for load-bearing areas.
45. Scrap view illustrating how multiple wires were assembled, (3-3.5mm piano wire was used). The sketch shows a triple wire example with strips of wood 20mm wide inserted between the wires and the whole bound with tape. This created a streamlined effect as well as ensuring some support if one or even two of the wires were severed. The double wires were of course made the same way.

46. Schematic view of Hazet-type radiators used with R-BVZ engines and occasionally with others. At least one Sunbeam-powered IM had Hazet radiators preferred by the Russians because they offered less head resistance despite their weight and vulnerability to damage from gunfire. The radiators were copied from an early German design which the originators were replacing by mid-1916.
Hot water from the engine rose up into the overhead expansion tank, it then drained down into the twin radiators and was drawn off at the bottom rear into pipes which led into the water pump on the engine. The radiators are shown here as parallel but in fact they were always fitted at an angle to the center-line to allow an unimpaired flow of air through the radiators. In plan view the radiators were arranged in a shallow arrow form (see 29).

Additional notes:

It should be noted that the IM was supplied with several instruments and items on which information is, at present lacking. In consequence, rather than fictionalize them they have been omitted from the drawings. There was a compass (possibly two) fitted within the pilot's sight and probably on the floor as the compass was also needed by the artillery officer while using the bomb sight. The actual position is not known, neither is the position of the throttles. A throttle for each engine was provided as well as a multiple control (Avtolog) to throttle down all engines simultaneously. The throttles were not operated by the pilot but by the mechanic or the deputy commander on instructions from the pilot.

Other items known to be fitted to Ship II were an arrow indicator operated by the artillery officer which resembled a ship's engine room telegraph in a way, he turned it and the action was repeated on a similar arrow in the pilot's sight. A stand was also provided for the camera. Extra bombs of smaller caliber could be carried in the bomb hatch or thrown out of the open door. These smaller bombs and missiles could be hand dropped through the open door.

The angular frame fitted on the nose (centrally in the case of Ship II but offset to port on other machines) was a simple artificial horizon devised by Igor Sikorsky. It had small horizontal strips fitted which helped the pilot to judge approach angles while landing, a critical period as far as handling the IM was concerned.

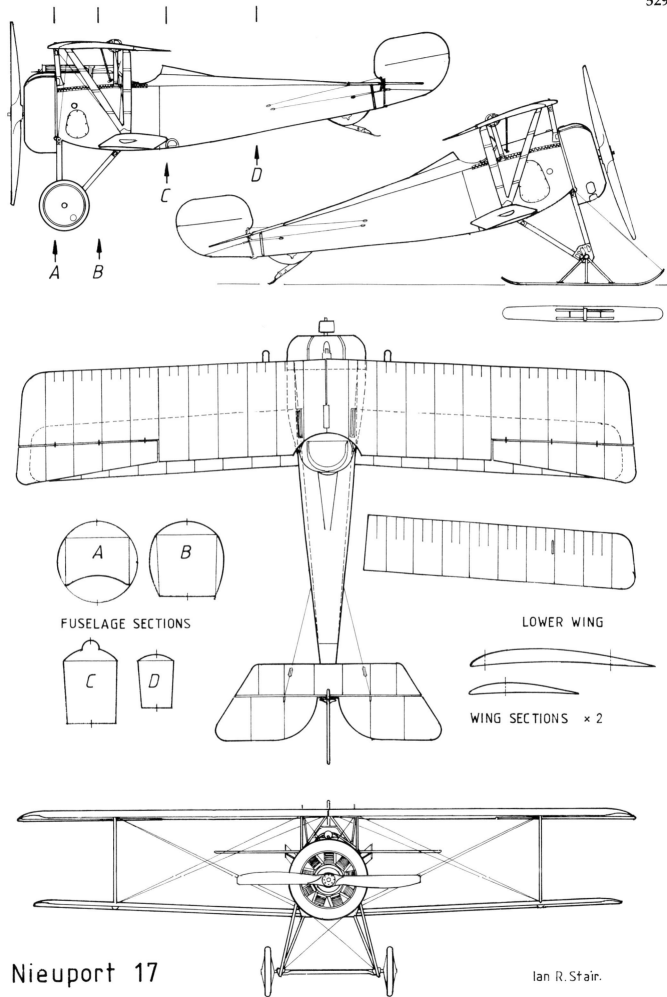

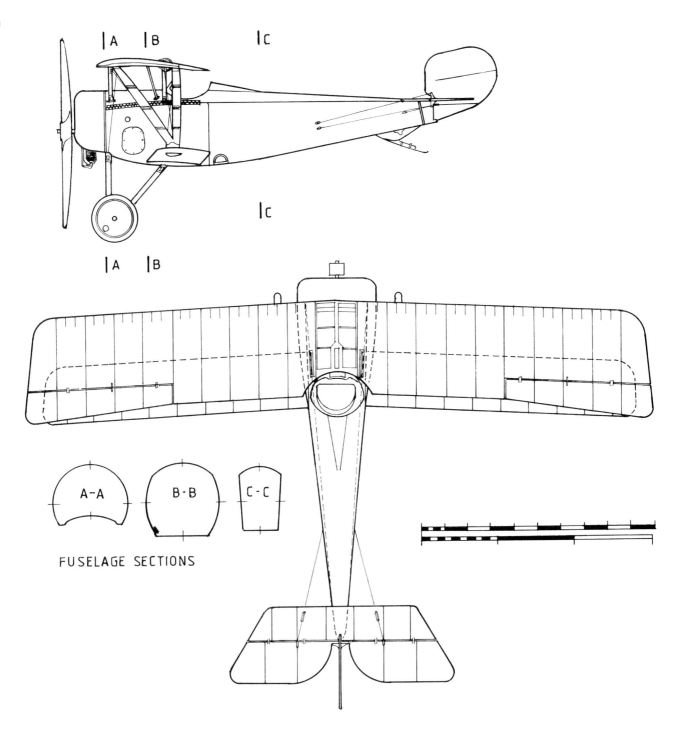
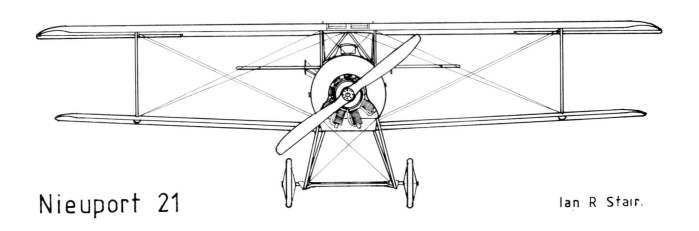

Nieuport 21 — Ian R Stair.

531

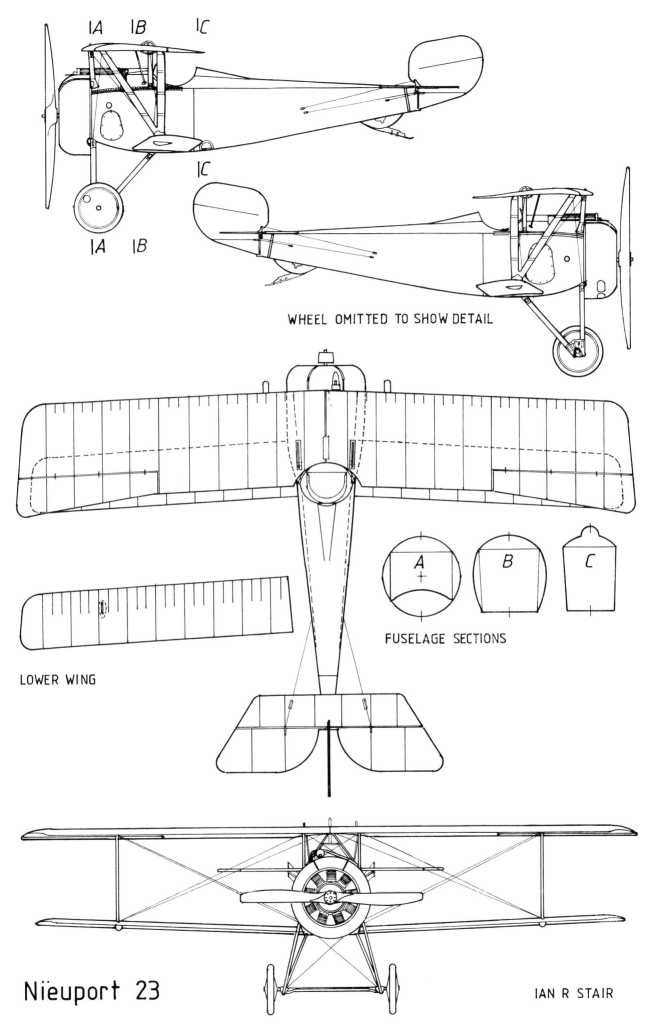

WHEEL OMITTED TO SHOW DETAIL

FUSELAGE SECTIONS

LOWER WING

Nieuport 23

IAN R STAIR

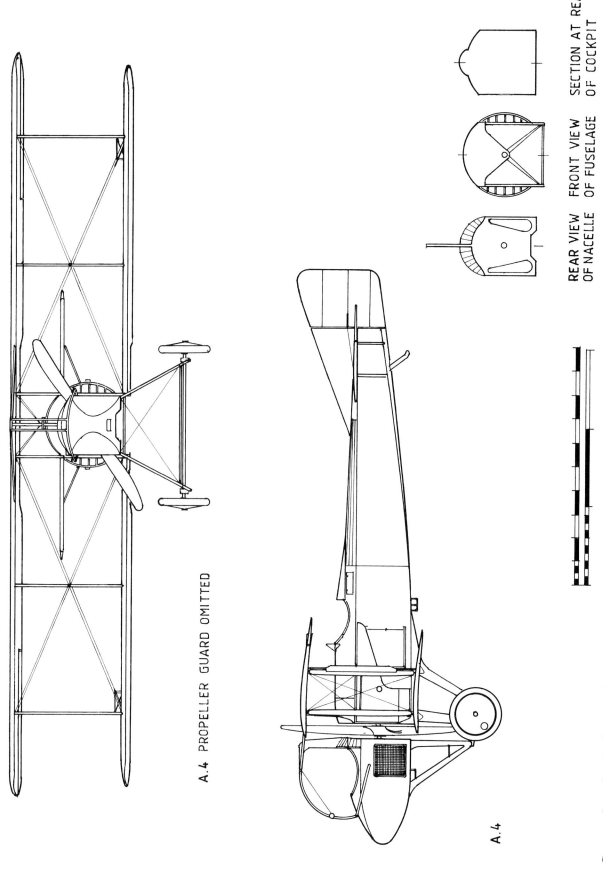

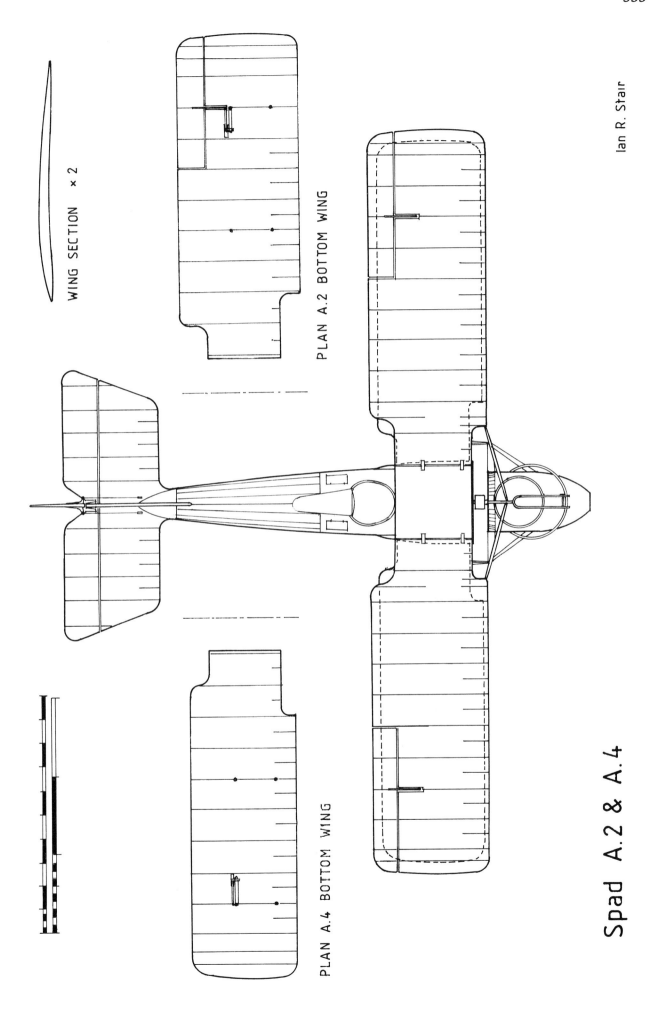

Spad A.2 & A.4

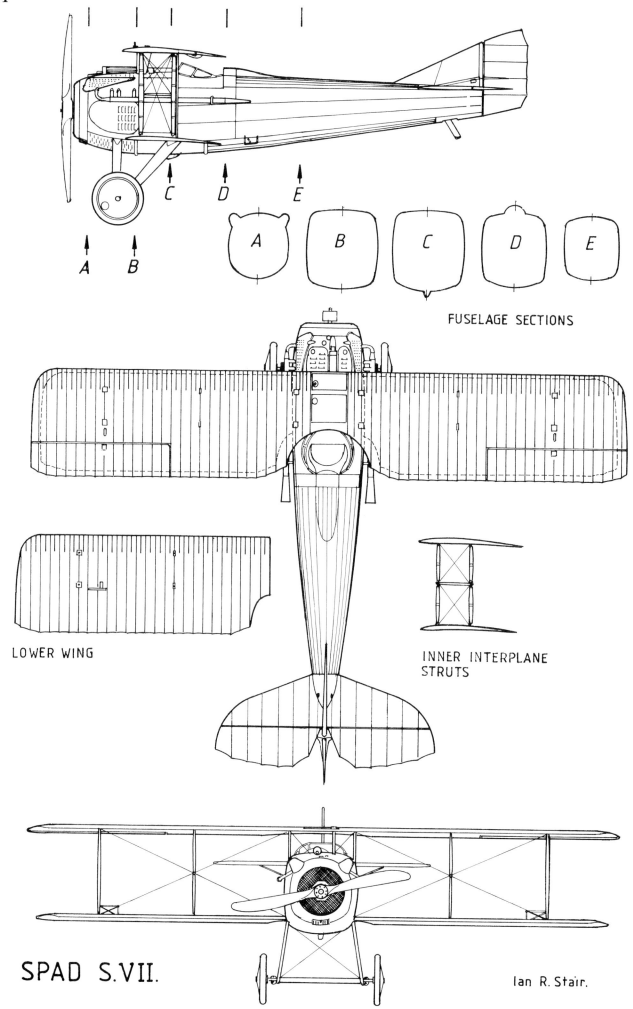

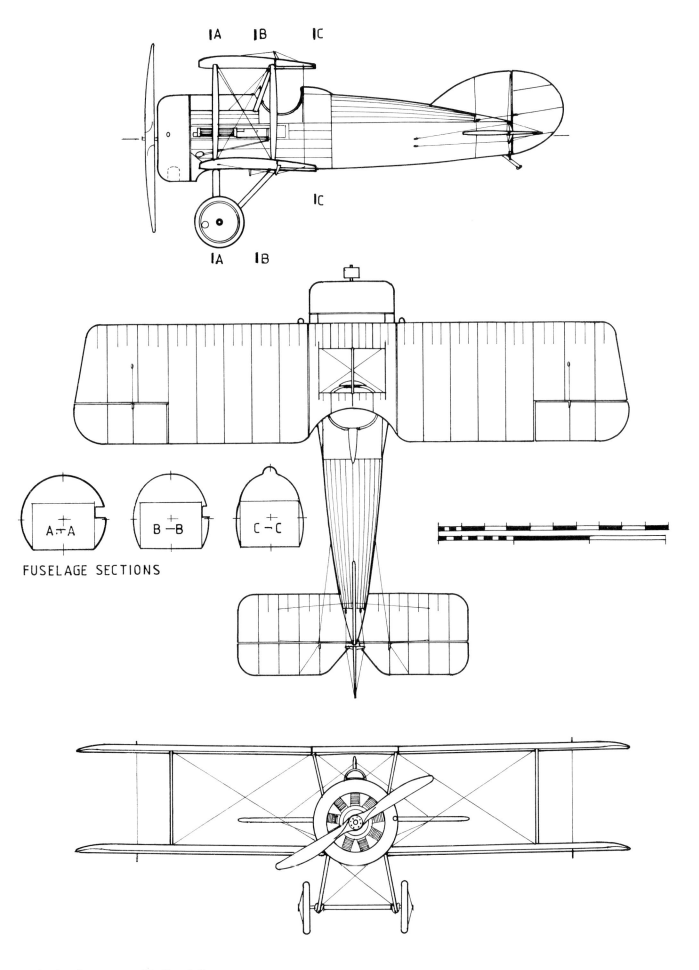

Vickers F.B.19.

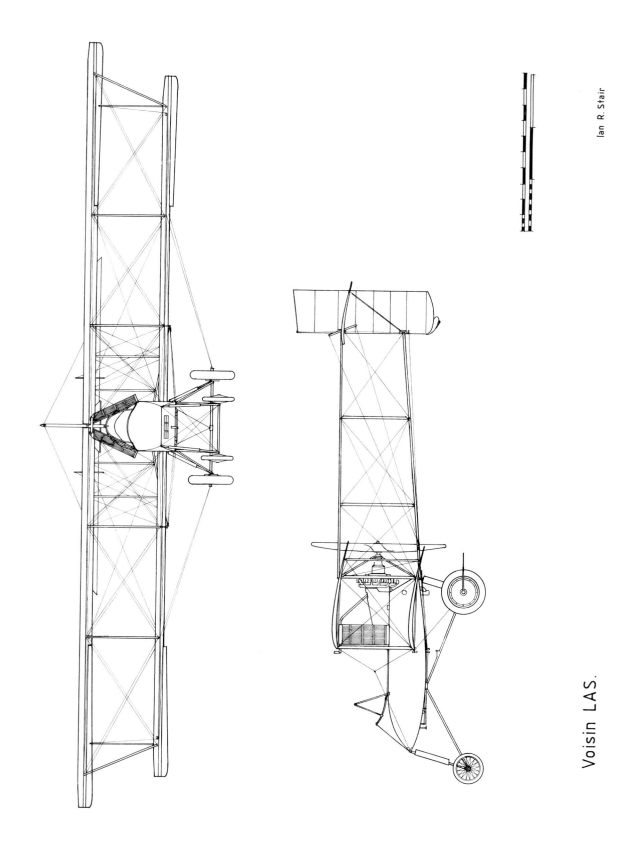

Voisin LAS.

Ian R. Stair

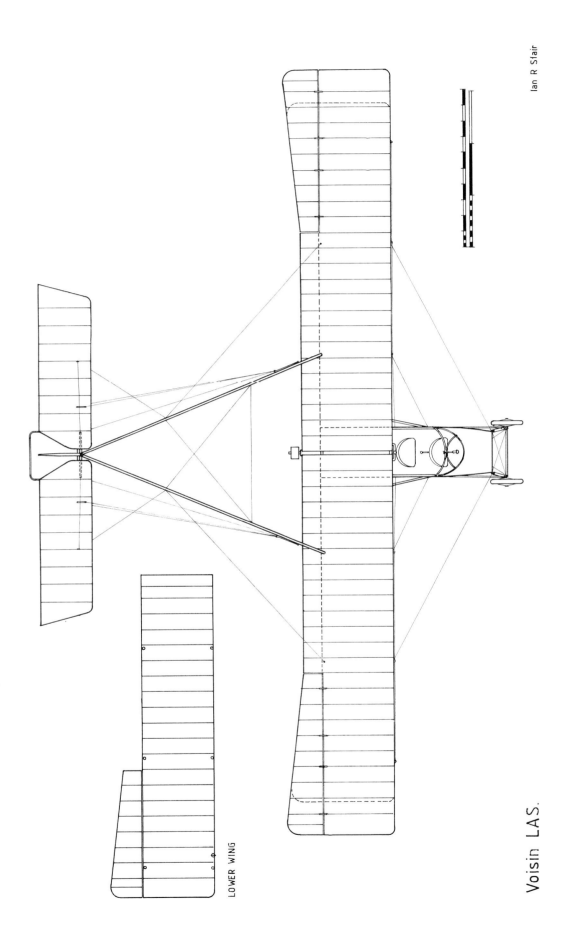

Voisin LAS.

DRAWN FROM LIMITED INFORMATION
BY - IAN R.STAIR.

Sikorsky S.12

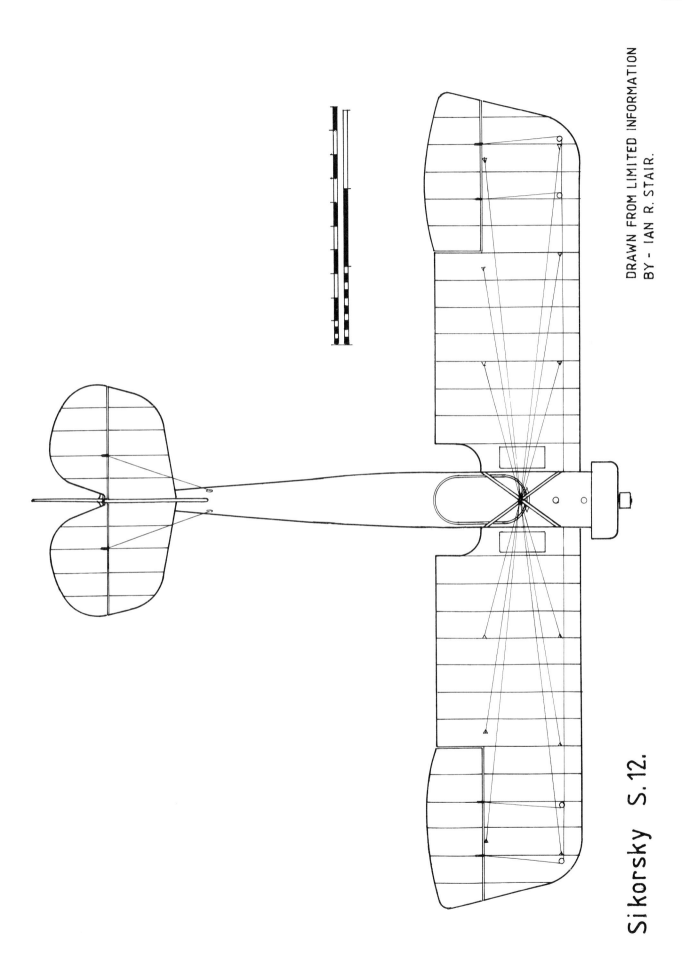

Sikorsky S.12.

DRAWN FROM LIMITED INFORMATION
BY - IAN R. STAIR.

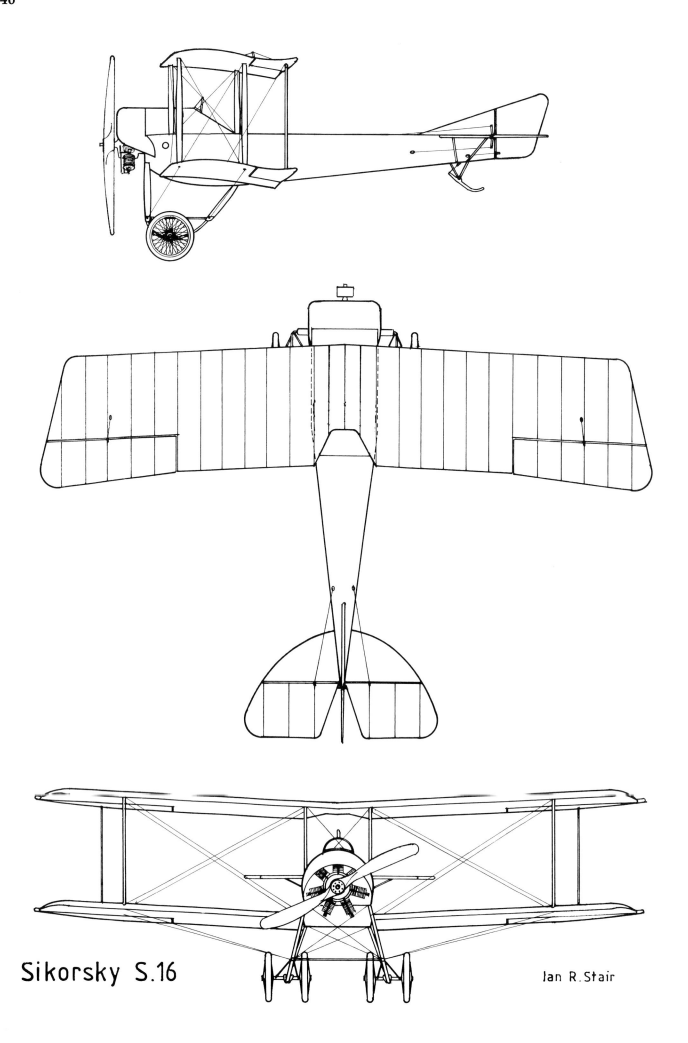

Sikorsky S.16

Jan R. Stair

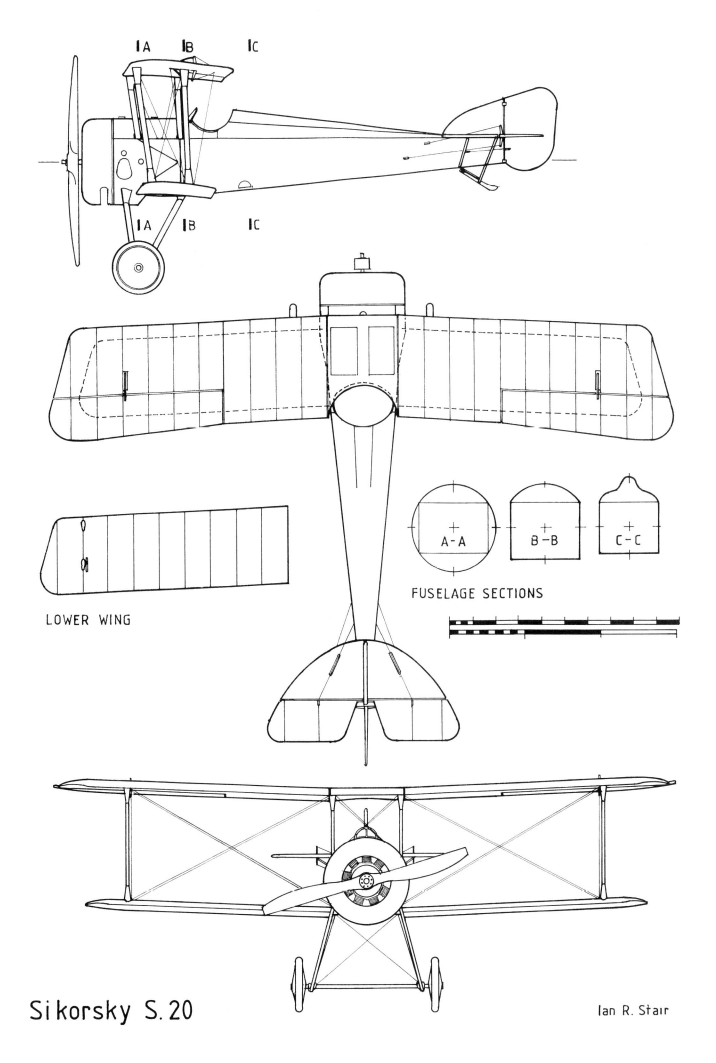

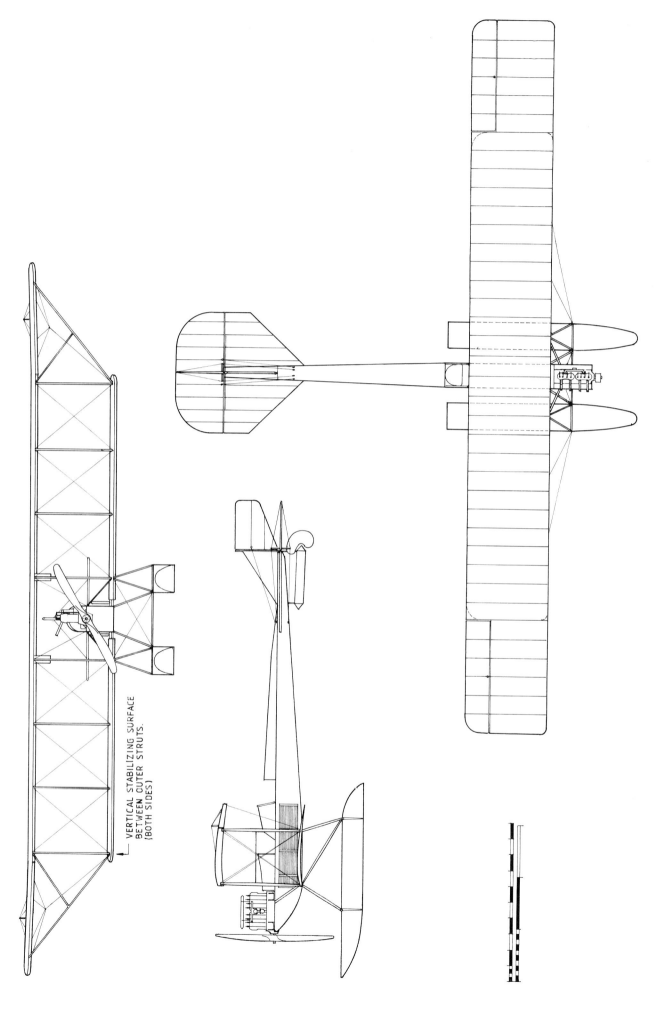

Sikorsky S.10 Hydroplane.

Glossary of Military and Nautical Terms

Adjudant: Warrant-Officer—France.

Aft (stern): At, near, or toward the back of a ship or aircraft.

Aviagruppa: Russian Combat Air Group.

Aviapark: Russian Air Service Park.

Beam: A vessel's greatest width.

Berth: A space for anchoring or tying up.

Bilge: The rounded, lower part of a hull.

Bow: The front part of a ship, boat, or airship; prow.

boyevye otryady: combat units.

Capitan: Captain—Romania.

Caporal: Corporal—France.

Chef de Battalion, Commandant: Major—France.

Chine: The ridge at the intersection of the bottom and sides of a flat or vee-bottom hull.

Colonel: Colonel—France.

Cornet: Second Lieutenant—Russian Cavalry.

der Reserve (d.R.): Reserve service—Germany and Austria-Hungary.

drachen: observation balloon (German slang, literally sausage).

Esaul: Captain—Russian Cossack.

Escadra Vozdushnykh Korablei: EVK-Squadron of Flying Ships of Il'ya Muromets bombers.

Escadrila: Romanian aviation squadron.

Escadrille : French aviation squadron.

Fähnrich: Ensign—Austria-Hungary.

Feldflieger Abteilung: German aviation field detachment.

Feldwebel: Sergeant Major—Austria-Hungary, or Sergeant—Germany.

Flieger Abteilung (A): Germany aviation unit specializing in artillery spotting.

Fliegerkompanie (Flik): Austro-Hungarian aviation squadron.

Fore (stem): A prefix denoting the front.

Frame: The skeletal structure of a boat, that which supports and stiffens the skin.

Gefreiter: Lance-Corporal—Russia.

General : General—Russia.

General Feldmareshal: Field Marshal—Russia.

General-Leitenant: Lieutenant-General—Russia.

General-Maior: Major-General—Russia.

Generale: General—France.

gidrokreisera: Russian seaplane (hydroplane) carrier.

gidroviotransport: hydroplane transport.

Hauptmann: Captain—Germany and Austria-Hungary

Hull: The body of a vessel including the frame and its covering.

Il'ya Murometsy: plural of Il'ya Muromets bomber.

Kapitan 1. Ranga: Senior Captain—Russian Navy.

Kapitan 2. Ranga: Captain junior grade—Russian Navy.

Kapitan: Captain—Russia.

Keel: The main longitudinal structural member extending the entire length along the bottom of a boat (normally along the centerline) and supporting the frame.

Korporal: Corporal—Austria-Hungary.

Leitenant: Lieutenant and Lieutenant Commander—Russian Navy.

Leutnant: Second Lieutenant—Germany and Austria-Hungary.

Lieutenant: Lieutenant—France.

Locotenent: Lieutenant—Romania.

Marechal-des-Logis: Sergeant—French Cavalry.

Michman: Ensign—Russian Navy.

Mladchi Unteroffizier: Corporal—Russia.

Morskoi: Naval.

Nijnichin: Private—Russia.

Oberleutnant: Lieutenant—Germany and Austria-Hungary.

Offizierstellvertreter: Warrant-Officer—Austria-Hungary.

Otryad: aviation detachment—Russia.

Palkovnik: Colonel—Russia.

Planing hull: Hull designed with a relatively flat underwater surface.

Planing step: A break in the horizontal line of the bottom of the hull. The step helps break the suction of the water on the hull during take-off.

Pod'Esaul: Staff-Captain—Russian Cossack.

Podpolkovnik: Lieutenant-Colonel—Russia.

Podporuchik: Second Lieutenant—Russia.

Podpraporshik: Warrant Officer—Russia.

pogoni: shoulderboard on Russian uniform.

Poruchik: Lieutenant—Russia.

Praporshik: Ensign—Russia.

pud: measurement of weight =16 kg or 35.3 pounds.

Rittmeister: Captain—German and Austro-Hungarian Cavalry.

Rotmistre: Captain—Russian Cavalry.

sajen : measurement of length = 7 feet.

Sergent: Sergeant—France.

Soldat: Private—France.

Sous-Lieutenant: Second Lieutenant—France.

Stabs-Kapitan: Staff-Captain—Russia.

Stabs-Rotmistre: Staff-Captain—Russian Cavalry.

Stabsfeldwebel: Staff Sergeant—Austria-Hungary.

Starshi Leitenant: Commander—Russian Navy.

Starski Unteroffizier: Sergeant—Russia.

Stavka: Russian Headquarters of the Commander-in-Chief.

Sublocotenent: Second Lieutenant—Romania.

Unteroffizier: Corporal—Germany.

verst: measurement of distance = 3500 feet, or 0.663 miles.

Vizefeldwebel: Sergeant Major—Germany.

Wachtmistre: Sergeant Major—Russian Cavalry.

Zugsführer: Sergeant—Austria-Hungary.

Bibliography

Alexandrov, Andrei. All-Russian Boats—Grigorovich Flying Boats 1913–1918, *Air Enthusiast*. 1995.

Aleksandrov, Andrew and Gennadi Petrov. "Captured Central Power Aeroplanes In Russian and Red Service 1914–1920—Part 1," *Windsock International*, Vol. 9, No.2, 1993, pp 7–14.

Aleksandrov, Andrew and Gennadi Petrov. "Captured Central Power Aeroplanes In Russian And Red Service 1914–1920—Part 2," *Windsock International*, Vol. 9, No.1, 1993, pp 5–11.

Anuchin, V.V. "Prominent Russian Pilot P.N. Nesterov," *Journal On Military History*. Number 2, 1987.

Bailey, Frank W. "L'escadrille Jeanne D'Arc—Spa.124," *Cross & Cockade Journal USA*, Vol. 19. No. 4 , pp344–359, 1978.

Bailey, Frank W. "L'Escadrille Spa.48." *Cross & Cockade Journal USA*, Vol. 24. No. 1, 1983, pp. 1–33.

Bailey, Frank W. and Paul Chamberlain. "L'Escadrille De Chasse SPA 57," *Cross & Cockade Journal USA*, Vol. 26. No. 1, 1985, pp. 1–23.

Blume, August G. "The Eastern Front War Episodes Of Russian Aviation 1914–1917," *Over The Front Journal USA*, Vol. 5. No. 4, 1990, pp 340–355.

Bruce, J. M. *Warplanes of the First World War*, Volume 1–5: Fighters. Macdonald: London, 1972.

Cain, Claude W. "Flying for the Czar: Alexander Riaboff, Imperial Russian Air Service. A Photo Essay," *Cross and Cockade USA*, Vol. 11, no.4, pp.305–332, 1970.

Casari, Robert B. *Encyclopedia Of U.S. Military Aircraft 1908 To April 6, 1917*, Vol. 2. Ohio: Casari, 1970.

Casey, Louis S. *Curtiss The Hammondsport Era 1907–1915*. New York: Crown Publishers, 1981.

Celms, R. "The Cheerful Flyer Olgerts Teteris," *Atputa*.

Chalif, Don. *Military Pilot & Aircrew Badges of the World (1870–Present)* Vol. 1. San Jose: Bender, 1982.

Clark, Charles U. *United Romania*. New York: Dodd, Mead & Co. 1932.

Cynk, Jerzy B. *History of the Polish Air Force 1918–1968*. Reading: Osprey, 1972.

Davilla, James and Arthur M. Soltan. "French Day Bombers 1914–18," *Over The Front Journal USA*, Vol. 4. No. 3, 1989, pp 196–234.

Delear, Frank J. *Igor Sikorsky: His Three Careers in Aviation*. New York: Dodd, Mead & Company, 1969.

de Seversky, Alexander P. *Victory Through Air Power*.

d'Orey, Ladislau. *Airships of the World*. Century Co. 1917.

Dorling, H. T. *Ribbons and Medals*. London: Osprey, 1983.

Duz', P.D. *Istoriya vozdukhoplavaniya i aviatsii v SSSR, 1914–18* [A history of aeronautics and aviation in the USSR for the period 1914–1918]. Moscow: OBorongiz, 1944, 1960, and 1979.

Duz', P.D. *A history of aeronautics and aviation in the USSR, pre-1914*. Moscow: Mashinostroyeniye, 1981.

Elman, H.J. and H.D. Hastings, B.F. Hardesty, A.D. Toelle. "The Standard French Camouflage System of 1918—Part 1," *Cross & Cockade Journal USA*, Vol. 9 No. 1, 1969, pp. 1–21.

"Escadrila Nieuport 3," *Jurnal de Front 1916–17*. Editura Militara, Bucuresti, 1986.

Farson, Negley, *The Way Of A Transgressor*, Harcourt Brace & Co., 1936.

Finne, Konstantin Nikolayevich. *Igor Sikorsky: The Russian Years*. Edited by Carl J. Bobrow and Von Hardesty. Washington, D.C.: Smithsonian Institution Press, 1987.

Flanagan, Brain P. "Operation Albion," *Cross & Cockade Journal USA*, Vol. 8, No. 3, 1967, p. 254–260.

Franks, L.R. and Bailey, F. W. *Over The Front*. London: Grub Street, 1992.

George, Mark and Vic Sheppard. "Russia's Air Forces In War and Revolution 1914–1920: Part 1," *Cross & Cockade Journal GB*, Vol. 17. No. 4, 1986, pp.145–153.

George, Mark and Vic Sheppard. "Russia's Air Forces In War and Revolution 1914–1920: Part 2," *Cross & Cockade Journal GB*, Vol. 18. No. 2, 1987, pp. 49–54.

George, Mark. "At War With The Soviets—The RAF In North Russia, 1914–1918," *Cross & Cockade Journal GB*, Vol. 18. No. 3, 1987, pp.119–125.

Gilbert, Martin. *First World War Atlas*. New York: Macmillan, 1970.

Guttman, Jon. "The Thrills And Perils Of Frying Sausages—Le Prieur Rockets In Action Over Three Fronts," *Over The Front Journal USA*, Vol. 1. No. 1, 1989, pp 76–80.

Guttman, Jon. "France's Foreign Legion Of The Air," *Windsock International*, Vol. Vol. 9, No.4, 1993, pp 33–36.

Graciansky, A.N. "Prominent Russian Pilot, E.N. Kruten," *Academy of Sciences of the USSR*, Issue 31, 1977.

Gregor, Michael. "Flying As It Was—Early Days in Russia," *The Sportsman Pilot*. 1939.

Griffiths, William R. *The West Point Military History Series—The Great War*. Avery Publishing Group, 1986.

Grosz, P. M. "Austro-Hungarian Aircraft Armament: 1914–18," *Cross and Cockade Journal USA*, Vol.15. No. 3 (1974).

Hastings. H.D. "French Escadrilles Of World War I," *Cross & Cockade Journal USA*, Vol. 7 No. 3, 1966, pp. 205–236.

Hardesty, Von. "Aeronautics Comes to Russia: The Early Years, 1908–1918," Research Report, National Air and Space Museum, pp.23–44. Washington D.C.: Smithsonian Institution Press, 1985. Illus.

Haythorthwaite, Philip J. *The World War One Source Book*. London: Arms and Armour Press, 1992.

Hurley, Christopher, *Russian Orders Decorations and Medals*, 1935.

Ivanov, N. I. *Aeroplanovdeniye* [Data on airplanes]. Moscow: MOV, 1915 and 1916.

Joly, Paul. "Sentinels of the Champagne—Escadrille Spa 38," *Cross & Cockade Journal USA*, Vol. 17 No. 1, 1976, pp. 1–33.

Katchinsky, V., *Aviation on the Black Sea (1912–1917)*, unpublished work.

Kerr, James. *A Condensed Chronology Of German Aerial Operations And Personnel Casualties*. Unpublished work.

Kilmarx, Robert A. "The Imperial Air Forces of World War I," *Airpower Historian*, Vol. 10, no. 3, pp. 90–95, 1963.

Kolankovsky, A. *A Short History Outline Of The Squadron Of Flying Ships—Ilya Muromets*. Unpublished work.

Kornerup, A. and Wanscher, J.H. *Methuen Handbook of Colour*, 3rd ed., London: Eyre Methuen, 1978.

Kulikov, Viktor. "Chronicle Of The Operations Of The 1st Corps Detachment Of The Imperial Russian Air Service, 1914–1917," *Over The Front Journal USA*, Vol. 10. No. 2, 1995, pp 149–161.

Lamberton, W.M. *Fighter Aircraft of the 1914–1918 War*. Letchworth: Harleyford, 1964.

Lamberton, W.M. *Reconnaissance & Bomber Aircraft of the 1914–1918 War*, Letchworth: Harleyford, 1962

Layman, R.D. *Before The Aircraft Carrier—The Development of Aviation Vessels 1849–1922*. Naval Institute Press, 1989.

Layman, R. D., "Euxine Wings—Russian Shipboard Aviation in the Black Sea: 1913–1917," *Cross & Cockade Journal USA*, Vol. 15, No. 2, 1974, p. 143–178.

Layman, R. D., "Allied Aircraft vs. German Submarines 1916–1918," *Cross & Cockade Journal USA*, Vol. 11 No. 4, 1970, pp. 289–304.

Layman, R. D., "Aviation Vessels of the World 1914–1918," *Cross & Cockade Journal*, Vol. 21 No. 2, 1980, pp. 146–174.

MacDonald Coupar, Anne Robertson, The Smirnoff Story, De Spiegel, *RAF Flying Review*, Vol. 13 No. 10.

Meos, Edgar. "Allies On The Eastern Front," *Cross & Cockade Journal USA*, Vol. 10. No. 4, 1969, pp. 314–327.

Meos, Edgar. "Amazon Pilots And Lady-Warbirds," *Cross & Cockade Journal*, Vol. 16. No. 4, 1975, pp. 375–379.

Mikheyev, Vadim. *Sikorsky S-16 Russian Scout*. Moscow: Polygon Books. 1995.

Mollo Andrew. *Army Uniforms of World War I*. New York: Arco, 1978.

Mollo, Boris and John Mollo. *Uniforms of the Imperial Russian Army*. Poole, Dorset: Blandford Press, 1979.

Nilsson, Thomson. "Groupe De Bombardement 1—A History," *Over The Front Journal USA*, Vol. 1. No. 4, 1986–87, pp 297–324.

Nowarra, H.J., and G.R. Duval, eds. *Russian Civil and Military Aircraft, 1884–1969*. London: Fountain Press, 1971.

Nowarra, Heinz J. *Marine Aircraft of the 1914–1918 War*. Letchworth: Harleyford, 1966.

O'Connor, Martin. *Air Aces of the Austro-Hungarian Empire 1914–1918*. Mesa: Champlin Fighter Museum Press, 1986.

Pantone Color Formula Guide. New Jersey, 1990.

Pares, Bernard. *A History Of Russia*. New York: Dorset Press, 1953.

Peter, Ernst. *Die k.u.k. Luftschiffer-und Fliegertruppe Osterreich-Ungarns 1794–1919*. Stuttgart: Motorbuch, 1981.

Pisano, Dominick A., T.J. Dietz, J.M. Gerstein, and K.S. Schneide. *Legend, Memory and the Great War in the Air*. University of Washington Press, 1992.

Porret, D. *Les AS francais de la Grande Guerre*. Tome I and II. Cedocar, 1983.

Purves, Alec A. *The Medals, decorations and Orders of the Great War 1914–1918*. London: J.B. Hayward & Son, 1975

Riaboff, Alexander. *Gatchina Days: Reminiscences of a Russian Pilot*. Edited by Von Hardesty. Washington, D.C.: Smithsonian Institution Press, 1985.

Robertson, Bruce. *Air Aces of the 1914–1918 War*. Letchworth: Harleyford, 1959.

Rodina Russian Military Museum. *The Uniforms Worn By Members Of The Russian Naval And Military Aviation 1913–18*. Unpublished work.

Rosignoli, Guido. *Air Force Badges and Insignia of World War 2*. New York: Arco, 1977.

Rosignoli, Guido. *Ribbons of Orders, Decorations and Medals*. Dorset: Blandford Press, 1976, 1979.

Safonov, Ludmila. *Only My Memories*. 1975. Unpublished work.

Schroeder, Walter, and Totschinger, Bernard. *Handbuch de k.u.k. Luftfahrtruppe 1914–1918*. Vienna: OFH Nachrichten Sonderheft, 1982.

Sergievsky, Boris. *Boris Sergievsky—An Autobiography*. New York: Russian Mutual Aid Society.

Shabashev, N. *Privyaznoe Vozdukhoplavanie 1914–1917* [Captive Ballooning During 1914–1917], Moscow, 1921.

Shavrov, V. B. *Istoriya Konstruktsii samoletov v SSSR do 1938 g*. [History of aircraft designs in the USSR for the period before 1938]. Moscow: Mashinostroyeniye, 1969; 3d ed., 1985.

Shipilov, I F. *Vydayushchiisy russikiy voyennyy letchik P. N. Nesterov* [Peter Nesterov: Outstanding Russian Military Pilot]. Moscow, 1951.

Sikorsky, Igor, I. *The Story of the Winged S: An Autobiography*. New York: Dodd, Mead and Company, 1938 (rev. ed. 1958)

Sikorsky, I. A. *The Technical History Of Sikorsky Aircraft And Its Predecessors (Since 1909)*. 1966. Unpublished Work.

Sikorsky, Sergei. *A Brief Review Of Sikorsky Aircraft Designs 1909 Through 1917*. 1987. Unpublished work.

Skelton, Marvin L. "The Use Of Special Ammunition," *Cross & Cockade Journal USA*, Vol. 23 No. 3, 1982, pp. 249–267.

Smirnoff, I.W. and Johan Visser. "Iwan Wasilicvich Smirnoff Number Two Star Ace Of The Tsar," *Over The Front Journal USA*, Vol. 3. No. 2, 1988, pp 134–143.

Stone, Norman. *The Eastern Front 1914–1917*. New York: Charles Scribner's Sons, 1975.

Stokesbury, James L. *A Short History Of World War I*. London: Robert Hale Limited, 1981.

Tarnstrom, R. *Handbooks Of Armed Forces—The Balkans Part II—Yugoslavia, Bulgaria, Rumania*. USA, 1981.

Taylor, A.J.P. *The Struggle for Mastery in Europe 1848–1918*. Oxford: Oxford University, 1971.

Tegler, John H. "The Humble Balloon—Brief History—Balloon Service, AEF," *Cross & Cockade Journal USA*, Vol. 6 No. 1, 1965, pp. 1–42.

Toelle, A.D. and H.D. Hastings and B.F. Hardesty. "Project Butterfly—The Standard French Camouflage System of 1918—Part 2," *Cross & Cockade Journal USA*, Vol. 13 No. 2, 1972, pp. 150–183.

Toelle, A.D. and H.D. Hastings and B.F. Hardesty. "Project Butterfly—The Standard French Camouflage System of 1918—Part 3," *Cross & Cockade Journal USA*, Vol. 13 No. 4, 1972, pp. 325–341.

Trunov, K.I. *Petr Nesterov* [Peter Nesterov]. Moscow: Soveskaya Rossiya, 1971.

Vasicek, Radko. "Czech Pilot Rudolph Simacek," *Cross & Cockade Journal USA*, Vol. 21 No. 3, 1980, pp. 270–272.

Waligora, David. "Le Mission Aeronautique Francaise En Russie 1916 –1918," *Pegase*, no. 72, January 1994, pp 4—20

Werlich, Robert, *Russian Orders Decorations and Medals*. Washington D.C.: Quaker Press, 1979.

White, Christine A. "Gossamer Wings: Women In Early Russian Aviation, 1910–1920," *Proceedings of the Second Annual National Conference on Woman in Aviation*, 1991.

Williams, Sandra A. "The History Of Escadrille SPA 103," *Cross & Cockade Journal USA*, Vol. 21 No. 2, 1971, pp. 97–115.

Woodman, Harry. "Les Bombardies geants d'Igor Sikorsky," *Le Fanatique de l'aviation*, nos. 150 and 151, May and June 1982.

Woodman, Harry. *Early Aircraft Armament—The Aeroplane and the Gun up to 1918*. Smithsonian Institution Press, 1989.

Woodman, Harry. "The Big Il'ya, Part 1," *Windsock International*, Vol. 6, No.3, 1990, pp 16–25.

Woodman, Harry. "The Big Il'ya, Part 2," *Windsock International*, Vol. 6, No.4, 1990, pp 4–11.

Woodman, Harry. "The Big Il'ya. Part 3," *Windsock International*, Vol. 6, No.5, 1990, pp 4–11.

Woodman, Harry. "Hazet," *Windsock International*, Vol. 9, No.4, 1993, pp 10–13.

Woolley, Charles. "A Brief History of Escadrille 3," *Cross & Cockade Journal USA*, Vol. 15 No. 1, 1974, pp. 27–62.

Periodicals

1. *Air International*.

2. *La Guerre Aerienne Illustree*

3. *Morskoi Sbornik*, Russia, 1908–1916.

4. *Nachrichtenblatt der k.u.k. Luftfahrtruppen*, Vienna, July 1917–October 1918.

5. *OFH Nachrichten* (Informationsblatt der Osterreichischen Flugzeug Historiker). Vienna, 1977–1993.

6. *Osterreichische Flug-Zeitschrift*, Vienna, 1914–1918.

7. *WWI Aero*

Index of Names

Adamenko, V.F. — 332, 333
Anatra, Artur A. — 338
Anatra, Eudocie V. — 261
Argeyev (d'Argueeff), Pavel V. — 43–48, 65, 389, 467, 468, 485
Bagrovnikov, Ivan M. — 185–186, 482, 485
Bashko, Jezups S. — 187–196, 482, 485
Chudnovsky, Ensign — 225
Coudouret, Louis F. — 145–152, 389, 416, 468, 485
Degtereva, Nadeshda — 263
Dolgorukaya, Princess Sophie A. — 263
Fedorov, Victor G. — 153–157, 387, 409, 468, 485
Finne, Constantin N. — 195
Gilsher, Juri V. — 49–53, 137, 138, 386, 391, 392, 406, 430, 435, 436, 469, 485
Golanchikova, Lyubov A. — 262
Golubov, B.V. — 444, 446
Gond, Maurice R. — 158–164, 386, 387, 407, 469, 485
Gorshov, G.G. — 32, 187–189, 205
Grigorovich, Dimitry P. — 266, 268–283, 332
Grochowalski, Tadeusz — 388, 413
Iordan, V.V. — 59, 63
Kachinsky, Victorin — 390, 424
Kokorin, Nicholai K. — 54–57, 384, 397, 470, 485
Kozakov, Alexander A. — 44, 45, 58–71, 384–387, 389, 397, 403, 410, 416, 470, 471, 485
Kruten, Yevgraph N. — 72–78, 223, 386–388, 392, 409, 412, 434, 437, 472, 485
Lachmann, Georges M. — 165–173, 389, 416, 472, 485
Lanero, Pierre — 153–157
Lebedev, Vladimir A. — 359, 360
Leman, Ernst K. — 45, 65, 79–81, 389, 416, 473, 485
Lipsky, Longin — 119, 120, 389, 477
Loiko, Ivan A. — 82–85, 388, 473, 485
Mahlapuu, Jaan M. — 197–200, 386, 388, 404, 412, 482, 485
Makeenok, Donat A. — 86–89, 387, 411, 474, 485
Manchoulas, Henri — 386, 406
Meller, V.A. — 345, 346
Moska, F.E. — 332, 345, 346
Mrochkovsky, Anton E. — 131, 383, 385, 403

Nesterov, Petr N. — 201–204, 384, 385, 397, 402, 482, 485
Novak, Augustin — 126
Orlov, Ivan A. — 90–94, 474, 485
Pankrat'yev, Aleksei V. — 205–214, 482, 485
Pishvanov, Alexander M. — 95–97, 388, 475, 485
Plait, Marcel — 215–217, 483, 485
Pulpe, Eduard M. — 174–177, 386, 475, 485
Raiboff, Alexander — 392, 435
Revol-Tissot, Charles A. — 161, 178–182, 476, 486
Safonov, Mikhail I. — 26, 98–101, 390, 422, 425, 476, 486
Samsonova, Helen P. — 262, 263
Schmidt, Roman — 51, 88, 136
Shcherbakov, M.A. — 332
Shchetinin, S.S. — 332
Sergievsky, Boris V. — 218–227, 387, 410, 483, 486
Seversky, Alexander N.P. — 26, 102–111, 337, 390, 392, 412, 434, 476, 486
Seversky, Nikolas P. — 336, 337
Shakhovskaya, Princess Eugenie M. — 260, 261
Shidlovsky, Mikhail V. — 33, 206, 211, 266, 319
Sikorsky, Igor I. — 139, 187, 205, 206, 209, 232, 260, 266, 284–330, 332
Simacek, Rudolph — 68–70
Slyusarenko, V.V. — 258, 259, 332
Smirnov, Ivan V. — 112–121, 385, 388, 389, 399, 412, 415, 477, 486
Strizhesky, Valdimir I. — 122–126, 388, 478, 486
Suk, Grigory E. — 127–130, 388, 389, 479, 486
Sukhorzhevskii, D.S. — 444, 446
Sveshnikov, Alexander N. — 228–230, 384, 389, 397, 483, 486
Tereshchenko, F.F. — 332–334
Teteris, Olgert — 231–233, 483, 486
Texier, Jacques — 161, 162, 386, 406
Tkachev, Vyatcheslav M. — 120, 234–238, 384, 385, 398, 402, 484, 486
Tomson, Peter M. — 239–242, 384, 398, 484, 486
Utgoff, Victor V. — 243–257, 390, 421, 423, 424, 486
Vakulovsky, Konstantin K. — 131–133, 385, 399, 480, 486
Yanchenko, Vasili I. — 134–139, 384, 387, 392, 398, 410, 436, 481, 486
Zvereva, Lydia V. — 258–260, 332